A CARTOGRAPHIC HISTORY OF OUR
LIVES AND HISTORY FROM
THE BEGINNING OF RECORDED TIME
TO THE PRESENT DAY

EARTH is an epic publishing feat never to be repeated, proudly created by Millennium House

Western Europe

Locator box indicates location of map within world

Locator box indicates location of map within region

Color-coded bars make identifying each continent easy

Each page is edged with silver gilding to help in the preservation of the book over time

Comprehensive labelling with current data

Specially created state-of-the-art full-color background relief

Colored relief bar indicating elevation

Feature boxes throughout the book focus on milestone events in a country's history or take an in-depth look at a unique feature about a country

Exquisite full-color images are used throughout, with more than 800 images in total

Scale bar and map scale information

A profile of each country provides a snapshot of vital information, including official name, population, area, capital city

A map of each country shows the major cities, highest point, and neighboring countries

Handy map reference information will take you straight to the corresponding map for each country

A locator map pinpoints the location of the country within the region

This limited edition atlas—the world's largest modern atlas—is bound by hand in beautiful custom-dyed leather with silver-gilded pages for preservation and silver-plated corners for protection. *Earth* establishes a new benchmark in the world of atlases, with highly detailed mapping and comprehensive country profiles. With 580 pages, including 355 maps of 194 countries, more than 800 images, 4 breathtaking gatefolds, and information on every country, territory and dependency in the world, *Earth* will appeal to book collectors, libraries and institutions, map lovers, and anyone wishing to enjoy now, and preserve for the future, a record of our world today.

Earth can be ordered from all good book stores or contact Millennium House for your nearest supplier

www.millenniumhouse.com.au

A CARTOGRAPHIC HISTORY OF
OUR LIVES AND HISTORY
FROM THE BEGINNING OF RECORDED
TIME TO THE PRESENT DAY

Chief Consultant
Dr Geoffrey Wawro

MILLENNIUM HOUSE

FIORENZA

First published in 2008 as *Historical Atlas* by
Millennium House Pty Ltd
52 Bolwarra Road, Elanora Heights
NSW, 2101, Australia

ISBN: 978-1-921209-71-0

SALES
For all sales, please contact:
Millennium House Pty Ltd
52 Bolwarra Road, Elanora Heights
NSW, 2101, Australia
Ph: (612) 9970 6850 Fax: (612) 9913 3500
Email: rightsmanager@millenniumhouse.com.au
Website: www.millenniumhouse.com.au

Printed in China
Color Separation by Pica Digital Pte Ltd, Singapore

AUTHORS
Millennium House would be happy to receive
submissions from authors. Please send brief
submissions to: editor@millenniumhouse.com.au

PHOTOGRAPHERS AND ILLUSTRATORS
Millennium House would be happy to receive
submissions from photographers or illustrators.
Please send submissions to:
editor@millenniumhouse.com.au

COVER (FRONT AND BACK): Seventeenth-century
illustrated map of the world with a small brass
drawing compass and telescope. The top band
features images of rulers of the time. From left:
Grand Duke of Tuscany, Grand Duke of Savoy, Louis
XIV of France, Carlos II of Spain, Anne Marie of
Orléans, Pope Innocent XI, Holy Roman Emperor
Leopold I, King of Sweden, King of Poland, and
Ottoman sultan Mahomet I.

PAGE 1: Italian explorer, Sebastian Cabot, along with
his father John, attempted to find an easy sea route
to Cathay via the Northwest Passage. Neither did
much to record their journeys but they are credited
with discovering Newfoundland, Canada. This portrait
of Sebastian Cabot can be found in the Bristol City
Museum and Art Gallery, UK.

PAGE 3: This magnificent panorama of Firenze
(Florence), the cultural heart of the Renaissance, is
part of the *Carta della Catena* (1490), at the Museo
de Firenze Com'era, Florence, Italy.

PAGES 4-5: *Christopher Columbus in the Monastery
of La Rabida* is an oil on canvas painted by Eduardo
Cano de la Pena around 1856. It can be found at the
Prado, Madrid, Spain.

PAGES 6-7: This map is a colored engraving drawn
by Juan de la Cosa around 1500, showing nineteenth-
century rulers and kingdoms of Africa. It resides in
the Royal Geographical Society, London, UK.

PAGES 8-9: This actual photograph taken around 1940,
shows the British Armed Forces operations room with
military personnel grouped around a map of Great
Britain. The operations room was used to determine
strategy and planning during World War II.

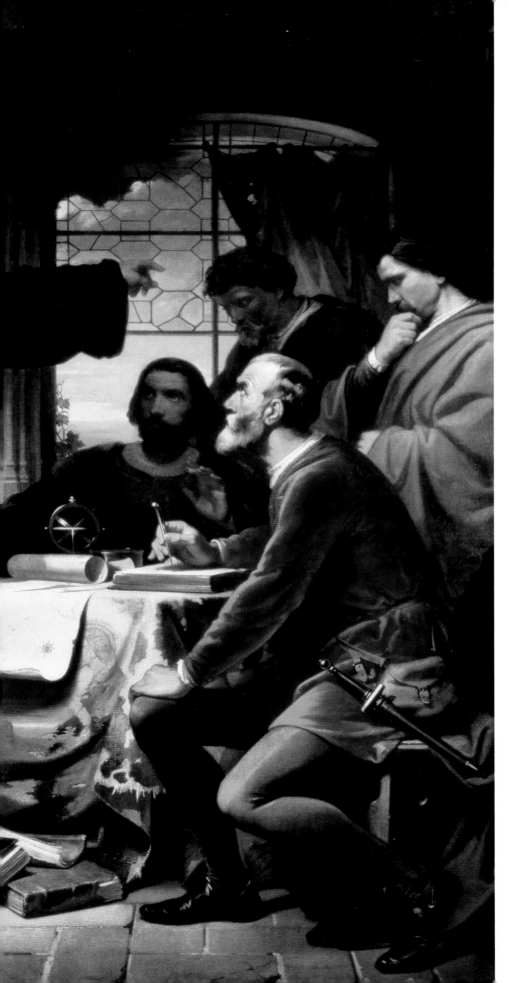

Publisher
Gordon Cheers

Associate Publisher
Janet Parker

Art Director
Stan Lamond

Project Manager
Carol Jacobson

Chief Consultant
Geoffrey Wawro

Contributors
Zoë Anderson, Carolina Armenteros, Serwan M. J. Baban,
Anthony J. Barker, Ivan T. Berend, David Cahill, Malcolm
Campbell, Emma Cavell, Robert R. Coenraads, Sally Cove,
Michael H. Creswell, Michael Crouch, Chris Dixon, Peter
Edwell, Norman Etherington, William R. Fowler, Thomas
F. Glick, Jonathan A. Grant, Dr. Matthew Gray, Sue Hart,
Kerry Hickson, Dexter Hoyos, Hans Hummer, Cindy Lane,
Jessica Lenney, Cecilia Leong-Salobir, Sophie Loy-Wilson,
Janette McWilliam, Ryota Nishino, Prashant H. Prasad,
Sonia Puttock, D. R. SarDesai, Jamie A. Smith, Alice
Stevenson, Tom Stevenson, Denis Stonham, G. Bruce
Strang, Mike Thompson, Blanca Tovías, Chad Van
Dixhoorn, Elisabeth van Houts, Jelle van Lottum,
Richard Von Glahn, Geoffrey Wawro, Steven A. Wernke

Designer
Avril Makula

Cover Design
Stan Lamond

Editors
Loretta Barnard, Helen Cooney, Chris Edwards,
Kate Etherington, Denise Imwold, Heather Jackson,
Melody Lord, Jonathan Nally, Anne Savage,
Marie-Louise Taylor

Picture Research
Kate Etherington, Carol Jacobson

Illustrators
Andrew Davies, Warwick Jacobson, Glen Vause

Cartographic Consultant
Damien Demaj

Cartographers
Warwick Jacobson, Alok Pathak, Max Peatman

Chief Map Editor
Susan Page

Map Editors
Loretta Barnard, Sally Fitzgerald, Denise Imwold,
Heather Jackson, Nick Jackson, Michelle DiStefano

Index
Diane Harriman

Typesetting
Dee Rogers

Production
Alicen Hunter, Bernard Roberts

Production Assistants
Louise Buchanan, Sam Diacos, Scott Quin

International Private Collections
Suzanne Gross

Publishing Assistant
Elissa Dempsey

Contributors

Zoë Anderson
Ph.D. candidate History,
University of Western Australia

Carolina Armenteros
Postdoctoral Research Fellow, British Academy,
University of Cambridge

Serwan M. J. Baban
BSc, MSc, Ph.D., FRGS, FGS, FRSPSoc;
Professor of Environmental Geoinformatics,
Director, the Centre for Geoinformatics Research
and Environmental Assessment Technology
(GREAT), Southern Cross University

Associate Professor Anthony J. Barker
Senior Honorary Research Fellow in History,
University of Western Australia

Ivan T. Berend
Distinguished Professor of History,
University of California, Los Angeles

David Cahill
Professor of Modern History,
University of New South Wales

Associate Professor Malcolm Campbell
Ph.D., University of New South Wales;
University of Auckland

Emma Cavell
D.Phil., Oxon.; Junior Research Fellow,
Wolfson College, University of Cambridge

Dr. Robert R. Coenraads
BA (Hons), M.Sc. Ph.D. FGAA, Dip DT., F.Aus.IMM

Sally Cove
Ph.D., University of New South Wales;
The Emanuel School

Michael H. Creswell
Ph.D., University of Chicago;
Florida State University

Michael Crouch
Ph.D. candidate History,
University of Western Australia

Chris Dixon
Ph.D., University of New South Wales;
University of Queensland

Dr. Peter Edwell
Ph.D.; Macquarie University

Professor Norman Etherington
Ph.D., Yale University;
University of Western Australia

William R. Fowler
Associate Professor of Anthropology,
Vanderbilt University

Thomas F. Glick
Professor of History, Boston University

Jonathan A. Grant
Ph.D., University of Wisconsin-Madison;
Associate Professor of History,
Florida State University

Dr. Matthew Gray
Centre for Arab and Islamic Studies, The
Australian National University, Canberra

Sue Hart
Ph.D. candidate History,
University of Western Australia

Kerry Hickson
Ph.D., London School of Economics;
University of Cambridge

Dexter Hoyos
D.Phil., Oxon.; University of Sydney

Hans Hummer
Ph.D. University of California, Los Angeles;
Wayne State University

Cindy Lane
Ph.D. candidate History,
University of Western Australia

Jessica Lenney
B.A. (Hons), Dip. Ed.,
University of Western Australia

Cecilia Leong-Salobir
Ph.D. candidate History,
University of Western Australia

Sophie Loy-Wilson
Ph.D. candidate History,
University of Sydney

Janette McWilliam
Ph.D., University of Cambridge;
University of Queensland

Ryota Nishino
Ph.D., University of Western Australia

Prashant H. Prasad
BA/LLB Undergrad., University of Auckland

Sonia Puttock
Ph.D.; University of Queensland

Dr. D. R. SarDesai
Emeritus Professor of History,
University of California, Los Angeles

Jamie A. Smith
Ph.D., University of Toronto;
Alma College

Alice Stevenson
BA, MA, Ph.D., University of Cambridge;
Egypt Exploration Society

Tom Stevenson
Ph.D., University of Sydney;
University of Queensland

Denis Stonham
BA (Hons)

G. Bruce Strang
Ph.D., McMaster University;
Lakehead University

Mike Thompson
Ph.D. candidate and tutor History,
University of Sydney

Blanca Tovías
Ph.D., University of New South Wales;
University of New South Wales

Chad Van Dixhoorn
Research Fellow, Wolfson College,
University of Cambridge

Dr Elisabeth van Houts
LittD (Cambridge), Ph.D. (Groningen);
Lecturer in Medieval History, Emmanuel
College, University of Cambridge

Jelle van Lottum
MA, Ph.D.; University of Cambridge

Richard Von Glahn
Professor of History,
University of California, Los Angeles

Geoffrey Wawro
Ph.D., Yale University; Director of the Military
History Center, University of North Texas

Steven A. Wernke
Ph.D.; Assistant Professor, Department of
Anthropology, Vanderbilt University

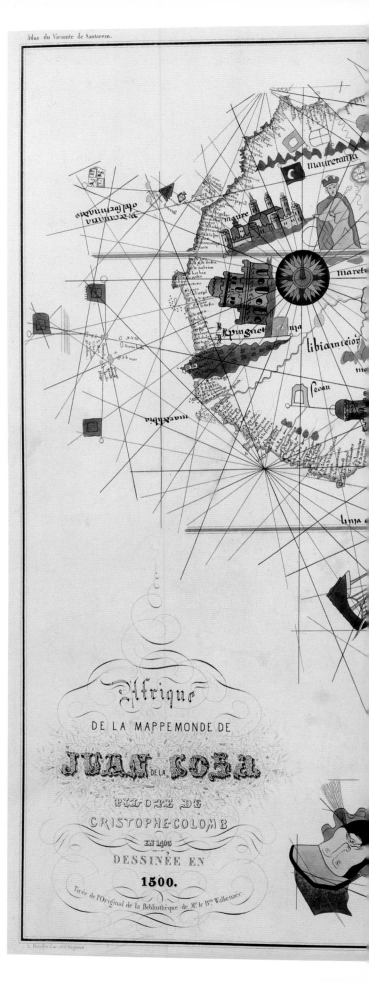

Atlas du Vicomte de Santarem.

Afrique
DE LA MAPPEMONDE DE
JUAN DE LA COSA
PILOTE DE
CRISTOPHE-COLOMB
EN 1493
DESSINÉE EN
1500.

Tirée de l'Original de la Bibliothèque de Mr. le Bon. Walkenaer.

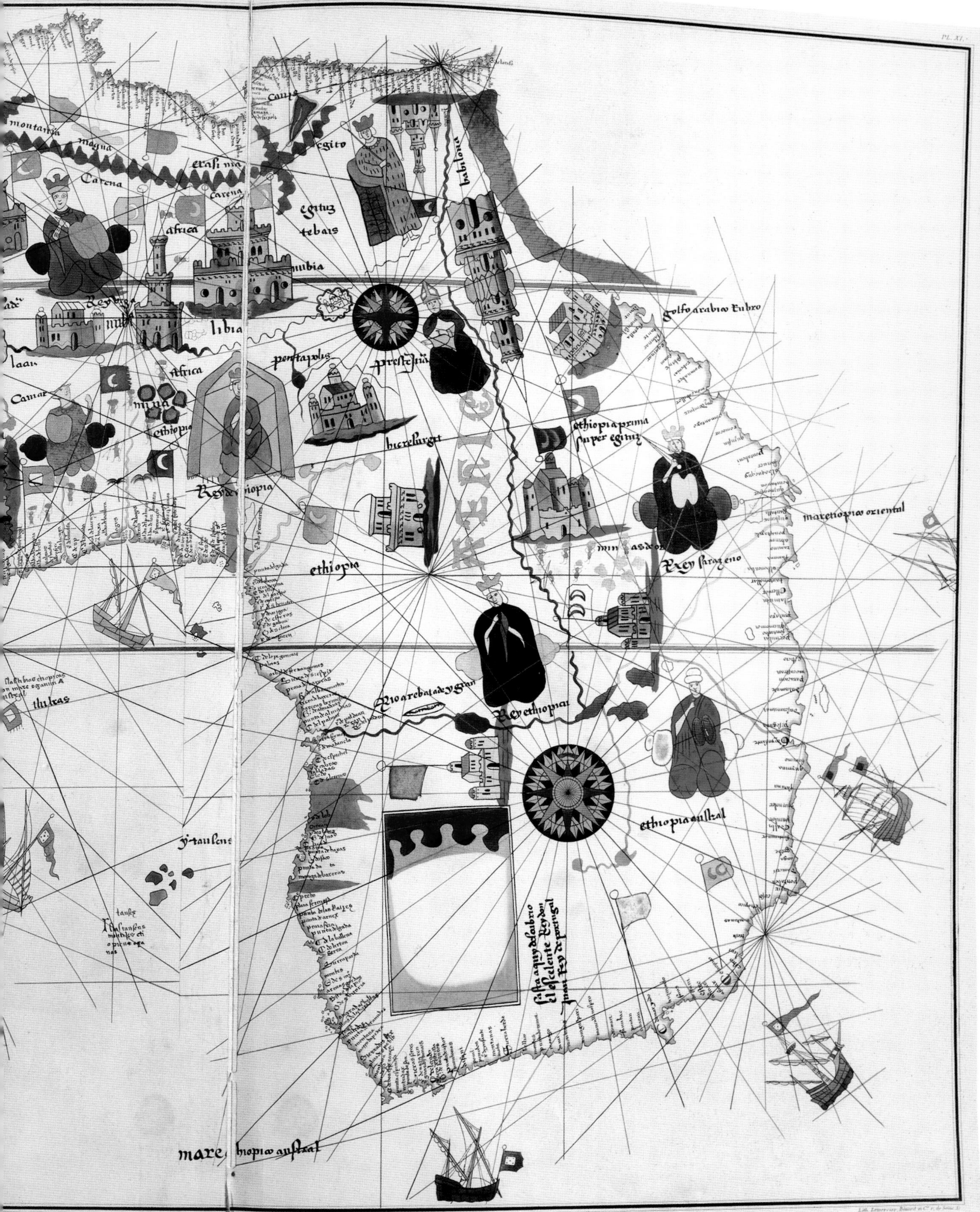

montania magna

erasi nia

carena

africa

egito

egitis

tebais

babilonia

carena

nubia

libia

africa

pentapolis

minia

ethiopia

hierusalem

Reydethiopia

ethiopia

Golfo arabico Rubro

Preste Juan

ethiopia prima
super egitu

Camar

Ylaau

Reyes

min casdei

Rey sarazeno

mare thiopico oriental

ethiopia

Yraulens

Rio arebata dy San

Rey ethiopia

ethiopia austral

tauxe

fafta aquy descobrio
el excelente Reydon
Juan Rey de portugal

Contents

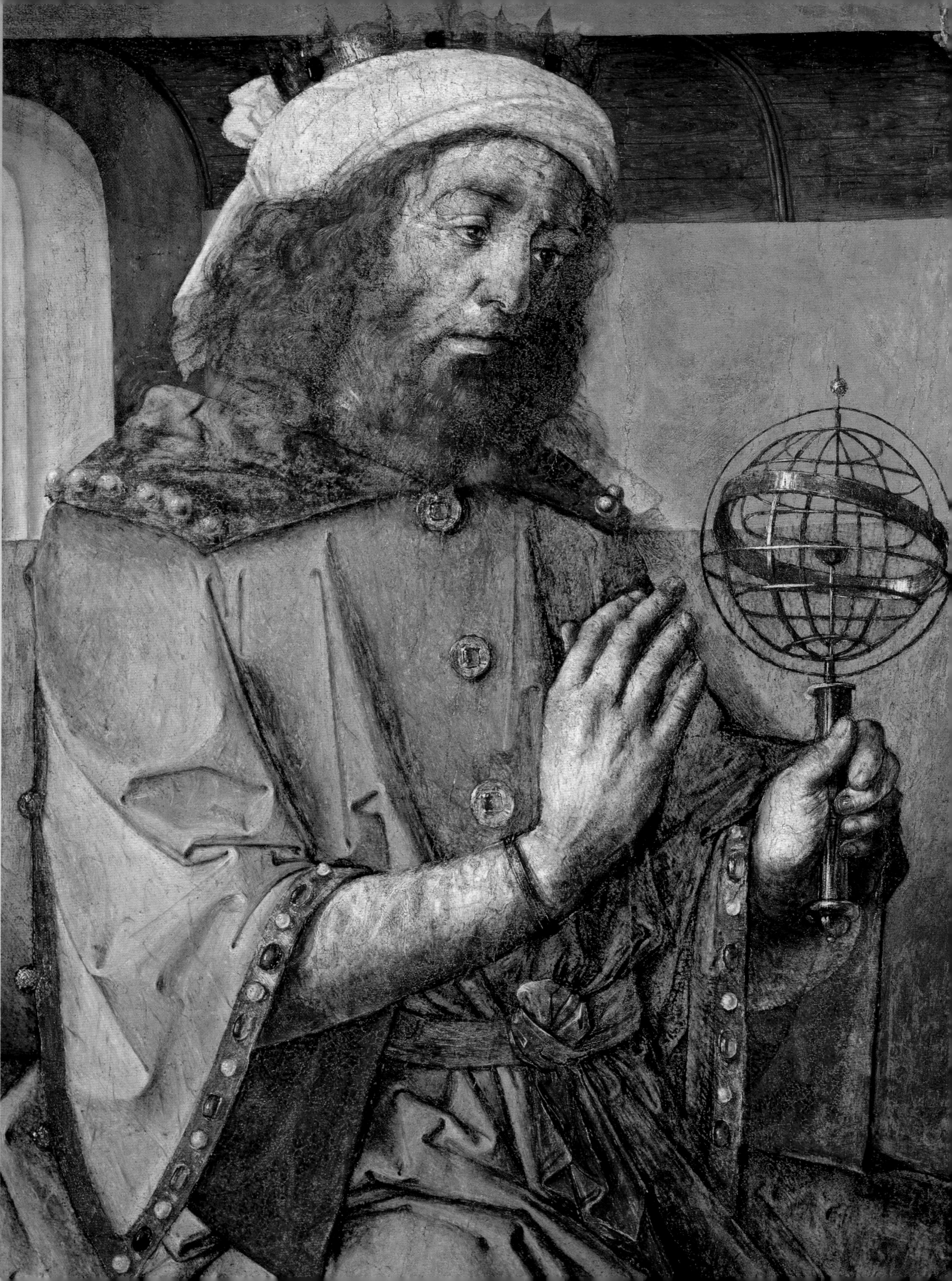

Finding our Place in the World

Maps better than any other medium describe the ebb and flow of barbarism and civilization. Maps flick the switch of civilization in our brains. They are an inherently civilized tool, for they represent man's attempt to order and make sense of the world.

Maps are the opposite of the new enemies of modernity—GPS and satellite images—which return us to the dawn of humanity, when we reconnoitered our world and our history using crude directions—turn left at the stump, walk till you see a pond, wade across, and then stop at the cave. Maps are the work of enlightened people who desire an overview— your route, but also those of others as well as your own alternatives—and the maps in this exciting volume provide as good and entertaining an education on world history as one is likely to find anywhere.

They show us the origins of Earth itself, which rippled, folded, and tore itself into continents, islands, and oceans. They carry us back to 10,000 BCE when people began hunting, herding, planting, and later warring in Europe, Africa, Asia, America, Australia, and New Zealand. The *Historical Atlas* reveals the remarkable diversity of life and history on Earth.

Athens and Sparta

We watch the emergence of the Western civilizations on these maps—the Western Greek world forms in opposition to mighty Eastern Persia. While Persia annexes land from Afghanistan to the Balkans and molds the new satrapies into tame tributaries, the Greek world is remarkable for its diversity—small city-states that defend their interests and identities. Sparta and Athens are first among equals, and *Historical Atlas* depicts their descent into war. The Athenian coalition and finances were ruined, and a balance of power returned to the Greek world. Athens lost its superpower status and rubbed along with the rest of the city-states, which would be gobbled up by Philip of Macedon and his son Alexander the Great.

Rome

New historical interpretations of the Roman Republic and Empire cast it as a relatively benign "empire of trust" that shielded and developed its subject peoples. Here we see Rome expanding and gathering in territory. The Tiber wended through the heart of Rome, but the Mediterranean washed through the empire, dividing its European and African halves.

Decadence and barbarians didn't dismantle the Roman Empire, Christianity did. Constantine had shifted the capital, Nova Roma, to Byzantium 100 years before the Visigoths swarmed over the walls of Old Rome. The new creed displaced the old Roman will to power, and opened a path for the German invasions. The Byzantine Empire became a repository of Greek and Roman culture, and stabilized the Mediterranean world through the Middle Ages with its laws, culture, solid gold currency, and military.

Arabia and India

The Dark Ages—when western "Romans" such as Charlemagne chafed at the pretensions of the Byzantines—were anything but dark outside of Europe. *Historical Atlas* unfurls the color and luxury of the Arabian Empire, with its hanging gardens, perfumed palaces, treasures, and breathtaking cities, like Damascus and Baghdad. Arab caliphates pushed the borders of the Arab world in this period from Pakistan all the way to Spain. India shone brightly too—the Gupta dynasty fostered India's "Golden Age," when the great minds of the subcontinent made lasting discoveries in mathematics, science, and philosophy.

China

On Russia's eastern frontier, China was a different world. The "Middle Kingdom" still regarded itself as culturally superior to the barbarians who inhabited the rest of the globe. The ancient Chinese

ABOVE The Comte de Vaudreuil, aged 18, is seen pointing out his place of birth on a map in 1759.

LEFT Ptolemy, Egyptian geographer and astronomer, was the author of several scientific works. He is portrayed here in a painting by Joos van Gent, c. 1475.

RIGHT This 1673 painting depicts the Battle of Hydaspes (326 BCE) in which Alexander the Great defeated the Indian king, Porus. Impressed by Porus's valor, Alexander spared his life.

PREVIOUS PAGES This nineteenth-century oil on canvas painting shows Napoleon being presented by General Bertrand with plans to throw a bridge over the River Danube at Ebensdorf. The painting now hangs in the Château de Versailles, outside Paris, France.

were big, powerful, and cultivated. They pushed out to Korea, Vietnam, and Mongolia, and cut the Silk Road across Central Asia.

Europe

In Europe, the Renaissance, the Reformation, and Enlightenment propelled Europe into a golden age that cemented Western power, and the casual, enduring assumption of "Western" superiority.

Historical Atlas details the spread of art, science, and literature across Renaissance Italy, and it dusts off the fissure between Catholicism and Protestantism, which superficially shattered the Christian world, but really strengthened it.

New faiths—a reformed Catholicism and a vigorous Protestantism—bonded new states, which strode into the early modern world with a sense of mission.

BELOW Babur, founder of the Mughal Dynasty, was a descendant of Genghis Khan through his maternal bloodline. This miniature lithograph shows him at the head of his army.

BELOW RIGHT The French Revolution saw the overthrow of the monarchy and the death, by beheading, of King Louis XVI. The catchcry of the new French Republic was "Liberté, Egalité, Fraternité" ("Liberty, Equality, Fraternity").

New Worlds

This mission began at sea, drawn in the lines of European exploration and conquest. Bartolomeu Dias sailed around Africa and charted the sea route to India and China, which slashed the once-great revenues from the Silk Road.

Christopher Columbus weaved through the Caribbean and crashed into the Bahamas, which he took for India. The Native Americans—ever after "Indians"—goggled at this Italian explorer, who has been credited from then on with discovering an America that, the atlas conclusively demonstrates, had been ably discovered, cultivated, and populated in its "Pre-Columbian" epochs.

Still, there was something thrilling and chilling about the Europeans. They came in waves—Columbus, John and Sebastian Cabot, Vasco da Gama, Ferdinand

Magellan, Jacques Cartier, Francis Drake, Willem Barents, Abel Tasman, James Cook. Their courageous questing—they had scant hope of surviving their voyages—reflected a drive and enterprise that were increasingly traits of the West. Their circumnavigations and restless search for a "northwest passage" from Europe to China were like early modern science fiction. Exploring the unknown oceans and hostile shores of the planet and braving the Arctic ice was like voyaging to Jupiter. Only a knave, a hero, or a European would do it.

Mapping the European mind is as difficult as it was for Magellan to pick his way through the Strait of Magellan, which the modest Portuguese navigator called the Strait of All Saints. We gasp at the achievements of European explorers, turn the page, and come face to face with European slave trading and the nearly genocidal fighting of the Thirty Years' War—the Czech and German populations reduced by 30 percent or more, half the males of Germany liquidated.

Revolutions

With its religious wars sorted out and peace arranged in 1648, the "New Europe" of securely constituted "great powers"— Britain, France, Austria, Russia, and Prussia—began to grow and compete. Now, the fights were different. France and Britain competed for primacy in America, and Britain won, only to lose all to the American colonists, who were rescued in their hour of need by the avenging French. *Historical Atlas* makes the point—best understood through

UNITE·INDIVISIBILITE
DE·LA·RÉPUBLIQUE
LIBERTE·EGALITE
FRATERNITE·OU·LA·MORT

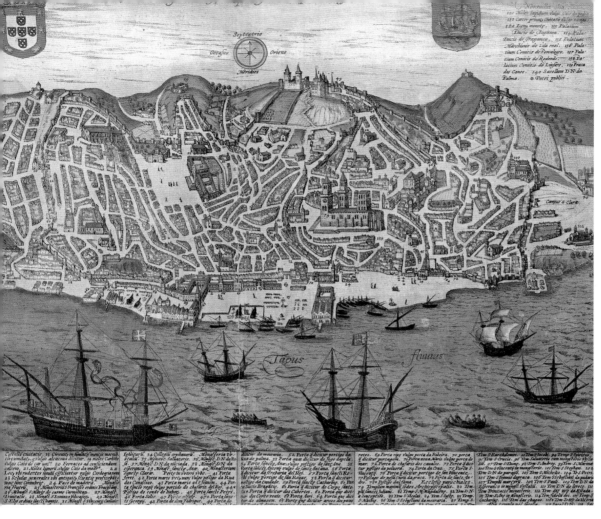

LEFT This is a colored engraving of a map of Lisbon from *Civitates Orbis Terrarum* by Georg Braun and Frans Hogenberg, published c. 1572. The fifteenth and sixteenth centuries proved to be the golden age of Portuguese exploration.

BELOW Here Amerigo Vespucci (1454-1512) is seen navigating by the stars. He was the first person to point out that Christopher Columbus had not found Asia, but a new fourth continent.

BELOW LEFT In 1770, English navigator and explorer Captain James Cook (1728-1779) claimed the east coast of Australia for Great Britain. Cook explored most of the world, traveling as far as Newfoundland, Australia, New Zealand, the Barents Sea, and the Sandwich Islands where he met his death at the hand of natives.

maps—that the American Revolution was a world war. The battles that sank the British were waged from the shores of India and the Mediterranean all the way to the Caribbean and the Virginia Capes.

The French Revolution masked a French bid for hegemony in Europe and the world. Where the goals of the revolution—liberty, equality, and fraternity—were not welcomed, they were bitterly contested. The French slaughtered luckless generals and herded barely trained draftees into storm columns that shattered themselves against the well-aimed fire of monarchical mercenaries.

We see old monarchies and duchies converted to "republics" by battle, but the back-story is often less edifying. These maps show the spread of French power, but are less good at coloring in the *mer de sang*—the "sea of blood"—that sloshed around the new French "republican" tactics.

Napoleon Bonaparte inherited the gains of the French Revolution, and bundled them into his Great Empire. Countries that didn't fit

inside the new aggrandized France were clamped onto its borders like pilot fish. Poles, Jews, and Neapolitans did better, but the Dutch, Germans, and Milanese were not so sure that they had passed to a better world.

Colonies

Australia was settled in this period as the convicts streamed in, and Matthew Flinders circumnavigated the "unknown land of the south"

for the first time in 1814, when Napoleon was abdicating and heading off to his own southern island. The British governor of New South Wales began using the term "Australia" in his dispatches for the first time in this period, and recommended in 1817, successfully, that Australia be adopted as the formal name for the colony.

The map of Latin America we recognize today was wrought by the Napoleonic Wars. Bonaparte's

invasion of Spain in 1808, and dethronement of the dynasty in Madrid, emboldened South American revolutionaries to oust their royal governors and proclaim their republics.

United States of America

The new United States added the "Louisiana Purchase" to its territory thanks to the Napoleonic Wars. His treasury drained by war, Bonaparte sold off that vast tract

FAR RIGHT A magnificent map from the sixteenth century shows natives paying homage to the Venetian explorer Alvise Cadamosto. He was a trader along the African coast in the 1400s.

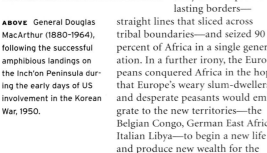

ABOVE General Douglas MacArthur (1880-1964), following the successful amphibious landings on the Inch'on Peninsula during the early days of US involvement in the Korean War, 1950.

RIGHT The first Gulf War (1991-1992) was fought between Iraq and a United Nations-led coalition following the invasion of Kuwait by Iraqi forces. Oil was the issue and in the conflict many oil wells were blown up, leading to severe pollution of the atmosphere and the loss of billions of barrels of oil.

of land stretching from the Florida panhandle all the way north to the present state of Montana, for about 5 cents an acre. The slavery question made it difficult for the United States government to absorb the new territories. Would the new land be slaveholding, or "free soil" and abolitionist? That debate would also be settled by war—the bloody, attritional American Civil War, which raged from 1861 to 1865. *Historical Atlas* makes clear that this was an industrialized modern war won by the ability of the Union to master geography. The Civil War and Reconstruction allowed America's rapid rise to great power and eventually to superpower status.

Africa

The last gasp of the Europeans may have been their vigorous carve-up of Africa between 1882 and 1902. They drew deplorable lasting borders— straight lines that sliced across tribal boundaries—and seized 90 percent of Africa in a single generation. In a further irony, the Europeans conquered Africa in the hope that Europe's weary slum-dwellers and desperate peasants would emigrate to the new territories—the Belgian Congo, German East Africa, Italian Libya—to begin a new life and produce new wealth for the motherlands. They emigrated all right, in droves…to America!

Asia

The Russians and the Japanese saw the American colossus approaching and fought a war with each other to secure their own futures.

The Russo-Japanese War of 1904–1905 was about geographical advantage. The Russians wanted to stake their future on control of Korea, the China trade, and a flourishing port at Vladivostok— their "window to the East." So they pushed the Trans-Siberian railway far across wastelands to conquer geography and to repel what the Tsar called "the yellow peril."

The Japanese felt shrunken and even betrayed by geography. Hence they lunged into Korea and Manchuria to gain a hinterland, to weaken China, and to attenuate the power of the Anglo-Saxons in Asia.

World War

World War I destroyed the German Empire, along with three others— Russia, Austria-Hungary, and the Ottoman Empire.

Russia's communist revolution and physical movement into the west—by the creation of Poland and the Baltic states—attenuated what had been the greatest check on German power, namely, the Russian steamroller on Germany's eastern border.

Historical Atlas depicts the spread of German power into the spaces vacated by the Habsburgs and the Romanovs, and the near victory of German arms in World War II. Hitler's Holocaust aimed to exterminate the Jews, enslave the Russians, and make "the Heartland" ring to the sound of folksy German Lieder.

The stakes were almost as big in East Asia. In World War I and World War II, Japan fought to expand and increase its power. Successful in World War I— raking in the German leaseholds in China and island groups in the Pacific—Japan overreached in World War II. China emerged, first as an American ally against Japan, and then as a competitor, which it remains to this day.

The Korean War broke out because no one in the communist camp grasped that America had interests in Korea, largely because even the Americans—focused on Prague, Berlin, Belgrade, Athens, and Ankara—didn't know either, until North Korean tanks were rampaging through Seoul.

Washington would not make the same mistake in Vietnam, where the atlas sketches determined American war plans that invariably foundered amid Vietnamese apathy. The big coalition of the first Gulf War—the whole world with America, against Mauritania and the PLO with Iraq—suggested that a "new world order" had come into existence. The internet, which roped the continents together, reinforced the impression of a "flat world" that had "globalized" itself.

New Order

But history did not end in the 1990s. History never ends, a fact brutally rammed home to all of us on September 11, 2001.

We see maps of human movement—hungry, poor, uneducated third world peoples pushing desperately into Europe and America. Immigration debates now rock all the Western powers. In the Middle East, Islamic fundamentalism spreads, borne on a wave of petrodollars. The oil and gas burned to achieve those dollars has wrought climate change, which makes for interesting, if quite alarming, maps.

The topics of war, conflict, and invasions—from the all-conquering Mongols to present-day Iraq— are examined in *Historical Atlas*. Worldwide, the amount of money invested in warfare is astronomical, and when nations finally turn their attention back to the more serious environmental problems sketched in the last chapter, what will they have left "in the tank?"

GEOFFREY WAWRO

HENRICO PRINCIPI LUSITANO NOVAS
TERRAS PERQUIRENTI MAGNO ADIU=
MENTO FUIT ALOYSIUS A MUSTO QUI
ANNO MCCCCLVI. INSULAS PROMONTORII
VIRIDIS AUT PRIMUS INVENIT AUT INTER
PRIMOS INVISIT. HINC ITERATO CURSU
PERLUSRATA AFRICAE PARTE DETECTAS A
LUSITANIS REGIONES TUM SUIS
TUM ALIENIS ITINERARIIS EVUL=
GATIS IN PUBLICAM LUCEM
EDUXIT.

MADERAE INS.

Porto Santo
Madera
Funcial
Infulae defertae

CANARIAE INS.

Salvage
Palma
Teneriffa
Laguna
Gomera
Ferro
Vigie
Bojador
Canaria

S. Clara
Rocca
Lanceroti
Forte Ventura
C. de N.
Banh

HILE
Rio dell'O
Inf. de Heronf
Lituf Angriae ubi
mutatur pulvif

Primul Meridianuf
Aloyfii a Mufto

Tropicul Cancri

Bot Rougeff
Angora dof Cavallof

C. delaf Barbu

GUALATA

C. Carvo
Lobof I.
C. BLANCO

Salinae
Infula & Arx Arguin

Hoden
Rio S. Antonio feu S

OCEANUS

INS. CAPITIS VIRIDIS,

S. Vincentii I.
S. Antonii I.   I. S. Nicolai
S. Luciae I.
Salif I.

Buenavista I.

S. Jacobi I.
Mayo I.

Fuego I.
Brava I.

Ribeira Grande

Refouer
Doyano
S. Annae Po
C. daf Arenaf
Portendic feu Forte Peñi
Palma minor
Granar
BUDO

Palma maj
Portuf Ba
Salinae
Mamillae R.
Rufifco
Joala
Palmerin
Bara

GENEHOA
Senega
Infula & Arx S. Aloyfii
Byurth
JALOPH
Barbacini
BARBACINI
SERRERI

C. Almadi
G. orge
C. R.
C. S. M
S. Annae

Caput Viridis
Katamanza I.
Rio Cacheo
Cacheo

ATLANTICUS.

In the Beginning

In the beginnings of the Universe, before history, before time as we know it, planet Earth formed from a spinning disk of debris, allowing landforms, oceans, and finally life to form on its surface.

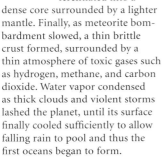

Some 4.6 billion years ago, planet Earth began to condense from the spinning solar disk. Earth steadily grew in size through meteorite bombardment as its orbit cut a swathe through the debris-laden solar disk. The planet continued to heat up, finally becoming a molten ball during a time aptly named the Hadean eon. Gravity drew the heavier elements like iron towards the center of the planet, allowing the lighter ones such as silicon and aluminum to rise, and planet Earth differentiated into a dense core surrounded by a lighter mantle. Finally, as meteorite bombardment slowed, a thin brittle crust formed, surrounded by a thin atmosphere of toxic gases such as hydrogen, methane, and carbon dioxide. Water vapor condensed as thick clouds and violent storms lashed the planet, until its surface finally cooled sufficiently to allow falling rain to pool and thus the first oceans began to form.

First Spark of Life

The first spark of life was not long in appearing, adapting to the harsh conditions. Simple life—single-cells without any nucleus (prokaryotes)—flourished in the early oceans, and even built massive reef-like limestone colonies, called stromatolites. Already the "feedback" loop between Mother Earth and her developing life forms had begun—oxygen, the byproduct of prokaryote cell respiration, began to build in concentration. This, in turn, converted free iron into insoluble oxides that deposited as massive heavy bodies—today's major iron ore mines. Excess free oxygen then built up in the primitive atmosphere, along with ozone that protected the planet's surface from harmful solar radiation, and new, more complex life was able to evolve. Cells with a nucleus and other internal structures—the eukaryotes—appeared by the Ediacharan period, about 630 million years ago. Complex soft-bodied organisms exploded in numbers around the world.

Evolutionary "Arms Race"

The Cambrian period marked the beginning of the Palaeozoic era 542 million years ago and saw the start of life's "great evolutionary arms race," with the entire incredible story recorded in the massive stone pages of Earth's geological history book. The story tells of the rapid evolution of predators and prey, with each becoming progressively more sophisticated in order to outdo the other and survive to reproduce. Predatory hard parts such as teeth and other grabbing appendages were equally matched by defensive armor plating, shells, and external skeletons. Eyesight evolved in the Cambrian, offering a tremendous tactical advantage to predators and prey alike. Life gained a tenuous foothold on the barren continents in the Ordovician period, when mosses evolved from algae near the shoreline. Plants then spread inland during the Silurian and Devonian periods.

Humanity's Rapid Rise

The period from 10,000 BCE to 600 CE encompasses the shadowy beginnings of human history. The first writing—hieroglyphics on clay tablets—appeared about 5,000 years ago (3,000 BCE) in the region of Iraq and Egypt, considered the "cradle of civilization." Before then, archeological evidence is the only way to piece together the developmental stages reached by humans in different regions.

Ten thousand years ago takes us back to the beginnings of agriculture, when humankind began to move away from its hunter–gatherer origins and into more permanent settlements with complex social and trade relationships. Their early gods evolved too, changing from animal totems to more relevant deities of sun, wind, rain, and earth.

The 5,000 year period of written human history, and indeed the entire 200,000 year period in which anatomically modern humans—*Homo sapiens*—have existed on earth, is incredibly short compared to the 3,800,000,000 years of time in which life has been evolving on the planet. We are uniquely in tune with the planet on which we live—its daily, seasonal, and longer-term cycles—and we depend heavily on the plants and animals around us for our survival. It is the extraordinary lengths of time involved in the evolution of life that has allowed the development of this finely balanced symbiosis.

Emerging Life

The Devonian period saw the first amphibians evolve from lobe-finned fish. Living on the mudflats of shallow estuaries, their limbs began to strengthen and they evolved a simple lung in order to survive occasional exposure. Eventually they lumbered onto the land and advanced into the swamps.

BELOW Littered with the fossils of ancient marine life, Los Mogotes Carsticos (the Karstic Hummocks) in Viñales Valley, Cuba, were formed millions of years ago during the Jurassic Period. Upheaval and air and water erosion have sculpted their interiors as well as their outer shape, creating limestone caverns with subterranean rivers, such as the Grand Caverns of Santo Tomas. Tobacco and various other crops are cultivated on the valley floor, mostly by traditional agricultural means.

Warm conditions worldwide saw giant tree ferns and horsetails thrive in swampy regions and later evolve into the extensive tall conifer forests of the Carboniferous Period. Most of the world's major coal deposits had their beginnings as peat in the swamps of this period. With such fervent photosynthetic activity, and the locking away of so much carbon in the swamps, atmospheric oxygen levels on Earth soared, reaching an extraordinary 35 percent compared with today's 21 percent. Gigantic arthropods, including mayflies, millipedes, spiders, and scorpions, thrived in the forests. *Arthropleura* was a millipede-like creature that measured up to 10 feet (3 m) in length, while *Meganeuropsis*, the largest dragonfly that has ever lived, had a wingspan of over 2 feet (75 cm). The warm conditions and extremely high oxygen levels, as well as the lack of predators, are believed to have been the principal drivers of this Carboniferous gigantism.

Reptiles and Dinosaurs

As the Carboniferous swamps began to dry out, amphibians gave way to reptiles during the Permian Period. Reptiles were better able to survive independently out of water than the amphibians because they had evolved a thicker, impermeable skin; they were the first vertebrates to lay amniotic, or shelled eggs.

These eggs resisted drying out, so for the first time vertebrates did not have to return to water to lay eggs and reproduce. Reptiles rose to dominance during the Triassic Period before splitting into divergent branches, the marine reptiles (ichthyosaurs, plesiosaurs, and pliosaurs), and the flying reptiles (pterosaurs). Reptiles were in turn overshadowed by dinosaurs in the Jurassic and Cretaceous periods.

The diversity of dinosaur types was amazing, including some of the largest land animals that have ever lived. Some dinosaurs developed warm blood and feathers for insulation, and as these feathers evolved further, they developed adaptations

LEFT Dinosaur tracker Martin Lockley investigates brontosaur tracks near the Purgatoire River in southeastern Colorado, USA. The parallel tracks, along an ancient lake shoreline of the Morrison Formation, are evidence that sauropods were social.

intelligent genus, *Homo*, appeared about 2 million years ago, at the start of the Quaternary Period, and one of their line evolved into the anatomically modern human, *Homo sapiens*, about 200,000 years ago in northeastern Africa.

Here to Go
More recently it has been realized that the evolution of life on Earth was not a slow and steady affair, but one punctuated by often-violent and calamitous global disasters. In these periodic "mass extinctions," most of Earth's existing species are wiped out, due to causes ranging from natural climate change and glaciation, to much more dramatic and sudden phenomena—episodic supervolcanic activity or chance meteorite impacts. The end of almost every one of the traditional geologic periods is marked by a major extinction event.

Significant mass extinctions took place 488 million years ago at the end of the Cambrian Period, 444 million years ago at the end of the Ordovician, 359 million years ago at the end of the Devonian, 251 million years ago at the end of the Permian, 200 million years ago at the end of the Triassic, and just 65 million years ago at the end of the Cretaceous Period.

> Nature is relentless and unchangeable, and it is indifferent as to whether its hidden reasons and actions are understandable to man or not.
>
> –Galileo Galilei (1564-1642),
> Italian astronomer and physicist.

BELOW Geological time is conventionally divided into eons, and smaller subdivisions called eras, periods, and epochs, based on the appearance and disappearance of major life forms. Many period boundaries represent significant, often worldwide, catastrophes—"mass extinctions"—in which most life on Earth was killed.

for gliding and flight, giving rise to *Archaeopteryx* and the first birds. All up, reptiles and dinosaurs ruled Earth for over 200 million years—throughout the Mesozoic Era—before calamity befell them.

The Rise of Mammals
In the wake of the extinction of the dinosaurs, the Cenozoic Era saw the rise to dominance of mammals. Their success went hand in hand with the spread of flowering plants and grasses during the Tertiary (or Paleogene and Neogene) Period. This was linked to the cooling and drying climate, which prompted open woodlands and grasslands to expand at the expense of forests.

Grass represented a new and very important renewable food source for grazing herbivores. Unlike most plants, which grow from their tips, grasses grow from the base of their stem, so the tops of the leaves can be grazed off continuously without killing the plant. Grazing herbivores prospered and grew larger on the open plains, developing tough grinding teeth and strong stomachs to process their diet of grass. Predators—saber-toothed cats, pack-hunting wolves, and bears—soon evolved to take advantage of the increasing herbivore numbers. The first primates also appeared at about this time—ancestors of the monkeys, apes, and humans. The

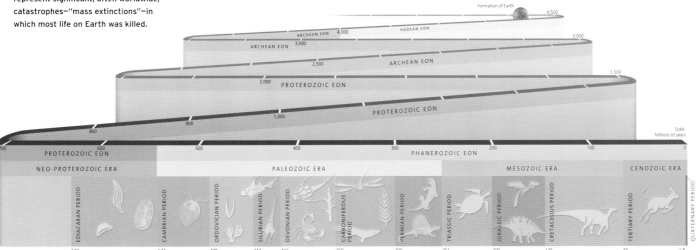

The World

North American Plate

Pacific Plate

Caribbean Plate

Cocos Plate

Nazca Plate

South American Plate

Scotia Plate

Antarctic Plate

ARCTIC OCEAN

NORTH ATLANTIC OCEAN

NORTH PACIFIC OCEAN

SOUTH PACIFIC OCEAN

SOUTH ATLANTIC OCEAN

Pacific Plate   Antarctic Plate   Juan de Fuca Plate   Nazca Plate   Cocos Plate   Caribbean Plate   North American Plate

Eurasian Plate

ARCTIC OCEAN

Eurasian Plate

Pacific Plate

Philippine Plate

Arabian Plate

NORTH PACIFIC OCEAN

African Plate

INDIAN OCEAN

Indo-Australian Plate

Indo-Australian Plate

SOUTHERN OCEAN

Antarctic Plate

South American Plate

Scotia Plate

African Plate

Eurasian Plate

Arabian Plate

Indo-Australian Plate

Philippine Plate

25

PREVIOUS PAGES The outermost part of Earth is made up of two layers: the lithosphere—the crust and rigid uppermost part of the mantle—and the asthenosphere, which flows like a liquid on geological time scales. The lithosphere is broken up into seven major and many minor tectonic plates. These plates move around the globe, jostling one another at convergent or collision boundaries, divergent or spreading boundaries, and transform boundaries—all of which are major locations for earthquakes, volcanic activity, mountain-building, and oceanic trench formation.

RIGHT The mid-Jurassic period was pretty much a black hole in dinosaur research until the 1970s, when a road crew building a highway near Zigong, China, found a treasure trove of Jurassic dinosaur fossils, now preserved as Zigong Dinosaur Museum.

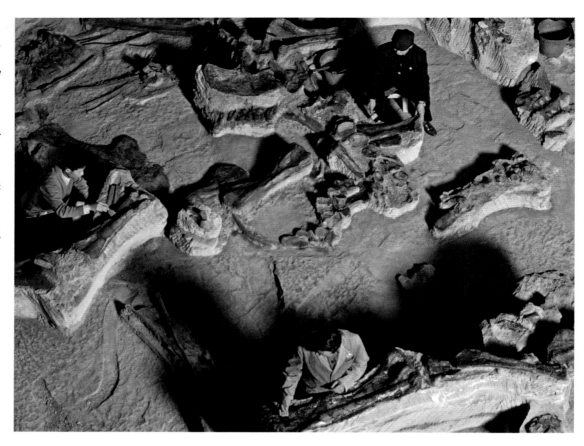

ABOVE The giant Galapagos tortoise, the largest living tortoise, is endemic to nine islands of the Galapagos Archipelago. Adults sometimes weigh over 660 pounds (300 kg) and can measure up to 4 feet (1.2 m) in length. Their life expectancy is estimated to be 150-200 years, and their diet consists of cactus, grasses, leaves, vines, and fruit. Fresh young grass is their favourite food, but they also devour the poison apple (*Hippomane mancinella*), the endemic guava (*Psidium galapageium*), the water fern (*Azolla microphylla*), and a bromeliad (*Tillandsia insularis*).

The Biggest Extinction Ever

The Permian mass extinction was by far the worst catastrophe ever suffered by life on Earth, with an unbelievable 90 to 95 percent of marine species becoming extinct along with 70 percent of terrestrial species, including plants, insects, and vertebrate animals. All around the world, fossil-rich "death beds" mark an event that left the land and seas practically empty. Severe global climate change may have been the cause. The geological record shows evidence of extreme drying in the form of thick strata of desert sand dunes and salt beds. The reasons for this are uncertain, but extensive volcanic eruptions in Siberia and China that pumped enormous quantities of gas and ash into the atmosphere may have been responsible. Glaciation on the great southern continent of the time, Gondwana, similar to that which brought about the Ordovician and Devonian mass extinctions, has also been cited as a possibile cause.

Meteorite Impact

Large impacts have the momentum to crack Earth's brittle crust, initiating worldwide chain reactions of earthquakes and volcanic activity. Dust- and ash-darkened skies, lasting for months or even years on end, would deprive plants of vital sunlight, slashing most food chains at their base and starving all life above out of existence. Only the strongest and most adept species would be able to survive. Perhaps without such disasters periodically clear-felling life on the planet, certain species may not have had a chance to diversify and evolve in the way they did. Life on today's planet could have been very different, for example, if a few chance events had not occurred. A savage meteorite impact on Mexico's Yucatan Peninsula some 65 million years ago saw the end of both the Cretaceous Period and some 200 million years of dinosaur rule. Without that meteorite strike, the nocturnal rodent-like mammals that had remained hidden and insignificant in the Mesozoic forests during the age of the the dinosaurs would not have had the chance to evolve into new niches. Mammals could at last diversify and would eventually dominate the expanding grasslands. Hence the evolution and rise of bipedal primates.

Human Impact

Today, we are in the midst of another great mass extinction caused by just one species. The rise of *Homo sapiens* to a position of dominance has taken place at the expense of the habitat of most other species. Early casualties included the megafauna, the giant animals that began to disappear from each continent shortly after the arrival of humans, surviving only in the legends and rock art of different migratory peoples. Today, species loss is occurring at a rate equal to that of any of the previous great extinctions, as forests and other natural ecosystems fall prey to the bulldozer, tractor, and chainsaw, in order to feed and house the growing human population. Life in the last natural strongholds, such as the Amazon forests and the great plains of Africa, is disappearing, in some cases even faster than we can record its existence.

Evolutionary Driving Force

Why is it that life on Earth is so unstoppable? Try clear-felling a forest and paving the ground over; before long, tufts of grass and tiny plants will begin to appear in the

RIGHT A saline lagoon nestles inside the crater of Rocas Bainbridge off the coast of Santiago Island, Galapagos Archipelago, Ecuador. Cores taken from this and the many other saline lagoons found in the Galapagos provide some of the oldest and most complete records of the frequency of intense *El Niño* events.

ABOVE Lava flows are streams of molten rock that pour onto Earth's surface from an erupting vent, hardening as they cool. The surrounding topography, as well as the type of vent and the varying speeds of different lava types (basalt, andesite, dacite, and rhyolite) help to determine their shapes and sizes. This black, whorled pattern, studded with bubbles, is found on Santiago Island in the Galapagos.

BELOW The most recent of Earth's supercontinents, known as Pangea, was formed about 275 million years ago. Our present continents are all fragments moving outward from its break-up. At a future time, all of today's continental fragments will once again come crashing together to form a new supercontinent.

cracks—a new community of life producing new soil and nutrients, slowly rebuilding a complex living ecosystem conducive to higher life. The process seems slow at first, but examples such as the reclamation of great Mayan cities by Mexico's Yucatan forests testify to its power.

Hidden within life's building block—the cell—is an incredibly powerful adaptive force. The cell's coded genetic information or "life blueprint" is stored in helicoidal deoxyribonucleic acid (DNA) molecules. The code can undergo minor change (mutation) as it is passed to successive generations through cell division and reproduction. Such changes make it possible for species to adapt over time to gradually changing environmental conditions, rather than simply dying out.

Through careful observation of life in the wild during the mid-nineteenth century, both Charles Darwin and Alfred Wallace independently recognized how minor genetic changes can be propagated in a population by the process of "natural selection" or "survival of the fittest." What this means is that individual members of a species that are stronger, better at sourcing food, more agile, or more intelligent, are more likely to survive under difficult conditions, and thus more likely to reach reproductive age and pass on advantageous traits to the next generation. In prey and predator species alike, attributes such as better eyesight, speed, or camouflage increase the chances of an individual's survival.

Evolutionary change is a slow and involuntary process. And as Alfred Wallace puts it: "Neither did the giraffe acquire its long neck by desiring to reach the foliage of the more lofty shrubs, and constantly stretching its neck for that pupose." Rather, "those with a longer neck than usual at once secured a fresher range of pasture than their shorter-necked companions, and at the first scarcity of food were thereby enabled to outlive them."

Moving Continents

Ever since its thin, brittle crust first hardened around Earth's semi-molten interior, land masses have been moving about, driven by the hot currents rising from Earth's core. Continental drift is slow—about the same speed as a growing fingernail—but over the fullness of geological time, the continents have drifted from equator to pole many times over. Life on the continents has thus always been on the move and has either adapted to changing conditions or perished. Over time, living communities have been moved in and out of contact with one another, and have been subject to climatic conditions varying from glacial to desert. Biodiversity reaches a maximum when there are many smaller continents separated by ocean, and a minimum when the continents are pushed together into one large supercontinent.

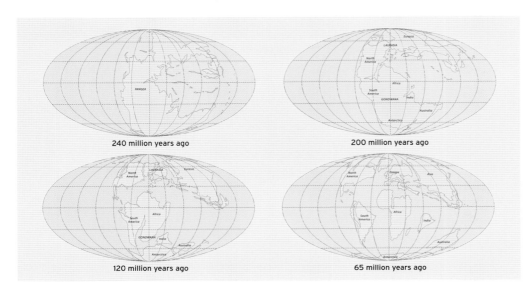

240 million years ago

200 million years ago

120 million years ago

65 million years ago

One Species

The history of the human race before the invention of writing can only be guessed at using evidence provided by archeological excavations and the study of modern human biology.

Employing a variety of chemical and biological techniques, scientists study fragments of bones, tools, and rubbish preserved at a few widely scattered sites throughout the world. Until recently it was believed that the oldest examples of our genus date back to about 4 million years ago. If we suppose that the human race had 4 million years to evolve then it is not surprising that people today display so many differences in physical appearance. In the nineteenth and early twentieth centuries, many respectable scholars believed that these physical differences were paralleled by differences in behavior and intellect. Thus different races were supposed to have had distinctive ways of life.

Evolution

No respectable scientist nowadays would link racial type to culture or

BELOW Humans probably followed these migration paths from our origins in Northeast Africa.

ABOVE Some natural historians attribute the extinction of large animals like woolly mammoths (pictured) and saber-toothed tigers to the arrival of human hunters.

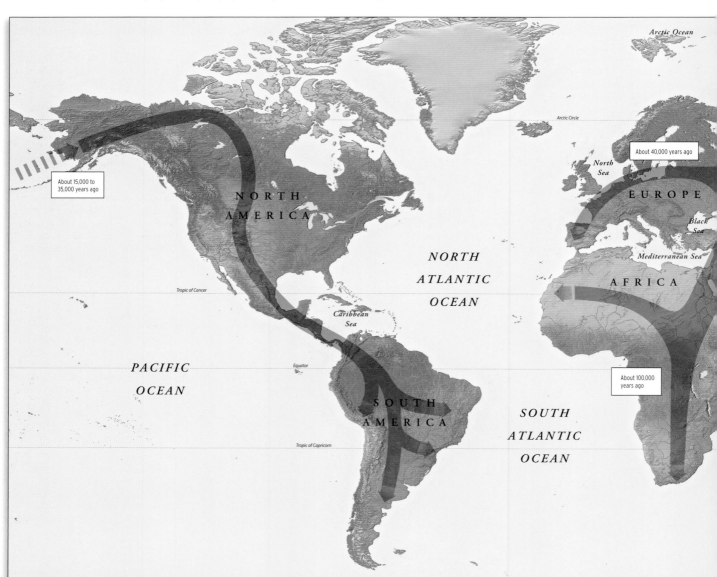

About 15,000 to 35,000 years ago

About 40,000 years ago

About 100,000 years ago

Arctic Ocean

Arctic Circle

NORTH AMERICA

EUROPE

North Sea

Black Sea

Mediterranean Sea

AFRICA

NORTH ATLANTIC OCEAN

Tropic of Cancer

Caribbean Sea

PACIFIC OCEAN

Equator

SOUTH AMERICA

SOUTH ATLANTIC OCEAN

Tropic of Capricorn

behavior. However, some continue to believe that human evolution occurred very slowly among tiny populations separated by vast distances and millions of years of time. A big problem with this theory is the ability of all present-day human populations to interbreed with each other—a sure indication that we all belong to the same species.

The hypothesis of slow evolution is now massively challenged by new kinds of data which indicate that all the human beings on our planet are descended from a single group of people who lived in a small region of Northeast Africa about 100,000 to 150,000 years ago. The study of mitochondrial DNA in present-day humans demonstrates that at the microbiological level we are so similar to each other that we must all be descended from a single group that lived not so very long ago. Thus other human-like creatures whose million-year-old bones have been found in such widely scattered sites as China, Java, and South Africa are not our ancestors but our very distant cousins—different species to our own.

Colonization

Why, when, and by what paths people from the core population spread from Northeast Africa to other regions is not known. Possibly the discovery of fire or developments in language, which enabled people to communicate more effectively with each other, made colonization of new territories easier.

> ### It is not the strongest of the species that survives, nor the most intelligent that survives. It is the one that is the most adaptable to change.
>
> –Charles Darwin (1809–1882), English naturalist and geologist.

Some people pursued adventurous paths to extremely distant new homes at an early date. For example, people found their way to Australia at least as early as 60,000 years ago and soon spread to all parts of the continent. By 30,000 years ago human settlement had reached Japan. Colonization of North and South America, on the other hand, appears to have come relatively late, most probably via the Bering Strait where Siberia comes closest to Alaska.

We must bear in mind that this view of human origins and migrations is likely to change as archeologists find new sites. One discovery of human remains can drastically alter our view of the past.

Agriculture

What is not in doubt is that populations and technical innovations exploded, beginning about 10,000 years ago, following the domestication of animals and the beginnings of agriculture in North Africa, the Middle East, South Asia, and China. By about 3,000 years ago agriculture had been independently invented in Central America. Compared with hunting and gathering, agriculture involved longer hours of backbreaking work; it also brought social stratification, more starkly marking off the wealthy few from the laboring many. But it did encourage the discovery of new technologies: Writing, metallurgy, bows and arrows, pottery, wheeled transport, organized religion, and urbanization emerged suddenly. Prehistory ended and history began.

c. 150,000 BCE *Homo sapiens* appears in Northeast Africa

c. 71,000 BCE Mount Toba on Sumatra erupts, possibly causing a change in climate

c. 70,000–10,000 BCE Ice Age inhibits the spread of humans in Europe, northern Asia, and North America

c. 60,000 BCE Migration to the Australian continent takes place

c. 30,000 BCE Humans settle in Japan

c. 13,000 BCE Early settlements appear in North America, probably via the Bering Strait from Siberia through Alaska

c. 10,000 BCE Climate improves enough for colonization to increase in Europe

BELOW This prehistoric rock art found in North Africa depicts warriors and a horse. Early humans used such art to represent both mundane and ritual aspects of their daily lives.

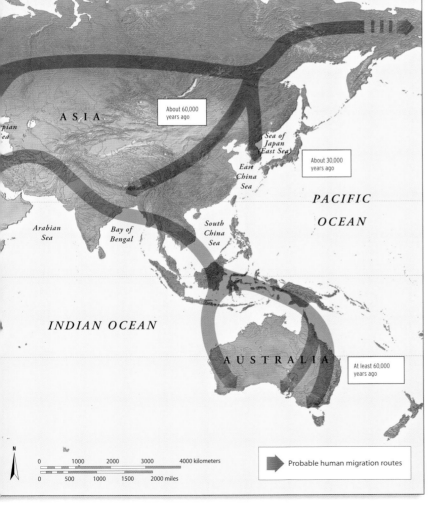

ASIA

About 60,000 years ago

Sea of Japan (East Sea)

About 30,000 years ago

East China Sea

PACIFIC OCEAN

Arabian Sea

Bay of Bengal

South China Sea

INDIAN OCEAN

AUSTRALIA

At least 60,000 years ago

N

| 0 | 1000 | 2000 | 3000 | 4000 kilometers |

| 0 | 500 | 1000 | 1500 | 2000 miles |

Probable human migration routes

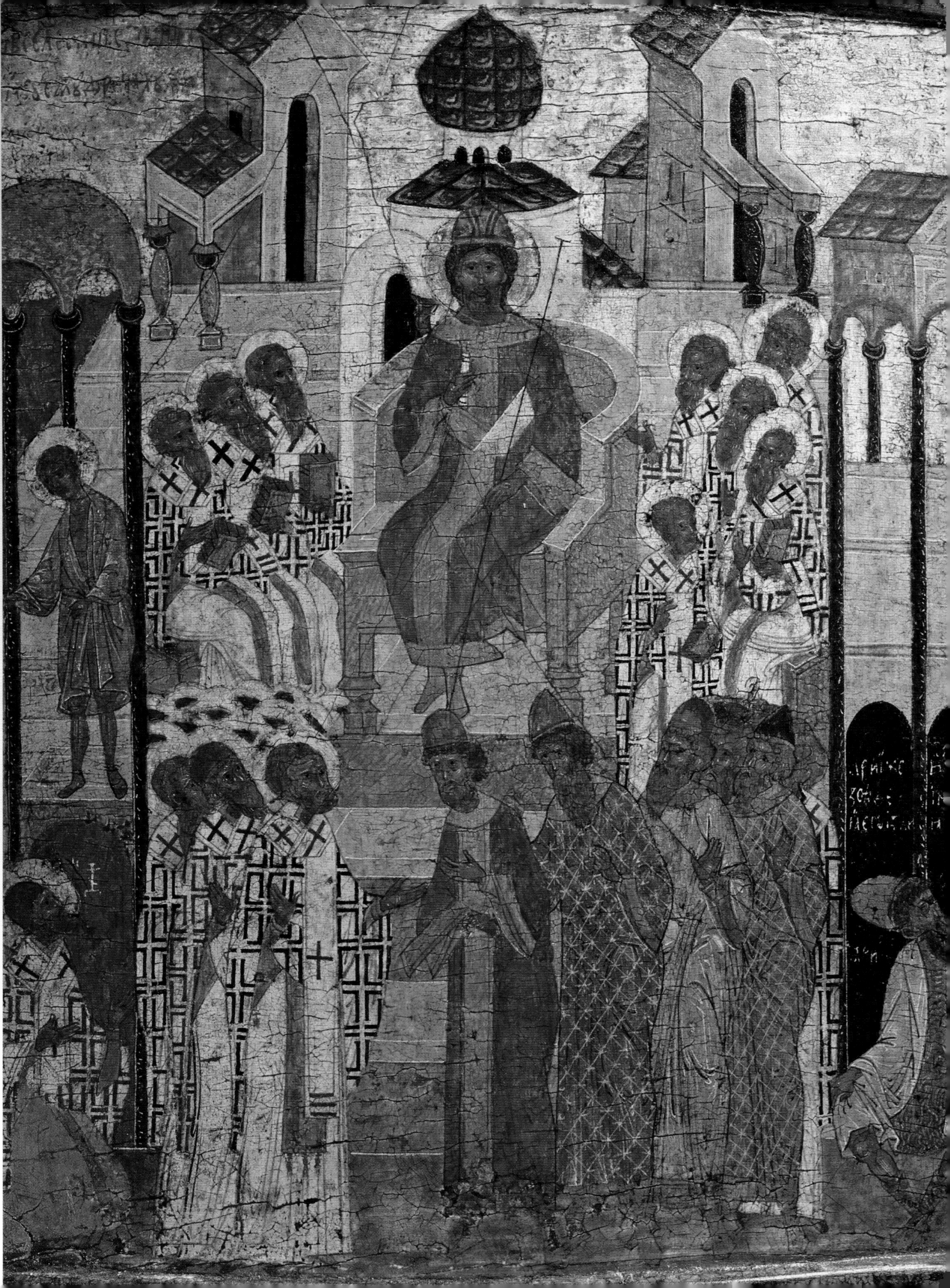

Creating Legacies

The sweep of ancient history has always fascinated and instructed us. The development and interaction of these societies in turn created the modern world, which has repaid the debt by bringing to light far more knowledge of ancient times than anyone living then ever had.

ABOVE The extraordinary craft of our ancestors as seen in this magnificent marble bust is the legacy of our forebears.

LEFT From the Banca Intesa Collection, this painting depicts Constantine, Holy Roman Emperor, at the First Council of Nicea in 325 CE.

RIGHT Intense color has stood the test of time in this fresco of cup bearers from the walls of the palace of Knossos, in Crete.

PREVIOUS PAGES The eerie light of the Seti I temple in Abydos, Egypt, is reflected on the elegant wall relief which depicts Seti, Osiris, and Isis.

The earliest identifiable organized societies lived up to 10,000 years ago, in widely separated regions of the world—notably Israel and Mesopotamia, Egypt, north China, and north India. The most obvious feature of ancient times, though not always the most important one, is the rise and fall of empires—conquest-states spreading over large and varied regions, typically due to one founding community imposing its control on others.

City-states

But an equally important feature was the number and variety of other states, large and small, which flourished in almost every era of the ancient world. Empires themselves began with above-average successes by certain states—the Hittites starting from their Anatolian heartland, China's empire from the central Yellow River plain, the Romans from a small but energetic city on seven hills by the lower Tiber. This basic pattern would recur in modern times, for instance with the British and Dutch empires.

Monarchy and Republics

Perhaps the very earliest type of political system, in states large and small, was monarchy in some form. Even Athens and Rome had kings in their primitive past. But a further significant characteristic of ancient states was that many of the most successful and creative had evolved into republics. In practice this usually meant oligarchies— fairly small ruling elites that largely monopolized political and other offices, and citizen bodies that invariably excluded women from voting and normally restricted their other rights too.

The Roman ruling élite, for example, had a membership very different in 44 BCE from what it had been in 509 BCE when the Roman republic began—as well as a vastly different competitiveness within its ranks, which eventually brought Rome into the grip of a new kind of monarchy.

Slavery

All states of the ancient world, without exception, used slavery as a standard form of labor, though not the only form. It was accepted that battle captives, defeated enemies, and weak communities preyed on by their stronger neighbors supplied slaves. Even philosophers took slavery for granted—at best, they argued that slaves should be humanely treated. The Romans were unusual—their freed slaves joined the citizen body. This illustrates a broader point. Slaves were very often similar in race, culture, and religion to their owners, especially in imperial capitals and major cities—a point that sometimes worried observers. Thus, ancient slavery both resembled and contrasted with modern slave-owning societies.

Religion

In languages and religions the ancient world showed an almost countless variety. One feature shared by almost all religions, though, was that each worshipped numerous divinities. Again, it was natural for different societies to see one another's gods and goddesses as their own in foreign guises. The Jews, who developed a one-god religion in which their deity could not even be portrayed, were judged quite strange, and so were Christians later. Persecution of religious believers was mercifully very rare, although Druids and Christians were two notorious exceptions.

Lineage

Our debts are immense to these sophisticated civilizations. Art and architecture are only part of their legacies. Towering works of literature, history, and law; complex philosophic thought; great religions; and political systems ranging from monarchic absolutism to extreme democracy are others. Nor can these achievements be thought of purely in the abstract. They were all the work of men and women like ourselves, some of whom lived lives and left achievements still memorable today. Their creations and the civilizations in which they flourished are their legacies to humankind.

Tribal Populations

The distribution of human populations across our planet during the last 10,000 years has not been determined by technology alone. It has also depended on the character of available resources, soil fertility, topography, climate, ease of communication, and disease.

c. 5,700 BCE Towns develop in Egypt

c. 4,600 BCE Cities and towns develop in the Indus Valley

c. 3,800 BCE State and city organizations develop in China

c. 2,700 BCE The first Greek and Estruscan city-states emerge

c. 1,800-1,200 BCE Maya civilization begins to emerge

c. 800-400 BCE First stirrings of Inca culture in South America

It used to be commonly thought that humankind developed in a series of stages, each successively more advanced than the previous one. European philosophers of the eighteenth century hypothesized that the lowest and earliest stage was characterized by dependence on hunting for food production. Next came societies organized around the herding of animals. These gave way to the increasingly advanced societies that engaged in agriculture, and top of the heap were societies that had developed industrial methods of production.

Not All Grass Is Greener

We now know that such conceptual frameworks oversimplify and distort our understanding of the processes by which people gradually spread across the globe and began to adapt to new environments. Where metals were scarce, stone and wood provided the best tools for pioneers. Some places are home to endemic diseases that make the herding of animals impossible, and agriculture cannot succeed where poor soils, permafrost, or excessive rain resist planting, or rot stored grains. Even the invention of the wheel had few advantages for people who lived in mountainous terrains or had no access to beasts of burden.

Africa

Following the birth of agriculture, populations grew rapidly along river systems suited to farming. Social organization and land use varied according to the crops. In the Nile Valley of Egypt and also the Tigris-Euphrates region of modern Iraq, conditions favored grains such as wheat, barley, and sorghum.

Asia

The Chinese river systems led to the development of rice culture. The Indian subcontinent drew on both Middle Eastern and East Asian agricultural experience. In all these environments, a variety

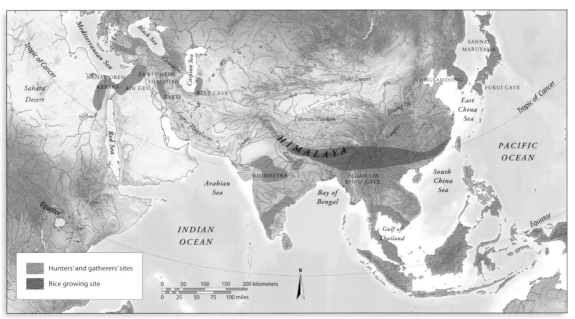

ABOVE The Amazon River region in South America was home to indigenous cultures quite distinct from those found in the Andes. After colonization, it became a refuge for indigenous people from all over South America.

LEFT Wild rice was first domesticated in southern China (*Oryza sativa japonica*), and eastern India or Indonesia (*O. sativa indica*).

Hunters' and gatherers' sites

Rice growing site

> The savage's whole existence
> is public, ruled by the laws of his
> tribe. Civilization is the process
> of setting man free from men.
>
> –Ayn Rand (1905-1982), in *The Fountainhead* (1943).

of domesticated animals provided additional sources of food and vital assistance in transport. Southeast Asian agriculture adapted Chinese rice strains to the monsoonal rain patterns and mountainous terrains, where terraced paddies made best use of the land. Water buffalo and poultry made sense in such regions; horses, mules, and camels did not.

America

Across the Pacific Ocean in Mexico and Central America, agriculture was based on the staple of maize, which thrives wherever soils are fertile and rainfall is reliable. Ingenuity in plant cultivation enhanced the diet of the Maya, Inca, and Aztec populations with locally domesticated potatoes, chilies, tomatoes, bell peppers, and sweet potatoes. The use of animal power in cultivation was not possible as their only domesticated animals were dogs, cats, and llamas.

Fishing, Hunting, and Herding

Where agriculture could not be practiced, human societies had to develop other specialized means of food production. For example, people who settled in the frozen Arctic and sub-Arctic regions of North America, Europe, and Asia depended on fishing, hunting, and herding. Large-scale social and political organization was out of the question in these latitudes. The ability to quickly put up and take down shelters was vital to groups following migrating herds. Sleds, snowshoes, and skis aided mobility in the long winter, while wheeled vehicles were useless before the invention of motorized transport.

Along the Inside Passage, stretching from southern Alaska to Puget Sound, canoe-borne trade flourished, as did sculpture, oratory, ritual, music, and dance. But the nature of the climate and terrain decreed that neither agriculture nor wheeled transport would gain a foothold. And to this day roads are few and far between along the coast between Vancouver, British Columbia and Juneau, Alaska.

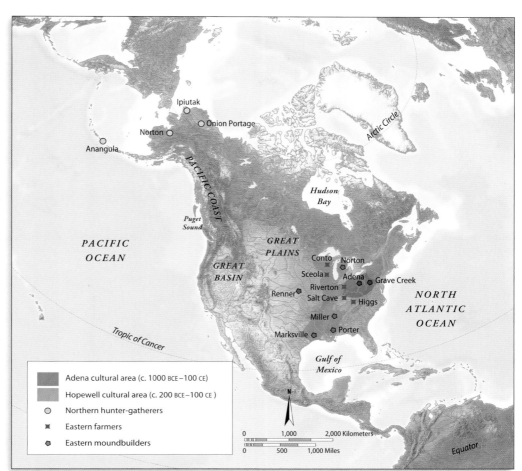

ABOVE Indigenous crop economies began to emerge in the eastern part of North America between c. 200 BCE and 200 CE.

LEFT In Mesoamerica, from c. 8000-2000 BCE, many bands of hunters and gatherers began to cultivate wild plants.

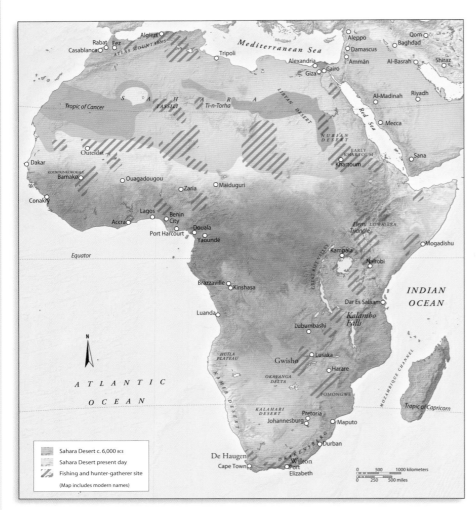

Sahara Desert c. 6,000 BCE
Sahara Desert present day
Fishing and hunter-gatherer site
(Map includes modern names)

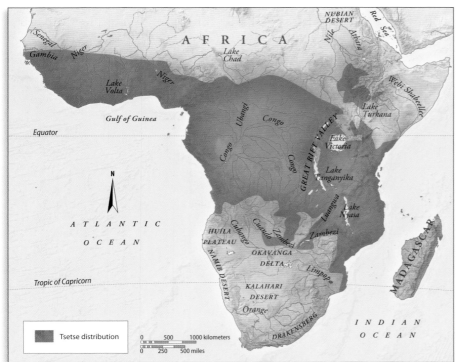

Tsetse distribution

LEFT The climate of the Sahara has undergone great variation between wet and dry over the last few hundred thousand years. During the last ice age, it was bigger than it is now, but between these periods of dryness were a few millennia of plentiful rain and lush vegetation when prehistoric humans left the congested Nile Valley and established settlements around rain pools, green valleys, and rivers.

BELOW Tsetse flies of all species tend to avoid the Sahara and Kalahari deserts. Their numbers are highest in the wetter central and western parts of the African continent. This small biting insect, which feeds on the blood of vertebrate animals, did much to impede human settlement in the region.

Pastoralism

On grasslands too arid to sustain agriculture or impossibly distant from urban markets, pastoralism developed as the predominant way of life following the domestication of animals. Seasonal variations in rainfall and plant growth led most groups to move their herds and tents from place to place over the course of each year.

Over time, the pastoral way of life encouraged the development of the skills in mounted warfare that made the societies of Central Asia such formidable enemies to the settled populations to the west, south, and east of them.

On the Great Plains of North America, an entirely new way of life grew up after the Spanish conquerors of Mexico introduced horses. People who had formerly lived in small settlements in river valleys learned to ride bareback and to shoot arrows while mounted, and with their newfound mobility they could follow the annual migrations of the bison. Within two centuries they had developed the military skills that made Chief Sitting Bull so dangerous to the US cavalry.

The rising demand for wool in the later Middle Ages led many rich landowners in Britain to cut

relationship between the language spoken there today and the languages of Malaysia and Indonesia proves that one or more voyages across the Indian Ocean occurred.

Language also provided the clue that led to the discovery of another stupendous episode in the history of human migration—the peopling of Oceania. When British navigator James Cook traveled from New Zealand to Tahiti and Hawaii, he found that the languages spoken in each island group resembled each other so closely that speakers of any one of them could make themselves understood on any other island.

Although some have advanced other hypotheses, ranging from chance settlement by fishermen blown off course, to colonization from South America or western Canada, it is now generally agreed that the islands were peopled by successive generations of seafaring folk who grew progressively more skilled in the arts of navigation. Linguistic studies, radiocarbon dating of human sites, studies of pottery types, and re-examination of the reports of early European travelers have established that people from Southeast Asia had island-hopped their way as far as Fiji by about 1300 BCE. From there, the distances to be negotiated inhibited further movement until the development of more reliable techniques, but by the end of the first millennium CE, Polynesian sailors had gone as far as Hawaii, New Zealand, and Easter Island.

A little later, the development of long-distance sailing techniques by Scandinavian seafarers led to a similar process of island settlement stretching across to the Orkney Islands of northern Scotland and eventually to the North American coast via Iceland and Greenland.

Populating Africa

Paradoxically, Africa, cradle of the human race, was one of the last continents to be fully peopled from Egypt to the Cape of Good Hope. This was probably due to the many obstacles thrown up by climate, disease, and topography. The least of these was the Sahara Desert, which, until about 2,000 years ago, had not reached its current state of aridity. Below the Sahara, however, poor soils, fearsome parasites, and diseases kept populations low as far south as the Zambezi. Humans could neither herd nor keep animals other than poultry wherever the moisture-loving tsetse fly—which is harmless to African game but deadly to domestic animals apart from poultry—is endemic. Pioneering migrants with herds had to travel through the high country of the Great Lakes region, skirting the East Coast and Congo River basin before spreading out across the modern countries of Botswana, Zimbabwe, and South Africa. Some managed this more than 2,000 years ago, but the southern regions remained sparsely populated until the arrival of the agriculturalists, beginning c. 200 CE.

down forests and enclose land for sheep grazing, at the expense of the peasants who used to live there. This example shows that herding was not the fixed primitive stage in the evolution of human societies that many eighteenth century theorists had imagined.

Maritime Migration

One aspect of the peopling of Earth that depended on new technology was the colonization of islands far from continental landmasses. It is possible, though not certain, that the first humans reached Australia by boat 60,000 or more years ago (alternative theories suggest that they crossed via a land bridge that once existed). It is equally possible that the continent was reached the same way many times before two-

way navigation became common in the eighteenth century. In other cases we can be more definite. Sometime in the first millennium BCE, seafarers from the Indonesian archipelago reached the island of Madagascar off the East African coast. Although we cannot be sure of the exact process by which this feat was accomplished, the close

ABOVE Very early fishing techniques are seen in this painted limestone fresco from the tomb of Ipy, a sculptor during the reign of Rameses II during the nineteenth dynasty in Egypt.

RIGHT Australian natives (Murray River region), as seen through the brush of the Scottish surveyor-general of New South Wales, Thomas Livingstone Mitchell (1792-1855).

ABORIGINAL TOOLS

Prior to colonization, Aboriginal people living in what is now Australia, used a range of tools, some for day-to-day living and others for ceremonies. The basic implements were spears, boomerangs, and woomeras—throwing sticks or clubs—for hunting kangaroos, emus, wallabies, wombats, etc. and stone tools for scraping and digging. Aboriginal tools had to be portable as tribes moved often. Adzes—rather flat roundish hard stones—were used in woodworking. Bifacial points—oval pointed stones—were often used as spear heads. The use of these tools was important to sustain life. Stone tools were also used to scrape out shellfish, resulting in shell middens, and also for treating bark and animal skins. Large flat millstones were also used for grinding seeds and sharpening stones.

Pharaoh—Keeper of the Great House

Ancient Egyptian civilization is one of the most widely recognized cultures of the ancient world. Yet the very term "ancient Egyptian civilization" glosses over four millennia of cultural development.

Its diversity can be seen across the three distinctive kingdoms, which are the conventional way that Egyptologists divide the history of ancient Egypt. These are the Old Kingdom (c. 2686–2125 BCE), Middle Kingdom (c. 2055–1650 BCE), and the New Kingdom (c. 1550–1069 BCE), during which Egypt was a unified country.

The intermediate periods separating these kingdoms are characterized as periods during which the country's rule was contested. These kingdoms and intermediate periods are divided into 31 dynasties, according to Egyptian priest Manetho, writing in the third century BCE.

BELOW Mural from the wall of the tomb of Tutankhamun, in the Valley of the Kings, discovered intact by Howard Carter in 1922.

Predynastic and Early Dynastic Egypt

Even before the dynasties were established, however, many of ancient Egypt's characteristic traits had already developed in prehistory. This occurred during the fourth millennium BCE, which Egyptologists call the Predynastic, and the early part of the third millennium BCE, otherwise known as the Early Dynastic period.

Origins and Early Rulers

By 3800 BCE, a vibrant culture had established along the Nile's banks in southern (Upper) Egypt, known as the Naqada I period. One of the most important communities in Egypt at this time lived around a site called Hierakonpolis, which in ancient Egyptian times was known as Nekhen—City of the Hawk. Excavations there have uncovered the first known painted tomb, the first evidence of ancient Egypt's trademark practice of mum-mification, and one of the earliest Egyptian temple complexes known.

The rulers buried at the Umm el-Qa'ab probably controlled most of Upper Egypt with their influence spreading northwards. Political unification is often attributed to Narmer, the first king of the first dynasty around 3100 BCE, at which time the capital of Memphis was probably founded.

Tombs and Burial Rituals

One of the most important aspects of rule ideologically, for the king as well as for most social strata, was the mortuary cult. A monumental architecture of tombs and mortuary cult structures became symbolic of the state and its government. Some of these tombs were surrounded by burials of sacrificial victims. For example, King Djer's burial was surrounded by over 300 subsidiary burials. This is the only time in ancient Egyptian history that the practice of human sacrifice occurred. The Second Dynasty kings no longer subscribed to this ritual and many are not buried at the sacred city of Abydos.

Not much is known about them and it is not until the Third Dynasty that the historical period of Egypt really comes into clear focus. Nevertheless, it is clear that throughout the course of the Early Dynastic period, royal control was consolidated and its institutions strengthened, so that by the beginning of the Old Kingdom, the monuments of the state represented a new form of control with vast resources, both human and material, in the "Age of the Pyramids."

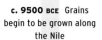

c. 9500 BCE Grains begin to be grown along the Nile

c. 8000 BCE People migrating to the Nile region form societies

c. 6000 BCE Rowing boats and small ships are built in Egypt

c. 4400 BCE Finely woven linen and cloth is evident

c. 4000 BCE Evidence of cosmetics and alchemy

c. 3500 BCE Musical instruments appear

ABOVE The Narmer Palette, dated c. 3100 BCE, is thought to depict the unification of Upper and Lower Egypt.

RIGHT This wooden fresco shows a Seker boat. Seker was patron god of the Memphite necropolis from Predynastic times.

BELOW The borders of the Predynastic and Early Dynastic periods of Egypt have been estimated using archeological finds.

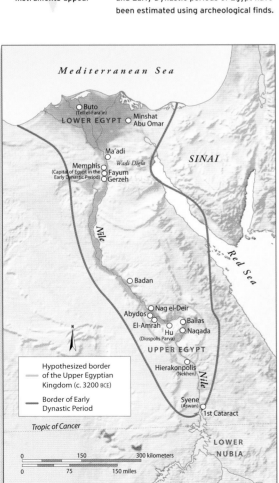

HIEROGLYPHICS

The process of social differentiation in Egypt accelerated between 3500 and 3300 BCE—Naqada II period—and it is from this period that the burial place of the first rulers of Egypt, or a part of Egypt, can be identified in an important cemetery at Abydos. It is in the graves of one of these anonymous rulers, known only by the excavator's number U-j, that the first unequivocal evidence for hieroglyphic writing has been found inscribed on small square ivory labels. They were probably tied to cloth or some other craft product, perhaps identifying its source. While these objects do not reveal the names of the tomb owners, it is nevertheless clear that from the outset, writing was associated with the elite, and literacy was never common amidst the general population of ancient Egypt.

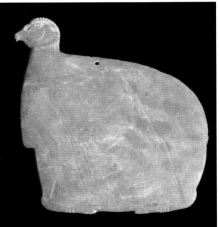

ABOVE A schist ceremonial palette in the shape of a large ram with a small horned head, dated around the Naqada II period, c. 3500–3300 BCE.

ABOVE Exquisite painted limestone from the Fifth Dynasty, Old Kingdom, showing the kneading and baking of bread.

Old Kingdom (c. 2686–2125 BCE)

The Old Kingdom is often called the Pyramid Age, as this was when the largest and most famous pyramids were constructed. Although in modern times Egyptologists often separate it from the less well-documented Early Dynastic period it is clear that it developed directly from the practices of this earlier phase. Central to the political organization of the Old Kingdom was the institution of kingship. The sun god Ra was the most prominent deity at this time and his cult was to influence the development of royal architecture during the Old Kingdom, especially the pyramids.

Pyramids

The Old Kingdom pyramids are testament not just to the power of the king, but to the organizational abilities of the civil service, which was an extension of the royal household. They were able to organize teams of workers from all over Egypt, who worked seasonally and were paid in rations by the state. The pyramids that they built were more than just tombs for the kings. They also contained temples devoted to the perpetuation of the king's cult.

Great Pyramid of Giza

It is Sneferu's son, Khufu, who is credited with the construction of the biggest and most accomplished pyramid of them all—the Great Pyramid at Giza—that stands 481 feet (146 m) tall. The base of the pyramid covers an area of 19 acres (5.3 hectares) and the pyramid's sides are aligned to the cardinal points, with only a slight deviation on each side. The level of the base on each side deviates by only 1 inch (2.5 cm). Much of the temple complex that accompanied this pyramid is gone, but three queens' pyramids, as well as two boat pits complete with dismantled boats, have survived. Also recently excavated is the settlement of the pyramid builders nearby, which contains bakeries and breweries that would have provided food and drink for the workers.

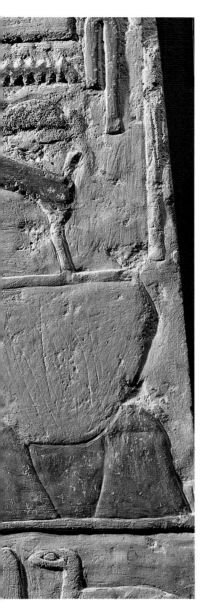

RIGHT The Great Pyramid of Giza was built over a 20-year period and is almost perfectly level across its massive 19 acre (7.7 ha) base. For almost 3,000 years it was the tallest man-made structure in the world.

ABOVE Made of sycamore, this is a life-size statue of Ka-aper (Sheikh el-Beled), dating to the Fifth Dynasty, Old Kingdom.

RIGHT Towns and villages began to flourish during the Old Kingdom, concentrated mainly around the Lower Nile.

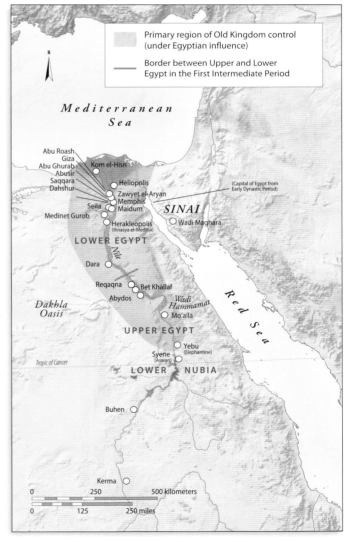

Pyramid Texts

The pyramids of the Fourth Dynasty were undecorated inside, but the tombs of the highest officials in the land at Saqqara were decorated with scenes of everyday life and offerings being brought to the deceased. Later pyramids of kings and queens in the Old Kingdom—smaller than the Fourth Dynasty—were also decorated on the inside but this time with magical spells. Called the Pyramid Texts, they are the earliest religious philosophical writings in Egypt, intended to protect the dead king from danger in the afterlife. In the Fifth Dynasty, royal patronage of the sun cult was expressed in sun temples with obelisks.

Old Kingdom Collapse

The Old Kingdom collapsed around 2180 BCE. Egyptologists disagree as to the causes, but a combination of factors was probably responsible. These included low Nile floods, famine, and a destabilized royal succession following the exceptionally long 90-year reign of King Pepi II in the Sixth Dynasty. The country began to break up and rather than a single king ruling the whole of Egypt, local governors established themselves as rulers within their own regions. This period from 2160 to 2055 BCE is known as the First Intermediate Period and was characterized by conflicts between the south and north of Egypt for control of the whole country. Many texts describe the bleak state of affairs in Egypt in this time and the First Intermediate Period is often seen as a sort of dark age. Yet, while kingship was certainly weakened and divided, local arts and crafts flourished and many of the experiments in religious practice, such as specially made tomb equipment, became important components of the culture of the subsequent Middle Kingdom.

Middle Kingdom (c. 2055–1650 BCE)

Following many years of hard fighting, the First Intermediate Period ended when the country was reunited by a ruler called Mentuhotep from Thebes in southern Egypt, around 2016 BCE. The ensuing 400-year-long Middle Kingdom was to become the classical age of Egyptian civilization with a flowering of art and literature in a time of peace and prosperity. This was to end, however, when Asiatic groups established themselves in the north of Egypt towards the end of the Middle Kingdom, instigating the Second Intermediate Period.

Reunification

Following reunification, King Mentuhotep II ruled for 51 years and undertook extensive building work across the country prompting innovation and renaissance in the arts. This included his funerary temple near Karnak where the bodies of 60 soldiers who may have died during the fighting at the end of the First Intermediate Period were buried. Despite his strong reign, the country lapsed into civil war following his death. It was only in the reign of Amenemhat I, the first king of the Twelfth Dynasty, that full stability was restored.

Coffin Texts

Despite the strengthening of royal authority, the notion of kingship had been damaged by the uncertainties of the end of the Old Kingdom and the First Intermediate Period. The king was no longer seen in the same divine light as before and there was a loss of religious authority.

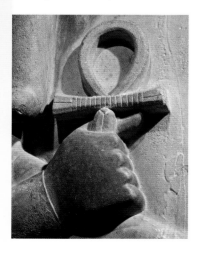

LEFT An ankh (symbol of life) from the Twelfth Dynasty, Middle Kingdom. It was found at the Temple of Amon, Karnak.

ABOVE A gold funerary mask from the Middle Kingdom.

LEFT Sobekhotep IV and his wife, painted on a limestone stela from the Middle Kingdom.

RIGHT The Middle Kingdom brought an expansion of territorial control reaching as far as the second cataract on the Nile.

This is evident in a form of democratization of the afterlife, and religious knowledge such as contained in the Pyramid Texts was no longer the sole prerogative of kings and queens, but was now carved onto coffins of all those who could afford them. These are known as the Coffin Texts.

The kings compensated for this loss in authority by cultivating a new iconography that portrayed them as "good shepherds" who protected the Egyptian people. This change in the image of the king can be seen in the statuary of the period, particularly from the reign of King Senusret II.

Writing and Language

In the Middle Kingdom there was a proliferation of texts, and these sources allow the voices of Middle Kingdom Egyptians to be heard in a more direct manner than those of the Old Kingdom. The language of this period became the standard "classical" form of ancient Egyptian—Middle Egyptian.

Narrative works of literature stand out as one of the great cultural achievements of the Middle Kingdom and include prophecies, moral tales, and hymns. The most famous of these are the *Story of Sinhue* and the *Tale of Shipwrecked Sailor*, both of which remained popular long after the end of the Middle Kingdom.

Middle Kingdom Collapse

The last ruler of the Middle Kingdom was a woman called Sobekneferu, who reigned for about four years. She was, however, reigning over a much weakened Egyptian state. The civil service had been slowly slipping out of royal control and another period of irregular Nile floods may have damaged royal authority further.

> And I shall go in before Pharaoh, I shall bring the gifts which I have brought from this isle into the country.
>
> –from *Tale of Shipwrecked Sailor*, a narrative written during the Middle Kingdom.

During the Middle Kingdom, people from Palestine had been filtering into Egypt, and Asiatic names are found in some Middle Kingdom texts. It seems that they were able to take advantage of a weakened Egypt. The Egyptians began to lose control of the eastern Delta in the Thirteenth Dynasty and these Asiatic groups came to rule the region from their capital at Avaris (Tell el-Daba). They are usually called the Hyksos, a Greek form of the Egyptian meaning "rulers of foreign lands." With the Hyksos in the Delta, and Egyptian rulers at Waset (Thebes), the Second Intermediate Period began.

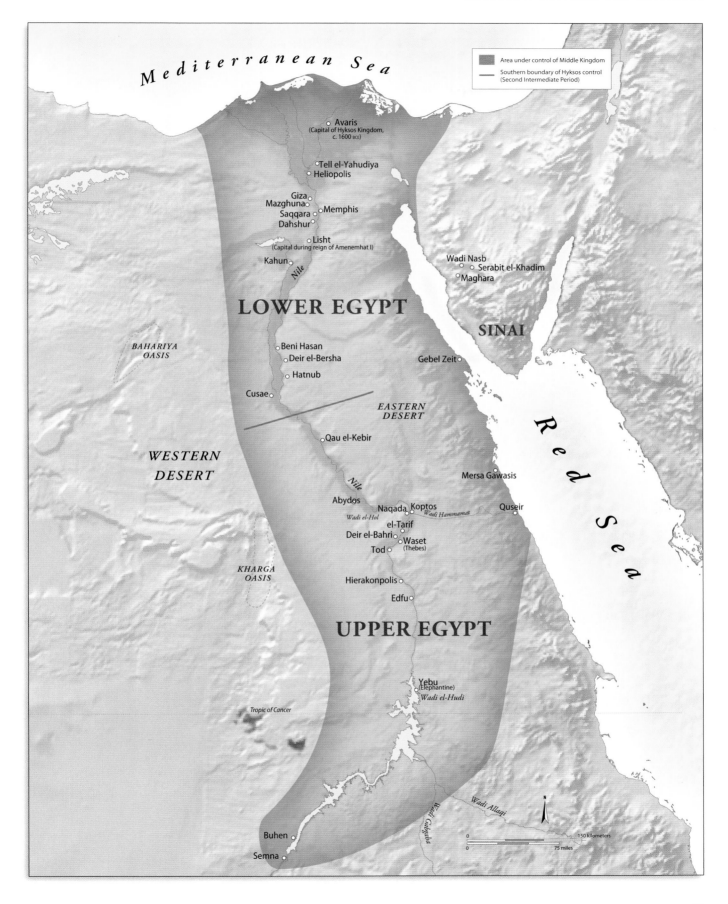

Mediterranean Sea

Area under control of Middle Kingdom

Southern boundary of Hyksos control
(Second Intermediate Period)

Avaris
(Capital of Hyksos Kingdom,
c. 1600 BCE)

Tell el-Yahudiya
Heliopolis

Giza
Mazghuna
Saqqara   Memphis
Dahshur

Lisht
(Capital during reign of Amenemhat I)

Kahun

Nile

Wadi Nasb
Serabit el-Khadim
Maghara

LOWER EGYPT

SINAI

*BAHARIYA
OASIS*

Beni Hasan
Deir el-Bersha

Gebel Zeit

Hatnub

Cusae

*EASTERN
DESERT*

**WESTERN
DESERT**

Qau el-Kebir

Nile

Mersa Gawasis

Abydos

Naqada   Koptos
Wadi Hammamat

Quseir

Wadi el-Hol
el-Tarif

Deir el-Bahri   Waset
Tod   (Thebes)

*KHARGA
OASIS*

Hierakonpolis

Edfu

UPPER EGYPT

R e d   S e a

Yebu
(Elephantine)
Wadi el-Hudi

Tropic of Cancer

Wadi Allaqi

N

Wadi Gabgaba

0   150 kilometers
0   75 miles

Buhen

Semna

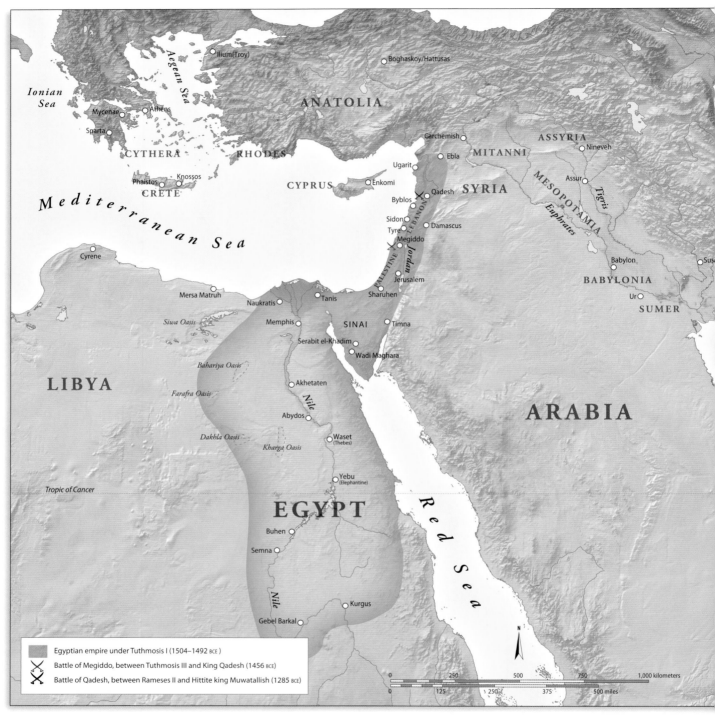

Egyptian empire under Tuthmosis I (1504–1492 BCE)

Battle of Megiddo, between Tuthmosis III and King Qadesh (1456 BCE)

Battle of Qadesh, between Rameses II and Hittite king Muwatallish (1285 BCE)

ABOVE At its peak, the New Kingdom controlled areas farther north than previous kingdoms, including most of the eastern coast of the Mediterranean.

New Kingdom
(c. 1550-1069 BCE)

The New Kingdom was founded upon the military expulsion of the Hyksos and it was this military prowess that allowed the Pharaohs of the New Kingdom to push the frontiers of the country further out into Syria-Palestine than ever before. Consequently, the New Kingdom is often described as the Age of Empire, one that was concurrent with the other large empires of the ancient world—the Mitanni in north Syria and Assyria, the Hittites in Anatolia, and Mesopotamia.

Pharaohs

As the Greek form of the ancient Egyptian phrase *per-aa* (Great House) the term "pharaoh" was used to refer to the royal palace, but in the New Kingdom it was often used to refer to the king himself. The pharaohs rode forth on their campaigns in the name of the god Amun, whose cult at Waset (Thebes) had become one of the strongest and influential. The massive temple at Karnak was built to Amun and almost all pharaohs of the New Kingdom built here.

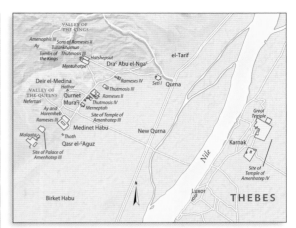

Amarna Period

In the reign of Amenhotep IV, polytheism was challenged. He changed his name to Akhenaten and established a new capital at Akhetaten (el-Amarna) where the old gods were replaced by the sole worship of the Aten—sun-disk. During this time of religious heresy—the Amarna period—Egyptian art became very stylized. This is seen in the depictions of Akhenaten and his wife Nefertiti, with elongated heads, thin necks, paunchy bodies, and thin arms and legs. The old order was restored by one of his sons (or possibly son-in-law), Tutankhamun, who, despite his short reign, is famous for his small, but intact, tomb in the Valley of the Kings. His successor, General Horemheb, became the last king of the Eighteenth Dynasty.

The Rameside Period

The subsequent dynasties, the Nineteenth and Twentieth, are often referred to as the Rameside period because many of the pharaohs were called Rameses. The most famous was Rameses II, whose self-promotion has meant that his name is found on monuments throughout Egypt. He reigned for 66 years, had over 100 children by several wives, and oversaw a great battle with the Hittites, the most powerful people in Asia Minor. He claimed a single-handed victory over them at Qadesh in Syria, but as the Hittites still controlled the area after the battle, the outcome was probably less favorable. The empty victory of Qadesh, however, was followed by a greater achievement, an international peace treaty with the

Hittites, a copy of which is on the wall of the General Assembly building of the United Nations.

End of the New Kingdom

Royal power collapsed around 1100 BCE in the face of the increasingly powerful priesthood of Amun at Thebes, who eventually came to rule the south of Egypt, while the last king of the New Kingdom, Rameses XI, ruled from the north. Once again Egypt was no longer controlled by a single ruler. By 1000 BCE, all of the New Kingdom empire had been lost and, in 716 BCE, Egypt itself was conquered by the Nubians of Kush. Periods of Nubian, Assyrian, and Persian rule were interspersed by brief periods of native rule, but following Alexander the Great's conquest in 332 BCE, Egypt was continually under foreign rule.

ABOVE LEFT The creator god Ptah is depicted on this limestone tomb decoration.

TOP This detail of the Valley of the Kings shows the proximity of the various tombs.

ABOVE The vast area of ruins that were the homes of the artisans working in the Valley of the Kings during the New Kingdom.

VALLEY OF THE KINGS

Instead of being buried in pyramids, New Kingdom pharaohs chose tombs hidden in the cliffs at Thebes. Today this is known as the Valley of the Kings. It contains tombs covered with paintings and texts about the king's journey with the sun-god through the underworld in the 12 hours of night. Notable amongst these are the impressive tombs of Seti I and Rameses II, as well as the beautifully decorated tomb of Rameses's chief wife Nefertari in the Valley of the Queens. An enormous tomb (KV5) was also prepared for sons of Rameses II.

Europe's First Civilization

The Minoans, a Bronze Age people of the island of Crete, became a major sea power in the eastern Mediterranean in the early part of the second millennium BCE. They left ruins that depict a life of plenty.

ABOVE This undeciphered Linear A inscription on a stone tablet, dated c. 1500–1400 BCE, is from the palace of Knossos, Crete.

This civilization was given its modern name by the English archeologist Arthur Evans in 1899 as a tribute to Minos, the legendary king of Knossos who is mentioned in the Homeric epic poems of the eighth century BCE. Yet the majority of modern knowledge of these people is based on archeological interpretation even though the Minoans have left symbols incised into clay tablets that appear to be palace records. These symbols form a script called Linear A that has yet to be fully deciphered.

Mediterranean Confederation

Crete was comprised of individual small city-states or kingdoms based on the fertile plains. Knossos was the largest, and later it may have been the leader of a broad confederation of the smaller kingdoms. Other cities included Mallia, Zakro, and Phaistos, and a network of roads linked all major centers.

The geographical position of Crete, on the trade routes between Greece, Egypt, and the cultures of the Near East, made the island a major trade center and generated a market for their goods and provided a source for raw materials. This created the wealth that is evident in the remains of the palaces.

Sophisticated Culture

The Minoans had kings who were the rulers of all secular, religious,

> There is a land called Crete, in the midst of the wine-dark sea, a fair, rich land, begirt with water, and therein are many men, past counting, and ninety cities.
>
> –Homer, *Odyssey* 19.172–174, eighth century BCE

and state matters within their particular city and its hinterland. Each lived with his family in a large well-appointed palace around which were clustered private brick and timber houses, some of which may have been several stories high. These were the homes of the wealthy courtiers or administrators. Less affluent homes of laborers and farmers were in smaller villages and rural areas and are almost absent from the archeological records.

Existing wall paintings depict young and graceful Minoan men and women with carefully arranged hair. The men wear kilts or short loincloths and are clean-shaven, while the women are depicted with long flounced skirts, open bodices, and gold jewelry.

The palaces provide evidence for the religious beliefs of the Minoans. Shrines decorated with stylized bull horns or "Horns of Consecration," vessels in the shape of a bull's head, and wall-painting

showing the sport of bull-vaulting by young men and women all point to the cultic significance of the bull. The combination of the painting, the mazelike corridors, and the character of King Minos suggest an association with the myth of the Minotaur.

Some rooms had small areas with a few steps leading down into them. These areas were originally known as "lustral basins," and might possibly have held water for the ritual washing needed for religious ceremonies. However, some may have been cult rooms symbolizing the underworld.

Decline

By somewhere around the middle of the second millennium, Minoan Crete was in decline. It is unknown whether the explosion of Thera had an impact on this, but by about 1500–1450 BCE, the Mycenean people from mainland Greece were in control of the island.

By 1375 BCE, the palaces had been burned and the townhouses were falling into disrepair. The decline of the Minoan civilization continued and power was then transferred to mainland Greece.

c. 2000 BCE
The first palaces are built on Crete

c. 1850 BCE
First invasions by Myceneans

c. 1628 BCE
Volcanic eruption on Thera causes massive destruction

c. 1500 BCE
The Myceneans conquer Crete

c. 1425 BCE
The palace of Knossos is destroyed

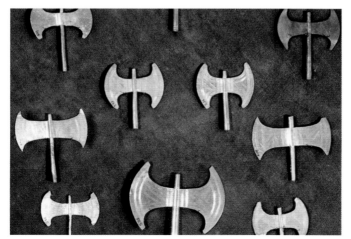

RIGHT The double ax is a symbol of Minoan culture. These miniatures, dated around 1500 BCE, are made of gold and were found in the cave of Arkalochori.

ABOVE This map of Crete, showing the seaport of Herakleion, was drawn by Frederick de Wit around 1680.

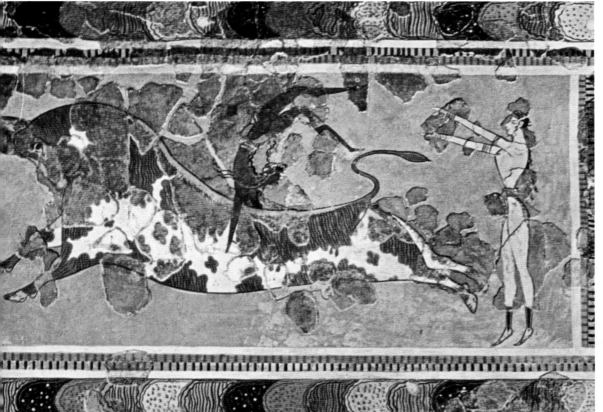

LEFT The Toreador fresco from Knossos Palace, Crete, shows athletic young people engaged in the dangerous sport of bull-vaulting.

Dawn of the Subcontinent

The Indus-Saraswati civilization is unique in the ancient world for being the first major urban civilization with architectural town planning, and a drainage system.

The rediscovery in 1921–22 of two major urban archeological sites, at Harappa on the banks of the Ravi River in Punjab and Mohenjo Daro on the lower Indus in Sind, put it beyond doubt that India is one of four major riverine civilizations of the ancient world, the others being Egypt, Mesopotamia, and China. A lull in digging activity lasting approximately a quarter century followed the first excavations of these sites, but the archeological departments of India and Pakistan have in more recent years uncovered some 1,500 settlements along the Indus and Saraswati river valleys. Most—about 1,000—are on the old Saraswati River, in the Hakra-Ghaggar river region, straddling India and Pakistan.

> An ancestor of the game of chess has been unearthed at Lothal. Children too were not forgotten, judging from the exquisite care with which toys were fashioned.
>
> –Michel Danino, in a lecture on the Indus-Saraswati civilization, 1999.

Exploding Theories

The finds made since 1947 also demonstrate the vastness of the Indus–Saraswati civilization. The stark similarities in the artifacts in a region covering over 1.5 million square miles (3.9 million km²) makes the Indus–Saraswati civilization more extensive than any of the other three riverine civilizations.

The presence of domesticated wheat and barley, cattle, sheep, and goats in Mehergarh, according to Jean-Francois Jarrige, Director of the French Excavation Project from 1974 to 1986, indicates not only that the agricultural/neolithic stage may have started there as early as c. 8000 BCE, but also explodes the previous theory that these grains and animals had spread from Mesopotamia into the Indus Valley. Archeologists affirm that the high point of the Harappan/Mohenjo Daro urbanization extended from c. 2600 BCE–1900 BCE and that the decline and disintegration of the Indus–Saraswati civilization must have taken place in the period c. 1900 BCE–1300 BCE.

LEFT Head of dignitary in limestone, excavated from Mohenjo Daro. The artwork discovered there and at other sites has generally been small, which leads archeologists to conclude that it was mostly for personal possession.

Harappa—a Model of Urban Civilization

Most of the cities excavated so far have been on the Harappan pattern, with a Citadel and a Lower Town, including a granary. The streets, forming a grid pattern along east–west and north–south corridors, are a unique feature among the ancient riverine civilizations, but the most notable feature of town planning, also unique for ancient times, was an underground drainage system, with "soakage jars" placed outside each structure. Houses usually opened on the sides, not onto the streets, thereby keeping out the traffic dust. Most houses also had a courtyard in the center which acted like an atrium, admitting fresh air and light.

The Indus–Saraswati civilization did not have palaces or the very large residences we generally associate with powerful kings of large kingdoms. The absence of weaponry suggests a lack of warfare and efforts to create large political entities under a single ruler. Though the dwellings were of different sizes, suggesting social stratification, there were also such common facilities as the Great Bath, which, in Harappa, measured 30 feet (9 m) long, 23 feet (7 m) wide, and 8 feet (2.5 m) deep. It had verandahs backed by galleries and rooms on all sides with a flight of steps leading to the bath.

The people in this extensive civilization were multi-ethnic and multi-linguistic, but used a single

4300-3200 BCE
Calcolithic cultures develop

3500-2700 BCE
Early Harappan civilization begins

2700-1900 BCE Middle Harappan civilizations continue to develop

1900-1500 BCE Late Harappan (Lothal, Bet Dwarka) civilizations

ABOVE This board game suggests that in the Indus-Saraswati civilization, fun and games were legitimate parts of everyday life.

LEFT Overlooking Mohenjo Daro, the Citadel included an elaborate bath, a giant granary, a large residence, and at least two aisled assembly halls.

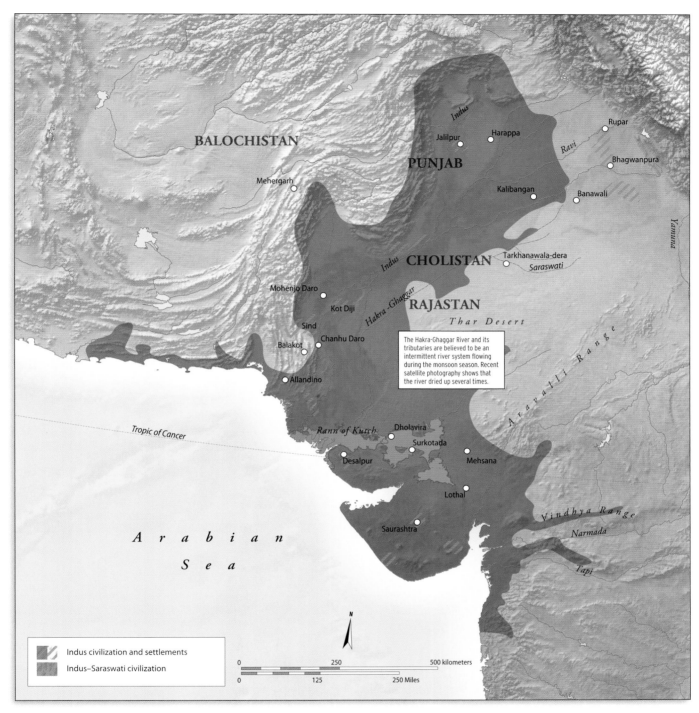

BALOCHISTAN

PUNJAB

Indus

Jalilpur

Harappa

Rupar

Ravi

Bhagwanpura

Mehergarh

Kalibangan

Banawali

Yamuna

CHOLISTAN

Tarkhanawala-dera

Saraswati

Indus

RAJASTAN

Mohenjo Daro

Hakra-Ghaggar

Thar Desert

Kot Diji

The Hakra-Ghaggar River and its
tributaries are believed to be an
intermittent river system flowing
during the monsoon season. Recent
satellite photography shows that
the river dried up several times.

Aravalli Range

Sind

Chanhu Daro

Balakot

Allandino

Tropic of Cancer

Rann of Kutch

Dholavira

Surkotada

Desalpur

Mehsana

Vindhya Range

Lothal

Narmada

Saurashtra

Tapi

A r a b i a n
S e a

N

Indus civilization and settlements

Indus–Saraswati civilization

| 0 | 250 | 500 kilometers |
| 0 | 125 | 250 Miles |

script. They engaged in extensive
domestic and international trade,
using a common system of weights
and measures—a binary system for
the lower denominations of weight,
a decimal system for larger weights,
and a standard measure for linear
measurements. Despite much effort,
their script remains undeciphered,
so one can only base conjecture as
to their religion on artifacts. Seals
have been found showing Shiva,

one of the trinity of Hindu gods,
seated like a Yogi in a meditative
posture, as well as terracotta figurines depicting a Mother Goddess,
which some scholars identify as
Shiva's consort, Parvati. A large
number of figurines in limestone,
steatite, alabaster, and bronze show
dancing girls, animals of different
kinds including fantasy creatures
(one of which resembles a unicorn),
toys, chariots, and carts.

There is currently no way of
knowing how the Indus–Saraswati
civilization began to decline or why
it disappeared, but there is general
agreement that it was not due to
external aggression. A more likely
cause is a major natural disaster or
series of disasters such as flooding,
earthquake, or tsunamis. When the
Saraswati changed its course eastward to Ganga and Yamuna, the
old bed dried up completely.

ABOVE It seems likely
that when the Saraswati
River, which was in full
flow between c. 3000 BCE
and c. 1500 BCE, began to
flow eastward to join the
Yamuna, and its old bed
began to dry up, surviving
inhabitants of the region
moved to the vast fertile
plains of the Yamuna and
the Ganga, further east.

Between the Rivers

Some of the most important developments in the history of humanity took place in southern Mesopotamia from c. 5000 BCE to 2300 BCE. These developments include the earliest examples of urban civilization, states, sophisticated irrigation techniques, and writing, which were all to have a profound effect on the history of the human race.

The term Mesopotamia, which means "between the rivers," derives from the ancient Greek language and refers to the area between the Euphrates and Tigris Rivers in modern Iraq. Of particular importance was the region which became known as Sumer in southern Mesopotamia in the vicinity of the Persian Gulf. The earliest evidence for permanent agricultural settlement in southern Mesopotamia has been found at the ancient site of Eridu dating to around 5000 BCE.

The Fertile Crescent

Over the next millennium, a considerable increase in population in southern Mesopotamia was the primary catalyst for the emergence of technological innovation, cities, and writing. Scholars believe that part of the population from the area known as the Fertile Crescent stretching across northern Syria, southern Turkey, northern Iraq, and into Iran, which relied more on cereal farming and domesticating animals, moved to southern Mesopotamia as a result of drier conditions across the whole of the Near East and Mesopotamia. While the Fertile Crescent became less productive, the drier regional conditions made agricultural practices in the delta of the Euphrates and Tigris Rivers more effective than they had been before due to decreased seasonal flooding.

Cities and Towns

Evidence suggests that over the next 1,000 to 1,500 years human populations in southern Mesopotamia became denser due to intensified agriculture and migration. As population density increased, settlements in the form of cities grew. Their population density resulted in strengthened political and social hierarchies and the need to establish clearer ownership of resources—probably the catalyst for the invention of writing.

5000 BCE Evidence of early human culture

c. 4400 BCE Pottery is evident during the Halaf period; also some evidence of metal

c. 3900 BCE Southern Mesopotamia culture with temples and early architecture

c. 3400 BCE Gawra and Ninevite periods

RIGHT The Fertile Crescent played a crucial role in human history. Today, however, this once rich and important farming land is mostly desert.

LEFT Dating from the second millennium BCE, this fresco piece comes from the Mesopotamian city of Mari. Archeological evidence shows that Mari was an influential artistic and ceremonial urban center in ancient times.

BELOW This fragment of a stele (stone marker) found in the Akkad region of Mesopotamia, dates to the third millennium BCE.

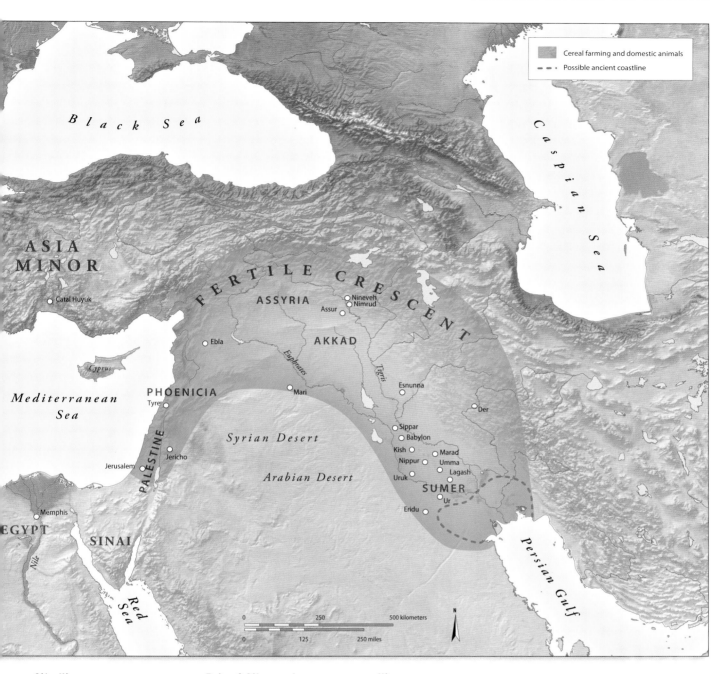

City Kings

At this time, Sumer was ruled as a state comprised of the various cities led by their individual kings. It appears that one city at a time held the seat of the kingship of the land of Sumer and that this power was challenged on occasion by the other cities. It is interesting to note that some cities outside the southern alluvial plain of Mesopotamia also exercised such power at times. The most interesting of these is Mari, which is located a considerable distance to the north on the Middle Euphrates.

Epic of Gilgamesh

The most famous struggle for power in the Early Dynastic period is recorded in the legendary poem, the *Epic of Gilgamesh*. The city of Kish had received the kingship, or supremacy, over the other cities of Sumer after a great flood that occurred c. 3000 BCE, and this may form the basis of the Biblical flood story. It did not take long for the city of Erech (Uruk), located well to the south of Kish, to threaten Kish's power. The *Epic of Gilgamesh* tells the story of two assemblies which met at Erech at this time.

Nippur

In the Early Dynastic 1 period (3000–2750 BCE), we also see the emergence of Nippur as an important city in terms of its religious significance; this was linked to the city's role in conferring political legitimacy on whichever king became the leading king of "The Land" of Sumer. Nippur's rise to prominence was most likely associated with its location in the central plain, and the city appears to have become an important factor in the collaboration of the cities of the alluvial plain.

> Supreme over other kings, lordly in appearance, he is the hero, born of Uruk, the goring wild bull.
>
> –from *Epic of Gilgamesh*, Tablet I.

Colonization of the Pacific

Now commonly referred to as Oceania, the lower western area of the Pacific Ocean consists of Australia, New Zealand, and Polynesia. The early inhabitants of these lands are some of the oldest populations on Earth.

Certain areas in Polynesia and New Zealand have migration histories about which we know little. What we do know is primarily based on archeological and spoken evidence. Though much early colonization of the Pacific was possible by means of land migration, there was also a great deal of travel by sea.

Australia

Australia's first human inhabitants are thought to have arrived around 60,000 years ago. Aboriginal settlement in Arnhem Land in the north is placed at this time, with estimates for the southern regions extending over the next 20,000 years.

By 20,000 years ago there were people living all over the continent. Around 6,000 years ago, although Aboriginal settlements were still situated largely on the coast, the central areas were becoming more important as a source of natural resources. However, populations on small islands failed to survive and they became uninhabited. The last 5,000 years were characterized

by the development of a sophisticated tribal culture. Aboriginal people lived off the land, and had intricate relationships to their environment. They made tools out of wood and stone, in what is now known as the Australian Small Tool Tradition. They held ceremonies and had a highly organized social system, though there were significant regional differences in culture.

Polynesia

Polynesia could be described as a triangle with its corners at New Zealand, Easter Island, and Hawaii. The other main island groups within it are Tonga, Samoa, and the island chains that form the Cook Islands and French Polynesia.

Polynesia's first settlements occurred around 3,200 years ago, by traders carrying Lapita pottery, including its characteristic highly colored earthenware pots. A new and distinct Polynesian culture emerged from geographic isolation in the Pacific Ocean, with early Polynesian people demonstrating

> We are all visitors to this time, this place. We are just passing through. Our purpose here is to observe, to learn, to grow, to love...and then we return home.
>
> –Australian Aboriginal proverb.

incredible similarities in ethnicity, language, and culture. From around 300 BCE, they began spreading from Fiji, Samoa, and Tonga as far as the Marquesas, Tahiti, and the Cook Islands. The Marquesas islands served as a key site, between about 400 BCE and 800 CE, from which settlers could distribute flora and fauna, tools, and ornaments, to islands in the "Polynesian triangle." Voyaging was done in canoes built with tools of stone, bone, and coral.

Easter Island, located more than 1,000 miles (1,600 km) from the nearest island, was first settled around 400 CE. Its inhabitants were the only Polynesians to develop a

ABOVE Bark painting by Lipunja from Milingibi, Australia. Bark painting by Aboriginal people is a long tradition, extending back thousands of years.

form of writing. They were also highly skilled in stone carving, as can be seen in the monumental stone statues, or *moai*, that still stand on the island.

New Zealand

Though the exact date of Polynesian settlement of New Zealand remains unknown, both archeological and linguistic evidence suggests that several waves of migration came from Eastern Polynesia to New Zealand between 800 and 1300 CE.

Settlement of New Zealand came very late in comparison to other regional areas. The pattern of site expansion indicates a large group of settlers, with the first Polynesians settling mainly around the coast—especially the east coast of the North Island, which was more hospitable and temperate in climate. Due to the differences in climate, flora and fauna in New Zealand, the settlers were forced to adapt their traditional Polynesian hunting methods and implements.

These Polynesian settlers became the original Indigenous Maori. Maori oral history describes the arrival of their ancestors from Hawaiki—a mythical homeland in tropical Polynesia—in large canoes, in what Maori tradition refers to as the "Great Fleet."

LEFT Linguistic and other clues suggest that Indonesia and Malaysia are the most likely origins of the Polynesian people.

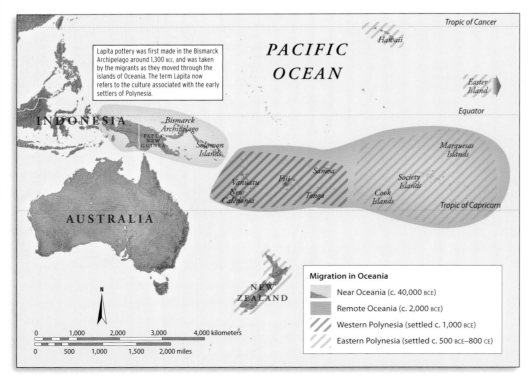

Lapita pottery was first made in the Bismarck Archipelago around 1,300 BCE, and was taken by the migrants as they moved through the islands of Oceania. The term Lapita now refers to the culture associated with the early settlers of Polynesia.

PACIFIC OCEAN

Tropic of Cancer

Hawaii

Easter Island

Equator

INDONESIA

Bismarck Archipelago

PAPUA NEW GUINEA

Solomon Islands

Marquesas Islands

Vanuatu New Caledonia

Fiji

Samoa

Society Islands

Tonga

Cook Islands

Tropic of Capricorn

AUSTRALIA

N

NEW ZEALAND

0   1,000   2,000   3,000   4,000 kilometers
0   500   1,000   1,500   2,000 miles

Migration in Oceania

Near Oceania (c. 40,000 BCE)

Remote Oceania (c. 2,000 BCE)

Western Polynesia (settled c. 1,000 BCE)

Eastern Polynesia (settled c. 500 BCE–800 CE)

GOBI DESERT

Sea of Japan
(East Sea)

JAPAN

East
China
Sea

ASIA

CHINA

Tropic of Cancer

South
China
Sea

PACIFIC
OCEAN

Sulu
Sea

Probable migration route to Australia
● Aboriginal shelters
● Fossils
● Aboriginal paintings
● Aboriginal stone tools
● Aboriginal middens

Up until about 10,000 years ago the sea level
was lower and the landmass of Southeast
Asia (known as Sunda) and the landmass of
Australia and New Guinea (known as Sahul)
were separated by a narrow channel. From
about 60,000 years ago people from the
north began crossing over to Sahul.

Borneo

SUNDA

Banda
Sea

New Guinea

Equator

Java

Arafura Sea

Cape
York

Coral
Sea

Timor
Sea

Arnhem
Land

Malakunanja
(Rock shelter—c. 30,000 BCE)

c. 60,000 BCE
Aborigines settle in
Australia

INDIAN
OCEAN

Kimberley
Plateau

Miriwun
(Midden—c. 16,000 BCE)

Nauwalabila
(Rock shelter—c. 30,000 BCE)

c. 32,000 BCE Cremated
skeleton of "Mungo Man"
left at Lake Mungo, New
South Wales, Australia

Dampier Archipelago
(Petroglyphs—at least 17,000 years old)

Great Sandy
Desert

SAHUL

Great Dividing Range

Great Barrier Reef

Pilbara

Tropic of Capricon

Gibson Desert

Kenniff Cave
(Adzes and bifacial points
collection—c. 17,000 BCE)

c. 400 BCE Polynesian
travelers arrive in the
Marquesas

Ashburton

Murchison

AUSTRALIA

Uluru

Shark Bay

Mandu Mandu Creek
(Shelter—c. 35,000 BCE)

Puntutjarpa
(Shelter—c. 10,000 BCE)

Cuddie Springs
(Megafauna fossils—c. 30,000 BCE)

c. 300 CE First
Polynesian people arrive
in Hawaii from the
Marquesas

Great Victoria Desert

Koonalda Cave
(c. 20,000 BCE—paintings)

Lake Mungo
(Human fossils—c. 32,000 BCE)

Darling

c. 1000–1500 CE Stone
statues on Easter Island
are carved out of vol-
canic rock

Nullabor
Plain

ABOVE It is possible that
early migration occurred
across land bridges at a
time when sea levels were
lower, and New Guinea,
Australia, and Tasmania
formed a single landmass.
But the first settlers were
probably also among the
earliest known seafarers.
By around 6,000 years
ago, the seas had risen
to their present levels.

Devil's Lair
(Megafauna fossils—c. 41,000 BCE)

Great
Australian
Bight

N

Murray

Kow Swamp
(Burial site—c. 13,000 BCE)

Tasman
Sea

c. 800 CE The Great
Migration—the first
Polynesian peoples land
in New Zealand

| 0 | 500 | 1,000 | 1,500 | 2,000 kilometers |

| 0 | 250 | 500 | 750 | 1,000 miles |

The Assyrian Empire

The emergence of Assyria as a regional power early in the second millennium BCE was closely linked to its centrality to trade between Iran, southern Mesopotamia, Anatolia, and the Levant.

RIGHT Two Assyrian dignitaries are portrayed on this rich fresco in Til Barsip (Tell Ahmar), Syria.

FAR RIGHT During its rather short existence, the Assyrian Empire stretched from a small homeland to encompass a vast area of the known world.

4750 BCE The first temple of Ashur is built, marking the beginning of the Assyrian calendar

1307 BCE Adad-Nirari I establishes the first Assyrian Empire

935 BCE Ashur-Dan II establishes the Assyrian Empire from Egypt to the Caspian Sea, under one rule

609 BCE The Assyrian Empire collapses after a successful attack by Medes, Scythians, and Babylonian tribes

The wealth generated from trade soon led to imperial ambitions and by 1800 BCE, under King Shamshi-Adad I (r. 1808–1776 BCE), the Assyrians controlled territory from western Iran to the Mediterranean coast. This was a very short-lived empire as the Babylonians to the south succeeded in subjugating Assyria by 1750 BCE.

Independence
For the next 400 years, the region of Mesopotamia was the scene of invasions from the north and internal struggles for control that saw Assyria ruled by various kings and powers. In the fourteenth and thirteenth centuries BCE, a series of Assyrian kings succeeded in establishing Assyrian independence.

RIGHT This gypsum relief shows men with bows and arrows hunting birds. It is from the late Assyrian period and was found in the Palace of Sargon II, in northern Iraq.

> Tell me your friends, and I'll tell you who you are.
> —Assyrian proverb

Assurnasirpal II
From 970 to 883 BCE, Assyria was ruled by a series of monarchs who succeeded in maintaining the kingdom's position in northern Mesopotamia. It was during the reign of Assurnasirpal II (883–859 BCE), however, that Assyria once again established imperial dominance throughout northern Mesopotamia. Assurnasirpal undertook many military campaigns and conquered all of the territories surrounding Assyria.

Shalmaneser III
Under Assurnasirpal's successor, Shalmaneser III (858–824 BCE), military activity to secure the Assyrian kingdom continued over a broader area. In 853 BCE, Shalmaneser's forces met an army of 46,000 men at Qarqar, formed from a confederation of southern Syrian principalities. They drove back the Assyrians but success was shortlived, as by 841 BCE the confederation had fallen apart.

Assyrian homeland

Empire of Sargon (c. 705 BCE)

Empire of Assurbanipal (c. 627 BCE)

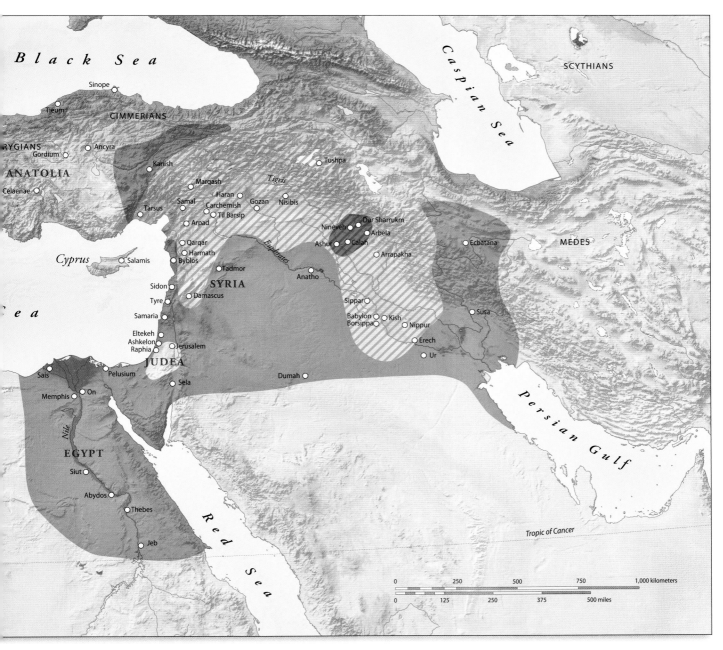

Internal Division

Over the following eight years Assyria suffered internal division that brought about a period of relative decline. This began to change, however, when Tiglath-Pileser III (r. 744–727 BCE) took the throne in 744 BCE. He established a permanent standing army and the city of Nineveh on the Tigris, by now the seat of imperial authority in the Assyrian kingdom, became the mustering point for many imperial campaigns.

Having lost control of Syria and Anatolia during the previous 50 years, the Assyrians now retook control of these areas and also turned their attention to Babylonia. In 729 BCE, Tiglath-Pileser captured the city of Babylon and was crowned Lord of Asia.

The successors of Tiglath-Pileser continued in his footsteps with Sargon II (r. 721–705 BCE) capturing Carchemish on the Euphrates from the Hittites and subduing territory in Media. His son Sennacherib (r. 704–681 BCE) experienced considerable problems with ongoing revolts in Babylon that saw him eventually raze the city in 691 BCE. Under his son, Esarhaddon (r. 680–669 BCE),

Babylon was restored and during 670 BCE a remarkable invasion of Egypt was undertaken. The invasion was successful but the empire of Egypt would prove too difficult for the Assyrians to retain for any length of time.

Decline

The spectacular rise of the Assyrian kingdom was eclipsed only by its dramatic decline. A civil war between the sons of Essarhaddon's successor, Assurbanipal (r. 668–627 BCE), made the kingdom vulnerable to attack from all sides. Syria was lost in 626 BCE and over

the following decade the Medes captured Assyrian territory in Iran before capturing important parts of the Assyrian kingdom itself. Assur was captured in 614 BCE and Nineveh fell two years later. An Assyrian general commanding western armies based at Harran in southern Turkey crowned himself king as Assur-Uballit II (r. 611–609 BCE) in an attempt to consolidate the last vestiges of Assyrian military power. This was short-lived and in 609 BCE an allied force of Babylonians and Medes captured Harran, formally putting an end to the Assyrian Empire.

Mediterranean Traders

The Phoenicians are famed as merchants and seafarers, operating throughout the Mediterranean from as early as the twelfth century BCE. Their trading activity had a significant impact on the development of Mediterranean culture in the first millennium BCE and they were increasingly drawn into military conflicts during this period.

10,000 BCE to 600 CE

The area of Phoenicia comprised part of the northern coastline of modern Syria, modern Lebanon, and parts of northern Israel. The cities which would emerge as the most important were all trading ports and included Tyre, Sidon, Byblos, and Beirut. There is evidence that all of these cities were emerging as important trading ports from c. 1100 BCE, with Sidon taking a leading role throughout the eastern Mediterranean.

BELOW A traditional Phoenician trading ship is shown arriving at Alexandria in Egypt in this nineteenth-century watercolor by Albert Sebille.

Tyre

The city of Tyre emerged as the most important Phoenician city politically in the tenth century BCE. The Tyrian king, Hiram I (r. 970–936 BCE), established formal diplomatic ties with King Solomon of Jerusalem (969–930 BCE) that were associated partly with the provision of cedar for Solomon's construction of the temple in Jerusalem. By 850 BCE Tyre and Sidon came to an arrangement to form a joint kingdom ruled by Ethbaal's successor, Ittobaal, who was called the king of the Tyrians and the Sidonians. This appears to have taken place due to the arrival of the Assyrian armies under Assurnasirpal in 866 BCE.

Trading Colonies

The ongoing invasions of Syria, including Phoenicia, by Assyrians in the ninth and eighth centuries BCE were important catalysts for

RIGHT The Phoenicians controlled most of the territory along the eastern coast of the Mediterranean in modern Jordan, Israel, Lebanon, and Syria.

FAR RIGHT This beautiful fragment of a female bust was carved by Phoenicians around the sixth century BCE.

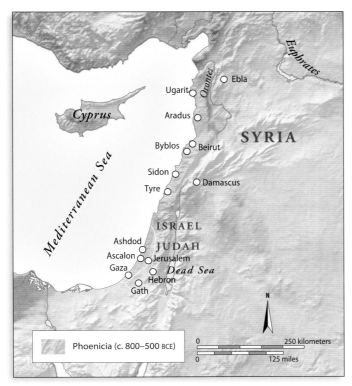

2750 BCE Tyre is established as a major settlement

c. 1500 BCE The Phoenicians settle Cyprus

1200 BCE Tyre becomes the chief Phoenician city. The Trojan wars begin.

c. 970 BCE King of Tyre, Hiram, builds the Temple of Solomon

c. 860 BCE Princess of Tyre, Jezebel, marries Ahab, King of Israel

c. 854 BCE The Phoenicians are defeated by the Assyrians

c. 814 BCE Carthage is founded

The son of a woman of the daughters of Dan, and his father [was] a man of Tyre, skilful to work in gold, and in silver, in brass, in iron, in stone, and in timber, in purple, in blue, and in fine linen...

–quote from the Bible describing the fine artisans of Phoenicia.

the Phoenicians establishing new trading colonies throughout the Mediterranean. In the ninth century BCE, when Assurnasirpal II and Shalmaneser III invaded, the cities of Byblos, Tyre, and Sidon were able to avoid political conflict by paying tribute to the Assyrian kings. Increasingly, the Phoenician trading cities, especially Tyre, looked to found colonies in other parts of the Mediterranean as a result of instability due to the Assyrian presence. The best known of these was the legendary founding of Carthage in North Africa in c. 814 BCE by Tyrian refugees.

The Phoenician cities were increasingly affected by the Assyrian presence, especially when the Assyrians formally organized territory in Syria in the eighth and seventh centuries BCE. Despite the political and military conflict which would take place from this time, Phoenician trading activity continued to prosper.

The city of Tyre played a leading role in resisting the Assyrians because Tyre was still an island at that stage.

By 701 BCE, the Assyrians had taken control of all of the Phoenician cities except Tyre, when the Tyrian king, Luli, escaped to Cyprus, signaling the capitulation of Tyre to the Assyrians. The city of Sidon

emerged as the more important Phoenician city early in the seventh century BCE but it was razed by the Assyrians in 675 BCE when its king revolted against Assyrian authority.

Decline

The Neo-Babylonian king, Nebuchadnezzar II, placed Tyre under a 13-year siege between 585 and 572 BCE which was eventually lifted when the Tyrian king recognized Babylonian authority.

Alexander the Great began campaigns along the Phoenician coastline in 332 BCE as part of his war of vengeance against the Achaemenid Persians. The Phoenician cities mostly capitulated, except Tyre, which held out for seven months while Alexander's forces constructed a land bridge to the island that still exists.

RIGHT The siege of Tyre, as depicted in a tenth-century CE miniature. Although the Tyrians defended their island city with great ingenuity, Alexander the Great eventually prevailed.

Swifter, Higher, Stronger

The Olympic Games in ancient times (776 BCE–394 CE) were fundamentally religious in character, for it was believed that the athletes were inspired by Zeus, the ruler of the Greek pantheon.

ABOVE Pelops and his wife Hippodameia are depicted in this Roman marble relief. Legend says that many of Hippodameia's previous suitors were killed by her father.

c. 2000 BCE The first palaces are built on Crete

776 BCE Hippias of Elis (c. 460 BCE- 399 BCE) calculates from inscriptions recording Olympic victories that the first Olympic Games must have been held in 776 BCE. Coroebus of Elis wins the first stade (sprint) race

752 BCE A wreath from the sacred olive tree is awarded for the first time to an Olympic victor

720 BCE At the 15th Olympiad a new event, the Dolichos—long race—is introduced. Acanthus of Sparta is the first winner, and Orsippus probably ran in the nude for the first time

594 BCE Athens starts a special training program designed to stop the dominance of Spartan athletes at Olympia

490 BCE Athens defeats a Persian army at the Battle of Marathon

472 BCE The Olympic Games are extended to five days' duration

336–323 BCE Alexander the Great reigns as King of Macedon. A palm branch is introduced as the immediate symbol of victory at the Olympic Games

Athletic competition, therefore, honored the god by acknowledging and reflecting his great power. The games were held every four years at Olympia in western Greece; more precisely, they were held in a sacred wooded area known as the Altis. Athletes journeyed there from all corners of the Greek world, and it was understood generally that conflicts between Greeks had to cease for the duration of the games. This was a dramatic requirement, since citizens of the Greek cities tended to think of war as a natural feature of life, but it is a clear indication that all Greeks thought it was the right thing to do to honor the god with regular games. It would have been very dangerous to offend him by interfering with athletes who were traveling to his sacred games.

Winner Takes All

Religious considerations aside, athletes and spectators had other reasons for traveling to Olympia every four years. The individual athletes, for instance, sought glory

O my soul, shall we sing of crowns and contests? Then know this—The sun warms more than any lesser star, and no festival outshines Olympia.
– from Pindar's *Olympian Ode* 1.

for themselves and lucrative rewards from their proud cities. Athenian victors could receive meals at public expense for the rest of their lives. Diplomats used the occasion of the games to negotiate with rival cities; merchants took the opportunity to display their wares and seek new trading opportunities; cultural activities of various kinds took place, including musical recitals, plays, and readings of poetry and history. This was a gathering of the whole Greek world in microcosm and it is no wonder that marginal communities in Italy and Sicily who wanted to be recognized as part of the Greek world sought admission to the games at Olympia.

Origins and Myths

Lists of victors in the games date from 776 BCE, and there is a tradition that credits Herakles as the founder. The most famous origin myth, however, is undoubtedly that involving the hero Pelops and the evil king Oinomaus. A number of versions have survived, but the central elements are consistent: Pelops, a grandson of Zeus, wanted to marry Hippodameia, the beautiful daughter of the king; the arrogant Oinomaus challenged Pelops to a chariot race, with his daughter as the prize; Pelops won the race, during which Oinomaus was thrown from his chariot and killed—an example of the justice of Zeus.

The Olympic Oath

Although this story is woven around the anticipation, excitement, and danger of a chariot race, it seems that a foot race was the original event at Olympia. This race took place down the length of the stadium, a distance of roughly 220 yards (200 m). In later times the games were conducted over five days and a variety of other events were added. These included boxing, wrestling, jumping, javelin- and discus-throwing, and races for single horses and chariots. The running races were conducted over distances quite similar to those of modern track meets. In ceremonial terms, the high points were the athletes' oath, the judges' oath, and the sacrifice to Zeus of 100 oxen;

LEFT Athens held the first modern Olympic Games in 1896. The games have been held every four years since then, except during the First and Second World Wars.

RIGHT These ruins of the Palaestra at Olympia date to around the third millennium BCE. The central courtyard, with its sand floor, would have been used for wrestling or boxing matches.

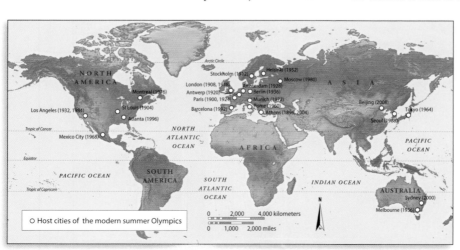

O Host cities of the modern summer Olympics

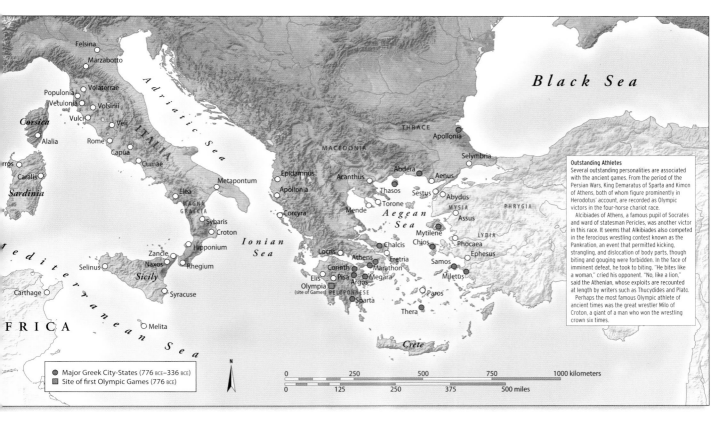

Outstanding Athletes

Several outstanding personalities are associated with the ancient games. From the period of the Persian Wars, King Demaratus of Sparta and Kimon of Athens, both of whom figure prominently in Herodotus's account, are recorded as Olympic victors in the four-horse chariot race.

Alcibiades of Athens, a famous pupil of Socrates and ward of statesman Pericles, was another victor in this race. It seems that Alkibiades also competed in the ferocious wrestling contest known as the Pankration, an event that permitted kicking, strangling, and dislocation of body parts, though biting and gouging were forbidden. In the face of imminent defeat, he took to biting. "He bites like a woman," cried his opponent. "No, like a lion," said the Athenian, whose exploits are recounted at length by writers such as Thucydides and Plato.

Perhaps the most famous Olympic athlete of ancient times was the great wrestler Milo of Croton, a giant of a man who won the wrestling crown six times.

- Major Greek City-States (776 BCE–336 BCE)
- Site of first Olympic Games (776 BCE)

the meat from these animals was used in a great feast that was held at the conclusion of the games.

The Laurel Wreath

Spartans appear to have dominated the victors' lists before the sixth century BCE. Their prize was not a medal but a crown of wild olive—the tree which Herakles had supposedly brought to the region from the River Istros (Danube). Only the victors were honored, there were no team sports, only males were permitted to compete, and women of the general public were not permitted within the Altis for the duration of the games. No records were kept of winning measurements or times; it only mattered that you won on the day. The marathon race, a prominent part of the modern games, did not feature in ancient times. This race represents, in fact, a modern attempt to commemorate the extraordinary courage exhibited by the Athenian runner Pheidippides, who ran multiple times between Athens and Sparta—a distance of roughly 150 miles (240 km)—carrying messages about the Persian landing at the town of Marathon in 490 BCE.

ABOVE By the time the first Olympic Games were held in 776 BCE, Greece had colonized the Mediterranean and Black Sea region to establish a great empire.

BELOW This plan of the ancient Olympic Games site shows its growth from archaic times to the period of Roman rule.

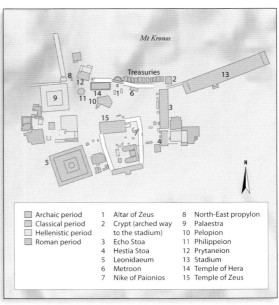

Archaic period	1 Altar of Zeus	8 North-East propylon
Classical period	2 Crypt (arched way to the stadium)	9 Palaestra
Hellenistic period		10 Pelopion
Roman period	3 Echo Stoa	11 Philippeion
	4 Hestia Stoa	12 Prytaneion
	5 Leonidaeum	13 Stadium
	6 Metroon	14 Temple of Hera
	7 Nike of Paionios	15 Temple of Zeus

Neo-Babylonian Empire –In the Lion's Den

The empire established in 616 BCE in Babylon in rebellion against Assyrian rule is referred to in modern scholarship as the Neo-Babylonian Empire.

The Assyrian Empire had emerged in the middle of the eighth century BCE, and by the middle of the seventh century BCE it was in control of southern Mesopotamia, Iran, the Near East, and Egypt. This control broke down quickly in the second half of the seventh century BCE. The emergence of the Neo-Babylonian Empire was a major contributor to the collapse.

Nebuchadnezzar II

Nebuchadnezzar II, the most important of the Neo-Babylonian rulers, came to power in 605 BCE. Nebuchadnezzar was the son of Nabopolasser, and instrumental in the Babylonian campaigns in Syria against the Egyptians. In the battle of Carchemish (modern Jerablus) in northern Syria in 605 BCE, the forces of Nabopolasser inflicted a major defeat on the Egyptians. Nabopolasser died soon after the battle and Nebuchadnezzar returned to Babylon where he formally took the throne.

Old Testament

Following an unsuccessful attack on Egypt itself in 601 BCE, Babylonian power in Syria was challenged in some regions, Judah in particular. In 597 BCE, Nebuchadnezzar removed the King of Judah, Jehoiakim, from power in Jerusalem and replaced him with a puppet ruler. This action was accompanied by deportations of very large numbers of Judeans to Babylon. Among those deported to Babylon during this period were the Old Testament figures Ezekiel and Daniel.

The Bible story of Daniel in the lion's den is set in Babylon. Other important stories from the Old Testament emerge from the Judean captivity in Babylon indicating the madness of Nebuchadnezzaar, inflicted on him by the Jewish God as punishment for mistreating the Jews, and telling of the escape of Shadrach, Meshach, and Abednego unscathed from the fiery furnace, protected by an angel.

Siege of Tyre

The rebellion of Judah against Babylonian rule and the ensuing suffering of its population, especially that of Jerusalem, is better known than other events during this period due to the survival of the Old Testament stories. We know that other kingdoms in Syria rebelled against Babylonian rule during this time, most notably the Phoenician city of Tyre in modern Lebanon. Nebuchadnezzar's forces put Tyre under siege for 13 years (585–572 BCE) before the two sides finally reached a compromise in which Tyre agreed to recognize some aspects of Babylonian rule. By 567 BCE, however, Nebuchadnezzar appears to have tired of the ongoing conflict with Egypt and eventually agreed to a type of border in Syria with Egypt.

Hanging Gardens

While Nebuchadnezzar II is well known for the wars he conducted against Egypt and for attacks on Judah, he is also remembered for the transformation of the city of Babylon into one of the great cities of the ancient world. It was during his reign that the famous Hanging Gardens were constructed and the city was provided with a circuit wall said by some ancient writers to have been more than 45 miles (70 km) in length.

Teima

Nebuchadnezzar II died in 561 BCE and in the following six years there was considerable turmoil with three short-lived Babylonian kings. In 555 BCE, an obscure individual named Nabonidus, who was not a royal relative of Nebuchadnezzar, assumed the Babylonian throne.

Three years later he chose to abandon Babylon as the capital of the empire, moving the court to Teima, a rich oasis on the trade routes in the Arabian desert. This move was probably designed to establish the capital of the empire closer to Syria where problems with the Egyptians continued.

End of Empire

The most significant problem to confront Nabonidus, however, was the emergence of Cyrus in Persia in 559 BCE. In 553 BCE, Cyrus succeeded in taking control of Media and over the following decade his power continued to grow. In 539 BCE, Cyrus inflicted a major defeat on Babylonian forces at the confluence of the Tigris and Diyala rivers in northern Iraq before taking control of Babylon in October of the same year. The Neo-Babylonian empire was now effectively at an end and the rest of its territory quickly fell to the Persians.

...came Nebuchadnezzar king of Babylon unto Jerusalem, and besieged it.
–Bible, the Book of Daniel.

LEFT This seventeenth-century painting by Frans Francken shows the building of the Tower of Babel, an event from the Bible's Book of Genesis.

587 BCE Judah becomes a province of Babylonia

—

586 BCE Nebuchadnezzar II conquers Phoenicia

—

581 BCE Nebuchadnezzar II burns Jerusalem

—

539 BCE Cyrus conquers Babylonia, absorbing it into the Persian Empire

—

539 BCE Cyrus frees the captive Jews from Babylonia

ABOVE LEFT Detail of a bronze portal made around the twelfth century CE, depicting Nebuchadnezzar II on the throne.

LEFT Foundations are all that remain of the Hanging Gardens of Babylon, built by Nebuchadnezzar to please his wife. They are counted as one of the original Seven Wonders of the World.

RIGHT At its height, the Neo-Babylonian Empire stretched across much of the modern Middle East.

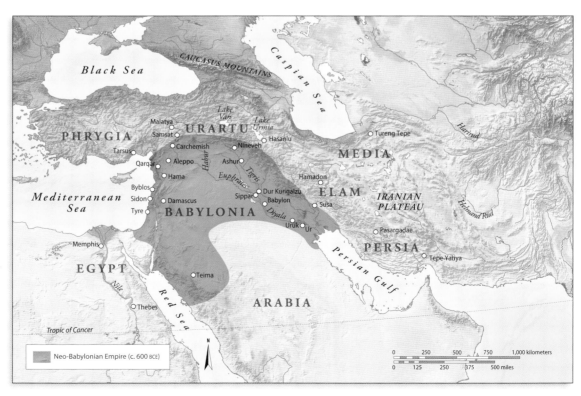

Neo-Babylonian Empire (c. 600 BCE)

Persian Empire

The rise to power in Iran of the Achaemenid Persians is obscure, as it took place quickly and few contemporaries could have foreseen how significant their rule would become.

ABOVE Darius I, Achaemenid King of Persia, sits on his throne in this bas-relief on the wall of the audience hall in the Achaemenid Citadel, Iran.

2000 BCE The game of chess–*shatranj*–develops in Persia

539 BCE Cyrus of Persia sacks Babylon and frees the Jews

521 BCE Darius becomes king of Persia and expands the empire west beyond the Indus River

331 BCE Alexander the Great conquers Persia

460 CE King Firuz of Persia persecutes Jews, who emigrate to Arabia

632 CE Abu Bakr declares war on the Roman and Persian (Sassanid) empires

650 CE Arabs conquer the whole of Persia

In 559 BCE, Cyrus succeeded as the dynastic ruler of Fars in the southwest of Iran and quickly set out to expand the influence of his kingdom. In 539 BCE, Cyrus marched against Babylonia in Mesopotamia, capturing the city of Babylon itself.

Expansion

Under Cyrus' successor Cambyses, who ruled for only a short period (529–522 BCE), Egypt was added to the Persian Empire. Conquered in 525 BCE, Egypt was ruled by Cambyses as its king, signaling the intent of the Persians to occupy Egypt in a more direct way than the Neo-Babylonians had. Indeed, Egypt became a Persian satrapy, just as most of the territory under Persian rule was divided into individual satrapies.

Darius I

Cambyses's long-reigning successor, Darius I (r. 521–486 BCE) conquered Libya in North Africa and succeeded in adding the western parts of India to the Persian Empire.

Thus, the Persian Empire now controlled a vast territory stretching from the southern coast of the Mediterranean, through Syria, the Near East, Mesopotamia, and Iran, to parts of Central Asia and even India. Darius's Persian Empire was by far the most significant empire to have emerged in southwest Asia by this time.

RIGHT
The Persian Empire spread through the succession and consequent invasions by its kings.

[Map showing the Persian Empire with locations including: Olbia, Black Sea, Sinop, THRACE, MACEDON, Byzantium, Granicus (334 BCE), GREECE, LYDIA, Sardis (546 BCE), Pteria (547 BCE), CAPPADOCIA, CILICIA, Issus (333 BCE), ARMENIA, Caspian Sea, Nisibis, Gaugamela (331 BCE), MEDIA, Nineveh, Hatra, PARTHIA, Hecatompylos, Salamis, ASSYRIA, Ctesiphon, Ecbatana, Sidon, Tyre, Damascus, Seleucia, Behistun, SAGART, Mediterranean Sea, Pelusium (525 BCE), Jerusalem, Memphis, BABYLONIA, Opis (539 BCE), Babylon, Susa, PERSIA, Spasinou Charax, Pasargadae (Cyrus the Great's capital, 550 BCE), Corma, LIBYA, Persepolis, PERSIS, EGYPT, ARABIA, Red Sea, Persian Gulf, Syene, MAKA]

Empire of Achaemenid (c. 559 BCE)
Territory added by Cyrus (529 BCE)
Territory added by Cambyses (525 BCE)
Territory added by Darius I (500 BCE)

0 250 500 750 1,000 kilometers
0 125 250 375 500 miles

Xerxes

Darius I died in 486 BCE and was succeeded by Xerxes, who reigned from 485 to 465 BCE and attempted an invasion of Greece in 479–478 BCE. Despite numerous attacks by both land and sea on Greek territory, Xerxes was not able to defeat the Greek forces and eventually withdrew after both his army and navy were defeated. This effectively marked the end of Achaemenid Persian attempts at expansion of their vast empire, as a series of internal power struggles after Xerxes' death made this more difficult.

Combined Forces

One of the difficulties confronted by Persian military commanders was the composition of the army. A whole range of peoples from the empire was represented in the army, contributing different skills, but making command difficult. There were skilled horsemen from Central Asia, slingers from Babylonia and considerable numbers of Greek mercenaries.

> Good poetry makes the universe reveal its secret.
> –Hafiz of Persia, poet.

Darius III

Most of our sources for events in the Persian empire in the fifth and fourth centuries BCE are Greek and, therefore, hostile to the Persian rulership. This should be remembered when dealing with the history of the Achaemenid Persians in the lead-up to their most difficult challenge—the war with Alexander the Great. The last Achaemenid ruler, Darius III, came to power in 336 BCE after the murder of both Artaxerxes III and Arses. Darius III, a distant relative of the Achaemenids, was distinguished in battle.

Decline

In May, 334 BCE, the Persian forces under Darius III met the invading army of Alexander the Great for the first time at the battle of the Granicus River, and were easily defeated. The two forces met again at Issus in Cilicia in November, 333 BCE. Darius was forced to flee for his life, which became the subject of the famous and beautiful Alexander mosaic found at Pompeii in the nineteenth century. After Alexander had taken control of all the Achaemenid possessions in Asia Minor, Syria, and Egypt, the Macedonian and Persian forces met for a third time in northern Iraq in 331 BCE.

Darius was again soundly defeated and fled to Iran where he was murdered by Bessus, the Satrap of Bactria, in summer, 330 BCE.

ABOVE LEFT A gryphon (winged lion) decorates a sixth-century BCE drinking horn from the Achaemenid period.

ABOVE *The Battle of Issus* by Jan Brueghel (1568-1625) records the Persian forces' defeat by Alexander the Great.

BELOW King Xerxes, son of Darius, at the foot of the Hellespont, the narrow passage between Turkey and Europe.

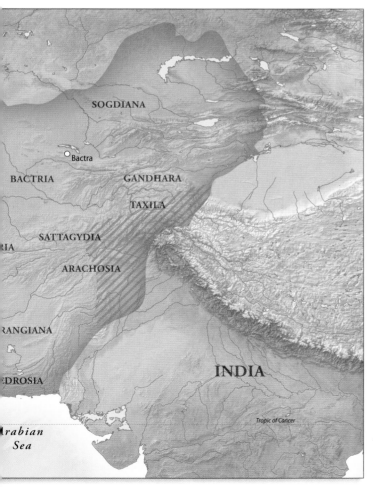

Empires of Ancient India

When Alexander invaded India (327-325 BCE), it was a land of mainly small kingdoms, principalities, and republics.

The invasion acted as a catalyst to political consolidation and the rise of the first Indian empire, that of the Mauryas. Though the Mauryan empire lasted only 136 years (321–185 BCE), its sway covering most of the sub-continent and Afghanistan created an example for future rulers. Mauryans were succeeded, though briefly, by the Sungas and the Kushanas. It was not until 320 CE that an empire sub-continental in scope rose under the Guptas (320–550 CE). Historians have rightly designated the period from 321 BCE to 550 CE as the Age of Empires.

Maurya (321-185 BCE)

One of the individuals shaken by the debacle at Alexander's hands in northwest India was Chanakya, or Kautilya, a most highly regarded scholar at Takshashila University (near Rawalpindi). Chanakya made Chandragupta, his best student, who was adept both in the military arts and diplomatic skills, the spearhead of a proposed confederacy against any foreign invader. After overthrowing the hated Nandas, Chandragupta made Magadha and its premier city, Pataliputra, the base of his political expansion. Toward the end of his life, Chandragupta became very spiritual and abdicated the throne in favor of his son, Bindusara (297–272 BCE). Chandragupta became a Jain monk and migrated to Sravanbelagola, a very sacred spot to the Jains.

Historians have showered Ashoka, Chandragupta's grandson, with praise as the ablest and noblest ruler of ancient India. Initially ruthless, Ashoka underwent a dramatic transformation in 260 BCE when at the battle of Kalinga (in Orissa), he witnessed a carnage of more than 100,000 deaths. Thereafter, he chose conciliation over conflict, forgiveness over revenge. Yet, he was not a pacifist—he maintained a very large force to ensure domestic peace and protection against external enemies. His empire extended from the Oxus in Afghanistan to North India, Deccan, and Konkan.

Mauryan Administration

The extensive Mauryan Empire had a combination of a centralized government co-existing with village autonomy. The courts at different levels collected fines and the officials in charge of trade and industry collected toll taxes and excise duties. All appeals for justice, from the village onward through the hierarchy of officials, lay with the king. As a paternalistic state, the Mauryan administration maintained homes for the aged, destitute widows, the handicapped, and orphans. There were programs for famine relief, refugees, and those affected by epidemics. At the local level, there were programs to help the peasants with seeds or cattle to tide over droughts or floods.

The Mauryan empire collapsed within 50 years of Ashoka's death, the last ruler overthrown by his commander-in-chief, Pushyamitra Sunga in 187 BCE. The Sungas ruled a much smaller territory, from the Indus to Magadha. After Pushyamitra's death, this was divided among Sunga feudatories.

Kushanas (165 BCE-c. 233 CE)

Meanwhile, northern India was wracked by invaders from the northwest, including the Kushanas, a branch of the Central Asian tribal Yueh-chi, who had settled in northeastern Iran.

Under their leader, Kujula Kadphises, they conquered northwest India in the first century CE. Kujula's grandson, Kanishka (78–101 CE), became the mightiest Kushana ruler with control over an extensive region, from Central Asia to Oudh in the east, and Kashmir. With their capital at Purushapura (modern Peshawar), the Kushanas

ABOVE This molded votive plaque of a mother and child was made of terracotta around the second century. It is from the Sunga Dynasty.

remained a power until the third century CE. The contribution made by the Kushanas to Buddhism was enormous.

Kanishka in particular was a great patron of the Buddhist faith, which under his rule spread to Central Asia and China through the Bamiyan Valley, as evidenced by the numerous Buddhist shrines in that valley.

Guptas (320-550 CE)

A political consolidation comparable to the Mauryan did not occur again until Chandra Gupta established the Gupta dynasty in 320 CE. This dynasty marked the Golden Age of ancient India. The period also saw the phenomenal extension of Indian culture to Southeast Asia. The greatest ruler of the dynasty was Samudra Gupta, whose empire stretched from the Punjab to Kamarupa and South India up to Kanchi. The successors of Chandra Gupta II (375–415 CE) were plagued from the middle of the fifth century CE by Hun invasions, which weakened the empire militarily, financially, and politically.

By the middle of the sixth century, the Gupta power was limited to Magadha and Bengal.

> The Indians all live frugally, especially when in camp. They dislike a great undisciplined multitude, and consequently they observe good order. Theft is of very rare occurrence.
>
> –Magesthenes (c 350-290 BCE), Greek traveler.

BELOW This maps shows the territories added to the Indian Empire during the Gupta dynasty.

HIMALAYA

Indus

Tropic of Cancer

Yamuna

Ganges

Brahmaputra

Narmada

DECCAN
PLATEAU

WESTERN GHATS

EASTERN GHATS

Godavari

Krishna

*Arabian
Sea*

*Bay
of Bengal*

N

- ▨ Empire of Chandra Gupta I
- ▤ Territory added by Samudra Gupta
- ▥ Territory added by Chandra Gupta II

0   500 kilometers

0   250 miles

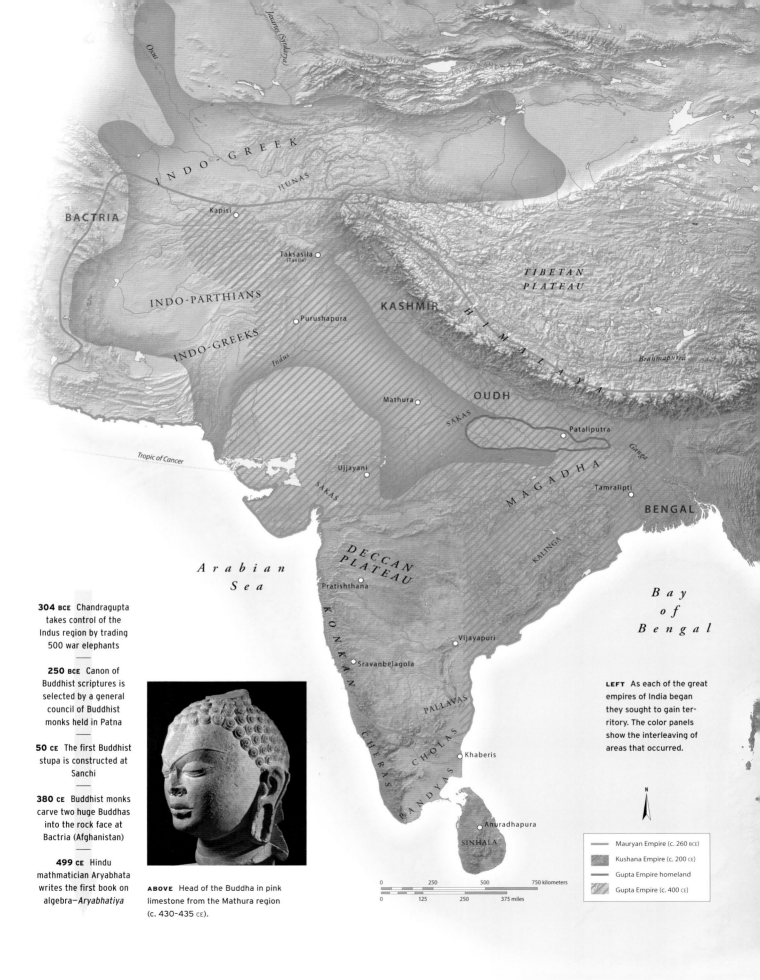

INDO-GREEK

BACTRIA

HUNAS

Kapisi

INDO-PARTHIANS

Taksasila
(Taxila)

INDO-GREEKS

Purushapura

Indus

KASHMIR

*TIBETAN
PLATEAU*

H
I
M
A
L
A
Y
A

Brahmaputra

Mathura

OUDH

SAKAS

Pataliputra

Ganga

MAGADHA

Tamralipti

BENGAL

Tropic of Cancer

Ujjayani

SAKAS

*Arabian
Sea*

DECCAN
PLATEAU

Pratishthana

K
O
N
K
A
N

KALINGA

*Bay
of
Bengal*

Vijayapuri

Sravanbelagola

PALLAVAS

C
H
E
R
A
S

C
H
O
L
A
S

Khaberis

P
A
N
D
Y
A
S

Anuradhapura

SINHALA

304 BCE Chandragupta
takes control of the
Indus region by trading
500 war elephants

250 BCE Canon of
Buddhist scriptures is
selected by a general
council of Buddhist
monks held in Patna

50 CE The first Buddhist
stupa is constructed at
Sanchi

380 CE Buddhist monks
carve two huge Buddhas
into the rock face at
Bactria (Afghanistan)

499 CE Hindu
mathmatician Aryabhata
writes the first book on
algebra–*Aryabhatiya*

ABOVE Head of the Buddha in pink
limestone from the Mathura region
(c. 430–435 CE).

LEFT As each of the great
empires of India began
they sought to gain ter-
ritory. The color panels
show the interleaving of
areas that occurred.

N

| 0 | | 250 | | 500 | 750 kilometers |
| 0 | 125 | | 250 | | 375 miles |

Mauryan Empire (c. 260 BCE)

Kushana Empire (c. 200 CE)

Gupta Empire homeland

Gupta Empire (c. 400 CE)

ANCESTRY, EMPIRES, AND ARTIFACTS

End of the Golden Age

The Peloponnesian War is often seen as representative of the end of a golden age in Greek culture and politics that had existed during the sixth and fifth centuries BCE.

The war brought out the tensions and problems in the Greek city-states that were beneath the surface during this golden age. It was fought essentially between Athens and Sparta and our most important source for the history of the war is the historian and retired Athenian general, Thucydides.

Land versus Sea

At the time the Peloponnesian War broke out, Athens dominated the Aegean Sea, having developed a powerful navy. This was achieved under the leadership of Pericles during the 20 years before the Peloponnesian War began. While Athens exercised its naval power, Sparta and the members of the Peloponnesian League possessed strong land armies that Athens was not capable of matching.

The Peloponnesian League

Pericles seems to have deliberately caused difficulties for Sparta and its allies from around 433 BCE as a way of advancing Athens' interests. These actions included banning traders from Megara from accessing markets throughout the Aegean and meddling in colonies that were subject to Corinth. Those states affected by the Athenian's actions lobbied Sparta as the head of the Peloponnesian League to take action; eventually—with support

> The ability to understand a question from all sides meant one was totally unfit for action. Fanatical enthusiasm was the mark of the real man.
>
> –Thucydides (c. 460–395 BCE) in the *History of the Peloponnesian War*.

from Boeotia, Phocis, Megara, and Locris—the Peloponnesian League, with Sparta at its head, decided on a course of war with Athens.

Spartan Invasion

The first phase of the Peloponnesian War (431–421 BCE) began with a Spartan invasion of Attica. The Spartan *hoplites* (infantrymen) were clearly superior to those of Athens; however, Athens had a considerable naval advantage, which meant that over time the war became inconclusive and ended with the Peace of Nicias in 421 BCE.

Syracuse

With Athenian expansion basically checked by the terms of the treaty, the peace established in 421 BCE continued until problems emerged in the Greek colonies of Sicily. Eager to take the opportunity to expand its influence, the Athenian assembly voted to send a large force to Sicily in 415 BCE under the

joint command of three generals, including Alcibiades and Nicias. The venture was a disaster from the beginning. Alcibiades was requested to return to Athens in order to face charges of profaning the Eleusinian mysteries (religious initiation ceremonies) and, rather than returning to Athens, where he almost certainly would have been executed, Alcibiades fled to Sparta where he encouraged the Spartans to come to the aid of Syracuse. The Corinthians eventually led the support of Syracuse and, over time,

431 BCE Spartans invade Attica. Plague of Athens begins

429 BCE Death of Pericles. Plague continues.

424 BCE Battle of Delion. Athens is defeated by the Thebans. Thucydides is exiled

421 BCE The Peace of Nicias

411 BCE Subversion of democracy in Athens, with political assassinations and reign of terror

410 BCE Alcibiades victorious in the Aegean

406 BCE Antiochos is defeated by Lysander in Battle of Notium (Cape Rain). Alcibiades is deposed. Spartans offer peace

405 BCE Siege of Athens begins

404 BCE Starvation compels surrender

Withstanding the Siege
An important means by which Athens held out against repeated Spartan invasions of Attica and the superiority of the Spartan hoplites was its defensive walls constructed some 25 years earlier. The Athenian walls extended all the way to the port of Piraeus allowing the port to remain open for regular provisioning during the Spartan siege.

Athens and allies (405 BCE)

Sparta (405 BCE)

LEFT From about 412 BCE, Sparta built up its naval and military forces, allowing it to defeat Athens after a series of attacks.

FAR RIGHT The 415 BCE naval attack on Sparta was disastrous for Athens. Around 6000 men died and Athens experienced political instability in the following years.

PLAGUE

The Athenian defense walls, which extended to the port of Piraeus, housed the large rural populations of Attica who were forced to flee from the Spartan advance. The resulting significant increase in the population of Athens led to the outbreak of the infamous plague of Athens, which ran in varying degrees of intensity from 430 BCE to 426 BCE. The plague claimed tens of thousands of victims, including Pericles in 429 BCE; the writer and historian Thucydides contracted the disease but managed to survive it.

ABOVE This fifteenth-century fresco by an unknown artist shows a doctor treating victims of the plague.

the Athenian siege became bogged down despite reinforcements arriving from Athens in 413 BCE. Eventually Nicias ended the siege and retreated, at which time his army was completely destroyed.

ABOVE The Aegean Sea region, represented in this sixteenth-century map by Abraham Ortelius, was the staging ground for the Peloponnesian War.

Surrender

Taking advantage of Athens' significant commitment to war in Sicily, many who were subject to its dominance in the Aegean rebelled, and Sparta seized the opportunity to lead a campaign against Athens. Athens enjoyed some success initially, but in 412 BCE Persia entered the conflict and financed the Spartans in the construction of a large fleet. The Spartan naval commander, Lysander, inflicted a number of quite devastating defeats on the Athenian fleet in 405 BCE and in the spring of 404 BCE the Athenians had no choice but to surrender to Sparta. While many of Sparta's allies wanted Athens to be permanently destroyed, Sparta refused the request. The walls between Athens and Piraeus were destroyed and the Athenians were deprived of their navy. According to the Greek historian Xenophon, the Spartans claimed that the destruction of Athens' power marked the beginning of the liberty of Greece.

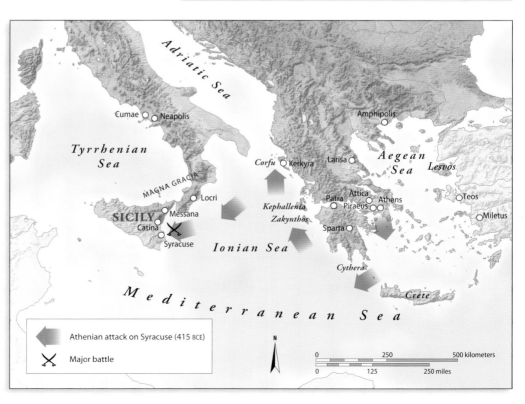

The Greek World

The period between the end of the Peloponnesian Wars in 404 BCE and the emergence of Macedonia as the dominant power in Greece is important in Greek history. A number of events which took place during this period explain the explosion of Greek armies and culture into the Near East, Mesopotamia, Central Asia, and India under the initiative of Alexander the Great.

ABOVE A classic bust of Leonidas, King of Sparta for a decade, from 490 to 480 BCE, a Greek hero.

BELOW The vast theater of Tholos at Epidaurus seats 14,000 people and was built in the fourth century BCE. It was designed by the architect Polykleitos the Younger.

The Peloponnesian Wars had been protracted affairs and by the time they concluded many of the Greek city-states were exhausted. The devastation of the Athenian fleet, which took place during the wars, made Greek trade more vulnerable to attack in the Aegean and left Greece itself more open to attack by Persia.

Sparta

As the leading power in the fight against Athens in the Peloponnesian Wars, Sparta was now dominant in the Greek city-states, but this dominance quickly became unpopular. Sparta placed a governor, garrison, and governing board in a number of cities including Athens. In Athens, the garrison was located on the Acropolis and a board of 30 leading men was appointed to oversee the running of the city. In 403 BCE, the board demonstrated its harshness toward the Athenian population when it ordered the execution of 1,500 citizens and the exile of 5,000 others as punishment for anti-Spartan activities during the Peloponnesian Wars.

In 401 BCE, the Persian King Cyrus led an army against his brother in Mesopotamia that comprised approximately 10,000 Greek mercenaries. Following Cyrus' defeat by his brother at the battle of Cunaxa, the Greek mercenary soldiers made their way back via Armenia. The story of this adventure by Xenophon, one of the mercenary generals, seems to have been a catalyst for mounting a significant attack on Persia.

Fall of Sparta

In the wake of the expedition by Cyrus and the Greek mercenaries, Sparta attempted to reassert itself as the protector of the Greeks in Asia Minor but this was only partially successful. By 395 BCE, a confederation of Greek city-states had gathered to challenge Sparta's dominance throughout Greece. Attacks by cities including Thebes, Corinth, and Athens resulted in the death of Sparta's leading general, Lysander, in 394 BCE. This marked the beginning of Sparta's demise, which would be virtually complete in only 25 years. In 371 BCE, the Spartan army suffered a major defeat by a Theban-led army at Leuctra, only a few miles from Thebes itself. Sparta never recovered from this loss as it was unable to raise the soldiers required to replace the casualties.

Thebes

At the time of Sparta's demise, Greece had become so divided that Persia was able to exploit the situation to wield considerable power throughout the Greek world. The Persians were not only in control of the Greek cities of Asia Minor but had been called upon to act as arbiters of disputes between the various city-states. The city that would emerge as the most powerful of the Greek city-states from 371 BCE to 362 BCE was Thebes. Thebes was the leader of the Boeotian league at this time and sought to strengthen its hand throughout Greece through this vehicle. Thebes was fortunate during this period to have capable military and political leadership. Its leading general, Epaminondas, and most persuasive political leader, Pelopidas, worked well together and were jointly responsible for the success Thebes enjoyed during its decade of supremacy in Greece.

The death of both these men by 362 BCE, at which time Thebes was defeated by a coalition of Athens, Achaea, Sparta, and others, saw the fortunes of the city wane so that by 360 BCE, the Greek world was in a state of considerable turmoil and unpredictability.

> A hero is born among a hundred, a wise man is found among a thousand, but an accomplished one might not be found even among a hundred thousand men.
>
> –Plato (c. 424 BCE–c. 348 BCE), Greek philosopher and teacher

Corsica

Sardinia

Tyrrhenian Sea

Motya
Egesta
Himera
Carthage
Acragas
Sicily
Catania
Gela
Syracuse
Camarina

Mediterranean

AFRICA

Greece (c. 404 BCE)

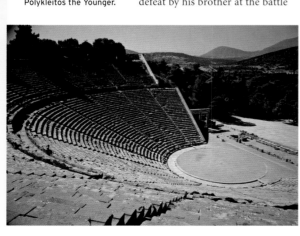

399 BCE Master philosopher Socrates dies

388 BCE Plato, founds his Academy—a school of philosophy—in Athens

338 BCE Philip II of Macedonia defeats the combined Greek army at Chaeronea

336 BCE Philip II of Macedonia is assassinated; his son Alexander succeeds him as king

LEFT Depicting the School of Athens, this fresco in the Vatican shows Plato and Aristotle at the center. It was painted by Raphael for Pope Julius II.

BELOW The Greek world and its surrounding area, in 404 BCE.

RIGHT The Parthenon, on the Acropolis, was built between 450 and 430 BCE as a temple to the Greek goddess Athena. It still dominates the landscape of Athens.

BELOW From the atlas *Theatrum Orbis Terrarum* of 1570 by Abraham Ortelius, this ancient map shows the Mediterranean islands of Sicily, Sardinia, Corfu, Zerbi, Elba, Malta, and Jerba.

RIGHT This sixteenth-century fresco honors three famous Greek philosophers—Plato, Solon, and Pythagoras, depicting them as kings.

BELOW King Philip II of Macedonia was a superb general. His well-trained professional soldiers defeated the Greek army at the Battle of Chaeronea in 338 BCE.

Expansion

Clearly, Greece was in turmoil by the middle of the fourth century BCE. Modern scholars often point to this as a reason for the extraordinary expansion that Greece underwent in the following centuries.

Firstly, the exhaustion which the Greek city-states had inflicted upon one another in the preceding 40 years allowed the rise to dominance of Macedonia in the 350s and 340s BCE under the leadership of its brilliant and ruthless king, Philip II.

While this dominant position of Macedonia under Philip was resented by many of the Greek city-states, in particular Thebes and Athens, it also addressed ongoing concerns regarding the power of Persia throughout Greece, and led to rising anti-Persian feeling.

Panhellenism

The unwitting outcome of the wars and disintegration of the previous century was the emergence of what modern scholars call Panhellenism. Panhellenism was the notion that a broader and shared Greek culture existed beyond the individual city-states.

One of the persons most responsible for promoting this concept was the influential Athenian orator Isocrates, who for many decades called for a Panhellenic war against Persia. When he died in 338 BCE, aged almost 100, the reality of a Greek war against Persia led by Macedonia was in the early stages of development.

Sicily and Carthage

The island of Sicily had been the key point of dispute between Sparta and Athens in the second phase of the Peloponnesian Wars and the outcome had been disastrous for Athens.

The dispute allowed Carthage to become more involved in Sicily, with the leader of the Carthaginians, Hannibal Mago, sending a force in 409 BCE to take control of the island. This expedition met with partial success and another was sent in 405 BCE, designed to capture Syracuse.

Dionysius, the recently appointed tyrant of Syracuse, had undertaken projects at the city that

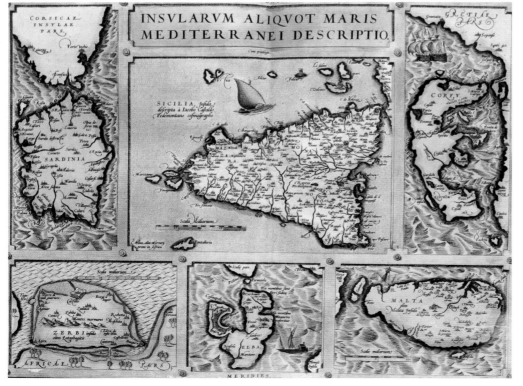

were designed to assist it in resisting future Carthaginian attacks. Howwever, during the Carthaginian attack in 405 BCE, the outbreak of plague across the armies of both protagonists forced a compromise to be struck in the form of a treaty.

By 398 BCE, Dionysius had gathered enough strength to mount attacks on some of the Carthaginian possessions in Sicily, especially Motya. In the following year, the new Carthaginian leader, Himilco, responded by laying siege to Syracuse before the onset of plague once again interrupted military operations.

Dionysius attempted to expand the power of Syracuse on the Italian mainland in 387 BCE. This resulted in Syracuse gaining control over the Straits of Messina which separate Sicily and the mainland.

Dionysius' growing strength led him to attack Carthaginian interests in Sicily again in 383 BCE. This sparked a new set of conflicts that lasted until 378 BCE when yet another treaty was signed, in which Syracuse fared badly.

Plato

Dionysius died in 368 BCE and was replaced as tyrant by his son, Dionysius II. In 367 BCE, problems emerged within the family that were eventually to spark a civil war in Sicily. Dionysius's uncle, Dion, was accused of treason against his nephew and banished.

Dion had invited his friend Plato to Sicily to act as an advisor to Dionysius II when he succeeded his father. Dion's exile forced Plato back to Athens but he returned to Syracuse in 361 BCE and effectively treated Sicily as a type of democratic experiment. In 357 BCE, one of Plato's pupils advised Dion to return to Sicily as Dionysius II was becoming increasingly unpopular and Plato backed Dion to replace Dionysius II because of Dion's reputed leanings toward democracy. Dion succeeded in capturing eastern Sicily from the Carthaginians and then marched to Syracuse, which he captured, apart from its citadel. Unfortunately, Dion did not support democracy but ruled as an oligarch. In 354 BCE, he was assassinated and democracy was instituted in Syracuse.

Dionysius II returned to Syracuse in 347 BCE to exact revenge on those who had opposed him. In desperation, members of the elite appealed to Corinth and even Carthage for assistance.

Corinth sent an able general, Timoleon, who between 344 and 336 BCE succeeded in restoring democracy in Syracuse and defeating the Carthaginians. He then helped restore the city.

Alexander the Great and his Empire

In 334 BCE, at the age of 19, Alexander left Macedonia with an army of approximately 45,000 men with the aim of conquering the vast Persian Empire. He was never to see Macedonia again.

343 BCE Aristotle is invited to become Alexander's teacher in Macedonia

336 BCE Phillip II, Alexander's father, is assassinated. On accession, Alexander has all those responsible killed.

332 BCE Alexander is crowned Pharoah of Egypt at the capital Memphis

c. 331 BCE The city of Alexandria is founded by Alexander

327 BCE Alexander marries the Bactrian princess, Rhoxane

323 BCE Alexander dies

310 BCE Rhoxane and her son Alexander IV are imprisoned and murdered

The emergence of the Kingdom of Macedonia from obscurity in the middle of the fourth century BCE, to control territory as far east as India by 323 BCE, is one of the most dramatic and important historical developments in the ancient world.

Hellespont

The Persian Empire comprised Asia Minor, Syria, Egypt, Central Asia, Mesopotamia, and Iran. Alexander's invasion of Persian-controlled territory began when his army crossed the Hellespont (the Dardanelles)—a narrow body of water usually identified as separating Europe and Asia. When the fleet carrying the army was about to land on the Asiatic shore of the Hellespont, Alexander hurled a spear onto the beach, symbolically claiming Asia as a "spear-won land." This was done in emulation of Heracles, a god Alexander identified with closely and sought to outdo throughout his campaigns against the Persians. Not long afterwards, at the river Granicus in northwest Asia Minor, Alexander's army scored a significant victory over the Persian King, Darius III.

Following his defeat, Darius III fled with his army to Damascus in Syria where he waited to see how the invasion would progress.

Asia Minor

Following the defeat of Darius, Alexander and his army marched down the coast of Asia Minor and captured important cities including Miletus and Ephesus. In late 333 BCE, at Issus in the extreme south of modern Turkey, Darius engaged in another major battle with Alexander in an effort to halt the invasion before it reached Syria and Egypt.

Alexander scored another decisive victory and Darius was again forced to flee with what was left of his army.

RIGHT Aristotle is shown teaching morality to a young Alexander in the fourteenth-century Italian manuscript, *Book of Treasure*.

> There is something noble in hearing myself ill spoken of when I am doing well.
> –Alexander the Great, on hearing criticism of himself.

ABOVE The success of Alexander's campaign strategies can be seen in the vastness of his empire at the time of his death at only 32 years of age.

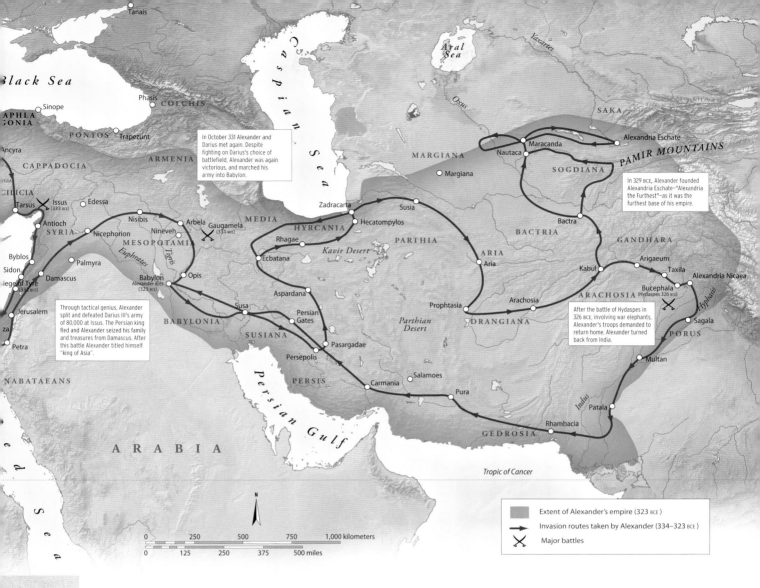

Tanais

Black Sea

Sinope
APHLA
GONIA
Phasis COLCHIS

Caspian Sea

Aral Sea

Oxus
Yaxartes
SAKA

Alexandria Eschate
PAMIR MOUNTAINS

PONTOS Trapezunt

Ancyra

CAPPADOCIA

ARMENIA

MARGIANA

Nautaca Maracanda

SOGDIANA

CILICIA
Tarsus
Issus
(333 BCE)
Edessa

MEDIA

Margiana

In October 331 Alexander and
Darius met again. Despite
fighting on Darius's choice of
battlefield, Alexander was again
victorious, and marched his
army into Babylon.

Bactra

BACTRIA

In 329 BCE, Alexander founded
Alexandria Eschate–"Alexandria
the Furthest"–as it was the
furthest base of his empire.

Antioch
SYRIA
Nicephorion

Nisibis
Nineveh
Arbela Gaugamela
(331 BCE)

Zadracarta

Susia

HYRCANIA

PARTHIA

ARIA
Aria

GANDHARA

Byblos
Sidon
iege of Tyre
(332 BCE)

Palmyra

Euphrates
Tigris

MESOPOTAMIA

Rhagae
Ecbatana

Hecatompylos

Kavir Desert

Arigaeum
Taxila
Kabul
Alexandria Nicaea
Bucephala
(Hydaspes 326 BCE)
Hyphasis

Jerusalem

Damascus

Babylon
Alexander dies
(323 BCE)
Opis

Aspardana

ARACHOSIA

za
Petra

Through tactical genius, Alexander
split and defeated Darius III's army
of 80,000 at Issus. The Persian king
fled and Alexander seized his family
and treasures from Damascus. After
this battle Alexander titled himself
"king of Asia".

Susa

BABYLONIA

Persian
Gates

SUSIANA

Prophthasia

DRANGIANA

Arachosia

Parthian
Desert

After the battle of Hydaspes in
326 BCE, involving war elephants,
Alexander's troops demanded to
return home. Alexander turned
back from India.

Sagala

PORUS

NABATAEANS

Pasargadae

Persepolis

PERSIS

Salamoes

Carmania

Pura

Multan

Persian Gulf

ARABIA

Indus
Patala
Rhambacia

GEDROSIA

Tropic of Cancer

d
S
e
a

0   250   500   750   1,000 kilometers
0   125   250   375   500 miles

N

Extent of Alexander's empire (323 BCE)

Invasion routes taken by Alexander (334–323 BCE)

Major battles

Tyre

Early in 332 BCE, Alexander and
his army advanced along the
Mediterranean coastline of Syria
capturing most of the major cities
along the way. One of the most
important cities in the eastern
Mediterranean, however, refused
to surrender. The city was Tyre
and it was situated on an island
close to the Syrian coastline.

Following Tyre's refusal to
surrender, Alexander had his army
construct a ramp out to the island
and captured the city. The siege
had lasted for seven months.

Egypt

After the siege of Tyre, Alexander
moved on and captured Gaza before advancing on Persian-held
Egypt. Arriving at the end of
332 BCE, Alexander was welcomed
by the Egyptians—contrary to his
expectations—as Persian rule of

Egypt had been very unpopular
and he was considered a liberator
throughout the kingdom. The Persian satrap of Egypt, Mazaces, surrendered immediately. The capital
of Egypt at this time was Memphis.
Upon Alexander's arrival there, he
was offered the Egyptian crown.

On returning to the Nile region,
Alexander and his army left Egypt
in April, 331 BCE, and made their
way towards Mesopotamia and
Iran in an effort to permanently
destroy Darius and his army.

Mesopotamia

Alexander's army marched through
Syria into northern Mesopotamia
where his forces would meet those
of Darius III for the last time. This
battle took place at Gaugamela in
modern northern Iraq on October 1,
331 BCE. It was, once again, a serious defeat for Darius and he fled
for his life from the battlefield.

Following this crushing victory,
the important cities of Babylon
and Susa in southern Mesopotamia
fell easily. Alexander then marched
into Persia where he captured the
royal capital of Persepolis late in
331 BCE. Darius III was murdered
by Bessus, satrap of Bactria, who
hoped to succeed him as king of
Persia. On Alexander's orders,
Darius's body was sent to Persepolis
to be properly buried.

Central Asia

Alexander invaded Bactria following Bessus's organization of a
revolt in Bactria and Central Asia.
Due to the mountainous terrain
and the freezing winter conditions,
this was a very difficult campaign.
Nevertheless, Alexander easily took
control of Bactria, while Bessus
was betrayed by his bodyguard. He
was later sent to Ecbatana in Media
where he was executed.

ABOVE Young, handsome,
and a master campaigner,
Alexander the Great is
portrayed here in a marble
bust copied from an early
Greek statue by Eufranor
in 338 BCE.

73

Tropic of Cancer

India

Alexander was now in control of a vast territory including Asia Minor, Syria, Egypt, Mesopotamia, Persis, Media, and Bactria. He did not stop at this point, however, and during 329–325 BCE spent much of the time invading India and Central Asia.

Alexander's battle-weary troops finally mutinied at the Hyphasis River in northern India. His angry reaction was not enough to convince them to continue so he was forced to turn back. On reaching the Hydaspes River, the army was transported by a large fleet down the river to the area around Karachi in modern Pakistan.

From there the army returned to Persia, making part of its return journey through the harsh Gedrosian desert. The army arrived at Susa and Persepolis in March 324 BCE, having captured them six years earlier. In the spring of 324 BCE, Alexander left Susa to return to Babylon, the city he planned to make the capital of his empire. Early in 323 BCE he received embassies from all over the known world offering gifts and congratulations for his exploits.

Babylon and Death

Alexander spent most of his time in Babylon preparing for an expedition to the Arabian peninsula. He unexpectedly fell ill towards the end of May.

There are two main traditions regarding the cause of the illness and how it ultimately contributed to his death. In one he is said to have drunk himself to death, consuming more than 10 pints (6 liters) of wine before collapsing unconscious. The other, which is generally more accepted, is that Alexander contracted a fever after a banquet held by one of his close associates. He went about his royal duties with increasing difficulty and made daily sacrifices to the gods. By June 8, 323 BCE, Alexander's fever was so serious that he was confined to bed and could not talk. With the end clearly drawing near, Alexander's distraught army filed past the barely conscious king before he finally died in the early evening of June 10, 323 BCE.

Significantly, Alexander had not established a succession plan. He was only 32 years old so he had probably not expected to die at this young age. On his deathbed

ABOVE Alexander the Great visiting the Oracle at Delphi, above, and taming a horse, below. The painting is taken from a fourteenth-century Cretan version of *Romance of Alexander*.

RIGHT Italian painting depicting the wedding of Alexander the Great and Bactrian princess Rhoxane, in 328 BCE. The artist is Mariano Rossi (1730-1807).

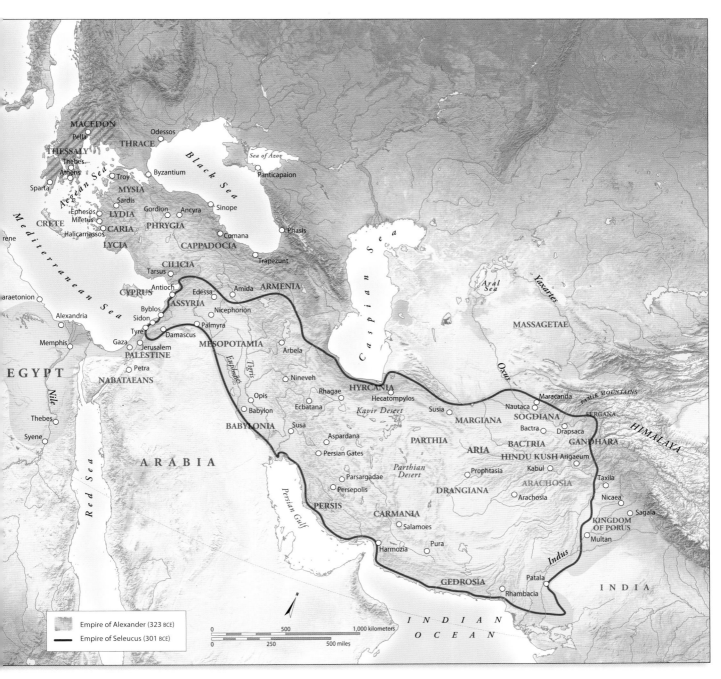

Empire of Alexander (323 BCE)
Empire of Seleucus (301 BCE)

Alexander is said to have left his empire simply "to the strongest." He did not have a male heir but his Bactrian wife, Rhoxane, was pregnant at the time of his death and some months later she gave birth to a son, also named Alexander.

Sharing the Spoils

It took more than 20 years of conflict between Alexander's family, generals, and associates before what was left of Alexander's vast empire resembled anything stable or permanent. In short, one of his

generals, Ptolemy, took control of Egypt while another, Seleucus, emerged in control of a very large empire that encompassed Syria, Iran, Bactria, and northern India. Antigonus and his son Demetrius took control of Macedonia and Greece. These men emerged as kings, establishing dynasties which ruled over these three kingdoms for centuries to come.

The cultural changes that emerged as a result of Alexander's conquests were fundamental in the region for the next thousand years.

ABOVE Seleucus eventually gained control of much of Alexander's empire.

LEFT Alexander the Great and Bucephalus, his battle charger. Many stories are told of the bond between the man and horse.

Gifted Strategies

Lasting almost 118 years, the conflicts between Rome and Carthage are known as the Punic Wars. Probably better known is the name of the Carthagian general, Hannibal, who defeated the Roman legions by crossing into the Po Valley using war elephants.

Carthage was initially founded as a Phoenician trading colony in the eighth century BCE. Its inhabitants came to be known as the *Poeni*, hence the term "Punic" used to describe the Carthaginians.

First Punic War

The immediate catalyst of the First Punic War was the establishment of a garrison at Messana in Sicily by Carthage in 264 BCE. Roman attempts to eject the garrison marked the beginning of the war. At its outset, Carthage had the greater naval strength of the two, the Romans a stronger infantry. But the Romans recognized their naval weakness and in 261 BCE constructed a fleet of 120 ships that, together with the army, allowed them to capture most of Sicily by the following year.

In 256 BCE Rome attacked Carthage itself. Following initial successes against the Carthaginian leader Hamilcar, the Romans suffered a serious defeat when one of their consuls, Regulus, was captured and the Roman army withdrew. In the years that followed, the Roman navy also suffered serious losses, primarily due to bad weather. By 241 BCE both sides were exhausted, but the Carthaginians accepted an agreement that gave Sicily and a large annual indemnity to Rome.

Second Punic War

Over time Carthage strengthened its position in Spain under the leadership of Hamilcar, Hasdrubal, and finally Hannibal. By 226 BCE, the Romans became so concerned about this expansion that they negotiated an agreement limiting Carthaginian influence at the Ebro River. Rome, however, continued to support Saguntum, south of the Ebro, and that led Hannibal to take the town by siege in 219 BCE. The Romans responded by demanding

RIGHT Hannibal, it has been said, taught the Romans (fierce descendants of Mars) the real meaning of fear. His impact still lingers in the phrase "Hannibal is at the gates!"–signifying imminent disaster.

195 BCE After defeat by the Romans, Hannibal flees to Tyre and then to Ephesus to join Antiochus III of Syria

192 BCE Hannibal assists Antiochus III to land in Greece

189 BCE Hannibal is defeated by the Romans at Thermopylae and Magnesia before fleeing to Crete and then back to Asia Minor to assist Prusias I of Bithynia

c. 183 BCE Hannibal takes poison–long carried in a ring–in Bithynia, rather than be extradited by the Romans

We will find a way–or we will make one.
–Hannibal on his quest to cross the Pyrenees.

ABOVE When Hannibal embarked on his famous crossing of the Pyrenees and the Alps into northern Italy in 218 BCE, his army numbered 20,000 infantry, 6,000 cavalry, and 37 war elephants.

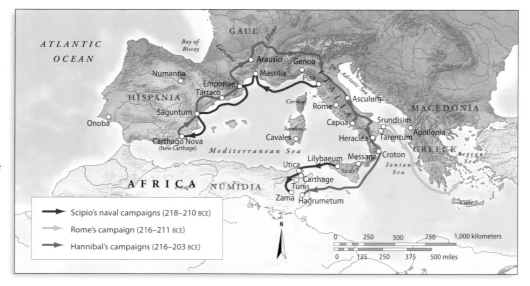

Scipio's naval campaigns (218–210 BCE)

Rome's campaign (216–211 BCE)

Hannibal's campaigns (216–203 BCE)

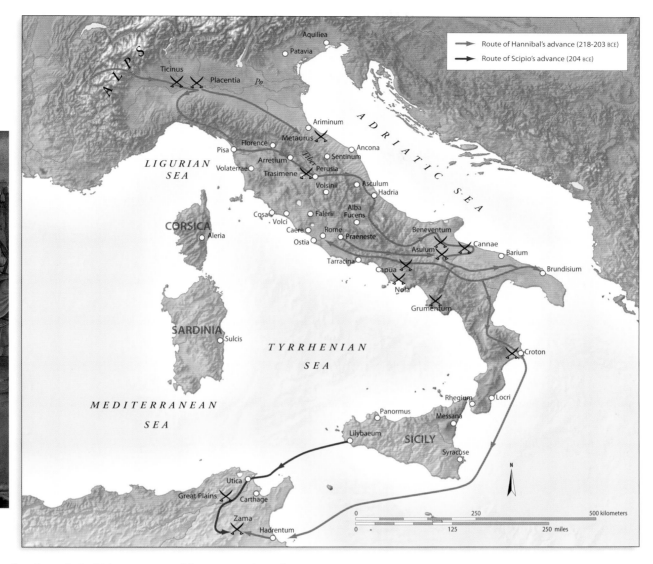

Route of Hannibal's advance (218-203 BCE)

Route of Scipio's advance (204 BCE)

the surrender of Hannibal, which the Carthaginians refused, and in March 218 BCE, Rome declared war. This conflict came to be known as the Second Punic War. Using its naval strength, Rome sent one force to Spain and another to conquer Carthage itself. But Hannibal took the Romans by surprise, marching across the Pyrenees and the Italian Alps into the Po Valley in September 218 BCE. The army he assembled there numbered 20,000 infantry and 6,000 cavalry. When both Roman consuls rushed to meet Hannibal's forces they were dealt a crushing defeat.

Over the following two years, Hannibal inflicted further serious defeats on the Roman army, particularly at Lake Trasimene, to the north of Rome, where the consul Flaminius and two legions were destroyed in 217 BCE.

One of the great questions of history, however, is why Hannibal did not attack Rome at this time. He probably thought it was better defended than it actually was; also, he had not won the support of the Roman subjects in central Italy. So Rome managed to survive, whereas Hannibal eventually found it very difficult to supply his armies.

Hannibal's brother Hasdrubal was killed in battle in northern Italy in 207 BCE. With Hannibal himself confined to the extreme south of the Italian peninsula, the Romans now had the upper hand. In 204 BCE, Scipio Africanus landed a force in Africa and in a peace deal secured Hannibal's withdrawal from Italy the following year. But the peace was broken soon after Hannibal's return, and in 202 BCE Scipio inflicted a final crushing defeat on the Carthaginian leader

ABOVE The Second Punic War came to a decisive end with Scipio's victory over Hannibal at Zama. Masinissa, who had changed sides the previous year, played a key role by strengthening Rome's cavalry.

at Zama. Subsequently, Rome gained two provinces in Spain.

Third Punic War

Masinissa of Numidia, an ally of Rome in the battle at Zama, continued to harass the reduced Carthaginians, who eventually attacked him in 150 BCE. Rome then declared war on Carthage at the instigation of Cato. Carthage managed to withstand the Roman siege until 146 BCE when Scipio Aemilianus, son of Scipio Africanus, destroyed the city and formed the Roman province of Africa out of the Carthaginian domains.

ABOVE Hannibal is said to be one of the finest military commanders and tacticians in history. Only 43 when defeated by Rome, he went into voluntary exile from Carthage and continued to put his skills to use until his death at age 64.

Han—The Great Empire of China

The Han Dynasty (206 BCE–220 CE), based in present-day Xian, was one of the longest in Chinese history—a period of unification and imperial expansion ushering in a radical reformation of governance influenced by Confucian values.

206 BCE–9 CE Period known as the Western or Former Han with the capital Ch'ang-an in the present-day Shaanxi Province

c. 101 BCE Emperor Wudi regains control of territory lost in southern China and the northern part of Vietnam. He also sets up commands in Korea. He seizes horses and gives China control of trade routes—the Silk Roads.

25–220 CE The Eastern Han Period is ruled from Loyang, a new capital in present-day Henan Province

57–107 CE Envoys arrive from Japan and Central Asia

132 CE Sundials, water clocks, astronomical instruments, and paper are developed

166 CE Reported arrival of an emissary from Andun (the emperor Marcus Aurelius Antoninus) bringing ivory, rhinoceros horn, and tortoiseshell, suggesting a link to Rome.

ABOVE RIGHT The Han Dynasty empire can be seen stretching west. Parts of the Great Wall are evident along the northern border.

RIGHT Three kingdoms were formed after the collapse of the Han Dynasty.

In 206 BCE, the Han dynasty—the namesake of the most populous ethnic group in China, the Han—replaced the Qin dynasty when an illiterate peasant rebel called Liu Bang defeated Qin armies near the Yangtze (Yangzi) river valley, and was crowned the Gaodi Emperor.

Emperor Wudi
Emperor Wudi, who reigned from 142 to 87 BCE, was a scholar, poet, and Confucian philosopher who revolutionized Chinese society with the following proclamation: "Heroes Wanted! Exceptional work demands exceptional men!" This proclamation was a call for applicants for the Imperial bureaucracy heard throughout China, and open to men from all classes.

Sima Qian, the Grand Historian (145–85 BCE)
The way that the Chinese have conceived of their past—and thus of themselves—was profoundly

> The King charged [his general] Nan Zhong to go and build a wall in the region.
>
> –translation adapted from Legge, *The Chinese Classics, Vol. IV, The She King.*

shaped by a book written in Han times—*The Historical Records (Shi Ji)* by Grand Historian Sima Qian. Following the work of his father, Sima Qian combed the Imperial Archives compiling 130 chapters documenting Chinese history.

Death and the Afterlife
The Han period saw a refinement of beliefs and practices concerning the dead that is reflected in the type of goods found in burials, such as the tomb of Countess Dai (who lived around 168 CE) located in present-day Hunan. The mummified body of the princess, covered in a jade coat, was buried with talismans allowing her to make the journey to the afterlife.

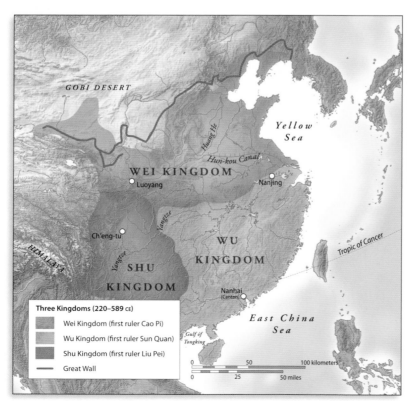

Three Kingdoms (220–589 CE)
- Wei Kingdom (first ruler Cao Pi)
- Wu Kingdom (first ruler Sun Quan)
- Shu Kingdom (first ruler Liu Pei)
- Great Wall

Red Eyebrow and Yellow Turban Rebellions
Near the end of the Han Dynasty, a series of peasant revolts attempted to overthrow the Han leadership. One such revolt broke out in Rizhao, Shandong, in 17 CE, under the leadership of a woman known as Mother Lu. The revolt occurred after a destructive flood was caused by the Han government's neglect of the rural dyke system.

Known as the Red Eyebrow Rebellion, it spread all the way to the central plains of China. The

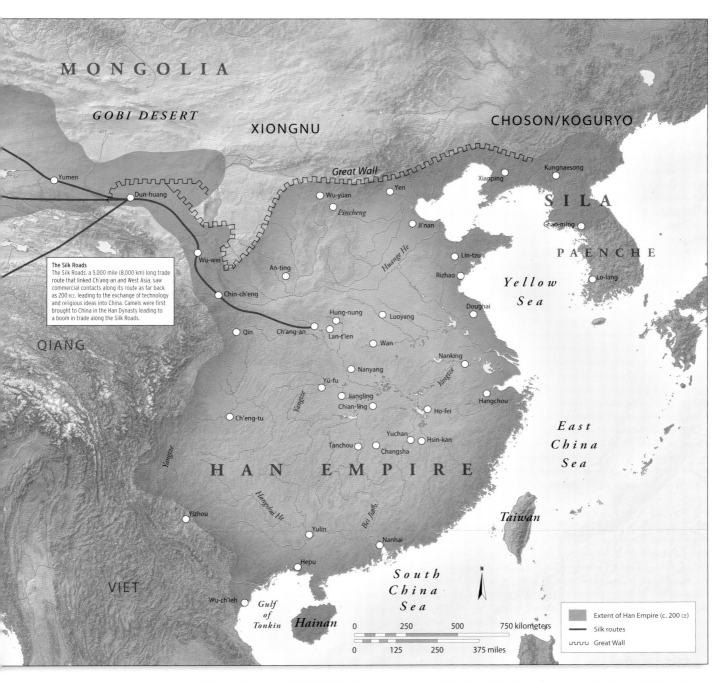

The Silk Roads
The Silk Roads, a 5,000 mile (8,000 km) long trade route that linked Ch'ang-an and West Asia, saw commercial contacts along its route as far back as 200 BCE, leading to the exchange of technology and religious ideas into China. Camels were first brought to China in the Han Dynasty leading to a boom in trade along the Silk Roads.

▨	Extent of Han Empire (c. 200 CE)
—	Silk routes
⏜⏜	Great Wall

rebels made up their faces to look like demons and became known as the Red Eyebrows.

In 184 CE, a similar movement began in Hubei province, led by the Daoist sect called the Yellow Turbans. Yellow Turban communities practiced religious rituals, fasts and collective confessions—trances which resulted in mass hysteria. At the height of its popularity the Yellow Turbans had 360,000 followers, many of whom were peasants protesting the govenment policies that impoverished farmers.

Three Kingdoms (220–589 CE)
Following the fall of the Han Dynasty, China was divided into three states—the Wei, Shu, and Wu—the Three Kingdoms.

The Chinese empire had fallen apart at the end of the Eastern Han dynasty, when the last Han Emperor, Xiandi, abdicated the throne to Cao Pi, ruler of the Wei Kingdom. His father, General Cao Cao, had led a rebellion against the Imperial government supported by Chinese gentry families populating the northern frontier regions.

The second kingdom, Shu, led by a distant member of the Han Imperial family, Liu Pei, was in the southwest and included the modern province of Sichuan.

The region of Wu was in the southeast, ruled by Sun Quan, who followed the previous two warlords and claimed the Wu Dynasty.

The Great Wall
The Great Wall of China—begun probably in the sixth century— winding its way across China's northern border, is the most

recognizable image of China in the modern world. Although the tradition of wall building in China is ancient, most of the structures only date back to the Ming Dynasty (1368–1644). Myths abound about the Wall's origin. In one folklore it was created when an exhausted dragon fell to the ground and turned to stone, forming a winding barrier across the northern borders of China. In truth, no single wall has ever existed, but rather a series of lesser walls, built at different points in Chinese history.

Ides of March

By the Late Republic (mid-second century BCE), Rome had brought much of the known inhabited world under control. Yet internal struggles would tear apart the traditional *res publica* (Republic) and pave the way for one man to gain total control of Rome and the Empire less than 20 years after the murder of Julius Caesar in 44 BCE.

RIGHT Marble bust of Julius Caesar, an accomplished general who greatly extended Rome's territory, and later became dictator for life.

43 BCE Following the assassination of Caesar, the third Roman civil war breaks out. Octavian, Antony, and Lepidus form the Second Triumvirate.

31 BCE After ending their peace, Octavian defeats Antony and Cleopatra in the Battle of Actium

30 BCE Antony and Cleopatra commit suicide and Egypt becomes a province of Rome

27 BCE Octavian becomes Augustus Caesar, Emperor of Rome

RIGHT Julius Caesar sends a Roman colony to Carthage. This painting by Claude Audran the Younger is part of a ceiling vault in the Chateau of Versailles, France.

In the decades preceding 200 BCE, Rome began the formation of an empire that at its height in the second century CE would spread across 1.2 million square miles (5 million km²) and boast a population of 60 million people.

Oligarchy

During the second century BCE, the government of Rome functioned along traditional republican (oligarchic) lines. Wealthy members of the elite dominated the Roman senate and most senior government positions. The two most powerful men in Rome's government were the consuls, who were responsible for affairs of state and could be given fixed-term military commands if the need arose. They were elected annually from a pool of men who had held the praetorship (the office below the consulship) and who were at least 42 years old. Men seeking public office in the second century BCE were required to serve as junior officers in the Roman army, and they were richly rewarded with the spoils of war.

Cracks in the Republic

Rome's army was mighty, and her empire growing rapidly. However,

Spartacus
Spartacus (c. 109–71 BCE) was a former auxiliary soldier who had been forced to train as a gladiator in Capua. He led a small scale revolt in 72 BCE that unexpectedly gained momentum as he found support among the displaced peasants and slaves of southern Italy. Ancient sources estimate that between 70,000–120,000 men joined in the uprising. After 2 years, Crassus, Roman Commander, finally ended the conflict, crucifying any remaining survivors, and Spartacus became a hero.

ABOVE Julius Caesar led many campaigns on behalf of Rome. They included the Gallic Wars of 58–51 BCE, during which a million Gauls were killed and a further million were enslaved.

this success was having unexpected effects on both the economy and society of Italy. The elite began to invest their new wealth in large landed estates worked by war captives forced into slavery. Although the nature and spread of these estates varied across Italy, their establishment resulted in the widespread displacement of peasants, the men who formed the backbone of the Roman army. Prolonged military service made it difficult

for peasant farmers to maintain their farms and led to a major problem for the Roman government. Displaced and impoverished peasants could not be recruited into the army because, without their farms, they were unable to meet the minimum property qualification required by the law.

Risky Precedents
In the opening decades of the last century BCE, Rome's military

supremacy was challenged in every part of the empire. Faced with war in Numidia (111–106 BCE), invasions by the Cimbri and Teutones (107–101 BCE), and the Sicilian slave revolt (103–101 BCE), the Senate, whose members were unwilling to give up their new luxurious lifestyles, began to crumble. Gaius Marius, a man without traditional family connections in the Senate, took control. He solved the military crisis and temporarily settled

the upheaval in Rome. Marius achieved this by being granted an unprecedented number of consulships year after year. Never before had one man been given so much power in Rome—this was in total contravention of the traditional republican constitution, and set dangerous precedents.

Marius also reformed the recruitment process of the Roman army, repopulating its depleted ranks. Henceforth the Roman

10,000 BCE to 600 CE

LEFT This nineteenth-century painting shows Queen Cleopatra, who wooed Julius Caesar in order to gain political power in Egypt.

BELOW According to his biographer, the scholar Gaius Suetonius Tranquillus, Caesar was stabbed 23 times before he died on the Ides of March, 44 BCE.

RIGHT Rome aimed to dominate the Mediterranean and Western Europe by invading the territories of competing powers in the region.

BELOW RIGHT By the end of his reign (44 BCE), Julius Caesar had expanded the Roman Empire. Octavian added Egypt in 30 BCE.

army became a professional body. Although Marius had solved one problem, he had unintentionally created another. The new recruitment process meant that army loyalty was now directed toward individual legionary generals rather than to Rome. Individual generals recruited soldiers by personally guaranteeing army pensions—land and funds at the end of their term of service provided from war booty. This would have another unforeseen and devastating effect on the republican system of government as ambitious men realized that the army was a powerful weapon that could be used to help them rise to prominence.

Allied Revolt

By 91 BCE, Rome had extended its control to include almost the entire Mediterranean seaboard. However, the government had done little to address the social and economic problems facing Italy, which was organized into provinces or allied territories of Rome. So after many years of hardship, the Italian allies finally took up arms against Rome, in the Social War (91–89 BCE).

Sulla

Realizing that Rome would be occupied at home with the Social War, Mithridates VI, king of Pontus in northern Anatolia, began to ravage Roman territories in the

East. In 88 BCE, Lucius Cornelius Sulla, protégée of Marius, was given the job of dealing with Mithridates by the Senate. However, Sulla's appointment was overturned by the tribune Publius Sulpicius Rufus and command given instead to the popular Gaius Marius. The city of Rome erupted into violence. Sulla decided to use the Roman army to win back his command by offering the men—five legions of Rome's new professional army—land and rich rewards. By 81 BCE, Sulla had systematically eliminated all political opponents through a series of bloody proscriptions—as many as 1,600 upper class Romans were slaughtered. Sulla became the sole dictator of Rome.

In 79 BCE, Sulla unexpectedly stepped away from politics. Although he had made changes to the Roman constitution, they proved ineffectual, and Rome began to slide from one crisis to another. Rome was even faced with a serious slave revolt led by the legendary Thracian gladiator Spartacus (73–71 BCE).

Pompey the Great

Rome turned to the services of a competent young soldier, Pompey the Great, who was well below 42 years of age and had never held any public office at Rome—by law he was not eligible for a military appointment. Nevertheless, in

> ...but when it comes to [civil] war and armies, it is the stronger side that men should follow—and they should judge the better side the one where greater safety lies.
>
> –M. Caelius Rufus to Cicero, early August 50 BCE (Cicero, *Letters to Friends* 8.14.3).

67–66 BCE Pompey was given, first, an overriding command against the pirates who were disrupting trade in the Mediterranean, and second, the charge of the war against Mithridates VI, who had by now been causing problems for a remarkable 22 years. During these campaigns Pompey proved himself an outstanding military general and was hailed as the savior of Rome and the East.

First Triumvirate

However, at home, the government itself was unable to function effectively. Factions were operating within the Senate, and both stalling tactics and threats of violence were increasingly used to block the career paths of certain men. Such behavior forced Pompey, Licinius Crassus, and the new rising star of Roman politics, Julius Caesar, to enter into an informal pact—the so-called First Triumvirate. They

pooled their resources and worked together for the benefit of the Senate as a whole. For Julius Caesar this was a very important move. He was appointed consul in 59 BCE and given governorship of the important provinces of Gaul and Illyricum, beginning in 58 BCE. Unrest among the tribes of Gaul and neighboring Germany gave Caesar the opportunity to fight a major war—the Gallic Wars of 58–51 BCE—during which he proved

himself to be a brilliant military strategist and charismatic general.

Back in Rome, problems continued. Caesar's enemies, angered by his success, made moves to have him prosecuted at the end of his governorship. They also plotted to drive a wedge between Pompey and Caesar. They succeeded, sealing the fate of the Roman republic. Unable to secure his future by negotiation, Caesar, backed by his loyal troops, marched on Rome in

49 BCE. Once again the empire was in the grip of civil war; citizen was pitched against citizen, Pompey against Caesar. Caesar would emerge victorious a year later.

Caesar's new government did look toward a brighter future for Rome. Yet, despite programs and reforms that heralded him as visionary and an excellent administrator, Caesar failed to make his supporters feel valued members of his new government. His actions

were viewed as monarchical, and his liaison with Queen Cleopatra of Egypt was judged un-Roman. Cleopatra was the embodiment of Eastern luxury and vice, thus a threat to the moral character of Rome. On March 15, 44 BCE, Caesar was stabbed to death by a group of senators, among them his close friends Brutus and Cassius. Despite the might of the Roman Empire, the traditional republican government was in ruins and beyond repair.

The Early Spread of Christianity

With its roots in a marginal Jewish sect, Christianity became a world religion that shook the foundations of what was undoubtedly the greatest empire in history—the Roman Empire.

Jesus of Nazareth is perhaps one of the most divisive and yet most-loved figures in world history. Though his public career lasted only about three years, and though he was executed for allegedly being a treasonous criminal, Jesus left an indelible mark on the world.

The Messiah

Jesus' career started in about 27 CE in rural Galilee. For centuries foreign invaders had oppressed the Jewish people and they were on the lookout for a messiah to rid Israel of foreign rulers and restore the nation to its rightful state.

Many came before him, but Jesus' message was different and his extraordinary popularity made him a threat to the religious leadership. To them, he was placing himself above the Law of Moses and some felt it better to quash this popular movement before Rome came to punish the whole nation.

During a trip to Jerusalem Jesus was captured and tried for blasphemy by the Jewish council, called the Sanhedrin. Unable to exercise the death penalty, they called on Pontius Pilate, the Roman governor of Judea. With his agreement, Jesus was severely beaten and crucified, and the movement around Jesus seemed to have dissolved.

Early Church

In fact, it came to pass that Jesus' death was the foundation of Christianity as we know it. Rather than running scared, Jesus' followers claimed that he was actually the Messiah. Soon Jesus-followers grew into thousands. This early "church" ran into very strong opposition in

> Faith is to believe what we do not see, and the reward of this faith is to see what we believe.
>
> –Saint Augustine (354–430 CE), patron of the Augustinian religious order.

26 CE John the Baptist begins his missionary work

57 CE Paul writes his Letter to the Romans

60 CE Peter, the apostle of Jesus Christ, dies

336 CE Constantine the Great dies

380 CE Christianity is made the official religion of the Roman Empire

LEFT While traveling on the road from Jerusalem to Damascus, Paul had a vision of Jesus Christ and converted to Christianity.

BELOW During the Last Supper, Jesus correctly predicted that one of his 12 apostles would betray him. That man was Judas.

NORTH ATLANTIC OCEAN

HISPANIA

Cordova

Seville

Jerusalem and around 35 CE great persecution took place there.

Around this time, one of the most decisive turning points in world history occurred. The early church began to accept those who were not of Jewish origin—the Gentiles. However, while most agreed that Jesus' message applied to Jew or Gentile, many disagreed on whether they had to become Jewish to follow the Jewish Messiah.

Spreading the Word

Paul of Tarsus, more than anyone else, influenced the future of Christianity on this question. "Saul," as he was known, was an educated Jew and a citizen of Rome. Part of the persecutions and arrests of the 30s, Saul was turned to their cause after he had a vision of Jesus and became convinced he was fighting on the wrong side. He changed his name to "Paul" and the one who had been a leader in suppressing the early church thus set about building it.

Paul's first mission was to go into the synagogues, to persuade the people there that Jesus was the Christ—the anointed one. First he had to explain that the Christ was

actually a man who had been executed as a criminal, and second that Gentiles did not need to become Jewish to be a Christian. The message was revolutionary.

On his first trip between 46 and 48 CE, Paul traveled with Barnabas around Cyprus and Galatia, visiting Antioch, Lystra, and Derbe. On his second trip in 49–52 CE, Paul visited Galatia before opening up

new ground in Macedonia and Greece. He founded churches in Philippi, Thessalonica, and Corinth. During 53–58 CE, Paul moved to Ephesus, continuing to visit churches and cities around the Aegean and write his letters.

Paul returned to Jerusalem in 58 CE, where he was arrested. Two years later, he was taken in chains to Rome; by 67 CE Paul was dead.

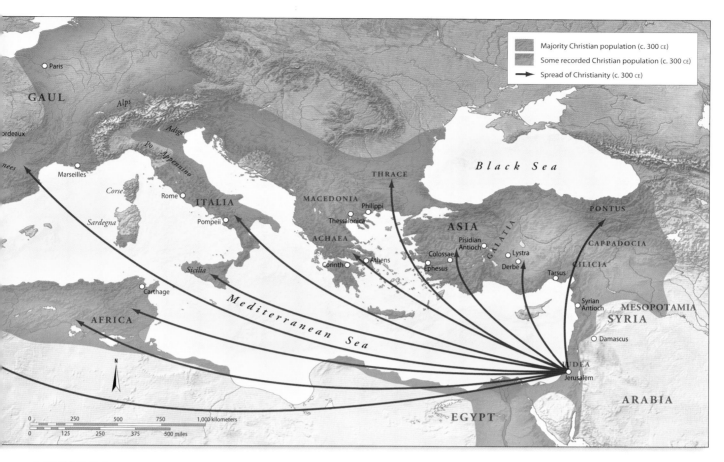

Legend:
- Majority Christian population (c. 300 CE)
- Some recorded Christian population (c. 300 CE)
- → Spread of Christianity (c. 300 CE)

A World Religion

Despite persecutions for the next 150 years, the new Christian church spread into France, Spain, North Africa, and Mesopotamia. The once small sect devoted to Jesus Christ grew to between 5 and 6 million by 300 CE. By 350 CE the number of Christians in the Roman Empire was over 33 million, and Christianity had become a universal religion.

PUNISHMENT SEVERE ENOUGH?

The Roman historian Cornelius Tacitus reported that Nero punished Christians for their alleged role in the April 64 CE fire in Rome's Circus Maximus using the following means:

- He had them covered with animal skins and let them be eaten by dogs.
- He had them nailed to crosses.
- He had them burned as torches for light after sundown.

"Nero offered his gardens for the spectacle, and was exhibiting a show in the circus, while he mingled with the people in the dress of a charioteer or stood aloft on a car."

From *Tacitus Annals* 15.44

ABOVE This map shows just how far Christianity had spread by around the end of the second century CE.

BELOW Following his conversion on the road to Damascus, Paul journeyed great distances to spread the word of Christ. His last trip, to Rome, was as a prisoner.

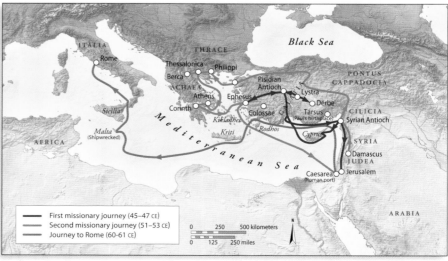

Legend:
- First missionary journey (45–47 CE)
- Second missionary journey (51–53 CE)
- Journey to Rome (60-61 CE)

Africa—Land and Language

Once the practice of agriculture reached Egypt about 8,000 years ago, it spread rapidly southwards along the Nile Valley to other parts of the African continent suited to cultivation.

Agriculture may even have been independently invented in the Horn of Africa and the Western Sudanic region. Because no documents exist to provide information, historians rely on archeologists to help them make educated guesses.

Agriculture and Herding
After the Nile Valley, the most significant developments before the Common (Present) Era occurred along the Niger River and in the Horn of Africa. It appears that agriculture spurred population growth in all three regions. Substantial towns sprang up at many points along the Niger River and trade routes developed to link them with North African cities on the other side of the Sahara. Grain production flourished across the central Sahelian savannahs stretching from Senegal to Ethiopia.

This development went hand in hand with the herding of animals in a system known as transhumant agriculture. Herders moved their cattle, sheep, and goats north during the wet seasons to avoid the tsetse flies that carried the disease trypanosomiasis (sleeping sickness), which is fatal to introduced species of domestic animals in Africa. In the dry seasons, as the flies retreated, the herders moved south to take advantage of new pastures. Grain growers welcomed the seasonal arrival of the herders, whose animals' manure enhanced soil fertility—a system that survives in some places to this day.

Common Language of Bantu
It is more difficult to say exactly how agriculture spread south of the Congo River Basin. A clue was provided by nineteenth-century

RIGHT An exquisitely detailed 1878 illustration by Caton Woodville portrays a young Bantu chief from Cape Province, South Africa.

linguists who discovered that the vast majority of people living between South Africa and Kenya speak closely related languages belonging to what is called the Bantu language family. These have a common word for man *(ntu)* and form plurals by adding prefixes to words, rather than suffixes like the English -s and –en in "cows" and "children." Thus the word for "people" is *ba + ntu = bantu.*

Bantu Advance
The nineteenth-century explorer and scholar, Harry Johnston, was the first to suggest that the spread of the Bantu language was associated with iron and agriculture. He speculated that population pressure caused a pioneering group of Bantu-speakers from the Niger–Congo region to move eastwards toward the Nile Valley, where they acquired knowledge of

300 BCE Use of iron increases across Africa

100 CE Camels introduced to North Africa for trans-Saharan trade

100-200 CE People along the east African coast start trading with Romans and Arabs

350 CE Crops such as bananas and yams begin to grow in east Africa

646 CE Egypt is conquered by the Arabs

RIGHT The spread of agriculture throughout Africa was accompanied by a growth in population. In this painting from an Ethiopian manuscript, a man plows using oxen.

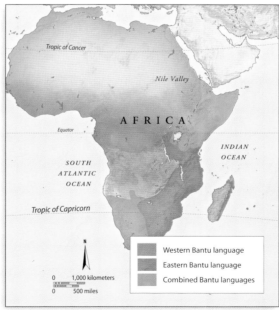

> Every beast roars
> in its own den.
> –Bantu proverb.

agriculture and iron working. This made some sense because the approximate date at which iron technology came to Africa is known—when an Assyrian army using iron spearheads defeated Egyptians in the seventh century BCE. Johnston's idea was that learning how to make iron weapons enabled the Bantu pioneers to sweep southward, pushing aside all resistance. He thought they would have skirted the eastern edge of the Congo River Basin to avoid tsetse flies, disease, and other obstacles. Once the Bantu reached the savannah country of modern Zambia and Tanzania, they would have been able to spread themselves rapidly over most of the rest of southern Africa.

While acknowledging Johnston's ingenuity, present-day scholars believe that he was far too much under the spell of European militarism when he conceived the Bantu advance as a single rapid migration spearheaded by warriors. They are far more inclined to the hypothesis that a peaceful process gradually carried Bantu-speaking groups by many different routes into the regions where their language group now predominates. Some of them may have known techniques of iron smelting, while others did not.

It is also quite possible that small groups of Bantu speakers had already reached the southern savannahs before diffusion of knowledge acquainted them with the ability to refine iron ore.

Iron Working

That said, recent radio-carbon dating of iron-age sites is broadly consistent with the hypothesis that agriculture and iron working spread southwards from the Nile Valley beginning in the seventh century CE. By 200 CE at the latest, it had reached the Zambezi River valley and by 300 CE had cropped up south of the Limpopo River. The process was assisted by the arrival of additional cultivatable crops from other sources, such as

bananas and the plantain family from Southeast Asia, yams and cassava from West Africa, and maize from the New World sometime during the sixteenth or seventeenth centuries.

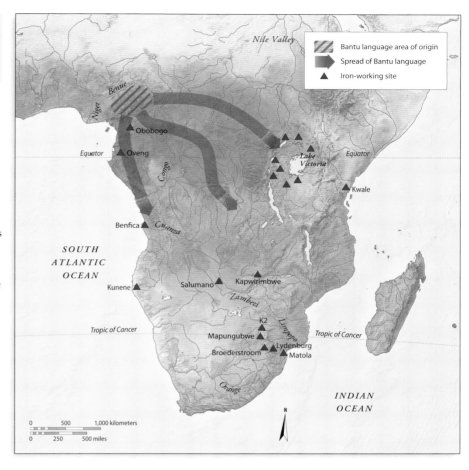

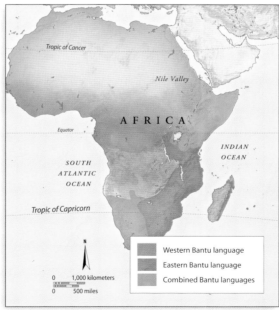

ABOVE Archeologists hypothesize that agricultural practices and iron working spread from the Nile Valley southwards at the beginning of the seventh century CE.

LEFT The movement of Bantu speakers toward the Nile Valley allowed them to acquire knowledge of agriculture and iron smelting. These skills were then disseminated as the Bantu swept southwards.

BELOW An Asante funerary mask, Ghana.

Barbarians

During the early Middle Ages (400–1000 CE), Germanic tribes from northeastern Europe entered the Western European part of the Roman Empire. These nomadic tribes destroyed much of Roman civilization and Roman institutions in the West.

> If it were easy to be a Chieftain, everyone would be one.
> –Attila the Hun (406–453 CE).

ABOVE Attila the Hun was a brutal man. Some believe he killed his brother, Bleda, who died about 12 years into the brothers' joint rule of the Hunnish Empire.

The warlike nature and uncivilized behavior of these tribes earned them the name "barbarians," a Greek term meaning "illiterates," "strangers," and "wanderers." An ethnically diverse people who were united by transient tribal confederations, they included, among others, the Visigoths, Vandals, Ostrogoths, Franks, and Huns.

Visigoths

Central to this were the Visigoths. The Goths were a Germanic tribe that, in the late fourth century, split into the Ostrogoths of the east and the Visigoths of the west. After expanding into Eastern Europe, the Huns pressured the Goths, absorbing the Ostrogoths and threatening the Visigoths. The latter fled and, according to long-standing treaty provisions, took refuge in the Roman Empire. The Romans dealt with the Visigoths the way most empires handle peoples on their borders—pursuing policies of accommodation and assimilation.

Still, the Visigoths revolted, convinced the Romans had failed to honor their obligations. They routed the Roman army in the Battle of Adrianople (378 CE) and then went on a rampage in Greece; however, the new Roman emperor, Theodosius I, pacified them by making them part of his army. On the death of Theodosius, the Visigoths moved west, leading to the Sack of Rome (410 CE) and a Visigothic kingdom in the Iberian Peninsula and southern Gaul.

Vandals

The Vandals, another East Germanic tribe, migrated at the same time as the Visigoths. Overcoming Frankish resistance, the Vandals crossed into Gaul at the close of 406 CE and by 409 CE traversed the Pyrenees into the Iberian Peninsula. Later, they conquered the rich lands of North Africa where they established a Vandal kingdom.

Ostrogoths

Following the pattern established by the Visigoths, the Ostrogoths, at first part of the Hunnish Empire, also crossed the Danube into Roman territory. In the 480s CE, the Ostrogoths, freed of Hunnish rule, entered the empire and were sent to Italy, to serve the emperor there and to keep them out of the East. This led to the creation of the Ostrogothic kingdom in Italy under Theodoric the Great (454–526 CE).

Franks

Another prominent tribe was the Franks. Following the collapse of Roman authority in the west, Clovis (466–511 CE) united the various Frankish tribes. He then founded the Merovingian dynasty, which ruled the ancient Roman province of Gaul—modern France and much of western Germany—

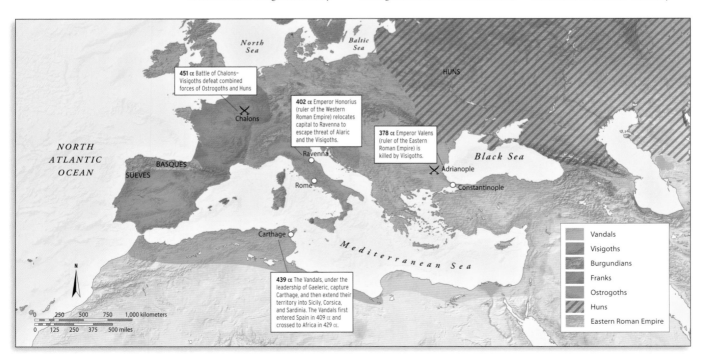

451 CE Battle of Chalons–Visigoths defeat combined forces of Ostrogoths and Huns

402 CE Emperor Honorius (ruler of the Western Roman Empire) relocates capital to Ravenna to escape threat of Alaric and the Visigoths.

378 CE Emperor Valens (ruler of the Eastern Roman Empire) is killed by Visigoths.

439 CE The Vandals, under the leadership of Gaeleric, capture Carthage, and then extend their territory into Sicily, Corsica, and Sardinia. The Vandals first entered Spain in 409 CE and crossed to Africa in 429 CE.

	Vandals
	Visigoths
	Burgundians
	Franks
	Ostrogoths
	Huns
	Eastern Roman Empire

C. 100 CE
Lombards settle along the lower Elbe

C. 200-533 CE Vandals establish a kingdom along the Danube River

238 CE Goths cross the Danube

250-275 CE Franks begin raids through the Western Empire

375 CE Ostrogoths are conquered by the Huns.

410 CE Visigoths sack Rome

555 CE The Ostrogoths disappear

from the mid-fifth to the mid-eighth century. His conversion to Roman Catholicism would powerfully influence the subsequent history of France and all of Europe. Thus by 500 CE, we see a Visigothic "state" in Spain and southern Gaul, a Vandal state in north Africa, a Frankish state in most of Gaul, as well as an Ostrogothic state in Italy.

Huns

Another group from Asia arrived to rove Rome-controlled territory. The Huns, who likely emerged from a union of nomadic Central Asian and European tribes, reached the Danube River frontier of the Roman Empire around 376 CE. By the fifth century, the Hunnish Empire stretched from the steppes of Central Asia to the western borders of modern Germany and from the Black Sea to the Baltic Sea. The empire ended in 469 CE with the death of Dengizik, the last Hunnish King.

The Huns provided history's most famous barbarian—Attila (406–453 CE). Known as "Attila the Hun" or the "Scourge of God," he led the Hunnish Empire (initially with his brother, Bleda) from 434 CE until his death. A cruel and brutal man, Attila sought to claim half the Western Roman Empire. He and his forces invaded Gaul, but they were driven out in 451 CE at the hands of a Roman-Visigoth alliance. Attila died two years later on his wedding night.

Grandeur and Decline of the Roman Empire

The traditional date for the start of Rome's decline and fall is 180 CE, but a more significant year was 238 CE when, for the first time, people from beyond the lower Danube—the Goths—clashed with Roman frontier forces, beginning four decades of destructive attacks on every frontier by peoples and states from outside, plunging the empire into a near-death crisis.

192 CE Commodius is murdered by the Praetorian Guard

235-285 CE Continuous civil war breaks out against Persians, as well as Barbarian raids

313 CE Constantine and Licinius, the Eastern ruler, agree to end persecutions. Christianity is legalized.

361-363 CE Emperor Julian the Apostate attempts to ban Christianity. He dies while fighting the Parthians.

410 CE First Sack of Rome

455-476 CE Barbarians become Roman generals and puppet emperors

During two decades of intermittent civil war, the assertive and short-lived dictatorship of Julius Caesar—terminated on the Ides of March 44 BCE—was followed by power struggles between his chief lieutenant Marcus Antonius (Marc Antony) and his great-nephew and adopted son, Gaius Octavius, who became Gaius Caesar Octavianus. Even dividing the empire between them, with Antony ruling the east—where he married Egypt's Greek pharaoh Cleopatra—and Octavian the west, brought only a brief respite. In 31–30 BCE, Octavian finally defeated his rival, annexed Egypt, and united the Roman world under his sole rule.

Politics and Power

Octavian, taking the portentous extra name of Augustus, ruled for 44 years (30 BCE–14 CE) as the leading man *(princeps)*—an open, yet undeclared, monarch whom

Provinces of the Late Roman Empire (c. 120 CE)

RIGHT A dying Marc Antony is brought to Cleopatra in this painting by Ernest Hillemacher.

we call the first "emperor" from his military title *imperator*. The Senate and the other institutions of state followed where he led, making Rome simultaneously both re-public and monarchy.

Augustus was succeeded by four kinsmen, the "Julio-Claudian" emperors. But after Nero's suicide in 68 CE, emperors—still adding Caesar and Augustus to their own names—came from an ever-widening range of aristocratic families.

Peace within the empire—the famous though not always unruffled *pax Romana*—reigned for most of the two-and-a-half centuries after Augustus's victory over Marc Antony, and again for most of the fourth century. This did not mean the end of wars abroad. Augustus himself masterminded conquests of new lands across

Europe from the North Sea to the Black Sea, almost doubling the extent of the empire. Although he counseled against further expansion, those who followed ignored him. Claudius invaded Britain in 43 CE. Trajan annexed Dacia—modern Romania—and, briefly, ancient Armenia, Mesopotamia, and Babylonia. Then Severus took back northern Mesopotamia from the declining Parthian empire. After this, expansion more or less halted, but not the militaristic self-idealism of an ever-victorious Rome, superior and invincible to all foes, which endured almost to the end.

Culture

Society was essentially civilian, with literary and rhetorical education the benchmark of social achievement. In the western half of the empire, knowing Greek was another standard feature of education—though Latin was less common in the east. Literacy was open to everyone, though only a minority of people enjoyed it. Except for Druids and Christians—both seen as anti-social elements—there was complete religious freedom.

Some features of the Roman world would be less attractive today—above all the persistence of slavery, especially as slaves were often badly treated. There was the institutional violence of some judicial punishments, like condemning criminals—and sometimes Christians—to be killed by wild animals in the arena, and the bloodstained gladiatorial sports. Officials at every level in every region were often harsh or incompetent or both, acted illegally, and took bribes. Women endured limited and domestically-focused roles.

Rome, as both state and idea, was an always-evolving reality. The Roman state drew no lasting ethnic, racial, or geographical lines around itself. All Italy by 80 BCE was part of it and then a growing number of provinces. In 417 CE, the poet Namatianus wrote, "You have made a city of the world."

RIGHT Regulations concerning the development of Roman territories in Africa are recorded on this stone tablet, dated around 209 CE.

ABOVE The Late Roman Empire included most of the known world, controlling trade and influencing culture until Germanic tribes began to infiltrate and plunder the world's great power.

BELOW The Roman emperor Nero is shown here sending Vespasian to Judea to avenge the Jewish insult to him, in a detail from a fifteenth-century manuscript.

Society and Stresses

In modern terms, Rome and its empire were technologically and economically limited, like all societies until recent times. Children could die before they were even a year old. The energy for agriculture, manufacturing, transport, and daily needs came mainly from human or animal muscle—hence the phenomenon of slavery, though this was less extensive than often supposed. The legions and other forces, mostly stationed on the European and eastern frontiers, brought spending power and Roman ways to distant regions. As the remains of Pompeii and Ostia in Italy, Silchester (Calleva) in England, and Italica in Spain show, Roman towns had well-ordered amenities, from paved streets and running water, to supervised shopping centers and impressively adorned temples, basilicas, and houses.

Invaders

From 238 CE on, troubles came almost unendingly. The European tribes gathered into large, changeable, and militant confederations—Alemanni, Saxons, Goths, and Franks—which swept up many peoples. The old Parthian monarchy was replaced by an invigorated Persian dynasty. In the 250s and 260s CE these forces all fell on the embattled empire. Compounding these ills, the Roman state itself was wracked by palace and army coups on an unheard-of scale, and after 260 CE by a plague epidemic that killed millions. First Gaul, Spain, and Britain in the west, then eastern provinces led by the desert city of Palmyra, set up their own separatist empires to cope with the invasions, splitting the empire for more than 15 years (258–274 CE).

Because of military needs, there were from now on two—and sometimes more—emperors entitled "Augusti," one governing the east and one the west, at times assisted by junior emperors termed "Caesars." Administration was rearranged, taxes and coinage reformed—Constantine's gold solidus became ancestor of the bezant, florin, ducat, and shilling—and Christianity not only tolerated but now promoted. As a match for Rome, Constantine transformed an old Greek city, Byzantium, into his new city of Constantinople.

NORTH ATLANTIC OCEAN

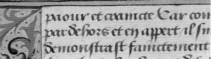

ABOVE A solid gold coin bearing the profile of Marcus Aurelius, Roman emperor 161–180 CE, was used as currency during his reign. The Romans had vast trading routes across the empire and currency was used extensively.

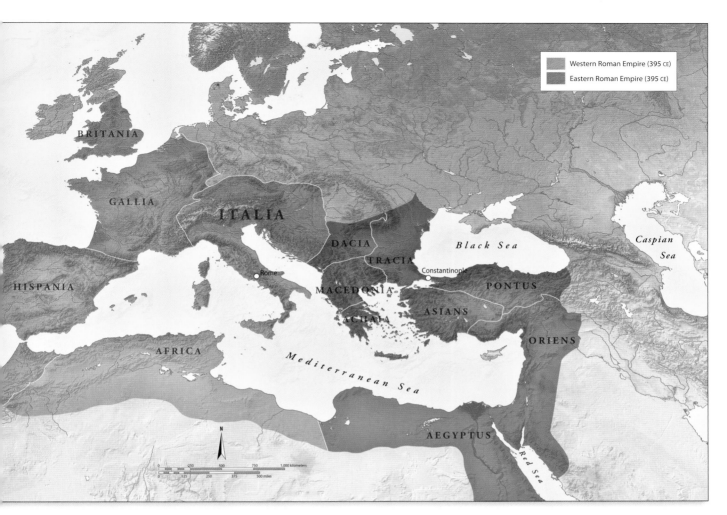

Map legend:
- Western Roman Empire (395 CE)
- Eastern Roman Empire (395 CE)

BRITANIA

GALLIA

ITALIA

HISPANIA

DACIA

TRACIA

Black Sea

Constantinople

Caspian Sea

Rome

MACEDONIA

PONTUS

ACHAIA

ASIANS

ORIENS

AFRICA

Mediterranean Sea

AEGYPTUS

Red Sea

N

0   250   500   750   1,000 kilometers
0   125   250   375   500 miles

ABOVE The Roman empire had vast resources of wealth that allowed the people to enjoy a rich culture and the improvement of living standards.

LEFT This relief, from the Temple of Neptune, Campo Marzio, Rome, shows an early census taker recording his numbers. The census was taken every five years.

Decline

The Late Empire is commonly judged morally and economically degenerate, culturally inferior, indeed ripe for overthrow. Modern studies are correcting this illusion. Despite outside pressures, violent controversies among Christians, fiscal problems, and periodic civil wars, it continued to be powerful and prosperous—the east more so perhaps than ever.

A fresh Gothic invasion, victorious at Adrianople in 378 CE, was tamed by 383 CE. A generation later came great German invasions of the west in 406–412 CE, with a relatively polite Gothic ransacking of Rome itself in 410 CE. Yet the situation in the west was largely restored by brilliant if now forgotten generals, the emperor Constantius III and Aetius the Patrician. Meanwhile the eastern provinces returned to enjoying peace.

After 420 CE, the west's strength did lessen. Britain was given up. Goths and others were granted virtually independent enclaves in Gaul and Spain, while the Vandals more intransigently seized the wealthy provinces of North Africa.

Yet Roman authority remained powerful across Gaul, Spain, Italy, and the upper Danube lands. Attacks by the Huns under Attila (441–453 CE) were checked, then repulsed by Aetius with Gothic help. This was, however, the western empire's last achievement.

Even though legions still watched the Rhine and Danube frontiers, political instability and strife recurred, allowing much of Gaul and Spain after 468 CE to fall under Gothic occupation.

On September 4, 476 CE, Odovacar, commander of the mostly German-born Roman army of Italy, sacked the last western Augustus—ironically a boy named Romulus—to become master of Italy under nominal authority of Constantinople. In effect, the western Roman empire now ended—not with a whimper, but a thud.

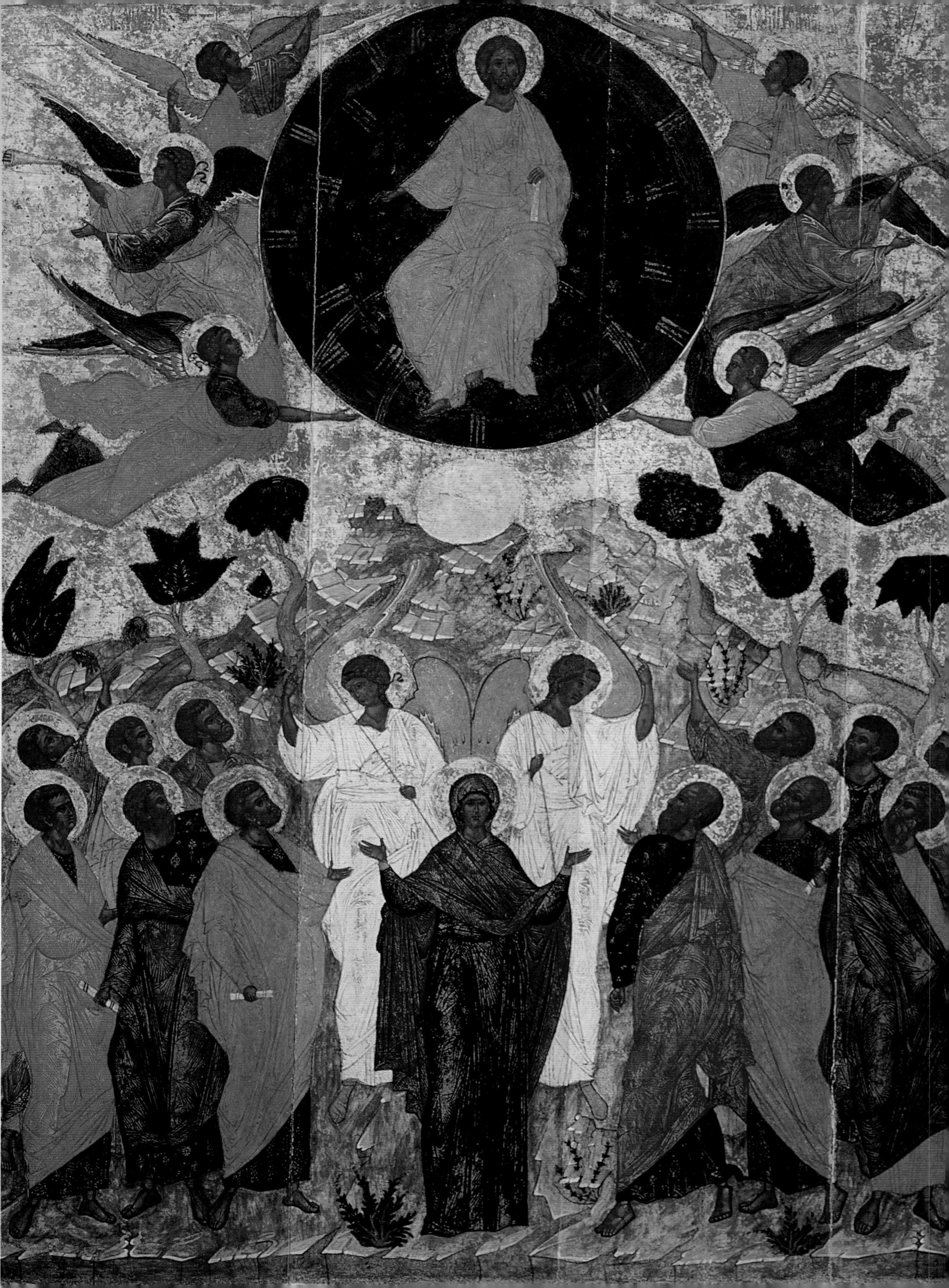

Divine Conquering

From 601 to 1300 new groups of conquerors established vast empires. Some of these were driven by religious zeal, others by the need for new lands.

RIGHT A Crusader and a Muslim warrior battle it out in this painting dated c. 1250.

LEFT Christianity continued its spread throughout Europe. The Ascension of Jesus Christ is shown in this panel, c. 1543.

RIGHT Buddhism became the dominant religion in India. This painting of an elephant shows various Buddhist figures.

PREVIOUS PAGES This exquisite representation of Constantine the Great and St Helena is made of hundreds of mosaic tiles.

The Roman Empire initially split into halves. In the east, Byzantine Emperors tried to remake the old empire, but they had to face many threats. In the early 600s CE, war between the Persian Sassanid and Byzantine empires exhausted both sides without leading to any decisive result. Leaders in Constantinople could not prevent the tribes of Lombards from settling in northern Italy and various Slavic tribes from conquering the Danube region. Ultimately, Constantinople lost its ties with the western half of the old Roman Empire, ensuring that the eastern rites of the Church would not hold sway in Western Europe.

Mohamed

The resulting weakness of the Byzantine Empire created the opportunity for the rapid expansion of a new religion rooted in the Judaic and Christian traditions. A new prophet, Mohamed, called for believers' personal submission to a great and merciful God. His holy work, the Qur'an, provided a moral and legal code, as well as a banner under which Mohamed and his followers were able to unite Bedouin tribes in the Arabian Peninsula. After Mohamed's death in 632 CE, highly skilled warriors motivated by religion and the desire for the spoils of war were able to conquer a vast new empire, encompassing North Africa and southern Spain, the whole of the Middle East, and the entirety of the Sassanid Empire. Islamic warriors fought long wars against the Byzantine Empire and eventually against Christian crusaders from across Europe.

Charlemagne

The western half of the Roman Empire faced similar issues. Roman Gaul transformed into the Merovingian Kingdoms, and Charlemagne used that power base to forge a new empire that at its height covered most of western and central Europe. Charlemagne's heirs could not keep the empire together, as family intrigue and eventual civil war led to the 843 CE

Treaty of Verdun that split the empire in three—the western third would eventually become France, the eastern third the Germanic empire, while the middle third would gradually lose some of its territory to France and Germany, with the remainder coalescing into Belgium, the Netherlands, Luxembourg, Switzerland, and northern Italy.

Charlemagne's kingdom also served to link the Christian church with political elites, and Christianity spread rapidly throughout the remainder of Europe, often at the point of a sword, through conquest and forced conversion.

The ties between kings and the Church in Rome were very uneasy, however, and struggles between the popes and temporal rulers over control of the population, taxes, territory, and spiritual matters would continue unabated until modern times.

Mongols

In the 1200s, the Mongols, compelled by climate change that reduced the grazing for their animals, and inspired by Genghis Khan's vision of conquest, swept from their steppeland homes, destroying the Song dynasty in China, conquering Persia and the Middle East, and dominating Russia. The Mongols used heavy

savagery to intimidate the enemy, but also realized that it was sometimes wiser to demand tribute from conquered peoples rather than massacre them.

Genghis Khan eventually turned more to lawmaking, establishing a legal code and judicial system. In China, Kubilai Khan ruled through Mongol administrators, but also honored Chinese rites and customs. Perhaps the most enduring effect of the Mongols' conquest was their inadvertent creation of communication between China and the west, allowing for greater trade. Traders like Marco Polo brought back knowledge of paper-making, gunpowder, and better navigation—technological innovations that transformed Europe and the world.

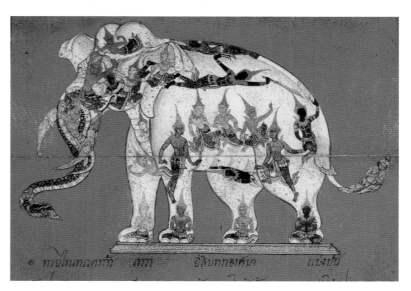

Human Encounters

After the colonization of the world in the preceding millennia, around 600 CE there were very few places on the globe left without established communities.

Even though the world was still sparsely inhabited—with an estimated population of 260 million in the year 1000 CE—population movements increasingly resulted in different cultures coming in contact with one another. These encounters were often of a friendly character, for instance in the case of trade contacts, but increasingly population movements also resulted in violent encounters.

Iceland

At the beginning of this period there were, however, still some areas in the world left where no people lived at all.

In Europe such a place was the island of Iceland. Although the island had been visited before, for the first time settlers from present-day Norway in 874 CE would settle permanently on the uninhabited and hostile shores of the volcanic island in the Atlantic.

Oceania

Perhaps the last time new travelers discovered genuine *terra incognita* was when Polynesian settlers reached Hawaii and New Zealand. The exact time of the Polynesian arrival at Hawaii is unknown, but there is consensus among scholars that between 500 and 1000 CE

the first settlers from the Marquesas and Tahiti must have crossed the ocean and arrived on the shores of the Hawaiian island group.

America

On the American continent, before the arrival of Europeans, the populations were also far from sedentary. Continuously in search of better hunting grounds, in North America there were various wandering groups who migrated—often back and forth—from one valley to another in an area that stretched from Utah in the northwest to the southeastern parts of Mexico. Some groups founded

> Treat the earth well. It was not given to you by your parents. It was loaned to you by your children.
> –Native American Proverb

settlements in certain valleys, such as the Hopi tribe in present-day Arizona, and in the Valley of Mexico a settlement arose at Teotihuacán where, according to some scholars, around 500 CE no less than 250,000 people lived. However, after about 250 years, the city was completely abandoned.

RIGHT Called the Psalter map (c. 1250) because it accompanied an early edition of the Book of Psalms, this map shows the city of Jerusalem as the center of the known world and is one of the earliest maps to depict Biblical events.

LEFT The Pyramid of the Sun, seen from the Temple of Quetzalcoatl, in the ancient city of Teotihuacán in present-day Mexico. The story of the city's builders is not known, although many theories exist.

700 CE The Arabs conquer Tunis

c. 1000 An early Andean culture of Huari uses complex irrigation systems to cultivate crops

1000 Château de Goulaine vineyard in the Loire Valley, France, is founded. It is thought to be one of Europe's oldest and continuous family businesses.

1100-1200 Serbs occupy already inhabited parts of northern and eastern Albania

1200 The Anasazi tribe begin building cliff dwellings in southwest Colorado, USA

BELOW Although discovered earlier, it wasn't until 874 CE that a settlement was established on Iceland.

Africa

Pastoralist societies are often mobile by nature, moving their livestock in search of fresh pasture and water. In Africa from the first century CE, cattle-keeping groups originating from the middle Nile region migrated upstream of the river Nile in a southward direction. They penetrated the lands of the Bantu societies in the area of present-day Uganda, often dominating the existing cultures there.

Asia

Another migration movement that also had a pastoralist background was to be found in the western parts of Asia.

The Arabs, a Semitic-speaking tribe from the Arabian Peninsula consisting largely of groups of pastoralists, would form an army united under the faith of Islam. Using horses and camels to move quickly over large distances, they would conquer large parts of Asia Minor, the Iberian Peninsula, then onto North Africa. Their migrations not only resulted in the actual movement of people, but also in the spread of religion, culture, and science.

Europe

In Europe, one of the most extraordinary population movements was that of the Vikings. They left fewer traces than Arabic conquests during the same period, but Viking migrations were nonetheless impressive and without precedent in the region. First invading the British Isles, then the Low Countries and France, Viking influence slowly spread around the Mediterranean—encountering the expanding Arab societies—while penetrating Slavic territories in the east. Viking merchant settlements could be found as far south as Sicily, while in the east, Viking settlers founded the city of Kiev—the capital of present-day Ukraine.

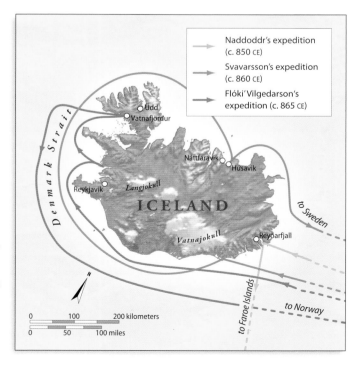

Naddoddr's expedition (c. 850 CE)

Svavarsson's expedition (c. 860 CE)

Flóki'Vilgedarson's expedition (c. 865 CE)

Denmark Strait

Udd
Vatnafjördur

Náttfaravík
Húsavík

Reykjavík
Langjokull

ICELAND

Vatnajokull

Reydarfjall

to Sweden

to Faroe Islands

to Norway

N

0   100   200 kilometers
0   50   100 miles

GOD AND COUNTRY

Islam—Message of the Prophet

The religion of Islam is typically seen as beginning with the preaching of the prophet Mohamed although it has antecedents in Arabia in the sixth century. The spread of Islam can be attributed to the vast empires of the Caliphs.

Mohamed first began to preach his message at Mecca (in modern Saudi Arabia) but it was not well received there, as its monotheistic tone threatened polytheistic tendencies of entrenched Arabian religious traditions in the city.

In 622 CE, Mohamed moved to the oasis of Yathrib, north of Mecca, due to the lack of acceptance of his teachings in Mecca. Yathrib later became known as Medina and the move—known as the *hijrah*—was seen as being so significant that it marks the beginning of the Islamic calendar.

Mohamed

Mohamed is claimed to have received revelations from God that were later preserved in the Qur'an. In Islam, Allah is held to be the only god and Mohamed is considered to have been the messenger of Allah. In practicing the Islamic faith, believers are called to observe the Five Pillars of Islam which are to say prayers five times daily, publicly affirm the faith, give alms to the needy, fast during the month of Ramadan, and undertake a pilgrimage to Mecca at least once during the believer's lifetime.

The community of believers was referred to as the *ummah* and was the main institution, rather than the church or state, as in the Roman world. Mohamed himself was the leader of the *ummah*, but he was not a monarch in the way Roman emperors were. Mohamed not only received revelations from God which were recorded to form the Qur'an but also set an example by his way of life, which is recorded in the *hadith*.

Mohamed died in 632 CE, only 10 years after the move to Medina, but he had succeeded in establishing Islam so that it would continue to flourish after his death. By this time, Mecca had become part of the *ummah* and was now central to the Islamic faith.

Of great importance at Mecca was the Ka'bah, which became a shrine and was claimed to have been an altar built originally by

Abraham. Mecca became a center of pilgrimage and the direction in which all Muslims were expected to face when they prayed.

Caliphs

Following the death of Mohamed, four successors or caliphs emerged who had been his companions. The third caliph, Uthman, was from the Umayyads clan and his murder in 656 CE set off a civil war. Developments during the war marked the beginning of two major sects of the faith that remain significant to this day.

Shia and Sunni

In Medina, Mohamed's cousin Ali was appointed Caliph by those responsible for killing Uthman, and it was from this group that the Shia sect emerged. The Shia claimed that Ali had been appointed by Mohamed as his successor before his death in 632 CE.

This appointment was challenged by a group supported by Mohamed's most important wife, Aisha, and also by the remaining leadership of the Umayyads. It was from this second group that the Sunni tradition emerged.

In another civil war that ran from 744–750 CE, the Umayyads were overthrown by a revolutionary group of Shia Muslims who had become concerned at the permissiveness of the Umayyads. They supported the Abbas family and their victory over the Umayyads marked the beginning of the Abbasid Caliphate that was to last for the next 300 years.

It was under the rules of the Umayyads and the Abbasids that two of the greatest cities of the Islamic world were to emerge—Damascus and Baghdad.

c. 610 CE Mohamed has a vision in a cave near the city of Mecca

632 CE Death of Mohamed, who is succeeded by Abu Bakr

c. 650 CE Qur'an is recorded by order of Caliph Uthman

c. 661 CE Damascus becomes the capital of the Umayyad Caliphate

754 CE Baghdad becomes the capital of the Abbasid Caliphate

LEFT A pilgrimage to Mecca, one of the Five Pillars of Islam, is shown in this Ottoman manuscript.

RIGHT In the space of a few hundred years, Islam spread across the Arab world and the Middle East.

> Even as the fingers of the two hands are equal, so are human beings equal to one another. No one has any right, nor any preference to claim over another.
> —Mohamed (c. 570–632 CE), prophet.

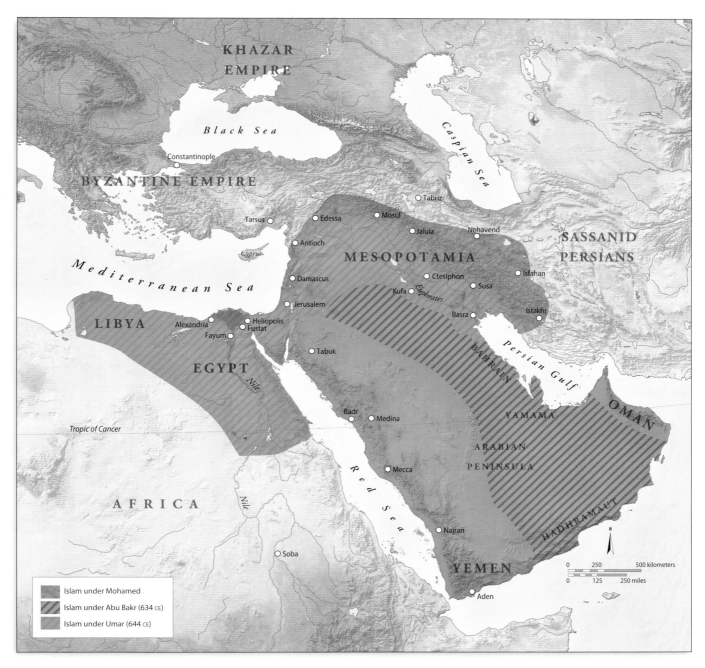

Islam under Mohamed
Islam under Abu Bakr (634 CE)
Islam under Umar (644 CE)

Damascus and Baghdad

The Umayyads had based themselves in Damascus and it was during their rule that Damascus flourished, with the construction of the famous mosque representing one of their great achievements.

The Abbasids based their Caliphate at Baghdad and that also became a magnificent city, with eyewitness accounts from the period describing its opulence.

When the Fatimids of North Africa established themselves at Cairo in the tenth century, another important Islamic city was born.

RIGHT Mohamed is shown preaching to followers in the desert in this painting by Domenico Morelli (1826–1901).

Judaism–The Beginning of the Jewish Faith

According to Jewish tradition, the history of Judaism begins with the Covenant between God and the Jewish patriarch Abraham.

Christians and Muslims also share the traditions of Abraham and the Old Testament prophets, and the followers of all three faiths are accordingly known in Muslim lore as the "People of the Book." But just as Christians and Muslims adhere to their own respective religions, so Orthodox Jews insist that Judaism is the only true faith. One must be born a Jew, or have Jewish antecedents, or be converted.

Origins

Jewish history now encompasses nearly 4,000 years, and hundreds of different populations throughout the modern world. It has been suggested that the earliest Jews were not Semitic at all, but descendants of the Sumerians who created the earliest civilization in recorded history, in Mesopotamia. The known Jewish past dates back as far as Abraham, who is said to have migrated from a tribe in Aoor, in what is now Iraq, to Palestine, sometime between 1950 BCE and 1920 BCE. More importantly, it is possible, though it has not been confirmed empirically, that the first Jewish settlements were established on what is now the West Bank as far back as 1200 BCE. Other stories from the Old Testament are questionable. For example, Jericho,

some archeologists believe, was abandoned at least 300 years before the Hebrews emerged.

Persecution

In ancient times, Jews migrated to various parts of the Middle East and Arabia, then to Europe and Asia. It is also possible that they moved with Arab armies across northern Africa and into southern Europe at the time of the Islamic invasions of Saladin—and that they moved thenceforth into the rest of Europe. Until the 1400s CE, the Iberian Peninsula, North Africa, and the Middle East were all controlled by Muslims, who generally allowed Jews to move freely, although they were sporadically

LEFT Rabbi reading the Torah, also called the Five Books of Moses. Said to be the inspired Word of God as revealed to Moses, these books are known to Christians as the Pentateuch: Genesis, Exodus, Leviticus, Numbers, and Deuteronomy.

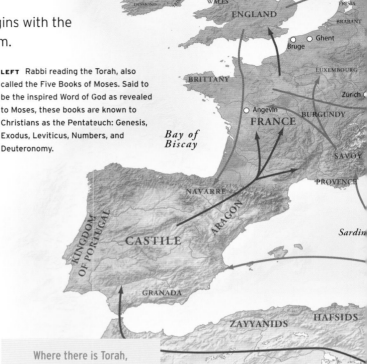

> Where there is Torah, it sustains the world.
> —Ovadia Yosef, former Sephardic Chief Rabbi of Israel.

persecuted. But in Spain between 610 CE and 641 CE, following a prophecy that the Roman Empire would be overthrown by a circumcized people, there was an attempt by Heraclius to exterminate them, and between 637 CE and 644 CE, the Saracens drove most Christians and Jews out of Arabia.

In 1146 CE and between 1346 CE and 1353 CE, Jews were massacred in Germany, following religious enthusiasm for the Crusades. In 1189 CE, the coronation of King Richard the Lionheart of England, imbued with Crusader fanaticism, incited a violent outbreak of Jewish persecution. A century later, King Edward I of England—another zealous Crusader who detested all unbelievers—accused Jews of adulterating the coinage and hanged

LEFT Jerusalem, from a sixth-century Byzantine mosaic (the oldest extant map of Palestine), Church of Saint George, Madaba, Jordan. Jerusalem was captured by the Byzantines from Persia in 629 CE.

280 unfortunates in London for this offence. Edward prohibited Jews from moneylending, and from owning property; he also imposed a poll tax and made Jews wear a special badge, as did the Turks.

Structure

Judaism, the religion of the Jews, is a complex expression of religious and ethnic communities—a way of life as well as a set of basic beliefs and values discernable in patterns of action, social order and culture, religious statements, and concepts. Among the oldest religious traditions still in practice today, it differs from many religions in that central authority is not vested in a person or group, but in sacred texts and traditions. The focus of Jewish religious affirmations is to experience God's presence in human events, affecting and fashioning lifestyle and mode of existence. The pattern of life for Jews is based on a "Covenant" between God and the people, via obedience to God's teaching—the Torah.

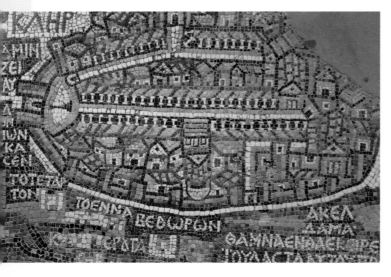

SWEDEN

Baltic
Sea

NOVGOROD

DENMARK

PSKOV

RUSSIAN
PRINCIPALITIES

HOLSTEIN

OSTSIEDLUNG

TEUTONIC ORDER

OKA BASIN

MAZOVIA

POLAND
(AND DUCHY OF
LITHUANIA)

RYAZAN

GOLDEN HORDE

HOLY
ROMAN
EMPIRE

MEISSEN

BOHEMIA

BAVARIA

HUNGARY

MOLDAVIA

REPUBLIC OF
VENICE

AUSTRIA

Venice

BOSNIA

Genoa

Florence

RAGUSA

WALLACHIA

SERBIA

Caspian
Sea

PAPAL
STATES

Adriatic Sea

Rome

Black Sea

GEORGIA

TREBIZOND

Naples

OTTOMAN EMPIRE

ERZINCAN

AK KOYUNLU

DOMINION OF
EMIR TIMUR

Sicily

Crete

Cyprus

RAMAZAN

DULKADIR

KARA
KOYUNLU

ILKHANATE

Mediterranean Sea

MAMLUK
SULTANATE

Red Sea

Persian
Gulf

N

0   250   500   750   1,000 kilometers

0   125   250   375   500 miles

Jewish area

Jewish diaspora (700–500 BCE)

Jewish diaspora (to 1350)

Jewish expulsions (to 1394)

c. 1500–1200 BCE
Exodus. Jews wander
in the desert.

1200–1050 BCE
Occupation of the
Promised Land

1050–920 BCE Jews
united under Saul, David,
and Solomon form a
capital at Jerusalem

722 BCE Assyria
conquers Israel

586 BCE Babylonians
burn Jerusalem

ABOVE In ancient times,
Jews migrated to various
parts of the Middle East
and Arabia, then to Europe
and Asia.

LEFT The Ark of the
Covenant housed the
stone tablets containing
the Ten Commandments.
This painting offers an artist's impression of its journey back to Zion after it
had been returned by the
Philistines, King David
dancing before it.

103

Christianity– Eternal Salvation

Christianity was one of the key political and social factors in the development of the Medieval West and the Byzantine East.

LEFT Sixteenth century fresco showing Emperor Constantine I (280–337 CE) and his mother, St Helena (c. 250–330 CE), who is traditionally credited with finding the relics of the True Cross in Jerusalem, together with the nails used in the crucifixion.

ABOVE By the sixteenth century, Christianity had extended its area of influence from its beginning in the Middle East to Europe, part of Africa, and the Americas.

> I believe in person to person. Every person is Christ for me, and since there is only one Jesus, that person is the one person in the world at that moment.
>
> –Mother Teresa (1910-1997), Roman Catholic nun, missionary, and humanitarian.

c. 6 BCE Birth of Jesus

c. 26 CE John the Baptist begins his ministry.

c. 27 CE Jesus begins his ministry.

c. 30 CE Jesus is crucified.

c. 46 CE Paul begins his missionary journeys and spreads the word of Christianity.

One of the important features of Christianity, right from the very beginning, was the universal message of salvation and the conveying of that message through vigorous missionary activity. This feature, together with the church's ability to grow even stronger during periods of persecution, gave Christianity its opportunity to move from relative obscurity at the beginning of the fourth century CE to political and cultural dominance in the medieval and Byzantine periods.

Church and State

Originally a marginalized, sometimes persecuted sect, Christianity moved to a position of imperial favor beginning with the reign of Constantine (ruled 306–337 CE). This had profound ramifications, and not only for the Christian church. Christian theology and leadership became major political issues that would later play very

important roles in the development of medieval Europe and Byzantium. By the early fourth century CE, there were already bitter theological divisions in the church that had on occasion spilled over into violence. For political purposes, Constantine became involved in some of these theological disputes, emphasizing the need to resolve them for the sake of unity. Church unity would assist the growth of Christianity and the unity of the Roman Empire under his rule. Importantly, later emperors would take the same approach—but the more they attempted to achieve theological unity the more divisions emerged. Emperors also legislated against

pagan practices from the reign of Constantine, and the banning of many elements of pagan practice in the 380s CE has led many to refer to Christianity as the state religion of the Roman Empire from this time.

The Bishop of Rome

The Roman world was changing politically during this time and Christianity played an important part in these changes. The Roman emperors had found it increasingly difficult to maintain military and political control over the western provinces of the empire and in 476 CE, the last of the western Roman emperors abdicated. The various tribal groups in Western

ARCTIC OCEAN

Barents Sea

Arctic Circle

Iceland

EUROPE

Black Sea

Caspian Sea

Rome

Mediterranean Sea

Jerusalem

AFRICA

Red Sea

Arabian Sea

ASIA

Sea of Okhotsk

East China Sea

PACIFIC OCEAN

South China Sea

Equator

INDIAN OCEAN

SOUTH ATLANTIC OCEAN

Tropic of Capricorn

AUSTRALIA

Europe, such as the Goths and Visigoths, had converted to Christianity in the fourth century, and although their leaders now replaced the Roman emperor they maintained an emphasis on Christianity as an important political force. This gave the Bishop of Rome enormous power, and the bishops of the church throughout Western Europe wielded not only theological power, but also political and economic power. As the kingdoms of Western Europe emerged in the post-Roman period, the Popes were called on to confer legitimacy on them by formally investing their heads of state. This was most evident in 800 CE when Charlemagne, the Frankish king of modern France, Spain, Italy, and Germany, was crowned Holy Roman Emperor by Pope Leo III in Rome.

The role of Christianity in the Byzantine Empire was different in some ways to the role it played in medieval Europe. While the Roman Empire in the west had effectively collapsed by the end of the fifth century CE, it continued in the east with varying levels of success until 1453 CE as the Byzantine empire. Constantine had in some senses heralded that the future of the empire lay in the east when he founded the city of Constantinople in 330 CE. Constantinople was also known as New Rome and over time it would supplant Rome as the imperial capital.

The Byzantine Empire faced its most significant challenge in the 630s CE when invading Islamic armies captured Egypt, Arabia, and Syria. Christianity continued to play an important cultural role in these societies but had little of the influence it once had on government. The eastern church also became increasingly estranged from the church in the west, to the point where a formal split occurred between the western and eastern churches in 1054 CE.

BELOW Sandro Botticelli's painting *The Adoration of the Magi* (c. 1473) shows the infant Jesus being presented to various members of the Medici family (Cosimo kneeling), the philosopher Pico della Mirandola (in red cap), and the painter himself (far right, gazing at the viewer).

N

| 0 | 1,000 | 2,000 | 3,000 kilometers |
| 0 | 500 | 1,000 | 1,500 miles |

Buddhism–Seeking Nirvana

Buddhism was born in India in the sixth century BCE as a revolt against Brahmanism, which had become predominantly ritualistic and emphasized sacrifices for different occasions.

Instead, Buddhism sought a deeper solution to the problems of inner life without the intervention of priests. Though rejecting the authority of the Vedas, Buddhism borrowed from later Vedic literature the twin doctrines of Karma and Samsara, the cycle of births, deaths, and rebirths. Buddha, however, taught an independent morality that could liberate the soul from the bondage of Samsara and help it attain Nirvana.

Buddha

The son of Suddhodana, chieftain of a principality on the India–Nepal border, Buddha was born Gautama Siddhartha. When his mother, Mahamaya, was pregnant with him, she had a dream in which an elephant with a lotus flower entered her side. The court astrologer interpreted the dream to mean that the child would be a son who would be either a Universal Emperor or a Universal Teacher, the latter if he saw misery. As Gautama grew up, he was trained in all arts appropriate to a prince. He was married to the beautiful and accomplished Yashodhara, and his father kept him from misery and provided him with comforts. Despite such precautions, one day, during a chariot ride, Gautama experienced four "sights," three of them—an aged man, a sick man, and a corpse—all representations of pain and misery. The fourth

LEFT Buddha in Nirvana. *Nirvana* is a Sanskrit word meaning "to extinguish." In a Buddhist context it means more specifically to extinguish ignorance, hatred, and all forms of earthly suffering.

483 BCE Buddha dies at Kusinara

c. 200 BCE Trading with Arabia, Indians begin to spread the word of Buddha

120 BCE Two golden statues of Buddha are presented to the Chinese Emperor Han Wudi

68 CE The building of the White Horse Temple officially establishes Buddhism in China

c. 538 CE Buddhism is introduced to Japan via Korea

"sight" was an ascetic, who was calm and serene. With the last sight, Gautama felt relieved, but also determined to resolve the question of pain and misery and bring about an end to suffering.

On the same night, Gautama abandoned the palace and his family and left for the forests. He spent the next 14 years trying to solve the riddle of misery. One sage, Alara Kalama, agreed to teach him Vedic lore but Gautama was disappointed that knowledge and self-discipline did not offer a solution that would end human misery.

He then tried asceticism, fasting, and self-mortification for six years. Instead of becoming enlightened, he fainted. Finally, he tried meditation under a large *pipal* tree at Gaya in Magadha—today's Bihar—and at the end of 49 days of meditation, resolved the riddle of suffering. Gautama attained Enlightenment; he became the Buddha. In Buddhist parlance, Buddha's First Sermon in the Deer Park at Sarnath (near

LEFT An attendant of Fudo Myo-o, one of the warlike emanations of Buddha. Of the Myo-o, Fudo is the most revered in Japan.

Benares or Varanasi) set in motion the Wheel of Law and enunciated the Doctrine of Righteousness (*Dharmachakrapravartan*).

Buddhists regard four events as most important and sacred in the life of the Buddha—his Birth, Enlightenment, the First Sermon, and Death. He talked of the Four Noble Truths: (1) Existence is suffering (manifestation of pain); (2) suffering is born of desire; unfulfilled desire leads to rebirth (cause of pain); (3) detachment from desire leads to the end of pain; (4) when desire ceases, rebirth ceases; one attains Nirvana.

Cessation of desire and attainment of Nirvana is achieved by pursuing the 10 injunctions and the Eightfold Path. The injunctions are: Not to kill, or steal, or commit adultery; not to lie, or speak ill of other people; not to indulge in fault-finding or profane language; to abstain from covetousness and hatred, and to avoid ignorance. The Eightfold Path (*Asthangika marga*) comprises: Right Belief, Right Thought, Right Speech, Right Action (non-violence), Right Means of Livelihood, Right Effort, Right Mindfulness, and Right Meditation.

Great Schism and the Spread of Buddhism

At the Fourth General Council in 78 CE, Buddhism split into two sects—Mahayana or the Greater Vehicle (conveyance to salvation), and the Theravada (faith of the elders). The latter was called the Hinayana, or Lesser Vehicle, by the Mahayanists, whose concept of *bodhisattva* held that a meritorious person could "save" others.

The Mahayana faith spread via India's northwest to the imperial court of China, beginning in the second century CE. From China, it spread readily to Korea, Japan, and Vietnam, countries traditionally receptive to anything Chinese.

On the other hand, Theravada Buddhism, having spread to Lower Myanmar from Sri Lanka, also spread to North Myanmar in the eleventh century and from there to Thailand, Laos, and Cambodia. In India, the gap between Hinduism and Mahayana Buddhism narrowed over the centuries; by the seventh and eighth centuries CE, Buddha himself was absorbed by Hinduism as an incarnation of Vishnu. Many Buddhist temples were converted to Hindu places of worship.

RUSSIAN FEDERATION

Sakhalin

Amur

Hokkaido

KAZAKHSTAN

MONGOLIA

GOBI DESERT

Sea of Japan (East Sea)

NORTH KOREA

JAPAN

Honshu

SOUTH KOREA

Kyushu

PAMIR PLATEAU

TAKLAMAKAN DESERT

CHINA

Huang He

Yellow Sea

NDU KUSH

KUNLUN SHAN

East China Sea

Yangtze

TIBETAN PLATEAU

LEFT While Mahayana Buddhism traveled north from India to China, then on to Vietnam, Korea, and Japan, Theravada Buddhism spread south through Sri Lanka to Myanmar, Thailand, Laos, and Cambodia.

THAR DESERT

H I M A L A Y A

NEPAL

BHUTAN

Brahmaputra

Yamuna

Ganga

BANGLADESH

LAOS

Taiwan

PACIFIC OCEAN

Narmada

Tropic of Cancer

MYANMAR

Hainan

Luzon

I N D I A

DECCAN PLATEAU

Godavari

Krishna

Irrawaddi

Salween

THAILAND

VIETNAM

South China Sea

PHILIPPINES

CAMBODIA

Mindanao

Mekong

SRI LANKA

INDIAN OCEAN

BRUNEI

M A L A Y S I A

SARAWAK

Celebes

SINGAPORE

Borneo

Equator

Sumatra

I N D O N E S I A

Java

> All that we are is the result of what we have thought. The mind is everything. What we think we become.
> –Buddha.

N

| 0 | 50 | 100 | 150 kilometers |

| 0 | 25 | 50 | 75 miles |

☐ Theravada Buddhism
☐ Mahayana Buddhism
☐ Tibetan Mahayana Buddhism
(Map contains modern country names)

Hinduism—Rebirth and Karma

Hinduism is not a static religion. Like all religions, the interpretations of it over time depend greatly on the psychological and moral conditioning of the scholars and scriptural authorities.

Today, Hinduism is an inclusive religion of nearly a billion people, mostly in India, with approximately 20 million in the Indian diaspora around the globe. It is difficult to define Hinduism in precise terms. Among its essential features are the doctrine of transmigration of souls—*samsara*; the doctrine of re-birth and karma; and worship of numerous gods and goddesses, subsumed in a monotheism by the doctrine that all lesser divinities are subordinate aspects of the one God.

Social Structure

Hinduism includes a social hierarchical structure signified by *varnas* and castes. By the second century CE, those who were deemed to have "lost their caste" were considered as outcastes or untouchables. In historical terms, the Hindu beliefs are found in the Vedic literature, 1200–600 BCE—the *Vedas*, the *Brahmanas*, the *Aranyakas* and the *Upanishads*; two epics—*Ramayana* and *Mahabharata*; the *Bhagwad Gita* and the *Dharmashastras*. All these texts relate to the society and thought from the Vedic times to about 300 BCE to 200 CE, when they were finally put into writing.

Doctrine of Rebirth and Karma

Integral to Hinduism were the twin doctrines of *samsara* (the cycle of existence) and karma. The *Vedas* and the *Brahmanas* did not speak of transmigration of soul, rebirth or karma. The growing uncertainty and misery of the masses of the people from around the sixth to fourth century BCE, caused by political upheavals and constant warfare, needed an explanation. It was provided by the doctrine of rebirth and karma. It was held that one was born with his/her karma, yet his/her rebirth depended on the karma during the present life. The cycle of births and rebirths would repeat itself endlessly until one's superior karma helped in breaking the cycle and attaining *moksha* (liberation). To break the cycle, the seers suggested that people follow

LEFT The eight-armed goddess Parvati, wife of Shiva, cradles her elephant-headed infant son, Ganesha.

RIGHT Built around 1268 CE by the Hoysala Empire in southern India, the Keshava Temple features layers of intricate decorations.

1200–900 BCE The earliest Vedas are compiled

c. 1000 BCE Hinduism begins to gain followers in the south

c. 500 BCE Numerous Hindu texts are composed including *Shrauta, Mahabharata, Sutras,* and *Puranas*

c. 400 BCE Panini composes Sanskrit grammar—Ashtadhyayi

	Hindu population
	More than 60 percent Hindu population
	10–20 percent Hindu population
	1–9 percent Hindu population

> That which we call the Hindu religion is really the Eternal religion because it embraces all others.
> —Sri Aurobindo (1872-1950), Indian scholar, yogi, and guru.

one or more of the four *margs* (paths)—knowledge (*dnyana*), meditation (*dhyana*), devotion (*bhakti*), or self-discipline (*yoga*).

The scriptures also delineated the four ends (*purusharthas*) of life—*dharma, artha, kama,* and *moksha. Dharma* included Vedic ritual, ethical conduct, maintaining the varna and caste system and observance of laws. *Artha* or material gain was important but it must be pursued along ethical lines. *Kama* or love and pleasure must be pursued in a balanced way. The final end was the *moksha,*

involving a totally spiritual life trying to understand the nature of the Ultimate Reality.

Class and Caste System

The Indian social structure had its authority in the *Rig Veda*, which spoke of a cosmic sacrifice, the *Purushasukta*. The latter stated that Prajapati (Lord of Beings) (not unlike in many other early societies) was a primeval man or *purusa*. Prajapati made an offering of the cosmic being, *purusa*, as a sacrifice to himself. From the body of the sacrificed *purusa*, the whole

universe was believed to have been created, including the four classes of the society, each being made from different parts of his body: mouth—Brahman; arms—*Kshatriya*; thighs—*Vaishya* and feet—*Shudras*. These indicated four main professions, an open class system, which regarded the Brahmans as the highest and the *sudras*, who were mostly menials, at the bottom. By switching one's profession, one could move upward or downward on the social ladder.

Over the centuries, the broad four-fold class system came to be

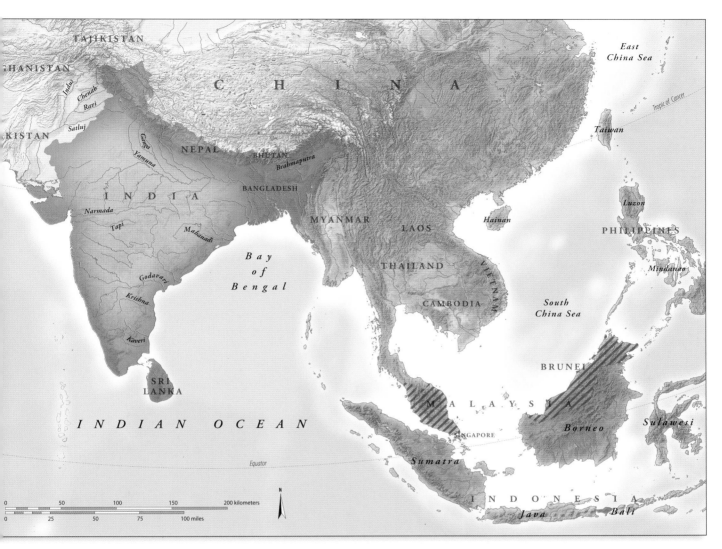

ABOVE The third largest religion in the world, Hinduism dominates in the Indian population at approximately 890 million.

RIGHT Painted during King Rama I's reign (1782–1809), a fresco from Wat Phra Leo Palace in Bangkok shows a scene from the Hindu Sanskrit epic *Ramayana*.

sub-divided into several thousand castes or *jatis*. Most of the time, the jatis belonging to a given varna are operative within a geographical and linguistic region.

Many of the practices and beliefs of Vedic times, whether in the form of rituals or the conception of the universe or the world order, or norms for the life of the individual, family, and society, remained integral parts of Hinduism. Most spiritual thinkers and religious reformers have regarded Vedic thought and life as the purer form of Hinduism.

The Frankish Realm

The Frankish conquest of the Paris basin, the middle Rhine region, and the territories in between, initiated a far-reaching geo-political reorganization that laid the foundations of European civilization.

LEFT Fourteenth century French depiction of Clovis, founder of the Frankish kingdom at the dawn of the sixth century, with Queen Clothilde and their sons Clodomir, Childebert, Theodoric, and Clotaire.

BELOW When he died in 814 CE, Charlemagne's empire encompassed what today forms the core of continental Europe, with Frankish influence also extending into Denmark and the Slavic regions.

Hitherto, the western portion of Europe had been an appendage of the vast Roman Empire built around the ancient Mediterranean and Near Eastern civilizations. The Frankish kings refashioned the northwestern parts of the Roman Empire into a new polity, added to them the territories east of the Rhine that the Romans had never succeeded in conquering, and thus for the first time centered political power on Europe itself.

This was an arduous process. Clovis (481–511 CE), the first of the Merovingian line of kings, succeeded his father, Childerich, who had commandeered the Roman province of Belgica Secunda. In a fateful battle at Zülpich near Cologne, Clovis defeated an Alemmanic host, allegedly after raising his arms to Heaven and promising that he would convert to Christianity if granted victory. The story, probably apocryphal, nonetheless underscores one of Clovis's most far-reaching decisions—to reject the Arian Christianity of neighboring barbarian kings and convert to Orthodox Christianity, a choice that fostered warmer cooperation between the Franks and the provincial senatorial families who controlled the wealthy cities of old Roman Gaul. Clovis, reportedly bothered by heresy, subsequently launched a campaign against the Arian Visigothic kingdom that saw him conquer much of Aquitaine.

Divisions

Initially, Clovis's realm was divided among his four sons, whose kingdoms were organized around the city hubs of Paris, Orleans, Soissons, and Rheims, a division that reflected the lingering Roman imprint. But by the early seventh century, the Merovingian realm had coalesced into three core kingdoms—Neustria, the "new lands" between the Loire and the Meuse; Austrasia, "the eastern lands" between the Meuse and the Rhine-Main region; and Burgundy, encompassing the upper Rhone and Saône valleys. Surrounding

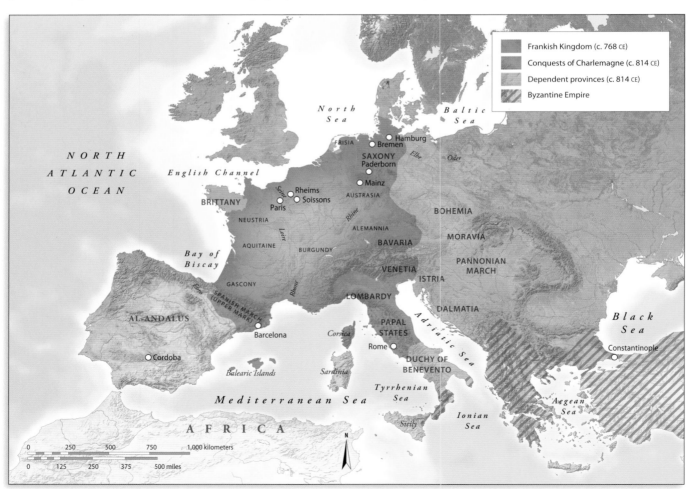

Frankish Kingdom (c. 768 CE)
Conquests of Charlemagne (c. 814 CE)
Dependent provinces (c. 814 CE)
Byzantine Empire

North Sea
Baltic Sea
FRISIA
Hamburg
Bremen
SAXONY
Paderborn
Elbe
Oder
Mainz
AUSTRASIA
North Atlantic Ocean
English Channel
Seine
Rheims
BRITTANY
Paris
Soissons
Rhine
BOHEMIA
NEUSTRIA
ALEMANNIA
MORAVIA
Loire
BAVARIA
AQUITAINE
BURGUNDY
PANNONIAN MARCH
Bay of Biscay
VENETIA
ISTRIA
Rhône
LOMBARDY
DALMATIA
Adriatic Sea
GASCONY
Ebro
SPANISH MARCH (UPPER MARK)
AL-ANDALUS
Black Sea
PAPAL STATES
Barcelona
Corsica
Rome
Constantinople
Cordoba
DUCHY OF BENEVENTO
Balearic Islands
Sardinia
Tyrrhenian Sea
Aegean Sea
Mediterranean Sea
Sicily
Ionian Sea
AFRICA

0   250   500   750   1,000 kilometers
0   125   250   375   500 miles

LEFT In 732 CE, at the Battle of Tours (also known as the Battle of Poitiers), Frankish ruler Charles Martel defeated Abd-er-Rahman, Muslim governor of Spain, thus extending his authority in the south.

751 CE Pepin the Short becomes King of the Franks

800 CE Charlemagne is crowned as Holy Roman Emperor by Pope Leo III

814-40 CE Louis the Pious succeeds Charlemagne as Holy Roman Emperor

843 CE Treaty of Verdun partitions the Carolingian Empire

870 CE Treaty of Mersen allows the Frankish kingdoms to absorb the fragmented middle lands to the east and west

the core kingdoms were peripheral dukedoms: Aquitaine, Provence, Alsace, Alemannia, Bavaria, Thuringia, Saxony, and Frisia.

Peripheral Territories
These hostile peripheral territories were pacified by the Carolingian line of Frankish rulers. Charles Martel (714–741 CE), and his son Pepin the Short (741–768 CE), who usurped the Frankish kingship in 751 CE, suppressed and reintegrated the dukedoms; while Pepin's son Charlemagne (768–814 CE), dubbed the "father of Europe" by a courtier, became emperor in 800 CE and enlarged the Frankish empire with new conquests of the Lombard kingdom, northeastern Spain, the Avar Khanate, and, after 33 years of brutal warfare, the Saxon lands of northern Germany.

Formation of Europe
The partitioning of the Frankish empire into regional kingdoms by Charlemagne's three grandsons at

> I take it very hard that these Arians hold part of the Gauls. Let us go with God's help and conquer them and bring the land under our control.
>
> –Clovis, from *History of the Franks* by Gregory of Tours.

Verdun in 843 CE was momentous. Charles the Bald's (829–877 CE) west Frankish kingdom included Francia, the Frankish lands west of the Meuse which roughly corresponded to old Neustria, as well as Aquitaine. Louis the German (825–876 CE) styled himself "king in east Francia," the mid-Rhine districts and the lands beyond the Rhine. Lothar (817–855 CE), who enjoyed the patrilinear title, claimed the lands between his brothers' kingdoms, as well as Provence and Italy.

Lothar's northern territories, granted to his son Lothar II (855–869 CE), became known as "Lothar's realm," or in modern German

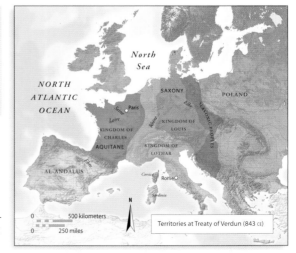

and French, Lotharingia and Lorraine. In the late ninth century, Lotharingia became a client kingdom of the east Frankish kings. Burgundy, which had disappeared during the Carolingian period, was revived as a subordinate realm in the empire of Otto I (939–972 CE).

ABOVE The kingdoms of Charles and Louis laid the foundations for medieval France and Germany, while Lothar began a tradition that linked the possession of Italy with a hold on the imperial title.

111

The Byzantine Empire

The Byzantine Empire rose out of Emperor Constantine's decision to build an eastern capital on the site of Byzantium on the Bosporus Strait, foreshadowing the eventual division of the Roman Empire.

ABOVE A contemporary mosaic portrait of Emperor Justinian, the so-called "Last Roman." One of the most important figures of late antiquity, Justinian is considered a saint by some Orthodox Christians. His rule constitutes a distinct epoch in the history of the Byzantine Empire.

And so the streets, squares, houses of two and three stories, sacred places, nunneries, houses for nuns and monks, sacred churches, even the Great Church of God and the imperial palace, were filled with men of the enemy, all of them maddened by war and murderous in spirit.

–The Bishop of Ephesus commenting on the Crusaders' sacking of Constantinople, 1204.

ABOVE In the sixth century, under Justinian, military campaigns saw the Byzantine Empire gain control over the Italian peninsula, Dalmatia, and parts of North Africa.

During the third, fourth, and fifth centuries, barbarian invaders continually harassed the western half of the Roman Empire, eventually sacking Rome. But because the eastern half of the empire could afford to hire mercenaries and pay the tributes necessary to fend off the barbarian attacks, it was able to maintain its imperial structure.

Between 527 ce and 565 ce, Emperor Justinian I, the last Latin-speaking emperor, launched what proved to be a long campaign to recover the western parts of the Roman Empire, those that had succumbed to barbarian invasion. After spending a fortune and fighting a series of brilliantly successful military campaigns, Justinian successfully re-conquered Dalmatia, the Italian Peninsula, and North Africa, but in the long run these conquests were indefensible.

Under Seige

The Byzantine Empire faced too many foes. Justinian had made peace with the Sassanid (Persian) Empire, but the Sassanids invaded in 603 CE, taking Damascus and Egypt. It became a recurring theme, however, that just as the future looked grim for the empire, a strong ruler stepped forward, reorganized the empire, and counter-attacked. In this case, Emperor Heraclius eventually repelled the invasion and defeated the Sassanids, but the war exhausted both sides. Later, the Lombards, a Germanic tribe, occupied the Po Valley and parts of Southern Italy, and various Slavic tribes raided the Danube Valley. But the greatest threat came from the expanding Arab Empire. Arab armies seized most of the Middle East, North Africa, parts of Anatolia, and endangered Constantinople.

Arab Attacks

Emperor Leo III rallied the imperial forces in 718 CE and repulsed the Arab attack on Constantinople, defeating the Arab fleet with Greek fire, a weapon that would burn on water, and benefiting from military reforms introduced in the previous century. Rather than relying on an expensive centrally-controlled army, the empire instituted the *theme* system—providing free land to local soldier–farmers. These men would fight on behalf of the empire but would pay no taxes on their land. Through this method, the empire could maintain strong forces in each region, quickly rallying a defense against raiding Slav or Arab armies, without tying up the enormous tax revenues that were involved in equipping a large professional army. The theme system served to secure the empire's

FRANKISH KINGDOMS

ATLANTIC OCEAN

SUEVES

Ebro

Caesarea Augusta

VISIGOTHS

Cordoba

Balearic Islands

Corsica

Sardinia

Hippo

AFRICA

Genoa

Verona
Florentia
DALMATIA
Zara
Rome
Danube
MOESIA
THRACE
Adrianopole
Naples
Thessalonica
Constantinople
Traianopolis
Panormus
Sicily
Messina
Cyzicus
Nicaea
Syracuse
Corinth
Ephesus
Sardes
Aphrodisias
Perga
Leptis Magna
Crete
Gortyn

Black Sea
Trebizond
PONTICA
CAPPADOCIA
Caesarea
Melitene
GALATIA
Tarsus
Antioch
Beroea
Edessa
SYRIA
Cyprus

Mediterranean Sea

Caspian Sea
IBERIA
ARMENIA
PERSIAN EMPIRE
Amida
Dura
Tigris
Euphrates

Damascus
Jerusalem
Alexandria
Heliopolis
Memphis
Aila
ARABIA
Nile
EGYPT
Red Sea
Philae

	Byzantine Empire (527 CE)
	Territory gained by Justinian (565 CE)
	Territory under dispute
✕	Major battle

N

0   250   500   750   1000 kilometers
0   125   250   375   500 miles

defense, but it also signaled an important shift within the now much smaller empire. It allowed the empire to stave off multiple threats from its enemies and even allowed it to retake some territory. Between 850 CE and 1025 CE, soldiers of the empire conquered Antioch, Greece, Crete, Bulgaria, Croatia, and Serbia.

In the case of Bulgaria, to take just one example, warfare could be brutal. The Bulgarians captured and executed Emperor Nicephorus, and their leader Khan Krum lined Nicephorus's skull with silver and used it as a drinking cup. In turn, Emperor Basil II reputedly blinded some 14,000 captured Bulgarian soldiers and forced the Bulgarian leader to convert to Christianity under the aegis of the Byzantine Patriarch, at least temporarily ending their long conflict.

The empire's history was marked with bitter warfare, court intrigue, and a long decline masked by occasional revivals and military victories. Outside Constantinople, however, the former splendor of the Roman Empire seemed like a distant memory.

The Long Decline
By the early days of the eleventh century, the empire had grown to its largest extent since the rise of Islam nearly 400 years earlier. It had resisted attacks from the Russian steppes, and the leaders of Kiev had converted to Christianity under the auspices of the Eastern Church. Scholarship in Constantinople increased, as wealthy patrons subsidized philosophers' and historians' research into the classical texts of Plato and Aristotle. Sculptors created statuary, and artists

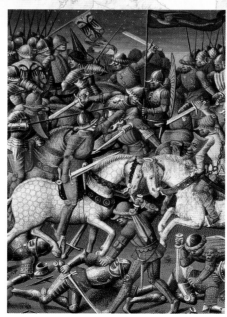

LEFT Emperor Heraclius defeating the Sassanids, as depicted 800 years after the seventh-century event. Heraclius later restored the True Cross to Jerusalem.

Thessalonica

Aegean Sea

Athens

Crete

Rhodes

Mediterranean Sea

Constantinople

Black Sea

ANATOLIA

Sinope

Caesarea

Trebizond

Iconium

KINGDOM OF
CYPRUS

Antioch

Euphrates

Tigris

ISLAMIC
CALIPHATE

Acre

Damascus

Cairo

Hattin

Nile

Jerusalem

Territory gained by Crusaders (c. 1099)

Byzantine Empire (c. 1095)

Route of First Crusade (1096–1099)

Major battle

| 0 | 10 | 20 | 30 | 40 | 50 kilometers |

| 0 | 5 | 10 | 15 | 20 | 25 miles |

RIGHT Byzantine Emperor Constantine IX Monomachus, 980–1055 CE. The threat posed by the Seljuk Turks began in his last years of power.

312 CE Constantine the Great defeats Marcus Aurelius at the Mulvian Bridge

324 CE Constantine establishes Byzantium as his new capital and moves his court. He has his name chiseled on the portal.

330 CE Constantine renames the town of Byzantium "New Rome which is Constantine's City." It became known as Constantinople.

335 CE Emperor Constantine builds the Church of the Holy Sepulcher in Jerusalem

527 CE Justinian rules the Byzantine Empire

c. 560 CE Justinian returns the treasure of Jerusalem, plundered by the Romans in 70 CE, to the Church of the Holy Sepulcher in Jerusalem

636 CE Arabs gain control of most of Palestine from the Byzantine Empire

painted religious icons. Trade throughout the Mediterranean flourished, and Constantinople served as a meeting place between Europe and Asia. The empire seemed strong.

The tough military campaigns that restored former territories, however, carried grave risks for the empire. The theme system worked well when farmers sought to defend their own homes, but the wars of conquest had increasingly relied on expensive mercenary armies, and the theme system began to decline. Emperors needed higher tax revenue, and supported wealthy provincial elites who could pay taxes on profitable land, rather than local soldiers who paid no taxes.

Seljuk Turks

By 1050, the rise of the Seljuk Turks, a fierce warrior people, threatened the eastern borders of the empire. Emperor Romanus IV raised a great army to try to end the threat, but the Seljuk Turks defeated the Byzantine army and captured the Emperor at the battle of Manzikert in 1071. The Seljuk Turks gradually overran the Anatolian plain and pushed towards the gates of Constantinople.

Crusades

The threat posed by the Muslim Seljuks eventually led Emperor Alexius I to appeal to his Christian co-religionists in the West for support against the Islamic armies that had occupied the Holy Land and imperiled the empire. Pope Urban II responded, but the Crusaders from Western Europe did not place themselves under Byzantine control, as Alexius had hoped. Instead, after they attacked the

Holy Land, seizing Antioch, Jerusalem, Tripoli, and Edessa, Western knights established independent kingdoms rather than adding their conquests to the Byzantine Empire. These isolated pockets of Christian military orders faced a continuing threat from the Seljuk Turks, and they eventually succumbed to the Islamic armies. Alexius, deprived of Western support, increasingly relied on mercenaries rather than peasant-soldiers, and gave further concessions to the great families of the empire who could afford to underwrite the large tax revenues needed to pay for the army.

The Fourth Crusade in 1202, undertaken at the behest of Pope Innocent III, dealt a mortal blow to the Byzantine Empire. Too few Crusaders turned out for the expedition. They could not afford to

pay the Venetians the required price for transport, so they agreed to sack the city of Zara, a port town whose merchants competed with the Venetians. Worse still for the empire, an ousted member of the Byzantine imperial family convinced the Crusaders to install him on the throne in Constantinople as Alexius IV. In truth, Alexius had little support, and an outraged courtier killed him. In retaliation, the Crusaders laid siege to the capital. On April 13, 1204, they broke through, sacking the city in an orgy of looting and violence against their fellow Christians. They installed Baldwin of Flanders on the imperial throne. The Byzantine Empire fragmented. Although one of the successor states, Nicaea, was eventually able to wrest control of Constantinople back from the Latin usurpers in 1261, the Byzantine Empire was a spent force. By the early 1300s, it controlled only Constantinople, a small part of Western Anatolia, Thrace, and a strip across the Northern Peloponnesus to Albania. In 1453, the vast host of Ottoman ruler Mehmed II would breach Constantinople's walls, putting an end to the empire.

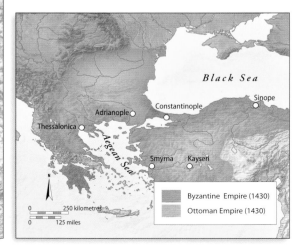

Black Sea

Sinope

Constantinople

Adrianople

Thessalonica

Aegean Sea

Smyrna   Kayseri

N

| 0 | 250 kilometres |
| 0 | 125 miles |

Byzantine Empire (1430)
Ottoman Empire (1430)

LEFT By the time it was engulfed by the Ottoman Empire, the Byzantine Empire controlled only a few scattered regions.

FAR LEFT The territory gained by Western Crusaders was under threat from the outset from various Islamic forces.

The Arabian Empire

Beginning in the seventh century CE, a new religion, Islam, sparked a decisive change in the Arab world. By the time of Mohamed's death, it dominated the Arabian Peninsula, and it soon spread further afield, transforming the political landscape.

745 CE Plague breaks out in Iraq, upper Mesopotamia, and Syria

747 CE Abu Muslim of the Abbasids begins revolution

749 CE The Abbasids gain control of Persia

749-750 CE The Caliphate of the Umayyads is ended by revolution

755 CE Al-Mansur has Abu Muslim murdered

In 600 CE, the Arabian Peninsula held a variety of peoples. In the south, Yemeni farmers used advanced irrigation and farming techniques, and towns served as centers of trade and commerce. Fierce Bedouin tribesmen roamed the interior desert, trading and raiding in order to capture slaves, grain, and dried fruit. Bedouin culture exalted masculinity—bravery in battle, pride, and honor. The need to avoid shame and dishonor led to revenge attacks against perceived enemies, often leading to generations-long cycles of violence.

Rise of Islam

A new religion, however, sparked a decisive change in the Arab world. Mohamed, a caravan merchant of the powerful Hashemite clan of the Quraysh tribe, heard a messenger from God telling him to convey God's message to the people. The result was Mohamed's recitation, the Qur'an, the holy book of Islam, which spoke of a great and merciful Allah—God in Arabic—and laid out God's laws for the people.

Mohamed gained adherents slowly, converting his family and close associates to the new faith. The Quraysh tribe controlled Mecca, the home of the Kaaba, a large black stone that had long served as a center of worship. Most of the tribe did not accept the new religion, leading Mohamed and his followers to move to Medina, where the people welcomed this dynamic leader so that he could settle long-standing disputes among feuding clans. In Medina, Mohamed came to wield political, legal, and religious authority, uniting the previously disparate local tribes. Having secured control in Medina, Mohamed and his followers attacked and seized Mecca in 630 CE. By the time of Mohamed's death in 632 CE, Islam dominated the Arabian Peninsula.

Expansion

Mohamed's successors took to heart the call for war against unbelievers. Launching a dramatic expansion, they seized control of a vast empire. Arab tribesmen, who were excellent fighters, were also able to travel rapidly thanks to their camels' ability to carry large loads and go for days without the need to drink water. The vicious war between the Sassanid (Persian) and Byzantine empires had exhausted both, leaving them easy prey for the swords of Islam. Arab armies rapidly conquered Syria, then Egypt, and then spread west across North Africa. Eventually they crossed into Spain, seizing most of the Iberian Peninsula. In 637 CE, they succeeded in

Tropic of Cancer

conquering the Persian capital Ctesiphon, and by 661 CE they had conquered the entire Sassanid Empire. Islamic fighters also swept eastward across the Jaxartes and Indus Rivers. Eventually, they met tough resistance. Charles Martel, the Hammer, stopped the invasion at Poitiers in France, and the Nubian kingdom halted attacks south of Egypt. In the east, the Islamic army fought victoriously against China's Tang dynasty but decided to halt further expansion there.

Arab leaders built upon the remains of the Byzantine and Sassanid empires, constructing garrison towns and using local officials to collect taxes and administer laws. Trade grew, with caravans and ships linking China in the east with Spain in the west. A small Islamic elite ruled over conquered peoples. Imperial decree made Arabic the language of government, and this language gradually replaced local tongues. The Qur'an prohibited forced conversions of Jews and Christians, so the new empire tolerated religious diversity, although those who did not accept the new faith paid heavier taxes and faced legal discrimination. Yet by 750 CE, Muslims made up only ten percent of the population of the empire.

LEFT This painting, *Reading the Sacred Word*, by Turkish artist Osman Hamdi Bey (1840-1910), reinforces the importance of the Qur'an, the holy book of Islam.

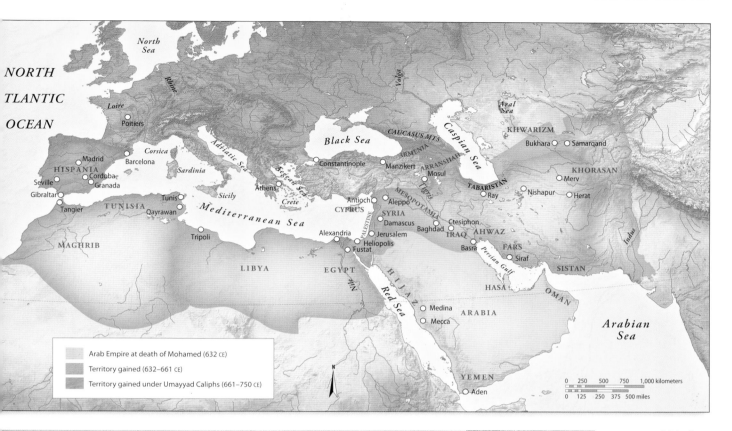

North Sea

NORTH
TLANTIC
OCEAN

Rhine

Loire

Poitiers

Corsica

Madrid

Barcelona

HISPANIA

Seville
Cordoba
Granada

Gibraltar

Tangier

TUNISIA

Tunis

Qayrawan

Sardinia

Sicily

Athens

Crete

Mediterranean Sea

Tripoli

MAGHRIB

LIBYA

EGYPT

Nile

Alexandria

Heliopolis

Fustat

HIJAZ

Red Sea

Medina

Mecca

ARABIA

YEMEN

Aden

Adriatic Sea

Aegean Sea

Black Sea

Constantinople

CAUCASUS MTS

ARMENIA

Manzikert

ARRANSHAH

Mosul

MESOPOTAMIA

Antioch

Aleppo

CYPRUS

PALESTINE

SYRIA

Damascus

Jerusalem

Tigris

Ctesiphon

Baghdad

IRAQ

Basra

Persian Gulf

FARS

Siraf

HASA

Volga

Aral Sea

Caspian Sea

KHWARIZM

Bukhara

Samarqand

KHORASAN

TABARISTAN

Merv

Ray

Nishapur

Herat

AHWAZ

Indus

SISTAN

OMAN

Arabian Sea

Arab Empire at death of Mohamed (632 CE)

Territory gained (632–661 CE)

Territory gained under Umayyad Caliphs (661–750 CE)

N

0   250   500   750   1,000 kilometers

0   125   250   375   500 miles

ABOVE LEFT Originally constructed as a Christian Visigoth church c. 600 CE, then refashioned into a mosque from 784 CE, the Mezquita (Great Mosque) of Cordoba, Spain, boasts many striking features, including a stunning honeycomb dome, its tiles studded with stars.

ABOVE The century after Mohamed's death in 632 CE saw a dramatic expansion of territories controlled by Islamic forces.

LEFT left The Fatimid Caliph of Egypt was determined to make Cairo a city that would rival Baghdad as the most important and influential city in the Muslim world. He built a new port, repaired the roads, sewers, and canals, and built high walls around the city, with two forbidding gates, Bab al-Nasr (the Gate of Victory) and Bab al-Futuh (the Gate of Conquest) on the northern side, and Bab al-Zuwayla on the south side.

Migration and Warfare

The Umayyad Caliphs ruled until the mid-700s CE, but they faced rebellions from Shi'ites and from the Abbasid clan, descended from Mohamed's uncle. The Abbasids and Shi'ites allied against the Umayyad leadership, allowing the defeat of the last Umayyad Caliph in battle. The Abbasids secured their succession to the Caliphate, but the alliance with the Shi'ites collapsed, while the Abbasids continued to hunt down the surviving members of the Umayyad clan. Only one Umayyad leader escaped to Spain, establishing a separate Caliphate in Córdoba, as the Arab Empire fragmented.

Baghdad

The Abbasids moved the capital east to Baghdad in order to be closer to their strongest base of support in Persia. Initially, Abbasid control was strong, but it too began to decline, as the Abbasid leaders maintained a large and expensive army. They found it increasingly difficult to ensure that provincial chieftains submitted their tax revenues. As revenues declined, soldiers began to support different Caliphs who could pay better and more regular salaries. Ethnic and regional differences exacerbated the empire's problems, and local leaders established essentially independent states within the larger empire. Abbasid Caliphs became mere figureheads as local rulers operated independently.

Fatimid Caliphate

In the early 900s CE, a group of Shi'ites based in Tunisia dealt a severe blow to the Abbasid Empire, establishing the Fatimid Caliphate. The Shi'ite Ubayd Allah claimed to be the Imam, a direct descendant of Ali and a divinely inspired ruler. The Fatimids eventually took control of most of North Africa, Egypt, some parts of Syria, and the vitally important holy city of Mecca. The Fatimids moved their capital to Cairo, and maintained widespread trade networks throughout the Mediterranean and Southeast Asia.

The Fatimid dynasty ruled for two centuries, until it too fell, to challenges from the Seljuk Turks and from crusading armies from Western Europe.

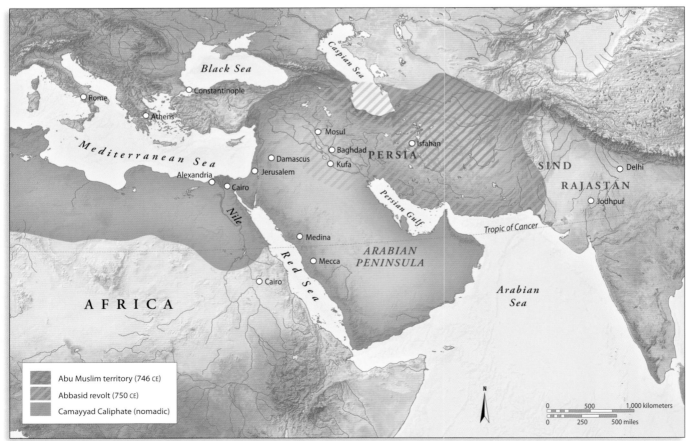

Abu Muslim territory (746 CE)

Abbasid revolt (750 CE)

Camayyad Caliphate (nomadic)

LEFT Originally an Aramean temple to Hadad, god of storms, then a Roman temple to Jupiter, and later a Christian church, the Umayyad Mosque of Damascus, Syria, houses the tomb of Saladin, the famous Muslim general.

RIGHT A page from the seventeenth-century *Book of Chants*, an Ottoman miniature, after a painting in the 1237 copy of *The Maqamat (or Assemblies)* of al-Hariri (1054–1122), an Arabic poet from Basra, showing a satirical view of a caravan of pilgrims en route to Mecca.

LEFT The Umayyad Caliphs ruled until the mid-700s CE, when they were overthrown by the Abbasid clan (descended from Mohamed's uncle) and their Shi'ite allies. The Abbasids moved the capital east to Baghdad in order to be closer to their strongest support base in Persia. In the early 900s CE, the Abbasid Empire would in turn be replaced by the Fatimid Caliphate.

Seljuk Turks

The nomadic Seljuk Turks, who originated in the Kirghiz steppe and migrated south into Persia, had a fierce warrior culture. In 985 CE, their leader converted to Islam. They established control over the Abbasid Caliphs by seizing Baghdad, and carved out an empire of their own, ranging into Anatolia, south to Jerusalem, and east into Central Asia. After they defeated a Byzantine army at the battle of Manzikert in 1071, the danger they posed to Constantinople prompted the Crusades, which blunted the expansion of the Seljuk Empire and alleviated the pressure on Constantinople, but provoked a determined Islamic response.

Ottoman Empire

Edessa was re-conquered in 1144 by a Seljuk chieftain, Zengi. The heroic Islamic warrior Nur ad-Din united Syria against the Christian invaders, and the general Saladin, Zengi's successor, took Jerusalem back in 1187. Saladin went on to conquer Egypt, ending the Fatimid Caliphate and limiting the extent of Shi'ite control to the areas covered by modern-day Iran. In the 1200s, as the Mongols swept through Asia, they destroyed the last vestiges of the Abbasid Caliphate and took most of the Seljuk Empire, confining the Seljuks themselves to a small principality in Anatolia that served as the birthplace of the Ottoman Empire. The violent rise of the Arab empire forged a new world in the Mediterranean and the Middle East. Islam aimed to be a world religion. The *jihad* swept away the remains of the Roman and Sassanid empires, and Muslim armies fought centuries-long campaigns against Christians of the Byzantine Empire and Western Europe. Periods of religious growth, scientific advance, and increased trade did little to stop the sporadic violence and civil wars that toppled dynasties and both made and fragmented the empire. The rise of the Seljuk Turks destroyed Arab control and paved the way for the Ottoman Empire that would dominate the Arab world for centuries.

601 CE to 1300 CE

Khmer—Harnessing Nature

From the middle of the ninth century to the 1430s, a remarkable empire—the Khmer Empire—appeared in Southeast Asia.

RIGHT Jayavarman VII (r. 1181–1219), the last of the great kings of Angkor, built the walled city of Angkor Thom—and its geographic and spiritual center, the temple known as the Bayon—over the ruins of an older capital city, Yasodharapura.

BELOW The temples of the Angkor area number over one thousand, ranging from nondescript piles of rubble to the magnificent Angkor Wat. Part of the legacy of Suryavarman II (r. 1113–1150), it is dedicated to the god Vishnu.

In the first millennium of the current era, several principalities and kingdoms arose in Southeast Asia, particularly in areas where agricultural surpluses were available to finance the growing maritime trade between China, India, the Arab world, and the Mediterranean. Agriculture abounded wherever state power was applied to human ingenuity to harness water from the monsoon, rivers, and lakes.

One such major area was the region around the Tonle Sap River, which received its water supply from the mighty Mekong. The Tonle Sap backed up into Western Cambodia and formed a huge lake. The Khmer Empire rose around the northern edges of the Tonle Sap Lake, an area of approximately 100 square miles (260 km²), generally identified as the Angkor region. After the much-reduced empire's capital was moved eastward to Phnom Penh in 1434, the Angkor region, home to thousands of structures and statues, was damaged by forces of nature. Although the local people, occasional travelers, and some Western missionaries were aware of the historical riches there,

the discovery of Angkor is usually ascribed to the French explorer, Henri Mouhot, in 1860.

The present-day Cambodians call themselves Khmers and claim to be the descendants of people who once ruled the southern part of mainland Southeast Asia, from Northern Thailand to Southern Laos, Cambodia, and South Vietnam. The progenitors of the Khmer people were believed to be the wise hermit Kambu and the celestial nymph Mera—their kingdom was called Kambuja, hence the French name, Cambodge, for Cambodia.

Funan and Chenla Kingdoms

The ancient Cambodian kingdoms of Funan (first century to mid-sixth century CE) and Chenla (sixth to eighth century CE) predated the Khmer Empire. With its capital at Vyadhapura—near present-day Phnom Penh—Funan ruled over central and southern Cambodia and the Mekong Basin in South Vietnam. Its mythical founder was Kaundinya, an Indian Brahman, who had married the princess Soma, and in the first century CE established a Hindu royal line.

The Funanese were probably an early Mon-Khmer people. The accounts of visitors and a plethora of inscriptions attest to the overwhelming Indianization of the royal court in script and literature, art and architecture, music and dance, philosophy and statecraft. This bedrock remained even when the Khmers supplanted Funan and established the kingdom of Chenla, which in turn split in 706 CE into Upper (Land) Chenla and Lower (Water) Chenla.

Khmer Empire

Late in the eighth century, the Sailendras conquered the divided Chenlas, but their decade of rule was brought to an end in 802 CE by the Khmer leader, Jayavarman II (r. 802–850 CE), who united the Chenlas, threw out the Sailendras, and shifted the political center to the area around Tonle Sap Lake, which gave control over the passes leading to Korat Plateau and further western and northern expansion.

Among the great Khmer emperors was Suryavarman II (r. 1113–1150), builder of the majestic Vishnu temple at Angkor Wat. Occupying an area of one square mile (2.5 km²), Angkor Wat may well be the largest single religious edifice in the world. Mirroring the Hindu cosmos, it was surrounded by a vast moat and long balustrades in the form of the bodies of the

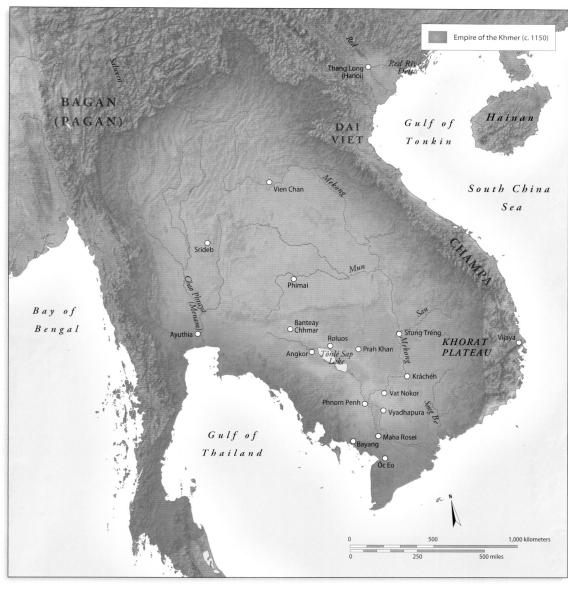

Empire of the Khmer (c. 1150)

BAGAN (PAGAN)

Saluen

Red

Thang Long (Hanoi)

Red River Delta

DAI VIET

Gulf of Tonkin

Hainan

South China Sea

Vien Chan

Mekong

CHAMPA

Bay of Bengal

Srideb

Mun

Phimai

Chao Phraya (Menam)

Ayuthia

Banteay Chhmar

Roluos

Angkor

Tônlé Sap Lake

Prah Khan

Stung Trêng

Mekong

San

KHORAT PLATEAU

Vijaya

Krâchéh

Vat Nokor

Phnom Penh

Vyadhapura

Song Bé

Maha Rosei

Bayang

Óc Eo

Gulf of Thailand

N

0   500   1,000 kilometers
0   250   500 miles

802 CE Jayavarman II declares independence from Java

1150 CE Suryavarman II trades elephant tusks and feathers with China in return for gold

1186 CE The monastery at Ta Prohm is finished. Inscriptions say it took thousands of servants to maintain it.

1431 CE Invasion by Thai armies sees the end of the Khmer civilization at Angkor Thom, with the court eventually moving to Phnom Penh

LEFT The Khmer built the largest empire in Southeast Asia. From what is now Cambodia, they ruled parts of modern-day Laos, Thailand and Vietnam.

BELOW As the empire developed, so did close cultural, political, and trade relations with Java and with the Srivijaya kingdom to the south.

divine *Nagas* (cobras). The Wat's towers, copied by modern Cambodia on its flag, dominate the sky; its central tower, shaped like a blooming lotus, rises 213 feet (65 m).

Emperor Jayavarman VII made Mahayana Buddhism the religion of the state and proclaimed himself a *Bodhisattva*—a future Buddha. As well as 102 hospitals, 101 rest houses for pilgrims, and 20,000 shrines, he built extensive edifices in Angkor Thom. He also paid for the upkeep of some 300,000 priests and monks. All this and continued warfare in Champa and Thailand weakened the state.

In the late thirteenth century, Theravada Buddhism took hold in the Khmer Empire; its egalitarian features did not permit *Bodhisattvas*

> For the prosperity of the people in this perfectly pure royal race, great lotus which no longer has a stalk, he rose like a new flower.
>
> –Text inscription about Jayavarman II, first king of the Khmer Empire (r. 802-805 CE).

or the divine basis of kingship. In the fourteenth century, the Thais and Chams took large chunks of the Khmer Empire, and in 1431 the Thai kingdom of Ayuthaya took Angkor itself. Though the Khmers regained the capital, they thought it prudent to shift it to Phnom Penh in 1434, effectively marking the end of Khmer power and glory.

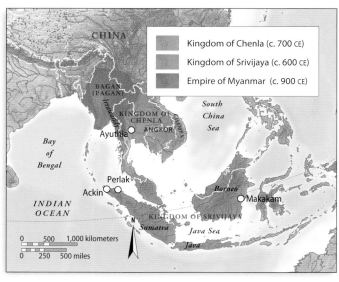

CHINA

Kingdom of Chenla (c. 700 CE)
Kingdom of Srivijaya (c. 600 CE)
Empire of Myanmar (c. 900 CE)

BAGAN (PAGAN)

Irrawaddy

KINGDOM OF CHENLA

ANGKOR

Mekong

South China Sea

Bay of Bengal

Ayuthia

Perlak

Ackin

INDIAN OCEAN

Borneo

Makakam

KINGDOM OF SRIVIJAYA

Sumatra

Java Sea

Java

N

0   500   1,000 kilometers
0   250   500 miles

Pagan Hordes

During the ninth century, Europe was subjected to a three-pronged attack from three different groups of invaders—the Vikings from the North, the Saracens from the South, and the Magyars from the East.

The Vikings from Scandinavia not only plundered settlements on the European coast, extending as far as the Mediterranean, but also set up trading routes through Russia to Byzantium, and established settlements in Britain, Ireland, northern France, Iceland, and Greenland. Meanwhile, the Saracens occupied the islands of the western Mediterranean and the greater part of Spain, and also ventured into Italy and southern France, while the Magyars of Hungary ravaged northern Italy and Germany.

Vikings

Whether as colonizers, traders, or warriors, the Vikings reached almost every part of the known world and discovered new lands along the way. From the Nordic kingdoms, their ships penetrated the western European coast, sailed through the Strait of Gibraltar into the Mediterranean Sea and from there journeyed to Italy, Spain, Morocco, and the Holy Land.

From the Baltic they penetrated the continent, traveling up Russian rivers and waterways to the Black Sea and the Caspian Sea, and all the way to Baghdad. In Asia, they met caravans from China and traded walrus ivory and furs for spices, silver, and exotic goods. They also sailed the entire North Atlantic, discovering the Faeroes, Iceland, and Greenland, and settled parts of England, Scotland, Ireland, and Normandy—an area that still bears their name. Even more remarkably, the Vikings, under Leif Eriksson, reached North America, with putative expeditions to present-day Canada, Maine, and southeastern

> Never before has such a terror appeared in Britain as we have now suffered from a pagan race, nor was it thought possible that such an inroad from the sea could be made.
>
> – English scholar Alcuin of York in 793 CE when he heard of the first Viking raid in England.

Massachusetts in the tenth century. These significant achievements are known both from contemporary written sources and through archeological discoveries.

Saracens

Though Saracen raids into Sicily and southern Italy had been common occurrences since 652 CE, it wasn't until 740 CE that the first true conquest expedition was launched, resulting in the brief capture of Syracuse. The Saracen conquest of Sicily and southern Italy lasted for just over a century.

In 711 CE, the Saracen leader Tariq ibn-Ziyad crossed from northern Africa to Gibraltar, and by the end of his campaign the majority of the Iberian Peninsula was brought under Saracen control. This campaign's decisive moment was the Battle of Guadalete, where the last Visigothic king Roderick was defeated and killed on the battlefield. After this eight-year campaign, Saracen forces tried to move northeast across the Pyrenees Mountains toward France, but were defeated by the Frankish Christian Charles Martel at the Battle of Tours in 732 CE.

Magyars

Around 830 CE, a civil war broke out in the Khazar khanate. Consequently, three Kabar tribes from the Khazars joined the Magyars

of Hungary in a move to what the Magyars call the Etelköz—modern-day Ukraine. From 862 CE onwards, the Magyars and their allies, the Kabars, embarked upon a series of looting raids from the Etelköz to the Carpathian Basin, mostly against the Eastern Frankish Empire, Germany, and Great Moravia, but also against Bulgaria and the Balaton principality. From there, they intensified their looting raids across the European continent. In 900 CE, they moved from the upper Tisza River to Transdanubia–Pannonia, which later became the core of the rising Hungarian state.

All these separate expansions disrupted royal authority and triggered political fragmentation. In the Carolingian empire, the Frankish kings practically surrendered to the Vikings, leaving defense to the local elite who rapidly established their own centers of power. In England the Vikings were met with determined resistance by Alfred the Great of Wessex (871–899 CE), but a second wave of Viking invasions a century later proved irresistible. In the eastern half of the Frankish empire, Otto I's defeat of the Magyars at Lechfeld (995 CE) proved to be a defining moment, one that resulted in Germany becoming the first country in Europe to recover from the invasions. This in turn led to its predominance in Europe for almost three centuries.

LEFT This thirteenth-century fresco in Anagni Cathedral, Italy, shows the Bishop of Atri awaiting the return of a reliquary of Saint Magno taken by Saracens in 877 CE.

789 CE The first Viking attack on England

798 CE Viking attacks on France begin

c. 813 CE The magnificent Oseberg ship is built

827 CE The Saracens conquer Sicily

844 CE A Viking raid on Seville is repulsed

866 CE Danish Vikings establish the kingdom of York, England

871 CE Alfred the Great becomes king of Wessex and the Danish advance is halted in England

882 CE Saracen base established at Garigliano, Campania, Italy

898 CE Magyars make a raid into Italy

983 CE Vikings establish a settlement in Greenland under Erik the Red

RIGHT Whether as raiders or invaders, the Vikings, Saracens and Magyars traveled far in search of plunder and new territory.

Viking settlements in Scandinavia were concentrated around the southern coastline and in Denmark. Plying sea and river routes in their longships, the Vikings ventured east, west, and south. Their journeys took them to Asia, the Mediterranean, Greenland, and North America. They conquered parts of England, Scotland, Ireland, and northern France, and established settlements there.

Originally from the east, the Magyars first established themselves in the area of present-day Ukraine, before settling in the Transdanubia-Pannonia region in around 900 CE.

The Saracens sent out raiding parties across the Mediterranean for many years, before taking Syracuse in Sicily in 740 CE. The proximity of the Iberian Peninsula to northern Morocco saw the Saracens easily cross the Strait of Gibraltar and take control of much of the region.

ICELAND

Arctic Circle

Faroe Islands

Shetland

Orkney

ATLANTIC OCEAN

NORSE

SWEDES

Gulf of Bothnia

Staraya Ladoga

Novgorod

VIKING LANDS

ETELKÖZ

Inishmurray
Lindisfarne
Jarrow

IRELAND
Kells

North Sea

DANES

Baltic Sea

BRITAIN

Kiev

Lincoln

Derby
London

Hamburg

KHAZAR KHANATE

Aachen
(Aix-la-Chapelle)

HOLY ROMAN EMPIRE

BRITTANY   NORMANDY

Trier

Reims

Regensburg
Passau

Pressburg

FRANKISH EMPIRE

TRANSDANUBIA-PANNONIA

MAGYARS

Bordeaux

Gijon

Black Sea

IBERIAN PENINSULA

Pisa

Corsica

Adriatic Sea

BYZANTINE EMPIRE

Karmona
Granada

Rome

Constantinople

Balearic Islands

Sardinia

Bari
Taranto
Otranto

Aegean Sea

Sicily

Athens

SARACENS

Tunis

Syracuse

Mediterranean Sea

AFRICA

N

■ Viking settlements
▶ Viking raids
■ Magyar settlements
▶ Magyar raids
▶ Saracen raids

0   250   500 kilometers
0   125   250 miles

Kievan Rus'

The Grand Duchy of Kiev, also known as Kievan Rus', emerged
from the fusion of Viking military and political elites with a
Slavic population of merchants and peasants.

The ruling dynasty is said to have been founded in 862 CE by a Viking leader named Rurik, branches of whose descendants continued to rule in some form or another into the sixteenth century. Up until the tenth century, the relationship between Vikings and Slavs focused mainly on the river trade routes from Scandinavia through the Black Sea to Constantinople.

Integration

The group of Vikings known as Varangians who passed through this area acted at the outset as marauders, levying tribute on the settled populations as they made their way downriver. Eventually, however, they began to settle down and intermarry with the Slavs to such an extent that the ruling elite became Slavic-speaking. The rulers' names are one sign of this process: Prince Sviataslav (c. 962–972 CE) was the first Grand Prince of Kiev to have a Slavic name. By his time, each town had its own prince from the Rurikid dynasty, and each prince had a retinue of military henchmen known as a druzhina. Princes gained loyalty from their druzhina by distributing booty and arbitrating between henchmen.

First Rulers

The first great ruler of Kiev was Vladimir (c. 980–1015 CE), who fought against the Poles, Pechenegs, Byzantines, and Bulgars, but who left his most important historical mark by converting to Orthodox Christianity. This choice of religion carried political significance, and Vladimir's policies were an attempt to create some unity and common bond among the peoples of his multi-ethnic realm. By the time of Vladimir, Rus' had become a geographic designation, but he sought to give it a cultural unity as well by finding a single common religion. His first choice was pagan, and when this proved unsatisfactory he considered Judaism, Islam, and Latin Christianity. By choosing Orthodox Christianity, he gained the recognition of neighboring Christian powers in Sweden, Poland, and Hungary, while forging an alliance with the Byzantine Empire, thus differentiating his realm from his western neighbors.

Peak of Power

Under Grand Prince Yaroslav the Wise (c. 1019–1054 CE) Kievan Rus' reached its military and cultural apex. He ordered the translation and production, as well as the collection, of many books, especially religious works. He also oversaw construction of the magnificent St Sophia Cathedral in Kiev, aided the development of the Russian church, and helped compile the first written law code, the *Russkaia Pravda*—Russian Justice.

State against State

Strong rulers such as Vladimir and Yaroslav were the exception rather than the rule for Kievan Rus'. Internecine strife between princely city-states was more typical. As each princely state developed, leaders in Novgorod, Galicia-Volhynia, Kiev, Pereyaslavl, Chernigov, Smolensk, Tver, and Vladimir-Suzdal acted as separate political actors with their own alliances and interests.

Each principality consisted of three political institutions—Rurikid princes, boyars, and the veche (town assembly). However, the balance of power among the three varied by region. In southwestern principalities such as Galicia-Volhynia, the boyars proved strongest and behaved as landowning aristocrats. The princes held dominance in the northeast principality of Vladimir-Suzdal, while the veche exercised the most power in Novgorod in the north. In Novgorod, uniquely, the veche could hire and fire the city's prince, and princes were prohibited from owning land in that town.

The Rurikid princes conducted war against each other to promote their own authority and compete for the title of Grand Prince. In 1169 CE the prince of Vladimir-Suzdal, Andrei Bogolyubsky, sacked Kiev, claimed the title of Grand Prince, then returned to his own principality. Kiev was not so important anymore.

Self-defeating

These internal conflicts prevented any kind of unified foreign policy or common defense for Rus' as each principality pursued its own best interest. When the Mongols invaded from the east there was no coordinated response and the Rus' principalities were easily defeated between 1236 and 1240 CE.

c. 988-989 CE Vladimir, having adopted Orthodox Christianity, commissions the creation of religious icons and architecture

1019 CE Yaroslav is made Grand Prince of Kiev

1037 CE Construction of St Sofia Cathedral in Kiev begins

1072 CE Princes Boris and Gleb are canonized

1146 CE The first mention of Moscow appears in documents

1156 CE The first Kremlin walls are built in Moscow

1223 CE Mongols have first victory over Kievan Rus'

LEFT The miracle-working saints of Kiev Monastery of the Caves. Since its foundation in 1015 CE, the monastery has been a key center for Orthodox Christianity in Eastern Europe.

Barent Sea

White Sea

SAMOVED

PERM

Arctic Circle

KARELA

VYATIKA TERRITORY

CHUD

SCANDINAVIA

Gulf of Bothnia

Onega

Ladoga

Belo Ozero

VOLGA BULGARS

Neva

Kopor'ye

Gulf of Finland

Ladoga

Yaroslavl

Volga

ESTS

Peipus

Veliky Novgorod

VLADIMIR-SUZDAL

Yuriev

NOVGOROD

Toropets

Rostov

Riga

Pskov

Suzdal

SMOLENSK

Moscow

Vladimir

Baltic Sea

Vitebsk

Smolensk

Koselsk

Ryazan

DENMARK

POLOTSK

CHERNIGOV

MURÓM -RYAZAN

Volga

Minsk

KIEVAN RUS'

Listern

TUROV -PINSK

NOVGOROD -SEVERSK

Lyubech

Dnieper

Novgorod-Severskiy (862 ce)

Vladimir-Volynsk

Turov

Chernizov

Kursk

VLADIMIR -VOLYNSK

Don

Volga

Peremyshl

KIEV

Kiev (879 ce)

PEREYASLAVL

Belgorod

Pereyaslavl

Galich

Dniester

Caspian Sea

POLES

PECHENEGS

GALICIA-VOLHYNIA

Dnieper

Sea of Azov

Adriatic Sea

Black Sea

Constantinople

N

BYZANTINES

RIGHT There was a built-in expansionist impulse in Kievan Rus' because the leader of each principality needed a constant supply of booty to satisfy his henchmen and to attract more supporters.

| | Kievan Rus' (c. 1054) |

0   250   500   750 kilometers

0   125   250   375 miles

Cultural Renaissance of China

The fall of the Tang dynasty marked the end of China's supremacy in East Asia. It was followed by the Song dynasty, during which many of the most characteristic features of Chinese society and economy took shape.

c. 1044 Book published with a written formula for gunpowder as well as describing an early form of compass

1127 Jurchen soldiers besiege the capital of the Song dynasty and kidnap the emperor and other members of the imperial court

1215 Mongols attack northern China and continue their quest south

1271 Marco Polo begins his journey to China

The Song dynasty found itself beset by powerful adversaries on the steppe frontier. Yet the Song also presided over unprecedented economic growth and a cultural renaissance as the southward shift of the increasing population and the rise of the rice economy transformed Chinese livelihood and material culture.

Five Dynasties (907–960 CE)

By the time the last Tang emperor was deposed in 907 CE much of the empire had already been carved into quasi-independent regions controlled by military governors, and North China became a battleground fought over by rival Turkic and Chinese armies. Civil wars laid waste to the Tang capitals of Chang'an and Luoyang. Strategically located on the North China Plain where the Grand Canal joins the Yellow River, Kaifeng emerged as a new northern political center. Five successive regimes claimed Kaifeng as their capital—hence the name of this period—but none lasted longer than 16 years.

South China was more fragmented politically and more stable economically during this time. The south was divided among six major kingdoms whose rulers frequently clashed, though none was able to add substantially to his territory.

Founding of the Song (960–1279)

Zhao Kuangyin (927–976 CE), a battle-hardened general, came to power in a coup d'état in 960 CE, in which he deposed the child-emperor on the throne of the last of the Five Dynasties. He took the

dynastic name of Song, in honor of his ancestral homeland in Hebei, but retained Kaifeng as his capital. Mindful of warlordism, which had brought down the Tang dynasty, Zhao tried to consolidate military power in the hands of the emperor, but it was not until 978 CE, under his successor, that the Song defeated the last of the southern kingdoms and reestablished unified imperial rule. The Song faced formidable rivals to the north. Powerful confederations of pastoral nomads, the Khitan (Liao) in the northeast and the Tangut (Xia) in the northwest, who occupied strategic areas south of the Great Wall, posed a constant menace. In 1004, the Song suffered a devastating defeat at the hands of the Khitan and had to accept a humiliating peace treaty and pay annual tribute of silk and silver.

> To be first in worrying about the world's troubles, and last in enjoying its pleasures.
>
> –Song statesman Fan Zhongyan (989-1052 CE) in an essay musing on the responsibilities of the Confucian scholar-official, *Commemoration for the Yueyang Tower* (1045).

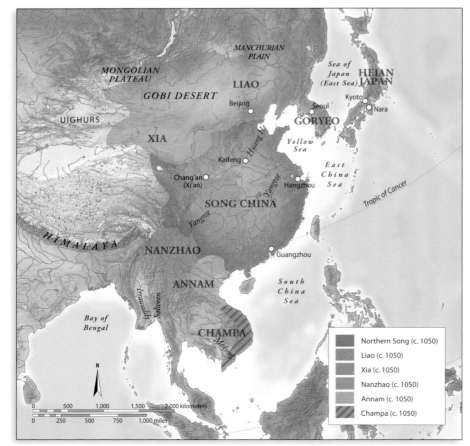

Northern Song (c. 1050)
Liao (c. 1050)
Xia (c. 1050)
Nanzhao (c. 1050)
Annam (c. 1050)
Champa (c. 1050)

LEFT The Song's rivals, the Khitan (Liao) and the Tangut (Xia), occupied strategic areas south of the Great Wall, and posed a formidable threat.

ABOVE Confucian scholar-officials flourished under the Song dynasty's need for an educated civil service, and the demand for education increased.

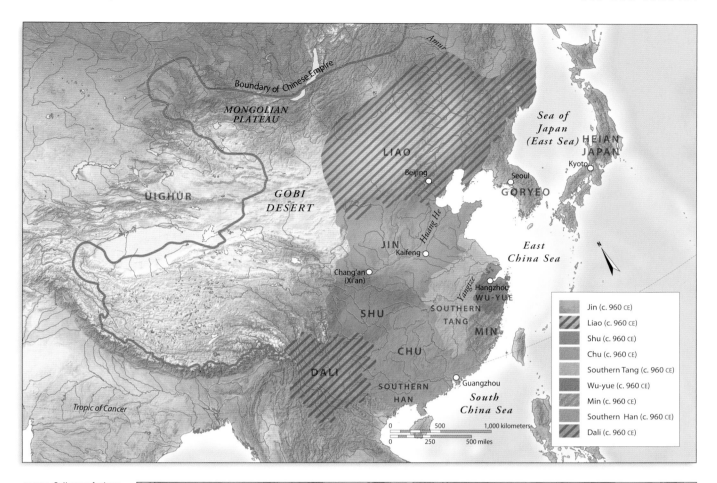

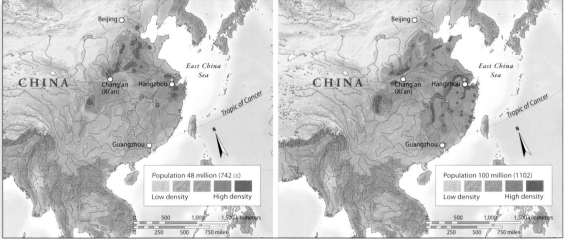

Legend:
- Jin (c. 960 CE)
- Liao (c. 960 CE)
- Shu (c. 960 CE)
- Chu (c. 960 CE)
- Southern Tang (c. 960 CE)
- Wu-yue (c. 960 CE)
- Min (c. 960 CE)
- Southern Han (c. 960 CE)
- Dali (c. 960 CE)

Population 48 million (742 CE)
Low density · High density

Population 100 million (1102)
Low density · High density

ABOVE Salt manufacture, mining, tea cultivation, and maritime trade all began to flourish in the south after the fall of the Tang dynasty. But it would be a northern warlord who succeeded in rebuilding a unified empire.

RIGHT The southward shift of the population and the rise of the rice economy saw China's population soar from 48 million in 742 to over 100 million people by 1100. Two-thirds lived in the south.

Rise of the Confucian Scholar-Official

Following in the footsteps of Zhao Kuangyin, the Song emperors strove to establish the primacy of civil authority over military power. Government officials were recruited through a civil service examination system that required many years of study—of history, poetry, current affairs, and above all the Confucian classics. The intense competition produced a highly literate ruling class dedicated to selfless public service. Both the civil service examinations and the spread of printing contributed to a revival of Confucian learning. Song scholars championed the idealist philosophy of the ancient Confucian sage Mencius, who proclaimed the goodness of human nature and the potential for each individual to achieve moral excellence. Among the educated elite, a reinvigorated Confucian commitment to family and society overshadowed any Buddhist religious concerns.

Economic Revolution

Civil wars and invasions wracked north China from the eighth to the twelfth centuries. During this time many people migrated from the north, the traditional heartland of Chinese civilization, to the frontier territories south of the Yangtze River. The irrigated rice-growing regions of the south could feed many more people, but also needed more labor and capital. China's population soared to more than 100 million people by 1100. Two-thirds of them lived in the south.

Agriculture and Industry

Newly developed seed varieties, irrigation techniques, and cropping systems dramatically increased the productivity of rice farming, but the wet, humid environment of south China had other advantages. Tea, which first became popular in the Tang dynasty, was

BELOW The Song had a strong economy and introduced paper money or "strings." A string was worth 1 ounce (28 g) of silver.

well suited to the rainy climate and soils of the rugged, mountainous areas of the south. Sugar cane and tropical fruits such as litchi, longan, and tangerines also flourished there, and the abundant natural waterways facilitated the movement of goods and people. South China's evergreen hardwood forests also contributed timber and pitch for shipbuilding and paper and ink for the burgeoning printing industry. During this period, China's

maritime trade with Japan, Southeast Asia, and the Indian Ocean eclipsed that of the overland Silk Road across central Asia. Industrial production also underwent a revolution during the Song. Innovations in mining and metallurgy vastly increased the output of coal, iron, and steel. Advances in pottery manufacture produced the first true porcelain wares, which became China's most important export. New machinery and techniques

also improved the quality and variety of silk fabrics. Silk weaving became a highly specialized industry employing skilled male artisans in urban workshops.

Although at its peak the Song state minted six billion bronze coins per year, it could not generate enough coin to satisfy the market demand. Gradually much of its cumbersome bronze and iron coins were replaced with the world's first paper money, known as "strings."

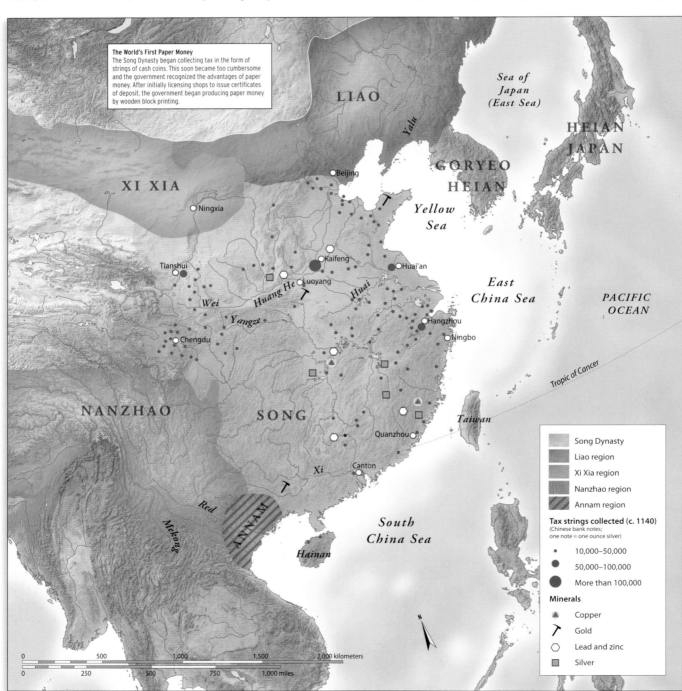

The World's First Paper Money
The Song Dynasty began collecting tax in the form of strings of cash coins. This soon became too cumbersome and the government recognized the advantages of paper money. After initially licensing shops to issue certificates of deposit, the government began producing paper money by wooden block printing.

LIAO

XI XIA

Ningxia

Tianshui

Wei

Huang He

Yangze

Chengdu

Luoyang

Kaifeng

Huai'an

Huai

Beijing

Yalu

GORYEO
HEIAN

Sea of
Japan
(East Sea)

HEIAN
JAPAN

Yellow
Sea

East
China
Sea

PACIFIC
OCEAN

Hangzhou

Ningbo

NANZHAO

SONG

Quanzhou

Xi

Canton

Taiwan

Tropic of Cancer

Red

Mekong

ANNAM

Hainan

South
China
Sea

N

	Song Dynasty
	Liao region
	Xi Xia region
	Nanzhao region
	Annam region

Tax strings collected (c. 1140)
(Chinese bank notes;
one note = one ounce silver)

- · 10,000–50,000
- ● 50,000–100,000
- ⬤ More than 100,000

Minerals

- ▲ Copper
- ⚒ Gold
- ⬡ Lead and zinc
- ◼ Silver

| 0 | 500 | 1,000 | 1,500 | 2,000 kilometers |
| 0 | 250 | 500 | 750 | 1,000 miles |

Inventions

Among the important inventions that came into widespread use during the Song dynasty were gunpowder, the compass, and printing. No longer merely an explosive for fireworks, gunpowder was applied to weaponry ranging from cannon to fragmentation bombs. The nautical compass along with innovations in the design of deep-keeled ships enabled mariners to venture across the oceans out of sight of land. The Mongols introduced gunpowder weapons to the Islamic world and the West, while most likely it was Arab navigators who spread knowledge of the compass.

Urban Life, Popular Culture

Commercial prosperity stimulated the growth of cities and the emergence of a vibrant urban popular culture. The Southern Song capital of Hangzhou, which Marco Polo deemed "the City of Heaven, the most beautiful and magnificent in the world," numbered more than one million inhabitants. Exotic goods from many lands poured into Hangzhou's markets; more than 100 trades were required to supply goods and services to the imperial palaces and ministries. The city's entertainment quarters, frequented by high and low alike, teemed with taverns, restaurants, brothels, and teahouses. Storytellers, bards, and opera performers gave birth to a new vernacular literary culture. Imperial officials and Confucian scholars formed poetry clubs, hosted wine-drinking parties in their gardens, and developed ink painting into a refined art. Despite its growing wealth and prominence, however, the merchant class lacked the political power and social prestige of the scholar-official elite.

The Jurchen Conquest and the Southern Song

In the early twelfth century, the balance of power among the Song and its northern rivals was upset by the abrupt rise of a new tribal confederation, the Jurchen, in northern Manchuria. After declaring themselves the Jin dynasty in 1115, the Jurchen overthrew their Liao overlords and then invaded the Song territories.

During the Southern Song period (1127–1279) the northern half of China remained under foreign rule. In 1235, the Jin state was conquered by a Mongol army. The Southern Song endured repeated attacks by the Mongols until 1279, when Kubilai Khan captured Hangzhou and completed the Mongol conquest of China.

ABOVE Confucius (c. 551–479 BCE) was a thinker and social philosopher whose teachings emphasized personal and governmental morality, correctness of social relationships, justice, and sincerity.

COMMERCIAL PUBLISHING

Printing was invented in China by the early eighth century at the latest, but became widespread only in the Song period. The Song government produced standard editions of the Confucian classics, as well as the Buddhist and Daoist religious canons, dynastic histories, law codes, philosophical writings, and treatises on mathematics, medicine, warfare, and agriculture. During the Southern Song period private schools and commercial publishers supplemented official printing projects, catering to the growing markets for almanacs, divination manuals, religious texts, reading primers, and above all handbooks helpful for civil service examinations. By broadening access to knowledge, printing encouraged innovation, especially in agricultural and medical techniques.

ABOVE Painting from *The Six Paths to Rebirth and the Ten Kings*, Bodhisattva Ksitigarbha, c. 983 CE.

BELOW After the fall of Kaifeng to the Jin in 1126, the Song emperor moved south and re-established his court at Hangzhou.

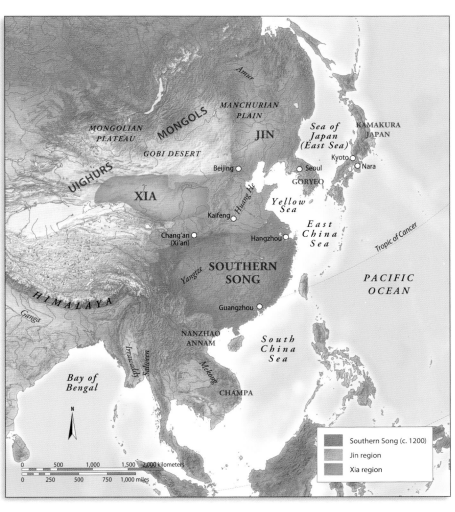

Germany–Beginning of the Holy Roman Empire

Germany in the early Middle Ages was a collection of principalities that became known as the Holy Roman Empire because its kings, who were crowned as emperors, were seen as the leaders of Western Christendom.

> They [my words]...merely relate, plainly and in order, the lives and mores of the pious kings of Saxony...in their times, our land rose up, as the towering cedar, and inspired fear far and wide.
>
> –Thietmar of Merseburg on the kings of the Holy Roman Empire, c. 1020.

The imperial title had first been acquired in 800 CE by Charlemagne (d. 814 CE), but with the demise of his Frankish empire, the eastern part covering the German lands which he had conquered—Saxony as far as the Elbe and Bavaria in the south-east—fell under the influence of a succession of dynasties—the Ottonians (dukes of Saxony) until 1024, the Salians (from Bavaria and Swabia) from 1024 to 1152, and then the Hohenstaufen (dukes of Swabia) until the death of Frederick II in 1250.

Church and State

The borders of this massive realm extended enormously under Otto I (936–973 CE), who, as a result of marriage, added the kingdom of Italy, reaching almost as far south as Rome, an acquisition which enabled him, in 962 CE, to persuade the Pope to crown him as emperor and thereby effect a *translatio imperii*—transfer of imperial rule—from Carolingians to Ottonians. But his move set in process an imperial–papal relationship that for centuries was an uneasy alliance of two men, each of whom claimed to be the representative of God on earth.

Numerous clashes over their relative place at the top of the world's hierarchy caused great dramas, such as Henry IV's submission to Pope Gregory VII at Canossa in the winter of 1077. Due to their imperial ambitions the German rulers had their sights on prosperous southern Italy, where Sicily's grain meant cash wealth in gold.

After two centuries of failed military campaigns against the Greeks and the Normans, Henry VI (d. 1197) at last received his prize as a result of marriage to the heiress Constance of Sicily. This paved the way for the glittering career of the most famous medieval German emperor Frederick II, *stupor mundi*—wonder of the world. As a result the Pope in his Roman enclave felt under imperial siege from both from the north and the south.

The king-emperors remained a relatively weak political force in Germanic lands, primarily because royal succession was usually determined by election—hereditary kingship never lasting more than two or three generations within one dynasty. Due to the frequent dynastic changes, very few lands had accrued to the crown.

As a result, kings relied primarily on their own inherited lands for income from taxation and recruitment of troops, of which there were never enough to enable the rulers to impose their will on their neighbors. Within Europe, Germany never saw the rise of a centralized administrative kingship such as emerged gradually in England and France, where kingship was hereditary and relatively stable.

Culture and Education

Culturally, the Church provided education and learning of the highest quality. The Ottonian and Salian nunneries were led by abbesses who were all impressively learned, such as Matilda, abbess of Quedlinburg, dedicatee of Widukind's history of Saxony,

LEFT In this eleventh-century German manuscript, Otto II is seen receiving homage from his subjects. He was Holy Roman Emperor from 967 CE.

From 500 CE Language changes cause a shift in High German consonants that separates it from other Germanic languages

800 CE Charlemagne is crowned Emperor of the Romans

955 CE Otto I defeats the Hungarians in the Battle of Lechfeld

962 CE Otto I is crowned Emperor of the Romans, beginning the Holy Roman Empire

German Empire (c. 1000)
(Holy Roman Empire)

ABOVE Pope Gregory VII blessing King Henry IV of Germany in a very detailed drawing by Italian artist Federico Zuccari.

LEFT The Holy Roman Empire was referred to as the Holy Roman Empire of the German Nation from the late fifteenth century. Although it encompassed much of northern Italy, Rome was never included.

or the nun Hrotsvitha of Gandersheim who wrote Latin dramas. Two centuries later Abbess Hildegard of Bingen, the author of medical and spiritual literature, exchanged over 200 letters with a wide variety of people, including kings and popes, across Europe. The libraries of these monastic houses were treasure troves of illuminated manuscripts, ivories, and gold and silver work.

Yet the Church did not have a monopoly on learning. The interests of Frederick I included an impressive knowledge of Roman law. His grandson Frederic II himself wrote a book on falconry and was so intrigued by multilingualism that he set up an experiment with small children and their wet nurses to see how they acquired the skill to speak.

RIGHT This painting by nineteenth-century artist Albert Bauer, depicts Frederick I at Aachen in 1171.

Warriors and Emperors

We often think of Japan as a singular state. However, much of Japanese history revolves around the struggle for political domination and territorial acquisition between the Imperial family and the nobility, or later, the warrior clans.

> This world, I think, is indeed my world. Like the full moon I shine, Uncovered by any cloud.
> –Japanese poet Fujiwara no Michinaga.

BELOW Japan at the end of the twelfth century saw the decline of the Imperial family and the commencement of provincial division leading to almost four centuries of feudalism.

Steady flows of immigrants from the Korean peninsula were the first settlers on Japanese islands. These original inhabitants were hunter-gathers who later introduced rice cultivation that led to powerful clans conquering the weaker clans to gain control of agriculture.

Imperial Rule

In 645 CE, the Imperial family established a bureaucratic state, modeled after the Chinese state. To run it, the central government took a family register, allocated land to each individual on the register, and levied taxes on their produce. It also conscripted troops to expand the territory and to subjugate the indigenous peoples.

In 794 CE, during the Heian period, Emperor Kemmu established a new capital in Kyoto to make a fresh start and also to consolidate his rule. However, the government's taxation system was failing and many peasants deserted the allocated land and sought refuge on privately owned estates.

Shogun

As a result, clans emerged, with the Fujiwara clan disrupting the Imperial family and causing infighting. Seizing this political vacuum, Taira no Kiyomori, a warrior clan leader,

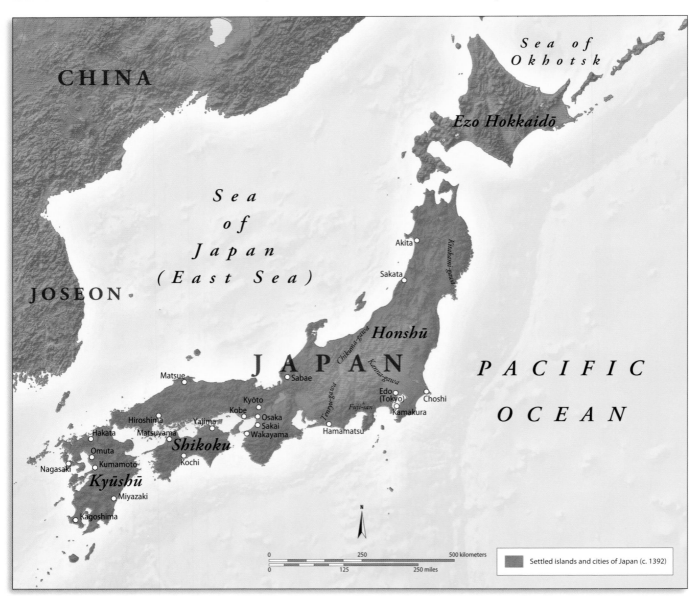

Settled islands and cities of Japan (c. 1392)

supported the Imperial family and rose through the ranks. His defeat of the rival clan, Minamoto, in 1159, earned him the political chieftainship, ushering Japan from aristocratic to military rule. Later, the Minamoto clan leader, Yorito-mo, defeated the Taira clan in 1185. In exchange for the policing of eastern Japan, Yoritomo secured from the Imperial family the title of shogun, or supreme military commander, and established the Kamakura regime.

Kamikaze

The regime faced challenges from various quarters. In 1221, Emperor Gotoba launched a revolt with the help of warriors siding with him, but he was defeated. A further blow came from two Mongol attacks in 1274 and 1281 on Kyushu Island. The Japanese were overwhelmed by the sheer volume and firepower of the Mongol troops, but the attacks failed because fortuitous typhoons repelled the Mongol forces. These typhoons later became known as *kamikaze*, the divine wind, and

ABOVE Minamoto Yorito-mo, the founder of the Shogunate, wearing full ceremonial robes.

RIGHT This extraordinary image shows the love affair of Niou-ni-miya and the prince's sixth daughter. It is part of a manuscript on paper, written c. 1000 CE, called *The Tale of Genji*, by Murasaki Shikibu, a female writer. It was the first novel written in any language.

formed the basis for the widely believed notion that Japan was a special land protected by nature's providence.

Rival Factions

Inside the Imperial family, tension over imperial succession ran high. The legitimacy of Emperor Godaigo's imperial lineage—the southern court—was challenged by a rival faction—the northern court. The clash between the two factions resulted in a five-decade civil war sweeping across Japan, plunging the country into turmoil. The conflict ended in 1392 when the third Ashikaga shogun, Yoshimitsu, brokered a compromise. This restored stability, re-established the Ashikaga as the head of the Bafuku (military government), and put the Imperial family in a subordinate position.

Culture and Scripts

During the Heian period culture thrived. Scholars from Japan had studied and brought back knowledge from China. The central government ceased to send scholars to China in 894 CE, giving Japan the opportunity to integrate the new and foreign with the old and local forms of artistic styles and religions. Most significant were the new forms of writing. To this day, in addition to the Chinese script, *kanji*, the Japanese language uses two kana scripts: *hiragana* and *katakana*. The renowned female novelist of the Heian period, Murasaki Shikibu, used the kana in the classic saga of court life, *The Tale of Genji*.

ABOVE The Battle of Ichi-no-tani of 1184 is one of a series of battles from 1180 to 1185 between the Taira clan and the Minamoto clan known as the Gempei War.

500 CE Japan adopts the Chinese alphabet

c. 607 CE Prince Shotoku builds a Buddhist temple in the Asuka Valley

794 CE The Emperor moves the capital to Kyoto

858 CE Emperor begins the rule of the Fujiwara clan

1227 CE Zen Buddhism is introduced into Japan by a monk called Dogen

GOD AND COUNTRY

Expanding Europe –Three Dynasties

The central European principalities of Poland, Hungary, and Bohemia were formed in the late ninth and early tenth centuries around three family dynasties of the Piasts, Arpads, and Premyslids, respectively.

Their nucleus was formed by the various peoples who coalesced in the three main language groups of Polish, Hungarian (Finno-Ugric), and Czech. Their political history waxed and waned depending on: The personality of inspiring military leaders who managed a unifying influence; the aggression of neighbors—the Holy Roman empire in the west, the Kiev principality in the East, and Byzantium in the south—which often led to border provinces being overrun;

as well as internal divisions along fault lines which had roots going back to the period before the rise of the three main dynasties.

Ruling Families
The comparative similarity in the rise of the three principalities explains why their ruling families felt great affinity with each other, resulting in alliances and marriage pacts between themselves and their neighbors—Kiev dynasty and Holy Roman Empire families. Of the

three, only Hungary emerged early as a kingdom, being ruled consistently by a king after the ascent of King Stephen I (c. 975–1038).

Christianity
At around the time of the formation of the three principalities, all three were introduced to Christianity as a result of calculated conversion campaigns launched from the Holy Roman Empire in the west, though Bohemia and western Hungary were converted by the

Slavs whose liturgy was part of the eastern Byzantine orthodoxy. As part of the Christian world each principality took on modes of government administration through the written word, especially Latin, in order to acquire taxes and tribute but also to enable the rulers to grant land through charters and to codify local customs in the form of written laws.

Previously unknown in these areas, cities sprang up, not least in order to provide the Church with archbishoprics and bishoprics, where church and state based their administrative centers; Cracow, Wroclaw, Poznan, Gniezno (Poland), Buda, Pecs and Varad (Hungary), as well as Prague and Brno (Bohemia). In Poland an important role was played by the Teutonic Knights of the Baltic, whose order colonized vast tracts of land in Pomerania and exploited the trade opportunities with Scandinavia and northern Russia and, through the Russian river system, with Byzantium in the south.

Literature
Culturally, the three principalities fostered ideas of nationalism and ethnicity that found expression in

> So if we write about holy men and good work and miracles we also have to write about secular kings and princes. We talk about saints in churches, [but] in schools and courts we read about kings and princes and victories.
>
> –Anonymous, *Deeds of the Polish Princes*, Book III.

903 CE Good King Wenceslaus, Duke of Bohemia, is born

966 CE Duke Mieszko I of Poland converts to Christianity when he marries Dabrowka of Bohemia

997 CE Saint Adalbert of Bohemia is martyred

997 CE King Stephen rules over the Arpad dynasty of Hungary

1100 Boleslaw Krzywousty divides Poland among his sons

1055 The foundation charter for the abbey at Tihany in Hungary is the earliest writing in the Hungarian language

ABOVE LEFT Known after his death as Saint Stephen Confessor, King Stephen I of Hungary was a genuine Christian, rather than an expedient one.

LEFT Saint Stanislaus of Cracow, bishop and martyr, died on May 8, 1079. This Gothic painting by an unknown artist depicts him on his deathbed.

RIGHT Some of the Bohemian dukes were granted royal titles by the Holy Roman Emperor. Frederick Barbarossa, seen here invading Italy in 1157, became Duke Wladislav II in 1158.

ABOVE The political boundaries in place in eastern Europe by the end of the thirteenth century highlight the dominance of Poland and its ally, the Hungarian Empire.

national histories. The earliest is *The Deeds of the Polish Princes* written c. 1116–1120 in the reign of Boleslav III (1102–1138) by a foreign author whose name is unknown. He (the writer was most likely male, but one cannot be absolutely certain) dedicated the chronicle to the archbishop and three episcopal colleagues. At around the same time, and perhaps inspired by him, his contemporary Cosmas of Prague produced the *Deeds of the Bohemians*. Hungary's first national chronicle on the same scale, the *Deeds of the Hungarians*, dates from much later (c. 1200). It was written by a notary in the royal chancery—the Hungarian Anonymous. Written in Latin, these narratives are the ultimate expression of national identity within the framework of Latin Christianity. Copies in manuscript formed part of the large output in writing of Christian texts like the Bible, Biblical commentaries, and saints' lives.

Saints

The three countries produced their own saints. The most important are: King Stephen I (Hungary); Bishop Wojciech (Adalbert) of Prague (d. 997 CE) who, following his exile from Bohemia, became Poland's first saint; and Bishop Stanislaus of Cracow (1030–1079).

Denmark–1,000 Years of Monarchy

From the tenth century on, Denmark has been a remarkably stable entity. It was here that the Danish people became an established state, retaining a variant of "Old Norse" as the Danish language.

690 English missionaries arrive

810 King Godfred is murdered

831 Danish Vikings invade Ireland

1016 King Cnut (Canute) defeats the English

1350 Plague ravishes the country

LEFT This Viking mask appears on the runic stone erected by Toke the blacksmith to thank a man by the name of Troels, son of Gudmund, for giving him gold and saving him.

Geographically, Denmark consisted of the Jutland peninsula—which in the south bordered the Holy Roman Empire—with the islands of Fyn and Sjelland to the east. From c. 1150, the Danish kingdom also occupied the southwestern strip of modern Sweden. Danish power was underpinned by the economic activity of its various fortified trading places like Hedeby (southeast tip of Jutland) and Ribe (west coast of Jutland), and by the Viking expeditions southward, raiding and settling coastal areas of Britain (the Danelaw), Ireland, and Carolingian France (Normandy).

Royal Dynasty

The Danish principality became a stable kingdom from the mid-tenth century onward when Harald Bluetooth (c. 930–c. 988 CE) converted to Christianity in about 965 CE.

> Harald had these monuments erected in memory of Gorm his father and Thyre his mother, that Harald who won for himself all Denmark and Norway and Christianized the Danes.
>
> –Memorial stone of Harald Bluetooth at Jelling, c. 965 CE.

He and his son Sven Forkbeard (c. 988–1014 CE) established themselves as the most feared royal dynasty in Scandinavia.

From the mid-twelfth century onward, however, the focus for conquest turned to the southeast where Danish kings Valdemar I (1157–1182) and his sons Cnut (1182–1202) and Valdemar II (1202–1241), organized expeditions against the Wends, a Slav people who lived between the Elbe and the Oder on the northern

fringe of the Holy Roman Empire. They also extended their empire as far as Lübeck, another important trading port in the west Baltic. In Scandinavia, the Danish kings were the first to issue a continuous silver coinage, from about 1075.

Christianity

Denmark was Christianized from Harald Bluetooth's reign onward. His own conversion is celebrated in the famous runic inscription on his memorial stone at Jelling, which he

erected together with a burial mound for his parents. For at least another century most bishops were foreigners—English or German—and, instead of having fixed sees, they traveled round as part of the royal retinue. By the mid-eleventh century the Danish church had established bishoprics, with an archbishopric established at Lund (then part of Denmark).

When in 1170 Valdemar I became the first Danish king to be crowned at a lavish ceremony at

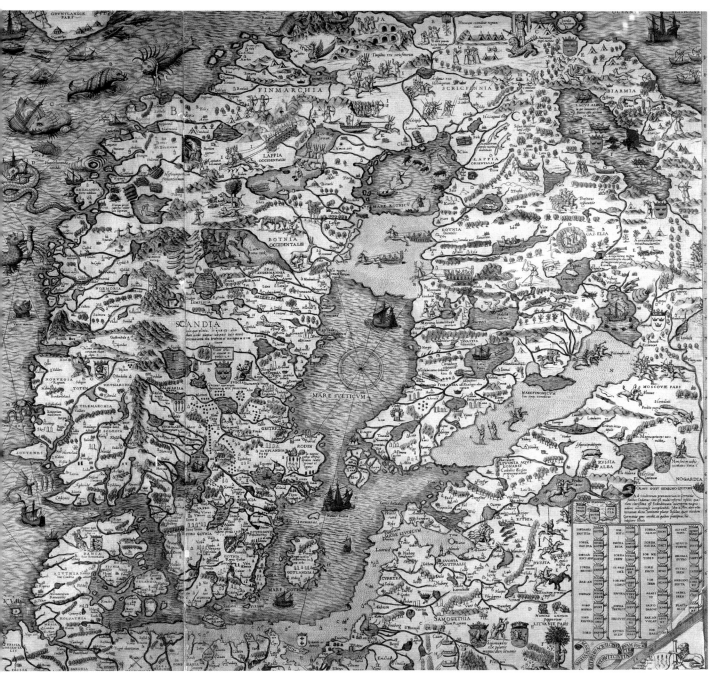

Ringsted, he not only had his eldest son associated with him in power—in keeping with the tradition of the Ottonian kings in the Holy Roman Empire—but also had his father Cnut III Lavard (who was murdered in 1134) declared a saint.

Recorded Histories

The most famous of all histories in Latin were the two composed in the period 1170 to 1220 by Saxo Grammaticus and Sven Aggesen. Saxo's *Deeds of the Danes* was dedicated to King Valdemar II, even though the chronicle stops early in the reign of his brother Cnut, and makes it clear that his aim was to eulogize the king "for overleaping the reputation of his predecessors," and to justify the rule that had started when the king's grandfather, Valdemar I, brought unity to the extended Danish kingdom. These narratives all emphasize Christianity as the true religion, whose only God saved them from a pagan past featuring chaos, violence, and uncertainty.

ABOVE Detail from *Carta Marina*, an intricate map of Scandinavia by Swedish geographer and historian Olaus Magnus.

LEFT Harald Bluetooth's runic stone at Jelling is 8 feet (2.4 m) high. The three sides are: Front page, Lion's page (facing here), and Christ's page.

137

Anglo-Saxons

"Anglo-Saxons" is a collective term applied to the Germanic-speaking peoples, who began migrating from continental Europe to the south and east of the British mainland around the beginning of the fifth century CE.

Related both linguistically as well as ethnically, these peoples were said by Bede, a Benedictine monk, to have been the descendants of three powerful tribes from northern Europe—the Angles and the Jutes, from the Jutland Peninsula, and the Saxons, from what is now Lower Saxony in Germany. They may also have included Frisians, Franks, and others.

Migration (400–600 CE)

It is not clear why Bede's "Angles, Saxons, and Jutes" came to Britain, but some sources say that they were invited in by the Romano-British, the Romanized Celtic peoples of Britain, to help defend the island at the end of Roman imperial rule. Despite difficulties in determining the precise demographic composition of England in the sixth century, overall, this period witnessed the formation of new, relatively coherent regional identities among Germanic newcomers. These were the roots of the earliest kingdoms in Anglo-Saxon England.

Heptarchy

"Heptarchy" is the term usually applied by scholars to the Anglo-Saxon kingdoms of south, east, and central Britain during the seventh, eighth, and ninth centuries that eventually unified into a single "Angle-land"—England. It refers to the seven main kingdoms of south Britain—Northumbria (including the sub-kingdoms Bernicia and Deira), Mercia, East Anglia, Essex, Kent, Sussex, and Wessex. However, we now know that further kingdoms were important in this period—Hwicce, Lindsey, Middle Anglia, Magonsaete, and others.

Christianization (600–800 CE)

The Christianization of the Anglo-Saxon kingdoms began around 600 CE, and was influenced by Celtic Christianity from the northwest and the Roman Catholic Church from the southeast. The conversion became a top-down process, as the ruling elites were encouraged to adopt the new religion and introduce it to their subjects.

Around 601 CE, Æthelberht of Kent, who had married a Christian Frankish princess, became the first kingly convert when he was baptized by Augustine, the Archbishop of Canterbury. Nevertheless, certain kings vacillated, apostasised, or remained resolutely pagan until the mid-seventh century.

Vikings

The *Anglo-Saxon Chronicle* records that the Viking Age in England began with a vicious and brutal attack on Lindisfarne by Norsemen on June 8, 793 CE—monks were slaughtered, thrown into the sea, or taken into slavery. The contemporary Northumbrian scholar, Alcuin of York, declared that it was the worst atrocity ever witnessed, and the event colored history's perception of the Vikings and their conduct for the next 1,200 years. Not until the end of the nineteenth century did scholars outside Scandinavia begin seriously to reassess the cultural and technological achievements of Vikings.

ABOVE Saint Bede, the Benedictine monk, depicted writing a manuscript c. 1175. Saint Bede is considered to be the "father of English history."

Yet by the sack of Lindisfarne the Vikings were probably well established in Shetland and Orkney. The Norsemen soon began to winter, then settle, on the British mainland, and by the 860s CE had embarked upon a mission of total conquest. They seized the southern part of the kingdom of Northumbria in 867 CE, and what is now York (Jorvik) became one of the key centers of Norse-controlled England, known as the Danelaw.

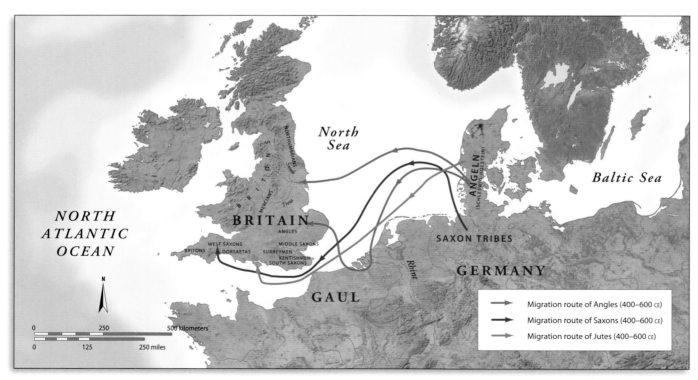

NORTH
ATLANTIC
OCEAN

Lewis

Skye

PICTS

Mull
○ Iona

Arran

N o r t h
S e a

Edinburgh ○

Tweed
Lindisfarne

BERNICIA

GALLOWAY

STRATHCLYDE
NORTHUMBRIA

RIGHT The seven Anglo-
Saxon kingdoms that
unifed to become England
are called the Heptarchy.

Dublin ○

IRELAND

Isle of Man

DEIRA

York ○
○ Stamford Bridge

Manchester ○

I r i s h   S e a

Chester ○

LINDSEY
Lincoln ○

Derby ○
Trent

Wexford ○

Lichfield ○
MIDDLE
ANGLES

"The Heptarchy" (c. 800 CE)	
	Northumbria
	Mercia
	East Angles
	Wessex
	Essex
	Kent
	Sussex

NORTH
WALES

Severn

MERCIA

Leicester ○

EAST
ANGLES

Warwick ○

Hereford ○

Huntington ○

SOUTH ANGLES

Buckingham ○

EAST SAXONS

MIDDLE
SAXONS

ESSEX

LEFT The Angles and
Danes traveled on similar
sea routes to reach their
destination, England.

Wedmore ○   ○ Edington

Thames   London ○

Glastonbury ○

WESSEX

○ Winchester

KENT   ○ Canterbury

Dover ○

WEST WALES

Southampton ○

SUSSEX
SOUTH SAXONS

Totnes ○

Hastings ○

Calais ○

English   Channel

FRANCE

c. 720 CE King Ine of
Wessex builds a stone
church at Glastonbury
Abbey

c. 729 CE The
Northumbrians sign
a peace treaty with
the Picts

835 CE The Isle of
Sheppey comes under
Viking attack

c. 955 CE Archbishop
Oda of Canterbury
rebuilds Canterbury
Cathedral

1052 Edward the
Confessor founds
Westminster Abbey

1067 Construction
begins on the Tower
of London

N

0		250		500 kilometers

0		125		250 miles

Rise of Wessex (800–900 CE)

During the ninth century, Wessex became the pre-eminent kingdom of Anglo-Saxon England, its ruler presiding over a dominion that incorporated the former kingdoms of Wessex, Sussex, and Kent and exacted tribute from Cornwall, western Mercia, and several Welsh kings. The victory of Alfred the Great of Wessex over the Danes at Edington in 878 CE curbed the threat for a time. However, by now the face of mainland Britain had changed irrevocably. The Danelaw stretched across the north and east of modern-day England, while in the far north of Britain, the Norwegian Vikings were one reason behind the formation of the Kingdom of Alba, which eventually evolved into Scotland.

English Unification

Alfred the Great died in 899 CE and was succeeded by his son Edward the Elder who, with his brother-in-law Æthelred of Mercia, began a program of building works and expansion following Alfred's example. When Edward died his son Æthelstan (d. 939 CE) succeeded to the Mercian kingdom and, after some uncertainty, to Wessex.

BELOW The "Treaty of Wedmore" was where the Viking Guthrum accepted Alfred as his adoptive father in 878 CE. At the time, Viking- and English-held territories were roughly equal.

BELOW RIGHT Graphic reproduction of the Battle of Hastings, October 14, 1066. Savage fighting inflicted heavy casualties with an estimated 6,000–8,000 deaths.

England at Treaty of Wedmore (878 CE)
Anglo-Saxon controlled territory
Viking controlled territory

NORTH ATLANTIC OCEAN

North Sea

Orkney

Lewis

Skye

KINGDOM OF SCOTLAND

Mull
Iona

Tay

Arran

Edinburgh

STRATHCLYDE

NORTHUMBRIA

GALLOWAY

Isle of Man

Dublin

Irish Sea

IRELAND

THE DANELAW

York
Stamford Bridge

Manchester

Chester

ENGLISH MERCIA

Wexford

Lichfield

DANISH MERCIA

Leicester

Huntington

WALES

Hereford

Severn

Buckingham

KINGDOM OF GUTHRUM

Edington

Isle of Sheppey

Wedmore

London

Canterbury

WESSEX AND ITS DEPENDENCIES

Winchester

Southampton

Dover

Hastings

Totnes

English Channel

FRANCE

N

0   250 kilometers
0   125 miles

Æthelstan continued the military support of his father and Edward's sister, Æthelflæd, and was the first king to achieve direct rulership of what we now consider England.

Danish Succession

At the turn of the century, Norse attacks resumed. King Æthelred II the Unready (d. 1016) had a long but troubled reign, as Danish campaigns had weakened his authority. In 1013, Æthelred lost his kingdom to Sweyn Forkbeard of Denmark. He recovered it following the latter's death in 1014, but only to be challenged by Sweyn's son Canute.

For the first half of the eleventh century, rule over England alternated between the descendants of Æthelred and Canute. By 1066, several very different characters wanted the kingdom. In early January 1066, the West Saxon earl, Harold Godwinson, became king, possibly appointed by Edward the Confessor on his deathbed. Waiting in the

> The more that is known of any period in the history of Anglo-Saxon England, the more we can appreciate the limitations of our knowledge.
>
> –Simon Keynes, *The New Cambridge Medieval History*, vol. III.

wings were William, Duke of Normandy, a descendant of Æthelred and his second wife Emma of Normandy, Harald Hardrada of Norway (aided by Harold Godwinson's estranged brother Tostig), and Edgar Ætheling, the underage grandson of Edmund Ironside. Edgar probably enjoyed the strongest claim, and was proclaimed king by the witan —assembly of royal advisors—in October 1066, aged around 14. He was never crowned and submitted to William several weeks later.

Norman Invasion (900–1066 CE)

The Norman invasion arose out of this complex situation. In late September 1066, King Harold of England defeated Harald Hardrada and Tostig at what became known as the Battle of Stamford Bridge (in Yorkshire), but was immediately compelled to march his army south and confront William in Sussex. Struck through the eye with an arrow and cut to pieces by Norman swords, Harold died at the famous Battle of Hastings on October 14, and following this, his army quickly disintegrated.

William the Conqueror was crowned at Westminster Abbey on Christmas Day, 1066 and soon began a program of consolidation.

Aftermath

Bitter and desperate local resistance marked the immediate aftermath of the Conquest. In 1067, rebels in Kent launched an abortive attack on Dover Castle in combination with Eustace II of Boulogne, while the Anglo-Saxon landowner. Meanwhile, Eadric the Wild raised a revolt against the Normans in western Mercia, attacking the Norman castle at Hereford in alliance with certain Welsh rulers.

Over ensuing years, uprisings occurred across the country. Most were quickly and brutally supressed by the Norman king. A large fleet sent by Sweyn II of Denmark had arrived off the coast of England by late summer 1069, sparking a new wave of rebellions across the country and an alliance between the Danes and Northumbrian dissidents. William was able to buy off the Danes, who agreed to leave England, and through the winter of 1069–70 his forces systematically subdued all resistance. There was a final outburst of rebel activity in the fenlands in 1071, but its suppression marked the effective end of resistance. The Anglo-Saxon aristocracy had been almost completely eliminated. English losses at Hastings, and the rebellions that followed, left only a handful of pre-Conquest thegns—military tenants —still in possession of lands. By the time of the *Domesday Book* (1086), only two English landowners of note had survived the takeover, and 10 years on no church see or bishopric was in English hands. Few medieval European conquests had such devastating consequences for a defeated ruling class.

Jerusalem Lost

The Crusades were a series of military conflicts of a religious character waged by much of Christian Europe against external and internal threats.

The Muslim presence in the Holy Land began with the Arab conquest of Palestine in the seventh century. Western Europeans were at first lukewarm in their reaction to the loss. The Holy Land lay far from Western shores, the invasion did not interfere greatly with Christian pilgrimages, and the Eastern Orthodox Byzantine Empire discouraged interference by the Western barbarians. Attitudes began to change in 1009, however, when the Fatimid caliph al-Hakim bi-Amr Allah ordered the destruction of the Church of the Holy Sepulchre. By this time, too, the Muslim Seljuk

Turks were on the rise beyond the eastern frontier of Byzantium.

Great Schism

Around the turn of the millenium, Western Europe was subject to its own pressures. Estrangement between eastern and western Christianity resulted in the "Great Schism" of 1054, while the western Church itself was riven by dispute between the papacy and secular leaders over the right to appoint churchmen. The collapse of the Carolingian Empire during the late ninth century, as well as the relative stabilization of local European

borders after the Christianisation of the Vikings, Slavs, and Magyars, had produced a large class of armed warriors who were in need of an outlet for their skill.

One outlet was the *Reconquista* of Muslim Hispania (al-Andalus), which had fallen to the Umayyad caliphate in the early eighth century. Officially sanctioned in 1063 by Pope Alexander II, who promised Heavenly reward to those who were killed in battle, the struggle against the Moors became both a military and an ideological focus for Iberian knights and adventurers from all over Western Europe.

The mounting religious fervor was fuelled by reports of Seljuk atrocities against Christian pilgrims in Jerusalem, and by papal propaganda. In 1074, Pope Gregory VII called upon the "soldiers of Christ" *(milites Christi)* to rally to the aid of Christian Byzantium against the Turks; in 1095 Pope Urban II, calling for a general campaign to recapture Jerusalem, whipped the crowds into a chant of "God wills it!"

> It is necessary to look for the origin of a crusading ideal in the struggle between Christians and Muslims in Spain and consider how the idea of a holy war emerged from this background.
> –Norman F. Cantor (1929-2004), Canadian historian.

People of the First Crusade
Pope Urban II urged his bishops and legates to preach in their own dioceses in France, Germany, and Italy. He tried to forbid certain people–including women, monks, and the sick–from joining the Crusade, but the people's enthusiasm was overwhelming. The majority of those who answered the call were not knights, but peasant workers–men and women whose millennial and apocalyptic yearnings found release in the call to holy war and generated an outpouring of emotional personal piety that was not easily harnessed by the ecclesiastical and lay aristocracy.
The planned day of departure was August 15, 1096, but a number of makeshift armies of peasants and lesser knights set off early, led by a charismatic monk named Peter the Hermit of Amiens.

Legend:
— Godfrey of Bouillon
— Adhemar of Le Puy and Raymond of Toulouse
— Bohemond and Tancred of Taranto
— Robert of Flanders and Hugh of Vermandois
— Combined forces from Constantinople

RIGHT Raymond IV of Toulouse (also known as Raymond de Saint-Gilles) receives the blessing of Pope Urban II. He was one of the first to respond to Pope Urban's call to recapture Jerusalem.

BELOW During the First Crusade (1096–1099), armies from several places in Western Europe gathered at Constantinople. In mid-1097, they marched from there to their final destination, Jerusalem.

LEFT This map shows the extent of the Byzantine Empire and of the Seljuk Turk Empire in the period leading up to the First Crusade. The Eastern Orthodox Byzantine Emperor feared territorial expansion by the Muslim Turks, and sought the Pope's assistance.

1095 Pope Urban II calls for the First Crusade

1099 Jerusalem is captured by Crusaders. El Cid, the great Moorish leader, is killed.

1163 Construction of Notre Dame Cathedral in Paris is begun

1189 Richard I is crowned King of England, then leaves on crusade.

1191 Richard is captured near Vienna

1194 After release at Mainz, Richard returns to England and captures Nottingham Castle, thus ending John's revolt. Richard is again crowned King of England.

LEFT *Entry of the Crusaders into Constantinople* was painted by Eugene Delacroix. The original aim of the crusades was to liberate the Holy Land from Muslim rule.

First Crusade

In March 1095, the Byzantine Emperor, Alexius I Comnenos, sent a request to Pope Urban II for aid against the Turks. Urban was only too willing to assist because he hoped to reunite the Christian Church under papal primacy and began to lay plans for a crusade. At a great assembly in the heart of France on November 27, 1095, known as the Council of Clermont, Urban gave an impassioned sermon to a large audience of French nobles and clergy. He called upon people to turn their swords to the service of God and wrest the Holy Lands from the infidel.

Led by a charismatic monk by the name of Peter the Hermit of Amiens, a migrating horde of up to 100,000 ordinary individuals, the "People's Crusade," soon ran into difficulty in eastern Europe. Supplies were problematic, skirmishes broke out between crusaders and local populations along the Danube, and about a quarter of Peter's followers died en route.

The rest reached Constantinople in August where they joined with crusading armies from France and Italy. A dismayed Alexius quickly ferried the hordes across the Bosporus, whence they split into two opposing camps. Most of the "People's Crusade" were slaughtered on entering Seljuk-controlled Asia Minor. Another army of Saxons and Bohemians did not make it past Hungary before splitting up.

The First Crusade also heralded the first organized violence against Jewish communities in Europe. Some religious leaders in Germany understood holy war against the infidel to apply equally to Jews within their own lands. Setting off in the early summer of 1096, the so-called "German Crusade," made up of about 10,000 soldiers, proceeded northward through the Rhine valley, away from Jerusalem, and began a series of pogroms which some historians refer to as "the first Holocaust." Thousands perished, and attacks against Jews followed each crusade.

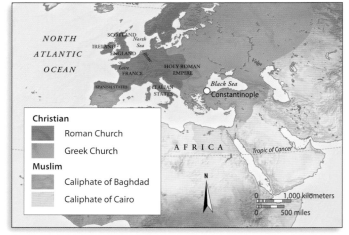

The Leaders

The main crusading contingent set out later in 1096. Raymond IV of Toulouse, with the papal legate, Adhemar of Le Puy, represented the knights of Provence; Bohemond of Taranto, with his nephew Tancred, represented the Normans of southern Italy; the brothers Godfrey of Bouillon and Eustace

ABOVE Eastern (Greek) and western (Latin or Roman) Christianity were separated in the Great Schism of 1054. This map shows that division at the time of the First Crusade.

and Baldwin of Boulogne led the men of Lorraine; and the Northern French followed Count Robert II of Flanders, Robert of Normandy (elder brother of King William II of England), Stephen of Blois, and Hugh of Vermandois (younger brother of King Philip I of France), who bore the papal banner.

The various leaders and their warbands took different routes to Constantinople and assembled outside the city walls in May 1097.

The crusaders' first objective was the old Byzantine city of Nicea, now the capital of the Seljuk sultanate of Rüm under Kilij Arslan I. Unable to blockade the main lake on which Nicea was built, the crusaders were forced to maintain a prolonged siege. On June 18, fearful that the crusaders would sack Nicea, Alexius secretly negotiated the Turks' surrender and barred the crusaders from entering the city, except in small escorted bands.

The march to Jerusalem began, with Stephen of Blois writing home that he expected it to take about five weeks. In fact, it took two years.

As men and horses died and leaders bickered, the crusaders finally reached Antioch in October. The city was so large that they could not block all the supply lines, and the siege endured nearly eight months. In May 1098, as a Muslim army under Kerbogda of Mosul approached, Bohemond bribed his way into Antioch. The crusaders slaughtered most of the city's inhabitants but soon found themselves besieged by Kerbodga.

In December, the Arab town of Ma'arrat al-Numan was taken after a seige, and the first reports of cannibalism by crusaders were heard.

Jerusalem had been recaptured from the Seljuks by the Fatimids of Egypt only the year before the crusaders arrived. It was now put to a lengthy siege, during which the

crusaders themselves suffered badly from lack of food and water. Of the estimated 7,000 knights in the main crusader army, only 1,500 or so remained. On July 15, buoyed by the divine visions of another priest in their midst, Peter Desiderius, the crusaders seized Jerusalem and butchered almost every inhabitant—Muslim, Jew, and eastern Christian. The crusaders returned home, leaving the kingdom of Jerusalem in a precarious position.

Second and Third Crusades

Relative peace between Muslims and Christians endured in the Holy Land for nearly 50 years, until Edessa succumbed to the forces of Nur ad-Din (Nureddin) of Aleppo and Mosul in 1144. A new crusade was called for by various preachers, most notably Bernard of Clairvaux, and French and South German armies, under the kings Louis VII and Conrad III respectively, marched to Jerusalem in 1147.

Despite some successes in the Mediterranean, the Second Crusade failed in the Middle East—

once again the leaders were divided, while the new arrivals in Jerusalem were resentful of the resident crusaders, whom they viewed as too accommodating of the Muslims.

Pope Gregory VIII launched a Third Crusade, led by several of Europe's most important leaders: Philip II of France, Richard I "the Lionheart" of England, as well as Frederick I Barbarossa, the Holy Roman Emperor.

Frederick drowned in the River Saleph on the way to Antioch, leaving an unstable alliance between Philip and Richard. They took Acre in 1191, defeated the Muslims near Arsuf, took the port city of Jaffa, and advanced to within sight of Jerusalem; but they got no further.

Richard the Lionheart

On the way home Richard was captured by his enemy Leopold, Duke of Austria, handed over to the Holy Roman Emperor, Henry VI, and forced to become Henry's vassal and pay a heavy ransom for his release. By now crusading had become little more than a cynical means of making one's fortune. The Fourth Crusade (1204) resulted in the sack of Constantinople and the partition of the Byzantine Empire between Venice and the crusaders.

The Sixth Crusade (1228) was the first to set sail without the Pope's official blessing, establishing the precedent that rulers other than the Pope could initiate a crusade. But Jerusalem was lost forever.

The Largest Empire on Earth

The Mongol Empire became the largest contiguous empire in the history of the world, and the only steppe empire that expanded after the death of its founder or tribal leader.

Under Genghis Khan—birth name Temujin—the Mongols surpassed all conquests made by earlier steppe powers, and his successors ruled over the entire Eurasian area of steppe contact.

Genghis Khan

Driven by a desire to dominate, Temujin's early career showed an increasing ambition. He began by seeking to dominate his own clan,

and by murdering his stepbrother he succeeded in that ambition. He then moved on to establish his dominance over the clan alliance within his own tribe through his marriage to Borte, his first wife, before pressing on to dominate all the Western Mongol tribes and clans. After defeating his former blood-brother, Jamuka, in a civil war, he was recognized as the Mongol leader in 1206.

Law and Order

Having achieved the unification of the Mongol nation, Genghis Khan pursued domestic policies designed to strengthen unity and reduce the potential for strife between the various nomadic tribes. Having established customary law—Yasa—based on shamanist principles, over all Mongols, he reorganized the tribal system into new administrative-military units by assigning specific

ABOVE At an assembly of Mongol tribes in 1206, one man was chosen Khan and given the name "Genghis," meaning fearless and unshakable. This was the first time the Mongols had chosen a single leader.

1135 Mongols raid northern China

1224 Genghis Khan splits his empire into khanates, to be ruled by his four sons

1227 Genghis Khan dies and is succeeded by Ogedei who moves the capital to Karakorum

1241 Ogedei dies and the Mongols retreat from Europe. Ogedei's widow Töregene takes over as regent.

1260 Kubilai is appointed Khan and declares Buddhism the state religion. Mongols are defeated for the first time in Palestine.

1267 Kubilai Khan moves the Mongol capital to Dadu (Beijing) and founds the Yuan Dynasty

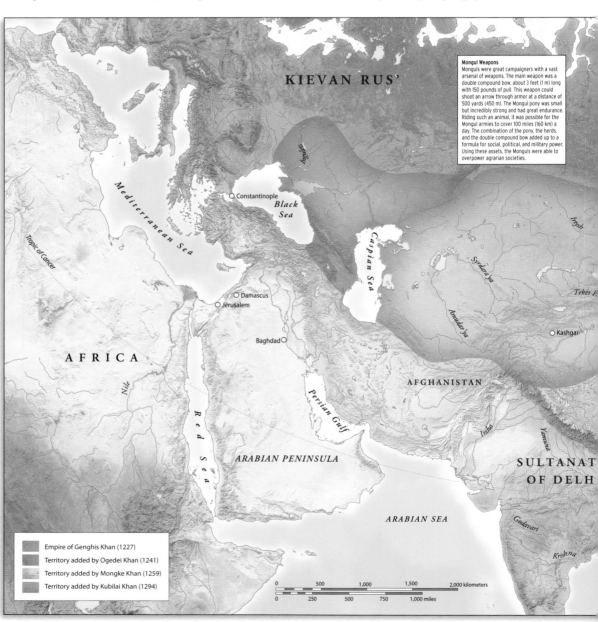

Mongul Weapons
Monguls were great campaigners with a vast arsenal of weapons. The main weapon was a double compound bow, about 3 feet (1 m) long with 150 pounds of pull. This weapon could shoot an arrow through armor at a distance of 500 yards (450 m). The Mongul pony was small but incredibly strong and had great endurance. Riding such an animal, it was possible for the Mongul armies to cover 100 miles (160 km) a day. The combination of the pony, the herds, and the double compound bow added up to a formula for social, political, and military power. Using these assets, the Monguls were able to overpower agrarian societies.

KIEVAN RUS'

Mediterranean Sea

Constantinople
Black Sea

Caspian Sea

Damascus
Jerusalem

Baghdad

AFRICA

Nile

Red Sea

Persian Gulf

AFGHANISTAN

Indus

Kashgar

Syrdar'ya

Amudar'ya

Tekes

Irtysh

SULTANAT OF DELH

ARABIAN PENINSULA

ARABIAN SEA

Godavari

Krishna

Yamuna

Tropic of Cancer

- Empire of Genghis Khan (1227)
- Territory added by Ogedei Khan (1241)
- Territory added by Mongke Khan (1259)
- Territory added by Kubilai Khan (1294)

0   500   1,000   1,500   2,000 kilometers
0   250   500   750   1,000 miles

pastures for grazing to support each unit of 1,000 mounted warriors. In effect, he broke up the old tribal rivalries by distributing members of the same clan throughout the organization, and fusing members of various clans into each unit.

Great Khan

Genghis sought to create unity through the absolute authority of the new institution of the Great Khan. He managed to create a new legitimacy by decreeing that only his male descendants by his wife Borte could ever be chosen as Great Khan. The territory of the empire was considered under the control of the Great Khan to distribute as he saw fit. Even though Genghis Khan designated patrimonial lands for each one of his four sons and their male heirs, there would be one ultimate lord whom everyone would obey. This would be the case until the last Great Khan, Kubilai, died in 1294.

Genghis distributed his lands among his sons as follows: Jochi received the westernmost lands from Russia to Turkestan, Chagatai held the south and southwest up to the Tibetan border, Ogedei received the south up to northern China, and Tolui's domain stretched from the easternmost lands as far west as the Mongol homelands on the Onun and Kerulen rivers.

Expansionism

The newly organized Mongols launched their first forays into China in 1209. After subduing the Hsi Hsia dynasty in northwest China they campaigned against the Chin dynasty in northern China, beginning in 1211. The Mongol advance into Central Asia came about more by circumstance than by premeditation. Motivated to avenge the killing of a Mongol trade caravan in the town of Otrar in 1218, Genghis launched a punitive military campaign against the ruler Mohammad Khworezm Shah, and by 1220 Mongol armies had converged on Samarkand and conquered Bukhara. Their mission of punishment now over, Genghis dispatched a reconnaissance force of 30,000 under generals Jebe and Subedei. Between 1221 and 1223, this scout force won victories in the Caucasus over Georgian and Armenian forces and crushingly defeated Russian forces at the Kalka River in 1223. Having gathered their intelligence, they returned to Mongolia in 1225.

Supplies and Weapons

The Mongols practiced pastoral nomadism, a way of life that revolved around the herding of a variety of animals—sheep, goats, cattle, camels, horses—to provide the necessities of life throughout their seasonal migration to pastures as much as 500 miles (800 km) apart. Such mobility yielded great military potential. Mongol armies brought their herds with them on campaign so that they did not require a supply line. The everyday practices of herding large flocks and hunting from horseback over extended areas gave the nomads plenty of experience in using their weapons from the saddle.

> It is not sufficient that I succeed—all others must fail.
> —Genghis Khan on his conquests.

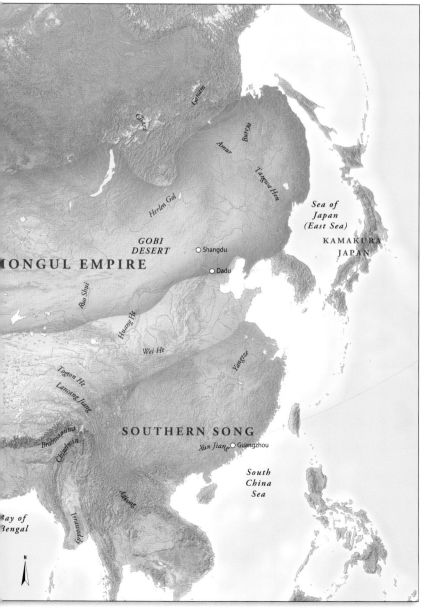

LEFT Having unified the Mongol nation, Genghis Khan distributed his lands among his four sons— Jochi, Chagatai, Ogedei, and Tolui—on the proviso that there would always be one Great Khan whom everyone would obey.

BELOW Genghis Khan orders a flogging. Though negative perceptions of him persist, his religious tolerance and promotion of exchange between Asia, the Middle East, and the West speak in his favor.

RIGHT After the death of Mongke, Kubilai Khan came to power. This art-work shows Kubilai Khan hunting–the Mongols were ruthless warriors, legendary horsemen, and skilled marksmen.

BELOW After Genghis died, the Mongol Empire kept expanding, reaching its peak under his son and successor Ogedei. Mongol armies pushed into Persia, finished off the Xi Xia, and battled the imperial Song Dynasty of China, starting a war that resulted in the Mongols controlling all of China.

Conquest of Russia

Under Great Khan Ogedei (r. 1229–1241), the Mongols launched a new and well-prepared attack against Kievan Rus'. The military operations that began in the winter of 1236–37 under the command of Batu, son of Jochi, resulted in the occupation of the South Russian steppe. The Mongols also captured the Russian towns of Riazan and Vladimir. Novgorod avoided direct conquest because flooding halted the Mongol advance, but the Prince of Novgorod, Alexander Nevsky, nevertheless voluntarily submitted. Eventually the Mongols reached the line of the Dnieper; in December 1240, they captured Kiev and ruthlessly sacked it as punishment for the city's resistance.

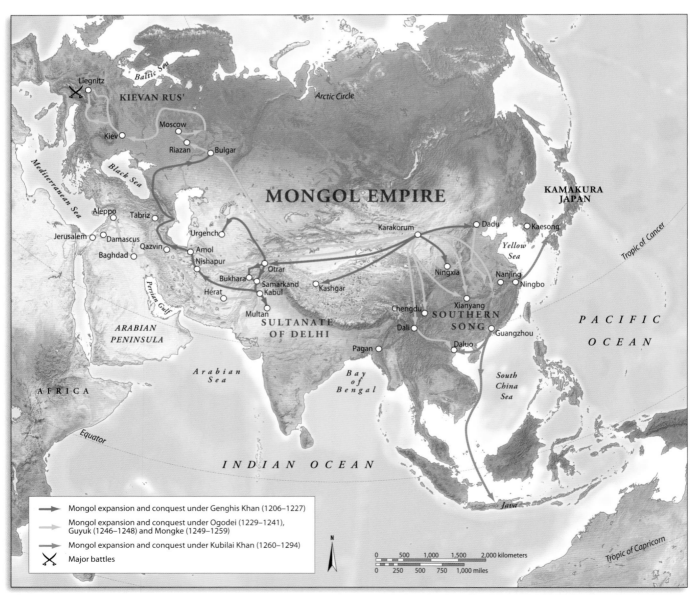

Astronomers at the observatory of al-Tusi in Maragha, founded in 1259 by Hulegu il-khan. The pursuit of knowledge was highly regarded and encouraged by the Mongol leadership.

European Advance

Having conquered Russia, Mongol forces continued westward along the steppe lands into Hungary, where resistance quickly collapsed. Meanwhile, the right flank of the Mongol army rode through Poland, defeating German forces from the Holy Roman Empire at the Battle of Liegnitz in April 1241. By the end of 1241, Mongol forces were approaching Vienna. They were also preparing for further advances into Western Europe; small raiding parties had already reached the Adriatic Sea and Spain as part of a reconnaissance operation. Future European campaigns never took place, however, because Ogedei died in December 1241, and Mongol advances were halted until his successor was determined. As was the case after the death of Genghis Khan, the Mongols also observed a year of mourning.

Golden Horde

Mongol rule over Russia continued under Jochi's son Khan Batu and his descendants, who increasingly acted as independent rulers; by the 1250s they had begun to refer to themselves as the Golden Horde to indicate their sovereignty. They established their capital at Sarai, east of today's Volgograd. Batu's son, Berke (r. 1257–1267), became the first Mongol ruler to convert to Islam, and the Golden Horde established strong links based on fraternal religious bonds with the Turkic Mamluks of Egypt. The alliance of the Golden Horde with the Mamluks opened the way for conflict between different parts of the Mongol empire over religious affiliations.

Family Empire

It fell to Great Khan Mongke (1251–1259) and his brothers Kubilai, Hulegu, and Arik Boge to resume imperial expansion, with such overwhelming success that, collectively, they built the largest land empire in world history. In East Asia, Mongke and Kubilai completed the conquest of southern China, Burma, and Vietnam, and Kubilai established his own ruling house over China—the Yuan Dynasty—between 1272 and 1368.

Simultaneously, at the other end of Eurasia, Hulegu campaigned in the Middle East between Iran and Palestine. He conquered Baghdad in 1258 and totally destroyed the city. The destruction of Baghdad also meant the termination of the Arab Islamic caliphate headed there by the Abbasid dynasty. By 1260, Hulegu controlled parts of Armenia, Anatolia, Mesopotamia, and all of Azerbaijan and Iran. Hulegu and his descendants were known as "il-khans" or secondary khans, subordinate only to the Great Khans in Mongolia.

The remaining patrimonial piece of the larger Mongol empire consisted of the Chagataid (1227–1370) lands in Central Asia which stretched from the Caspian Sea to the Tarim Basin. Chagatai had been given all the nomads and pastures between the Altai Mountains and the Amu Darya River.

Consequences

The Mongol conquest affected Russia in both the short term and the long term. In the aftermath of the military campaigns came physical devastation, destruction of markets, economic, and political isolation. Perhaps 5 percent of the population perished. The Mongols demanded a tithe of 10 percent on all goods, money, and movable property, and extended this to include mass deportations of Russian craftsmen, princes, horses, and livestock. Some deportees were used in military campaigns, others were sold as slaves. As a result of long association, the Mongol word for tithe—*denga*—first entered the Russian language as the modern Russian word for money—*dengi*. In the longer term, the Mongols affected Russian politics by fostering competition among princes for the privilege of being the lone prince responsible for collecting all taxes from Rus' lands. Eventually the princes of Moscow succeeded in securing the position, and Muscovite grand princes transformed themselves into autocratic tsars modeled on the Great Khan.

The World of Marco Polo

Traveling as a teenager to the far reaches of the Mongol Court, Marco Polo changed the world's perception of China.

LEFT The departure of Marco Polo and his family from Venice. This painting is from a manuscript dated c. 1400, held in the Bodleian Library, Oxford.

1251 Kubilai becomes governor of the southern territories of the Mongol Empire

1253 Kubilai attacks Yunnan and destroys the Kingdom of Dali

1259 Arik Boke, Kubilai's younger brother, is pronounced the Great Khan

1260 Kubilai declares himself the Great Khan, resulting in war with his brother and eventual destruction of the Mongolian capital of Karakorum

1263 Kubilai eventually wins after three years' battle with his brother and is declared the Great Khan

Fifteen-year-old Marco Polo must have been awestruck when his father, Nicolo, returned home to Venice from China, with his uncle, Maffeo, and was full of stories about their visit to the great Mongol Emperor, Kubilai Khan. The year was 1269 and it had been more than nine years since Marco had seen his father.

Brother Traders

The Polos were part of an elaborate network of missionaries and traders sprawled around the Byzantine and Mongol empires. So impressed was Berke Khan, of the "Golden Horde," after trading with them, that he sent them to see the Great Khan, Kubilai, ruler of the whole Mongol empire. The emperor interviewed them, and requested that they ask the Pope to send emissaries to him.

Maffeo and Nicolo Polo had returned just as Pope Clement had died, leaving it impossible to gain assistance to fulfil Khan's request. After two years of protracted elections, Pope Gregory X filled the office in 1271. He offered to send two friars, diplomatic letters, and gifts. More significant, perhaps, was the inclusion of Nicolo's 17-year-old son, Marco.

The Silk Roads

The Polos left Venice in late 1271, sailing to Constantinople and across the Black Sea. They then ventured overland through Persia, visiting Baghdad and Tabriz, with the aim of reaching the Persian Gulf and sailing. When this proved unviable they reverted to the overland trip. Crossing Afghanistan and the mighty Pamirs, the Polos traversed some of the trading routes known as the Silk Roads, linking China with the Mediterranean.

China

In September 1275, the party reached the capital of the Mongol Empire, Dadu—the present-day Beijing. Here Marco Polo records: "The city is full of fine mansions, inns, and dwelling-houses. All the way down the sides of every main street there are booths and shops of every sort."

Marco showed an aptitude for language, learning four of the languages in use. Soon Kubilai Khan appointed him as ambassador, and eventually as governor of Yangzhou.

The Return Voyage

After 17 years, Marco Polo and his family became anxious to return to Venice. The Great Khan was advancing in years, and they feared for their position should he die. Their desire to leave eventually coincided with his need to send a new bride to King Arghun of India. Marco Polo offered his seafaring skills to escort the young bride-to-be to India via the ocean.

In 1292, a fleet of 14 ships and 600 men set sail from Zaitun (Changchow) in China. They sailed the South China Sea, docking at modern-day Vietnam and Sumatra. They then ventured to Ceylon and finally India. Along the way, most of the 600 men were lost. In another change of plans, the princess had to marry King Arghun's son, as Arghun had by then died. The Polos continued to Persia where

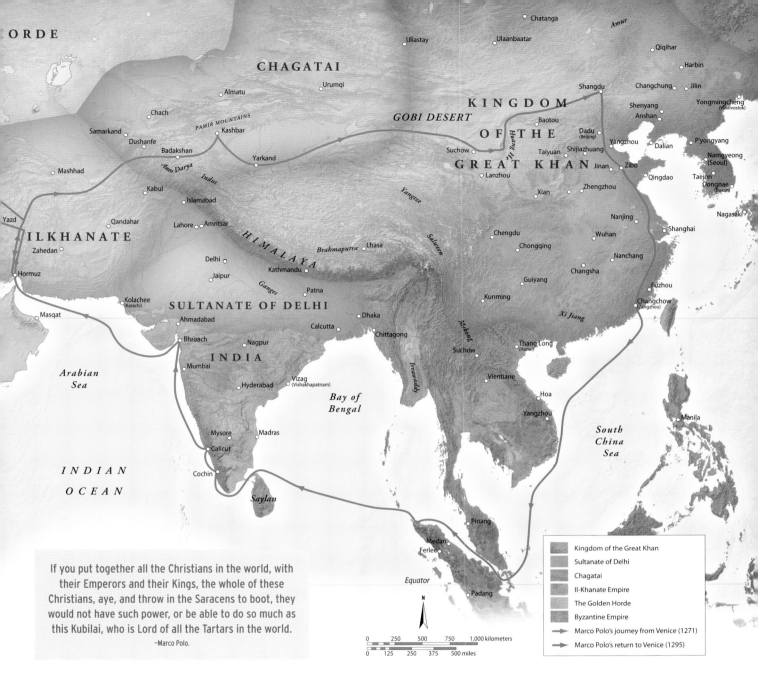

CHAGATAI

KINGDOM OF THE GREAT KHAN

GOBI DESERT

ILKHANATE

SULTANATE OF DELHI

INDIA

Arabian Sea

INDIAN OCEAN

Bay of Bengal

South China Sea

HIMALAYA

Saylan

Equator

Chatanga · Uliastay · Ulaanbaatar · Qiqihar · Harbin · Shangdu · Changchung · Jilin · Yongmingcheng (Vladivostok) · Shenyang · Anshan · Baotou · Dadu (Beijing) · Yangzhou · Dalian · P'yongyang · Suchow · Taiyuan · Shijiazhuang · Jinan · Zibo · Namgyeong (Seoul) · Lanzhou · Qingdao · Taejon · Dongnae (Busan) · Xian · Zhengzhou · Nagasaki · Nanjing · Wuhan · Shanghai · Chengdu · Chongqing · Nanchang · Changsha · Fuzhou · Guiyang · Changchow (Zangzhou) · Kunming · Xi Jiang

Almatu · Urumqi · Chach · Kashbar · Samarkand · Dushanfe · Badakshan · Yarkand · Mashhad · Kabul · Islamabad · Qandahar · Lahore · Amritsar · Yazd · Zahedan · Hormuz · Delhi · Jaipur · Kathmandu · Patna · Lhasa · Kolachee (Karachi) · Ahmadabad · Calcutta · Dhaka · Masqat · Bhroach · Nagpur · Chittagong · Mumbai · Hyderabad · Vizag (Vishakhapatnam) · Suchow · Thang Long (Hanoi) · Mysore · Madras · Calicut · Cochin · Vientiane · Hoa · Yangzhou · Manila · Pinang · Medan · Ferlec · Padang

Anu Darya · Indus · Ganges · Brahmaputra · Salween · Yangtze · Mekong · Irrawaddy · Xi Jiang · Huang He · Amur

ORDE

PAMIR MOUNTAINS

If you put together all the Christians in the world, with their Emperors and their Kings, the whole of these Christians, aye, and throw in the Saracens to boot, they would not have such power, or be able to do so much as this Kubilai, who is Lord of all the Tartars in the world.

—Marco Polo.

Legend	
	Kingdom of the Great Khan
	Sultanate of Delhi
	Chagatai
	Il-Khanate Empire
	The Golden Horde
	Byzantine Empire
→	Marco Polo's journey from Venice (1271)
→	Marco Polo's return to Venice (1295)

0 250 500 750 1,000 kilometers
0 125 250 375 500 miles

N

they learned the Great Khan had passed away too. Late in 1295, Marco, aged 41, reached Venice.

Recalling the Journey

It wasn't until a war between Genoa and Venice, when Marco was taken prisoner, that he dictated his journey to Rusticello da Pisa. Marco's account was published variously as *Le divasement dou monde*, *Il Milione*, or later, *The Travels of Marco Polo*.

The impact of the work, regardless of its fidelity to fact, may be partly seen by its influence on Christopher Columbus, who attempted to sail west to the lands Polo so meticulously described.

ABOVE The Polos' amazing trip across Asia made them the first European visitors to the court of Kubilai Khan.

LEFT The Polos are shown here outside Dadu (Beijing) recording the extensive structures of streets and shops.

Arab Conquest of Asia

The first conquest of part of India by Muslims took place in 712 CE in Sind, southern Pakistan, 90 years after Islam was born in Saudi Arabia. However, it was not India's first contact with the Arabs or with Islam.

Since at least the fourth century CE, commercial interaction had been taking place between Arabia and India's Malabar coast, with some of the Arab ships further bound for ports in Sri Lanka, Sumatra, and Southern China.

Arab Invasion

The first Arab military invasion of India occurred in 712 CE when the Arab governor of Iraq dispatched his 17-year-old nephew and son-in-law, Muhammad bin Kasim, to Sind at the head of a large army, ostensibly in retaliation for the harsh treatment meted out to some shipwrecked Arab families on their pilgrimage from Sri Lanka to Mecca. Kasim marched to India, crossed the Indus, killed King Dahir and, despite stiff resistance from Dahir's widow, annexed Sind. Soon after, he annexed Multan to the north.

Numerous Arab scholars, who took deep a interest in Indian scholarship, served as conduits for the transmission of Indian materials to Spanish universities and through them to France and England. In the process, some of India's contributions to the world were construed as Arab contributions. A number of Sanskrit texts in mathematics, science, medicine, and literature were translated into Arabic thanks to Khalifa Haroon-al-Rashid.

1026 Muhammad of Ghazni sacks the Somnath Temple

——

1190-1191 Prithviraj defeats the Muslim troops beyond Punjab. Muhammad of Ghur is severely wounded.

——

1192 Second battle of Tarain. Muhammad of Ghur captures the fortress of Uch.

——

1193 Muhammad of Ghur establishes a kingdom in India with its capital in Delhi.

——

1206 Muhammad of Ghur is murdered. With no successor, his throne is in disarray until Qutb-ud-din Aibak returns to India and declares himself Sultan.

RIGHT Tenth-century Arabic map by Abu Ishaq Ibrahim al-Istakhri showing the Indus River and Sind region. The cardinal points are also shown, with north in the left margin.

Muhammad of Ghazni's Raids

Except for Sind and Multan, there were no further Muslim territorial acquisitions on the subcontinent until the beginning of the eleventh century. This period of considerable political and military stability in the region from present-day Iran and Central Asia produced a number of adventurers who were also recent converts to Islam. One of them was Muhammad, the son of Sabuktigin, founder of Ghazni in Afghanistan. The young, ruthless Muhammad's ambition was to make Ghazni the most powerful kingdom in all of Central Asia. Whatever his dreams for Ghazni, Muhammad of Ghazni has gone down in Indian history as the epitome of cruelty and barbarism. He invaded India 17 times between 1000 and 1026 and, on the pretext of promoting Islam, raided temples and cities, killing innocent people, including women and children, and took an enormous amount of loot to Ghazni. An additional bonus for Muhammad was his misuse of prisoners-of-war as slaves.

Al-Beruni (973–1048 CE), the famous chronicler of the period, accompanied Muhammad to India. He praised Muhammad's conquests but condemned the devastating consequences of his invasions.

There were no major incursions from the west for quite some time, mainly because the Muslim potentates in Afghanistan and Central Asia were preoccupied with internecine struggles for power.

Muhammad of Ghur

Almost two hundred years later, Muhammad of Ghur, who by that time had conquered Ghazni and who was inspired by the same economic motivations that had moved Muhammad of Ghazni, decided to plunder the riches of India in order to build his own country. In 1182, he entered India through the Gomal Pass to the southern Indus region hoping to enlist the cooperation of a fellow Muslim, the ruler of Sind. But this did not materialize. Three years later, he tried attacking the northwest and the Punjab through the Khyber Pass, this time with the aim of going beyond plunder to build an Indian empire. Prithviraj Chavan of Delhi defeated and captured the Ghur leader at the battle of Tarain but, following the Rajput martial code, released his prisoner. A few months later, Muhammad returned with a larger force. This time he defeated Prithviraj and annexed the kingdom of Delhi.

Muhammad of Ghur returned to Afghanistan, leaving his trusted slave and companion, Qutb-ud-din Aibak, in charge of his Indian possessions. Muhammad himself was assassinated in Ghur by one of his lieutenants in 1206. In 1208, Aibak crowned himself Sultan of Delhi, thus founding the so-called Slave Dynasty (1208–1290).

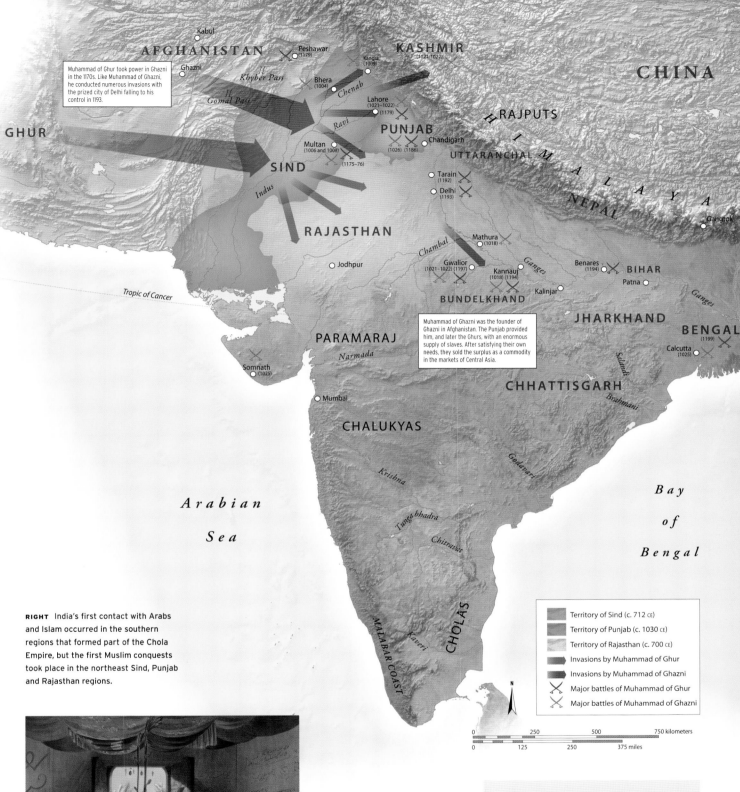

Muhammad of Ghur took power in Ghazni in the 1170s. Like Muhammad of Ghazni, he conducted numerous invasions with the prized city of Delhi falling to his control in 1193.

Muhammad of Ghazni was the founder of Ghazni in Afghanistan. The Punjab provided him, and later the Ghurs, with an enormous supply of slaves. After satisfying their own needs, they sold the surplus as a commodity in the markets of Central Asia.

CHINA

AFGHANISTAN
Kabul
Ghazni
Peshawar (1179)
Khyber Pass
Gomal Pass
Bhera (1004)
Chenab
Kangra (1009)
KASHMIR (1021–1022)
Lahore (1021–1022) (1179)
GHUR
Multan (1006 and 1008)
(1175–76)
SIND
Indus
Ravi
PUNJAB
(1026) (1186)
Chandigarh
RAJPUTS
UTTARANCHAL
HIMALAYA
NEPAL
Gangtok
Tarain (1192)
Delhi (1193)
RAJASTHAN
Jodhpur
Chambal
Mathura (1018)
Gwalior (1021–1022) (1197)
Kannauj (1018) (1194)
Ganges
Benares (1194)
BIHAR
Patna
Ganges
Tropic of Cancer
PARAMARAJ
Narmada
BUNDELKHAND
Kalinjar
JHARKHAND
BENGAL (1199)
Calcutta (1025)
Salandi
CHHATTISGARH
Brahmani
Somnath (1025)
Mumbai
CHALUKYAS
Godavari
Krishna
Tungabhadra
Chitravat
Arabian
Sea
Bay
of
Bengal
MALABAR COAST
CHOLAS
Kaveri

RIGHT India's first contact with Arabs and Islam occurred in the southern regions that formed part of the Chola Empire, but the first Muslim conquests took place in the northeast Sind, Punjab and Rajasthan regions.

	Territory of Sind (c. 712 CE)
	Territory of Punjab (c. 1030 CE)
	Territory of Rajasthan (c. 700 CE)
	Invasions by Muhammad of Ghur
	Invasions by Muhammad of Ghazni
✗	Major battles of Muhammad of Ghur
✗	Major battles of Muhammad of Ghazni

N

| 0 | | 250 | | 500 | | 750 kilometers |
| 0 | 125 | | 250 | | 375 miles | |

LEFT After his death, Muhammad of Ghazni was remembered in his own country as a national hero who established his father's small kingdom as a powerful empire, although elsewhere he was not so well regarded.

He seized all the gold and silver idols and ordered his soldiers to burn all the temples to the ground. The idols in them were deliberately broken into pieces. The city was pillaged for 20 days, and a large number of buildings were reduced to ashes.

– Al-Beruni (973-1048 CE), Muslim scholar, in his book *Indica* (c. 1030 CE).

East Meets West

By the end of the fourteenth century, the Ottomans had established an empire that stretched from the Balkans to the Euphrates River.

The emergence of the Ottomans had begun 150 years before in the context of the Mongol invasions and the instability they caused in Anatolia. This instability, together with that created in Asia Minor and the Balkans by the Mongol invasions of the thirteenth century, would contribute to the Ottoman Empire's development by the end of the fourteenth century.

Turkic Migrations

With the Mongol invasions of the thirteenth century, migrations of Turkic peoples reached western Anatolia on the borders of the Byzantine Empire. This frontier region also became important to the emergence of the Ottomans as various Muslim groups gathered there, first to challenge Mongol control and later the authority of the Byzantines.

Principalities

The Turkic peoples who had settled in western Anatolia declared a holy war—*ghaza*—against the Byzantine Empire, mainly in an attempt to take control of rich pastoral lands in the area. Between 1260 and 1320, the leaders of the holy wars—*ghazi*—established a number of independent principalities in western Anatolian territory they captured from the Byzantine Empire. The Byzantine preoccupation with problems in the Balkan territories during this period worked in favor of the leaders of the holy wars. One of these leaders, Osman, emerged in control of territory close to the Byzantines. In 1301 he besieged Nicaea (now Iznik), the former capital of Byzantium. It is from Osman's name that the term "Ottoman" derives and it is from this time that the Ottomans are considered to have emerged into history as an important regional power.

Balkans

The Ottomans were to eventually establish dominance in Anatolia in the fourteenth century; by the middle of the century they had succeeded in capturing territory in the Balkans. The immediate catalyst for their expansion lay in the annexation by Osman's son and successor, Orhan, of the territory of the Karesi on the eastern shore of the Dardanelles straits. In 1352 Orhan's son, Suleyman, went to the assistance of Cantacuzenus, who was fighting a war against a joint Serbian and Bulgarian invasion of the Gallipoli peninsula. Suleyman managed to take control of the great fortress at Gallipoli as well as other fortresses on the peninsula, and garrisoned them with Ottoman troops from Anatolia.

The Ottomans now controlled much of the territory of Thrace, giving them an important foothold on European soil, and the city of Constantinople itself was now thought by European Christian powers to be under threat.

ABOVE Sultan of Turkey, Osman I (1259–1326), laid the foundation for what became known as the Ottoman Empire.

LEFT The Central Asian empire of Timur (1370–1405) was gained by brilliant military strategy and ruthless tactics.

c. 1120 Seljuk Empire splits into principalities ruled by family princes

1258 The Mongols conquer Baghdad

1317 Osman lays siege to the city of Bursa

1326 After an extended battle, Bursa surrenders and is made the capital

Territory of Ottoman Beylik (c. 1300)
Territory expansion (1300–1359)
Territory expansion (1360–1451)

ABOVE During the fourteenth century the Ottomans established dominance in Anatolia and claimed suzerainty over most of the Balkan peninsula.

RIGHT The collapse of the Byzantine Empire brought Christendom face to face with a growing Islamic presence in the sultanates and empires to the east.

> No distinction is attached to birth among the Turks; the deference to be paid to a man is measured by the position he holds in the public service.
>
> –Ogier Ghiselin de Busbecq (c. 1521-1592), in *The Turkish Letters*, 1555-1562.

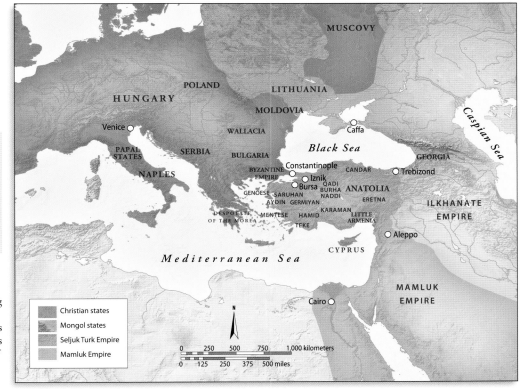

Christian states
Mongol states
Seljuk Turk Empire
Mamluk Empire

Using the communities they had established in Thrace as bases, the Ottomans set about conquering the Balkans. The Balkan territories were particularly fragmented at this time, with many small principalities and local lords vying for control of territory. They would not be conquered overnight, and though the Ottoman advance into the Balkans is sometimes seen as inexorable, it did face obstacles. The main opposition came from the kingdom of Hungary, which provided support to a range of rulers and principalities in the region which had united against the Ottoman advance. The Byzantines were also active in supporting opposition groups despite the fact that they were virtually Ottoman vassals themselves.

Notwithstanding these obstacles, over the next three decades most of the Balkan peninsula came under Ottoman suzerainty. This was a major success, and it strengthened the Ottomans' position in Anatolia. Indeed, their victories in Europe meant that the prestige of the Ottomans was significantly increased throughout the Islamic world. The emergence of Timur (Tamerlane) as ruler of a powerful empire in Central Asia and Iran at the end of the fourteenth century, however, caused some setbacks. In 1402, Ottoman ruler Bayezid I, who had succeeded Murad in 1389, was defeated and captured by Timur's forces at Ankara. It was only after Timur's death in 1405 that Bayezid's sons were able to successfully challenge the authority Timur had established and remove the mantle of suzerainty they had been forced to accept earlier.

Monarchy

During the Middle Ages, the monarchs of England and France not only battled within their own countries but also between themselves, until war gave impetus to ideas of both French and English nationality.

England

The Viking raids and settlements of the ninth century were followed by the emergence of the ancient kingdom of Wessex as the most powerful Anglo-Saxon dominion. Alfred the Great (d. 899 CE), king of Wessex, dominated a wide swathe of Anglo-Saxon territories beyond the borders of Wessex, but never ruled all of England. The kingdom was politically united for the first time in 927 CE under Æthelstan (d. 939 CE), and unification became permanent in 954 CE when Ædred (d. 955 CE) defeated Eric Bloodaxe.

The eleventh century witnessed a more stable English state, despite new conflict with the Danes and the advent of a Danish monarchy

> Uneasy lies the head that wears a crown.
> –William Shakespeare, *Henry IV*, Part II, 1597.

under kings Canute (d. 1035) and Harthacanute (d. 1042). The latter was succeeded by his half-brother Edward the Confessor, the son of Æthelred the Unready and heir to the native dynasty. "Angle-Land" was again an independent power. When Duke William of Normandy seized England from King Harold in 1066, he became the ruler of a kingdom with perhaps the strongest royal authority in Europe.

William I was succeeded by two of his sons—William II Rufus (the Red), then later Henry I. Under Henry I, England and Normandy, separated on the death of the Conqueror in 1087, were reunited, and a number of important judicial and financial reforms were implemented in England. When his son and heir, William, went down with the *White Ship* in 1121, Henry decided to name Matilda, his only legitimate child to survive the tragedy, heir to the throne. On Henry's death in

RIGHT The English succession was complicated when Henry I (1068-1135) lost his son, William the Aethling, in the wreck of the *White Ship* in 1120, and named his daughter, Matilda, as his heir to the throne. This proved to be an unpopular move, with the realm reluctant to accept the possibility of a female monarch.

1135, however, his nephew Stephen (who was a grandson of the Conqueror) took power, supported by most of the barons. His weak rule allowed Matilda to challenge his accession, and before long England had descended into a period of civil war known as "the Anarchy." Stephen clung precariously to power for the rest of his life, but ultimately agreed to a compromise under which he would be succeeded by Matilda's son, Henry. Consequently, in 1154, Henry II Plantagenet, son of Matilda and Geoffrey, Count of Anjou and Maine, became the first English monarch of the Angevin or Plantagenet dynasty.

Richard I (the Lionheart), who followed his father in 1189, spent the bulk of his 10-year reign on crusade. He was succeeded in 1199 by his infamous younger brother John Lackland, who was also the Irish sovereign and whose reign was marked by bitter conflict with the barons. In 1215, they coerced him into issuing the *Magna Carta*—the Great Charter—to guarantee the rights and liberties of the nobility. Soon after, however, John repealed the charter, thus plunging England into the First Barons' War (1215–1217). The war ended abruptly when John died in October 1216, leaving the crown to his 9-year-old son Henry III (d. 1272). When war broke out again in the 1260s, the result was a royalist victory.

Henry's son Edward I (d. 1307) successfully maintained royal power. He made legal and administrative reforms, conquered Wales in 1283, and increased English dominance in Scotland. Some of his gains were reversed under Edward II, who engaged in a disastrous conflict with the nobility and was deposed in 1327. Edward III (d. 1377) by, contrast, was one of the most successful English rulers of the medieval period—though his uncompromising claim to be the rightful king of France then set the stage for the prolonged and bloody war between the two kingdoms.

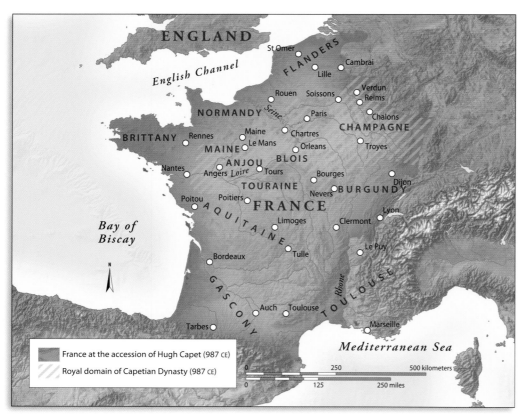

France at the accession of Hugh Capet (987 CE)
Royal domain of Capetian Dynasty (987 CE)

ENGLAND

English Channel

St Omer
FLANDERS
Lille
Cambrai
Rouen
Soissons
Verdun
Reims
NORMANDY
Paris
Chalons
CHAMPAGNE
Maine
Chartres
Rennes
Le Mans
Orleans
Troyes
MAINE
BLOIS
ANJOU
Nantes
Angers
Tours
Bourges
Dijon
TOURAINE
Nevers
BURGUNDY
Poitou
Poitiers
FRANCE
BRITTANY

Bay of Biscay

AQUITAINE
Limoges
Clermont
Lyon
Bordeaux
Tulle
Le Puy
GASCONY
Auch
Toulouse
TOULOUSE
Tarbes
Marseille

Mediterranean Sea

0   250   500 kilometers
0   125   250 miles

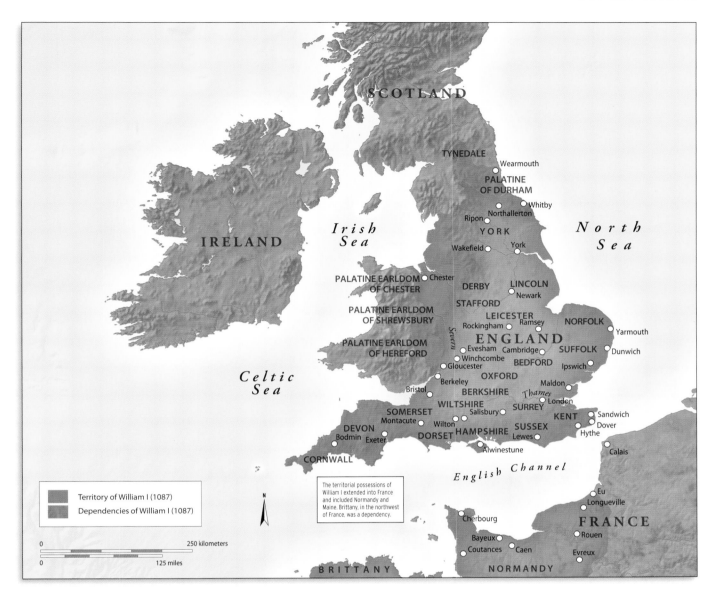

SCOTLAND

TYNEDALE
Wearmouth
PALATINE
OF DURHAM
Whitby
Northallerton
Ripon
YORK
Wakefield York

*North
Sea*

*Irish
Sea*

IRELAND

PALATINE EARLDOM
OF CHESTER Chester
DERBY LINCOLN
Newark
STAFFORD
PALATINE EARLDOM
OF SHREWSBURY
LEICESTER
Rockingham Ramsey NORFOLK
Yarmouth
PALATINE EARLDOM
OF HEREFORD ENGLAND SUFFOLK Dunwich
Evesham Cambridge
Winchcombe BEDFORD Ipswich
Gloucester
OXFORD
Berkeley Maldon
Bristol BERKSHIRE London
Thames
WILTSHIRE SURREY
SOMERSET Salisbury KENT Sandwich
Montacute Wilton SUSSEX Dover
DEVON HAMPSHIRE Hythe
Bodmin Exeter DORSET Lewes
CORNWALL Alwinestune Calais

*Celtic
Sea*

English Channel

Eu
Longueville

Cherbourg FRANCE
Rouen
Bayeux
Coutances Caen Evreux

BRITTANY NORMANDY

Territory of William I (1087)
Dependencies of William I (1087)

The territorial possessions of
William I extended into France
and included Normandy and
Maine. Brittany, in the northwest
of France, was a dependency.

0   250 kilometers

0   125 miles

ABOVE The Norman Conquest brought many changes to English politics, society, law, architecture, and—not least—language.

RIGHT Henry II (1133-1189) of England had many ambitious children, and few of them liked his plans for the succession. Here, he leads his wife Eleanor of Aquitaine and son Richard (later the Lionheart) into captivity after their rebellion in 1173.

FAR LEFT Though they only ruled directly over a rather small region, the Capetian kings were supported by the church, and the dukes of the various potentates often faced problems from their own subordinates. By 1270, however, at the death of Louis IX (on his way to beatification), France under the Capetians was the preeminent power in Western Europe. This largely continued under Philip III (1245-1285), and Philip IV (1268-1314).

France

Louis the Pious, son and successor to Charlemagne (d. 814 CE), did not find it easy to maintain the unity of his father's empire against attack from the outside or rebels within. The western realm, the kernel of modern-day France, was repeatedly targeted by Vikings, who sailed inland along the great waterways of the Seine and Loire rivers. Civil war between Louis's sons followed his death in 840 CE and ceased only with the Treaty of Verdun in 843 CE, which formally partitioned the empire into three distinct *regna* or "kingdoms." One of these was West Francia, the dominion of Charles the Bald until 877 CE.

Despite a short-lived attempt to restore unity in the empire (884–887 CE), the imperial title ceased to be held in the west. Here, the Neustrian Count of Paris, Odo, distinguished himself in the struggle against the Norse and in 888 CE secured recognition as ruler of an area roughly equivalent to West Francia as laid out at Verdun in 843 CE. Under Odo, the capital was fixed on Paris.

An emerging dynasty called the Robertines produced not only Odo, but also his younger brother Robert, king of West Francia 922–923 CE, and ultimately the Capetian dynasty. The Carolingians were not quite finished, however. Intermittently possessing the kingdom until 987 CE were the last of the Carolingians of West Francia: Charles the Simple (898–922 CE), Rudolph (923–936 CE), Louis IV (from Overseas) (936–954 CE), Lothar (954–986 CE), and Louis V (the Lazy) (986–987 CE).

The Capetians began with the grandson of Robert I, Hugh Capet (c. 940–996 CE), who was elected "king of the Franks"—*rex Francorum*—in 987 CE. Hugh had the strong support of the Church, which continued throughout most of the Capetian dynasty. Determined to make the throne hereditary, Hugh immediately demanded the coronation of his son Robert II. Upon Hugh's death, Robert II (972–1031 CE) continued his father's plans. The Capetians' holdings were small areas around the Île-de-France and Orléanais during a time of unrest and disorder. The rest of France was ruled by the duke of Normandy, the count of Blois, the duke of Burgundy, and the duke of Aquitaine whose territories were just as unsettled. The area around

the lower Seine, ceded to Norse invaders as the duchy of Normandy in 911 CE, became a particular source of concern when Duke William invaded England in 1066 and made himself and his heirs the Capetians' equal outside of France, where he was still at least nominally subject to the Crown.

Between 1154 and 1189, the English throne was occupied by Henry II (Plantagenet)—hereditary duke of Normandy, count of Anjou, and husband to France's recently-divorced ex-queen, Eleanor of Aquitaine, who controlled much of southwest France. Henry came to dominate the western half of France as a greater power than the French king himself.

From the time of the reign of Louis VI (the Fat) (1108–1137) onward, however, French royal authority became more deeply entrenched, and disputes among the descendants of Henry II of England over the division of his French territories, coupled with King John's lengthy quarrel with Philip II (Augustus) of France (1180–1223), allowed France to recover most English-controlled territories. Philip's son, the future Louis VIII (1223–1226), invaded

England during the troubles of John's reign and was briefly proclaimed king of England by a host of rebel barons. Although he was never crowned king of England, Louis seized Poitou and Saintonge from the Angevins in 1224.

France became a centralized kingdom under "Saint" Louis IX (1226–1270), who initiated several administrative reforms that were added to by Philip IV (the Fair) (1285–1314). Philip—who suppressed the Templars, formed an alliance with Scotland against England, and established the Parlement of Paris—was so powerful he could name popes and emperors. When his son Charles IV died in 1328, however, Capetian rule ended. The house of Valois came to the throne in the person of Philip VI (d. 1350).

Separate Nations

In 1337, England and France began a protracted conflict known today as the Hundred Years' War, over rival claims to the French kingdom. Punctuated by periodic outbreaks of peace, the conflict was to last 116 years, finally coming to an end in 1453 with the decisive expulsion of the Plantagenets from France, except for the Calais Pale.

ABOVE Under Louis IX (1214-1270), France enjoyed unprecedented prosperity and peace. A respected arbitrator, Louis tried to settle territorial claims with Henry III. In the Treaty of Paris (1259), he ceded Limoges, Périgueux, and Cahors, in exchange for Normandy, Touraine, Poitou, Maine, Anjou, and suzerainty in Aquitaine.

800 CE Charlemagne is crowned *Imperator Augustus* by the pope

936 CE Otto the Great is crowned king in Germany

955 CE John XII becomes pope at age 18 and rules for nine years

1125 German princes abolish hereditary claims to the throne and establish an election system

RIGHT When Philip II of France (1165-1223) met Henry II of England (1133-1189) at the sacred field of Gisors, France, on January 21, 1188, they engaged in battle around its central symbol, an elm tree–which Henry defended but Philip cut down, thus strengthening his hold on France.

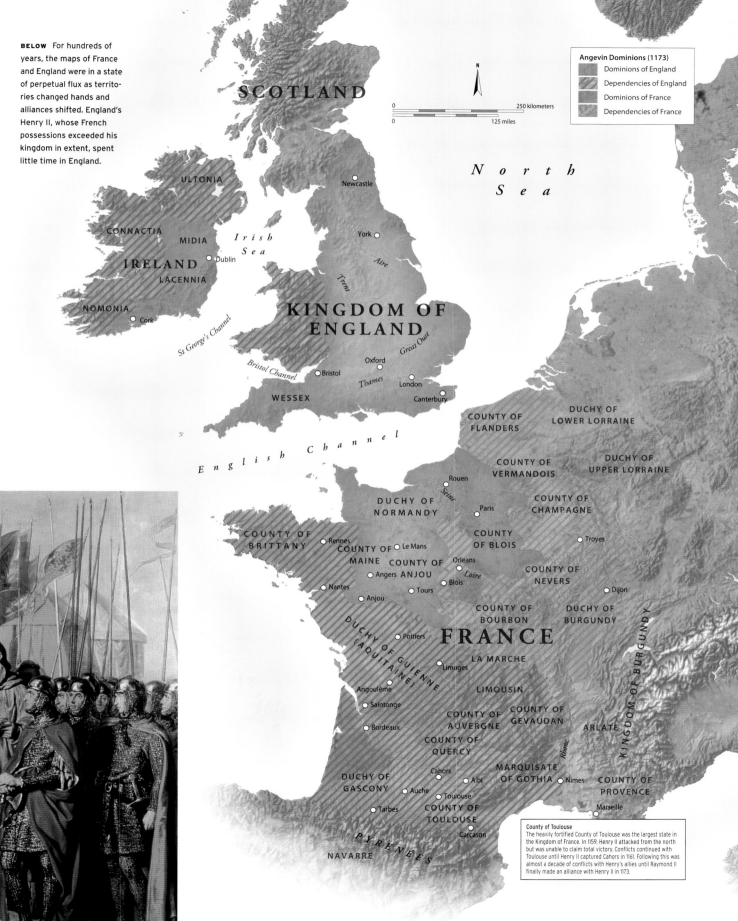

BELOW For hundreds of years, the maps of France and England were in a state of perpetual flux as territories changed hands and alliances shifted. England's Henry II, whose French possessions exceeded his kingdom in extent, spent little time in England.

Angevin Dominions (1173)
- Dominions of England
- Dependencies of England
- Dominions of France
- Dependencies of France

North Sea

SCOTLAND

Newcastle

York

Irish Sea

Aire

ULTONIA

CONNACTIA

MIDIA

IRELAND

Dublin

LACENNIA

Trent

NOMONIA

Cork

St George's Channel

KINGDOM OF ENGLAND

Oxford

Great Ouse

Bristol Channel

Bristol

Thames

London

Canterbury

WESSEX

English Channel

COUNTY OF FLANDERS

DUCHY OF LOWER LORRAINE

COUNTY OF VERMANDOIS

DUCHY OF UPPER LORRAINE

Rouen

Seine

DUCHY OF NORMANDY

Paris

COUNTY OF CHAMPAGNE

COUNTY OF BLOIS

COUNTY OF BRITTANY

Rennes

Le Mans

COUNTY OF MAINE

Orleans

Troyes

Angers

COUNTY OF ANJOU

Loire

COUNTY OF NEVERS

Nantes

Blois

Tours

Dijon

Anjou

DUCHY OF BURGUNDY

DUCHY OF GUIENNE (AQUITAINE)

Poitiers

COUNTY OF BOURBON

FRANCE

Limoges

LA MARCHE

KINGDOM OF BURGUNDY

Angoulême

LIMOUSIN

Saintonge

COUNTY OF AUVERGNE

COUNTY OF GEVAUDAN

ARLATE

Bordeaux

Rhône

COUNTY OF QUERCY

Cahors

MARQUISATE OF GOTHIA

COUNTY OF PROVENCE

DUCHY OF GASCONY

Albi

Nimes

Auch

Toulouse

Marseille

Tarbes

COUNTY OF TOULOUSE

PYRÉNÉES

Carcason

NAVARRE

County of Toulouse
The heavily fortified County of Toulouse was the largest state in the Kingdom of France. In 1159, Henry II attacked from the north but was unable to claim total victory. Conflicts continued with Toulouse until Henry II captured Cahors in 1161. Following this was almost a decade of conflicts with Henry's allies until Raymond II finally made an alliance with Henry II in 1173.

159

Supply and Demand

The rise of trade and of cities would forever alter the European landscape.
By the end of the twelfth century, surpluses in agriculture and a significant
increase in the population dramatically changed the face of European society.

> All men are by nature equal,
> made all of the same earth by
> one Workman; and however we
> deceive ourselves, as dear unto
> God is the poor peasant as
> the mighty prince.
>
> –Plato, Greek philosopher and teacher.

BELOW Rostock, in Germany's far north,
was settled by German traders and owed
its rapid economic growth to its membership of the Hanseatic League. In 1218, the
city began operating under the "Lübeck
law" form of self-government.

Formerly, land had been the backbone of the economy. Most Europeans lived in rural areas and
worked in pastoral and agricultural
occupations during the Middle
Ages. By the first millennium's end,
artisans and merchants also populated towns and organized themselves into guilds, which acted as
regulating bodies—prices, hours
worked, punishments—and as
informal kin networks. Guild members assisted other members who
fell on hard times and this aspect
would be particularly important as
migration to towns increased, and
those who came from the countryside voluntarily removed themselves
from the protection of their family.

Technological Advances

The rapid demographic growth has
been attributed to agricultural and

technological developments such
as the increased use of water power
and wind power, the horseshoe and
horse collar, the heavy plow, and
three-field crop rotation. These
advances took place on large tracts
of land that had been cleared and
drained, particularly in the east
and along the Baltic coast.

Fair System

Any excess product could be sold
at rural markets or seasonal fairs,
which local lords sponsored. In the
thirteenth century there were six
comprehensive fair systems; they
were in Champagne, England,
Flanders, northern Italy, and the
lower and middle Rhine.

Rise of Cities

The trade increase complemented
the rise of cities—in truth, the two

went hand-in-hand. Most cities
were not autonomous at first; however, as their economic power grew,
they forced further legal and economic privileges from their lord.
This was nowhere more apparent
than in northern Italy. The Italian
cities became veritable states by
1300 for two specific reasons. First,
their geographic location placed
them directly in the middle of the
constant struggles between secular

LEFT Peasants often revolted against the poor treatment they suffered throughout the Middle Ages. Peasant insurrections continued to occur in later times, including that of the Jacquerie in France illustrated here.

RIGHT Its location near the major trade routes of the North and Baltic seas led to Hamburg becoming a vital port city for members of the trade alliance known as the Hanseatic League. Hamburg's main export was beer.

c. 1100 Chinese kilns begin to mass produce ceramics for the imperial court

c. 1000–1100 Marrakech is founded on the junction of a trade route running southward to the Niger River and eastward to Cairo

1245 Cottage weavers in Flanders go on strike against cloth merchants

1250 Florence becomes a major center for commerce and industry

kingdoms and the papacy. Second, the economic power of the merchants was quite formidable.

The makeup of urban populations differed greatly from rural populations, and migration to cities challenged the former structuring of society in which people fit into one of the three states: Those who worked the land, those who fought, and those who prayed. As artisans and particularly merchants gained greater economic status, they successfully altered the power and authority structures of cities.

Trade Balances
North–south trading saw high-quality goods such as spices, drugs, incense, silk, porcelain, and slaves move north from Italian ports as the staples of cloth, wool, and grain traveled south. For southern Europe, trade continued along well-established routes in the Mediterranean Sea. Italian merchants pioneered European long-distance trade. The Crusades provided the occasion for Italian merchants, Genoese and Venetian in particular, to innovate. They created new mercantile techniques like book transfers, money changing, and promissory notes. They established themselves not just in the Levant but also all over Europe, particularly in the fair cities where they placed banking houses.

Trade Alliances
The northern European counterpart to the Italian maritime cities was the Hanseatic League. During the twelfth century, some northern merchants allied themselves to form companies and ensure safe passage to protect trade. German-controlled trade stretched from England to Russia. From the east merchants brought grain, wax, honey, wood, and furs in exchange for cloth, wine, salt, and herring. The Hanseatic League reached its height around 1350 and included approximately 200 towns. Lübeck, ideally situated on the Holstein isthmus that connects the North Sea to the Baltic Sea, served as the capital for the league.

The impact of increased trade and vibrant well-populated cities returned Europe to a position of prominence in the Mediterranean and poised European countries to make their influence felt around the globe in the coming centuries.

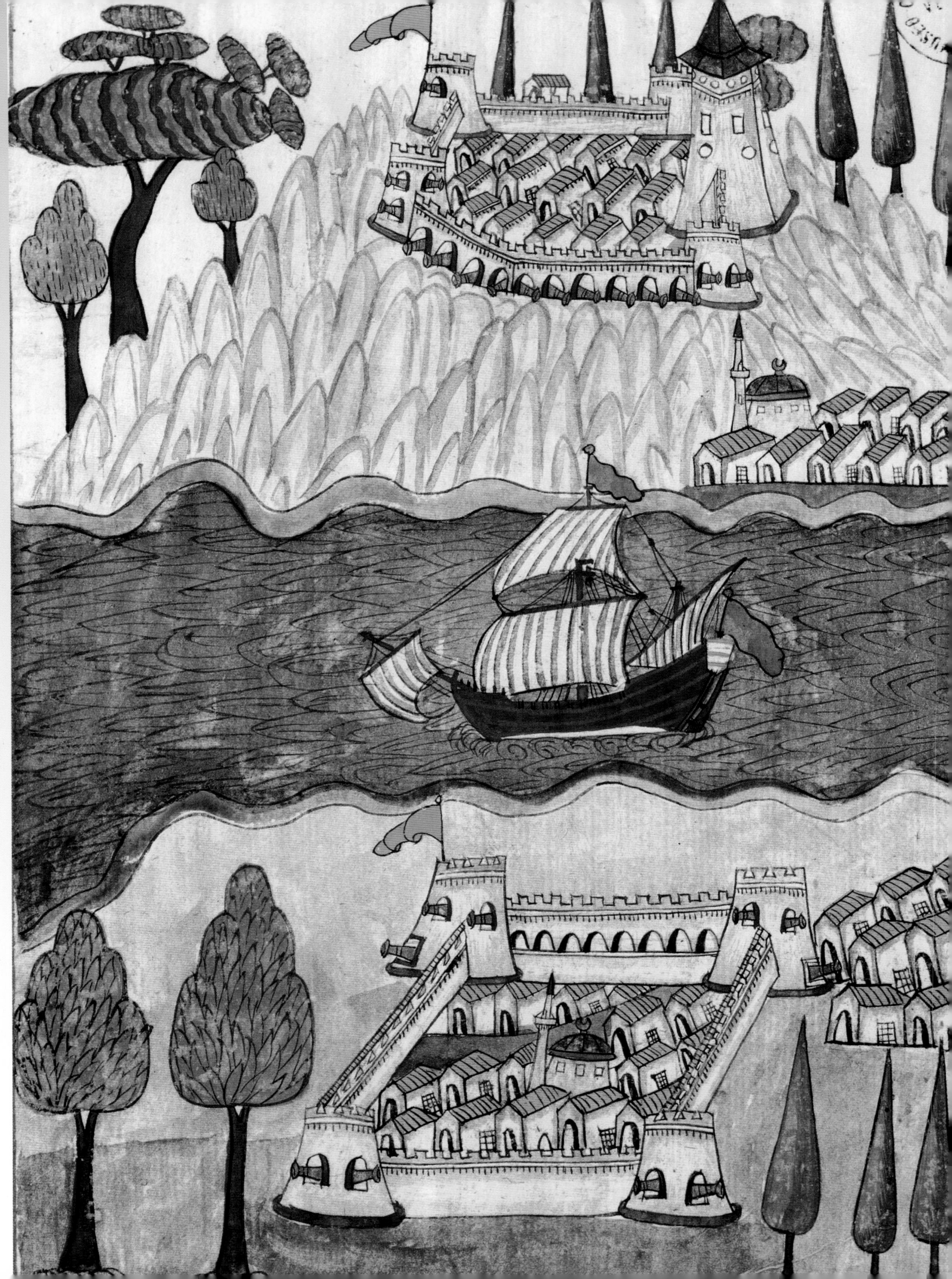

Cultural Awakening

The twelfth-century Renaissance, as scholars have labeled this period, marked no golden age. The 1300s saw continued warfare, the rise and fall of empires, and the savage calamities that the natural world inflicted on people little prepared to cope with disease, drought, and famine.

LEFT The Ottomans built fortresses to protect their territory. Here we see two Turkish fortresses on the Black Sea, one in Greece and the other in Anatolia.

ABOVE This silk painting shows two mandarins from the Ming Dynasty. The embroidered mandarin squares on their robes indicate their social or military rank.

RIGHT Medieval notaries march through the streets of Perugia. In the late 1200s, an administrative elite grew up in Italy to challenge the dominance of merchants and bankers.

PREVIOUS PAGES This French painting honors Eustace de Saint Pierre, one of six merchants who were willing to sacrifice their own lives to save the people of Calais from starvation and end Edward III's siege of the town. In 1347, the people of Calais surrendered to the English.

Eurasia suffered a series of calamities in the 1300s. A long-term rise in population and a decrease in temperatures and growing seasons strained the available food supply, creating widespread shortages.

Outside of the richest elite, those who could afford to eat still had poor diets, and much of the population was malnourished.

Plague

The bubonic plague broke out in central Asia and traveled to China, devastating its population. It spread west along the Silk Road and by ship through Southwest Asia and Europe, carried by the fleas that lived on rats. Between 1315 and 1317, crop failures led to famine, with some cities losing as much as 10 percent of their population. Those who survived were ready prey for disease, especially in the overcrowded and unsanitary conditions in cities. Siena lost half its population, and Florence two-thirds. Ironically, the mass death caused by successive waves of the plague improved life for many survivors. Labor shortages eased the lot of many peasants, as landlords and feudal lords had to grant concessions in order to secure sufficient labor, although the trend in Eastern Europe and Asia was to tighten control over the lower classes. Plague would continue to strike Europe until the 1700s.

Empires

In the Mid-East, the Ottoman Empire, named after the founder of the dynasty, Osman I, continued the long encroachment against the Byzantine Empire and an invasion of Southeast Europe. The Byzantine Empire found itself eclipsed because by 1400 it maintained only Constantinople, Thessalonika, and a narrow strip of territory in Greece. The Ottomans proved will-

ing to tolerate religions other than their own and to grant some local autonomy, and the combination of their military prowess and their relatively enlightened rule allowed them to dominate in Southeast Europe until the late 1800s.

China

China in the 1300s experienced great misery. The plague continued to sweep through the population until survivors developed some immunity in the latter part of the century. Drought struck the Yalu River basin, decreasing harvests and limiting trade. In 1351, an internal conflict over the succession to the throne boiled over into open rebellion, breaking the empire into many small states. One general, Zhu Yuan Zhong (Zhu Yuanzhang), arose from the chaos to conquer the Yangtze River basin. He called his dynasty the Ming Dynasty, in reference to the Chinese name for the Lord Maitreya, the mythical last of the earthly Buddhas. He skillfully balanced the power of the

Confucian elite, the Daoist and Buddhist religious leaders, the military, and the eunuchs who controlled the imperial household. Ming China sent vast fleets around the Pacific and Asian world, engaging in trade and even conquering some "barbarian" outposts.

New Learning

In spite of the disasters Europe endured, new forms of humanist thought expanded, transmitted by poetry and literature often written in vernacular languages rather than classical Latin, and aiming for a wider audience than priests and the court. This new scholarship originated in Italy, but gradually spread across the Christian world. Scholars aimed to revive historical learning. In visual art, new linear perspectives gave artists the freedom to depict more realistic scenes.

Humanists of the 1300s did not aim to challenge religious teaching, but rather sought to harmonize ancient and Arabic knowledge and skills with Christian beliefs.

Human Threshold

Between 1300 and 1400 the world stood at a threshold because the globe had virtually no uninhabited regions left. Even so, civilizations on the different continents still had little contact with each other.

1300 Paris is the largest city in the world, with a population of 200,000 to 300,000

1300 People from the Mississippi region of America build the earthen city of Cahokia

1349 Jews are expelled from Zurich, Switzerland

1350 Maori ancestors from Hawaii arrive in New Zealand on seven ocean-going canoes

BELOW An eagle on a cactus, with a snake in its mouth, was the prophesied sign that showed the wandering Mexica people they had found their new home, later known as Tenochtitlan.

Until the opening up of the transoceanic routes during the following century, Oceania and the American continents would remain cut off from the rest of the world. And although since Marco Polo's travels to China in the late thirteenth century trade routes between Asia and Europe were established, this did not result in large population movements between them.

Urbanization
In Europe, the main driving force of population movement was urbanization. Increasingly from the beginning of the fourteenth century, people settled in the safe confines of large towns and cities. Urban growth was strongly linked to economic development.

The need for supplementary workers was also great because the urban environment was far from healthy. As a result of the dismal conditions, more people died in early medieval cities than children were born, therefore every city needed migrants to maintain their population levels, let alone to grow.

Rural–Urban Migration
The process of urbanization and increasing rural–urban migration started in the north of Italy in the cities of Florence, Milan, and Venice. Halfway through the fifteenth

century, the combined cities would have a population of about 100,000 people. When, in the course of the fourteenth century and continuing in the century that followed, the economic center of Europe changed from Northern Italy to Flanders, the same development could be seen there as well, with booming cities such as Ghent and Bruges growing strongly through the inmigration from the countryside.

Cultural Migration
With the emergence of a new urban culture during the early Renaissance, many new cultural and academic institutions were

> Cities are the abyss of the human species.
> –Jean-Jacques Rousseau (1712-1778), French philosopher and writer.

ABOVE The growth of cities led to a corresponding growth in the demand for food and wine–good news for winemakers!

RIGHT This map shows the political situation in Europe in 1400. At around this time, economic power gradually shifted from Northern Italy to cities in Flanders such as Bruges and Ghent.

North Sea

SCOTLAND

IRELAND

WALES

ENGLAND

FRISIA

BRABAN

Ghent

Bruge

LUXEMBOURG

Zuri

BRITTANY

BURGUNDY

Angevin

FRANCE

SAVO

PROVENC

ATLANTIC OCEAN

Bay of Biscay

NAVARRE

ARAGON

KINGDOM OF PORTUGAL

CASTILE

GRANADA

ZAYYANIDS

HAFSIDS

MARINIDS

0   250   500   750   1,000 kilometers
0   125   250   375   500 miles

established, and increasingly artists and scholars traveled extensively, exchanging techniques and knowledge. At the same time, everywhere around the continent, merchant colonies arose, establishing a trade network that would ultimately form the fundament of the global commercial expansion of the century that followed.

America

At the time of the rise of the city-states in Northern Italy, large-scale migrations took place in Meso-america and South America.

Although very little is known about population movements in this part of the world during this period, scholars are certain that around the fourteenth century, the core of the Maya civilization shifted from Yucatan in present-day Mexico—having migrated there some four centuries before—to the area now known as Guatemala.

Slightly further to the north, a group of migrants invaded the highlands of Mexico. This group, the Mexica, settled near Lake Texcoco in the Valley of Mexico. An urban center arose at Tenochtitlan,

which would later become the heart of the Aztec Empire.

In the Inca and Aztec empires there was also considerable human mobility, albeit different to earlier migration on this continent. The conquests of both civilizations induced population movement that closely resembled the migrations resulting from the European conquest some centuries later.

First Clashes

In what an eminent American scholar has called "the best attempt yet to conquer the world," from the

first decades of the thirteenth century into the fourteenth century, Mongol armies conquered large parts of the Asian continent and dominated the steppes that stretched from China to Eastern Europe. Many of the armies consisted of Turks, and with the Mongol conquest, a migration flow of Turkish settlers poured into Europe, replacing or dominating the Slavic cultures of Eastern Europe. In this case in-migration resulted in extermination and repression of existing cultures—a forerunner of what would follow in the next century.

Political boundaries of Europe (c. 1400)

Holy Roman Empire

Although the electoral procedures of the empire that would dominate European affairs in later years were codified during the fourteenth century, the century would not be kind to the divided empire, which limped through the disasters of wars, the papacy in Avignon, and the Black Death no more easily than did its constituent parts.

The political system of the German lands east of the Rhine River were different from those of England and France, which had hereditary monarchies. Since the emperorship of Frederick II (r. 1212–1250), whose policies reinforced existing political divisions, local lords had wielded more influence than royal or imperial figures. While families like the Hohenstaufens, Habsburgs, and Luxembourgs built dynasties, Germany, like the papacy, kept alive the ancient tradition of elective kingship, whereby the king was chosen by dukes and bishops.

Succession

This system came under threat in the Interregnum (1254–1273) when no contender for the German throne could gain a clear advantage. Pope Gregory X threatened the electors that he would choose a king if they did not, so they instituted Rudolf I of Habsburg (r.1273–1291) who, although he was never crowned emperor, began the famed Habsburg dynasty. Rudolf married off three of his six daughters to lay electors who had supported him. The other daughters were also given in politically beneficial marriages.

> This agglomeration which was called and which still calls itself the Holy Roman Empire was neither holy, nor Roman, nor an empire.
>
> –Voltaire (1694-1778), French philosopher.

Rudolf did not concern himself, as had other emperors, with Italy. This suited the papacy, which had felt pressured by the Hohenstaufens in southern Italy. The Habsburgs would share the German crown with other houses throughout the fourteenth and into the fifteenth century until the election of Albert II (1397–1439), who assumed the throne in 1438. From 1438 until 1740, the Habsburgs ruled in unbroken succession.

Avignon

Italian intervention came when German king and Holy Roman Emperor Henry VII (r. 1308–1313) tried to revive imperial domination of European affairs in order to stem the tide of other rising secular powers, specifically France and England. French King Philip IV (the Fair) had undermined papal supremacy by kidnapping the never-popular Pope Boniface VIII in 1303. The aged Boniface died soon after, and his successor Pope Clement V transferred the Curia to Avignon in 1309—a move that seemed to strengthen France's rivalry with the German territories. England did not support the move, but the English king was unable to create an alliance against France with the Holy Roman Emperor and would engage France in a different kind of battle—the Hundred Years' War (1337–1453).

Clement V left northern Italy full of factional strife. The rivalry between the papacy and the empire had shaped northern Italian politics during the previous centuries, with most territories ruled by either a pro-papacy party (the Guelfs) or a pro-empire party (the Ghibellines). The exiles who found themselves on the losing side—Dante Alighieri being perhaps the most famous—continued to support their cause in other places until their fortunes were reversed. This led to ongoing political instability in most Italian cities. Some hoped that Henry VII would restore peace by uniting Europe once again. Given the state

LEFT Rudolf I, first Habsburg King of Germany and Holy Roman Emperor from 1273, focused less on Rome than on strengthening his position and that of his family in Germany. This suited the popes.

ATLANTIC OCEAN

Oviedo

Douro

Lisbon

Toledo

EMIRATE OF CORDOVA

Seville

Cordova

Cadiz

Granada

IRELAN

Baltic Sea

North Sea

KINGDOM OF ENGLAND

Hamburg

Bremen

SAXONY

ABODRITES

WILTZES

Munster

Magdeburg

Elbe

SORBS

English Channel

Boulogne

Aix-la-Chapelle (Aachen)

FRANCE

Rhine

THURINGIA

Rouen

Seine

Mainz

AUSTRASIA

BRITTANY

Paris

NEUSTRIA

Rennes

Chalons

BOHEMIANS

Angers

Tours

Strasbourg

MORAVIANS

EMPIRE OF CHARLEMAGNE

Poitiers

ALEMANNIA

Angouleme

Chalon

Salzburg

BAVARIA

AQUITAINE

BURGUNDY

RAETIA

CARINTHIA

Bordeaux

Lyon

Cahors

Rhone

Grenoble

FRIULI

GASCONY

Toulouse

PROVENCE

Milan

LOMBARDY

Venice

Danube

CROATS

Genoa

Modena

PYRENEES

Saragossa

Bologna

Ravenna

Pisa

Florence

SORABIA

Barcelona

Corsica

Perugia

Adriatic Sea

Tortosa

Ligurian Sea

PAPAL STATES

DUCHY OF SPOLETO

alencia

Rome

ante

Sardinia

Capua

DUCHY OF BENEVENTO

Salerno

Tyrrhenian Sea

Mediterranean Sea

Ionian Sea

N

AFRICA

Legend

- Empire of Charlemagne (c. 806 CE)
- Main residence of Charlemagne at Aix-la-Chapelle (Aachen)
- Territories under Charlemagne's control
- Papal states aligned with Empire of Charlemagne
- Emirate of Cordova

Charlemagne (747–814 CE), was crowned first Holy Roman Emperor on December 25, 800 CE. He and his successors extended the sphere of Frankish influence deep into the slavic regions of eastern and south eastern Europe. By his death in 814 CE, Charlemagne's empire encompassed the lands that today form the core of continental Europe.

0 250 500 750 1,000 kilometers

0 125 250 375 500 miles

of the papacy in Avignon—French-dominated anti-popes supported by other nations—this hope seemed quite rational in the first decades of the fourteenth century.

The century brought political changes that would solidify the empire's structure for centuries to come. For most of the century, the house of Luxembourg controlled German lands. Louis of Bavaria (1283–1347), who ruled from 1314 until his death on a bear hunt in July of 1347, struggled with papal interference. In 1338 and again in 1339 the German electors asserted their right to elect German kings without the approval of the papacy.

ABOVE By 800 CE, Charlemagne was the undisputed ruler of Western Europe and had restored much of the unity of the old Roman Empire, thus paving the way for the development of modern Europe.

LEFT Like most Florentines of his day, the poet Dante Alighieri (1265–1321) was embroiled in the Guelf–Ghibelline conflict. The Guelfs divided into two factions, the White Guelfs (Dante's party), who wanted greater independence from the pope, and the Black Guelfs. Due primarily to the machinations of Pope Boniface VIII, Dante found himself exiled from Florence and his assets seized by the Black Guelfs, at which point he formed a party of one and began work on *The Divine Comedy*.

Golden Bull

The fourteenth century empire faced a different Europe than the one it had dominated in previous centuries. The reasons are twofold. First, the empire itself had become fragmented; its divisions were codified in the middle of the century with the proclamation of the Golden Bull of 1356. Issued by Emperor Charles IV, the bull set forth the principles that would govern the Holy Roman Empire until its eventual demise during the Napoleonic Wars. It described the procedure for election of the emperor ("King of the Romans") and specified who had the right to vote. The electors, who remained fixed until the seventeenth century, decided the next king by a simple majority vote. This was significant since of the seven electors, only three were archbishops—Cologne, Mainz, and Trier. The others—the King of Bohemia, Duke of Saxony, Margrave of Brandenburg, and Count Palatine of the Rhine—could thus limit Rome's influence. Despite this challenge, the bull avoided the touchy subject of papal confirmation. Traditionally two coronations took place. In Aachen, the king of the German people was crowned, and in Rome, the pope made him emperor. Instead, the bull focused on the cities of election (Frankfurt), coronation (Aachen), and first general meeting, or diet, to be held in Nuremburg.

Roman Law

The second reason the empire faced a different Europe than it had before was the rediscovery and subsequent adoption of Roman law in other countries. This provided monarchs with a legal framework to justify denying the idea of "old Rome" and assert their supremacy. Ironically, it had been the Holy Roman Emperors, particularly Frederick Barbarossa, who had sponsored the revival of Roman law in the Italian universities. In the fourteenth century, the maxim "*rex in regno suo imperator est*" — the king is emperor in his kingdom—helped European monarchs override the Holy Roman Emperor to accomplish their own goals.

Hardship

At the beginning of the fourteenth century the Holy Roman Empire had a population of approximately 14 million people, spread unevenly through the empire. The opening decades of the century brought wet summers and hard winters. Crop failures resulted in a decline in population, one that would be exacerbated by the middle of the century with the advent of the Black Death, which claimed between 25 and 50 million lives in Europe. Within the Holy Roman Empire, the net effect of the Black Death was that the rich got richer and the poor grew even poorer.

Spirituality vs Religion

Like most other Europeans, the Germans turned to God during times of hardship. The Holy Roman Empire comprised a loose conglomeration of religious communities—mirroring their political situation. In the Rhineland in particular, however, a new spiritual movement began to flourish, which influenced Western Christians despite the trend away from ritual toward legal and administrative concerns, as seen in the formation of the Teutonic Knights (1190). Spiritual leaders and mystics like Meister Eckhart, Hadewijch of Antwerp, and Mechthilde of Magdeburg shaped contemplation into something approaching an art form. During a century in which religious leaders were preoccupied by political intrigue, Eckhart's message—that the church as mediator was not necessary for one to know God—struck a chord, though it also saw him excommunicated.

Great Western Schism

The end of the fourteenth century showed no more promise of unity than had the beginning, primarily because most European affairs were affected by the Great Western Schism (1378–1417), which saw first two, then three, popes claim the throne of St Peter simultaneously—each with the requisite support of various political leaders. Despite all this, the Habsburg dynasty, backed up by the wealth of 80 imperial cities and rich banking families like the Fuggers, would ensure that the Holy Roman Empire continued the mixed legacy of Rome, and would see to it that the imperial crown rested firmly on German heads.

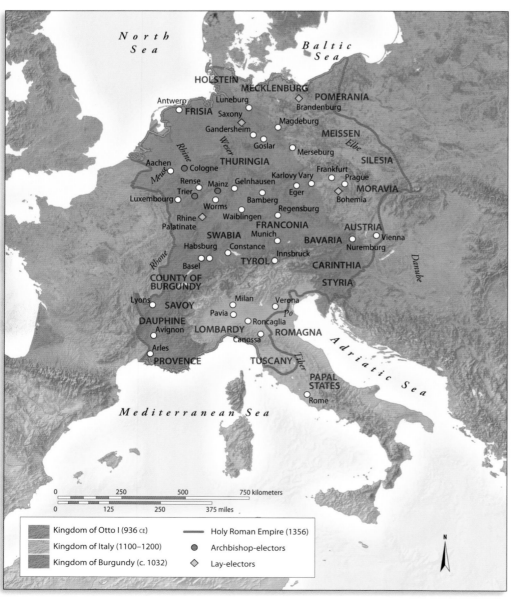

LEFT Otto I (912–973 CE), King of Germany from 936 and arguably the first Holy Roman Emperor from 962, brought Italy, Burgundy, and Lotharingia under German influence.

RIGHT Charles I of Spain (1500–1558), better known as Charles V, Holy Roman Emperor, ruled over extensive domains in Central, Western, and Southern Europe. He abdicated in 1556, dividing his realms between his son Philip II of Spain and his brother Ferdinand I, who became Holy Roman Emperor.

BELOW Sigismund of Luxembourg (1368–1437), King of Hungary and Bohemia and Holy Roman Emperor, was instrumental in resolving the Great Schism at the Council of Constance in 1414.

BELOW RIGHT After his defeat at Legnano in 1176, Holy Roman Emperor Frederick Barbarossa, shown here returning as a papal prisoner to Rome, recognized Alexander III as pope and acknowledged his sovereignty over the Papal States. In return, Alexander acknowledged the emperor as overlord of the Imperial Church.

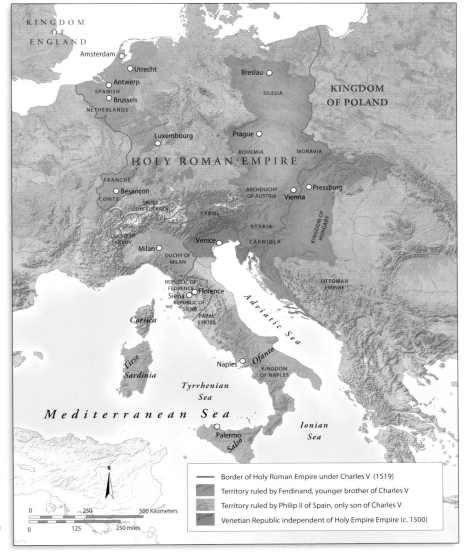

Border of Holy Roman Empire under Charles V (1519)

Territory ruled by Ferdinand, younger brother of Charles V

Territory ruled by Philip II of Spain, only son of Charles V

Venetian Republic independent of Holy Empire Empire (c. 1500)

1291 Three valleys in central Switzerland unite against the Habsburgs.

1303 King Philip IV of France kidnaps Pope Boniface VIII over the king's right to tax French clergy.

1346 In Germany, Charles IV of Luxembourg is elected Holy Roman Emperor.

1347 The plague (or Black Death) spreads throughout Europe, killing roughly one-third of the population.

1411 Sigismund becomes Holy Roman Emperor.

Black Death

Commonly thought to have been bubonic plague, the Black Death killed millions across the known world in a series of pandemics that decimated Europe.

The first plague pandemic ravaged the Middle East and Mediterranean regions, spreading from Egypt in 541 CE and lasting until the end of the eighth century. It is also known as the Justinian Plague because it ravaged the Byzantine Empire from 541–544 CE. Though a Byzantine historian reported that the plague was killing 10,000 people every day in Constantinople, modern estimates suggest perhaps 5,000 people per day died at the pandemic's peak. With no room to bury the dead, bodies were left stacked in the open air. By the eighth century, the plague had receded into the small scattered pockets of endemic disease thought to have been the origins of the second pandemic.

Second Wave

The second pandemic, later named the Black Death due to the black buboes (swellings) appearing on the bodies of those infected, swept into Europe from Asia in 1347. In 1346, Genoese merchants were besieged in the port of Kaffa by a plague-infected army who spread the disease to the Genoese by lobbing disease-ridden corpses over the city walls. From Kaffa, the disease was carried across the waters to Sicily by the traders. By November–December 1347 the plague had spread through southern Italy and France and by June 1348 it had spread into northern Italy, eastern Spain and as far as Paris in France. By December the epidemic had spread into southern Germany and had reached the shores of southern England. Accounts of the plague reaching western Germany, the Netherlands, and the midlands of England were heard by June 1349, and by December most of Ireland and all of England, Norway, and Denmark had succumbed. One year later, cases of the plague were being found in Sweden and northern Germany.

Cause

The Black Death is commonly identified as bubonic plague, a bacterium carried by the fleas infesting black rats. The bacterium *Yersinia pestis* is injected into humans by the flea *Xenophylla cheopsis*, then travels through the lymphatic system producing classic buboes. Two forms of the disease appear to have been present, the most common producing painful swellings in the groin, armpits, or neck. The second attacked the lungs, causing chest pains and the coughing up of blood, invariably proving fatal—unlike the first form, from which victims may recover.

Death Toll

According to many contemporary chroniclers, only one tenth of the population survived the plague. The best modern estimates, however, suggest a mortality rate of between 40 and 55 percent. Not all parts of Europe were as badly affected; in fact, some areas and communities escaped relatively lightly—which is not to deny the magnitude of the epidemic. In an eighteen-month period, roughly half the population of England died of plague.

> [the victims]...ate lunch with their friends and dinner with their ancestors in paradise.
>
> –Giovanni Boccaccio (c. 1313–1375), Italian poet and author.

Myth and Legend

Contemporary scientists came up with many explanations for the plague, ranging from astrological conjunctions to pollution in the atmosphere caused by earthquakes. When science failed to adequately explain the cause, religion was there to supply other answers: That the pestilence was caused by sinners, or by frivolous clothing that hampered the ability to kneel to God. Prayers and processions were in order, it was said, to drive away sickness and grant good health. Unfortunately, a large congregation of potentially infected people gathered in an enclosed space was more likely to spread the plague.

1320–1346 The Black Death ravages China and the Middle East

1346 The Black Death reaches the Crimea, including Kaffa

1348 Disease enters France through the port of Marseilles

1348, February The population of Avignon, France, is halved by the plague

1348, August The Black Death enters England through the port of Bristol

1348, September London is struck by the plague

1348, December Evidence of disease begins to disappear in Italy

1349 The Black Death continues to spread through England and into Ireland

LEFT With outbreaks continuing until about 1700, plague became the subject of art. Here, the Archbishop of Milan, St Charles Borromeo (1538-84), gives communion to sixteenth-century plague victims, in a painting by Sigismundo Caula (1637-1713).

RIGHT Brought back to Italy by Genoese traders from the Black Sea port of Kaffa, the Black Death spread through Europe with astonishing rapidity.

NORWAY

SWEDEN

Gulf of Bothnia

North Sea

DENMARK

Baltic Sea

○ Edinburgh

○ Belfast

IRELAND

○ Dublin

○ York

UNITED
KINGDOM

○ Leicester

○ Norwich

○ Bristol

○ London

○ Hamburg

NETHERLANDS

BELGIUM

Liège ○

Cologne ○

GERMANY

POLAND

English Channel

LUXEMBOURG

Erfurt ○

○ Paris

○ Würzburg

CZECH
REPUBLIC

○ Angers

○ Nüremberg

○ Strasbourg

SLOVAKIA

○ Zurich

FRANCE

SWITZERLAND

LIECHTENSTEIN

AUSTRIA

A L P S

HUNGARY

○ Bordeaux

SLOVENIA

Venice ○

CROATIA

SERBIA

P Y R E N E E S

Montpellier ○

○ Avignon

Genoa ○

Adriatic Sea

ANDORRA

○ Marseille

Pisa ○

A P E N N I N E S

SPAIN

○ Barcelona

Corsica

Florence ○
○ Siena

ITALY

○ Rome

Minorca

Valencia ○

Eivissa

Majorca

Sardinia

Naples ○

*Tyrrhenian
Sea*

*Ionian
Sea*

N

M e d i t e r r a n e a n   S e a

250

500 kilometers

125

250 miles

ALGERIA

Sicily

TUNISIA

	Early break-out (December 1347)
	Spread (June 1348)
	Spread (December 1348)
	Spread (June 1349)
	Spread (December 1349)
	Spread (June 1350)
	Russia (December 1350)
	Little or no disease
	Direction of pandemic spread

(Map includes modern borders)

Renaissance–Art and Culture in Italy

The word *renaissance* means "rebirth." The Italian Renaissance, born of a revival of classical knowledge, also saw the rebirth of cities, self-awareness, reason, and individualism.

1452, April 15 Leonardo da Vinci is born

1469 Leonardo da Vinci moves to Florence as Lorenzo de Medici becomes ruler

1497 Leonardo da Vinci paints *The Last Supper*

1498 Michelangelo, aged 24, begins his *Pieta*, completing it one year later

1504 Leonardo da Vinci paints *Mona Lisa*. Michelangelo creates the massive statue of David, begun 40 years earlier by Agostino di Duccio.

1508 Michelangelo begins painting the ceiling of the Sistine Chapel. He completes the composition four years later.

1519 Leonardo da Vinci dies in Amboise, France

1564 Michelangelo dies after designing the dome at St Peter's Basilica

LEFT Self-portrait of Leonardo da Vinci (1452–1519), polymath. Leonardo was the archetypical Renaissance man, as adept in science as he was in the arts.

RIGHT Giovanni Bellini (c. 1430–1516), *Pieta with Landscape*. Bellini's sumptuous colors and fluent, atmospheric landscapes had a great effect on Venetian painting.

The Renaissance is considered by most commentators to have begun in Italy during the fourteenth century and to have ended in the late sixteenth century, although these boundaries are rather blurred. A movement that affected all aspects of culture—literature, painting, sculpture, architecture, music, and scholarship—the Renaissance consciously sought to recover and revive the achievements of classical antiquity while maintaining a compromise between the classical and Christian traditions.

Classical Heritage

The Italians abandoned the Gothic style and intellectual habits of French theologians and turned to their indigenous classical heritage for inspiration, reviving Greco-Roman culture in a purer, albeit more self-conscious form. In sculpture, the calm spiritual nobility of stone saints gave way to classical emphases on the human body. Architects abandoned the Gothic spire and pointed arch, and created buildings featuring domes, round arches, and elegant classical facades. Humanist scholars turned from the logic of Aristotle and Aquinas to the aesthetic joys of literature, while painters pioneered techniques of linear and atmospheric perspective, imposing a classical unity on their lifelike figures and landscapes. The most common subject matter was found in the Bible; artists blended classical themes and techniques with Christian iconography.

Humanism

The study of humanities marked a decisive break with the traditional university curriculum of teaching logic and dry intellectual formulae. Emphasizing secular rather than transcendental values, scholars were less concerned with studying metaphysics and theology than with trying to understand human action and improvement; most were chiefly concerned with neo-Platonic philosophy. Neo-Platonism, which essentially united the spiritual and material worlds, greatly affected the artists of the High Renaissance, including such well-known figures as Leonardo da Vinci (1452–1519), Giovanni Bellini (c. 1430–1516), Michelangelo (1475–1564), Sandro Botticelli (1444–1510), and Raphael (1483–1520), whose compositions were based on harmony, symmetry, and geometrical exactitude.

> Carving is easy, you just go down to the skin and stop.
> –Michelangelo (1475–1564), Italian Renaissance sculptor, painter, and inventor.

Florence

Florence was to become the focal point of Italian Renaissance culture. Its large textile industry together with international banking allowed enterprising families such as the Bardi, Peruzzi, and Medici to grow very wealthy. The Medici, the city's de facto rulers and bankers to the pope, were the most important source of patronage for the arts.

Cultural Revolution

This was the great age of discovery. Cartography, travel, exploration, and the expansion of the known world ensured the diffusion of ideas and styles. The book trade rapidly became international, encouraged by such diplomatic gatherings as the various councils of the Church, and aided by the introduction in the 1460s of the new technology of printing by Johannes Gutenberg (c. 1396–1468) of Germany. Prior to this all works were laboriously copied.

Decline

The mood of superior confidence that characterized the Renaissance began to weaken in the sixteenth

MICHELANGELO

In 1508, Pope Julius II commissioned Michelangelo to paint the ceiling of the Vatican's principal chapel, the Sistine Chapel. The work took four years to complete. The composition evolved from its original schematic base to become a complex scene of nearly 300 figures with a narrative illustrating the creation of the universe and the story of humankind. Michelangelo's colossal statue of David, in Florence, is one of the most recognized symbols of the Renaissance.

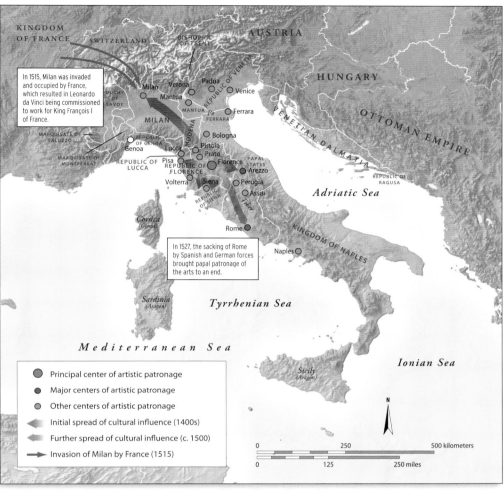

In 1515, Milan was invaded and occupied by France, which resulted in Leonardo da Vinci being commissioned to work for King François I of France.

In 1527, the sacking of Rome by Spanish and German forces brought papal patronage of the arts to an end.

● Principal center of artistic patronage
● Major centers of artistic patronage
○ Other centers of artistic patronage
➤ Initial spread of cultural influence (1400s)
➤ Further spread of cultural influence (c. 1500)
➤ Invasion of Milan by France (1515)

RIGHT From its inception in Florence, the Renaissance, helped by patronage from wealthy families like the Medici, spread gradually north, then south, through Italy.

BELOW Printing press (c. 1468) of Johannes Gutenberg, German craftsman and inventor of the method of printing from movable type. Printing revolution-ized the dissemination of knowledge.

century, when Christian pessimism returned and eroticism diminished. The Catholic Counter-Reformation accompanied a decline in Italian culture. Tastes changed in favor of the later styles of Mannerism and the Baroque. The openness of the Renaissance, with its emphasis on visual and intellectual experimen-tation, was discouraged. Technical achievements were put to new uses in more explicitly Christian arts.

RIGHT Many universities were established during the Renaissance. Some were under the thumb of the pope or a prince, while others were governed by civic agencies. Curricula were expanded to include medicine, philosophy, logic, arithmetic, astronomy, and "natural magic" (experimental science).

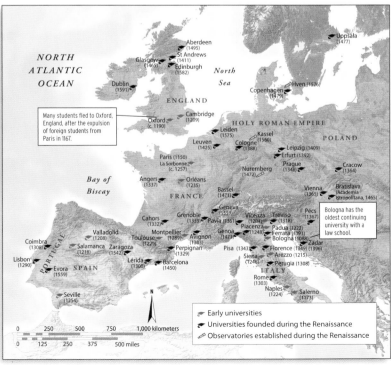

Many students fled to Oxford, England, after the expulsion of foreign students from Paris in 1167.

Bologna has the oldest continuing university with a law school.

➤ Early universities
➤ Universities founded during the Renaissance
➤ Observatories established during the Renaissance

Century of War

During the fourteenth century, amid natural disasters and political and religious crises, the monarchies of England and France entered into a struggle that would last for more than 100 years, with apocalyptic effects for both the people and the French countryside.

> Truly if you were to tear me limb from limb and separate my soul from my body, I would not tell you anything more.
>
> –Joan of Arc (1412-1431), during her trial.

After remarkable stability in the preceding centuries, the fourteenth century opened tumultuously for Western Europe. Poor weather conditions in the first decades exasperated a strained population that had grown beyond its ability to feed itself. In the first decade of the century, the papacy experienced a huge shock when Pope Clement V decided to move his papal seat from its traditional home in Rome to Avignon, where it remained for most of the century (1309–1377). Amid these crises, but before the onset of the pestilence known as the Black Death (1347–1349), a political struggle began.

The Three Edwards

Though he died just seven years after it began, King Edward I (r. 1272–1307) set the tone for England for the remainder of the fourteenth century. He had consolidated English domination over Britain by defeating the Welsh and causing Scotland briefly to submit, while also maintaining a stronghold over French territories—particularly Aquitaine—but the last years of his reign placed great economic strain on the kingdom and left political challenges that his son Edward II, who ruled for 20 years, was ill-suited to handle. Deemed by

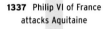

1337 Philip VI of France attacks Aquitaine

1340 Battle of Sluys decimates French fleet

1346 Up to one-third of all French noblemen killed at the Battle of Crécy, at which English longbowmen prevail

1360 Treaty of Brétigny confirms English possession of Aquitaine and Calais

1420 Treaty of Troyes declares Henry V of England heir to the French throne

1429 Joan of Arc's victory at Orléans turns the tide of war against the English

LEFT Having failed to ambush the English between the Seine and Somme rivers, the French faced them at the Battle of Crécy on August 26, 1346. One of the most crucial encounters of the Hundred Years' War, this battle involved a combination of new weapons and tactics that have led many historians to consider it the beginning of the end of chivalry.

Phases of War

Historians break the war into three distinct phases. The first period (1337–1360) saw the English score important victories; the second period (1369–1415) began with a French resurgence but ended in a stalemate; the third period (1415–1453) included clear victories on both sides, with England initially taking a decisive upper hand, but by 1453 Calais was the only English possession on the continent.

The Course of War

In 1340, Edward III of England began to refer to himself as King of France. War began in earnest with the English naval victory at Sluys, where English ships carrying troops to Flanders trapped and decimated a French force in the harbor. The skill of the English archers routed the French army, which twice outnumbered their English enemies. Edward advanced into France, more on a raiding mission than with conquest on his mind, six years later. Philip's troops overtook the English at Crécy, where a severe

ABOVE Council of the King of France at Sluys, June 24, 1340. The naval Battle of Sluys destroyed most of France's fleet, making a French invasion of England impossible and ensuring that the remainder of the war would be fought mainly in France.

ABOVE Edward III (1312-1377), who remained on the throne for 50 years, transformed England into the most efficient military power in Europe.

some (against fierce competition) to be England's most incompetent ruler, Edward II was succeeded in 1327 after a politically divisive rule (he had "favorites") by his son Edward III, who succeeded in re-establishing trust in and great respect for the English monarchy.

Catalysts of War

Philip IV, like his contemporary Edward I of England, put France on its own collision course at the start of the fourteenth century. Although it would be generations before France saw another king as powerful as Philip, he fought costly battles with England over southern France, and the Flemish—with the help of England—gained temporary, albeit informal, independence from their lord. Three sons ruled in brief succession after Philip's death, but all died without heirs.

By the 1330s, the preconditions for war had been set—dynastic and fiscal instability, political and economic rivalry, and social unrest. Edward III had been the closest male heir—his mother Isabella

was Philip IV's daughter—after the death of Charles IV in 1322. However, the Parlement of Paris had decided that Salic Law, which prevented women from inheriting land, precluded succession through a woman. The French throne had then passed to Philip VI, the first Valois king. Although Edward's claim, supported by the Flemish, would facilitate open war with the French, it was a small part of the impetus. Much deeper tensions had been mounting for decades.

When Philip insisted that Edward III owed him liege homage —entailing Edward's support for Philip against all enemies—instead of the simple homage that Edward had previously given, tensions escalated. Edward, as ruler of another realm, could not submit to Philip without surrendering his autonomy and so he denied Philip's request. In 1337, Philip declared that Edward had forfeited his fiefs and attacked Aquitaine, a move that put an end to diplomatic negotiations and strategic skirmishes. The result was full-fledged war.

177

BELOW In 1429, Joan of Arc persuaded Charles VII to let her lead a force to relieve Orléans, where she achieved a decisive victory that turned the tide of the war. When she was finally captured, however, Charles made no attempt to have her ransomed.

miscalculation ensured another English victory. In 1347, England gained Calais.

The French suffered an even greater defeat at Poitiers in 1356 at the hands of Edward's son, the Black Prince, who had first fought at Crécy. Exhaustion and plague led both sides to agree to the Treaty of Brétigny in 1360, confirming

English possession of Calais and Aquitaine. Edward then officially conceded the French throne.

The most noteworthy part of the second phase, often characterized as the war of attrition, is the devastation to the French countryside. In 1369 the French began to harass the English holdings in an attempt to slowly wear them down

without engaging in full-scale war. They succeeded, but the mercenary armies that had been employed by both sides plundered freely, laying waste to arable land and ruining crops and vineyards.

In the same year that the Council of Constance (1414–1418)—which would end the Great Western Schism (1378–1417)—burned religious reformer Jan Hus, England's Henry V renewed aggressive war with France. The famed longbowmen of England soundly defeated the French army at Agincourt in 1415. So decisive was Henry's victory and so weak was the French king, Charles VI, that Henry was able to impose the humiliating Treaty of Troyes in 1420. In the treaty, Henry insisted that the French king declare his son illegitimate and Henry his successor and regent of France. The treaty further provided that Henry's future sons—with his new bride, Charles's daughter Catherine, whose hand in marriage was also part of the settlement—would assume the French throne. Though Charles's son, the future Charles VII, mounted retaliations, they were unsuccessful, and by 1428 English capture of the strategically important city of Orléans seemed imminent.

During this time, Joan of Arc began her crusades. Her life, which testified to a growing sense of nationalism expressed in loyalty to the French king, inspired others and without further hesitation the French pushed the English off the continent. Although no formal treaty had been concluded, by 1453, only Calais belonged to England.

RIGHT The Hundred Years' War involved two royal houses fighting for the French throne. The House of Valois claimed the title King of France, while the Plantagenets, who had their roots in Anjou and Normandy, claimed to be Kings of France and England.

FAR RIGHT By 1453, only Calais belonged to England, and the war, together with plague, famine, and marauding mercenary armies turned to banditry, had reduced the French population by two-thirds.

BELOW The Battle of Agincourt saw the vastly outnumbered English army easily defeat the French due to their use of battle tactics and advanced weaponry. William Shakespeare centered his play, *Henry V*, around the battle.

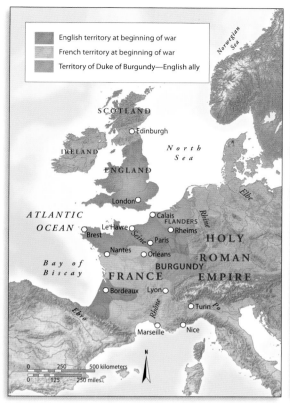

English territory at beginning of war
French territory at beginning of war
Territory of Duke of Burgundy—English ally

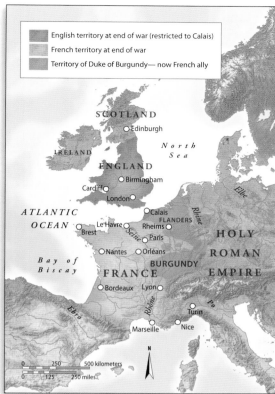

English territory at end of war (restricted to Calais)
French territory at end of war
Territory of Duke of Burgundy— now French ally

Lasting Effects

The Hundred Years' War had effects on both military technologies and the governmental structures of the warring parties. Infantry—armed with bow, pike, or gun—re-emerged as necessary for battle and gone were the days of knights on horseback who had dominated warfare since the invention of the stirrup.

Unfortunately, the kind of warfare fought during the second phrase—that of attrition—proved effective and would be used in future battles like the Thirty Years' War and World War II. In England, the Hundred Years' War resulted in the king ceding greater power and discretion to parliament over taxation, legislation, and decisions to go to war. In France, on the other hand, the French king decreased the power of the Estates Général and gained enough revenue to produce the first standing army since the Roman Empire.

JOAN OF ARC

One of the most fascinating characters of the Hundred Years' War was Joan of Arc (above). The tale of this young peasant woman from Domrémy who gained the trust of French commanders, the ear of the king, and the love of the French people has been recounted through the ages. Importantly for French interests, the Maiden—as she called herself—lifted the English siege of Orléans, ensured that the Dauphin Charles was crowned king in Reims, the traditional coronation city, and turned the tide of war. Joan's influence outlasted her life. She was captured by the Duke of Burgundy and sold to the English in 1430. The English had her tried, condemned, and burned for heresy, aged 19, in 1431.

ARCHITECTURE, ART, AND WAR

Mesoamerica

With a rich ecological and demographic base, the civilizations of pre-Columbian Mesoamerica were complex and diverse from very early in their development. At the time of the Spanish conquest in 1519, the area was inhabited by as many as 25-30 million people speaking 70 different languages.

ABOVE Stone funerary mask covered in a mosaic of jade, coral, turquoise and obsidian, from Teotihuacán c. 300 CE.

BELOW Mayan city with ball court. The ball game played by Mesoamerican people came in different versions depending on region, but all had ritual associations.

With highland basins at altitudes of 5,000–8,000 feet (1,500–2,400 m) almost adjacent to coastal lowlands, Mesoamerica supported an abundance of different life forms within relatively short distances.

Hunting and Fishing

The staple of life for Mesoamerican populations was (and still is) maize which, combined with beans and squash, provided the basis for a nutritious and satisfying diet. Other native Mesoamerican crops such as avocado, tomato, and chili peppers rounded out the vegetal portion of the diet. Hunting and fishing provided protein, as did the consumption of the main domesticated animals, the dog and the turkey. An interesting anomaly of ancient Mesoamerican civilization was the lack of large draft or cargo animals that could be consumed as meat, as cattle were in Europe and camelids in Andean South America.

Human porters were the means of transport for crops and goods.

Teotihuacán

As early as 1200 BCE in the tropical lowland regions, large Olmec and Maya chiefdoms dominated extensive riverine settlement systems. The pinnacle of these developments was reached at Teotihuacán where, about 25 miles (40 km) northeast of Mexico City, a stratified, urban, state-level society left its mark on virtually all Mesoamerica during the third and fourth centuries CE. This was a strategic location for passage to and from the Basin of Mexico, with permanent springs, an irrigable alluvial plain, access to obsidian sources (limestone and volcanic stone) as well as salt from Lake Tetzcoco in the eastern part of the Basin of Mexico, and clay for use in pottery-making. The city was laid out on a standardized grid plan with streets, residences, palaces,

> The Lords governed the town, settling disputes, ordering and settling the affairs of their domain, all of which they did by the hands of the leading men, who were very well obeyed and highly esteemed.
>
> –about the Maya, Diego de Landa, *Relación de las cosas de Yucatán.*

and temples all following an orientation determined by astronomical observations. The population of the multi-lingual metropolis has been estimated at approximately 125,000 at its peak in c. 400 CE.

Most of the male residents of Teotihuacán were peasant farmers who worked the fields on the outskirts of the city, while women tended the hearth and performed household tasks. Archeological evidence also indicates full-time

c. 1200 BCE Rise of Olmec and Maya civilizations

c. 0-150 CE Avenue of the Dead and Pyramid of the Sun established at Teotihuacán

c. 150-300 CE Grid pattern established at Teotihuacán

c. 650 CE Teotihuacán falls, Mesoamerica loses its unifying force

c. 1100 CE Rise of the Toltec empire

c. 1300 CE Rise of Mexica culture and Aztec empire

BELOW Fresco of Aztec priest praying, from the Tepantitla compound, Teotihuacán. Other murals show the god Tláloc rising from the ocean and distributing rain, and the paradise of the rain god. The artistry and sophistication of the Teotihuacános can be seen everywhere in the murals and carvings which adorn the palaces and apartment compounds of Teotihuacán. No writing system has been found there, however, despite the intricate iconography.

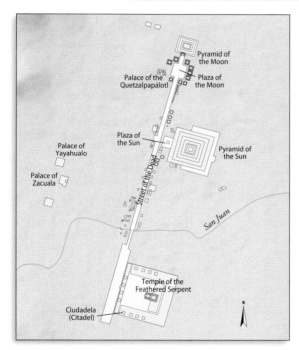

occupational specialization in the production of craft items made from obsidian, ceramic, jade, onyx, mica, shell, and feathers. Because it was a dominant economic and political power as well as a great pilgrimage center, Teotihuacán had a huge impact on Mesoamerican society over the course of several centuries. Monumental construction along the city's main avenue points to the presence of a strong, unchallenged central authority with the power to mobilize and direct workers and resources.

The Teotihuacán state also projected its might through the performance of sacrificial rituals at important temples in the city center. These are known through recent archeological research.

ABOVE Teotihuacán (a name that means "Birthplace of the Gods") is laid out on a grid offset 15½° from the cardinal points. A sightline over the top of the Pyramid of the Sun marks the meridian, allowing priests to fix the times of noon and midnight.

Tenochtitlan

The individual city-states of Classic Maya civilization collapsed almost in unison during the ninth century, falling prey to ecological deterioration, climate change, and social strife. Meanwhile, the Toltecs of Tula, Hidalgo, carried the mantle of civilization in what is now central Mexico by establishing their major

center of Tollan, north of the Basin of Mexico, in the tenth century. These trends were continued by the Mexica Aztecs of Tenochtitlan—the ruins of which, now referred to as Templo Mayor, may be visited in downtown Mexico City—from the fourteenth century until the arrival of Spanish invaders led by Cortés in 1519. At the time of the Spanish

conquest, Tenochtitlan was one of the world's most impressive cities, with a population of at least 300,000, a sophisticated market and tribute economy, a highly stratified society, an efficient legal system, a highly trained military organization with professional officers, and a complex, abstract religious and cosmological system.

Sultanates of India

Most historians of India regard the time span from 1206 to 1526 as a period largely dominated by the Sultanate of Delhi.

The period, however, witnessed the rule of seven different sultanates besides that of Delhi—Gujarat, 1407–1526; Khandesh, 1370–1510; Malwa (two dynasties), 1401–1531; Jaunpur, 1394–1479; Bengal (four dynasties), 1282–1533; Multan, 1444–1525; and the Bahamani Sultanate of Deccan, 1347–1482.

The Sultanate of Delhi
The Sultanate of Delhi itself was held between 1208 and 1526 by five different dynasties—the Slave dynasty, 1208–90; the Khaljis, 1290–1320; the Tughluqs, 1320–1414; the Sayyids, 1414–1451; and the Lodis, 1451–1526. Thirty-four sultans sat on the Delhi throne in a little over three centuries. The dynastic transitions were, without exception, marked by violence, bloodshed, and instability.

The Slave (Mamluk) Dynasty
The Slave dynasty was so called because the founder, as well as some of his successors, were slaves before they overcame their humble positions and became sultans. The most notable of the Slave dynasty sultans were Qutb-ud-din Aibak (1206–1210), Iltutmish (1210–1236), his daughter Razia (1236–1239), and Balban (1266–1287). Aibak, the founder, ruled for only four years, but his rule is notable for the construction of the famed Qutb Minar—built, according to historian Vincent Smith, using materials plundered from 27 Hindu temples. Aibak's able and powerful successor, Iltutmish, broke politically with the Islamic world, thus making the sultanate in India independent of the Caliphate.

The Khalji Dynasty
The Khalji dynasty produced a notable ruler, Alauddin Khalji (1296–1316), who was arguably the ablest of all 34 rulers of the Sultanate period. During his two-decade reign, Alauddin brought most of the subcontinent under his control, including territories south of the Vindhyas that had never before known Muslim rule. Four peninsular kingdoms became vassals of the Khaljis: the Yadavas of Deogiri, the Kakatiyas of Warangal, the Hoysalas of Karnataka, and the Pandyas of Tamil Nadu.

The Tughluq Dynasty
The most important ruler of the Tughluq dynasty was Muhammad bin Tughluq (1325–51). Two of his projects have evoked much controversy among historians. The first was his decision in 1326–1327 to transfer the capital from Delhi

to Deogiri—followed quickly by his abandonment of the project and return to Delhi, at the cost of immense hardship and loss of life. The second was his currency project. Because he introduced a token of copper and brass as the equivalent to existing silver coins, but did not withdraw the gold and silver coins, the project was a dismal failure. The population simply paid their taxes in token currency while hoarding the gold and silver coins.

Timur's Invasion
Timur, the ruler of a vast empire that included Afghanistan, Persia, Qurdistan, Syria, and Asia Minor, invaded India in 1399. Timur (also known as Tamerlane or Timur the Lame) had no plans to build an empire in India. Everywhere along his way, he left a trail of torture, mass killings, enslavement or conversion to Islam of women and children, and pillaging of an order that surpassed even Muhammad of Ghazni's bloodcurdling record three centuries earlier.

The Sayyids and the Lodis
Timur's invasion left the Tughluqs prostrate. After they were replaced by the Sayyids in 1413, the Sultanate of Delhi progressively atrophied until by 1451, when the Sayyid dynasty in turn came to an end, the authority of the Sultans barely extended beyond Delhi and its immediate environs. The next dynasty, that of an Afghan tribal family, the Lodis, put an end to the long-term primacy of the Turks.

The last of the Lodis, Ibrahim (1517–26), was weak and indecisive, qualities which prompted rebellion and serious discord within the royal family. Two discontented Lodis independently encouraged the Mughal adventurer, Babar, to attack India, remove Ibrahim and bolster their own authority over the Sultanate. But Babar had his own agenda. In a conclusive confrontation, his much smaller force trounced Ibrahim Lodi's army and established Mughal power in India.

LEFT Astrologers cast horoscopes during celebrations of Timur's birth (1336-1405). Timur, believing himself descended from Genghis Khan, slaughtered millions while trying to restore the Mongol Empire.

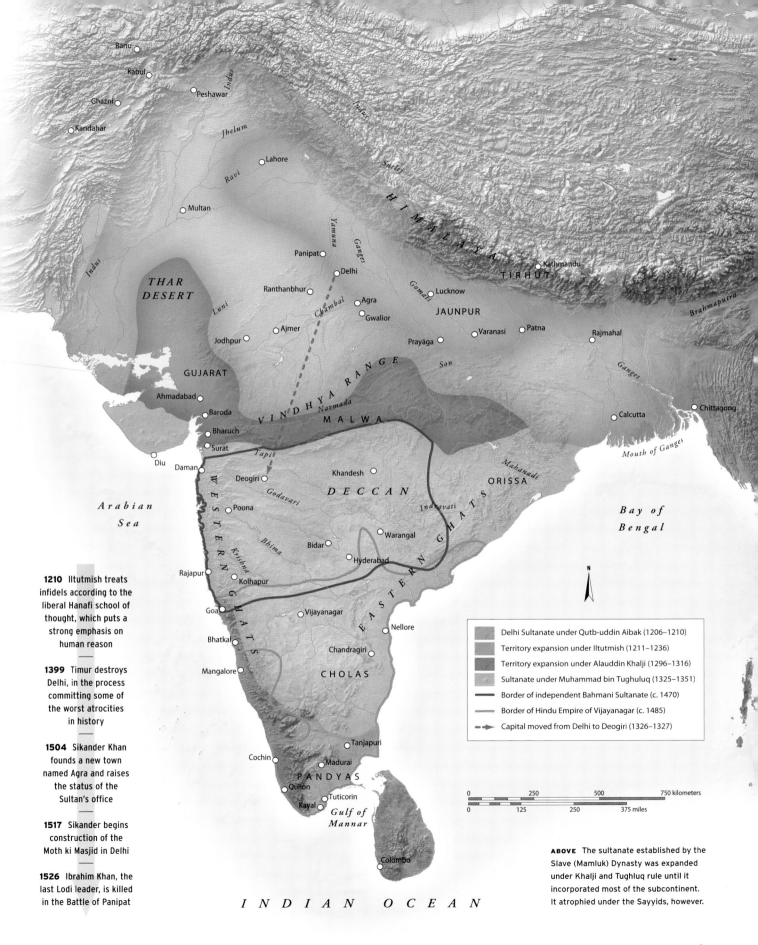

Banu

Kabul

Ghazni

Kandahar

Peshawar

Indus

Jhelum

Ravi

Lahore

HIMALAYA

Sutlej

Multan

Indus

THAR
DESERT

Luni

Panipat

Yamuna

Delhi

Ganges

Gomati

Kathmandu

TIRHUT

Brahmaputra

Ranthanbhur

Agra

Gwalior

Ajmer

Chambal

Lucknow

JAUNPUR

Jodhpur

Varanasi

Patna

Rajmahal

Prayāga

Son

Ganges

GUJARAT

VINDHYA RANGE

Narmada

MALWA

Ahmadabad

Baroda

Calcutta

Chittagong

Bharuch

Surat

Mouth of Ganges

Diu

Daman

Tapis

WESTERN GHATS

Deogiri

Khandesh

Godavari

DECCAN

Mahanadi

ORISSA

*Arabian
Sea*

Poona

Bhima

Krishna

Bidar

Warangal

Indravati

EASTERN GHATS

Rajapur

Kolhapur

Hyderabad

*Bay of
Bengal*

Goa

Vijayanagar

Nellore

N

Bhatkal

Chandragiri

Mangalore

CHOLAS

1210 Iltutmish treats
infidels according to the
liberal Hanafi school of
thought, which puts a
strong emphasis on
human reason

1399 Timur destroys
Delhi, in the process
committing some of
the worst atrocities
in history

1504 Sikander Khan
founds a new town
named Agra and raises
the status of the
Sultan's office

1517 Sikander begins
construction of the
Moth ki Masjid in Delhi

1526 Ibrahim Khan, the
last Lodi leader, is killed
in the Battle of Panipat

Tanjapuri

Cochin

Madurai

P A N D Y A S

Quilon

Tuticorin

Kayal

*Gulf of
Mannar*

| Delhi Sultanate under Qutb-uddin Aibak (1206–1210) |
| Territory expansion under Iltutmish (1211–1236) |
| Territory expansion under Alauddin Khalji (1296–1316) |
| Sultanate under Muhammad bin Tughuluq (1325–1351) |
| Border of independent Bahmani Sultanate (c. 1470) |
| Border of Hindu Empire of Vijayanagar (c. 1485) |
| Capital moved from Delhi to Deogiri (1326–1327) |

| 0 | 250 | 500 | 750 kilometers |
| 0 | 125 | 250 | 375 miles |

ABOVE The sultanate established by the
Slave (Mamluk) Dynasty was expanded
under Khalji and Tughluq rule until it
incorporated most of the subcontinent.
It atrophied under the Sayyids, however.

Colombo

I N D I A N   O C E A N

Ming Dynasty

The Ming Dynasty (1368-1644) began with the overthrow of the Mongol Yuan Dynasty by the Red Turban sect led by peasant rebel Zhu Yuan Zhong, signaling the end of 100 years of foreign rule in China.

Zhu, who became known as the Hongwu Emperor, came from a destitute family and had suffered under Mongol oppression, having witnessed Mongol soldiers destroy his home—a Buddhist orphanage.

Spies, Purges, and the Imperial Guard

Early Ming emperors, struggling to gain personal control over a large and highly complex empire, used terror to keep officials in line. Spies and purges became a regular part of court life. A web of eunuch secret police, known as the Imperial Guard, worked as informers across the Empire, gathering damaging

BELOW Ming Dynasty painters were told by the court to return to a more realistic style of painting, as can be seen in this c. 1500 silk painting of the Forbidden City.

information on both officials and ordinary people. By the end of Zhu's reign, around 40,000 people had lost their lives. The Ming culture of violence meant that penalties for failing or displeasing the emperor were terrifying.

Admiral Zheng He

In 1405, the Yongle emperor (Zhu's son) sent admiral Zheng He out with six huge junks on a mission of exploration and diplomacy to Java, Ceylon, even as far as Eastern Africa. His orders were to bring back exotic goods and animals, and to encourage diplomatic representatives from distant kingdoms to establish trade relations with China.

A New Capital—Beijing and the Forbidden City

On February 2, 1421, after 16 years of intense construction by more

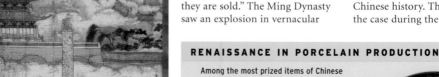

> ...the mind makes the world, the world does not make the mind.
> – Wang Yang Ming (1472-1529), philosopher.

than 200,000 laborers, the Yongle emperor inaugurated his new capital, Beijing, on the site of the former Mongol city of Dadu. At the center of Beijing was the imposing edifice of the Forbidden City, closed to all but specially selected members of the public.

The Philosophy of Wang Yang Ming

Path-breaking philosopher Wang Yang Ming (1472–1529) dominated Ming Dynasty intellectual life. He believed that the way to advance in one's understanding of the world was not through "the investigation of things" but through the discovery of one's own mind by a process of meditation or contemplation similar to Buddhist practice. To Wang Yang Ming's way of thinking, universal principles existed in every person's mind. People could discover them by clearing their minds of obstructions such as material desire and allowing their inborn knowledge of the good to surface.

Popular Culture

During his time in China, court adviser Matteo Ricci commented on "the exceedingly large number of books in circulation here and the ridiculously low prices at which they are sold." The Ming Dynasty saw an explosion in vernacular

ABOVE Zhu Yuan Zhong founded the Ming Dynasty in 1368, claiming the title "Emperor of China." By 1382, he had unified all of China.

literature, with a growing number of books published for the low-end market, cheap yet richly illustrated. Courtesan culture blossomed in this environment and a great many poems written by late Ming courtesans have been preserved. Full-length novels were published for the first time and included famous classics such as *The Dream of the Red Mansions, The Romance of the Three Kingdoms,* and *The Journey to the West.* The latter story featured Sun Wu Kong, a brave peasant also known as the "Monkey King."

Eunuchs and Corruption

Employed by each Chinese dynasty since the Shang—to guard the palace harems; later as functionaries and de facto prime ministers—eunuchs have gained a reputation for perpetrating political infamy in Chinese history. This was especially the case during the late Ming

RENAISSANCE IN PORCELAIN PRODUCTION

Among the most prized items of Chinese export trade was porcelain, labeled "China" in English. In the Ming period production on a considerable scale was undertaken in factories, notably at kilns in Jing de Zhen in the Jiangxi province. The quality of clay was so high in these areas that vessels could be made with walls thin enough to be translucent. Ming porcelain was particularly noted for pieces decorated in blue underglaze and polychrome enamels.

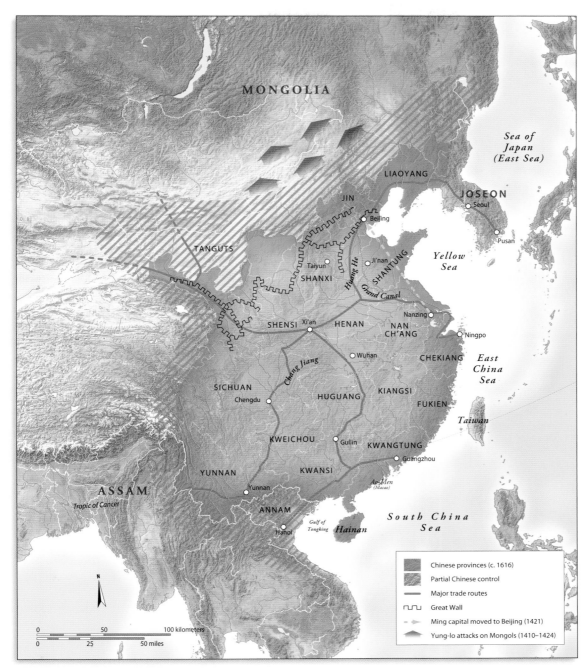

LEFT At its zenith, the Ming Dynasty controlled an enormous territory and had an impressive network of trade routes.

1368 The renovation of the Great Wall of China is begun

1421 Construction begins on the Forbidden City in Beijing

1583 Jesuit missionary Matteo Ricci arrives in China

1616 The Jurchens are unified and the state of Jin/Qing in northeastern China is established

1636 Hong Taiji changes the name of his people from Jurchen to Manchu, meaning "pure"

1637 Manchus invade Korea

1644 Manchus invade northern China and take Beijing, overthrowing the Ming Dynasty and establishing the Qing Dynasty

Map legend:
- Chinese provinces (c. 1616)
- Partial Chinese control
- Major trade routes
- Great Wall
- Ming capital moved to Beijing (1421)
- Yung-lo attacks on Mongols (1410–1424)

BELOW Ming Dynasty china vase with enamel glaze. High demand for Chinese goods such as silk and porcelain led China away from its isolationism and toward trade with the outside world.

Dynasty. The principal problem with eunuchs was that they were not taken onto the imperial staff through a regularized system of recruitment—unlike Confucian bureaucrats who toiled to pass the civil service exam—but on imperial whim. This meant they had no secure career ladder to climb and that their personal prospects depended on the emperor's favor.

During the Ming Dynasty their favor and status increased, leading eventually to their interference in policy decisions in the imperial government. When eunuch Liu Jin was arrested by provincial officials after attempting a coup against the government in the seventeenth century, 240,000 gold bars and 5 million silver bars were discovered among his confiscated property.

Management Problems

The later Ming Dynasty suffered management problems. More and more land was illegally annexed to a swelling imperial gentry, cutting down the amount of taxable land, and shifting China's tax burden to those least able to pay—the peasantry. By the seventeenth century, tax exemption allowances for the imperial family were eating up half the tax revenue from two major provinces: Shanxi and Henan.

The late Ming emperors surrounded themselves with sycophantic eunuchs and isolated themselves from the Chinese people. When the Manchus invaded China in 1644, the imperial treasury was empty, and the last Ming emperor had hung himself on Coal Hill, behind the Forbidden City.

Muslim World

With a common language through the use of the Qur'an, Muslims were provided with a passport quite as useful to travelers in unknown lands as any modern document. That language could readily be put to use for other purposes, such as keeping account books, writing letters of introduction, or presenting bills and promissory notes in distant places.

1325 Ibn Battuta, aged 20, begins his travels

1326 Battuta arrives in Mecca for the hajj

1328 After studying in Mecca for a year, Battuta travels the Red Sea to Aden, then East Africa

1331 Arriving in Turkey, Battuta finds the people well versed in the Sunni Muslim faith but is surprised to find that "they eat hashish and think no harm of it"

1334 Battuta reaches Delhi, after a time in the Golden Horde. He is made welcome by being given use of a house and being hired in service to the state, receiving a vast salary.

1349 Ibn Battuta arrives home in Tangier

1351 He travels to West Africa and Timbuktu, continuing to spread the Muslim word through the known trade routes

All the world's great religions are portable. That is to say that, unlike local cults built on natural features such as springs, rocks, and caves, they offer the same access to spiritual knowledge and ritual practice no matter where their followers might be located. Unsurprisingly, the monotheistic religion founded by Mohamed, merchant of Mecca, proved exceptionally portable.

HOLY ROMA
EMPIRE
Mediterranea
Tangier
Fez
Tlemcen
Casablanca
Marrakesh
Tunis
Tripoli
Ghat
Murzuq
SAHARA
Tandeni
MALI
EMPIRE
Timbuktu
Gao
Dakar
Ouagadougou
Niger
Accra
Lagos
Equator
SOUTH
ATLANTIC
OCEAN

RIGHT Islam, which spread rapidly along international trade routes, helped forge common bonds between people of many lands and cultures by giving them a common language, manners, and moral code.

Common Language

Unencumbered by a supreme pontiff claiming special access to God, or a priestly hierarchy to support him, Islam could be practiced wherever a merchant might choose to travel, even if no mosque was available. While not specifically designed to facilitate trade and commerce, Islam had many features which traders found useful. A follower advanced in holiness by memorizing verses from the Qur'an, written in Arabic. Mastery of the Qur'an entailed literacy in a language that could be read by other advanced Muslims, wherever they happened to live.

Mecca

Another feature of Islam that united people from diverse lands was the Prophet's injunction that believers should try to make a pilgrimage during their lifetime to the holy city of Mecca. International travel soared to hitherto unknown levels.

Expansion by Trade

For these secondary reasons, as well as for its religious attractions, Islam tended to spread rapidly along international trade routes. By 1400, it had spread from its Arabian home west as far as Spain, south as far as the coast of modern Mozambique, and east as far as China. Along Mediterranean sealanes it traveled to Granada and down the Red Sea as far as Somalia. It traveled with caravans across the Sahara Desert to the Niger River, and along the Silk Road to Central Asia and Kashmir. During the course of the fourteenth and fifteenth centuries, it went far toward establishing itself as the state religion of the Malay Peninsula and the Indonesian archipelago. Not long after, it was to dominate northern India as the religion of the expanding Mughal Empire. The Ottomans carried it with them into the old Roman city of Constantinople in 1453 and on to most parts of the Balkans. By 1526, the Ottomans were in Hungary, knocking at Vienna's door.

RIGHT Muslim pilgrims performing the *hajj* rituals at Mecca, from a miscellany manuscript produced for Timurid prince Iskandar Sultan, c. 1410–11, Shiraz, Iran. *Hajj*, the sacred pilgrimage, is one of the Five Pillars of Islam.

Ibn Battuta

It is not hard to understand why the thirteenth-century Europeans marveled at Marco Polo's daring trip from Venice to China, which carried him far outside the orbit of his religion. Things were very different for the Moroccan Ibn Battuta when he set out from his native city of Tangier in 1325 to make the pilgrimage to Mecca. In the course of his *hajj* he visited

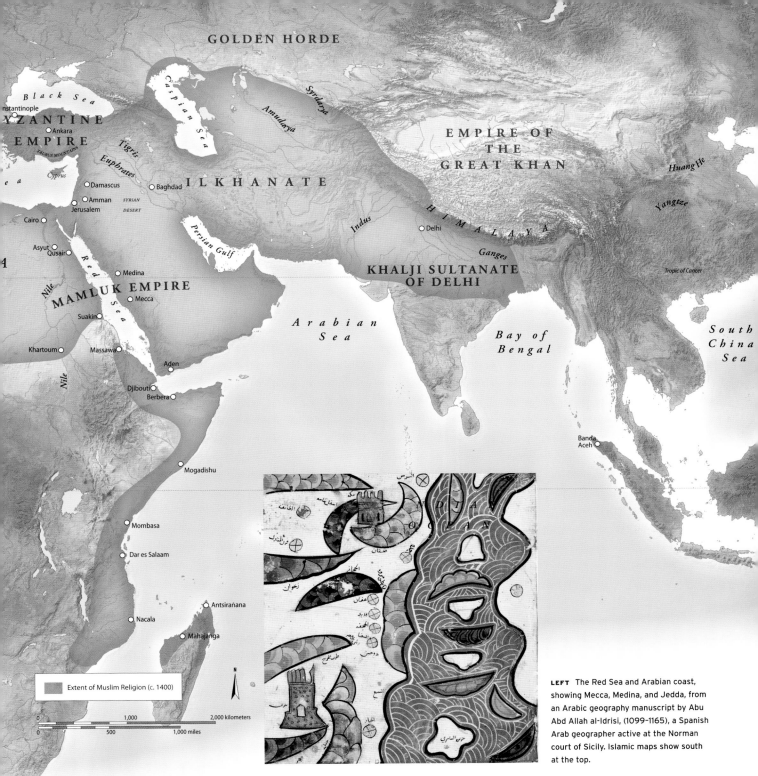

GOLDEN HORDE

BYZANTINE EMPIRE

EMPIRE OF THE GREAT KHAN

Black Sea

Constantinople

Ankara

Caspian Sea

Syr darya

Amu darya

Huang He

Yangtze

Cyprus

TAURUS MOUNTAINS

Tigris

Euphrates

Damascus

Baghdad

ILKHANATE

HIMALAYA

Amman

Jerusalem

SYRIAN DESERT

Delhi

Indus

Ganges

Cairo

Persian Gulf

Tropic of Cancer

Asyut

Qusair

Red Sea

Medina

KHALJI SULTANATE OF DELHI

Nile

MAMLUK EMPIRE

Mecca

A r a b i a n

S e a

Bay of

Bengal

South China Sea

Suakin

Khartoum

Massawa

Aden

Nile

Djibouti

Berbera

Banda Aceh

Mogadishu

Mombasa

Dar es Salaam

Antsiranana

Nacala

Mahajanga

Extent of Muslim Religion (c. 1400)

N

0 · 1,000 · 2,000 kilometers
0 · 500 · 1,000 miles

LEFT The Red Sea and Arabian coast, showing Mecca, Medina, and Jedda, from an Arabic geography manuscript by Abu Abd Allah al-Idrisi, (1099–1165), a Spanish Arab geographer active at the Norman court of Sicily. Islamic maps show south at the top.

Egypt, Palestine, and Syria, as well as Baghdad and Persia—and then, having caught the travel bug, made a further journey by sea down the east coast of Africa to Zanzibar, then on to Oman in Arabia and up the Persian Gulf. During eight years in India working for the Sultan, he was appointed to lead a diplomatic mission to China, and despite shipwreck and other misadventures he

did eventually reach China, having in the meantime seen something of southern India, Sri Lanka, and Burma. Not long after returning home to Morocco, he made a brief journey to the Spanish Muslim kingdom of Granada. Then in 1353 he set off on his final adventure by camel caravan across the Sahara to see the kingdom of Mali. Unlike Marco Polo, who had risked his life

by moving among hostile strangers, Ibn Battuta had seldom set foot anywhere where his religion did not provide a passport to hospitality. Traveling among fellow Muslims, he was constantly in the company of people with whom he shared his language, manners, and moral code. These were the factors that united the Islamic world at the beginning of the fifteenth century.

We made around it the seven-fold circuit of arrival and kissed the holy Stone; we performed a prayer of two bowings at the Maqam Ibrahim...
–from Ibn Battuta's account of his travels.

187

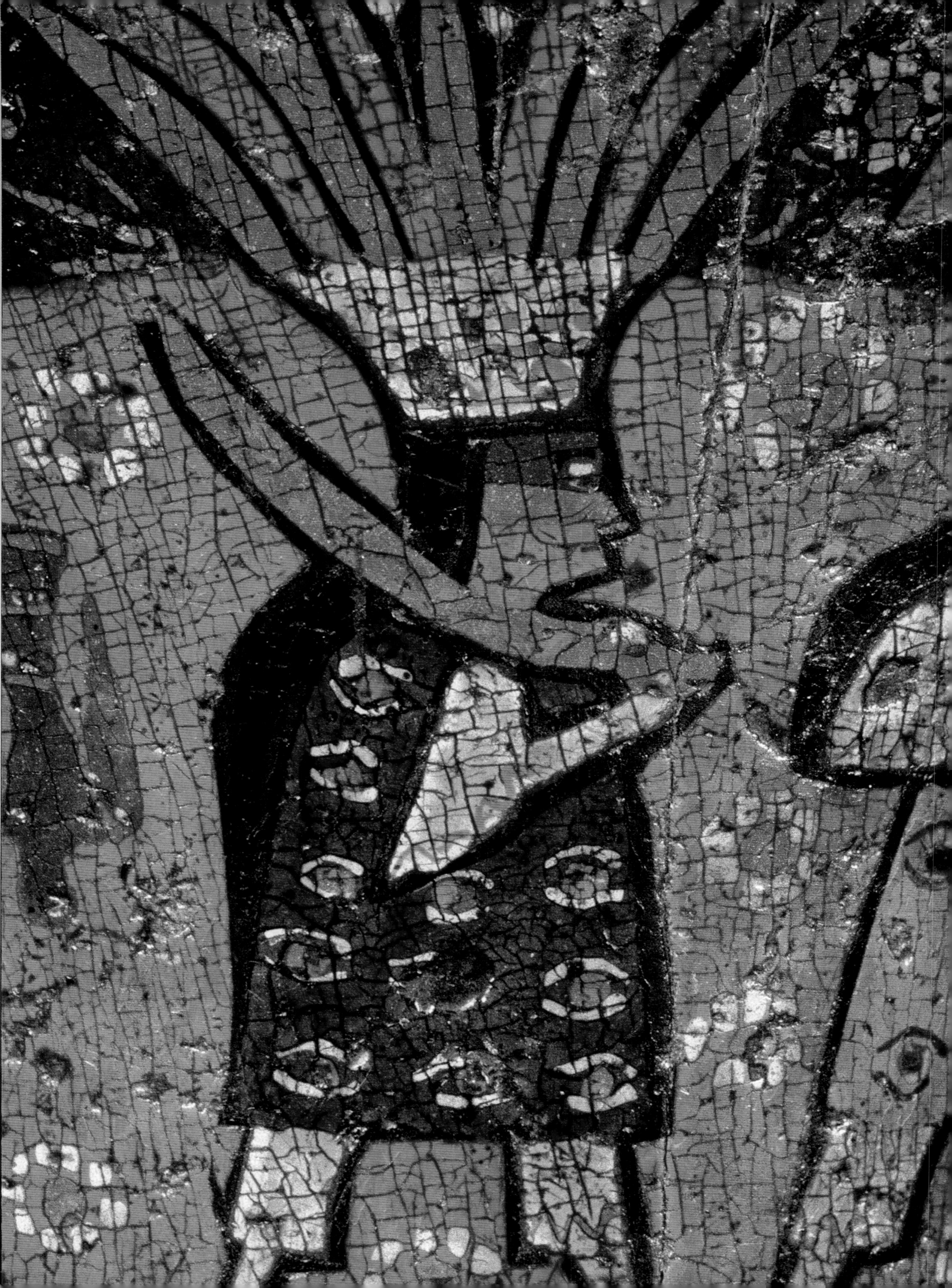

Seeking Riches

Although the period of the Middle Ages was one of brilliant scientific discovery and artistic creativity, it ran parallel to an era of religious intolerance, savage warfare, and brutal conquest of overseas empires.

LEFT *Kero* or painted wooden vase showing Inca warrior with headdress and spear, from Cuzco jungle, 1150–1550.

ABOVE A fifteenth-century Flemish-school depiction of Hell as a violent inferno. Dante's medieval vision of Satan as a ravening beast continued to exert a powerful influence on painting and on Christian theology.

RIGHT *Seaport (Villa Medici)* by seventeenth-century French painter Claude Gellée (Le Lorrain). The influential Medici family produced three popes, numerous rulers of Florence, and the patrons of some of the most famous works of Renaissance art.

PREVIOUS PAGES Mosaic from Cajamarca, Peru, of Conquistador Francisco Pizarro meeting Atahualpa, the last independent Incan emperor, in 1532. Pizarro used Atahualpa to control the Incan empire, but had him executed eventually by means of strangulation, thus bringing the era of the Incas to an end.

Improved navigation techniques and a better knowledge of wind patterns allowed European explorers to roam the world's oceans. One of the most destructive results was Europe's conquest of the so-called New World. Spain, a relatively impoverished country, occupied enormous amounts of new territory and, using indigenous American support, conquered two diverse empires—the Aztecs and the Incas.

America

The Incas had built an extensive and diverse empire based on expansion and trade that linked mountain, valley, and coastal communities, but faced hostility from the victims of their wars. For example, the Incas killed or deported the Chimú people from their homeland, eradicating their entire civilization as a grim warning for others. This produced resentment that Spanish invader Francisco Pizarro skillfully exploited to help him conquer the empire. Similarly, Hernando Cortez captured the Aztec capital Tenochtitlán through careful cultivation of the Aztecs' foes. Although it wasn't important in the initial stages of Spanish conquest, disease proved an even greater threat to local populations, who had little natural immunity to the European diseases such as smallpox that would ravage the Americas.

Spaniards and other European conquerors developed convenient rationales of racial and religious superiority in order to justify their devastation and exploitation of the people, land, and abundant natural resources of the Americas.

Divided Church

Roman Catholic leaders worked to heal the Great Schism that had divided the Church in the 1300s. The Council of Pisa in 1409 failed to settle the dispute and actually left the Church with three separate claimants to the title of Pontiff, but in 1417 the Council of Constance decided to depose Benedict XIII and John XXIII, while the Roman Pope, Gregory VII, accepted the Council's authority. Gregory made way for a universally recognized Pope, Martin V. Healing the rift, however, did not bring religious peace. Instead, it merely allowed the Catholic Church greater freedom to attack perceived heretics, dissenters, and Jews. Critics had long condemned what they saw as the excesses of the Church, such as the sale of indulgences that would reduce time spent in purgatory. The Church seemed to value earthly wealth more than Christian piety.

Martin Luther, who rejected the avarice of the Roman popes, dreaded the thought of dying outside a state of grace. According to Church doctrine he might not earn salvation, despite having lived a life of Christian devotion, so he promulgated a new doctrine—that faith alone, one's personal relationship to God, marked the true Christian. In 1520, he called the Roman Pope the anti-Christ. His views caught on, and the Protestant Reformation that followed shattered Western Christendom into diverse groups. Protestant denominations soon came to dominate England and Scotland, most of Northern Germany, Scandinavia, and the Baltic region, setting the stage for the Thirty Years' War in the early 1600s.

Art and Culture

Humanist thought continued to develop through the 1400s and 1500s in spite of the many religious conflicts that plagued Europe. European craftsmen learned advanced skills for making paper, and the development of the mechanical press made the printing of books and the reproduction of manuscripts easier and cheaper, allowing a broader dissemination of knowledge. Rich Italian patrons such as the Medicis and the Sforzas patronized and supported artists, with great results. Leonardo da Vinci and Michelangelo stretched the bounds of portraiture and sculpture, and their successors in Italy and Flanders developed ever more realistic visual perspectives.

1401 to 1600

Human Redistribution

The fifteenth century demarcated the start of an unprecedented redistribution of the population of the world.

The levels at which people moved over longer distances has for the most part been subject to the mode of transportation. Before the 1400s, most migrations were over short distances and usually on foot.

Things changed, however, with the dramatic improvement of maritime technology. As a result, from around 1400 a new system of global migrations emerged. No longer would long-distance migration consist only of isolated, regional moves, but increasingly the different migration systems would be linked up—migration slowly began to become a global phenomenon.

China

Around 1405, the great Chinese admiral and grand eunuch Cheng Ho (Zheng He)—and with him an estimated 300 ships and thousands of men—sailed off from mainland China on a maritime mission that would take him to India, the Arabian Peninsula, Ceylon, and East Africa. With the Chinese becoming more and more isolated during the fifteenth century—an outcome of a deliberate policy of its emperor—Europeans would, almost 100 years after Cheng Ho's extensive explorations and discoveries, dominate the conquest of the world for the centuries that followed.

Intercontinental Trade Routes

The great explorations would open up intercontinental trade routes. In the wake of the flow of goods, people followed.

Portuguese trade posts were founded on the African coast and in India, for example in Goa, a place where Portuguese influence is still apparent today.

America

Nevertheless, where the displacement of people is concerned, it was the crossing of the Atlantic by Columbus in 1492 that had the biggest impact on the movement of humans. Where the Portuguese

emigrants, without exception, were a minority in their settlements in the East, in the Atlantic settlements European settlers quickly gained the upper hand. The migration from the Iberian Peninsula in the fifteenth and sixteenth centuries was impressive and unparalleled. Between 1500 and 1600 an estimated 250,000 people left Spain and Portugal for South America—an annual migration of about 2,500 people.

Africa

The Atlantic settlements of the Portuguese and Spaniards also changed Africa forever. Although

c. 1400 The Toraja people arrive in Sulawesi and settle on the banks of the Sa'dan River

1413 Dried fish is used as currency in Iceland

1514 Approximately 1,500 Spanish immigrants settle in Panama

1539 Olaus Magnus, Swedish historian, produces a map of the world

1565 The first Spanish settlement in the Philippines is established in Cebu City

RIGHT The roots of the age of global migrations lay in the great maritime explorations of the fifteenth century. Admiral Cheng Ho's voyages were far reaching, predating similar European explorations by some 100 years.

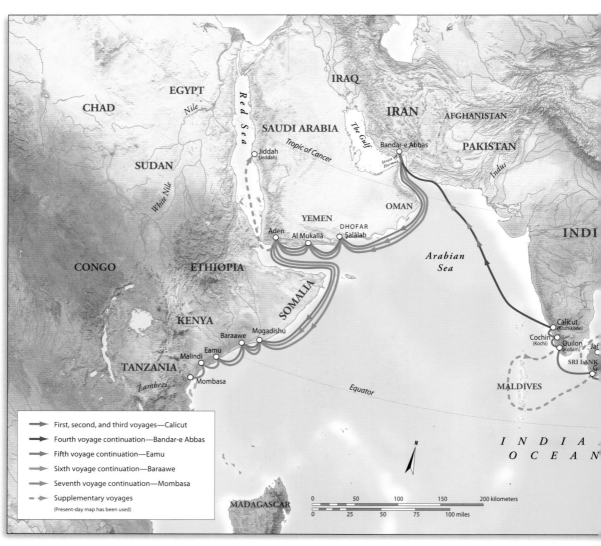

Legend:
- First, second, and third voyages—Calicut
- Fourth voyage continuation—Bandar-e Abbas
- Fifth voyage continuation—Eamu
- Sixth voyage continuation—Baraawe
- Seventh voyage continuation—Mombasa
- Supplementary voyages
(Present-day map has been used)

LEFT Artist Theodore de Bry's 1591 depiction of a Spanish expedition landing in the Americas. Natives were employed to carry equipment and supplies.

BELOW A 1493 German woodcut graphically details the practice of burning Protestants and Jews alive after they had been charged with heresy and witchcraft. Thousands fled to Africa and the Middle East to escape this gruesome fate.

a slave trade had existed in Africa for millennia, from around 1440–1450 the seemingly ever-growing demand for labor across the Atlantic made ever more international and it rose to an unprecedented scale. Although in the centuries that followed millions more slaves would be exported across the Atlantic, between 1450 and 1600 already an estimated 125,000 slaves had been transported overseas—about half the number of the free migrations to the Americas in the same period.

Jewish Diaspora

At the end of the fifteenth century, tens of thousands of so-called *conversos*—Jews who were forcibly converted to Catholicism—were ousted from Spain. The diaspora that followed saw Jewish refugees ending up in Portugal, only to be expelled from there a couple of years later. The Iberian Jews then fled to Muslim Africa, Syria, and to the Ottoman Empire. Other groups of *conversos*, who were often well off, settled in the Low Countries and would play an important role in financing the Dutch overseas trade, and thus in the expansion of the Dutch trading empire. One of the world's greatest thinkers of all time, Baruch de Spinoza, born in Amsterdam in 1632, was a descendant of these refugees. In many of the places the Iberian Jews fled to during this period, including the Muslim world, Jewish communities are still present today.

Indonesia—Dutch versus English

The Dutch presence and rule in Indonesia extended under two different entities from 1602 until 1948—the VOC and the Dutch Government. During this period the English East India Company also set about establishing a British presence in Southeast Asia.

The Dutch and the English, almost simultaneously, broke the Portuguese monopoly of discoveries and trade in the East granted to them by the Pope. The English East India Company (EIC) received a royal charter in 1600 but was not able to establish an outpost until 1615 in Surat, India. Several Dutch companies challenged the Portuguese and made their way to the East from 1595 but were compelled by the Dutch government to amalgamate as the Vereenigde Oostindische Compagnie (VOC) in 1602. Both the EIC and the VOC flew their respective country's flag, functioning as a state within a state. Neither the Netherlands nor Britain took responsibility for any acts of war initiated by the companies but legally retained the right of eminent domain to take over company territories when it pleased them.

Ports and Forts

As a private corporation, the VOC did exceedingly well for the first century and a half, declaring high dividends, averaging 30 to 40 percent, and in some years as high as 400 percent. Their territorial holdings in that period in India and Southeast Asia were limited to coastal areas.

The VOC also established outposts in the Moluccas—the real spice-producing region—and in Banda, Tidore, and Ambon. It soon came into deadly conflict with the EIC, with both parties vying for a monopoly in the spice trade with Europe. After an incident that took 10 English lives and was greatly

exaggerated in the EIC's records as the Ambon Massacre in 1624, the EIC resolved to withdraw from Indonesian waters with the exception of a factory in Sumatra, focusing their trading activities to India. The VOC was left to monopolize the archipelago trade.

Three Wars of Succession in Java (1704–1708, 1719–1723, and 1746–1755) witnessed growing anarchy on the prosperous island, which held two-thirds of the entire archipelago's population. The first war resulted in the Dutch protege, Pakubuwona, authorizing the VOC

to build forts anywhere in Java. By the Treaty of 1743, the ruler of Mataram ceded—officially styled "leased"—the entire north coast of Java along with the island of Madura to the VOC. The third war concluded with the division of the ancient kingdom of Mataram into

> Colonialism is known in its primitive form, that is to say, by the permanent settling of repressive foreign powers, with an army, services, policies. This phase has known cruel colonial occupations which have lasted 300 years in Indonesia
>
> –Ahmed Ben Bella, First President of Algeria.

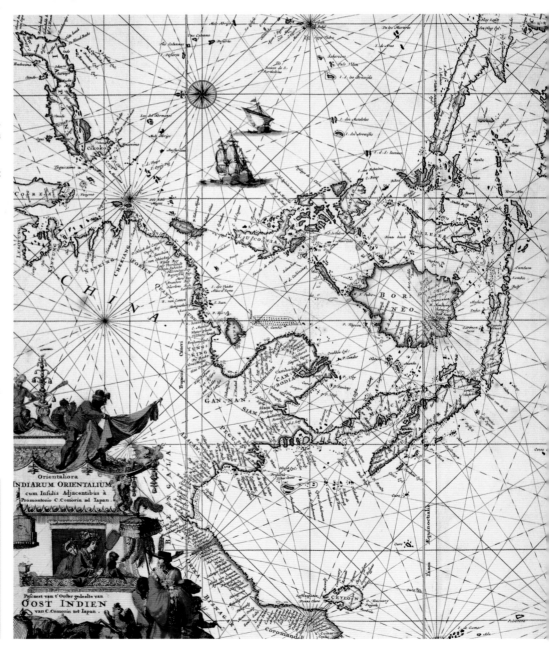

ABOVE This oil painting shows the Castle at Batavia, a leading port in Dutch trade.

RIGHT A busy street on the Molucca Islands is depicted in this engraving c. 1800.

LEFT This hand-colored engraving shows Southeast Asia and the East Indies. The map was published in Amsterdam around 1635.

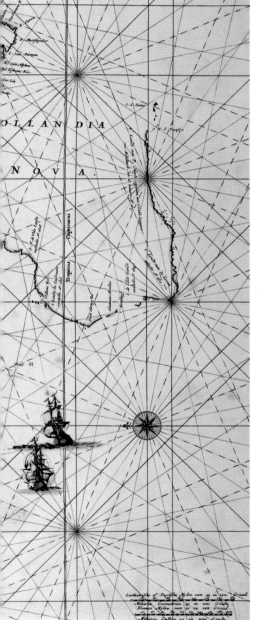

1600 West Timor is seized by the Netherlands

1607 Dutch take over from the Portuguese but the Portuguese retain control of East Timor

1616 Landing on Run, smallest of the Banda Islands, British merchant seaman Nathaniel Courthope persuades the residents to enter an alliance with England over nutmeg. Combining forces, they hold off the Dutch for over four years.

1621 Under Dutch control, Jakarta is renamed Batavia

Surakarta and Yogyakarta, both recognizing the VOC's authority over them in 1757.

British Interlude

During the French occupation of the Netherlands (1795–1814), the Dutch stadhouder, Prince William V of Orange, fled to England where he authorized the government to take over all Dutch possessions overseas. London, in turn, authorized the EIC to occupy the Dutch possessions in Ceylon (Sri Lanka) and the Indonesian archipelago. With Britain's policy to restore the monarchy in the Netherlands in 1814, all the Dutch possessions in the East, with the exception of Malacca and Ceylon, were restored to the Dutch government. By the Treaty of London in 1824, Britain and the Netherlands agreed to make the Straits of Malacca the dividing line for their mutual spheres of influence.

Looking Forward

In the second half of the nineteenth century, more so from 1860 to 1914, the Netherlands embarked on a policy of expansion. A protracted war (1871–1896) saw the Dutch defeat of Aceh and further expansion in the remainder of Sumatra and the neighboring small islands, notably for the exploration of oil and coal reserves. A new policy, the "Short Declaration" of 1898, initially applying to Aceh, was applied to over 300 chiefs all through the archipelago, confirming them in their possessions in exchange of recognition of Dutch suzerainty. In the eastern parts of the archipelago, Governor-General Lansberge (1875–1881) secured occupation of the Moluccas and the Sunda islands. By 1911, all of Indonesia, then called the Dutch East Indies, comprising over 12,000 islands, was brought under Dutch authority, direct and indirect.

Sons of the Sun

Ever since 1532, when Francisco Pizarro and his ragtag corps of conquistadores invaded their vast empire in western South America, the Incas have astounded and often confounded outside observers.

The sheer scale of the Inca (Inka in Quechua) realm, which they called *Tawantinsuyu*—"the fourfold domain"—was beyond anything previously achieved in the Americas; at its apogee during the fifteenth century, it was the largest empire on earth. Colossal in its expanse—covering the areas of five modern republics (Ecuador, Peru, Bolivia, Argentina, and Chile)—the territory administered by the Incas was, to say the least, geographically diverse, encompassing the driest desert in the world along the Pacific coast (the Atacama of northern Chile), the globe's second highest mountain range (the Andes), and parts of the world's wettest areas in the Amazon Basin. Equally remarkable are the size and diversity of the human populations brought under the Incas' imperial aegis—some 10 to 12 million people, divided among dozens of ethnic groups of disparate size, language, and organization. The empire was tied together by an intricate road network totaling some 25,000 miles (40,000 km), which connected a system of regional centers and provincial outposts to the imperial capital, Cuzco, the "navel of the world."

> As for my faith, I will not change it. Your own God, as you tell me, was put to death by the very men He created. But my God still looks down on His children.
>
> –Atahualpa, Incan king, on hearing Pope Alexander VI had declared Peru to be a possession of Spain.

Pachacuti, World Transformer

The beginning of the expansionist period of the Inca state is marked by the defeat of the Chankas by the prince Cusi Yupanqui in the mid-fifteenth century—conventionally dated to the year 1438. He would later take the name Pachacuti Inca Yupanqui. According to the dynastic historical retellings of the battle, his father, the Incan ruler Viracocha Inca, fled the scene and left Cusi

RIGHT After dispatching the Incan rulers in power at the time they arrived, the Spanish installed Manco Inca Yupanqui as emperor. Initially compliant, he soon rebelled and retreated to the mountains, where he and his successors ruled for 36 years. In 1572, the last of their strongholds was found and the last Inca ruler, Manco's son Tupac Amaru (pictured), was captured and executed.

Yupanqui outnumbered with only a small contingent of warriors to back him up. The young prince was said to have defeated the Chankas through the intervention of the solar deity *Inti* and the miraculous transformation of sacred stones (*pururaucas*) on the battlefield into warriors. After returning victorious to Cuzco and crowning himself king (*Sapa Inca*), Cusi Yupanqui took the name Pachacuti—"world transformer"—and embarked on

an ambitious campaign of imperial expansion. Incan domains soon included the Lake Titicaca Basin and beyond to the south, and the Andean highlands and coastal regions as far north as Ecuador.

The Unique Inca

The Incas did not, and could not, rule by force alone. The fact that they were able to expand so far so quickly is partly explained by the ideological basis of their rule, which played upon cosmological concepts shared by many Andean peoples. The Incan ruler, the *Sapa Inca,* or "unique Inca," together with his primary spouse—the *Qolla* or Queen—were considered divine rulers, literally living gods. Thus, by claiming to be "sons of the sun," the Incas affirmed their exalted status over other Andean peoples. Such claims, however, were rooted in traditional Andean attitudes to the proper relations between the living, the dead, and the gods that made up an animate landscape of deified rock outcrops, fields, springs, and mountains called *huacas.* The ancestors and *huacas* in the Andes —whether the actual mummified corpse of a known individual, or the mythified site of origin of an entire ethnic group—were considered the sources and guardians of

LEFT Ruins of an *acllahuaci,* a house where young women were isolated from daily life to be trained in weaving and making *chicha* and foods for festivals.

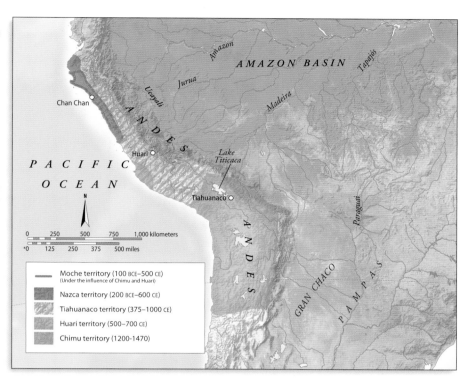

RIGHT By the time the Incas founded Cuzco about 1200 CE, various cultures had existed on the coastline for over 4,000 years. The Incas assimilated and amalgamated the cultures of those they defeated.

BELOW Connecting cities, villages, and ceremonial sites, the Inca trails of the Andes were dotted with inns providing food, shelter, and military supplies. Rope bridges allowed the deep valleys to be traversed.

BELOW RIGHT Wedding of Spanish noble Martin de Loyola to wealthy Inca Nusta (princess) Beatriz. Although he had many competitors, Loyola secured his claim to Nusta Beatriz by defeating and executing her uncle, Tupac Amaru, the last Inca king.

400 CE Inca tribe first mentioned in Peruvian myths and legends

1200 CE Manco Capac becomes the first ruler of the small city-state of Cuzco

1400–1500 Incas begin to expand and conquer other tribes

1471 Pachacuti, aged 80, abdicates in favor of his son

1525 Civil war breaks out between Huascar and Atahualpa, dividing the vast empire

Moche territory (100 BCE–500 CE) (Under the influence of Chimu and Huari)
Nazca territory (200 BCE–600 CE)
Tiahuanaco territory (375–1000 CE)
Huari territory (500–700 CE)
Chimu territory (1200–1470)

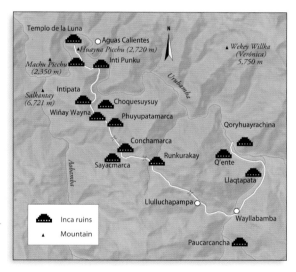

fertility and good fortune. Humans were bound to these spirits by ties of kinship and mutual obligation. Prosperity could only be realized through a reciprocal relationship; in order to receive, one had to give. By claiming descent from the sun, the Incas proclaimed descent from the ultimate and most powerful supra-local *huaca*. The *Sapa Inca*, a divine descendent of the sun and living *huaca*, was owed tribute.

The Spectacle at the Center

This ideological system was built into the actual configurations of Inca settlements and architecture.

Cuzco, a city of ceremonial plazas, courtly palaces, and sumptuous temples, was just one of several top-level centers established by the Incas at regular intervals along the highland and coastal highways. These great administrative sites, such as Huánuco Pampa, Jauja, and Tomebamba to the north, and Pumpu and Hatun Qolla to the south, were centrally planned settlements built around massive open plazas with central ceremonial platforms called *ushnus*. The plaza spaces were used as stages, where subject peoples reported to pay their tribute. In return, massive

state-sponsored processions and feasting events were held there as spectacles of state largesse. These centers were mostly populated on a rotating basis by households from surrounding ethnic groups paying their labor duties to the state.

Nodes and Networks

The regional centers functioned as nodes in the vast redistributive system of the Inca Empire which, rather than functioning through markets, supported and extended imperial prerogatives by redistributing labor and goods. Household and community economies were to

remain self-sufficient under Inca rule. But subject peoples also owed tribute to the state, and this was usually paid in the form of labor performed on a rotational basis. The produce generated by that labor was centrally collected in great storage complexes, often set in rows of regularly spaced and sized storehouses called *colcas*.

Advanced Accounting

Tribute obligations and the produce stored in *colcas* were managed by means of an accounting system far more sophisticated and accurate than anything in Europe at the time.

197

Population data, tribute levies, and the produce accumulated were all registered in complex knotted cord devices called *khipus* (or *quipus*), which were read and tallied by the state's official accountants, called *khipucamayoc* (*khipu* readers).

The Art of Co-option

Another key to the Incas' success in rapidly and vastly expanding their empire lies in the fact that it was administered for the most part indirectly. Many of the groups conquered by the Incas already constituted quite large territorial blocs, with populations in the tens of thousands. By co-opting pliant local leaders, the state minimized its investments and redirected local allegiances toward the Inca Empire.

From a global perspective, the Incas are especially fascinating because of the seemingly unusual means by which they administered their empire. Western observers often marvel at how the Incas were able to conquer and manage such a vast area so quickly "without" the wheel, writing, draft animals, or currency. But this overlooks the limited utility of such technologies in an Andean context, and ignores the cultural ingenuities elaborated by the Incas and their ancestors.

Deadly Pathogens

For all of the frenetic growth and success of the Inca Empire, the processes of imperial expansion and consolidation were nevertheless abruptly truncated by the Spanish invasion. Paralleling what happened in other parts of the Americas, it seems that the deadly pathogens that the Europeans had brought with them to the New World preceded Pizarro's arrival by nearly a decade. The Inca Huayna Capac, the last uncontested Inca ruler, appears to have fallen ill to smallpox while campaigning in Ecuador in 1428.

In one of many ironies of the Spanish conquest of the Incas, Huayna Capac's unexpected death sparked a bloody civil war of succession between two of his sons— Huascar and Atahualpa. On the eve of conquest, the two had essentially split the empire in two, with Atahualpa controlling the north from his "new Cuzco" in Quito, while Huascar controlled the south from Cuzco. The civil war had reached a climax just as Pizarro's ships began to drop anchor at Tumbes, providing a ready-made wedge to drive between competing dynastic factions and their allied forces, and marking the beginning of the end.

NORTH ATLANTIC OCEAN

PACIFIC OCEAN

SOUTH ATLANTIC OCEAN

Equator

Tropic of Capricorn

Backbone of the Empire
The imperial centers, bound by a series of networked roads, were populated largely by a rotating population of households from surrounding ethnic groups who were paying their rotational labor duties to the state. Evidence for specialized textile and ceramic production workshops, as well as areas for the production of mass quantities of maize beer that were consumed in state sponsored feasts at these centers, reflect their "company town" organization.

Securing an Empire
Though their empire was short lived, the origins of the Inca state came about through a longer-term process of political consolidation in the Cuzco area through strategic marriage alliances between Inca elites and those of neighboring ethnic groups, the elaboration of a pantheonic state religion centering on solar worship, and the development of an intricate system of ceremonial centers, fortresses, and interconnecting roads between the twelfth and fifteenth centuries. By the mid-fifteenth century, the Inca had thus consolidated their rule and orchestrated a coherent system of governance in the Cuzco heartland, but still faced threats by rival ethnic groups, especially their longtime foes, the Chankas of the Huamanga area to the southwest.

RIGHT The founder of the Inca Empire, Pachacuti Inca Yupanqui, is credited with forming the basis of Incan administration and city planning and with ordering the construction of Machu Picchu. His son Tupac Inca Yupanqui helped expand the empire both before and after his father's abdication, and Tupac's successor, Huayna Capac, expanded it even further.

Pachacuti and Tupac Yupanqui territory (1471)

Tupac Yupanqui territory (1417–1493)

Huayna Capac territory (1493–1525)

0   500   1,000 kilometers
0   250   500 miles

Faith Alone

Martin Luther was the most important theologian since Thomas Aquinas and probably the most original Christian thinker since the fifth century. His writings permanently divided Western Christianity and sparked revolts, wars, and the greatest flurry of literature the world had ever seen.

ABOVE Portrait of Martin Luther (1483–1546), the former German Catholic priest who led the Reformation movement in Europe.

Born in 1483 to a middle-class mining family, Luther was educated in the German university of Erfurt. Originally intended for a career in law, he diverged from his father's wishes and entered a monastery at Erfurt. Monks were deemed to be almost definite candidates for eternal salvation.

Early Teaching

Luther's health began to deteriorate from his unusually rigorous piety and his supervisor, Johannes von Staupitz (1460 or 1469–1525), decided to transfer him from Erfurt to the monastery at Wittenberg. By now no obscure monk, Luther was soon awarded a doctorate in divinity, and Staupitz urged him to take his own professorship at the new Wittenberg University. Initially reluctant, Luther finally accepted the appointment in 1512 and never looked back. Luther proved popular with his students and thus with the patron prince of the university, Fredrick III of Saxony (1463–1525). The approval of Fredrick proved critical when the professor and, from 1514 the town preacher, found himself a protestant reformer.

Protestant Reformation

From one perspective, the call for reform was initiated by exciting new developments in art and architecture. St Peter's in Rome, the immense basilica of the Pope, was being rebuilt as a monument to Renaissance ideals. The authorities in Rome determined to pay for the project by the sale of indulgences, whereby a payment of money promised forgiveness of sins for the living and, if properly designated, for the dead. When the papal indulgence salesman, Johann Tetzel (c. 1465–1519), came to Wittenberg, Luther used his position to criticize Tetzel's crass salesmanship. In producing *The 95 Theses* (against indulgences), Luther followed academic convention and informed his archbishop that he intended a public dispute on the topic. The disputation developed into a protestation when *The 95 Theses* was printed and distributed across Germany.

Luther's rise to fame began in the autumn of 1517 but as he saw it, the most important moment in his life had occurred in private. While wrestling with Romans 1:17, he suddenly saw that God's righteousness was not his judgment of sinners, but his gift to sinners.

"Here I felt that I was altogether born again and had entered paradise itself through open gates," Luther later testified. "A totally other face of the entire Scripture showed itself to me."

Jesus Christ had come into the world to keep the law that sinners break and to pay the penalty that they deserve. This was a righteousness earned for others, and it was Luther's core teaching that the way to be declared right or just by God was to trust this righteousness alone. It is here that Luther realized what became his most famous dictum, that sinners are justified by faith alone.

Luther spoke of himself as a sinner saved by grace—a humble preacher and not a magisterial reformer. But the impressive entourage of academics and preachers that surrounded him and developed his ideas said otherwise. He wrote letters to leaders everywhere and, harnessing the printing press, Luther produced the greatest flurry of literature that the world had ever seen, and rather more than any other person in the sixteenth century.

What Luther wrote, Europe read. Famously, he announced that it was his life's ambition to bring biblical literacy to every boy who could push a plow through a field.

LEFT Following the Reformation, religous fervor became violent. This painting by François Dubois depicts the St Bartholomew's Day massacre of Protestants in France, August 24, 1572.

Legend:
- Areas of reformed faith
- Areas of growing reform
- Areas of reformation influence
- Catholic areas

Papal Response

He was, of course, accused of heresy. When examined by Church authorities at Augsburg, Luther refused to repent and called for a Church council to decide the matter. When his doctrine was disputed in Leipzig, he still called for an ecumenical, Church-wide council, but declared that even Church councils could err, and argued that the only reliable judge in Christian teaching should be the Bible alone.

In 1521, Luther was called to Worms to confess his heresy before Emperor Charles V (1500–1558). Moving quickly, soldiers of Frederick "captured" Luther on his return from Worms—but only to whisk him away to the safety of Wartburg

> Faith is a living, daring confidence in God's grace, so sure and certain that a man could stake his life on it a thousand times.
>
> – Martin Luther (1483-1546).

ABOVE The growth of Lutheran teachings can be seen spreading across Germany and on to Britain and Scandinavia.

1401 to 1600

NORWAY

SWEDEN

KALMAR UNION

DENMARK

Baltic Sea

Konigsberg

North Sea

PRUSSIA

HOLSTEIN

POMERANIA

MECKLENBURG

Hamburg

BRANDENBURG

POLISH-LITHUANIAN COMMONWEALTH

ENGLAND

UNITED NETHERLANDS

Amsterdam

Berlin

MARCHE OF MAGDEBURG

Leipzig

SILESIA

SPANISH NETHERLANDS

BISHOPRIC OF LIEGE

Cologne

Wittenberg

SAXONY

LOWER PALATINATE

LUXEMBURG

Mainz

Prague

BOHEMIA

MORAVIA

Trier

Heidelberg

UPPER PALATINATE

Paris

LORRAINE

WURTTEMBERG

BAVARIA

Vienna

AUSTRIA

Augsburg

Munich

ARCH BISHOPRIC OF SALZBURG

STYRIA

FRANCHE COMTE

Basel

Zurich

TYROL

CARINTHIA

HAPSBURG HUNGARY

FRANCE

SWISS CONFEDERATION

CARNIOLA

Geneva

VENICE

Milan

OTTOMAN EMPIRE

Adriatic Sea

Bordeaux

Genoa

PAPAL STATES

Avignon

Florence

TUSCANY

SPAIN

Corsica

Rome

Mediterranean Sea

Sardinia

Sicily

N

	Territory under Catholic government (1648)
	Territory under Lutheran government (1648)
	Territory under Calvinist government (1648)

0   250   500   750   1,000 kilometers

0   125   250   375   500 miles

LEFT The division between church and state was very blurred at the time of the Reformation. Churches held sway with political decisions and government. The influence of the different faiths across Europe is shown on this map.

RIGHT The inaugural sitting of the Council of Trent, which was held on December 13, 1545, is depicted in this painting by Nicolo Dorigati.

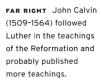

FAR RIGHT John Calvin (1509-1564) followed Luther in the teachings of the Reformation and probably published more teachings.

1519 Zwingli begins to preach through the Gospel of Matthew at Zurich; Luther debates with Johann Eck at Leipzig

1522 Luther's New Testament translation appears in German

1523 Calvin begins study in Paris and is soon influenced by Lutheran teaching

1524-25 Luther and Erasmus debate the freedom of the will

1529 Zwingli and Luther dispute the Lord's supper at Marburg

1536 Calvin's *Institutes of the Christian Religion* are published at Basel

1545 The Council of Trent begins

castle, where Luther initiated his translation of the Bible into German. Unwilling to remain in hiding, Luther made his way back to Wittenberg, where he continued his campaign of reform until his death in 1546.

When Luther could no longer be avoided, the papacy still delayed calling a council. The Pope managed instead to persuade the Emperor to force Protestants into submission. Coercion, counter-Reformation polemic from Jesuits, and the infamous Inquisition were only partially successful in addressing the Reformation. When the Pope, in 1545, finally did summon a council in the Italian town of Trent, it came too late to stem the flow of Protestants from the mother church.

"Radical" Reformation

The Lutheran reformation was radical in its approach to biblical authority and the way of salvation.

While Luther reduced the number of sacraments in the church from seven to two (the Lord's supper and baptism), and while he denied the authority of the papacy, his understanding of the sacraments and of church-state relationships

remained traditional, even medieval. For some in the reform movement, this was insufficient reform. Religious radicals called for immediate larger-scale changes in worship and church governance, and peasants demanded immediate changes in society.

Luther opposed both groups—which had overlapping constituencies. He worked to ban radical reformers from Saxony, and he wrote in favor of a negotiated settlement with peasants while publicly declaring that force could be used to crush open rebellion. The success of Luther's religious platform resulted in the exile of Anabaptists to Switzerland and elsewhere. His ill-timed pamphlet against revolt, although hardly influencing the course of events, left Luther to bear much of the blame when a peasant revolt in Thuringia was crushed by a bloody confrontation and prolonged persecution.

Spread of Reform

Within a few decades, Germany and most of Scandinavia became Lutheran, as did the northern part of Eastern Europe. In England, King Henry VIII was no admirer of Luther, but he respected Philipp

Melanchthon (1497–1560), the younger colleague of Luther. Many of the first generation of English Reformers and martyrs were Lutherans. To the south of Germany, Luther's genius and courage were admired, and his evangelical stance was accepted by a significant number of his contemporaries. Although working independently, the Renaissance scholar and Swiss patriot, Huldrych Zwingli, echoed many of the same themes as Luther and took the time to hold a personal, if futile, meeting to discuss the Lord's supper.

Calvin

While Zwingli was preaching in Zurich, John Calvin (1509–1564) was reading Luther and Erasmus in Paris, soon fleeing the city as a suspected Lutheran. His *Institutes of the Christian Religion* (1536) was the most read book of the Reformation. He came to differ from Luther on many points, for he advocated separation of church and state and a reformation of all aspects of theology, including worship. Although Zwingli and Martin Bucer (1491–1551) were more senior reformers, only Calvin would rival Luther's place in world history.

Students would spread his reformed version of the Protestant message across the Swiss cantons, through France (especially in the south) and the Netherlands. Scotland would adopt wholesale Calvin's teaching on church government, theology and worship.

Perhaps the most impacted were former followers of Jan Hus in Eastern Europe. It is there that the earliest Protestant universities were founded to advance a strong spiritual tradition that remains vibrant in many places of the world today.

The Wars of the Roses

The title of these wars was coined by nineteenth-century novelist Sir Walter Scott, and derived from a scene in Shakespeare's *Henry VI*, Part 1, depicting English nobility selecting roses, red or white, to signify their loyalty to the House of York or the House of Lancaster.

> And here I prophesy: this brawl today,
> Grown to this faction in the Temple garden,
> Shall send, between the Red Rose and the
> White, A thousand souls to death
> and deadly night.
>
> –William Shakespeare, *Henry VI*, Part One.

RIGHT This magnificent manuscript details the investiture of John Talbot with the sword of office as Constable of France, in 1436. John Talbot was the only Lancastrian constable of France.

BELOW The intermarriage and intrigue of the houses of York and Lancaster can be seen in the Line of Accession. The princes imprisoned in the Tower in 1483 are the last of their line on the bottom right.

Lasting from 1455 to 1487 between the royal houses of Lancaster and York, the Wars of the Roses resulted in the downfall of both and the emergence of the notorious Tudor dynasty that brought the Middle Ages in England to an end. There were actually two sets of Wars of the Roses and they stand in history as representative of anarchy at its absolute worst.

York versus Lancaster

The first set focused on the struggle for sovereignty between the houses of Lancaster and York, which began with the first Battle of St Albans in 1455, waged by Richard, Duke of York, and ended in 1471, with the death of Henry VI in the Tower of London.

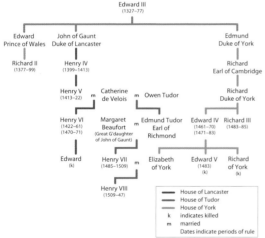

Causes

At the center of the first set of bloody faction fights driven by violence, treachery, and deceit was the feeble figure of Henry VI, whose mental instability and in-effectiveness in government gave rise to political volatility, public discontent, and discord between the landed nobility. Ultimately this led to war and a bitter battle over the throne itself.

Henry's chief rival was Richard Plantagenet, Duke of York, the man who should have been king according to the law of primogeniture as it was then understood. After York's death, his claim to the throne was inherited by his son, who became King Edward IV, and who would, in the end, ruthlessly finish off the House of Lancaster.

Henry was further undermined by his queen, Margaret of Anjou, taking up arms in the cause of Lancaster in her bitter fight for her son Edward's rights against accusations of being a bastard fathered by the Duke of Somerset.

York Victory

The conflicts erupted in some of the bloodiest and most dramatic battles on English soil—St Albans, Blore Hill, Towton—as both sides fought for control of the country. The crucial moment of the first wars came in March 1461, when York's son, Edward IV, defeated the Lancastrian forces at Towton and seized the throne. Fighting continued sporadically as Edward endeavored to secure full control of his kingdom. Henry VI was returned to power briefly for six months in 1470.

The death of Edward—son of Henry VI, Prince of Wales and heir to Lancaster, on the field of Tewkesbury in 1471, and the murder of his father, saw the decisive end of the first set of wars and victory for the house of York.

York versus Tudor

The second phase of civil war was launched in 1483 by the seizure of the throne by Richard III of York. These wars were then between the dynasties of York and Tudor, Henry VII of Tudor emerging as the rival claimant. His victory at Bosworth in 1485 gained him the throne but did not secure his dynasty until his second victory at Stoke in 1487.

Tudor Victory

Henry VII had married Elizabeth of York, daughter of Edward IV, in 1486, to strengthen his claim to the throne, and to try to unite the rival houses. He defeated several more Yorkist attempts to recapture the throne, including one at Stoke, and ostensibly united the two houses of York and Lancaster.

THE PRINCES IN THE TOWER

Upon Edward IV's death in 1483, his son Edward was proclaimed King Edward V. However within a month, Edward and his younger brother, Richard of York, were locked in the Tower of London by their uncle Richard, Duke of Gloucester, claiming it was for their safekeeping. The boys were never seen again, inspiring years of controversy over their disappearance. In 1674, during alterations to the Tower, two skeletons were found buried beneath a stone staircase. The bones were re-buried in the same year in the Henry VIII Chapel in Westminster Abbey. In 1933, the skeletons were disinterred and examined. It was concurred they were of two young boys, one aged about 10 and the other 13, and that they were those of the two princes, who probably died in the summer of 1483.

LEFT The series of battles making up the Wars of the Roses occurred throughout England.

BELOW Henry VI, a weak monarch, was ousted from the throne twice by his House of York rivals.

1455 First Battle of St Albans begins the Wars of the Roses

1462 Margaret of Anjou captures castles in Northumberland with the help of the French

1464 Second phase of the Wars of the Roses begins with a battle at Hexham

1465 Henry IV, although in exile, is captured at Clitheroe by Yorkists

1470 Edward V is born

1471 Henry IV is imprisoned in the Tower of London and killed

1483 Edward IV dies. Richard, Duke of Gloucester, locks away his heir Edward V and his younger brother Richard. Neither boy is ever seen again.

1485 Richard III is killed in the Battle of Bosworth

1487 Battle of Stoke ends Wars of the Roses

Maya and Aztec– Priests and Sacrifices

Two great civilizations occupied the area known as Mesoamerica before the time of the Spanish Conquest. While the Aztecs had no written language and used varieties of hieroglyphics to record their lives, the Mayans created the only true written language of pre-Columbian time.

Maya civilization began as a steady outgrowth of developments that began in the Middle and Late Formative periods (1000–200 BCE) through the lowlands and highlands in Chiapas, Yucatan, Belize, and Guatemala. What had been small agricultural villages were growing in size and political complexity. At sites such as Izapa, Kaminaljuyu, Chalchuapa, El Mirador, Tikal, and San Bartolo, archeological evidence reflects a demographic

> ...These great towns...and buildings rising from the water, all made of stone, seemed like an enchanted vision from the tale of Amadis. Indeed some of our soldiers asked whether it was not all a dream.
>
> –Bernal Díaz del Castillo,
> The True History of the Conquest of New Spain.

increase, increased competition and conflict, violence and warfare, and cultural and ethnic diversity. We also see increased economic, social, political, and ideological interaction. Triadic complexes of temple pyramids with stucco masks and flanking staircases are widespread. Polychrome murals were also executed at many centers.

Stela Cult

Another striking development was the development of the stela cult at many sites in the southern lowlands. This complex was directly descended from an earlier tradition derived from the southern highlands and the Pacific piedmont of Guatemala and Chiapas. Many monuments depict rulers with hieroglyphic texts and historical information reporting the feats and accomplishments of famous rulers. All these traits are expressions of an elite ruling ideology.

Tikal

By the Early Classic period, about 250 CE, Tikal had emerged as one of the primary centers in the central lowlands, the region that had now become the center of gravity for Classic Lowland Maya civilization. The dedication of a major stela at Tikal in 292 CE marks the center's achievement of primary-center status. Other central lowland sites asserted their importance and independence by erecting monuments soon after. All early dated monuments in the late fourth and early fifth century occur at sites in central lowlands.

Several dated monuments found at El Perú, Uaxactun, and Tikal attest to an invasion of the region by Teotihuacán in 378 CE, the great urban power of central highland Mexico.

After this event, we see the spread of Tikal's power throughout the lowlands with dynastic

foundations at places such Palenque, Copan, and Quirigua. Also significant is the evidence for close relationships during this period between the Teotihuacán and Kaminaljuyu in the highlands of Guatemala.

Abandonment

During the Late Classic period (600–800 CE) several major centers rose to power to challenge Tikal's dominance of the lowlands. Caracol became one of the dominant sites, having waged a successful campaign against Tikal resulting in the capture and ritual sacrifice of Tikal's king in 562 CE. At this time, many monuments in Tikal's Great Plaza were destroyed, and Tikal seems to have suffered a collapse that lasted about 130 years. At the same time, Caracol experienced an explosive period of growth until the eighth century. Endemic inter-elite warfare increased, exacerbated by population pressure, environmental degradation, and climate change.

These problems culminated with the Classic Maya collapse that led to the abandonment of the major centers throughout the lowlands during the period from about 800–900 ce. The individual city-states collapsed in unison

LEFT El Caracol observatory, with the Pyramid of Kukulkan behind, Chichen Itza. Astronomical observations were the basis of the amazingly accurate Mayan calendar.

ABOVE Mayan culture began as a series of small agricultural villages full of thriving trade. This painting of a Mayan fresco shows a variety of scenes from daily life.

RIGHT The bulk of the Mayan city-states disappeared in the eighth century due to environment and social problems.

falling prey to climate change, ecological deterioration, , and social strife. The small surviving populations in the lowlands reverted to village-level politics and small-scale agriculture.

Maya civilization continued in the northern lowlands of Yucatan where the collapse had little effect. The major Early Postclassic site of Chichen Itza had close relations with Tollan in Mexico. At the time of the Conquest, about a dozen major Maya city-states of Yucatan were vying for control of the trade routes around the peninsula.

Tropic of Cancer

Gulf of Mexico

Gulf of Honduras

PACIFIC OCEAN

Xcambo
Dzibichaltun
Chichén Itzá
Cobá
Mayapán
Mani
Tulum
Jaina
Uxmal
Mayapán
Ichpartún
Comalcalco
Uaxactun
Calakmul
Palenque
Tikal
Topoxte
Usumacinta
La Libertal
Nim Li Punit
Mezcalapa
Quirígua
Cahculá
Nabaj
Copan
Tajumulco
Solola
Kaminaljuyu

0   250   500 kilometers
0   125   250 miles

N

Central area of Mayan culture and settlements

207

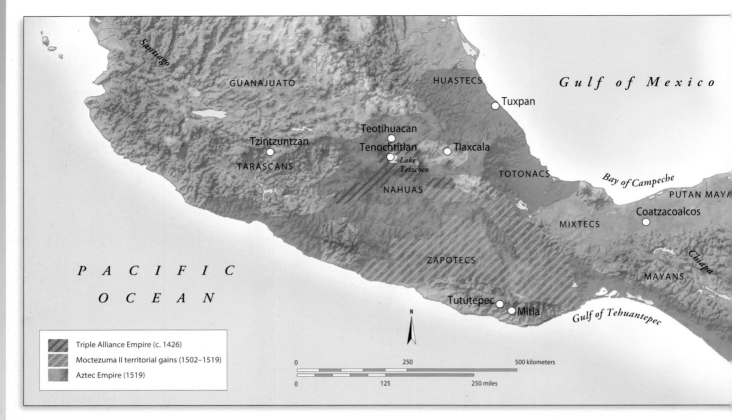

Aztec Civilization

No consideration of Aztec history is complete without the Toltec background. The first large group of Nahua speakers to inhabit central Mexico lived at the city of Tollan Xicocotitlan, known today as Tula, in the Mexican state of Hidalgo. The founders of the city had migrated from the northern desert region of Mexico. Although archeological evidence indicates an earlier population at the site, the native chronicles are traditionally interpreted to mean that Tollan was founded by the legendary priest and ruler Quetzalcoatl in 968 CE, who may have been descended from the royal house of the Epiclassic city-state of Xochicalco, Morelos. The chronicles assert that Quetzalcoatl was forced out of power by his rival Tezcalipoca, and he departed in disgrace. This is known as the "Toltec diaspora," and current thinking puts it at about 987 CE.

The collapse of the Toltecs paved the way for the entrance of many immigrant groups into the Valley of Mexico, most of whom were Nahua speakers known predominantly as Chichimecs, which translates as "barbarians." They had lived in a place known as Aztlan—hence the derivative, Aztec—on the northwest fringe of Mesoamerica during the Toltec period, and with the collapse of that state the groups began migrating into the Valley of Mexico in the late twelfth century. Among these were the ancestors of the Mexicas.

Tenochtitlan

Upon arrival in the Basin of Mexico, they served as mercenaries to the Epi-Toltec center of Culhuacan. Having become successful warriors, they began to threaten their hosts. Soon they were expelled by the Culhuas, and they moved to the island of Tenochtitlan where they founded a small fishing village in 1325 or 1345, although archeological remains suggest an earlier date. The site was strategically located in Lake Tetzcoco, and had good access to resources and water communication.

In 1372, the Mexicas, having restored relations with the Culhuas, obtained a prince of the Toltec-descended ruling family to become their first dynastic king. His name was Acamapichtli, and he ruled from 1372 to 1391. During this period, the Mexicas had paid tribute to the Tepanecs of Atzcapotzalco, on the west shore

RIGHT Moctezuma Xocoyotzin was the last king of the Aztecs and leader of the Triple Alliance.

of the lake. They remained under Tepanec control under the reigns of Acamapichtli's next two successors, Huitzilihuitl (1391–1415) and Chimalpopoca (1415–1426). Chimalpopoca was assassinated, perhaps in a palace coup because of his pro-Tepanec politics. Netzahualcoyotl, the son of the king of Tetzcoco, was then forced into exile. As a result, a coalition was formed between Tetzcoco, Itzcoatl, Chimalpopoca's successor, and the ruler of Tlacopan, himself a member of the Tepanec royal family and a pretender to the throne. Thus, the Triple Alliance empire was formed in 1426.

YUCATAN
PENINSULA

macinta

mché

RIGHT The capital of the
Aztecs, Tenochtitlan, was
a vibrant city situated
on an island in the Valley
of Mexico. This fresco by
Diego Rivera shows a doc-
tor or shaman working in
the street.

400 CE Maya high-
lands fall under the
domination of
Teotihuacán

500 CE Tikal becomes
the first great Maya city

600 CE The civilization
at Teotihuacán is
destroyed by an event
unknown. Tikal becomes
the largest city-state in
Mesoamerica, 500,000
inhabitants.

1325 Tenochtitlan
is founded and the first
temple is built

1519 Cortez conquers
Mexico and captures
Moctezuma II

Expansion

One of the keys in the Mexica
imperial expansion was that they
sought the protection of older
established groups, especially those
with Toltec dynastic ties, through
royal marriage alliance. By acquir-
ing a member of the Culhua royal
house as their first emperor, the
Mexicas could legitimately claim
Toltec descent. Another key was
the conquest of the rich chinampa
lands of the southern end of the
basin, which the Mexicas seized
from Atzcapotzalco after the revolt
of 1426. Expansion followed, but
in most cases other polities regarded the Triple Alliance armies as so
powerful that the use of force was
unnecessary. Thus the perception
of strength was often sufficient
to favor the expansion of power.
Much of their internal justification
for imperial expansion relied on
the belief that Huitzilopochtli had
to be nourished with the blood of
sacrificial victims captured in wars.

After a sustained war, the Triple
Alliance broke the power of Atzcapotzalco and soon came to be
dominated by Tenochtitlan. Four
other rulers would follow until
Moctezuma Xocoyotzin ascended
the throne in 1502. He would be
the ruler to meet Hernando
Cortés in 1519.

Spanish Colonization

The conquest of the Incas—marked by the execution of Atahualpa XIV on July 26, 1533—is often described as the watershed event marking the era of Spanish colonial domination of western South America.

> There lies Peru with its riches. Here, Panama and its poverty. Choose, each man, what best becomes a brave Castilian.
>
> –Francisco Pizarro (c. 1471-1541), Spanish conquistador and conqueror.

Pizarro was acutely aware of the precarious position of the colonists in the early years following the conquest, as the Spanish population represented a tiny minority amidst a vast and diverse landscape of sophisticated highland and coastal peoples. From the native Andean point of view, the Spanish, for all of their abuse and aggressiveness, represented yet another warring faction in a fragmented and confusing battlefield in the wake of the Inca civil war.

After Atahualpa was executed, rival dynastic factions jockeyed for alliance with the Spanish in hopes of eliminating their rivals and reuniting the empire. Though often described as a "puppet Inca" chosen by Pizarro, Manco Inca, scion of the dynastic rivals of Atahualpa, seized upon an alliance with Pizarro as he marched to Cuzco. This alliance was to quickly sour, however, and Manco Inca fled to the remote jungle region of Vilcabamba to form an Inca state in exile. By 1536, Manco mounted massive military offensives on Cuzco and the outskirts of Lima. The neo-Inca state was to remain a threat to Spanish colonial domination until the execution of their final ruler, Tupac Amaru, in 1572.

Disease

As elsewhere in the Americas, the diseases introduced by the European invaders—smallpox, measles, plague, whooping cough, among others—proved to be their most lethal weapons.

Populations were especially hard hit in the tropical coastal valleys—in some cases, total population extinctions occurred. In the highlands, overall rates of decline were generally lower, but still, declines of 80 to 90 percent were not uncommon by the middle of the eighteenth century.

Missionaries

During the first four decades of colonial rule, the Spanish presence in many provincial areas of the Peruvian viceroyalty was limited largely to Church clerics. The legitimacy of Spanish conquest rested on the precondition of Christianization, and a small but fervent pastoral corps quickly fanned out over the Andean landscape to establish mission settlements. Prior to the establishment of a formal parish system in the 1570s, evangelization was dominated by the mendicant orders, especially the Franciscans, Dominicans, and Augustinians.

Use of Labor

Early colonial Spanish governance was a hybrid system that left much of the intermediate levels of Inca provincial administration in place, siphoning labor and tribute through the native lords of the highland and coastal ethnic polities that had earlier constituted the great mosaic of the Inca geopolitical map. The labor of these populations was granted in trusteeship to the Spanish elite through the institution of the *encomienda*, a semi-feudal seigniorial arrangement in which the *encomendero*, beneficiary of native labor services, was reciprocally obliged—theoretically, at least—to Christianize and protect their native charges from undue abuse.

Stability

It wasn't until the arrival of the viceroy Francisco de Toledo in 1568 that a more formalized system of governance was established. His 12-year tenure began with a sweeping, viceroyalty-wide general inspection and tour, during which a complete census was conducted and much of the native population was resettled into compact, European-style villages built on a grid of regular blocks around a central plaza, church, and town hall. Although it disrupted indigenous patterns of settlement and land use and imposed onerous labor and tribute obligations on native society, this system of colonial governance and political administration endured largely intact until the wars of independence in the early nineteenth century.

ABOVE Francisco Pizarro, Spanish conquistador, sailed up and down the western coast of South America, conquering the Inca Empire and claiming land for Spain.

RIGHT This drawing is taken from *Atlas of South America* by Giullo Ferrario in 1827. It shows the capture of Atahualpa, Inca king, by Francisco Pizarro. After using him to control the Inca Empire, Inca Atahualpa XIV was executed by the Spanish in 1533.

ABOVE Francisco Pizarro, represented here by French artist Amable-Paul Coutan, began life as a soldier and became the Spanish governor of Peru.

RIGHT New Spain was the first Spanish viceroyalty, established in 1535. New Castilla (later known as Peru) came next in 1542, then New Grenada in 1717 and La Plata in 1776.

1513 Spanish explorer, Vasco Núñez de Balboa, crosses the isthmus of Panama and claims the Pacific Ocean for Spain

1520 Chocolate from Mexico arrives in Spain for the first time

1523 Turkeys are introduced to Spain and Europe from America by the conquistadors

1542 Gonzalo Pizarro, younger brother of Francisco, reaches the mouth of the Amazon River after having sailed its length as far as the Andes Mountains

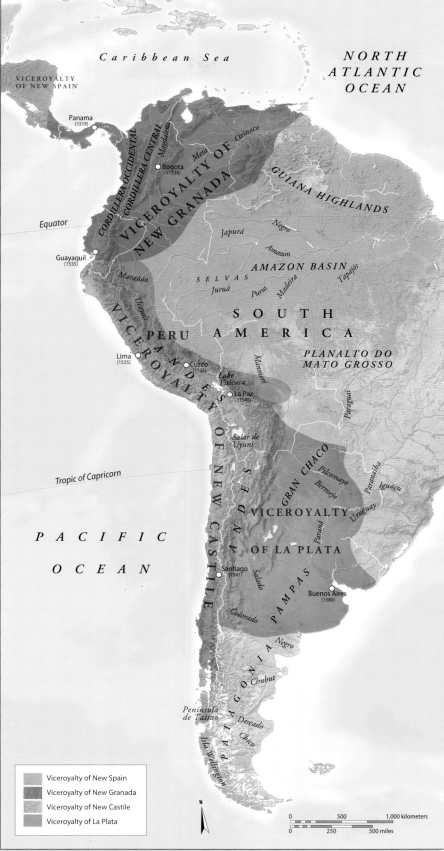

1401 to 1600

Sub-Saharan Kingdoms

Wherever trade sprang up alongside intensive agriculture, larger-scale political units tended to emerge. As it had been in ancient Egypt, so it would later be, south of the Sahara.

Thanks to the spread of Islam along trans-Saharan trade routes from c. 900 CE, literate observers documented kingdoms of considerable size and importance from Senegal to Darfur. Christian Ethiopia likewise documented the rise and fall of successive kingdoms.

Early Kingdoms
Exactly when the first substantial kingdoms arose in West Africa is difficult to say, as far too little archeological work has been done. The existence of rock art depicting wheeled chariots deep in the Sahara and excavations at Jenne on the Niger River suggest that trade routes and urban centers existed centuries before Roman rule ended in North Africa.

Arabic sources dating from the tenth century CE tell of a mighty kingdom, Ghana, which flourished for several centuries beginning about 600 CE. They also tell of other kingdoms bestriding the Niger River.

Mali dominated the central region from the twelfth to the fourteenth century. By the end of the fifteenth century the powerful kingdom of Songhay had based itself at Gao. Near the northernmost point of the Niger Bend, the city of Timbuktu had, well before 1500, acquired a worldwide reputation for riches and learning.

West Africa
After about 1581, when the sultan of Morocco staged a daring trans-Saharan raid in search of gold, kingdom-building declined. The next kingdoms to come to prominence made their headquarters a little inland from the coast—most likely because that was the best place to control trading routes.

Near the modern city of Lagos, Nigeria, the Portuguese found the flourishing Kingdom of Benin, which was probably already two centuries old. The seventeenth century would see the rise of Ashanti, Dahomey, and Oyo—all well placed to control trade in slaves and other goods from the interior to the coast.

East Africa
By the eighth and ninth centuries most of the coastal states had accepted Islam as their religion, and Swahili as the main language of trade. However, their glory days came to an end with the arrival of the Portuguese on the east coast

soon after 1500, fired with a thirst to monopolize trade and a crusading zeal to smash Islam. The important city of Mombasa was sacked and burned—on a bluff above the smoking ruins the Portuguese built their Fort Jesus.

Great Zimbabwe
Inland from the city of Sofala on the coast of Mozambique is a large complex of stone ruins, including the spectacular group at Great Zimbabwe. Similar ruins have been found further south at Mapungubwe on the Limpopo River.

Radio-carbon dating reveals that most building at Great Zimbabwe took place between the twelfth and fifteenth centuries. What other kingdoms might have been built in the region in earlier centuries can only be guessed at. Certainly, the prosperity of all of them declined as the Portuguese seized control of the coast.

LEFT Famous Moroccan traveler, Ibn Battuta, is depicted here at the court of Muhammad Tughlug, Sultan of Delhi.

RIGHT This bronze mask is of a king of Yoruba, a west African tribe. The headpiece is adorned with a coronet of Portuguese heads.

> Thence we went on to Tunbuktu, which stands four miles from the river [Niger]. Most of its inhabitants are of the Massufa tribe, wearers of the face-veil. Its governor is called Farba Musa.
> –Ibn Battuta in his account of his journeys.

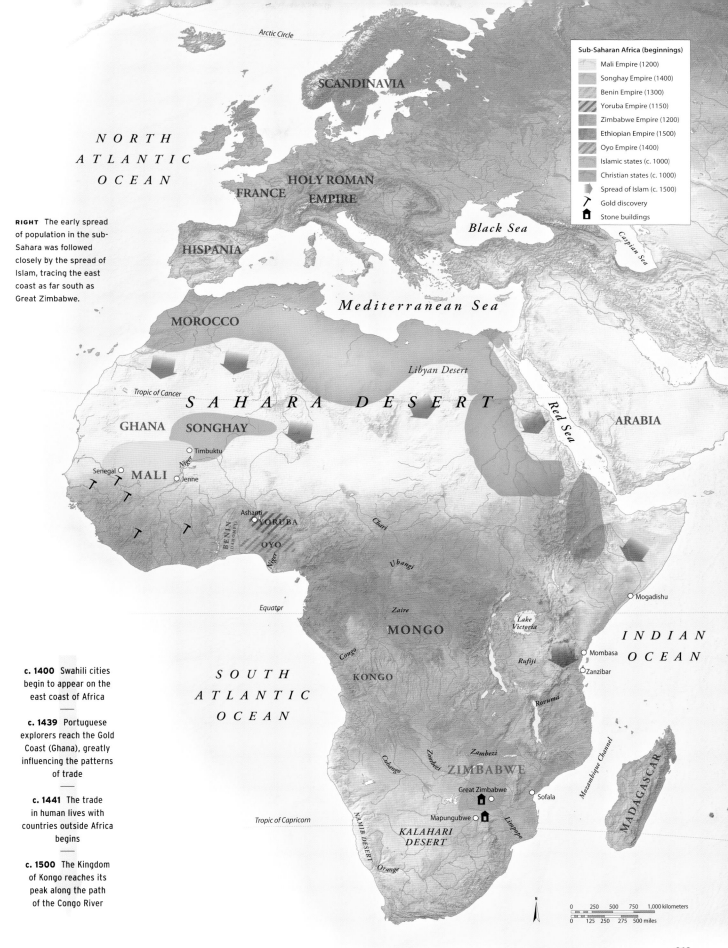

RIGHT The early spread of population in the sub-Sahara was followed closely by the spread of Islam, tracing the east coast as far south as Great Zimbabwe.

Sub-Saharan Africa (beginnings)

	Mali Empire (1200)
	Songhay Empire (1400)
	Benin Empire (1300)
	Yoruba Empire (1150)
	Zimbabwe Empire (1200)
	Ethiopian Empire (1500)
	Oyo Empire (1400)
	Islamic states (c. 1000)
	Christian states (c. 1000)
	Spread of Islam (c. 1500)
	Gold discovery
	Stone buildings

Arctic Circle

SCANDINAVIA

NORTH ATLANTIC OCEAN

HOLY ROMAN EMPIRE

FRANCE

Black Sea

HISPANIA

Caspian Sea

Mediterranean Sea

MOROCCO

Libyan Desert

Tropic of Cancer

SAHARA DESERT

Red Sea

ARABIA

GHANA SONGHAY

○ Timbuktu

Niger

Senegal ○

MALI

○ Jenne

Ashanti ○ YORUBA

BENIN (DAHOMEY)

OYO

Chari

Niger

Ubangi

Zaire

○ Mogadishu

Equator

MONGO

Lake Victoria

INDIAN OCEAN

Congo

Rufiji

○ Mombasa

KONGO

○ Zanzibar

SOUTH ATLANTIC OCEAN

Rovuma

c. 1400 Swahili cities begin to appear on the east coast of Africa

c. 1439 Portuguese explorers reach the Gold Coast (Ghana), greatly influencing the patterns of trade

c. 1441 The trade in human lives with countries outside Africa begins

c. 1500 The Kingdom of Kongo reaches its peak along the path of the Congo River

Cubango

Zambezi

Zambezi

ZIMBABWE

Great Zimbabwe ○

○ Sofala

Mozambique Channel

MADAGASCAR

Tropic of Capricorn

Mapungubwe ○

Limpopo

NAMIB DESERT

KALAHARI DESERT

Orange

N

0	250	500	750	1,000 kilometers

0	125	250	275	500 miles

Ottoman Empire

After the capture of Constantinople in 1453, the Ottoman Empire became one of the most powerful empires in the world.

1566 Suleyman dies

1571 The Spanish fleet overcomes the Ottomans in the Battle of Lepanto, ending supremacy in the Mediterranean

1683 Ottomans lose the Battle of Vienna which marks the end of expansion

1918 After two centuries of stagnation, the Ottoman Empire ends with the Armistice of Mudros in which it loses its Middle East territories, large areas of Anatolia, and almost all of Thrace

LEFT The army of Suleyman the Magnificent sets off to conquer Europe in this illustration from a manuscript dedicated to his military exploits.

RIGHT The map shows the Ottoman grab for territory. The inset is a detail of the navy positions in the Battle of Lepanto, 1571.

ATLANTIC OCEAN

The power established throughout Anatolia and the Balkans by the Ottoman Empire in the fourteenth century suffered a considerable setback at the beginning of the fifteenth century. It would take the first half of the fifteenth century for the Ottomans to restore the empire created under Osman and his immediate successors in the previous century. The culmination of this restoration and the beginning of a significant expansion was the capture of Constantinople in 1453 that signaled the end of the Byzantine Empire.

Civil War

Following the defeat and capture of Bayezid by Timur (Tamerlane) at Ankara in 1402, the Ottoman Empire was itself subject to the suzerainty of Timur's empire and during the following decades came close to extinction on a number of occasions. Eventually, under the leadership of Murad II, the Ottoman Empire returned to its former glory and by 1451 had completely recovered from the disaster of 1402.

Constantinople

With Murad II's death in 1453, Mehmed II came to power for the third time and from the very beginning set out to capture Constantinople and put an end to the Byzantine Empire. Placing the city under siege on April 6, 1435, with an army of approximately 50,000 men, the forces of Mehmed II

> In this world a spell of good health is the best state.
>
> –Kanuni Sultan Suleyman (1494-1566), longest serving sultan of the Ottoman Empire.

captured the city on May 29. Constantinople was renamed Istanbul and the heavily fortified city became an important base from which the Ottomans expanded their empire over the next 70 years. A significant element in this was strengthening of the navy.

Under the reign of Mehmed II, the Ottoman Empire developed a new strength and by the time of his death in 1481 he had established the nucleus of an empire

that would last for another four and a half centuries with its capital at Istanbul. The Ottomans controlled virtually everything south of the Danube as well as Anatolia as far east as the Euphrates.

Mehmed's rule was somewhat tyrannical and under his successor, Bayezid, there were many internal revolts to deal with. In 1484, Bayezid inflicted significant defeats over Moldavia and the Mamluk sultan of Syria and Egypt.

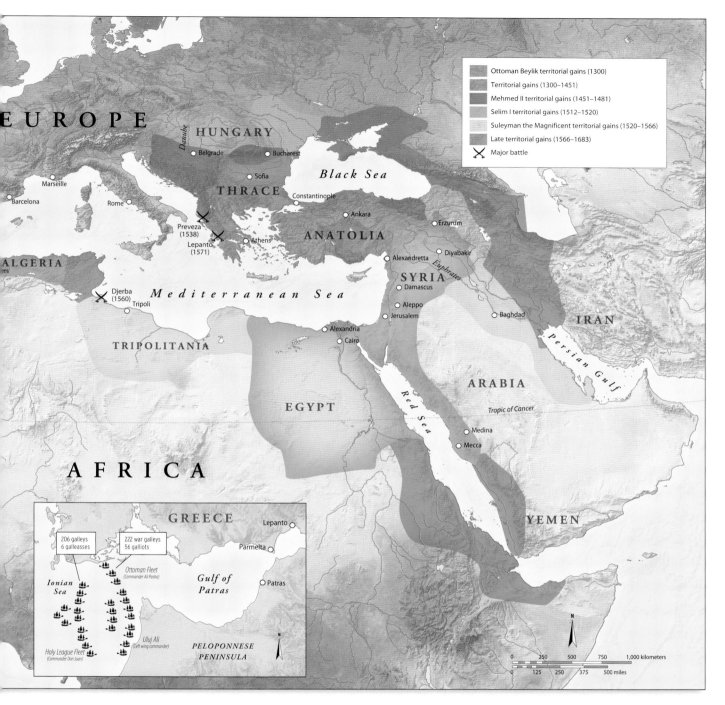

Western Expansion

During the sixteenth century, the Ottomans became directly involved in European politics and conflict. Developments on the frontier in Anatolia forced the Ottomans to a peace agreement with Venice and to direct their attention to the imperial activities of the Ismaili Empire in Iran. In 1512, Bayezid abdicated in favor of his son, Selim, who ruthlessly murdered other claimants to the sultanate and mounted a major campaign against Ismail. In 1514, he annexed territory from Erzurum to Diyabakir, and in 1516, he marched against Mamluks in Syria.

The Ottomans were, on the whole, welcomed in Syria with the city of Aleppo surrendering without a fight in August 1516. Later that month, Selim defeated the Mamluk Sultan, killing him on the battlefield. The Ottomans soon took control of Damascus and Jerusalem.

In January 1517, Selim marched on Egypt which was taken quickly from a recently established usurper. In July 1517, Selim received the submission of Mecca and Medina in Arabia and took control of all territory as far south as Yemen.

Suleyman

In 1520, Selim was succeeded by Suleyman I. During his long reign, which lasted until 1566, the Ottoman empire expanded even further.

Suleyman became known as the Magnificent and succeeded in extending Ottoman control in Europe, the Middle East, and Africa. By the end of his reign, the Ottoman Empire was the dominant power in the Mediterranean, the successor to the Islamic Caliphates in the Near East and Egypt, controller of former Byzantine territory in Asia Minor and Greece, and a major player in political and military developments in Europe.

215

Mughal India

In contrast with the period of multiple dynasties and centers of power during the Sultanate, power during the Mughal Empire emanated from a single center based on the Delhi-Agra region.

There were five great Mughal emperors—Babar (1526–1530), the founder; Akbar (1556–1605), meaning the Great, who lived up to his name; Jahangir (1605–1627), basically continuing the policies of his father; Shah Jahan (1627–1658), who was among the world's great builders; and Aurangzeb (1658–1707), whose reversal of Akbar's policies of tolerance and trust eventually destroyed the empire.

Babar and Humayun

The founder of the great Mughal dynasty was Babar from Ferghana, in Uzbekistan. He was descended from Timur on his father's side and from Genghis Khan on his mother's. Babar's ambition to find his fortune in India was helped by two separate invitations from members of the ruling family opposed to the reigning Sultan Ibrahim Khan Lodi. Babar died in 1530.

The second Mughal emperor, Humayun, is not known for any heroic exploits or administrative or artistic achievements. In 1540, he was easily defeated by Afghan nobleman, Sher Shah Suri, and spent the next decade in exile in Persia. He regained the throne with the help of the Persian monarch host in 1555 but did not live long. He died after stumbling from his library stairs in 1556.

Although Sher Shah Suri was on the throne for only five years—he died in an explosion during a siege of a fortress—he carved a place for himself in Indian history as an administrative genius.

Akbar

Humayun's 13-year old son, Akbar, succeeded him and extended his empire all over North India. Historians hail him as the greatest ruler since Ashoka because of his policy of promoting a harmonious relationship between the two principal

> The Taj Mahal is like a solitary tear suspended on the cheek of time.
> –Rabindranath Tagore (1861-1941), Indian poet and novelist.

communities, the Hindus and the Muslims. Akbar allowed the right of religious freedom to all his subjects. In 1581, he promoted a new syncretic faith, the Din-I-Ilahi, which was the result of his discussions with leaders of several faiths in the specially constructed Hall of Worship in his new capital of Fatehpur Sikri. Akbar's son Jahangir (1605–1627) did not disturb the political and religious balance of his father's time. The policy was continued also during his son Shah Jahan's rule (1627–1658) although the influence of the Muslim divines at his court increased visibly.

Aurangzeb

Aurangzeb was the last of the mighty Mughal emperors. His reign was marred by a large-scale and general intolerance towards people of non-Muslim, non-Sunni faiths. For the first time in a century, he imposed the discriminating zizya tax on non-Muslims, and desecrated and destroyed Hindu temples.

From the time of Aurangzeb's death in 1707 to the accession of the last Mughal "emperor," Bahadur Shah in 1837, there was less and less territory to rule. Bahadur Shah's writ was limited to the fort and its environs in Delhi.

By the time of the Persian Nadir Shah's "rape of Delhi" in 1739, the Mughal Empire resembled the political mosaic of the late Sultanate when a number of independent sultanates held power in parts of the subcontinent.

By 1765, when the Mughal Emperor granted the Diwani of Bengal to the East India Company, the British had emerged as the political arbiter on the subcontinent.

TAJ MAHAL

The Mughals have often been called fabulous because of the spectacular monuments they left behind. Shah Jahan was the greatest builder among them with the Taj Mahal being the best of the monuments. Basically a mausoleum to house the body of his wife, Mumtaj (and later, of Shah Jahan himself), the Taj Mahal stands on the right bank of the Yamuna River at Agra. With its 205 feet (63 m) high tomb and four four-level minarets, each 162 feet (50 m) tall, the Taj Mahal is known for both its massive majesty and its beauty. The monument took an estimated 20,000 artisans to build, from 1631 to 1653.

LEFT The last of the great Mughal emperors, Aurangzeb, is seen hunting lions in this painting on vellum dated about 1675.

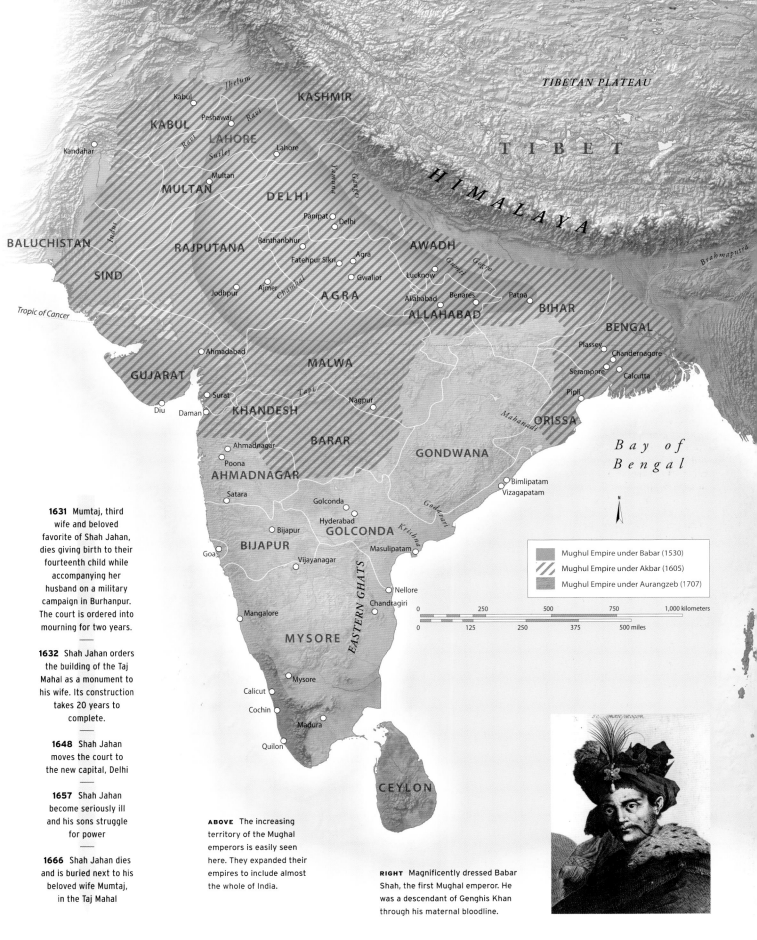

TIBETAN PLATEAU

Kabul
KABUL
Peshawar
Kandahar
KASHMIR
Jhelum
LAHORE
Ravi
Ravi
Lahore
Sutlej
Multan
MULTAN
BALUCHISTAN
SIND
Indus
RAJPUTANA
DELHI
Yamuna
Ganges
Panipat
Delhi
Ranthanbhur
Fatehpur Sikri
Agra
Gwalior
Jodhpur
Ajmer
Chambal
AGRA
Tropic of Cancer
AWADH
Lucknow
Gumti
Gogra
Allahabad
Benares
Patna
BIHAR
ALLAHABAD
BENGAL
Plassey
Chandernagore
Serampore
Calcutta
Pipli
ORISSA
Mahanadi
Ahmadabad
MALWA
GUJARAT
Surat
Tapi
Nagpur
Diu
Daman
KHANDESH
GONDWANA
BARAR
Bay of Bengal
Ahmadnagar
Poona
AHMADNAGAR
Godavari
Bimlipatam
Vizagapatam
Satara
Golconda
Hyderabad
Krishna
Bijapur
GOLCONDA
BIJAPUR
Masulipatam
Goa
Vijayanagar
Nellore
EASTERN GHATS
Chandragiri
Mangalore
Calicut
MYSORE
Cochin
Mysore
Madura
Quilon
CEYLON

HIMALAYA
TIBET
Brahmaputra

1631 Mumtaj, third wife and beloved favorite of Shah Jahan, dies giving birth to their fourteenth child while accompanying her husband on a military campaign in Burhanpur. The court is ordered into mourning for two years.

1632 Shah Jahan orders the building of the Taj Mahal as a monument to his wife. Its construction takes 20 years to complete.

1648 Shah Jahan moves the court to the new capital, Delhi

1657 Shah Jahan become seriously ill and his sons struggle for power

1666 Shah Jahan dies and is buried next to his beloved wife Mumtaj, in the Taj Mahal

ABOVE The increasing territory of the Mughal emperors is easily seen here. They expanded their empires to include almost the whole of India.

RIGHT Magnificently dressed Babar Shah, the first Mughal emperor. He was a descendant of Genghis Khan through his maternal bloodline.

Mughul Empire under Babar (1530)
Mughul Empire under Akbar (1605)
Mughul Empire under Aurangzeb (1707)

0   250   500   750   1,000 kilometers
0   125   250   375   500 miles

217

Great and Most Fortunate Navy

When the English and Spanish fleets met in combat in the English Channel during the summer of 1588, the result foreshadowed the centuries ahead.

It seemed unlikely at the time that the tiny island nation of England could defend itself from the military might of the Spanish Empire. But events perhaps reflected the sovereigns. The aging Spanish king was in decline, as was his empire. The beloved English Queen was at the height of her power.

Philip II of Spain

King Philip II of Spain (r. 1556–1598), an able administrator and model of virtue and devotion, had the unenviable task of defending the vast empire he had inherited, as well as a religion he believed under attack.

Elizabeth I of England

Queen Elizabeth I (r. 1558–1603), a supreme strategist in her own right, also carried the burden of inheritance. Her father Henry VIII (r. 1509–1547) had squandered monies from the royal coffers; her

> ...and think foul scorn that Parma or Spain, or any prince of Europe, should dare to invade the borders of my realm.
>
> –Elizabeth I in her address to the English army at Tilbury Fort, 1588.

brother Edward (r. 1547–1553) had allowed the nobility to regain authority; her sister Mary (r. 1553–1558) had reestablished the Catholic religion, plunging the country into revolt and disarray.

Cause

Philip did not lack reasons to subdue England's "virgin queen." However, it was Elizabeth's intervention in the Dutch Revolt in 1585 that convinced Philip to remove her from the throne. His determination only increased two years later when Elizabeth executed her Catholic cousin, Mary Stuart.

The king's plans for a naval victory suffered a significant setback with the death of the experienced commander Santa Cruz in February 1588. A reluctant Duke of Medina Sidonia replaced him at the helm of the 130 vessels, 18,000 soldiers, and 2,000 guns that comprised the Grande y Felicísima Armada (the great and most fortunate navy), which finally lumbered north on May 30, 1588, weathering storms and already fighting fatigue.

Battle Plan

The original plan had been for the Armada to meet up with the Duke of Parma's troops in Flanders.

While the Spanish galleons floated off the Flemish coast at the end of July, small squadrons of English ships troubled the Spanish and forced them up into the English Channel. Off Calais, Medina Sidonia and Parma were able to communicate, but only for Medina Sidonia to learn that it would be impossible to embark the Flanders army. Parma had no boats to ferry his men to the galleons and the great ships could not move closer to the shallows.

ABOVE Known as the Kitchener Portrait of Queen Elizabeth I, this image shows a determined and resolute ruler.

LEFT The *Ark Royal*, English flagship during the Spanish Armada, was a 38-gun frigate, bearing the Queen's and country's coats of arms.

RIGHT Although the Spanish chose what they thought was a safe route back to Spain to avoid further battle in the English Channel, many ships were lost during severe weather along the west coast of Ireland.

ATLANTIC OCEAN

Corunna
Oporto
PORTUGAL
Lisbon
Sevilla
Cadiz
Gibraltar
Tangier
Ceuta
Fez

Confrontation

The English took advantage of the situation by setting eight ships on fire on the night of August 7 and sending them drifting towards the resting Spanish. Recalling the havoc wrought by Dutch "hell burners" in 1585, the Spanish fleet panicked and cut their lines.

The following morning found the Great Armada scattered to the winds. Some of the ships managed to reassemble, and were duly attacked by the English, but by most accounts, the battles on August 8 were similar to any other day of fighting. However, the English had ships with greater maneuverability and firepower which, combined with bad weather, forced the Spanish east of the Channel. The Spanish chose to sail north around Scotland and Ireland to return home rather than risk another attack in the Channel. Despite the odds— lack of charts, weather, and illness—most of the fleet limped back to Spain.

The English continued to harass the Spanish, and Philip would send more armadas north. Nevertheless, the following centuries would see the power balance shift from the Mediterranean to northern Europe as economic power-houses, rather than military might, dominated European affairs.

ABOVE Queen Elizabeth I is seen here reviewing her troops at Tilbury Fort, in 1588. It was here she said she had "the body but of a weak and feeble woman"

1554 Mary I of England (Mary Tudor) marries Philip II of Spain

—

1558 Mary dies and is succeeded by her half-sister Elizabeth who refuses to marry Philip of Spain

—

August 1588 After years of political conflict, the English fleet destroys the Spanish Armada, killing 600 Spaniards and injuring around 800

—

September 21, 1588 Medina Sidonia's flagship arrives at Santander

—

October 23, 1588 After avoiding the English off the coast of Ireland, the remaining Spanish Armada returns to Santander

New France

Trading partnerships between French entrepreneurs and Native Americans laid the foundations of a French empire in North America, which eventually came to claim territory stretching from Hudson Bay and Labrador through the Great Lakes all the way down to New Orleans.

Under King Henry IV, the first permanent settlements took shape in the territory called Acadia (1604) and at Quebec City (1608). Several French chartered companies established forts and trading posts on the interior rivers and lakes that eventually consolidated into a single royal dominion, New France, in 1663.

This was not, by and large, a realm of European settlement and fixed frontiers. Apart from the villages of Quebec, Montreal, New Orleans, and the naval stronghold of Louisbourg, the French were thin on the ground.

Commercial and Religious Zeal

French traders known as *coureurs de bois* collected furs from the interior, and sped them along the rivers to the entrepots of the lower St. Lawrence. Competition for commercial advantage among Native American groups resulted in the spread of firearms and warfare. At the same time, idealistic French Jesuit missionaries began mounting a concerted and ambitious operation aimed at converting Indians to Christianity. Their written accounts of their endeavors over a period of nearly a century— the famous *Jesuit Relations*— occupy a high place among the annals of missionary zeal.

Conflict with Britain

Although they grew up during the same decades, the British colonies soon outstripped the French in population, urbanization, and wealth. When Louis XIV challenged Britain on a global scale in the long War of the Spanish Succession, the balance of power began to swing decisively toward the British. By the terms of the Treaty of Utrecht (1713), the French ceded territory they claimed on the southern shores of Hudson Bay, Newfoundland, and eastern Acadia (which the British renamed Nova Scotia. As part of an effort to consolidate their gains, British troops forced the migration of French-speaking Acadians to Louisiana.

The next great blow came in another worldwide conflict known in Europe as the Seven Years' War, which the colonists of British North America called the French and Indian War (1756–1763). British settlers had long regarded the French-Native American alliance as an obstacle to western expansion across the Appalachian Mountains. British troops and sea power combined to overwhelm French forces in a series of engagements culminating in the decisive battle of the Plains of Abraham at Québec in 1759. By the following year, French resistance had crumbled.

The Treaty of Paris that ended the war in 1763 put all of Canada under British rule, while Louisiana was transferred to Spain.

As Napoleon occupied Spain a flicker of excitement flared at the prospect of a renewed French empire in North America. However, scrambling to fund his wars, Napoleon sold the Louisiana territory, including all lands drained by the Mississippi River and its tributaries, to US President Thomas Jefferson in 1803. A French empire was extinguished as an American empire was born.

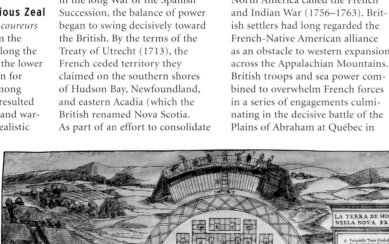

1524 Italian Giovanni da Verrazzano is the first European to discover present-day New York

1534 Jacques Cartier lands on the Gaspé Peninsula and claims the land for France, naming it Canada

1564 French settlement is established in Florida, south of Jacksonville

1608 Samuel de Champlain founds the city of Québec

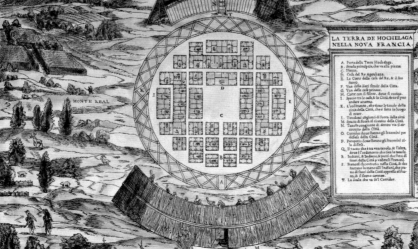

ABOVE This engraving from 1633 shows representations of First Nations peoples in New France.

LEFT This sixteenth-century engraving of New France, Canada, shows the meeting of people of the First Nations (Native Canadians) and Native Americans with early settlers outside a fort.

The real voyage of discovery consists not in seeking new landscapes but in having new eyes.

–Marcel Proust (1871-1922), French novelist and critic.

GREENLAND

Arctic Circle

Hudson Bay

LABRADOR

NEWFOUNDLAND

Plaisance

Fort Bourbon

Tadoussac

St Lawrence

Louisbourg

Québec

ACADIA

Fort Dauphin

Fort La Tour
(Fort St Marie)

Fort Richelieu

Port-Royal

Fort La Reine

NEW FRANCE

Montreal

Fort Chambly

Fort Saint Pierre

Fort Frontenac

Columbia

Missouri

Great Lakes

Fort Michillimakinac

Boston

Fort Orange
New York

Snake

Mississippi

Fort Beauharnois

Fort Detroit

Fort Duquesne

Philadelphia

Fort Crevecoeur

Baltimore

Missouri

UPPER LOUISIANA

Fort Orleans

Fort Saint-Louis

NORTH
ATLANTIC
OCEAN

Fort de Chartres

Arkansas

LOUISIANA

Canadian

APPALACHIAN MOUNTAINS

LOWER
LOUISIANA

Charleston

Colorado

Savannah

Fort Rosalie

Fort Toulouse

Mississippi

Baton
Rouge

Biloxi

Mobile

New Orleans

Tropic of Cancer

*Gulf of
Mexico*

PACIFIC
OCEAN

ABOVE The area known as Louisiana gave France a large portion of North America, much larger than that of the other colonial powers.

0   250   500   750   1,000 kilometers
0   125   250   375   500 miles

	French Territory
	British Territory
	French territory ceded to Great Britain in the Treaty of Utrecht (1713)
	Spanish Territory
	Fort

British Conquest

Encouraged by tales of rich lands of promise and wealth, British explorers headed off to settle and claim the great land of North America.

1584 Sir Walter Raleigh dispatches an expedition to explore the east coast of North America for settlement. The Outer Banks (North Carolina) are chosen.

1586 Sir Richard Grenville is assigned to further explore the possible colony. Ralph Lane is left in charge.

1587 Sir Walter Raleigh attempts a second expedition to North America

1589 Richard Hakluyt writes *The Principall Navigations, Voiages and Discoveries of the English Nation*, detailing eyewitness accounts of England's colonization

In 1584, the younger Richard Hakluyt's *Discourse of Western Planting* urged English colonization in North America, and Sir Walter Raleigh sent an exploratory voyage to Roanoke island. A second voyage in 1585 established a small colony under Ralph Lane that survived 10 months before being rescued in June 1586 by Sir Francis Drake.

Finally, in 1587, a settlement originally intended for Chesapeake Bay became the famous Lost Colony of Roanoke. A cryptic inscription on a tree, found by a relieving voyage in 1590, provided no explanation of the fate of 100 men, women, and children.

Plea for Assistance

A successful Roanoke colony had to be better funded than previous sixteenth-century expeditions, namely Martin Frobisher's scheme for temporary settlement in Newfoundland, Sir Humphrey Gilbert's project in the same area, and Sir Ferdinando Gorges' colony on the coast of Maine. Hakluyt's plea for royal finance for transatlantic voyages recognized that colonies needed more than was offered by merchants and companies seeking quick profits. But royal assistance continued to be confined to the granting of patents or licenses to hold on to what could be won.

However, inadequate funding did nothing to restrain optimism. If Frobisher's several voyages had dampened hopes of finding a northwest sea passage, ignorance of the breadth of the American continent kept alive hopes of easy westward access to the wealth of the Orient.

Propaganda

The Roanoke ventures were not mentioned explicitly in colonial promotional literature because the island appealed to some as a hidden base against Spain. So there could be no appeal for pioneering families more inclined to regard themselves as permanent settlers than adventurous plunderers. No matter what propaganda might say about humanitarian policies, Lane was more eager to emulate than shame Spain, believing "the discovery of a good mine…or a passage to the South Sea" would make the island worth development as a colony. Planners had always expected the Indians to be quickly dependent on the newcomers. But the English proved incapable of living without them, never managing to grow corn and never learning Indian techniques of building weirs to catch fish. They neglected agriculture in favor of an ambitious gold- and copper-seeking expedition that failed because it ran out of food.

Racial Disharmony

The only Indians favorably regarded were those who chose to assist the colonists by sowing corn and constructing new fish-weirs for them. When they refused to do more, Lane wrote of a treacherous "conspiracy." Although a report written by Thomas Hariot played down racial disharmony for promotional reasons, he admitted some of the

ABOVE Sir Walter Raleigh, a favorite of Elizabeth I, was a force behind the early attempts at colonization of the New World.

English " showed themselves too fierce, in slaying some of the people, in some towns, upon causes that on our part, might easily enough have been borne withal."

Ignoring History

The failures of would-be English colonizers in the sixteenth century might have been expected to make their seventeenth-century successors more realistic about the vast differences between North America and the rich civilizations of Mexico and Peru so spectacularly plundered by Spanish conquistadors. But the financial, administrative, and personnel failures of the early Roanoke colonies were largely ignored by future colonizers.

It was as if nobody involved in the Virginia enterprise had read the accounts of Lane, Hariot, or Hakluyt, as its settlers had failed to sow crops, wandered hopelessly in search of non-existent goldmines and gateways to the Orient, and fulminated against Indians who saved them from famine with food supplies before wreaking vengeance against their invasion.

LEFT Martin Frobisher, adventurer and colonizer, is portrayed in this artwork with his men, involved in a skirmish with Eskimos during one of his expeditions.

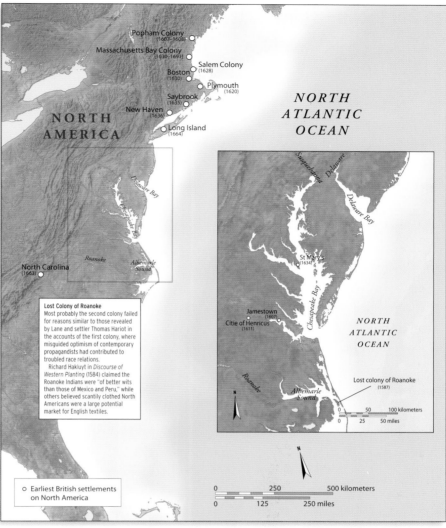

Lost Colony of Roanoke
Most probably the second colony failed for reasons similar to those revealed by Lane and settler Thomas Hariot in the accounts of the first colony, where misguided optimism of contemporary propagandists had contributed to troubled race relations.
Richard Hakluyt in *Discourse of Western Planting* (1584) claimed the Roanoke Indians were "of better wits than those of Mexico and Peru," while others believed scantily clothed North Americans were a large potential market for English textiles.

○ Earliest British settlements on North America

ABOVE Roanoke Island sits at the entrance to Chesapeake Bay on the east coast of North America. Over 100 men, women, and children perished in the second attempt at colonization.

LEFT Ralph Lane and his crew take on salt during their unsuccessful attempt to establish a colony at Roanoke Island.

223

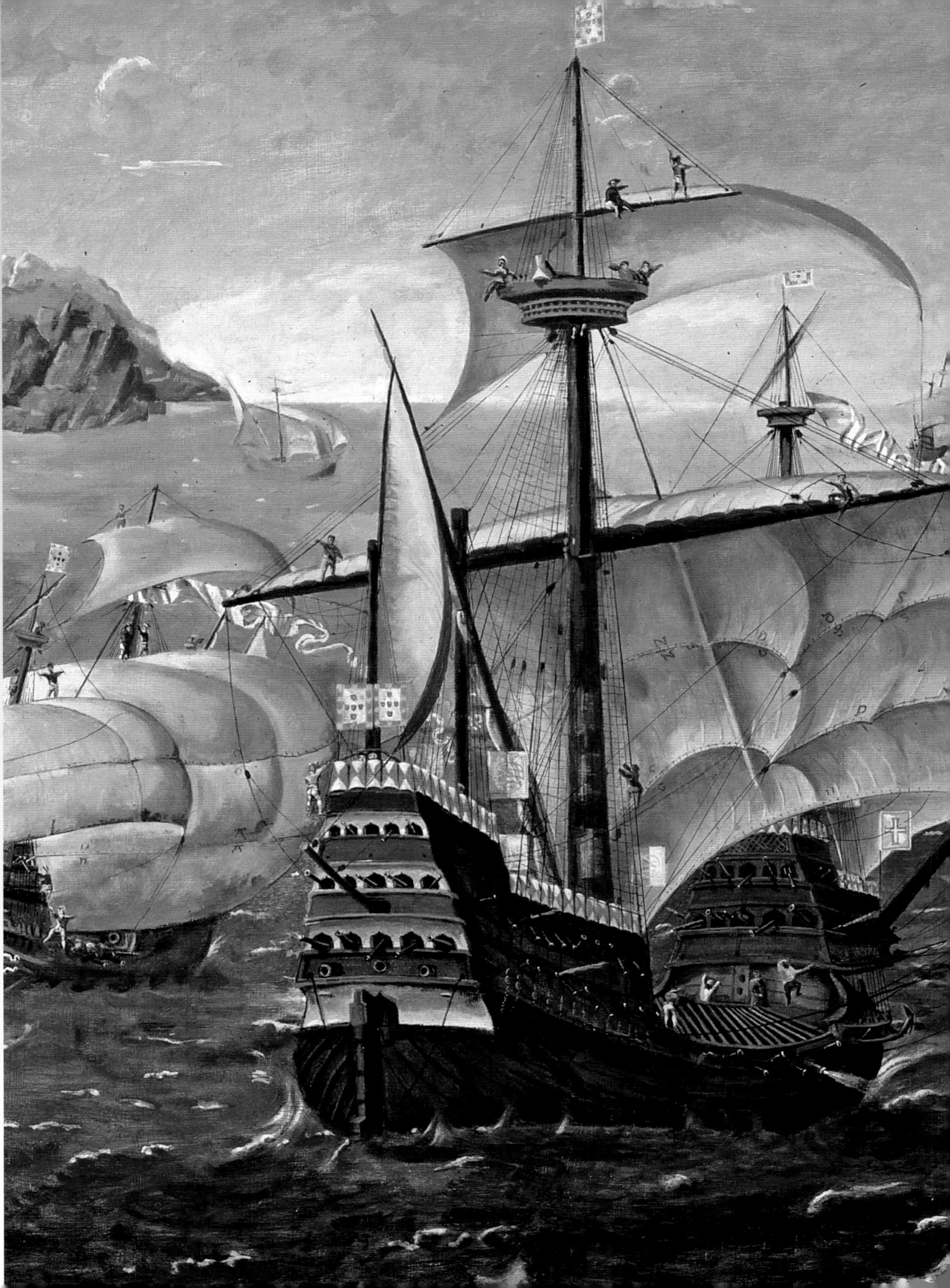

Favorable Wind

During the course of just four decades, beginning in the 1480s, expeditions by sea from the Atlantic seaboard of Europe changed entirely the medieval concept of the world, and established the feasibility of maritime trade routes to the East.

RIGHT This watercolor shows a Venetian carrack from the fourteenth century plying the trade routes to the East.

LEFT Portuguese vessels of the early sixteenth century are depicted here under full sail.

BELOW Fearful of bad winds and weather, many sailors sought protection and safekeeping from the Virgin of the Navigators.

PREVIOUS PAGES This altarpiece detail shows ships of the Spanish fleet at the time of the conquest of the New World.

The impetus for this remarkable seaborne enterprise was mainly commercial. European demand for spices from the East had existed since antiquity. Commodities such as pepper, cinnamon, cloves, and nutmeg were used to enhance the flavor of food, and like drugs, perfumes, and dyes, were extremely scarce in Europe and consequently very expensive.

Restricted Trade

The demand was met by a very complex network of overland caravan routes, and by small ships sailing the Indian Ocean, all converging on the Levant. As the spices were transported towards the Mediterranean, the trade was increasingly in the hands of Muslim merchants. This became of particular concern to the Christian nations of Europe when the Muslim faith spread to spice-producing regions in the fifteenth century.

In many ways the state of trade was unsatisfactory to European-consumers. Supplies of spices were occasionally cut off or restricted, and a papal ban on trading with Muslims was bypassed only by Venice and Genoa, which had commercial agreements with Muslim merchants. Other nations, initially those at the western end of the Mediterranean, sought to trade direct with those regions where spices were produced but in the mid-fifteenth century no direct sea route eastwards was known.

Ship Design

The largest ships at this time were inadequate for ocean voyaging but developments in naval architecture brought into being the three-masted ship, combining a strong capacious hull with a handy rig. By the mid-1400s the islands off the Atlantic coast had been visited and settled and Portuguese seafarers were pushing down the west African coast.

Patronage

With the patronage of Prince Henry the Navigator of Portugal, successive voyages led to a rounding of the Cape of Good Hope by Bartolomeu Dias in 1487 and the landfall of Vasco da Gama on the coast of India in 1498.

Six years before, in 1492, Christopher Columbus was successful in gaining backing for a voyage westward across the Atlantic that he expected would bring him to Cathay (China) and Cipangu (Japan) after sailing just 2,400 nautical miles from the Canary Islands. His first voyage was considered a success and evidence of a short passage to the East. This was shown later not to be the case and it was not until 1519 that Ferdinand Magellan passed round the tip of South America and established a route west to the spice islands.

Setting Course

Northern European nations were forced to look for other ways east, especially after the Treaty of Tordesillas had given papal authority to a division of the world into Portuguese and Spanish spheres of interest. The only alternative was to look in the high northern latitudes and attempt a passage either westwards across the top of the American continent or eastwards, passing to the north of Asia.

The search for the Northwest Passage had its origins in 1496 when King Henry VII of England granted authority to John Cabot to make voyages of discovery. In the course of his first voyage Cabot rediscovered Newfoundland, first sighted by Norsemen in the eleventh century, and thought it might be the northwestern extremity of Asia. Subsequent expeditions, notably under Cartier, Frobisher, Davis, Hudson, and Baffin, discounted this, but failed to find an open passage westwards.

Even as the hunt continued to the northwest, attention turned in the opposite direction and in 1553 an expedition, to be commanded by Sir Hugh Willoughby, was fitted out by merchants in London with the purpose of seeking a northeast passage. Over the course of the next 55 years similar expeditions with the same aim, led most notably by Willem Barents and Henry Hudson, met with equal disappointment.

The only practicable passage eastwards lay by way of the Cape of Good Hope and this became the established trade route until the opening of the Suez Canal in 1869.

Portuguese Crusade

In the fifteenth century, the Portuguese monarchy backed a highly rational strategy of exploration based on established facts—that the Indian Ocean lay east of the African continent.

The driving force of the Portuguese was the immense wealth and experience gained from expanding the monarchy's territory at the expense of the Muslim realms which had acquired control of almost the whole Iberian Peninsula between the eighth and eleventh centuries.

Battle of Ceuta

In the early fifteenth century, the Portuguese crusade went to sea. As water-borne trade had expanded between the Mediterranean Sea and northern Europe, the Portuguese had been well placed to keep up with the latest advances in maritime technology and naval gunnery. Their progress was signaled spectacularly when one of their naval expeditions took the port of Ceuta on the North African coast in 1415, a piece of valuable territory they were to hold for many hundreds of years.

Gold Coast

After reaching the island of Madeira in 1418, the Portuguese found little of value until they arrived at the Senegal River in 1446, where they learned that inland lay an important kingdom, Mali, supposed to be rich in gold and slaves. However, because its ruler was a Muslim, a certain enemy, it was clear that they would need to travel farther south in search of allies.

Only after they had passed Sierra Leone in 1460, and sailed on to the Bight of Benin, did they find non-Muslim rulers and richer possibilities for trade. The prospects of trading for precious metals sparkled brightly enough that they named this region the Gold Coast and the fort they established there São Jorge da Mina (The Mine).

Bartolomeu Dias

One of the members of the 1481 expedition to the Gold Coast was Bartolomeu Dias—in English, Diaz—a nobleman of the royal household, whose talents won him a far more ambitious and challenging commission in 1486. His orders were to sail south until he had rounded the southern tip of the continent and enter the Indian Ocean. If possible, he should establish friendly relations with a Christian land—probably Ethiopia—on the farther coast.

Diaz first made for the mouth of the Congo River—reached in 1482 by his countryman, Diogo Cão. Then he made his way south until reaching Walvis Bay—Whalefish Bay. From this point his ship was swept south for 13 days by ferocious storms that drove him out of sight of land. When the winds abated, he turned eastward but failed to regain the African coastline. Suspecting that he might have already achieved his first objective, Diaz set his course to the north, landing eventually at the place now known as Mossel Bay on February 3, 1488. After further progress up the coast as far as the Great Fish River, Diaz turned back, convinced that no further obstacle barred a passage to India. On his return voyage he rounded the Cape, which he named the Cape of Storms, but which his royal patron, King John II, insisted on calling the Cape of Good Hope.

Securing the Route

Diaz participated in another major discovery when, along with Pedro Cabral in 1500, the ship's initial course was set southwest in what proved to be a justifiable hope of finding more reliable winds to sweep them round the Cape. In the process, they touched the coast of Brazil. Within just a few years, the dreams of Henry the Navigator had been fulfilled and future Portuguese prosperity assured. The long and unprofitable business of following the African coast was over.

> No wind serves him who addresses his voyage to no certain port.
>
> –Michel de Montaigne (1533-1592), French philosopher and writer.

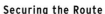

1419 Prince Henry the Navigator establishes an observatory and navigation school at Sagres

1439 Portuguese claim the Azores Islands

1451 Sailors from Portugal regularly visit the Senegal River

1460 Prince Henry the Navigator dies

1482 Portuguese erect a fort at El Mina (Elmina) on the Gold Coast (Ghana)

LEFT This rich fifteenth-century tapestry shows Portuguese soldiers led by King Alfonso V entering Tangiers, Morocco.

ABOVE Founded by the Portuguese in 1482, the Castelo de São Jorge d2 Mina still stands in the town of Elmina, Ghana.

SCOTLAND

IRELAND

WALES
ENGLAND

FRANCE

HOLY
ROMAN
EMPIRE

POLAND

HUNGARY

Black Sea

OTTOMAN EMPIRE

Caspian Sea

PORTUGAL

SPAIN

○ Lisbon

○ Sagres

Tangier ○○ Ceuta

MARINIDS ZAYYANIDS HAFSIDS

Madeira

Occupied in various ages by the Carthaginians, Romans, Visigoths, Byzantines, and Moors, Ceuta was seized by the Portuguese in 1415.

Mediterranean Sea

Porto Santo Island was discovered by two Portuguese captains, João Gonçalves Zarco and Tristão Vaz Terceira in 1418. Madeira Island was discovered a year later.

Libyan Desert

MAMLUK
SULTANATE
OF EGYPT

Red Sea

ARABIA

*Sahara
Desert*

MALI

Timbuktu ○ *Niger*

○ Jenne

Senegal

A F R I C A

Gulf of Aden

In 1460 Portuguese explorer Pedro da Cintra named the region Serra de Leão–Lion Mountains.

○ Sierra Leone

ETHIOPIA

Gold Coast

○ Owo

*Bight of
Benin*

Elmina ○

KINGDOM
OF BENIN

Mogadishu ○

Portuguese explorer Diogo Cão was the first European to sail this far south down the west coast of Africa. In 1482. he sighted the mouth of a large river, the Congo, and planted a cross ("padrão"). He sent envoys to the king of Mbanza-Kongo before returning to Portugal.

Malindi ○
(Portuguese ally 1512)

Mombasa ○

In 1471, the Portuguese were the first Europeans to land at present-day Elmina. In 1482, they built a fort called São Jorge da Mina, on land taken from the Fante people–the first permanent European construction in West Africa.

BELOW This portrait of Bartolomeu Diaz shows him holding an early compass.

Congo

Ponta Padrão ○

Zanzibar ○
(taken by Portuguese 1503)

*SOUTH
ATLANTIC
OCEAN*

KINGDOM OF
THE KONGO

Kilwa ○
(taken by Portuguese 1505)

NDONGO

Zambezi

Mozambique ○
(taken by Portuguese 1505)

Mozambique Channel

ZIMBABWE

MADAGASCAR

RIGHT Bad weather swept Diaz farther south than intended, took him around the Cape of Good Hope and showed him a clear passage to India.

In 1487, Bartolomeu Dias on his way south, sailed into a safe water haven he called Golfo de Santa Maria da Conceição. This deep-water natural harbor was later named Walvis Bay.

Walvis Bay ○

*Kalahari
Desert*

Limpopo

Return voyage

Bahia dos Vaqueiros (later named Mossel Bay) was the first landfall for Bartolomeu Dias after he had in 1488 sailed around the tip of Africa. He took on fresh supplies and sailed up to the Great Fish River before returning to Portugal.

Great Fish

*INDIAN
OCEAN*

Route of Bartolomeu Dias expedition to Indian Ocean (1486–1488)

Cape of Storms ○ Mossel Bay ○
(Cape of Good Hope)

N

0   250   500   750   1,000 kilometers

0 125 250 275 500 miles

229

The New World

Christopher Columbus (1451-1506) made four voyages to the "Indies." The first was the initial stage of the permanent colonization of the continent of America. The succeeding three enlarged on the area of discovery of the first voyage, embracing the whole Caribbean Sea.

BELOW The huge monument honoring Christopher Columbus in Barcelona, Spain, includes eight scenes from his life, in bronze bas-relief.

The very limited understanding of the world's oceans and continents before the great European expansion of the sixteenth century is illustrated by a remark of the astronomer Paolo Toscanelli who wrote "the shortest route to eastern Asia is due west from Lisbon across the Ocean."

Seeking Patronage

Born in Genoa in 1451, Christopher Columbus was at sea by the age of 14 and had a number of adventures before arriving in Lisbon.

For years Columbus persisted in attempting to raise interest in his "Enterprise of the Indies" but was turned down by John II of Portugal, Henry VII of England, and Charles VIII of France. Twice he was refused by Ferdinand and Isabella of Spain, before they agreed to his proposal in 1492.

In return for his endeavors Columbus asked for, and received, ennoblement, the rank of Admiral of the Ocean and the governorship of all islands and mainlands that should be discovered.

First Voyage

On August 3, 1492, Columbus sailed from Palos, on the Rio Tinto, in the *Santa Maria*, in company with the much smaller caravels *Niña* and *Pinta*. On September 6, after topping up with stores, the ships made their departure from Gomera, in the Canary Islands.

Columbus expected to sail less than 3,000 nautical miles to reach Japan, and on October 12, after sailing an estimated 3,466 nautical miles, he made landfall on an island of the Bahamas that he named San Salvador. This island Columbus considered to be an outlier of Japan.

From San Salvador, Columbus sailed southwest and on October 28, having touched at a number of other Bahamian islands on the way,

c. 1477-1484 A young Christopher Columbus begins his adventures sailing in merchant vessels to Iceland

1492 Columbus alters course on his first voyage, sailing to the southwest and missing Florida

November 15, 1492 Christopher Columbus makes the first recorded reference to tobacco

1494 Spain and Portugal sign the Treaty of Tordesillas establishing a line of demarcation 370 leagues west of the Azores. Portugal claims new land discovered to the east and Spain claims the west.

RIGHT On his first voyage Columbus thought he had reached Cipangu (Japan).

FAR RIGHT Admiral Christopher Columbus is portrayed here by Spanish artist José Roldan.

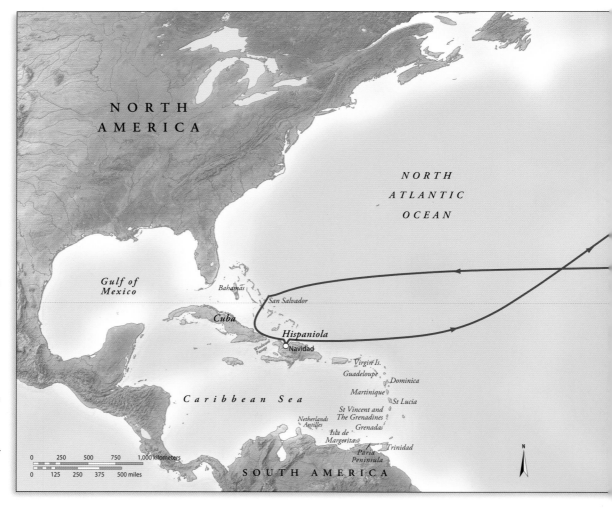

RIGHT During his first voyage, Columbus established the settlement of Navidad. Unfortunately, none of the original inhabitants survived.

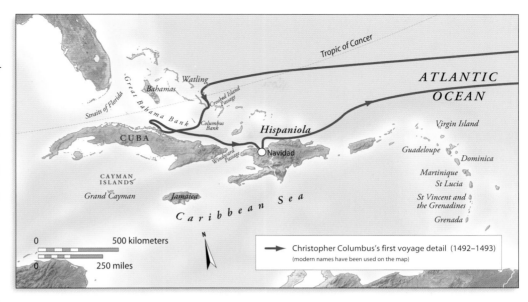

Christopher Columbus's first voyage detail (1492–1493)
(modern names have been used on the map)

went ashore on the island of Cuba which he believed to be Cipangu (Japan). After exploring part of the north coast, Columbus crossed the Windward Passage and found Haiti, naming it Hispaniola. It was here, while under sail in calm weather, that the *Santa Maria* ran on to a reef in Caracol Bay and had to be abandoned—an accident which created the first, although involuntary, European settlement in the New World.

Columbus named his enforced base ashore Navidad, commemorating Christmas Day, the date of his arrival. There he built a fort and decided that 40 men were to be left to man it, begin cultivation

Following the light of the sun, we left the Old World.
–Christopher Columbus.

of crops, and search for sources of gold. After further investigation of the north coast of Hispaniola, the *Niña* and *Pinta* made their departure on January 16, 1493.

The winter passage homewards proved more difficult than that outward. The wind that had served him then was now against him, and his two ships were worn and worm-eaten. On February 12, the

Niña and *Pinta* lost contact south of the Azores in heavy weather, and the *Niña*, with Columbus on board, found itself off Santa Maria, the most southerly of the Portuguese Azores, where he put in for shelter.

Setting sail again with some difficulty, Columbus was then forced to shelter again, this time in the Tagus River in Portugal.

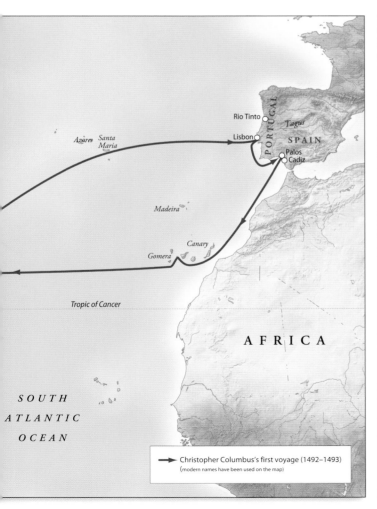

Christopher Columbus's first voyage (1492–1493)
(modern names have been used on the map)

On March 15, 1493, the *Niña* anchored off Palos. The *Pinta* arrived on the same tide. Columbus was received at the Spanish court where his privileges were confirmed. It was accepted that he had found Cipangu by the westerly route and plans for a second voyage, to capitalize on the discovery, were put in hand.

Second Voyage

The second voyage, on which Columbus sailed from Cadiz on September 25, 1493, was a much larger expedition than the first. Seventeen ships, including the *Niña*, left Spain with more than 1,200 men, many of whom were intended to be colonists. On November 3, after an uneventful voyage, the island of Dominica was sighted and the ships came to anchor off the nearby island of Maria Galante.

After sailing further and also naming each of the Leeward Islands, Columbus arrived back in Caracol Bay, on Hispaniola, but found no one alive of the garrison left at Navidad. A second settlement was established inland, at Isabela. On February 2, 12 ships were despatched home with quantities of gold and what were assumed to be spices. Columbus spent the next five months sailing west along the south coast of Cuba in an attempt to prove that the island was a peninsula of China but turned back shortly before reaching its western tip. During this passage the island of Jamaica was discovered.

Third Voyage

On his third voyage westward, Columbus achieved the first landing by a European on the South American continent, but the voyage ended in disgrace. He intended to make landfall further south than he had so far ventured, in the hope of discovering a new continent.

Just three ships sailed this time, making landfall in the vicinity of the island of Trinidad, which he named near the end of July 1498. While in the vicinity of Trinidad,

RIGHT On Columbus's return to the settlement of Navidad, he found no survivors. A second settlement was established at Isabela before the ships returned home with gold and spices.

Columbus noticed the massive amount of brown water pouring into the sea from the river Orinoco and guessed correctly that this could only be flowing from a continental river. He landed on the Paria Peninsula and became the first European to set foot on the South American mainland, although he was still convinced that he was in Asia.

Crossing the Caribbean, Columbus arrived in Santo Domingo—which had succeeded Isabela as the principal settlement on Hispaniola—to find a revolt in progress. Few remained loyal to him and he had to come to terms with the rebels. Columbus's privileges as viceroy and admiral were effectively ended when he was replaced as governor and his successor sent

him home in chains. He was, however, reconciled by the grant of a fourth voyage.

Fourth Voyage

This began at Cadiz on May 11, 1502, and had the object of exploring further west and discovering a passage through to the Indian Ocean. As yet the intervening Pacific Ocean was unknown.

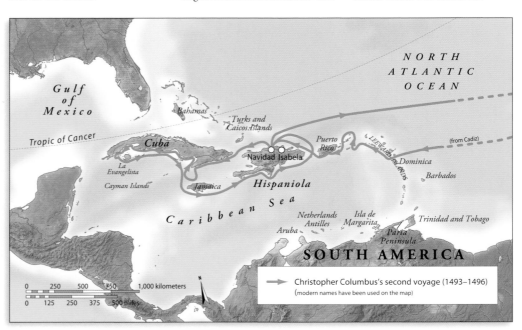

NORTH ATLANTIC OCEAN

Gulf of Mexico

Bahamas

Tropic of Cancer

Cuba

Turks and Caicos Islands

Puerto Rico

(from Cadiz)

Navidad Isabela

La Evangelista

Dominica

Cayman Islands

Barbados

Jamaica

Hispaniola

Caribbean Sea

Netherlands Antilles

Isla de Margarita

Trinidad and Tobago

Aruba

Paria Peninsula

SOUTH AMERICA

| 0 | 250 | 500 | 750 | 1,000 kilometers |
| 0 | 125 | 250 | 375 | 500 miles |

N

→ Christopher Columbus's second voyage (1493–1496)
(modern names have been used on the map)

LEFT The departure of Columbus on his first voyage, with the caravels *Santa Maria, Nina,* and *Pinta.*

RIGHT Convinced he was in Asia, Columbus was the first European to set foot in South America.

BELOW Columbus' fourth voyage was treated with some indifference and he died a few years later, still believing he had found a passage to Asia.

BOTTOM Later hailed as a glorious and hallowed event, the landing of Columbus in America is depicted by Spanish artist Dioscora de la Puebla.

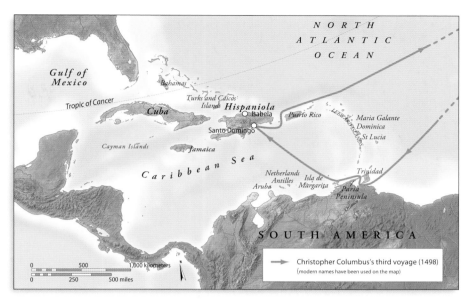

Christopher Columbus's third voyage (1498)
(modern names have been used on the map)

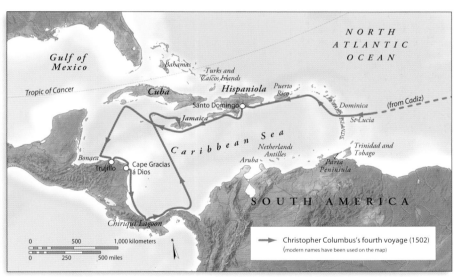

Christopher Columbus's fourth voyage (1502)
(modern names have been used on the map)

After passing through the islands of the Lesser Antilles, Columbus anchored off Santo Domingo before sailing on westward until he came upon Bonaca island, in the Gulf of Honduras. He met with the mainland at the point where the Honduran city of Trujillo now stands. Turning eastwards, he rounded Cape Gracias á Dios, which he named, and then sailed southward to anchor in Chiriqui Lagoon, in what is now Panama. Columbus was unaware that he was then only a short distance across the isthmus from a great ocean.

Homecoming

Disappointed at finding no passage further west, he turned back. In the two ships left to him he eventually made Jamaica, where these vessels were found to be unseaworthy. After many trials along the way, Columbus arrived back in Spain in November 1504. His principal patron, Queen Isabella, had died that year and King Ferdinand was now indifferent to him. It was, by then, becoming more commonly acknowledged that Asia lay much further to the west. Nevertheless, Columbus died in 1506 believing still that he had opened up a new route to the riches of the East.

North to the Unknown

Unlike Columbus, John Cabot and his son Sebastian failed to make proper accounts of their voyages. All we really know is that John made the first recorded landing on the North American continent since the Vikings.

> ...sayled in this tracte so farre towarde the weste, that the Ilande of Cuba bee on my lefte hande, in manere in the same degree of longitude.
>
> –John Cabot

Columbus was not alone in his belief that a way to Cathay lay open to the west. An Italian navigator named Giovanni Caboto had formed the same opinion and while Columbus was setting out for home on his second voyage to the Indies, John Cabot (c. 1451–1498), as he was known in England, was receiving from Henry VII authority to "to seeke out, discover, and finde" new lands.

Northern Passage

King Henry knew that any venture towards Cathay was likely to be resented by Spain and Portugal, so Cabot was limited to a northern passage to lessen the affront. This suited Cabot, who believed that Columbus had not yet approached the mainland of Asia, despite what he claimed.

North America

Little evidence remains to piece together the story of Cabot's voyage. After an initial aborted attempt to get away during the summer of 1496, when he had to put back to Bristol, Cabot sailed west in the *Matthew* in May 1497.

We do not know where it was that, on June 24, Cabot found land—most likely it was Newfoundland, which received the credit by being so named. Wherever it was that Cabot first touched on the North American continent, he went ashore and took possession of the land in the name of King Henry. He assumed he was standing somewhere in Cathay (China) or Cipangu (Japan), possibly on a peninsula or an offshore island. He had, in reality, made the first recorded landing on the continent since the Norse voyages to the region ceased in the eleventh century.

It is likely that Cabot coasted to the south for a month or so. Finding no sign that the country was rich in spices or the other exotic commodities of the East, he sailed for home in July, making a fast passage back. He returned empty-handed but the King was sufficiently impressed to grant him a second voyage.

Into the Unknown

In May 1498, Cabot sailed once more from Bristol. This time he had five ships. The intention was to establish a trading station and on board the ships were goods to be traded for the produce to be found in Cipangu.

One of the ships turned back due to stress of weather but the remainder sailed on into historical obscurity. No more is recorded of the fleet or of John Cabot himself. There are, however, intriguing fragments of inconclusive evidence that suggest he reached the American coast, but the voyage and the fate of Cabot and his crew remain shrouded in mystery.

Sebastian Cabot

It is thought that Sebastian Cabot (c. 1481–1557), one of John Cabot's three sons, may have sailed with his father on his first voyage.

Whether or not he did, he was able to use his family connections to raise the necessary financial backing to set out westwards in 1508. Again, there is little evidence for this voyage but it's possible that Sebastian sailed into Hudson Strait before being forced to turn back.

If this is so, it seems likely that Sebastian had realized that Cathay lay much further westwards and was attempting to discover a passage there north of the landmass his father had discovered. It is reasonable to suppose that his course, so much more northerly than that of his father, indicates this new appreciation.

On his return to Bristol in 1509, Sebastian found that Henry VII had died and interest in voyages of discovery was dormant. No further English expedition in search of the Northwest Passage was to be despatched until 1576.

ABOVE Henry VII is shown here with John and Sebastian Cabot. Henry funded their voyages in the hope of finding the Northwest Passage to Asia.

RIGHT John Cabot, together with his son Sebastian, receives the blessing of the Church before departing on England's first voyage to North America.

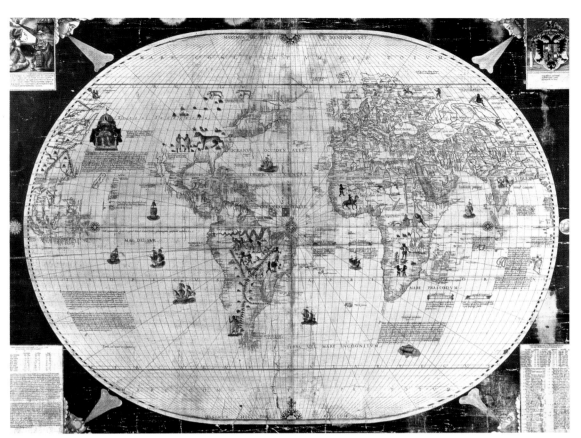

ABOVE In later life Sebastian Cabot (1474–c. 1557) became Spain's Pilot-Major and Great Pilot of England.

RIGHT Although he kept few records, Sebastian Cabot did design this map of the world in 1544.

1474 John Cabot marries Mattea and has three sons, Ludovico, Sebastiano, and Sancto

c. 1490 John Cabot and his family move to Bristol, England, where John hopes to gain patronage for his expedition

1497 Upon his return, John Cabot is given a gift of £3 for having found the new island. He is also granted a pension of £20 a year.

1499 Although there is no record of Cabot's death, his pension continued to be paid until this date

Vasco da Gama–World Trader

Born into a seafaring family, explorer Vasco da Gama (1460-1524) was the first to discover an ocean trading route from Portugal to India.

1415 Prince Henry the Navigator embarks on an expedition to Africa

1424 A Portuguese navigation chart is produced showing a land called Antilia near the West Indies

1492 Christopher Columbus discovers the Americas

1479 After a four-year war, Spain agrees to a Portuguese trade monopoly along the west coast of Africa

1521 Ferdinand Magellan begins his voyage to circumnavigate the world. He dies on the way and his crew complete the voyage

Vasco da Gama was born into a noble Portuguese family although his mother was of English origin. Little is known of Vasco da Gama's early life but it is thought that he formally studied mathematics and navigation and that he was accomplished in astronomy. He was certainly a proven seafarer and fighter.

Beyond the Cape

At the instigation of the king of Portugal, Manuel I the Fortunate, an expedition was mounted to ascertain whether there was a route to the Indian Ocean and beyond. Bartolomeu Dias had already rounded Africa's Cape of Good Hope in 1488, in an historic event that was the culmination of a generation of Portuguese sea exploration fostered by Prince Henry the Navigator.

In January 1497, the command of the expedition was conferred upon Vasco da Gama, and in July 1497, a fleet of four vessels sailed from Lisbon. Vasco was supported by a crew of about 150 men, his brother Paulo, and Nicoláo Coelho, both commanding separate ships, along with a supply ship. By the beginning of November they anchored in St. Helena Bay and, later that month, in Mossel Bay

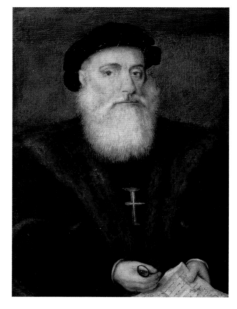

RIGHT During his many voyages to India, Vasco da Gama was often threatened by Arab traders. As a result he developed a deep suspicion of Muslims.

LEFT This portrait by an unknown artist shows Vasco da Gama in his later years. He was 64 years old when he died, in India.

> We left from Restelo one Saturday, the 8th day of July of the said year, 1479, on our journey. May God our Lord allow us to complete it in His service, Amen.
>
> –*Vasco da Gama: The Diary of His Travels through African Waters* by Eric Axelson, Stephan Phillips © 1988.

on the southern African coast. On December 16, the fleet arrived at the hitherto furthest Portuguese landing point, where they named the coast Natal, on Christmas Day, the day of discovery.

Rival Traders

By the end of January 1498, da Gama reached the mouth of the Zambesi River, then under the influence of Arab traders. They were later menaced by the Arabs in Mozambique and Mombasa who feared that commerce would be threatened. But the Portuguese were received in a friendly manner at Melinda—Malindi—East Africa. At Malindi, da Gama erected a pillar to record his landing that still stands there. They finally reached the harbor of Calicut, India, on May 20, 1498, with the guidance of an Arab pilot.

Da Gama was initially well received by the king of Calicut, the principal entrepot port on the Malabar coast of India. As a trading and transshipment center, Calicut's traders included many

LEFT Known as a cruel commander, da Gama is said to have attacked an Arab ship carrying Muslim pilgrims, all of whom were killed, on one of his voyages.

Ter

Cape Verde

Tropic of Capricorn

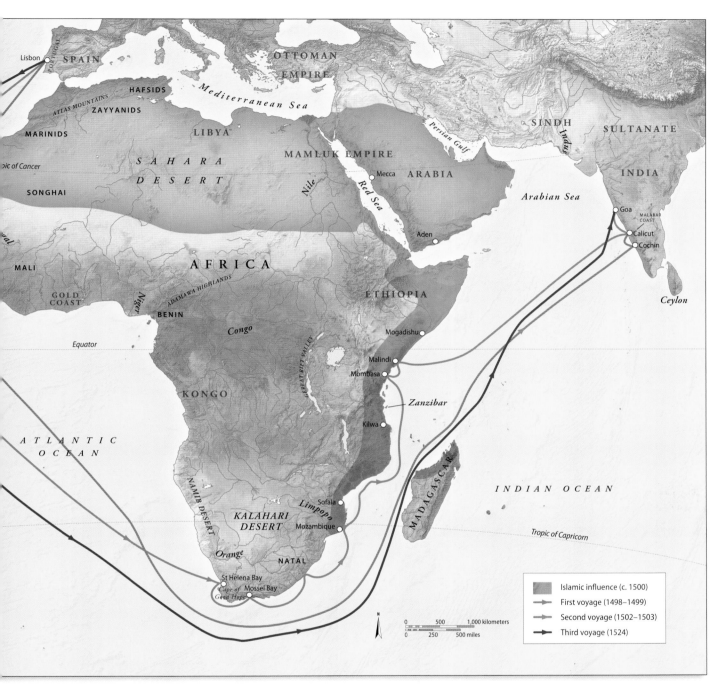

merchants from Mecca, Ceylon, Persia, Syria, Turkey, and Ethiopa. After some violent resistance from Arab merchants, da Gama was told to pay a large tax and leave all of his trading goods. Instead, the expedition left with da Gama taking his goods with him, along with some Indian hostages.

He arrived back in Portugal in September 1499 with many crew-members dying from scurvy along the way. Paulo, da Gama's older brother, also died on the expedition.

However, upon his return to Lisbon, da Gama was treated as a hero and was amply rewarded by the king.

Second Voyage
King Manuel sent da Gama, now an admiral, on another expedition to India in 1502. On this second trip he took 20 armed ships—anticipating problems from the Muslim traders—in order to demonstrate his military strength. The fleet reached Cochin in November 1502, and was given a favorable reception. After many negotiations with Muslim merchants who held the monopoly, prices for spices were agreed upon and a Portuguese agent remained behind to run a factory for the Portuguese. Da Gama later demanded a commercial monopoly over trade in the Indian Ocean and Malabar coast.

Suspicions and Cruelty
Vasco da Gama was known to be a very harsh commander. On his second voyage to India, it is said that he seized a ship returning from Mecca, embargoed all the cargo, then ordered the crew locked in the hold and the ship set on fire. It took four days to sink, killing everyone on board.

Return
After King Manuel's death, King John III sent da Gama again to India as a Portuguese viceroy. He died there of an illness, on December 24, 1524. His remains were returned to Portugal for burial.

Around the World

Ferdinand Magellan is recognized as having made the first circumnavigation of the world. However, he was killed in the Philippines, and his incredible voyage was completed by his crew, with one ship and only about 20 men surviving the hardships.

RIGHT This portrait of Ferdinand Magellan (1480–1521) is by an unknown artist. Magellan was the first explorer to lead an expedition around the globe.

BELOW The Magellan Strait is detailed in this drawing from folio 13 of the *Hydrographic Atlas of 1571* by Fernan Vaz Dourada.

In 1519, a Portuguese named Fernão de Magalhães approached Charles I, of Spain, seeking support for a voyage that would look for a way to the Spice Islands between the landmass of the supposed Great Southern Continent and the continent of South America. Magellan—as Magalhães is now better known—had sailed to India round the Cape of Good Hope and may have reached the East Indies. He believed that the coast of Cipangu (Japan) lay within reach of Panama and first put his notion of reaching those lands by the west-about

> The Church says the earth is flat, but I know that it is round, for I have seen the shadow on the moon, and I have more faith in a shadow than in the Church.
> —Ferdinand Magellan (c. 1480–1521).

route before King Manuel, the Portuguese monarch, but had been refused patronage. Turning to Spain, Magellan met with success when he petitioned Charles and was appointed captain-general of an expedition to prove his belief.

Departure

On September 20, 1519, the year in which Charles became Charles V, Holy Roman Emperor, Magellan sailed from Sanlúcar de Barrameda, near Cadiz, with five ships, the *Trinidad*, *San Antonio*, *Concepción*, *Victoria*, and *Santiago*. He sailed south down the African coast as far as Sierra Leone, possibly to avoid any Portuguese ships that might be sent out to intercept him, but certainly this gave him the shortest passage between the African and South American mainlands. On October 18, Magellan struck out west across the Atlantic.

Repairs and Refit

Six weeks later, on November 29, the coast of Brazil near Recife was sighted, and Magellan coasted southward. After spending two weeks in December refitting near where Rio de Janeiro now stands, and three weeks on the Plate River searching in vain for a strait leading westward, the ships arrived at Port St Julián, close to the latitude of the Falkland Islands, at the end of March.

It was then the beginning of the southern winter and Magellan decided to halt at Port St Julián to await better weather.

Mutiny

While on his way south in the Atlantic, Magellan had subdued a near mutiny, and at Port St Julián he faced another.

Some among his crews wished to return to Spain or to the Plate River where the winter climate would be more comfortable. Magellan suppressed the revolt firmly, executing one of the ringleaders and marooning ashore two more on August 24 when he sailed from Port St Julián.

During his stay there, one of his ships, the *Santiago*, which he had sent south to reconnoiter, was wrecked along the coast.

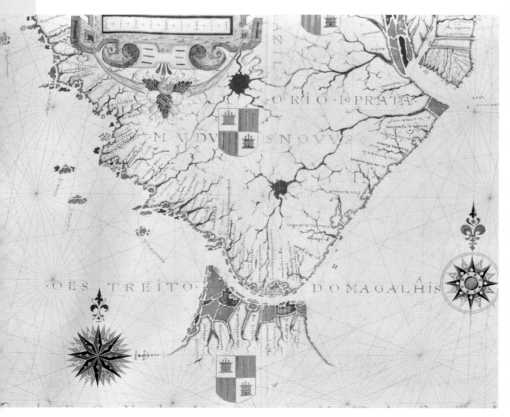

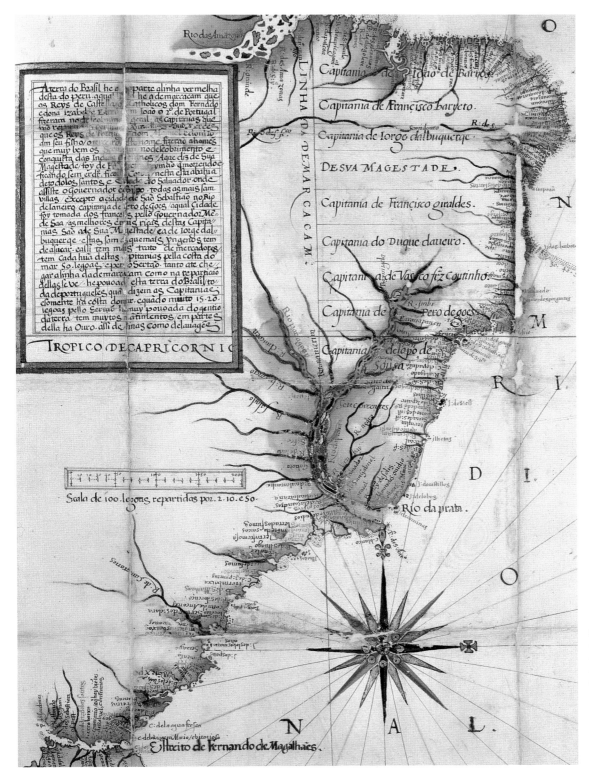

LEFT This Portuguese map shows the Brazilian coastline during the 16th century. Magellan chose to bide his time in safe harbors along this coast, awaiting suitable weather conditions for tackling the turbulent waters of the strait that would be later named in his honor.

Magellan Strait

In August, the four remaining ships arrived at Rio Santa Cruz where Magellan waited a further two months until October 18, when he set sail again. Three days later, a promontory—which Magellan named Cape Vírgenes—at the mouth of a likely-looking inlet, was sighted and Magellan entered the strait that now bears his name.

He split his fleet in order to investigate a number of promising openings and it was then that the *San Antonio* took the opportunity to desert the expedition and return to Spain. Time was wasted looking for the missing *San Antonio* but on November 28 the little squadron of now three ships passed into the Pacific, the first European vessels to do so. To Magellan's men this strait was named Todos los Santos to commemorate All Saints' Day—November 1—which passed while they were in transit. Soon, this stretch of water became known as Magellan Strait.

Pacific Transit

Emerging into the Pacific on November 28, 1520, Magellan was fortunate in encountering good weather, which prompted him to give the name Mar Pacifico to the newly-discovered ocean. Had he suspected how wide was this ocean he might have considered Mar Grande to be more appropriate. Once in the Pacific, Magellan sailed north on a course parallel to the coast of Chile until he met with a favorable wind—the southeast trade wind—that would carry him northwest. Now began the most arduous phase of the voyage as the vastness of the Pacific revealed itself for the first time to Europeans. A more westerly track would have taken the ships among the many islands that lie in the Pacific between Chile and Australia but Magellan's course was northwesterly, taking him into the empty seas north of the Tuamotu Archipelago, which was sighted in January, and the Marshall Islands.

Guam

Provisions, already short due to the treachery of ship chandlers in Spain and the desertion of the *San Antonio* with her supplies, gave out. The crews were reduced to eating rats and leather, and began to die from scurvy. At last, on March 6, 100 days from the Magellan Strait, the ships made landfall on Guam in the Mariana Islands. Here Magellan remained for three days, feeding and refreshing his men. He named the group of islands the Ladrones—*ladrón* means thief—honoring the overacquisitiveness of the inhabitants. When he departed the island he left the settlements in flames.

Philippines and Death

In April, the ships moved on to Cebu in the Philippines. In these islands it was noticed that Malay, a language common in the Indies, was understood. Here was proof that Magellan had achieved his goal and, by sailing west from

Spain, had reached the region where spices were to be had. He was not to live long to savor his triumph. At the end of the month he became unwisely involved in a local conflict, during which he was killed. Magellan died bravely, fighting to the last to give his surviving companions time to retreat to their boats. Although he failed to complete what was to become the first voyage of circumnavigation, Magellan had proved the existence of a route to the riches of the East, past the barrier of the American continent; had established the basis of a lasting, if exploitative, bond with the Philippine Islands; and had discovered the true extent of an immense new ocean.

Return Voyage

After further trials, including the murder of a number of Spanish officers by the ruler of Cebu, the now two remaining ships—the *Concepción* had been scuttled as there were no longer enough men to man her—arrived at Tidore, a tiny island in the Molucca Passage, where both vessels were loaded with cloves. Spain thus established a trading relationship in the Spice Islands to rival Portuguese interests.

It was decided that the ships would return to Spain by different routes. The *Victoria*, under Juan Sebastian del Cano, would sail for the Cape of Good Hope while the *Trinidad*, which had been damaged, would cross the Pacific to Panama where her cargo could be delivered into Spanish hands. An attempt at this crossing was abandoned in its early stages and the *Trinidad* returned to the Moluccas, to be captured by the Portuguese.

The *Victoria* sailed from Tidore on December 21, 1521, and arrived at Sanlúcar in September the following year. Only 20 or so of the 250 men that had set out with Magellan in 1519 returned, qualifying that small band as the first circumnavigators. The cargo of cloves in the surviving ship paid for the entire expedition.

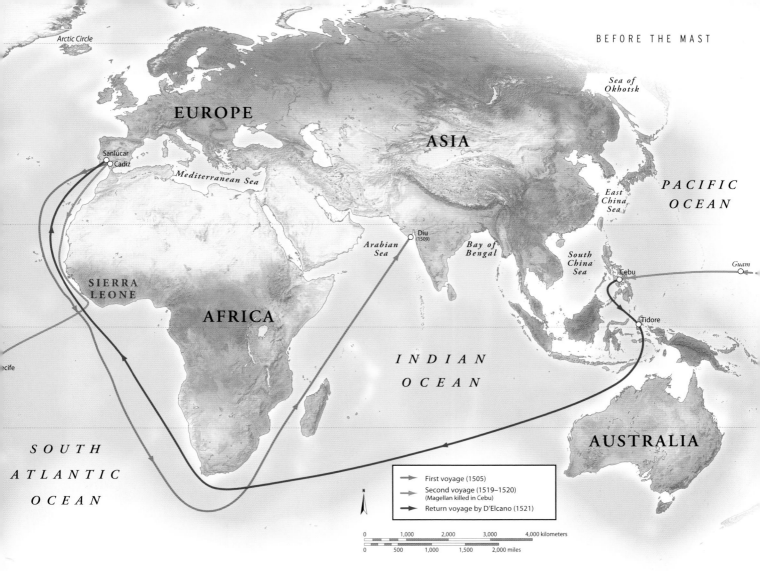

Arctic Circle

EUROPE

ASIA

Sea of
Okhotsk

PACIFIC
OCEAN

Sanlúcar
Cadiz

Mediterranean Sea

East
China
Sea

Diu
(1509)

Arabian
Sea

Bay of
Bengal

Guam

SIERRA
LEONE

Cebu

AFRICA

South
China
Sea

Tidore

ecife

INDIAN

OCEAN

PACIFIC
OCEAN

AUSTRALIA

SOUTH

ATLANTIC

OCEAN

First voyage (1505)

Second voyage (1519–1520)
(Magellan killed in Cebu)

Return voyage by D'Elcano (1521)

N

| 0 | 1,000 | 2,000 | 3,000 | 4,000 kilometers |

| 0 | 500 | 1,000 | 1,500 | 2,000 miles |

ABOVE Unfortunately
Magellan was killed half-
way around the world and
the trip was completed by
his remaining crew.

RIGHT This painting
depicts Magellan and his
ships passing through the
Magellan Strait and into
the Pacific Ocean—the
first Europeans to do so.

From Sea to Sea

The search for the Northwest Passage proved a challenge for centuries. Pack ice and the vast Arctic Archipelago prevented the route being discovered until the twentieth century.

RIGHT During Jacques Cartier's second voyage to Canadian shores he made detailed notes on the culture and manners of the indigenous Iroquois, including their scantily clad habits even in the face of the intense cold.

The interest among the countries of northern Europe in finding a route to Asia that avoided trespassing on those regions considered by Spain and Portugal as exclusively theirs under the Treaty of Tordesillas of 1494 was manifested by France when in the 1520s, Giovanni da Verrazano, a Florentine in French service, was despatched by Francis I to find a route westwards, across the Atlantic. Although he found what is now known as New York Bay and entered the Hudson River, none of Verrazano's three transatlantic voyages resulted in the discovery of a strait through to the Pacific.

BELOW One of the sixteenth-century maps of Pierre Desceliers, showing the bounty of animals, plants, and other riches to be found on the newly discovered Canada.

> I am inclined to believe that this is the land God gave to Cain.
> –Jacques Cartier on experiencing severe weather conditions in the new territory of Kanata.

Gulf of St Lawrence

Nevertheless, so great was the commercial imperative of finding such a passage that France persisted, and in 1534 Jacques Cartier (1491–1557), a Breton navigator, was commissioned by King Francis to continue the search. On April 20 that year Cartier sailed from St Malo with two ships—each of 60 tons (54 tonnes)—and 61 men. Three weeks later landfall was made at Cape Bonavista, on the eastern side of Newfoundland. He intended to look to the northwards and after spending 10 days refitting his ships Cartier set sail once more.

Entering the Strait of Belle Isle, which separates Newfoundland from the mainland, Cartier passed into the Gulf of St Lawrence. Had he coasted along the land lying on his right hand Cartier's course would have taken him into the mouth of the great St Lawrence River, but he turned to the south, down the west coast of Newfoundland, crossing the Cabot Strait to Prince Edward Island. Further to the west he took his ships into Chaleur Bay but to his disappointment found that after 80 miles (130 km) he was embayed.

While in Chaleur Bay Cartier met with fishing parties of the Huron and Micmac tribes. It was probably from them that Cartier heard of another great waterway some way to the north. But for the moment the voyage was over and

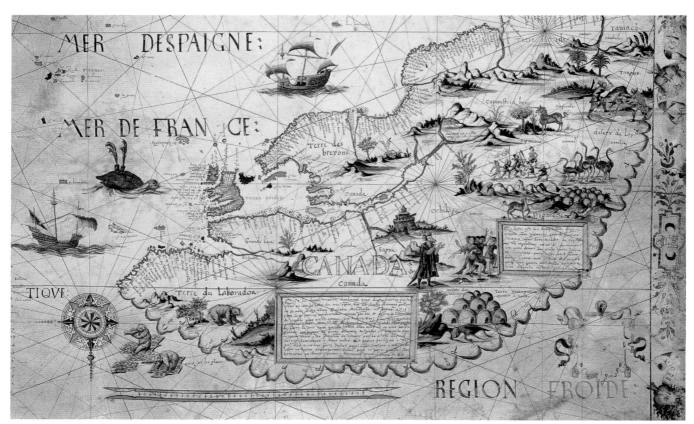

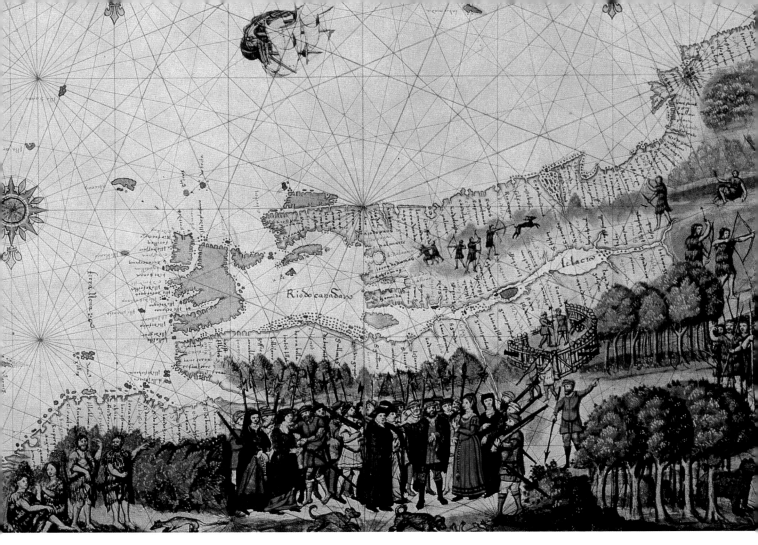

after touching at Anticosti Island, at the point where the St Lawrence flows into the Gulf, Cartier sailed for home, arriving back at St Malo in September.

Quebec

In May 1535, Cartier set sail once more, this time with three ships and more than 100 men, intent on finding and following the waterway of which he had been told. This time he had with him two Hurons, brought back from the first voyage. Passing again through the Strait of Belle Isle, he continued westwards and entered the St Lawrence. On September 7, the ships arrived at the Indian settlement of Stadacona, the site of the present-day city of Quebec. Here Cartier was told of the rich land of Saguenay which lay ahead so, transferring to the smallest of his vessels, the 40-ton (36 tonne) pinnace *Emerillon*, he continued upriver. Increasing difficulties with rapids and a strong ebb tide forced Cartier to transfer to longboats.

Montreal

At the beginning of October the explorers arrived at a village above which rose a considerable hill. From this height Cartier could see rapids that finally removed from his mind any lingering hope that this was the way to Asia. To the hill Cartier gave the name Mont Réal and it was there that the city of Montreal was later founded.

ABOVE Cartographer Nicholas Vallard's 1547 map shows Cartier flanked by settlers, as well as a more realistic representation of Newfoundland and Nova Scotia than had previously been rendered.

LEFT In his attempt to discover the elusive sea passage to the wealthy markets of Asia, Cartier made his way up the St Lawrence River in 1535, claiming the area for Francis I of France.

Turning back downriver, Cartier wintered at Stadacona, where his ships were frozen in for five months, their crews suffering greatly from the effects of scurvy. In the spring of 1536, he sailed for France. He was not finished with his Grande Rivière, though, and returned in 1541, this time not to seek a way to China but to assist with French colonization.

1401 to 1600

English Pirate

Before Francis Drake made his fame in the defeat of the Spanish Armada, Elizabeth I sent him around the world on a secret mission.

ABOVE This drawing by John Conyers of a seal in the Bay of Montevideo was based on a description provided by the chaplain on Drake's 1577–1580 voyage, Francis Fletcher.

RIGHT Francis Drake was the first Englishman to circumnavigate the globe. He continued his plundering sea voyages until his death in 1596.

1588 During the pursuit of the Spanish Armada up the English Channel, Drake forgoes duty in order to plunder the galleon *Rosario*, which was known to be carrying funds to pay the Spanish Army

1589 Drake fails in an attempt to capture Lisbon with a navy of 150 ships

1595 Elizabeth I sends Drake to pirate treasure from a wrecked Spanish galleon at La Forteleza

1596 Sir Francis Drake dies of dysentery off the coast of Panama and is buried at sea

The principal, most historically significant, achievement of Francis Drake's voyage of 1577 to 1580, during which he made the second circumnavigation and took much plunder, was to establish that the South American continent was not contiguous with an unknown Great Southern Continent, and that there was an open seaway joining the Atlantic and Pacific oceans.

This discovery was fortuitous, though a search for *Terra Australis Incognita* may have been included in the proposal for the voyage that Drake put before Elizabeth I. The plan was kept secret at the time, and remains unclear to this day.

Privateering

On December 13, 1577, Drake sailed from Plymouth in his ship the *Pelican*, in company with four smaller ships. An earlier departure, in November, was thwarted by bad weather. At the first opportunity, Drake embarked on his privateering and by early February had captured three ships, two Spanish and one Portuguese.

Mutiny

The secret nature of the voyage caused early trouble within the small fleet. Among the gentleman non-mariners sailing with Drake was Thomas Doughty, who was quite likely to have been acting secretly for Lord Burghley, Chief Secretary of State to the Queen. Burghley had been dismayed when he found out about Drake's intentions and wished the voyage prevented, thereby avoiding trouble with Spain. Doughty incited unrest and called Drake's authority into question. On arrival at Port St Julián, where Ferdinand Magellan had hanged a mutineer 58 years earlier, Doughty was tried and executed. On August 17, 1578, Drake sailed from Port St Julián, his authority reaffirmed, and three days later passed Cape Vírgenes, at the entrance to the Magellan Strait.

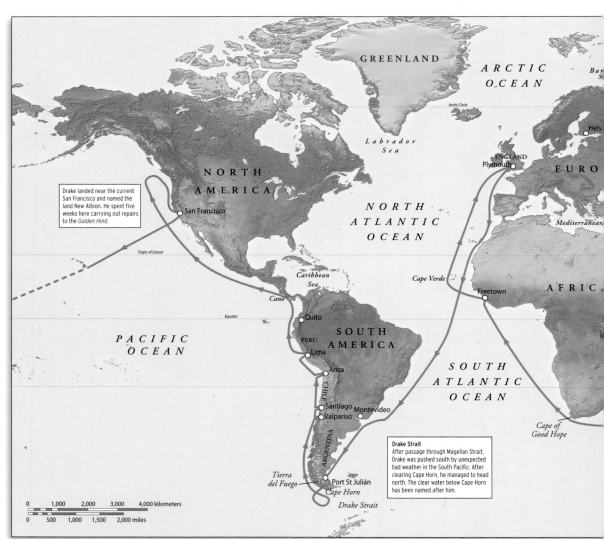

Drake landed near the current San Francisco and named the land New Albion. He spent five weeks here carrying out repairs to the *Golden Hind*.

Drake Strait
After passage through Magellan Strait, Drake was pushed south by unexpected bad weather in the South Pacific. After clearing Cape Horn, he managed to head north. The clear water below Cape Horn has been named after him.

GREENLAND

ARCTIC OCEAN

Arctic Circle

NORTH AMERICA

Labrador Sea

ENGLAND
Plymouth

EURO

Hels

NORTH ATLANTIC OCEAN

Mediterranean

San Francisco

Tropic of Cancer

Caribbean Sea

Cape Verde

AFRIC

Cano

Freetown

Equator

Quito

PERU

SOUTH AMERICA

Lima

Arica

PACIFIC OCEAN

SOUTH ATLANTIC OCEAN

CHILE

Santiago
Valpariso

Montevideo

Cape of Good Hope

ARGENTINA

Tierra del Fuego

Port St Julián
Cape Horn

Drake Strait

| 0 | 1,000 | 2,000 | 3,000 | 4,000 kilometers |

| 0 | 500 | 1,000 | 1,500 | 2,000 miles |

> There must be a beginning of any great matter, but the continuing unto the end until it be thoroughly finished yields the true glory.
> —Francis Drake on his plundering.

LEFT Sir Francis Drake's voyages have been a popular illustration topic. Here we see Drake and his ships in St Augustine, Florida, on America's east coast.

BELOW Born into a poor farming family in Tavistock, England in about 1541, Francis Drake was related to a wealthy family of ship-owners, the Hawkins of Plymouth. This connection gained Drake his first job on a ship and he never looked back.

Francis Drake's circumnavigation (1577–1580)
(Map includes modern names)

Drake Strait

The *Pelican*, together with her consorts, which by now were reduced to two ships, made a quick passage through the strait and entered the Pacific on September 6, 1578. Magellan had found calm weather and had given the ocean its name accordingly, but Drake met with strong gales, during which one of the ships was lost. Another ship—the *Pelican*'s last consort—turned back for England. Drake's vessel was driven southward, to approximately 57° South, below Cape Horn, where he found the open water now known as Drake Strait.

Search for Northern Passage

Drake's progress northward up the coast of Chile and Peru, during which he changed the name of his ship to *Golden Hind*, brought much plunder, ensuring a rich return for the promoters of the voyage. Realizing the danger in returning home via the Magellan Strait now that he had stirred up a hornet's nest on the coast, Drake resolved to look for the supposed Strait of Anian which would take him in an easterly direction through the North American landmass into the Atlantic. Having sailed north to about the latitude of present-day Vancouver and not found the strait, Drake had to accept that no passage existed. He went ashore near where San Francisco is today and named the land New Albion. After a stay of five weeks, during which repairs to the *Golden Hind* were made, Drake sailed again and struck out westward across the Pacific Ocean.

Returning the Spoils

His route homeward took him by way of the Spice Islands, where he took aboard a cargo of cloves only to lose it again when, on January 9, 1580, the *Golden Hind* ran aground in the Celebes. To lighten the ship, the cloves were jettisoned and the ship eventually floated off the reef.

The loss of the valuable spice mattered little. Nine months later, after crossing the Indian Ocean and sailing up the Atlantic, the *Golden Hind* arrived back in Plymouth, laden with the immense treasure that Drake had taken. The return to the investors in the voyage came to approximately 4,700 percent. Queen Elizabeth knighted Drake on the deck of the *Golden Hind*.

Strait to Cathay

Through the sixteenth century, successive expeditions in search of a Northwest Passage eliminated most of the North American coastline as the location of a strait leading to Cathay.

RIGHT In his search for the Northeast Passage from Europe to Asia, Willem Barents encountered many dangers. According to a book by Gerrit de Veer, Barents and his crew even had to defend themselves against polar bears.

BELOW Barents and his crew abandoned their icebound ship and set out in two open boats. A Dutch vessel eventually led the survivors home.

Attention soon focused further north. The extent of the northern ice was not comprehended and many maps of that time showed open water above both the American and Asian continents. In the closing two decades of the century, several attempts were made to discover westerly and easterly routes through Arctic seas.

John Davis

Englishman John Davis (c. 1550–1605) was one of the most distinguished of Elizabethan mariners. In the 1580s, he led three expeditions into the waters west of Greenland, extending the area that had been searched unsuccessfully by Martin Frobisher a decade earlier.

The first voyage began in June 1585 when Davis sailed from Dartmouth, England, with two small ships. The next month he reached Greenland, sailing about 400 nautical miles up the west coast as far as present-day Godthaab Fjord, which he named Gilbert's Sound in honor of one of his sponsors. Sailing west

across what is now the Davis Strait, Davis arrived on the coast of Baffin Island where he found a promising inlet which he followed for about 180 nautical miles before conditions persuaded him to turn for home, convinced that the inlet, which he had named Cumberland Sound, held promise.

The second voyage, beginning the following year, was not productive. Davis failed to recognize the opening to Cumberland Sound.

Despite the few results arising out of the first two voyages, backing was found for a third, and in May 1587, Davis sailed again for the waters between Greenland and Baffin Island. This time he penetrated Baffin Bay as far north as Upernavik before ice blocked his way. Turning south, and nearly losing his ship in the ice, Davis found Cumberland Sound again and eliminated it as a strait.

Davis turned for home after sailing down the Labrador coast as far as the Strait of Belle Isle. He had not found the way to the East.

> In all parts of the Old World, as well as of the New, it was evident that Columbus had kindled a fire in every mariner's heart. That fire was the harbinger of a new era, for it was not to be extinguished.
> —Charles Kendall Adams (1835-1902), American historian.

Willem Barents

Seven years after Davis set out on his third voyage, Willem Barents (c.1550–1597) sailed from the Dutch island of Texel on the first of his three expeditions in search of the Northeast Passage, following in the track of the Willoughby–Chancellor expedition of 1553.

The first voyage, departing in June 1594, took the Dutch navigator as far as the island of Novaya Zemlya, in the Arctic Ocean, before he was repulsed by ice. The next year Barents reached Vaygach Island, below Novaya Zemlya, when ice again forced a retreat.

On the final voyage, setting out in 1596, Bear Island and Spitsbergen were sighted before Barents's two ships parted. One ship, under the command of Jan Rijp, sailed northward, while Barents steered to the northeast, reaching Novaya Zemlya on July 17, 1596. Soon, however, his ship was beset by ice and the crew endured a winter of severe hardship. The following spring the ice failed to release the ship and the crew put to sea in two small boats. Barents died while sailing south toward refuge on the Kola Peninsula. The 12 survivors eventually reached Amsterdam.

Neither Davis nor Barents penetrated any distance toward their goal of sailing through northern waters to China and Japan, and neither of the Arctic passages they sought ever proved to be a practicable commercial seaway.

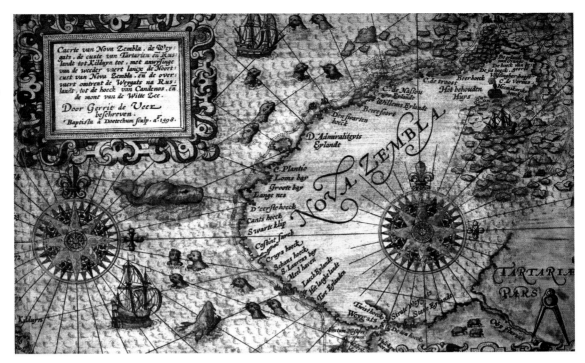

RIGHT This map of Nova Zembla (Novaya Zemlya) is from Gerrit de Veer's 1598 book, which tells the story of Willem Barents's final voyage. De Veer was one of only 12 survivors of the Arctic expedition.

1583 John Davis first proposes his expedition to find the Northwest Passage

1589 After completing three unsuccessful attempts to find the Northwest Passage, John Davis joins Thomas Cavendish on his last voyage

1592 After leaving Cavendish's expedition, Davis goes on to discover the Falkland Islands

1596 On his third voyage, Willem Barents's ship gets caught in pack-ice and the crew use timber from the ship to build a lodge

1597 By June, the ice has still not loosened and the crew take to two small boats to escape. Barents dies seven days later. Barents's lodge was discovered in 1871.

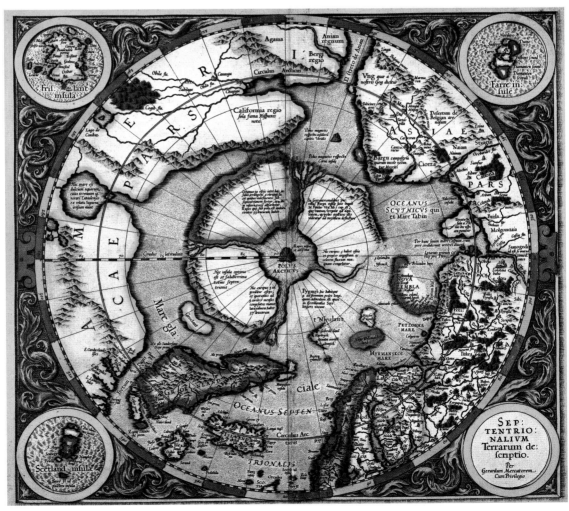

RIGHT Gerard Mercator's 1595 map of the Arctic shows the region explored by both John Davis and Willem Barents.

TECHNOLOGY, TRADE, AND TRANSITION

1601 to 1900

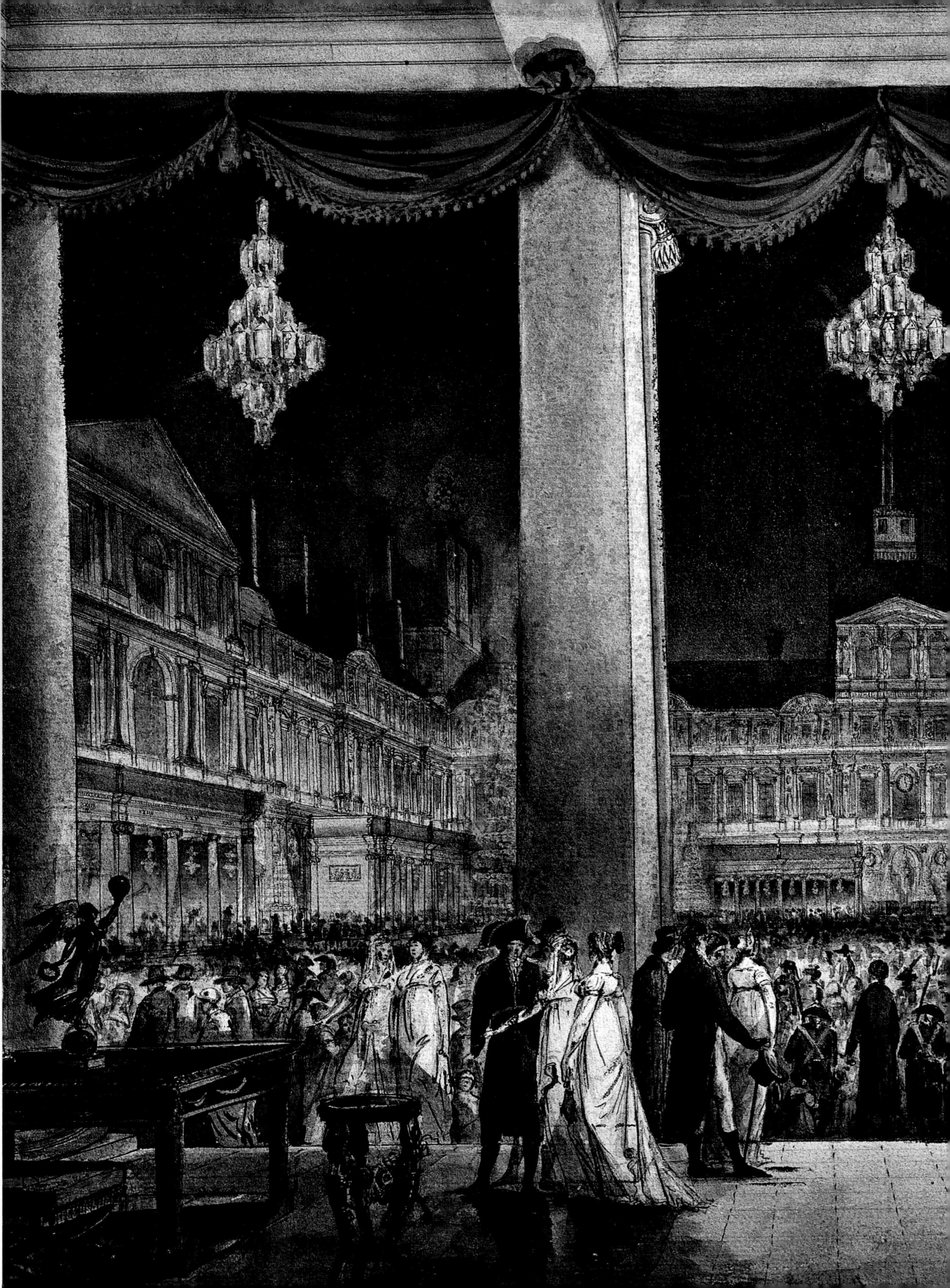

Nineteenth-century Changes

From 1601, the world began to expand due to exploration and the discovery of new worlds. The nineteenth century, in particular, was a turning point in history. Almost everything that had characterized human life for centuries suddenly began changing.

Changes in the nineteenth century included several "revolutions"—demographic, industrial, agricultural, transportation, banking, and educational. Their combined outcomes transformed and expanded human life. Population explosions doubled, in some cases quadrupled, the residents of countries in Europe, because death rates declined more than birth rates. Devastating medieval diseases such as cholera, plague, and smallpox disappeared because vaccinations and health services were introduced. Life expectancy at birth doubled in a century.

ABOVE Italian emigrants leaving Milan for a new life in Canada at the end of the nineteenth century.

LEFT This detail from a painting by an unknown artist depicts France's second industrial exhibition, held in the grounds of the Louvre in 1801.

RIGHT Opened in 1869, the Suez Canal enabled ships to sail between Asia and Europe without going around Africa. The canal connects Port Said (seen in this painting) on the Mediterranean Sea with Suez on the Red Sea.

PREVIOUS PAGES Jean Louis Bezard's painting depicts the taking of the Louvre during the 1830 July Revolution in France. This was a time of political upheaval across Europe.

Society

Social and occupational structures changed; traditional families of three generations began to be replaced by modern two-generation families. Mobility of people led to mass migration from the countryside to cities, and from one country and continent to another. Around 60 million people emigrated from Europe to America and elsewhere. British entrepreneurs established factories in other countries and continents, and skilled workers of advanced countries were employed in less developed ones.

Science and Technology

Nineteenth-century transformation, however, was by no means global. It emerged in northwestern Europe and gradually spread to the western half of the continent, further generating changes throughout the world over times to come. That was also true for the most dramatic change, the industrial revolution that introduced the mechanized factory and the steam engine. Mining of coal dramatically expanded and drilling crude oil began in this century. Later waves of technological revolution provided steel, electricity, and medicine, produced by newly-born pharmaceutical industries.

Transportation

For thousands of years the speed of transportation hardly changed at all, and did not surpass 12–15 mph (20–25 km/h). In the nineteenth century, railroads and, by century's end, cars increased the speed by five times and linked countries. Rivers were connected with each other and to the sea by canals—the Suez and the Panama canals cut distances by one-third—and sailboats were replaced by steamships. Cables were laid down on the ocean floor, joining continents, and at the end of the century telephone connections were introduced.

Education

This was the century when primary education became compulsory and free, and when for the first time in human history illiteracy disappeared in the most advanced parts of the world. However, that was only the beginning, because even within the European peripheries, forty to seventy percent of the population remained illiterate. Secondary education started to spread, and the concept of a modern university that combined teaching and research was invented and introduced in Germany. Modern science developed and new disciplines were established.

Government

The century became the cradle of the nation-state, and saw the introduction of citizenship and passports. Several nations as we know them now became independent, and others, such as Italy and Germany, were formed by uniting several small former states. Advanced countries introduced agreements and institutions that served the population and economic development. Parliamentary systems began to spread and the international gold standard was introduced. The wealthy industrialized European countries colonized most of the globe. They exploited and subordinated the people of conquered nations in Africa and elsewhere, widening the gap between rich and poor nations and continents.

Conflict

The nineteenth century was also the period of rising conflicts. It opened with the Napoleonic wars, followed by warfare between Germany and France, Russia and the Ottoman Empire, and Britain and Russia. The next century would begin with World War I, in which 8 million people were killed and 20 million wounded. The seeds of the tragedies of the twentieth century were sown.

Sourcing Labor

Large-scale long-distance movements of population were rare in human history until technological advances opened the way for the introduction of agriculture to new regions of the globe.

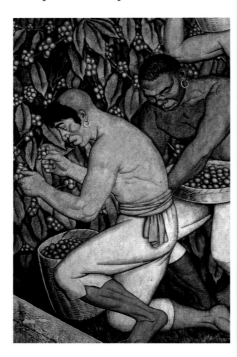

RIGHT This detail of a painting by the Mexican artist Fernando Leal shows slaves picking coffee beans in Venezuela in the early 1800s.

FAR RIGHT By 1772, five European nations had colonized much of the world. These conquered territories provided agricultural land and slaves to work it.

1615 The Privy Council of Britain sanctions the transportation of convicts to West Indian colonies and Virginia

1619 One hundred homeless children are sent to Virginia

1790 The US Congress passes an act requiring two years' residency before citizenship

1819 US Federal legislation requires the notation of vessel passenger lists

1862 The US *Homestead Act* grants citizens title to 160 acres, encouraging naturalization

1892 Ellis Island, in New York Harbor, is established as a screening station for immigrants

> I cannot make it better known than it already is that I strongly favor colonization.
>
> –Abraham Lincoln in his Second Annual Message to Congress, December 1, 1862.

The discovery of the Americas stimulated Europeans to explore ways of exploiting the potential of those continents for primary production. Early in the sixteenth century, British fishermen in Newfoundland began employing techniques for salting and drying fish for export back to Europe.

Labor Shortage

Unlike those in South and Southeast Asia, where cotton, sugar, and spices were also grown, American plantations could not draw on local workers because they were accustomed to wage labor. Spanish conquest and disease had drastically reduced the pre-Columbian populations of Mexico and Peru, so there were not enough local people to meet the planters' demands.

Native Americans could be coerced into working, but they escaped into territory they knew well. Experiments with recruitment of convict labor, indentured servants, and voluntary migrants from Europe also failed to meet the demand. Increasingly, planters turned to Africa as their main labor source.

Slavery

Portuguese navigators inching their way down the West African Coast in the fifteenth century had discovered they could buy human beings almost everywhere. As they experimented with growing sugarcane on offshore islands, African slave labor proved an ideal workforce. Not only had the Africans acquired childhood immunity to many tropical diseases, once

removed from their homeland they could not hope to escape into welcoming and familiar surroundings. Soon the unholy partnership between African slave traders and European dealers grew into a trade involving the movement of millions of people across the Atlantic.

Claiming Territory

So profitable was trade in people and plantation products that individual European countries scrambled to lay claim to territory along the West African coast, Brazil, the West Indies, and the southern Atlantic coastal regions of North America. While Africa's dangerous tropical climate made large-scale European migration unthinkable, forts built to protect European trading posts were the bases of

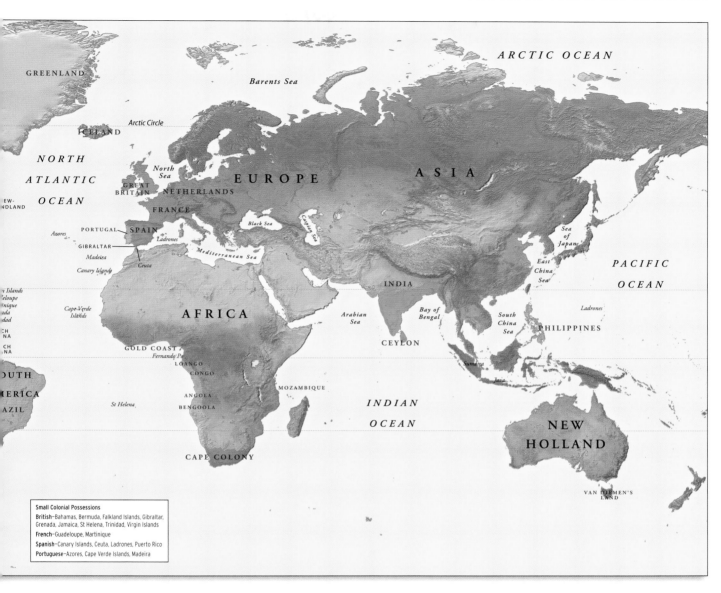

Small Colonial Possessions
British–Bahamas, Bermuda, Falkland Islands, Gibraltar, Grenada, Jamaica, St Helena, Trinidad, Virgin Islands
French–Guadeloupe, Martinique
Spanish–Canary Islands, Ceuta, Ladrones, Puerto Rico
Portuguese–Azores, Cape Verde Islands, Madeira

the countries that eventually took shape as Senegal, Sierra Leone, Ghana, Côte d'Ivoire, Dahomey, Togo, Nigeria, Congo, Cameroon, and Angola.

Transport

Growth of the fur trade on the North American Atlantic seaboard laid the foundations of the future Canadian provinces as well as some New England states, but the labor needed to get the furs came mainly from indigenous people. Thus, despite some settlement by people seeking religious freedom—like the Pilgrims in Massachusetts and the Quakers in Pennsylvania— migration to the northern colonies remained quite low until further technological advances occurred near the end of the eighteenth century.

Workplace Revolutions

Without industrial and agricultural revolutions in Europe, however, it is unlikely that the newly opened agricultural plains regions would have attracted enough settlers. The end of feudalism and the rise of large-scale agriculture in Europe, as well as the gradual development of labor-saving farm machinery, led to landowners pushing peasants from their ancestral homes. Millions of people chose to continue life on the land by migrating to the Americas, newly conquered French Algeria, Australasia, and South Africa. Others went to work in the factories that were springing up all over Western Europe.

Unable to grow their own food, these factory workers created an ever-expanding export market

RIGHT African slaves were usually confined below deck and shackled together. These slaves on the Spanish ship *Albanez* were set free by crew on the British anti-slavery vessel HMS *Albatross*.

for newly opened territories. This happened not only in the New World and Australasia—railroads also transformed parts of Russia and Eastern Europe, making the Ukraine, for example, a potent force on international grain markets.

Transformation of European agriculture resulted in human tragedies as well as great wealth, as when the failure of the Irish potato crop in the 1840s forced millions of starving peasants to seek new homes in one of history's largest documented mass migrations.

Shoguns and Samurai

Influenced at first by Europeans with their guns and trade, Japan's ruling classes battled each other for supremacy and control of the peasant population.

Political stability brokered by the Ashikaga shogunate in 1392 led Japan into a new epoch of a loose federation of domain lords. The Onin War, which began in 1467, split the warlords, rendered Japan rudderless, and brought conflict.

> If the cuckoo won't sing, kill it.
> –Oda Nobunaga
> If the cuckoo won't sing, I'll make it sing.
> –Toyotomi Hideyoshi
> If the cuckoo won't sing, I'll wait till it sings.
> –Tokugawa Ieyasu
> (poems depicting the styles of the three shoguns)

c. 1600
Japan begins to reunify after almost 100 years of civil war

1638 Shogun Iemitsu forbids any shipbuilding in Japan

1641 Shogun Iemitsu bans all foreigners, except Chinese and Dutch

1797 Mount Fuji erupts

1868 Emperor is restored to power and Japan becomes a nation with one ruler

1895 Japan rises to world power status after victories in both the Sino-Japanese and Russo-Japanese wars

Infighting

The warlord Oda Nobunaga came to power in 1568, in a rise often attributed to military innovation, such as the adoption of guns. His quest to unite the whole of Japan was curtailed when his subordinate, Akechi Mitsuhide, killed him in an act of treachery in 1582.

A former footsoldier of humble origin, Toyotomi Hideyoshi filled the political vacuum in 1590. His efforts included a land survey and civil registry to allot accurate tax quotas. He also prohibited the possession of arms by peasants, effectively pre-empting mounting protests and separating the samurai and the peasant classes. His reforms stimulated trade and commerce.

RIGHT Tokugawa Ieyasu's victory over the Toyotomi clan in 1600 at the Battle of Sekigahara–depicted here in a popular Japanese print–ushered in the Tokugawa era, which was to last for 250 years.

With an eye to conquering China, he invaded Korea (Joseon) in 1592 and 1597. This adventure strained diplomatic relations but was brought to a halt by his sudden death in 1598.

In 1600, Tokugawa Ieyasu won the battle of Sekigahara and paved the way for centralization. In 1603, he was given the title *shogun*, which marked the beginning of the 250-year long Tokugawa regime in the new capital, Edo, today's Tokyo.

Political Stability

The Tokugawa era is acknowledged for its political stability under the hereditary shoguns. The domestic economy was invigorated, especially in cities, literacy grew, and in the arts *kabuki* theater developed from the traditional *noh* theater.

Caste

Tokugawa rule ensured social order by implementing caste, and by restricting the power of domain lords. Caste was based on the Confucian idea that people had their rightful places in society. Those born into particular ranks were not allowed to marry into others, and so moving between tiers became unviable. The samurai occupied the top tier. Peasants, whom Confucianism favored, came next. Artisans and merchants, whom Confucianism disliked, occupied the bottom two tiers. Above these ranks were the nobles, monks, and priests, while underneath were the outcasts. The *eta*, the unclean, were butchers, tanners, and undertakers, while *hinin*, the non-humans, were prostitutes and entertainers. To this day, *burakumin*, the descendants of the *eta* and the *hinin*, are still unofficially and illegally discriminated against.

Periods of relative calm and stability reduced in the eighteenth century. Rice, the staple in Japan, became levied as taxes, and cycles of famines and natural disasters worsened the peasants' problems and tax burdens. As a last resort the peasants protested and broke into rice storage facilities. During the Edo period there were over 3,200 such protests, prompting reforms by the regime.

RIGHT A hanging scroll by Masanobu Okumura, showing the opulent women's quarters at the palace of the Shogun.

CHINA

Ezo Hokkaidō

Hakodate

MAP The Tokugawa Shogunate ruled nineteenth-century Japan, with other factions relegated to more outlying areas.

Akita

Kitakami-gawa

Sakata

Honshū

S e a
o f
J a p a n
(E a s t   S e a)

OSEON

Chikuma-gawa

J A P A N

Kanna-gawa

Mito

Matsue

Sabae

Battle of
Sekigahara
(1600)

Edo
(Tokyo)

Choshi

Tenryu-gawa

Nagoya

Kyōto

Kamakura

Hiroshima

Osaka

CHOSHU

Kobe

Sakai

Hamamatsu

Hakata

Matsuyama

Yajima

Wakayama

Tenryu-gawa

Omuta

Shikoku

Nagasaki

Kumamoto

Kochi

TOSA

Kyūshū

SATSUMA

Miyazaki

Kagoshima

P A C I F I C

O C E A N

N

| 0 | 250 | 500 kilometers |
| 0 | 125 | 250 miles |

Legend:
- Domains of Tokugawa shogunate
- Domains of shogun rivals
- Allied domains opposing the Tokugawa shogunate

Control and Conflict

The Tokugawas positioned their long-term and erstwhile allies close to the capital, while their former opponents were placed in far-flung domains. The regime also imposed a costly custom on each domain lord. In alternate years each lord had to pay a visit to Edo, give tributes to the central regime, and stay there for a year. Their wives and children could meet with them only when they were in Edo, thus effectively becoming hostages of sorts.

In 1637, a revolt occurred in Kyushu that involved about 37,000 Christian converts. The regime brutally suppressed it, banned Christianity, and persecuted the Christians. Thereafter, the rulers restricted foreign trade to only designated trading partners at regime-approved ports. Import of foreign, especially European, knowledge was banned or made available only to elite scholars, beginning a long period of isolation from the outside world.

Tearing Europe Apart

The long and devastating Thirty Years' War began as a religious
civil war in Germany between Catholics and Protestants.

> It is better that we tether
> our horses to the enemy's
> fence, than he to ours.
>
> –Swedish nobleman on learning that
> the Habsburgs wished to consolidate their
> hold on the shores of the Baltic Sea.

Ferdinand II, Emperor of the
Holy Roman Empire and King of
Bohemia, launched attacks against
the Protestants and forced a harsh
counter-reformation. Protestant
Bohemians and Protestant German
provinces and cities rose up against
Catholic Habsburg authority and
in 1608 a Protestant alliance was
established. It was counterbalanced
the next year by the foundation of
the Catholic League.

The war began in 1618 when
Protestant Bohemians attacked the
royal palace in Prague, igniting a
national uprising. In one of the
most damaging episodes of the
first phase of the war—the Battle
of White Mountain in 1620—the
Catholic League army under Count
von Tilly defeated Bohemia. By
war's end, the Czech nobility was
eliminated and half of the population of Bohemia had died.

Catholic victories generated
a strong Protestant reaction, but
in the second phase of the war
dynastic issues and power considerations took center stage. In 1625,
Christian IV, King of Denmark
and Norway, entered the war by
invading Saxony as a defender
of Protestantism, but he was
also aiming for territorial enlargement at the expense of northern
German territories.

After the Danish defeat in 1629,
and the Treaty of Lübeck that insti-
tutionalized Habsburg victory,
Gustav II Adolf of Sweden invaded
Pomerania to defeat the strong
Catholic power, but also to weaken
the overwhelming Habsburg rule.
He defeated the Germans in Breiten-
feld (Leipzig), and captured
Munich. Poland also attacked
Russia in a conflict concluded in
1634 by the Peace of Polyanov.

End of the Habsburgs

The peace of Prague in 1635 ended
the Danish-Swedish phase of the
war, but then France, allied with
Sweden, entered the war by invading Spain, the other major Habsburg domain, and the last phase
of the war began. Costly battles,
a Spanish invasion against French
territories, reversed by major
French victories against the Austro-
Bohemian army and the Bavarian-
Austrian army in 1644 and 1648
respectively, sealed the French

LEFT The rearrangement
of Europe after the war
established the new bal-
ance of power only for
a century. The outcome
of the conflicts that
strengthened France
also ignited a British-
French rivalry.

1619 Ferdinand
is elected Holy
Roman Emperor

1620 The Catholic
League and the
Protestant Union
enter into the Treaty
of Ulm pledging not
to battle each other
within the Empire

1622 Christian of
Halberstadt is defeated
by Count von Tilly and
Fernandez de Cordoba

1626 Count von Tilly
wins a crushing victory
against the Danes at
Lutter-am-Bamberg

1631 French and
Swedish forces enter into
the Treaty of Barwalde

1632 Count von Tilly
dies at Ingoldstadt,
Bavaria, from wounds
received in the battle
of Rain

Boundary of Holy Roman Empire (c. 1648)
Austrian Habsburg territory
Brandenburg territory
Church territory
Danish territory
Spanish Habsburg territory
Swedish territory
Major battle during Thirty Years' War

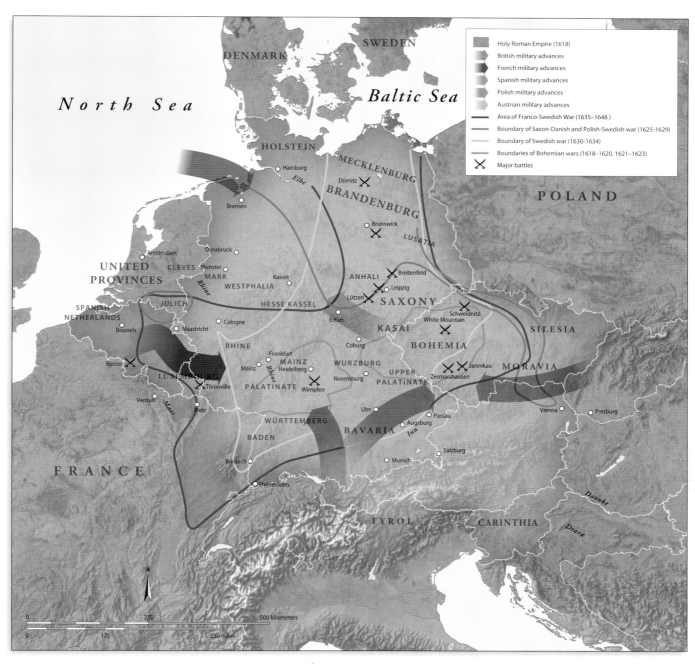

Holy Roman Empire (1618)
British military advances
French military advances
Spanish military advances
Polish military advances
Austrian military advances
Area of Franco-Swedish War (1635–1648)
Boundary of Saxon-Danish and Polish-Swedish war (1625-1629)
Boundary of Swedish war (1630-1634)
Boundaries of Bohemian wars (1618–1620, 1621–1623)
Major battles

victory over the Holy Roman Empire and marked the end of Habsburg domination over Europe. By the end of the Thirty Years' War, one of the most devastating wars in Europe, huge parts of Germany were ruined and half the population was killed. The Thirty Years' War transformed Europe.

The Treaty of Westphalia in 1648 changed the map of the continent, but even more the balance of power and the role of independent states. The treaty became a milestone for recognizing the absolute right of modern sovereign states within their borders. It also ended the religious tensions and created a more secular continent. Catholic Europe was practically ended. Most importantly, with the Habsburg power and the dominance of the Holy Roman Empire significantly curbed, member states of the latter became sovereign states, and Germany was divided for the next 200 years. Netherlands and Switzerland became independent. Denmark and Spain lost influence, Sweden gained control over the Baltic, and France emerged as the leading continental power.

TACTICS AND SUPPLIES

Feeding the thousands of men in the field meant taking livestock and other food supplies from the occupied land that deprived the civilians living there. Successful armies, such as the Swedes, used sustained attacks and offensive tactics to move an army quickly across ground. This professionalism began with what was called the caracole—a combined cavalry charged, assisted by fire-arms. Eventually these grew into full-scale cavalry charges. These, of course, called for well-trained and disciplined troops, leaving little time to pillage. Men in the successful armies were paid, and the Swedish army, under Gustavus, insisted that the men pay the locals for produce rather than stealing it as in the past.

ABOVE Throughout the duration of the the series of wars that made up the Thirty Years' War, country boundaries changed back and forth as territory was gained and lost. The Thirty Years' War claimed a huge human toll and transformed the political landscape of Europe.

257

Latitude 44°S

Setting sail to the most southerly latitude possible, Abel Tasman hoped to find the great land of *Terra Australis Incognita*. Weather forced him 10° further north, landing him on Van Diemen's Land–now Tasmania–the southernmost part of Australia.

> This land being the first land we have met with in the South Sea and not known to any European nation we have conferred on it the name of Anthoonij Van Diemenslandt.
>
> –Abel Tasman, journal entry on the discovery of Tasmania.

Dutch navigator Abel Janszoon Tasman (1603–1659) joined the Dutch East India Company around 1632 and patrolled in the Dutch East Indies. During this time, he engaged in skirmishes with smugglers and rebels, and was involved in various trading operations. In August 1642, he was commissioned by Anthony Van Diemen, the Governor-General of Dutch India

(Java), who was stationed in Batavia (Jakarta). As governor of the East Indies, Van Diemen concentrated minly on besieging the Portuguese outposts between Ceylon and Malacca, but he hired Tasman with instructions to explore the contours of the continent whose west coast had been sighted by Dutch ships on the way to Batavia, with some ending up wrecked upon its shores.

Van Diemen's Land

After a month refitting his ships, Tasman took a southern course from Mauritius and then struck eastward, well to the south of Cape Leeuwin. Heavy seas, bitter cold, ice, high winds, and fog were all against them as his ships swept east, until on November 24, 1642, they encountered the island of Tasmania, which Tasman named

1634 Abel Tasman is second-in-command of an expedition to Formosa in which half the crew dies during the voyage

1640-41 Tasman voyages to Japan and then southern Sumatra, where he makes a trade treaty with the sultan

1642 Tasman claims formal possession of Anthoonij Van Diemen's Land for the Dutch

1642 On sighting New Zealand, Tasman thinks it is connected to an island off Argentina

1643 Tasman's voyage takes him past Tonga and then Fiji

1649 Tasman, charged with unlawfully hanging a crew member, has his commission suspended

1651 Tasman's rank is restored and he enjoys his remaining years as a trader in Batavia

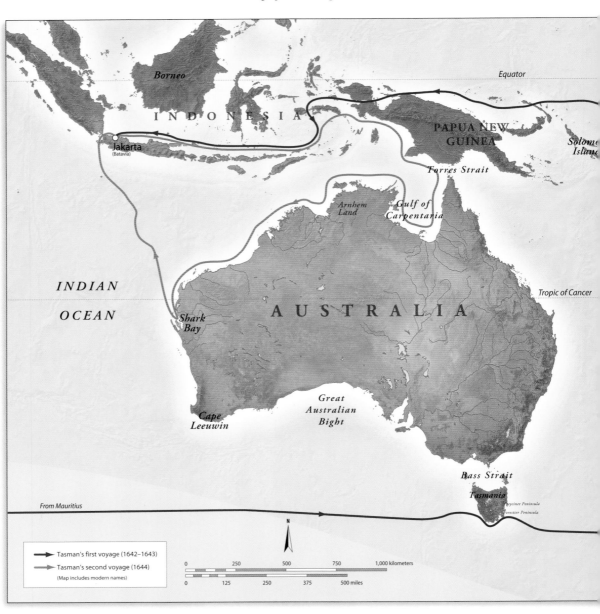

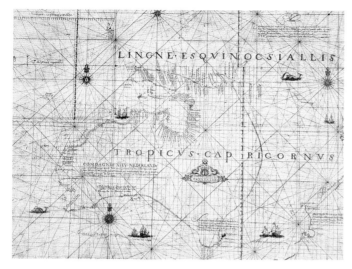

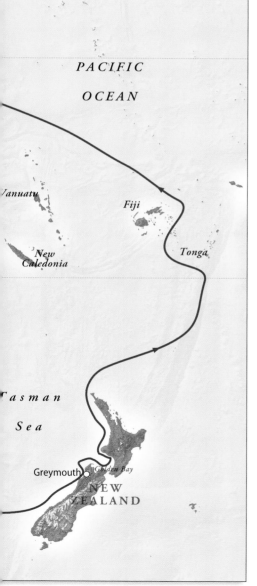

ABOVE Drawn on delicate Japanese paper, this 1644 Tasman map gives a surprisingly accurate general outline of Australia. Just below the Tropic of Capricorn, Tasman has marked the tracks of his two ships, *Heemskerck* and *Zeehaen*.

BELOW RIGHT Born in 1603 in Lutjegast, a village in Groningen in the Netherlands, Abel Tasman was a widower with a young daughter when he married his second wife Jannetjie Tjaers. They joined him when he went to work as a sea captain in Batavia.

LEFT Tasman's voyages were probably the first systematic attempts made by the Dutch to explore the Great South Land. The success of his expeditions was somewhat mixed. In 1642, Tasman mistook Cook Strait (between New Zealand's North and South Islands) for a bight (which he named *Zeehaen's Bight*), and named what he thought was a single island Staten Landt. In 1644, he missed the Torres Strait between New Guinea and Australia, and thus the opportunity to chart the east coast of Australia. However, Tasman did map the north coast, observing the new land, taking notes on its "natives" and "beasts."

Anthoonij Van Diemenlandt—Van Diemen's Land. After going ashore in Frederick Henries Baej (in the Forestier Peninsula), Tasman resumed his journey northeast, passing the Freycinet Peninsula. Deciding against any further exploration—and thus failing to find Bass Strait—he headed east.

New Zealand

On December 13, New Zealand was sighted. Tasman mistakenly assumed it was Staten Landt (State Land), an island earlier sighted by Schouten and Le Maire off Tierra del Fuego. He landed on the west coast of the South Island, near modern Greymouth, then sailed further north and rounded Cape Foulwind, anchoring in Moordenaars Baej—Golden Bay, Nelson—where four of his crew were killed by Maoris. Thinking Cook Strait an inlet, Tasman continued along the west coast of the North Island until he reached Amsterdam Islandt—Tongatapu—where he was given a friendlier reception by the inhabitants, and took on much-needed water and provisions.

Return Journey

On Tasman's return to Batavia, the council of the Dutch East India Company decided that he had not sufficiently explored the seas lying to the west of Chile. Although he had proved that Australia did not extend southward toward the Pole, and had been the first European to

sight Tasmania, New Zealand, and Tonga, he had not investigated the full nature and extent of these new lands he had sighted.

He was therefore commissioned to undertake a second expedition in 1644 to establish the relative geographical relationships of New Guinea, the known parts of the Great South Land (Western Australia), Van Diemen's Land, and the unknown parts of the Great South Land. He coasted past New Guinea as far as the Torres Strait, but failed to recognize the passage between New Guinea and Australia. He then proceeded south along the Gulf of Carpentaria and the north coast of Arnhem Land, before following the remaining northern coast of Western Australia as far as North West Cape (Shark Bay), and then returned to Batavia.

Decommission

Despite Tasman being made a commander and a member of the Council of Justice of Batavia, this voyage was also a disappointment to the company. The seventeenth-century Dutch were primarily interested in trade in gold, timber, or spices, and a land that could not trade was worthless. After an unsuccessful mission commanding a fleet of eight ships to capture a Manila galleon, Tasman left the Dutch East India Company under a cloud in 1653, and became an independent merchant, trading from Batavia. He died in 1659.

New Americans

The great majority of seventeenth-century immigrants to North America arrived independently of direct English authority, and the locally-born grew up in societies under largely local control.

1601 to 1900

1655 Massachusetts Bay Colony Puritans punish the first Quakers and later ban them from holding their meetings

---

1664 New Amsterdam becomes New York after Stuyvesant's surrender to the English

---

1670 Hudson's Bay Company is chartered

1676 Tobacco planter, Nathan Bacon, seeks permission to attack the Susquehannock Indians who are raiding settlements. When permission is refused, the colonists burn Jamestown and kill many Indians.

1684 The Charter of Massachusetts Bay is revoked after criticism reaches England

---

1699 Peace treaty at Maine ends hostilities between the Abenaki Indians and the Massachusetts colonists

This trend began to change in the middle of the century as a result of the English civil war that toppled the monarchy for a decade. In contrast to barely 3,000 settlers throughout all New France, the population of English North America in 1650 was 50,400.

The first English colony, at Jamestown in 1607, was formed by a Virginia company that failed for 15 years to provide returns to its investors. In 1622, when the worst of several Indian massacres killed 347 settlers, the company's charter was revoked, and Virginia became a royal colony two years later.

> Oh Newe England,
> Newe England, how much am
> I bound to the Lord for granting
> me so great mercy as to tread
> on thy grounds.
>
> –Edward Trelawney to Robert Trelawney
> in *A Letter from New England* (1635).

Tobacco

By then Virginia had found an economic lifeline in tobacco cultivation, using the labor of both indentured servants and convicts and, by mid-century, the first slaves from Africa. Tobacco and slavery were also taking root in neighboring Maryland, given by Charles I in 1632 to a Catholic proprietor, Lord Baltimore, who encouraged settlement by both co-religionists and Protestants.

Religious Differences

Religious toleration was not the goal of Protestants repelled by the quasi-Catholic tendencies of the Crown and Church of England. The Pilgrims, who founded Plymouth in 1620, were separatists already exiled in Holland. So too, in practice, were the Puritans who captured the charter of the Massachusetts Bay Company and led larger migration to the Boston area from 1630, while others stayed in England to "purify" the Church.

Colonial Entrepreneurs

Although the Crown claimed sovereignty over the whole eastern seaboard north of Spanish Florida, it had been unable to prevent the establishment of New Netherland in 1613, which acquired Manhattan Island from local Indians for its capital, New Amsterdam, in 1624.

The Dutch settlers were furtraders, like the small numbers of Swedes and Finns who established New Sweden on the Delaware River in 1638, and like those in New France.

Navigation Act

In 1651, the republican Commonwealth attempted to give substance to prevailing mercantilist theory that the function of colonial economies was to serve the interests of the mother country. Aimed at Dutch merchants supplying English colonies with European manufactures and carrying their agricultural produce to European markets, a *Navigation Act* decreed

RIGHT The site of New York was originally acquired by the Dutch as the capital of New Netherland, and named New Amsterdam. As New York, it became one of the original 13 colonies of the United States. This plan of New York was drawn in 1664.

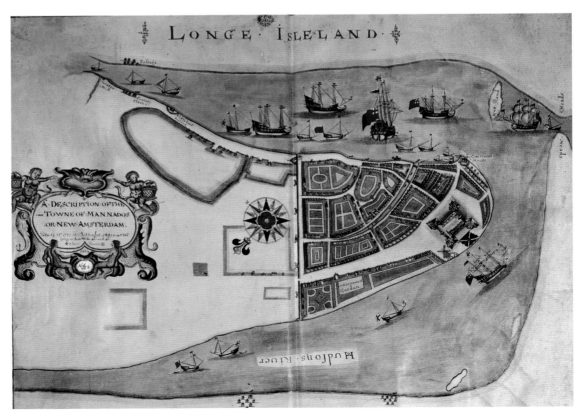

LEFT AND BELOW The European grab for land in North America is evident from the names given to the different areas. The earliest settlements were usually forts built to keep the settlers safe.

Territory acquired by fair purchase from Native Americans

Early forts

Early settlements

Virginia

Spanish territory

New Netherland

French Florida

RIGHT Religions continued their influence across the Atlantic Ocean. This lithograph shows early Americans on their way to church.

that all goods imported into England or the colonies must be carried in English ships.

Royal Interference

The intrusive trend accelerated after the monarchy was restored in 1660. Charles II attempted to create dependent European societies in new proprietary colonies, the Carolinas, New Jersey, and New York (renamed in 1664 after the conquest of New Netherland, which had absorbed New Sweden in 1655) and further tightened mercantilist controls.

New Settlements

Another *Navigation Act* in 1660 strengthened the ban on foreign shipping and decreed colonial produce be shipped only to English possessions. Huge land grants in the Carolinas in 1663, and New Jersey and New York in 1664, were royal rewards to aristocratic supporters. In Bacon's rebellion of 1675, poor frontier settlers in Virginia demanded the removal of the Indians, clashed with wealthy planters, destroyed Jamestown, and narrowly failed to overthrow Governor Berkeley.

Very different was Pennsylvania, founded in 1681 by William Penn as a refuge for pacifist fellow-Quakers persecuted in England.

In 1686, James II merged Rhode Island and Connecticut with Massachusetts Bay and Plymouth to form, with New York and New Jersey, an authoritarian royal Dominion of New England. This Dominion was quickly dissolved when the Stuart monarchy was deposed in 1688, but the new monarchs, William and Mary, retained close control of New England, combining Massachusetts Bay, Plymouth, and Maine into a new royal colony of Massachusetts.

TECHNOLOGY, TRADE, AND TRANSITION

Human Trade

Throughout human history, slavery has taken many forms, but is generally defined by two characteristics— the exploitation of coerced labor, and the ownership of laborers as property.

The abolition of slavery in the New World did not mean the end of it everywhere. During the twentieth century various forms of slavery survived, and although slavery no longer exists as a legal formalized set of labor relations, across the world millions of people, including children, are still forced to live and work in what the British Anti-Slavery Society describes as "conditions of slavery."

Ancient World

Ancient Asian, Egyptian, Greek, and Roman societies all made use of slave labor. People could be enslaved for a variety of reasons, including the inability to repay a debt, as punishment for a crime, or as a consequence of capture during war. The treatment of slaves varied widely in the ancient world, and while a minority achieved a social rank that accorded them some privilege, slaves who refused to work, or who ran away, could expect to be punished severely. In ancient Rome, which depended heavily on slave labor, runaway slaves might be crucified if they were recaptured.

Middle Ages

The Vikings also made use of slaves, whom they described as "thralls." Many of the Vikings' slaves were from Western Europe. Endemic warfare between Christian and Islamic societies produced steady supplies of slaves for both groups. Islamic societies also made use of African slaves. The distinction between slavery and freedom was less sharply drawn in Islamic societies, and some slaves were able to improve their status by conversion to Islam.

Modern Slavery

During the fifteenth and sixteenth centuries, Portuguese adventurers began exploring the coast of Africa. They also began transporting African slaves to Europe and later, in far greater numbers, to the Americas. Subsequently, other European

nations joined in this exploitative trade. Slavery had long been a part of many African societies, but the scale and unrestrained brutality of the European exploitation rendered the two systems very different. And while earlier forms of slavery had often relied upon differences between groups of people—"racial," ethnic, or religious—the modern slave system was explicitly racialized, with black skin becoming a marker of one's slave status, which was not only almost always a permanent condition, but was also likely to be the life-long condition of the slave's offspring.

According to estimates—and figures will never be precise, due to gaps in historical records—by the time of the eventual abolition of the African slave trade in the late nineteenth century, more than 12 million people had been transported from Africa. This number constitutes one of the largest, if involuntary, movements of people in human history.

RIGHT The west coast of Africa proved the ideal source for slaves as shipping times were short to the United States where there was an unlimited market for slaves.

No man can put a chain about the ankle of his fellow man without at last finding the other end fastened about his own neck.
–Frederick Douglass (1818-1895),
American abolitionist, statesman, and author.

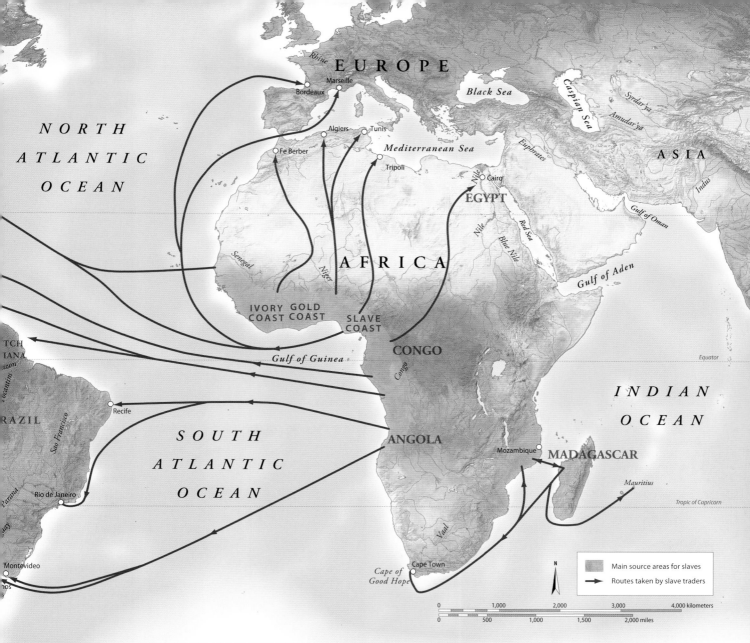

NORTH
ATLANTIC
OCEAN

EUROPE

Rhine

Marseille

Bordeaux

Black Sea

Caspian Sea

Syrdar'ya

Amudar'ya

ASIA

Algiers   Tunis

Fe Berber

Mediterranean Sea

Euphrates

Tripoli

Indus

Nile   Cairo

EGYPT

Red Sea

Gulf of Oman

Senegal

AFRICA

Niger

Blue Nile

Nile

Gulf of Aden

IVORY GOLD
COAST COAST

SLAVE
COAST

Gulf of Guinea

CONGO

Congo

Equator

TCH
IANA
zon

RAZIL

Recife

San Francisco

SOUTH
ATLANTIC
OCEAN

ANGOLA

Mozambique

MADAGASCAR

INDIAN
OCEAN

Mauritius

Parana

Rio de Janeiro

Vaal

Tropic of Capricorn

Montevideo
os

Cape Town

*Cape of
Good Hope*

N

Main source areas for slaves

Routes taken by slave traders

0   1,000   2,000   3,000   4,000 kilometers
0   500   1,000   1,500   2,000 miles

RIGHT Slave markets
were found all over the
world, including Persia,
as shown in this painting
on vellum by Al-Hariri.

LEFT One of the main
occupations for African
slaves in North America
was cotton picking. Huge
plantations thrived only
because of forced labor.

Horrors of the Slave Trade

Enslavement was a brutal process
from beginning to end. Slaves
bound for the Americas were
captured, either directly by European slave traders, or, more commonly, by other Africans working
on their behalf. They were then
marched to one of a series of "slave
pens," where they would be held
until they were purchased and
transported to the Americas.

The passage across the Atlantic
Ocean was one of the most dangerous aspects of slavery. Crowded
densely below decks in ships built
specifically for the purpose of
carrying large numbers of people,
the terrified Africans usually found
themselves packed alongside others

with whom they had no tribal or
linguistic connections. Mortality
rates on slave ships were very high,
but so cheap was their cargo that
most slave traders had no incentive—and felt no humanitarian
or moral obligation—to spend
money in order to improve the
conditions on board.

The Americas

Slavery became an important
part of economic life throughout
the Americas. In some places,
European colonists sought initially
to enslave Native Americans. Those
attempts were generally unsuccessful, as Native American men not
only resisted performing agricultural labor—which they often

1851 Frederick Douglass publishes the first of a series of newspapers

1862 Emancipation Proclamation issued by US President Abraham Lincoln. It comes into effect the following year.

1865 Thirteenth Amendment to the Constitution of the United States proposed. The amendment stated that: "Neither slavery nor involuntary servitude, except as a punishment for crime whereof the party shall have been duly convicted, shall exist within the United States, or any place subject to their jurisdiction."

regarded as women's work—but also found it relatively easy to escape into a familiar environment.

From the sixteenth century, the demand for agricultural labor throughout the Americas far outstripped the supply of white labor, including, in a number of colonies, the indentured labor provided by white men and women who bound themselves to work for a specific period of time in return for their passage across the Atlantic. There was a steady market, therefore, for African slaves.

Slave Life

Slave life varied according to time and place. Some slave owners took pride in their careful "management," and emphasized that it was not in their self-interest to mistreat their slaves. Others boasted that they were playing a part in "civilizing" and "Christianizing" the dark-skinned heathens from Africa. The law offered few protections to slaves. It was not surprising, therefore, that life expectancy for slaves was always far below whites, and in places—such as the French Caribbean colony Saint-Domingue—slave-owners treated their slaves with particular brutality. Slave women were often subjected to the worst abuses by their white master and valued solely for the ability to produce more slave children to add value to their owner's property.

Resistance and Rebellions

Despite their brutal mistreatment, slaves everywhere sustained ideas of freedom, and sought, in a variety of ways, to ameliorate the worst excesses of their situation. Resistance could take a number of forms. On the most fundamental level, slaves defended themselves by establishing and maintaining their own culture. Running away was a different form of resistance. Throughout the Americas, tens of thousands of slaves ran away. Although many were soon recaptured—and faced a range of brutal punishments—others succeeded in joining "maroon" colonies of ex-slaves. Slaves fleeing the Southern US states sought refuge in the North, where slavery was gradually outlawed in the period following the American Revolution.

The most assertive form of slave resistance was outright rebellion. Although slave-owners tried to persuade themselves that their slaves were content with their lot, they maintained their authority largely through violence, or the threat of violence, and lived in constant fear of rebellion.

A successful slave rebellion in the US was unlikely, because white Southerners had put in place a rigid system of control and authority. But when southern slaves did strike out violently against their white masters, such as in 1831,

when Nat Turner led a bloody, albeit unsuccessful uprising in Virginia, the white South reacted with predictable violence.

Abolition

During the late eighteenth and early nineteenth centuries, organized movements for the abolition of slavery developed in Britain and the United States. Under the leadership of people such as Thomas Clarkson, William Wilberforce, and William Lloyd Garrison, these movements demanded their emancipation. Later, in the US, the most

compelling arguments were made by ex-slaves, most notably Frederick Douglass, who left audiences in no doubt about either the brutality of slavery or the slaves' humanity.

Slavery throughout the British Empire was abolished by an Act of Parliament in 1833. In the USA, the Thirteenth Amendment to the Constitution (1865) formalized and extended Abraham Lincoln's earlier Emancipation Proclamation. The last slave society in the Americas to emancipate its slaves was Brazil, which formally abolished the practice in 1888.

CANADA

MAINE

VERMONT

NEW HAMPSHIRE

MINNESOTA

WISCONSIN

MASSACHUSETTS   Boston

NEW YORK

RHODE ISLAND

MICHIGAN

CONNECTICUT

Detroit

IOWA

Chicago

PENNSYLVANIA

NEW JERSEY

ILLINOIS   INDIANA   OHIO

DELAWARE

UNITED STATES OF AMERICA

MARYLAND

Cincinnati

St Louis

WEST VIRGINIA

VIRGINIA

MISSOURI

KENTUCKY

NORTH CAROLINA

TENNESSEE

NORTH ATLANTIC OCEAN

ARKANSAS

SOUTH CAROLINA

Charleston

ALABAMA   GEORGIA

Savannah

MISSISSIPPI

TEXAS   LOUISIANA

Percentage of Slave Population–1860

Arkansas	26	Florida	44
Texas	30	Alabama	45
Virginia	31	Louisiana	47
North Carolina	33	Mississippi	55
Georgia	44	South Carolina	57

New Orleans

FLORIDA

Gulf of Mexico

Bahamas   Tropic of Cancer

Cuba

N

Early states with approximately 50 percent slave population (1790)

Slave states (1860)

Underground slave escape routes (Underground railroad)

0	250	500	750	1,000 kilometers
0	125	250	375	500 miles

The Sun King

Louis XIV was the epitome of the absolutist ruler. He aimed to centralize power, reducing the influence and the rights of the nobility within France and fighting expansionist wars against his weaker neighbors.

Louis came to the throne at the tender age of four, with his mother and her reputed lover Cardinal Mazarin ruling as regents. Powerful nobles challenged the regency during the Fronde rebellion (1648–1653), and some members of the middle and lower classes joined in to protest their high taxes and Mazarin's arbitrary rule. Louis would not forget the humiliation that marked his childhood, later recalling that a mob of Parisians had once invaded his bedroom to make sure that the King remained in Paris.

After Mazarin's death in 1661, Louis took power into his own hands. He refused to appoint a First Minister to govern, choosing instead to make decisions for himself. He raised commoners to high office—such men would be entirely beholden to him. If he chose to dismiss them, they would have neither title nor inherited lands to support them.

Nobles also needed Louis's favor, and the leading peers of the realm competed for the right to hold his shirt while the King dressed, as this sign of preference would vastly improve their status at court, and that such a moment of intimacy might provide an opportunity to beseech a favor. Courtiers were acutely aware that the way to advance was to commit

RIGHT Louis XIV is often referred to as *Le Roi Soleil* (the Sun King), because of his belief that just as planets revolve around the Sun, so France should revolve around him. Though Louis engaged in numerous wars, his reign brought internal stability to the country, and a shift to a more sophisticated culture.

wholeheartedly to the crown and to Louis XIV's rule. It was also necessary to participate in the intrigues of Versailles and to earn Louis's attention.

L'état, c'est moi.
–Louis XIV's reputed remark to the Paris High Court of Justice.

Tetouan.

GIBRAL

DE

1660 Louis XIV marries Maria Teresa, daughter of Spanish king, Philip IV

1665 Louis XIV commissions architect Claude Perrault to design the eastern wing of the Palais du Louvre, then a royal palace. It is now Musée du Louvre, the most visited art museum in the world.

1682 Château de Versailles is opened

1685 Following the death of Maria Teresa in 1683, Louis marries Françoise d'Aubigne

RIGHT During his reign, Louis XIV spent a fortune waging war, at the cost of the nation. He sold rights to tax peasants as a way of gaining finances for further battles.

LEFT This grand engraving shows the capture of three Turkish vessels by the French in the Strait of Gibraltar in 1643.

France (1643)

Territory gained by Louis XIV (1715)

Château de Versailles

The chateau at Versailles served a number of roles. The elegant splendor of the Hall of Mirrors, the palace's precise geometric design, and the vast extent of its gardens symbolized the power of the French state and its monarch.

Louis's patronage of leading artists ensured a steady diet of theater, music, dance, and visual art, all carefully calculated to show the authority and grandeur of the Sun King. Louis himself danced in ballets if the role were sufficiently flattering. Jean-Baptiste Racine wrote plays depicting classical virtues of order and self-discipline that Louis admired. Paintings and sculptures of Apollo not so subtly tied the heroic Sun King to the mythical Sun God. Mock battles safely displayed the gallantry of the French nation.

Center of the World

In truth, Louis's power was far from absolute and he often had to cooperate with nobles and local elites. In order to finance his patronage of the nobility and the arts, the lavish life at Versailles, and his enormous appetite for war, Louis needed money, and lots of it. Without a centralized bureaucracy as we would understand it today, Louis had to sell contracts that allowed the buyer to collect taxes. The landed nobility often purchased such contracts, as they still had the political power in the provinces to exploit their new offices. Louis also received "gifts" from leading noble families, and he richly rewarded those who supported his treasury, providing social and political connections, arranging favorable marriages, providing Church or government posts, or positions in the Army. Of course, if Louis stopped the flow of patronage appointments and his largesse, he would have less money to fund his wars and less loyalty from his nobles.

While Louis's power was only theoretically absolute, his reputation ensured that French courtiers could flatter themselves that they lived at the center of the world. "There was nothing he liked so much as flattery," the Duc de Saint-Simon commented in his memoirs.

ABOVE Anne Marie de Montpensier, cousin of Louis XIV, seen entering Orléans, France during a protest against Louis.

RIGHT Maria Theresa of Austria, Infanta of Spain, was Queen Consort of France from 1660 to 1683. She was the mother of the Grand Dauphin, the only survivor of her six children.

Wars

Louis XIV was a warrior king, fighting a series of lengthy wars against his foes in Europe, seeking to expand his realm. Following the death of Philip IV of Spain, Louis used highly tenuous legal reasoning as a pretext to attack Spain, seizing both the Spanish Netherlands and the Franche-Comté. The abrupt French victory alarmed other European leaders. England, Sweden, and Louis's former ally, the Dutch Republic, formed the Triple Alliance in order to combat Louis's aggression. Louis prudently agreed to the Treaty of Aix-la-Chapelle in May 1668 rather than face this threat.

This war set the pattern for the following half-century. In 1672, Louis attacked the Dutch United Provinces, this time in alliance with England. Although the Dutch were able to negotiate a separate peace with England and recruit allies in Spain and the Holy Roman Empire, brilliant military campaigns allowed Louis' forces not only to fight off their combined enemies but to re-conquer the Franche-Comté and most of the Spanish Netherlands. Exhausted by war, the parties agreed to the Treaty of Nijmegen in 1778 that rewarded Louis with the Franche-Comté and much of the Spanish Netherlands, although he did return conquered Dutch territory.

By the mid-1680s, Louis had reached the height of his power. His ambitions led other European leaders to form the Grand Alliance, which at times included the Holy Roman Empire, England, Austria, Spain, Sweden, Portugal, the United Provinces, and various German principalities. Exceptionally skillful French generals and soldiers allowed Louis to stave off this Grand Alliance and often to defeat its armies on the battlefield, but despite money and expertise, Louis proved unable to achieve any lasting victory.

LEFT Louis XIV among troops at the siege of Tournal, June 21, 1667. This Flemish painting resides in the museum that was Louis's famous residence, Le Château de Versailles, outside Paris.

Defeat and Treaties

The war of the League of Augsburg from 1688 to 1697 led to French concessions at the peace table. The war of Spanish Succession from 1701 to 1714 bled France white. Defeats at the battles of Blenheim, Ramillies, Turin, and Oudenarde destroyed the myth of French invincibility and put Louis on the defensive. His last war dragged on until 1713, when exhaustion and the fear of a growing Austrian Empire induced England and the Dutch to sign the Treaty of Utrecht, followed by the Treaties of Rastadt and Baden in 1714 that put an end to the decades of Louis XIV's wars.

Louis's wars required a massive army, and the French army grew to roughly 300,000 soldiers by the early 1700s, which equaled the combined forces of Louis' enemies. The French army also became more professional, introducing tighter discipline and drill and modern innovations such as hospitals for wounded soldiers.

In 1693, at the height of the war of the League of Augsburg, Louis spent more than 114 million livres on the military, a figure almost ten times as much as his regents had spent in the early years of his reign.

In the end, Louis's incessant wars brought France relatively little reward; most French gains had occurred by the mid-1680s, and the following wars proved ruinously expensive. Philippe de Courcillon, Marquis de Dangeau, recorded in his memoirs that the dying King cautioned his heir: "Do not imitate me, but be a peaceful prince, and may you apply yourself principally to the alleviation of the burdens of your subjects."

Louis XIV proved unable to conquer Europe, but his armies dominated the European scene during his reign, and French power was ascendant, requiring the combined forces of the Grand Alliance to contain Louis's expansionism.

Treaties of Utrecht and Rastadt 1714

- British territory
- French territory
- Territory of Archduke of Austria—Holy Roman Emperor
- Savoy territory

LEFT European territorial divisions at the Treaties of Utrecht and Rastadt, 1714, limited Louis's expansion and ended his expensive wars.

The Greatness of Russia

Under Peter the Great and his successors, the Tsardom of Muscovy was transformed into the Russian Empire thanks to dramatic territorial expansion to the west.

LEFT Portrait of Peter the Great, in 1717, shows a man ready for battle. Peter expanded Russian territory during his reign.

FAR LEFT The luxurious Russian costume worn by Catherine the Great in 1770 is encrusted with precious gems. The Russian court was rich with the spoils of war.

1709 Russia scores a victory over Sweden at the Battle of Poltava

1711 Peter the Great establishes laws to allow the governing Senate to pass laws in his absence

1715 Peter forces his son Alexei to endorse his reforms or risk his right to the throne

1716 Alexei flees to Austria to avoid military service

1718 After returning to Russia on a promise of freedom, Alexei is put on trial, tortured, and dies in the Peter and Paul Fortress

1721 The Great Northern War ends with the Treaty of Nystad. Peter is declared Emperor of Russia.

The bulk of Peter the Great's reign (1682–1725) was taken up with the Great Northern War against Sweden, 1700–1721. The two rulers met in battle at Narva (1700), and although the Russians outnumbered the Swedes three to one, Charles XII routed Peter's forces. This humiliating defeat spurred Peter to greater action, and he began to mobilize more and more peasant conscripts to rebuild his army on western lines.

Peter's new army was equipped with state-of-the-art flintlock muskets, and trained in the discipline of the bayonet charge. Russian domestic weapons production increased sharply and Russia became self-sufficient in armaments by the end of Peter's reign.

St Petersburg

Tenaciously, Peter clawed his way back to the Baltic in 1703 when his forces captured the mouth of the Neva River on the Gulf of Finland. To secure this toehold, the Russians built the Peter and Paul Fortress, and around it Peter established a new city, St Petersburg. Despite the swampy terrain, poor agricultural land, and the lack of any local population, Peter decreed that St Petersburg would become his new capital city and his "Window on the West." He forcibly relocated thousands of Russian peasant serfs to the region to help lay the foundations of the city, with perhaps as many as 100,000 peasants dying in the process.

Victory at a Price

The decisive Russo-Swedish battle occurred at Poltava in Ukraine in 1709. Peter defeated the invading Swedes and forced Charles XII to flee south to the Ottoman Empire.

The Swedish king managed to stir up Ottoman resentments against Russia, resulting in an Ottoman declaration of war late in 1710. When Peter marched south to fight the Ottomans he stumbled into a Turkish trap and found his army surrounded at the Battle of the River Pruth in 1711. As terms of peace with the Ottomans, Peter had to abandon his earlier gains at Azov in Ukraine, and allow Charles XII to return to Sweden. Peace with Sweden came in 1721 with Russia gaining part of the Baltic coast including Latvia and Estonia.

> I have conquered an empire but I have not been able to conquer myself.
>
> –Peter the Great.

Catherine

Catherine the Great (r. 1762–1796) completed the westward expansion begun by Peter the Great. Under Catherine, Russian forces managed to conquer the Crimea and finally reach the Black Sea coast. More spectacularly, Russia, in cooperation with Prussia and Austria, participated in three partitions of the Kingdom of Poland (1772, 1793, 1795). As a result of the partitions, the Russian Empire expanded to include western Ukraine, White Russia (Belarus), and Lithuanian lands. These annexations added over seven million new inhabitants to the Russian Empire, including one million Jews.

Western Influence

Peter played a pivotal role in pushing Russian nobility towards westernization. In 1699, he changed the calendar to the western Julian calendar. Other decrees required that nobles shave their beards and dress in western-style clothing or face possible imprisonment. Official social functions had to include women as in the west. French literature and ideas readily flowed into the empire in the time of Catherine the Great, who corresponded with Voltaire and other luminaries of the Enlightenment.

Russia (1795)

Territory ceded to Poland (c. 1624), regained (c. 1686)

Territory gained from Poland (1645—1795)

Arctic Circle

Pechora

Ob

White Sea

URAL MOUNTAINS

Arkhangelsk

Deina

ARCHANGEL

Solikamsk

EN

FINLAND

CARELIA

Petrozavodsk

Perm

RUSSIAN EMPIRE

Nystad
(signed 1721)

Vyborg

Olonets

ulf of Finland

St Petersburg
(Peter the Great's capital - 1703)

NOVGOROD

Reval

ESTONIA

Novgorod

Neva

Riga

LIVONIA

Ural

MOSCOW

NIZHNIY
NOVGOROD

THUANIA

Vilna

Moscow

AST
USSIA

Smolenski

Tambov

WHITE
RUSSIA

Voronezh

Chemigov

Volga

aw

Astrakhan

OLAND

UKRAINE

Kiev

Poltava

ASTRAKHAN

Caspian Sea

L'viv

Dnieper

Don

Pruth

TAURIDA

AZOV

KHERSON

Azov

Dniester

KUBAN

Sea of
Azov

CRIMEA

Kerch

Black Sea

| 0 | 250 | 500 | 750 | 1,000 kilometers |
| 0 | 125 | 250 | 375 | 500 miles |

ABOVE Catherine the Great was responsible for further expansion after Peter and was successful in the division of Poland.

LEFT The complex of palaces, fountains, and gardens at Peterhof was built as the Summer Palace for the new capital city of St Petersburg.

271

The Senior Service

The oldest of the British armed services, the Royal Navy began its illustrious history in the sixteenth century during the reign of Henry VIII when the ships *Henri Grâce à Dieu* and the more famous *Mary Rose* battled the French at Solent.

1547 The Navy Royal, as it was then known, has a fleet of 58 vessels

1634 Charles I creates a "ship money" levy in order to build up the navy. The tax becomes the main cause of the English Civil War.

1759-1765 HMS *Victory* is built. It is the oldest naval ship still in commission. *Victory* now sits in dry dock at Portsmouth, UK.

1793-1815 The Royal Navy loses 344 vessels, 254 of which were shipwrecked, resulting in the loss of more than 100,000 seamen

1831 The Navy Board is abolished and the Admiralty takes charge of the Royal Navy.

The British Royal Navy held command of the sea for long periods of time from the eighteenth through to the early twentieth century, allowing Britain and its allies to trade, and to move troops and supplies easily in wartime while their enemies could not.

Naval Dominance

To maintain dominance during this early period, Britain battled any threats to her supremacy. Despite having signed the Treaty of Utrecht (1713), which ended the War of Spanish Succession, she sought to establish stability in Europe and overseas on the basis of a balance of power. This lasted until 1739 when the Royal Navy fought against Spain in the Caribbean and attacked Spain's possessions in the Pacific and the Philippines, as well as in modern-day Colombia at the 1841 Battle of Cartagena. These attacks were largely unsuccessful. The Navy also saw action in the Seven Years' War (1756–1763), which included the French and Indian war that enveloped both European and colonial possessions, and involved all of the major European powers of the period.

ABOVE The French flagship *Redoubtable* at the Battle of Trafalgar on October 21, 1805. Britain's Admiral Nelson was killed at the moment of victory over the French.

> **England expects that every man will do his duty.**
> –Last semaphore from Admiral Horatio Nelson's ship HMS *Victory* before the Battle of Trafalgar.

Victories

But it was later in the eighteenth and early nineteenth century that the Royal Navy fought its most bitter battles, nearly all of them against France and most of which Britain won. Britain had the advantage of being able to direct its main strength onto the world's oceans, whereas France had to divide its power between land and sea.

However, a series of the greatest naval victories over the French were fought during the 22 years of the Napoleonic Wars. The battles began in 1793, when war was declared against the young French republic by a powerful consortium of nations led by Britain, and which saw the Royal Navy rise to the peak of its power in the age of sail.

RIGHT The largest and most powerful navy in the world, the Royal Navy played a key role in establishing the British Empire as the dominant global force of the period.

The war with France continued until 1815. During this time, the Royal Navy's greatest contribution was the unremitting blockade preventing Napoleon from rebuilding his fleet and encouraging enemies in Europe to rise up against him. Disputes with America, made worse by the blockade because America was trying to trade with both Britain and France, erupted in war in 1812. The war mainly involved single-ship actions between small ships. Britain was able to deploy sufficient maritime strength along America's eastern seaboard, managing to disrupt merchant shipping and ending with peace in 1814. By 1815 Britain, through the Royal Navy, was clearly the unchallenged commander of the oceans.

GREENLA

Baffin Bay

DOMINION OF CANADA

Hudson Bay

NORTH AMERICA

Montreal

Halifax

Bermuda

Tropic of Cancer

Cuba

Bahamas

Cayman Islands *Jamaica*

WEST INDIES *Grenada* *Barbados* *Grenada* *Trinidad and Tobago*

Equator

PACIFIC OCEAN

SOUTH AMERICA

Tropic of Capricorn

Falkland Islands

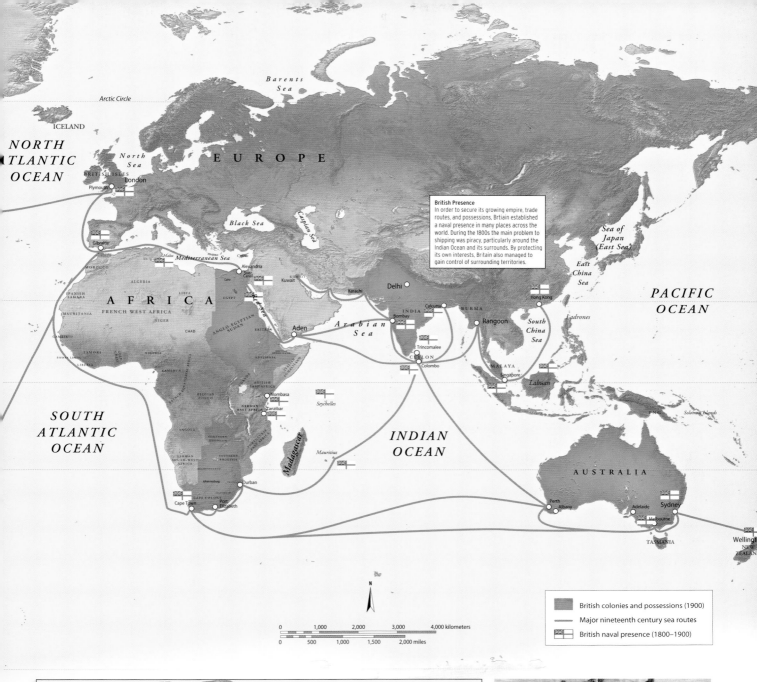

North Atlantic Ocean

ICELAND

North Sea

BRITISH ISLES
London
Plymouth

Barents Sea

EUROPE

Black Sea

Caspian Sea

Gibraltar

Malta *Mediterranean Sea*

Alexandria
Cairo

Suez Canal

Kuwait

MOROCCO

ALGERIA

LIBYA

EGYPT

Karachi

Delhi

Sea of Japan (East Sea)

East China Sea

PACIFIC OCEAN

British Presence
In order to secure its growing empire, trade routes, and possessions, Brtiain established a naval presence in many places across the world. During the 1800s the main problem to shipping was piracy, particularly around the Indian Ocean and its surrounds. By protecting its own interests, Britain also managed to gain control of surrounding territories.

SPANISH SAHARA

MAURITANIA

FRENCH WEST AFRICA

NIGER

CHAD

ANGLO EGYPTIAN SUDAN

Red Sea

Arabian Sea

Aden

INDIA

Bombay

Calcutta

Hong Kong

BURMA

Rangoon

South China Sea

Ladrones

A F R I C A

NIGERIA

CAMEROUN

ABYSSINIA

Trincomalee

CEYLON

Colombo

MALAYA

Singapore

Labuan

BELGIAN CONGO

Mombasa

GERMAN EAST AFRICA

Zanzibar

Seychelles

Solomon Islands

ANGOLA

GERMAN SOUTH-WEST AFRICA

NORTHERN RHODESIA

SOUTHERN RHODESIA

Madagascar

Mauritius

INDIAN OCEAN

SOUTH ATLANTIC OCEAN

Johannesburg

Durban

CAPE COLONY

Cape Town
Port Elizabeth

AUSTRALIA

Perth
Albany

Adelaide

Sydney

Melbourne

TASMANIA

Wellington NEW ZEALAND

N

0   1,000   2,000   3,000   4,000 kilometers
0   500   1,000   1,500   2,000 miles

▨	British colonies and possessions (1900)
—	Major nineteenth century sea routes
⚑	British naval presence (1800–1900)

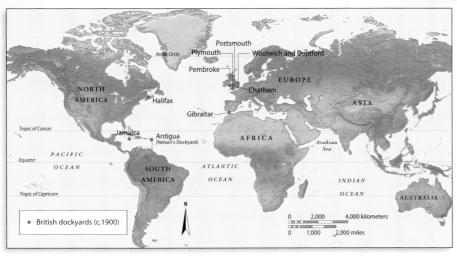

Arctic Circle

Portsmouth
Plymouth
Woolwich and Deptford
Pembroke
Chatham

NORTH AMERICA

Halifax

EUROPE

ASIA

Gibraltar

AFRICA

Tropic of Cancer

Jamaica

Antigua (Nelson's Dockyard)

Arabian Sea

PACIFIC OCEAN

Equator

ATLANTIC OCEAN

INDIAN OCEAN

SOUTH AMERICA

Tropic of Capricorn

AUSTRALIA

N

• British dockyards (c.1900)

0   2,000   4,000 kilometers
0   1,000   2,000 miles

LEFT By the turn of the twentieth century, Britain had established dockyards at several strategic locations around the world.

ABOVE The *Mary Rose* after she was rebuilt in 1536. The Royal Navy ship was originally built around 1511 by order of Henry VIII.

1601 to 1900

Atlantic Trade

At the start of the Industrial Revolution, the majority of British exports went to Europe. As the eighteenth century unfolded Britain increasingly traded with the Americas and the British West Indies, and by the end of this period trade with North America had become substantially more important due to the prominence of cotton.

In the European race for colonies Britain was a late starter compared to Spain and Portugal. By 1696, however, Britain had won many French Caribbean islands, which France had started colonizing as early as the 1650s. Other acquisitions included Jamaica in 1655, which had formerly belonged to Spain, and the eastern colonies in North America.

By 1800, Britain was conducting much trade that was dependent upon re-exporting goods from its colonies to Northern Europe. Sugar came from Caribbean islands and the Americas provided tobacco and cotton.

Right up until the nineteenth century the lush plantation islands of the Caribbean were the most valuable possession in the overseas imperial world.

Human Trade

Crucial in the production of the colonial powers' most important goods was slave labor. Hence, the slave trade expanded hugely when it was found that many of the Caribbean islands could grow sugar, a crop best handled on a big scale, on large plantations, requiring a great deal of labor. Following on from this, some of the biggest profits from trade during this period were made from slaving.

Asian Trade

During this period, Britain's role in trade became increasingly prominent compared to other European powers trading in Asia. The influence that Britain had at the close of the period was largely facilitated by her empire in India.

Outside India, British influence was more limited. In China, where trade had existed long before this period, Britain received no political concessions or favorable trade conditions and experienced a trade deficit up until the eighteenth century, which was a result of high demand for tea, silk, and porcelain in Britain and comparatively low Chinese demand for British exports.

This trade imbalance was made more equal by the trade in opium that was implemented to earn silver to finance British imports from China. During this period China had more valuable trade interests with the Philippines, Thailand, and the Indonesian archipelago. An increase in trade between America and China was achieved towards the end of this period.

Exporting the Industrial Revolution

One of the most exceptional features in Britain's industrial revolution was the magnitude of the cotton textile industry— iron, engineering, and coal were also remarkable. Given that the inputs and much of the market for the output of this industry involved overseas entities, there were important implications for trade.

Trade was conducted under a multilateral system whereby tropical primary products were financed by exports of manufactured goods. So extensive and successful was this process that it enabled Britain to hold the title of the world's greatest trading nation for the major part of this period and up until the twentieth century.

1792 The first trade union in the US is formed by shoemakers

1793 Eli Whitney invents the cotton gin, speeding up the production of cotton for export

1808 US Congress prohibits the importation of African slaves

1858 The first trans-Atlantic cable is completed

LEFT The Caribbean islands were the major source of the sugar that was exported to Europe. In this painting by William Clark, workers are seen rolling barrels of sugar aboard longboats for passage to trading vessels.

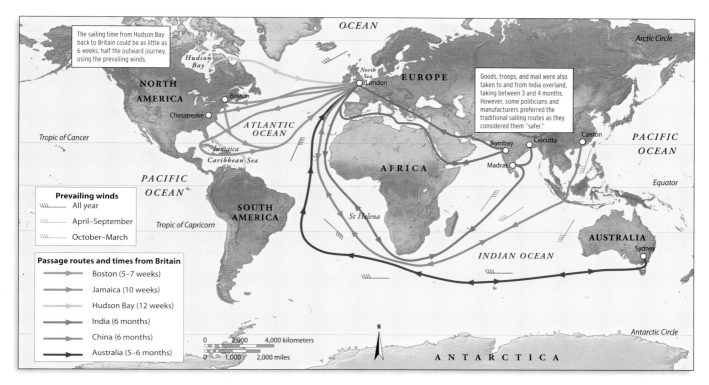

The sailing time from Hudson Bay back to Britain could be as little as 6 weeks, half the outward journey, using the prevailing winds.

Goods, troops, and mail were also taken to and from India overland, taking between 3 and 4 months. However, some politicians and manufacturers preferred the traditional sailing routes as they considered them "safer."

Prevailing winds
- All year
- April–September
- October–March

Passage routes and times from Britain
- Boston (5–7 weeks)
- Jamaica (10 weeks)
- Hudson Bay (12 weeks)
- India (6 months)
- China (6 months)
- Australia (5–6 months)

ABOVE The vast time and distance between ports made the need for good shipping imperative.

RIGHT By 1750, most of the world had been divided up by the seven leading trading nations.

- British Empire
- Danish Territory
- Dutch Empire
- French Empire
- Portuguese Empire
- Russian Empire
- Spanish Empire

(Colonial Possessions 1750)

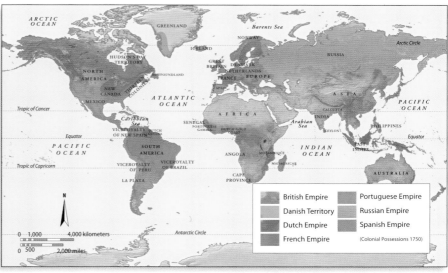

LEFT Customs House on Thames Wharf, London. All freight vessels had to pay duty on their goods at a customs house before the cargo could be unloaded.

RIGHT *New York City from Bedloe's Island*, painted in 1847 by James Pringle. By the mid-1800s New York was the busiest port in the country, handling more goods and passengers than the rest of the nation's ports together.

> By what means are the Europeans so powerful, or why, since they can so easily visit Asia and Africa for trade or conquest, cannot the Asiaticks and Africans invade their coasts, plant colonies in their ports, and give laws to their natural princes?
>
> –Samuel Johnson, *Rasselas* (1759).

The Course of Human Events

None of the 56 men who signed the Declaration of Independence on July 4, 1776, would have thought it remotely possible 13 years earlier that the American colonies would sever connections with Britain.

> The members of this Congress [declare that] it is inseparably essential to the freedom of a people, and the undoubted right of Englishmen, that no taxes be imposed on them but with their own consent, given personally or by their representatives.
>
> Resolutions of the Stamp Act Congress (October 19, 1765).

BELOW RIGHT American revolutionaries, opposed to the imposition of British duties, destroyed chests of tea as a protest—the famous Boston Tea Party.

When France ceded its vast, wild Canadian territory to Britain after the Seven Years' War in 1763, English-speaking America seemed on the threshold of a new prosperity. Military defeat had stopped the French from using their Indian allies to block the westward expansion of Britain's colonies.

British Control

A 1763 British royal proclamation that limited westward expansion was presented as an interim protective measure against a major Indian uprising. But Parliament's decision to make the colonies contribute financially to their own defense underlined the impression of tightening British control. So did the *Sugar Act* of 1764, seeking the necessary revenue through customs duties and restricting trade between New England and the foreign West Indies. The *Stamp Act* of 1765, which taxed every form of printed document, led to the first coordinated protests throughout North America, with the famous slogan "no taxation without representation" revealing common assumptions among otherwise divided colonies that local control should rest with local assemblies rather than the British Parliament.

Riot

In 1767, the *Townshend Acts* reignited American objections to direct taxation, voiced in the *Stamp Act* crisis, by once again using customs duties to raise revenue. A riot in Boston, when an accompanying tougher customs administration impounded a ship, led to the dispatch of 1,000 British troops. Their presence only raised tensions within the civilian population, culminating in the Boston Massacre of 1770— five locals were killed by soldiers firing into a riotous crowd. Yet not even this incident raised widespread support for independence.

Tea Act

When a partial repealing of the Townshend duties retained just one, on tea—to uphold Parliament's right to tax America—colonial protests and boycotts reduced and brought a two-year period of calm in Anglo-American relations. But the *Tea Act* of 1773 brought about renewed conflict. It offered the Americans a cheaper supply of their favorite drink, but its attempt to provide a captive market for the East India Company threatened the profits of Boston merchants

1774 The very First Continental Congress is held

1775 Paul Revere sent to warn John Hancock and Samuel Adams

July 8, 1776 Liberty Bell in Philadelphia rings to call out the people for a historic public reading of the Declaration of Independence

1783 John Adams helps write the peace treaty with England

1789 The Bill of Rights becomes the first ten amendments to the US Constitution

1789 Statesman George Washington becomes the first president of the United States

RIGHT The first shots were fired in the War of Independence at Lexington Common in Massachusetts, April 19, 1775.

BELOW A humble carpenter's hall in Philadelphia was the site of the first Continental Congress in 1774.

BELOW A boundary was declared around the colonies, ostensibly as protection against an Indian uprising.

smuggling tea from foreign sources in defiance of the Townshend duty. The Boston Tea Party saw 342 chests of tea thrown into the harbor to thwart the Massachusetts governor's plans to uphold the Act.

Rebellion

Punitive British responses to this event in December 1773 escalated protest into rebellion. The *Coercive Acts* of 1774 closed Boston's port, moved troops to the city, installed the British commander-in-chief as Governor of Massachusetts, and established trials in England for colonial offenders. Meanwhile, the *Quebec Act* permanently restricted westward expansion by extending that province into the area defined in the 1763 proclamation.

The American response, the First Continental Congress, promised more serious inter-colonial cooperation and aggressive anti-British commercial warfare than the previous shortlived attempts. In the most rebellious colony, Massachusetts, a six-month stalemate between the British army and the more numerous colonial militia ended in April 1775 with battles at Lexington and Concord, ambushes of British troops retreating to Boston, and a Second Continental Congress at Philadelphia in May. The war had begun, but it was not yet a war for independence—many of the rebels, while rejecting the authority of Parliament, still were loyal to the Crown.

Loyalists

On July 5, 1775, those Americans seeking independence were outvoted in the Second Continental Congress by moderates whose Olive Branch Petition asserted colonial rights but pledged loyalty to George III, even as George Washington's forces were fighting his armies. Victory was by no means certain in what some have called America's first civil war.

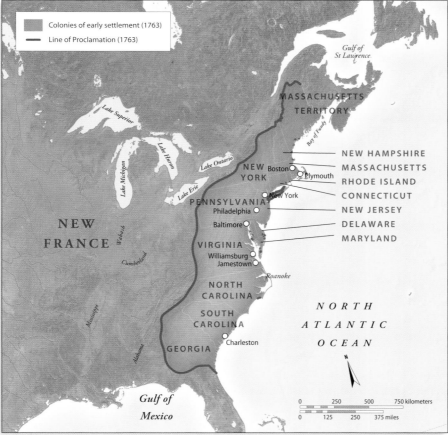

Colonies of early settlement (1763)
Line of Proclamation (1763)

Gulf of St Lawrence

MASSACHUSETTS TERRITORY

Lake Superior

Lake Huron

Lake Michigan

Lake Ontario

Lake Erie

Bay of Fundy

NEW YORK — Boston
Plymouth

NEW HAMPSHIRE
MASSACHUSETTS
RHODE ISLAND
CONNECTICUT
NEW JERSEY
DELAWARE
MARYLAND

NEW FRANCE

PENNSYLVANIA — New York
Philadelphia
Baltimore
VIRGINIA
Williamsburg
Jamestown
Roanoke

Wabash
Cumberland
Mississippi
Alabama

NORTH CAROLINA
SOUTH CAROLINA
GEORGIA — Charleston

NORTH ATLANTIC OCEAN

N

Gulf of Mexico

0   250   500   750 kilometers
0   125   250   375 miles

Continental Army

Washington's great achievement was to keep the continental army intact as a symbol of the Revolution, despite inadequate financial support from Congress, and the priority individual States placed on local militias. British forces— including German mercenaries and Iroquois Indians—were potentially much stronger. But General Lord William Howe was cautious in his pursuit after forcing the Americans into retreat in New York in 1776,

giving Washington the opportunity to achieve two victories with his counter-attacks in New Jersey. But more crucially, Howe then failed to implement his part of a three-pronged attack aimed to converge on Albany, New York, in a strategy intended to isolate the New England heart of the Revolution.

Valley Forge

In the winter of 1777–1778, George Washington's army underwent its most severe crisis at Valley Forge,

Pennsylvania. Harsh weather and poor supplies led to over 1,000 desertions and nearly 3,000 deaths from malnutrition and disease before the former Prussian military officer Baron von Steuben rallied morale with professional drills and maneuvers. By the time the continental army emerged in the spring, leaner but tougher, a victory at Saratoga had persuaded Britain's European rivals to support the war.

Turning Point

Direct intervention by France and Spain, and financial support from the Netherlands, were the war's major turning points. Not only did military support threaten to counter British power in America, but French threats to British interests in the West Indies and India—and even Spanish threats to Gibraltar— reinforced opposition to the war within Britain itself.

LEFT The historic Siege of Yorktown pitted Washington's forces and French forces against the army of English general, Lord Cornwallis–the outcome would determine the future of the nation.

ABOVE After being expelled from New York, US General George Washington led his army on a daring counter-attack across the Delaware River to seize New Jersey.

British Surrender

Following the conquest of Georgia in 1779, a series of victories established British control of South Carolina in 1780. But the arrival of 5,500 French troops in Rhode Island in July, followed by a series of American victories in the Carolinas later that same year, prompted the British commander, Lord Cornwallis, to concede the most southerly States and seek decisive victory in Virginia.

A combination of the military forces under the command of George Washington and the French Marquis de Lafayette, plus French naval control of Chesapeake Bay, led to Cornwallis's final surrender at Yorktown on October 19, 1781. This was effectively the end of the long war, though it wasn't until September 3, 1783, that the historic Treaty of Paris finally formalized American independence.

Lake Superior

Lake Huron

Lake Michigan

Lake Ontario

Lake Erie

NEW BRUNSWICK

MAINE

Bay of Fundy

VERMONT

NEW HAMPSHIRE

NEW YORK

MASSACHUSETTS

RHODE ISLAND

CONNECTICUT

Allegheny

PENNSYLVANIA

NEW JERSEY

MARYLAND

DELAWARE

VIRGINIA

Wabash

Cumberland

SPANISH
TERRITORY

INDIAN
TERRITORY

NORTH CAROLINA

SOUTH
CAROLINA

Savannah

GEORGIA

Mississippi

Alabama

Altahama

NORTH
ATLANTIC
OCEAN

WEST FLORIDA

EAST
FLORIDA

Rio Grande

Gulf of Mexico

N

0   250   500   750   1,000 kilometers
0   125   250   375   500 miles

Tropic of Cancer

CUBA

American colonies (1775)

Indian Territory

The Personalities

Over 100,000 Loyalists emigrated to Canada, the West Indies, or Britain as a result of the war. Few were as controversial as General Benedict Arnold, who remains to this day one of the most vilified figures in American history, after defecting to the British to escape Congressional scrutiny of his finances and a probable court martial.

Perhaps most unusual of the personalities was John Dickinson, anti-British pamphleteer, chairman of the Committee of Safety and Defense of the Continental Congress, and author of the *Declaration of the Causes and Necessity of Taking Up Arms*. He refused to sign the Declaration of Independence but was one of only two Congressmen to volunteer for armed service.

It is repugnant to reason, to the universal order of things, to all examples from the former ages, to suppose, that this continent can longer remain subject to any external power.

Thomas Paine,
Common Sense (January 1776).

ABOVE At the start of the American War of Independence, the former colonies occupied only the most eastern extent of the continent.

Restricted Powers

The United States in 1783 was more akin to the modern United Nations than a national state. The Articles of Confederation, drafted in 1777 but adopted only in 1781, protected the "sovereignty, freedom, and independence" of the individual states. Congress, with delegates from each state, was given powers essential in wartime, most vitally the conduct of foreign affairs, declaring war or peace, and maintaining an army and navy. But unable to collect taxes, regulate interstate commerce, or enforce laws, it was unable to deal robustly with major external and internal problems that would eventually lead to moves for a new Constitution.

Colonial Charter

Under the peace treaty of 1783, Britain ceded to the United States all territory westward to the Mississippi that it had gained from France 20 years earlier. But, arguing that the United States had not kept its promises to compensate Loyalists for confiscated property, Britain placed a second obstacle in

BELOW By 1783, most of the east coast had come under the firm control of the United States.

United States of America (1783)

Disputed territory (USA and Britain)

Disputed area (USA and Spain)

British forts within US borders

Camp of American Continental Army

the way by retaining forts within United States territory, thereby giving it residual military and economic influence among the Indian tribes in the northwest.

Local Leaders

Although the form of government inherited from Britain was retained, many new state constitutions gave substance to the "self-evident" truth proclaimed in the Declaration of Independence that "all men are created equal," by giving voting rights to people previously disfranchised by property qualifications.

One consequence of this was the emergence of new political leaders elected on very localized issues. For many prominent figures in colonial society, who had led the campaign against Britain, this parochialism was both an unwelcome distraction from the war and a harbinger of disturbing social change.

Electoral Representation

Black slavery meant that a regional factor also threatened the stability of the new nation. Despite private misgivings, both Thomas Jefferson,

WE THE PEOPLE of the United States, in Order to form a more perfect Union, establish justice, insure domestic Tranquility, provide for the common defence, promote the general Welfare, and secure the Blessings of Liberty to ourselves and our Posterity, do ordain and establish this Constitution for the United States of America.

– Preamble to the United States' Constitution (1787).

principal author of the Declaration of Independence, and the foremost military leader, George Washington, remained substantial Virginian slaveholders throughout their lives. Outside the South, however, where slavery was less economically vital, the Revolutionary rhetoric of equality began to erode the institution.

It would take a major compromise to overcome these regionally-based ideological divisions, with an

agreement that saw the southern slave-holding states commit to the new Constitution—the slave trade was to be abolished within 20 years, and two-thirds of slaves were to be included in counting a state's population to determine its numbers of representatives in a new national assembly. The major innovation, devised especially by James Madison, was to create a lower house elected at large, as well as a Senate giving equal representation to each state, regardless of its population. Even so, the process ended only in May 1790 when Rhode Island became the last state to ratify.

Constitutional Compromise

As the United States pushed out beyond its original western boundary on the Mississippi, the most fundamental weakness of the Constitution was exposed. The compromise that had allowed slavery to continue had been essential to the survival of the United States, even though it was blatantly at odds with the egalitarian rhetoric that had accompanied its fight for independence. The South's insistence that slavery expand into new areas, even where it was not economically viable, led to the calamitous Civil War from 1861 to 1865.

RIGHT First president of the United States, George Washington (1732-1799).

BELOW LEFT The drafting of the Declaration of Independence was a turning point in world history.

BELOW Flown at the Battle of Brandywine, and subsequently adopted by Congress, the Betsy Ross flag is allegedly the original Stars and Stripes. Thirteen stars and stripes represent the nation's 13 colonies, while the colors symbolize purity (white), hardiness and valor (red), and justice, perseverance, and vigilance (blue).

Ocean's Greatest Explorer

The three voyages of Captain James Cook are considered among the most remarkable undertaken during the "age of discovery," and created a new paradigm for scientific exploration that remains to the present day.

James Cook came to prominence by being the first explorer to map Newfoundland in Canada. His amazing expertise in mapping brought him to the attention of the British Admiralty and thus to his commission as commander of the HM Bark *Endeavour*.

Cook's voyages were considered "hydrographical" expeditions, whose primary task was to chart continental coastlines, islands, and harbors as an aid to British imperial and commercial strategy. He was also to search for a hypothetical land mass called Terra Australis Incognita—literally, unknown southern land (not to be confused with Australia). Cook believed his crew's diet was crucial for a successful voyage and he insisted that the ship carry fruit and vegetables.

Exploration and Science

The initial stimulus for the first voyage, that of the *Endeavour*, was to participate in a world-wide effort to observe a very rare transit of Venus across the disk of the Sun, which, if successful, would lead to a determination of the distance between the Sun and Earth. Cook took an astronomer, Charles Green, designated by the Royal Society, to study the transit, as well as a team of botanists led by the Englishman Joseph Banks, and Carl Linnaeus's disciple Daniel Solander, and two botanical painters. The ship was also loaded with scientific instruments chosen by the Royal Society, which included two reflecting telescopes and a portable observatory built under the supervision of Cook himself.

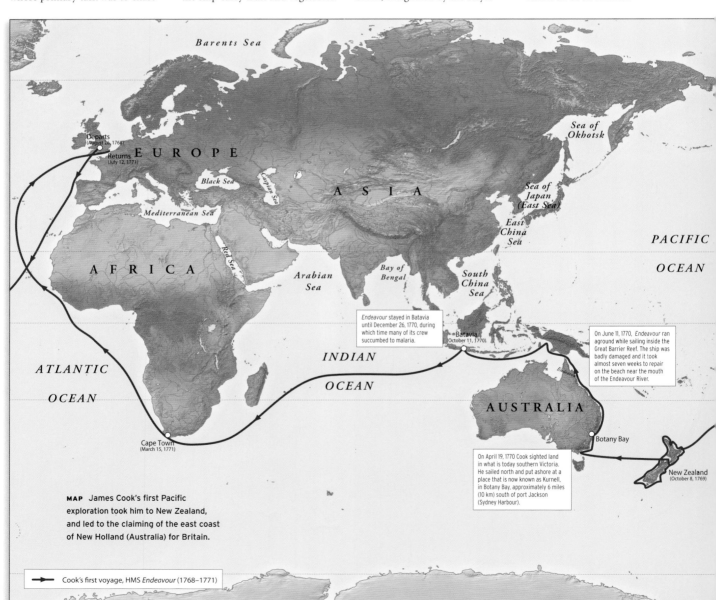

Departs (August 26, 1768)

Returns (July 12, 1771)

EUROPE

Barents Sea

Black Sea

Caspian Sea

Mediterranean Sea

ASIA

Sea of Okhotsk

Sea of Japan (East Sea)

East China Sea

PACIFIC OCEAN

Red Sea

Arabian Sea

Bay of Bengal

South China Sea

AFRICA

ATLANTIC OCEAN

INDIAN OCEAN

Endeavour stayed in Batavia until December 26, 1770, during which time many of its crew succumbed to malaria.

Batavia (October 11, 1770)

On June 11, 1770, *Endeavour* ran aground while sailing inside the Great Barrier Reef. The ship was badly damaged and it took almost seven weeks to repair on the beach near the mouth of the Endeavour River.

AUSTRALIA

Cape Town (March 15, 1771)

Botany Bay

On April 19, 1770 Cook sighted land in what is today southern Victoria. He sailed north and put ashore at a place that is now known as Kurnell, in Botany Bay, approximately 6 miles (10 km) south of port Jackson (Sydney Harbour).

New Zealand (October 8, 1769)

MAP James Cook's first Pacific exploration took him to New Zealand, and led to the claiming of the east coast of New Holland (Australia) for Britain.

➤ Cook's first voyage, HMS *Endeavour* (1768–1771)

Observing the Transit

Cook first made for Cape Horn, thereby avoiding the Strait of Magellan, in January 1769. Banks and Solander botanized at Tierra del Fuego, almost losing their lives in a snowstorm. The party then sailed straight to Tahiti from where Cook purposed to observe the Transit, which indeed took place on June 3, 1769. While there, Cook charted the entire island and Banks studied the social structure of Tahitian society.

The voyagers then made for New Zealand's North Island, where there was a skirmish and several Maoris were killed. After exploring the Auckland area, Cook and his men made for the South Island, where proof of cannibalism was found. Cook completed the circum-navigation of New Zealand in six months, mapping the entire coast-line. Banks concluded that those he called the "continent mongers" would have to admit that if Terra Australis existed, New Zealand was not a part of it.

Australia

Australia, then called New Holland, was next. Banks collected so many plants that Cook named a particu-lar anchorage Botany Bay—a large bay just south of what is now Syd-ney Harbour (Port Jackson). Cook claimed the whole of the east coast of Australia for Britain. By com-pleting a map of Australia, Cook exploded several myths about the southern continent theory. He also sailed inside the Great Barrier Reef, going aground and having to stop to repair *Endeavour*. Cook then made for Dutch Batavia to further repair his ship, but it was here that most of his crew became ill from malaria and 29 died. The *Endeavour* docked in Dover, England, on July 13, 1771, after three years at sea.

Second Voyage

Cook's first voyage caused quite a sensation in England. Two ships, the *Resolution* and the *Adventure*— each with an astronomer and bota-nist aboard—were then scheduled to make a second voyage, sailing from Plymouth on July 13, 1772. Cook had agreed to test four Eng-lish chronometers, one by Harrison and three by Arnold, and he car-ried garden seeds and live animals, believing an English-style diet would benefit Pacific islanders.

It was quickly realised that with accurate chronometers, longi-tude could be determined on sea voyages to within 1.5° accuracy. On January 17, 1773, Cook crossed the

> As we approached the Shore they all made off, except 2 Men who seem'd resolved to oppose our landing.
>
> –Captain James Cook (1728-1779), on arriving at Botany Bay, in his daily ship's log, April 29, 1770.

1755 James Cook joins the navy, hoping that participation in the Seven Years' War will advance his career

1757 Cook gains his Master's certificate and is qualified to navigate and captain a ship of the Royal Navy

1762 James Cook marries Elizabeth Batts. They have six children, only two of whom lived to adulthood.

1775 Cook is promoted to the rank of Captain and given honorary retirement from the Royal Navy. In addition, he is made a Fellow of the Royal Society.

1776 Cook is promoted from the rank of Master and Commander to Captain in the Royal Navy

BELOW James Cook, master explorer and navi-gator, in a painting by Sir Nathaniel Dance-Holland.

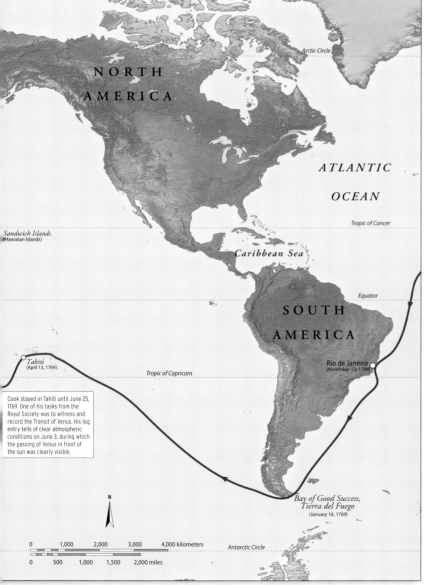

Sandwich Islands
(Hawaiian Islands)

NORTH AMERICA

ATLANTIC OCEAN

Arctic Circle

Tropic of Cancer

Caribbean Sea

Equator

SOUTH AMERICA

Tahiti
(April 13, 1769)

Tropic of Capricorn

Rio de Janeiro
(November 13, 1768)

Cook stayed in Tahiti until June 25, 1769. One of his tasks from the Royal Society was to witness and record the Transit of Venus. His log entry tells of clear atmospheric conditions on June 3, during which the passing of Venus in front of the sun was clearly visible.

Bay of Good Success, Tierra del Fuego
(January 16, 1769)

N

0   1,000   2,000   3,000   4,000 kilometers
0   500   1,000   1,500   2,000 miles

Antarctic Circle

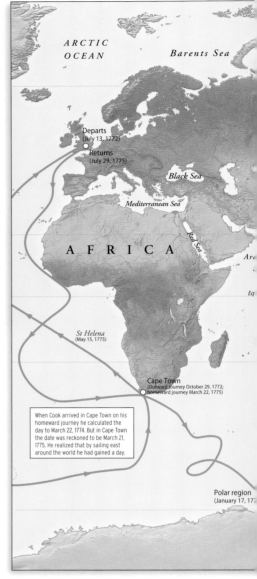

Antarctic Circle—no one had ever sailed that far south before. He did not find a continent, however, only lots of ice, so he made for New Zealand, where he planted a garden and released some livestock, before sailing for Tahiti.

From Tahiti he sailed to Tonga, whose society the English sailors deemed the most civilized of all they'd seen. Cook returned to New Zealand again, before heading south towards Antarctica once more. Then, sailing to the north again, he came upon Easter Island in March 1774, with its massive stone statues, discovered in 1722 by Jacob Roggeveen. Now Cook wanted to find the Marquesas, discovered by Mendaña in 1595, and then the New Hebrides, around 450 nautical miles southeast of which he found an inhabited, uncharted island, which he named New Caledonia. Sailing back past Cape Horn and into the South Atlantic in January 1775, Cook found another island— South Georgia, and more ice-covered islands and icebergs. He believed that icebergs were formed near land, so he deduced that a frigid continent must lie further to the south, surrounding the South Pole. The *Resolution* finally reached Plymouth on July 29, 1775.

Third Voyage

A third voyage was now planned to find the elusive Northwest Passage supposedly joining the Atlantic and the Pacific oceans from its western terminus. The *Resolution* made the voyage again, accompanied by the *Discovery*. Rounding the Cape of Good Hope, Cook made New Zealand in January 1777. In January 1778, they discovered Hawaii, which Cook called the Sandwich Islands, after his patron, the Earl of Sandwich. Cook had now visited the extremities of Polynesia—from Hawaii in the north, southwest to New Zealand, to Easter Island in the southeast, and all the major groups in between except for Samoa.

Cook called twice at Hawaii. The first time was in January 1778, when he arrived during a ritual according to which the "Year-God," named Lono, was expected to make his annual visit to renew the fertility of the soil.

Five weeks after leaving Hawaii, Cook's expeditionaries sighted the North American coast in northern Oregon. Finally he anchored near Vancouver Island in a harbor that he called Nootka Sound. As Cook sailed north, he realized the continent extended much further west than his maps had showed. June found him in the Bering Sea, where he visited the Aleutian Islands, and crossed the Bering Strait into the Arctic Sea, where ice flows turned him back at 70°10' N. He coasted the Asian side for a while, unsure of exactly where he was.

Cook's second visit to Hawaii, in February 1779, also happened

ABOVE James Cook met his fate at the hands of Hawaiian natives in 1779.

RIGHT Cook's second voyage took him far south, and through the middle of the Pacific Ocean.

to fall during the New Year festival of Lono–Makahiki. Cook began acting erratically, although the natives continued to look upon him as a god. He left in the first week of February but had to return for repairs, a fatal mistake, because a second appearance was not scripted in the ritual, and he lost the trust of the islanders.

Setting out to retrieve a stolen lifeboat on February 14, Cook fired into a crowd of natives, killing one, and when he turned his back, was set upon, clubbed on the head, stabbed in the neck, fell into the water, and died. His death at the hands of indigenous people was ironic because he was popular among the Pacific Islanders and had a reputation for dealing fairly with them.

On map:

ARCTIC OCEAN

Barents Sea

Departs (July 13, 1772)

Returns (July 29, 1775)

Black Sea

Mediterranean Sea

AFRICA

Red Sea

St Helena (May 15, 1775)

Cape Town (Outward journey October 29, 1772; homeward journey March 22, 1775)

When Cook arrived in Cape Town on his homeward journey he calculated the day to be March 22, 1774. But in Cape Town the date was reckoned to be March 21, 1775. He realized that by sailing east around the world he had gained a day.

Polar region (January 17, 17...)

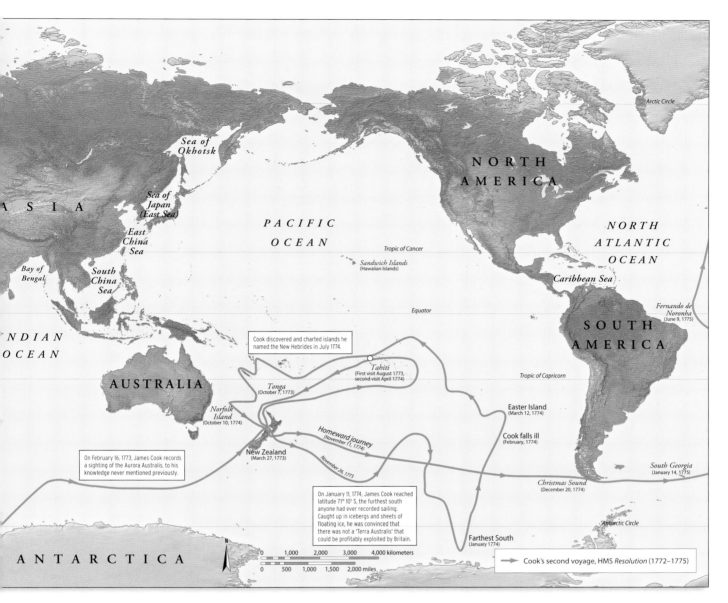

Sea of
Okhotsk

ASIA

Sea of
Japan
(East Sea)

East
China
Sea

Bay of
Bengal

South
China
Sea

INDIAN
OCEAN

AUSTRALIA

PACIFIC
OCEAN

NORTH
AMERICA

Tropic of Cancer

Sandwich Islands
(Hawaiian Islands)

Equator

NORTH
ATLANTIC
OCEAN

Caribbean Sea

Fernando de
Noronha
(June 9, 1775)

SOUTH
AMERICA

Cook discovered and charted islands he
named the New Hebrides in July 1774.

Tahiti
(First visit August 1773,
second visit April 1774)

Tonga
(October 7, 1773)

Tropic of Capricorn

Norfolk
Island
(October 10, 1774)

Homeward journey
(November 11, 1774)

New Zealand
(March 27, 1773)

November 26, 1773

Easter Island
(March 12, 1774)

Cook falls ill
(February, 1774)

South Georgia
(January 14, 1775)

On February 16, 1773, James Cook records
a sighting of the Aurora Australis, to his
knowledge never mentioned previously.

Christmas Sound
(December 20, 1774)

Antarctic Circle

On January 11, 1774, James Cook reached
latitude 71° 10' S, the furthest south
anyone had ever recorded sailing.
Caught up in icebergs and sheets of
floating ice, he was convinced that
there was not a 'Terra Australis' that
could be profitably exploited by Britain.

Farthest South
(January 1774)

ANTARCTICA

N

0   1,000   2,000   3,000   4,000 kilometers

0   500   1,000   1,500   2,000 miles

→ Cook's second voyage, HMS *Resolution* (1772–1775)

LEFT Vaitepiha Bay, Tahiti,
as painted by John Web-
ber, an artist accompany-
ing Cook on his final
voyage.

RIGHT Cook's third and
final voyage took him
through the Pacific to the
coast of North America.

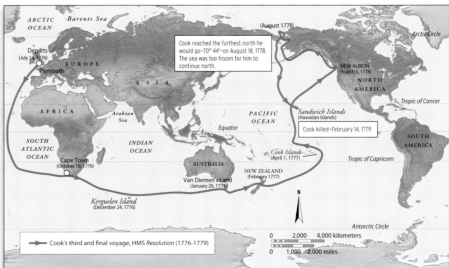

ARCTIC
OCEAN

Barents Sea

(August 1778)

Arctic Circle

Departs
(July 14, 1776)
Plymouth

EUROPE

ASIA

Cook reached the furthest north he
would go–70° 44'–on August 18, 1778.
The sea was too frozen for him to
continue north.

NEW ALBION
(March 6, 1778)

NORTH
AMERICA

AFRICA

Arabian
Sea

PACIFIC
OCEAN

Sandwich Islands
(Hawaiian Islands)

Tropic of Cancer

Equator

Cook killed–February 14, 1779

SOUTH
ATLANTIC
OCEAN

Cape Town
(October 18, 1776)

INDIAN
OCEAN

AUSTRALIA

Cook Islands
(April 1, 1777)

SOUTH
AMERICA

NEW ZEALAND
(February 1777)

Tropic of Capricorn

Van Diemen's Land
(January 26, 1777)

Kerguelen Island
(December 24, 1776)

N

Antarctic Circle

0   2,000   4,000 kilometers

0   1,000   2,000 miles

→ Cook's third and final voyage, HMS *Resolution* (1776-1779)

Conflict and Expansion in North America

In a mix of diplomatic intrigue, real-estate purchases, and bloodshed, 13 small British colonies hugging the east coast of North America expanded, and the people of the United States gained sovereignty over a land they already regarded as their own.

1601 to 1900

1787 The revolutionary US Constitution is adopted by the people of the new United States

1789 George Washington becomes the first President of the United States, John Adams is Vice-president, Thomas Jefferson is Secretary of State, and Alexander Hamilton is Secretary of the Treasury

1790 Congress meets in the temporary capital of Philadelphia. The US Supreme Court meets for the first time.

1800 Washington DC is chosen as the capital of the United States

1854 The US Supreme Court upholds slavery and denies Black Americans citizenship

1861 Abraham Lincoln becomes 16th President of the United States

BELOW Meriwether Lewis and William Clark's challenge to reach the Pacific finally paid off in 1805.

Since defeating France in 1763, Britain held all the territory between the Mississippi River and the Atlantic. The east coast colonies were still hemmed in, however, by a British Line of Proclamation, recognizing the right of native peoples' sovereignty and self-rule in "reservations." White settlement was forbidden in this so-called Indian Territory, which was perhaps three times the size of the 13 colonies combined.

Independence

After the War of Independence, things began to change. The newly sovereign USA stood to gain a large parcel of Britain's land to the west. Sure enough, the Paris Treaty signed in 1783 gave the new colonies all the land from the east coast to the Mississippi. Settlers began to move west, forcing the Native Americans to make way before them.

Real Estate

The French had held the territory bounded by the Missouri River in the west, the Mississippi in the east, and from the Gulf of Mexico into what is now Canada in the far

> The right of our manifest destiny [is] to overspread and to possess the whole of the continent which Providence has given us.
> –John L. Sullivan

north, since 1682, but in 1763 they ceded it to Spain. However, Spain had given it back to France around 1800. This raised anxieties about access to the Mississippi, leading President Jefferson to send diplomats to Paris to purchase an area around New Orleans and west Florida. Napoleon offered more than expected, however, and the whole Louisiana Territory was bought for a price of $15 million.

Go West

From 1803, thoughts turned west to the Pacific. This was further encouraged by the successful expedition of Meriwether Lewis and William Clark. President Jefferson had commissioned them to lead a "Corps of Discovery." They left in 1804, made it up the Missouri River, and crossed overland to the Pacific, reaching it in November 1805. The following spring they headed home, reaching St Louis on September 23, 1806.

Gaining Florida

The Spaniards were not happy with France's "sale," and some diplomatic wrangling followed. Spain, however, was in no position to bargain in North America. First, an uprising in the Spanish territory of west Florida resulted in US troops taking control. In 1812, Congress annexed the territory and absorbed half into the state of Louisiana, and half into Mississippi. Second, in the Seminole war of 1817–1818, President Monroe ordered Andrew

ABOVE The United States was born from many conflicts, exemplified by this battle between the frigate *L'Embuscade* and the *Boston* in the port of New York in 1793.

Jackson to invade Florida, claiming that the Spaniards were not controlling their Indian population. In effect, the United States warred against Spain and the Seminole Indians. Spain finally ceded Florida in the Adams-Onis Treaty of 1819. For the west, John Quincy Adams did a deal. The United States renounced its claim to Texas, and Spain recognized the Louisiana Purchase as reaching all the way to the Pacific.

BARGAIN REAL ESTATE

Much of the present-day territory of the United States was purchased the good old fashioned way—with money. Legend has it that the island of Manhattan was bought for a mere US$24.

- The Louisiana Purchase, a land parcel of 828,000 square miles (2,145,000 km²) went for US$15 million.
- California, Arizona, and Nevada were part of a 500,000 square mile (1,295,000 km²) package purchased from the Spanish for US$18.25 million in 1848—only months before the discovery of gold in California. The US also agreed to pay claims of US$3 million by American citizens against Mexico.
- A strip of land along the border with Mexico—now the states of New Mexico and Arizona—was purchased for around US$10 million in 1853.
- Alaska was purchased from the Russians in 1867 for a cool US$7.2 million.

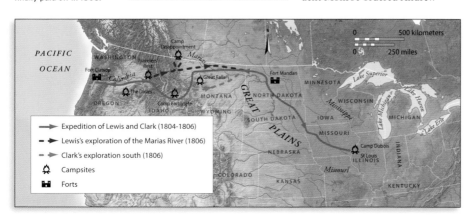

PACIFIC OCEAN

Camp Disappointment

WASHINGTON

Fort Clatsop

Travelers' Rest

Columbia

The Dalles

OREGON

IDAHO

Camp Fortunate

MONTANA

WYOMING

Great Falls

Marias

NORTH DAKOTA

Fort Mandan

SOUTH DAKOTA

GREAT PLAINS

NEBRASKA

COLORADO

KANSAS

MINNESOTA

Lake Superior

WISCONSIN

Mississippi

IOWA

MISSOURI

Missouri

Camp Dubois

St Louis

ILLINOIS

INDIANA

Lake Michigan

Lake Huron

MICHIGAN

Lake Erie

KENTUCKY

0   500 kilometers
0   250 miles

→ Expedition of Lewis and Clark (1804-1806)
➤ Lewis's exploration of the Marias River (1806)
➤ Clark's exploration south (1806)
⚑ Campsites
🏰 Forts

Arctic Circle

Hudson Bay

BRITISH TERRITORY

ROCKY MOUNTAINS

Border agreed with Britain in 1818

Columbia

OREGON COUNTRY

CASCADE RANGE

Missouri

GREAT PLAINS

FRENCH TERRITORY

Snake

Missouri

Louisiana Purchase
Hoping to buy an area around New Orleans and west Florida, American diplomats were very surprised when Napoleon offered this piece of land to them for $15 million.

INDIAN TERRITORY

APPALACHIAN MOUNTAINS

THIRTEEN BRITISH COLONIES

NORTH ATLANTIC OCEAN

SIERRA NEVADA

COAST RANGE

Colorado

Grand Canyon

Colorado

SPANISH TERRITORY

Mississippi

Land Grab
After independence in 1783, the new citizens of the United States moved westward into the lands their government was purchasing.

SPANISH TERRITORY

Tropic of Cancer

SIERRA MADRE OCCIDENTAL

SIERRA MADRE ORIENTAL

Rio Grande

Gulf of Mexico

RIGHT For many years, the North American continent was shared between the new United States of America and various European nations.

SIERRA MADRE DEL SUR

Caribbean Sea

Legend:
- Territory gained at Treaty of Paris (1783)
- Louisiana Purchase (1803)
- Shared British and US territory (1818–1846) Northern border undefined
- British Territory
- Oregon Country
- Spanish Territory
- ⬧ Native American occupation
- ◀ Initial waves of western settlement after independence (1783)

N

| 0 | 250 | 500 | 750 | 1,000 kilometers |
| 0 | 125 | 250 | 375 | 500 miles |

287

Nationalism

Aside from the success of the War of Independence, other victories were scoring morale boosts. In the War of 1812, Americans believed they had shown Britain a thing or two. Despite losing many battles in present-day Canada, and despite having the White House and Capitol burned down in 1814, General Andrew Jackson had defeated the British in the south. By 1819, Florida was American.

Lone Star State

In 1821, Mexico agreed to allow American settlement in Texas. But in 1835 this backfired as the settlers sought independence. In 1836, their leader, Stephen Austin, declared Texas an independent republic—the famous "Lone Star Republic." Eventually there were calls for the annexation, or inclusion, of Texas into the United States. But Mexico thought they owned part of it too. However, in 1845, Texas was formally incorporated into the USA. To make sure of the borders, President Polk sent armed forces down to the Rio Grande to press the US claim.

California

In May of 1846, the United States declared war on Mexico. During the ensuing Mexican–American War of 1846–1848, US troops engaged in bloody battles at Vera Cruz. Eventually they occupied Mexico City in 1847, which led to Mexican surrender. The Treaty of Guadalupe Hidalgo in 1848, saw not only Texas, but all of the Pacific territory of California incorporated into the USA.

Gaining the Rest

The ceding of Mexican territories left one area unclaimed. The issue of the Oregon Territory had been unresolved since John Quincy Adams had signed the Convention of 1818, in which Britain and the United States agreed to joint ownership for a period. In the Oregon Treaty of 1846, the British–American border was kept at the 49th parallel, and was extended to the Pacific through roughly equal distribution of the coastal waterways.

The territory of Maine was then settled with Britain in 1842. Mexico ceded a little more land—some of present-day Arizona—in the Gadsden Purchase of 1853, finalizing the US–Mexico border. Last, Alaska was sold off by the Russians for just US$7.2 million in 1867.

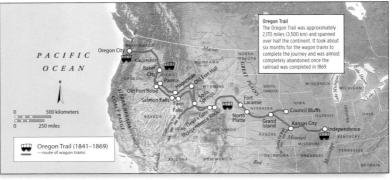

Oregon Trail (1841–1869)
—route of wagon trains

Oregon Trail
The Oregon Trail was approximately 2,170 miles (3,500 km) and spanned over half the continent. It took about six months for the wagon trains to complete the journey and was almost completely abandoned once the railroad was completed in 1869.

LEFT The Oregon Trail was a major migration route between the Atlantic and Pacific coasts.

BELOW Formation of the United States brought together individual colonies and regions, each with their own flag.

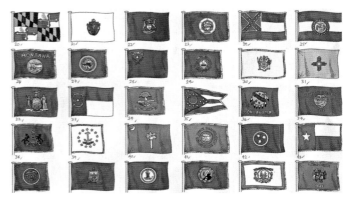

The Wealth and Heartache of Gold Discovery

In 1848, just as the war with Mexico ended, gold was discovered in California. Within two years the territory, indeed the whole west, was irreversibly transformed. The population in California grew exponentially, as did the required infrastructure. Gold required good transport and easy access to the northeastern commercial centers. Soon the first transcontinental railroads were built. More railways meant more rail towns, spelling disaster for Native American nations—land titles were eroded and buffalo hunting was reduced. However, by the close of the nineteenth century, the USA had reached the expanse it holds today.

The Cost

The blood-letting was perhaps worst in the so-called Plains Wars of 1850–1880, peaking in 1864 with the massacre of a friendly Cheyenne group at Sand Creek. The removal and killing of Native Americans had become a pattern —a result of westward expansion. Earlier, in the 1830s, whole groups were transported from the South to west of the Mississippi.

LEFT Lewis and Clark led the first official exploration of the western part of North America acquired by the Louisiana Purchase.

BELOW Many deaths occurred as Native Americans were forced to travel "The Trail of Tears" to Indian Territory.

Trail of Tears (1831)

GREENLAND

Arctic Circle

C A N A D A

Hudson Bay

LEFT Throughout the 1800s, the United States pushed further west, north, and south.

Oregon Treaty
Border agreed on by Britain and the United States in the Oregon Treaty of 1846, extending the 49th parallel from the Rocky Mountains to the Pacific Ocean.

Plains Wars
Between 1850 and 1880, Native American nations and the United States waged war across the Great Plains.

Gold!
Discovery of gold in California–near Sacramento–in 1848, triggered a "Gold Rush" of miners arriving by wagon from the north, and by sea from the south.

Sand Creek Massacre
In 1864, at Sand Creek, Colorado, over 200 Native American men, women, and children of the Arapaho and Cheyenne tribes were killed and mutilated. The brutality of the massacre shocked the nation.

Seminole Wars
In the Seminole War of 1817-1818, President Monroe ordered General Andrew Jackson to invade Florida claiming that the Spaniards were not controlling the Indian population. In effect, the United States warred against Spain and the native Seminole population. Spain ceded Florida to the USA in the Adams-Onis Treaty of 1819.

WASHINGTON
OREGON
MONTANA
NORTH DAKOTA
MINNESOTA
Lake Superior
WISCONSIN
MAINE
VERMONT
NEW HAMPSHIRE
MASSACHUSETTS
RHODE ISLAND
CONNECTICUT
NEW JERSEY
DELAWARE
MARYLAND
Lake Huron
Lake Ontario
NEW YORK
WYOMING
SOUTH DAKOTA
Lake Michigan
MICHIGAN
Lake Erie
PENNSYLVANIA
NEVADA
UTAH
NEBRASKA
IOWA
OHIO
INDIANA
ILLINOIS
WEST VIRGINIA
VIRGINIA
UNITED STATES OF AMERICA
COLORADO
KENTUCKY
NORTH CAROLINA
TENNESSEE
SOUTH CAROLINA
ARIZONA
NEW MEXICO
ALABAMA
GEORGIA
REPUBLIC OF TEXAS (1836–1845)
MISSISSIPPI
LOUISIANA
FLORIDA

N O R T H A T L A N T I C O C E A N

Gulf of Mexico

Battle of Buena Vista
Battle of Monterey
Tropic of Cancer

MEXICO

Amphibious landing at Vera Cruz

Caribbean Sea

PACIFIC OCEAN

N

Symbol	Legend
	Andrew Jackson invades Florida—war with Seminole Indians (1818)
	Adams-Onis Treaty (1819)
	Republic of Texas (1836-1845)
	USA and Mexico disputed territory (1845)
	USA and Mexico battlegrounds (1847)
	US troop movements—Mexican-American War (1847)
	Treaty of Guadalupe (1848)
	Gold discovered, California (1848)
	USA and Mexico shared territory (1848)
	Native American occupation (1850)
	Battlegrounds of the Plains Wars (1850–1880)

0   500   1,000 kilometers
0   250   500 miles

Waltzing Matilda

After a voyage of eight months, "The First Fleet"–11 ships under the command of Captain Arthur Phillip containing mostly inmates from English jails–sailed into Botany Bay on the east coast of the isolated southerly continent, *Terra Australis Incognita*. On that sparkling summer day, January 18, 1788, white settlement of Australia began.

1803 Matthew Flinders circumnavigates the continent

1808 The Rum Rebellion that breaks out after Governor Bligh tries to stop the barter and sale of spirits results in Bligh being returned to England

1817 The Bank of New South Wales opens in Sydney

1831 The *Sydney Herald* is first published–later *The Sydney Morning Herald*

1833 The penal colony of Port Arthur is founded in Tasmania

On January 26, now celebrated as Australia Day, Governor Phillip—as he became on arrival—moved his charges to Port Jackson, now known as Sydney Harbour, which had a more reliable water supply. Phillip founded the colony of New South Wales in the name of Britain, making no treaty with native peoples because the British government regarded themselves as settlers, not conquerors of the country—a view now disputed.

The Tyranny of Distance

The Aboriginal people of Australia numbered an estimated 750,000 in 1788, and had been living off the land for roughly 40,000 years, yet England's new colony had difficulty trying to feed itself. The seasons were "upside down," rainfall was erratic, and crops failed.

Relief from the mother country was over 12,000 miles (19,000 km) and many months away across the vast lonely oceans, and Governor Arthur Phillip had retained only two small ships.

Late in 1788, the *Sirius* sailed from Sydney around Cape Horn and on to Cape Town, taking seven months to return with supplies. Finally, in June 1790, with the population close to starvation, the *Lady Juliana* arrived from England, bringing more convicts to feed but also valuable food. By the end of June, four more English ships had arrived and the worst was over.

For 25 years, New South Wales faced intermittent food crises, but by about 1815 the colony was self-sufficient in essentials, and Australia soon had more colonies dotted around its vast coastline.

Building Self-sufficiency

At first, Australia was an English prison, governed by military rule, that received 162,000 convicts over 80 years. But its role changed greatly

ABOVE Arthur Phillip RN (1738-1814) was the first Governor of New South Wales, and chose the site which is now the city of Sydney. His suggestion that people with experience in farming, building, and crafts be included in the first batch of colonists was rejected. Most of the 772 convicts (of whom 732 survived the voyage) were petty thieves from the London slums.

LEFT Greek philosophers including Plato thought that, since there were lands in the northern hemisphere, there should be lands in the southern hemisphere too, lest the world be unbalanced. In the sixteenth century, as sailors reported new lands farther south, *Terra Australis* began appearing on maps as an imaginary land that might actually exist.

RIGHT Convicts were delivered to the First Fleet transports directly from hulks and jails. The transports then met up at Portsmouth, where the last convicts were loaded on the day the fleet sailed.

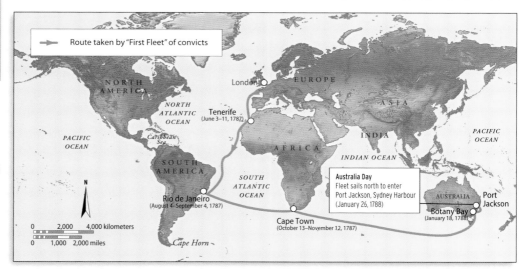

LITERATURE

Australian literature in the nineteenth century reflected many of the concerns of a settler society in an unfamiliar country. The poems of "Banjo" Paterson, together with Henry Lawson's stories, helped create the image—yet a woman, Dorothea Mackellar, wrote the stirring poem "My Country." Marcus Clarke's *For the Term of his Natural Life* (1874) has retained popularity as an account of convict life. Rolf Boldrewood's *Robbery Under Arms: A Story of Life and Adventure in the Bush and in the Goldfields of Australia* tells the story of Captain Starlight, a famous bushranger, or highwayman. The many skilled women writers concentrated on more domestic themes, in a recognizably Australian context. Ada Cambridge, Rosa Praed, and Barbara Baynton all wrote about the conflicts women faced at a time when the only viable career was marriage.

over time. British and American whalers used Australia as a base, while ships sailing between Europe, the Americas, China, and India traded goods in Australia. Free settlers arrived, many with farming skills and experience. Australians also began to harvest the country's natural resources, including seals and timber, and above all, whales.

It was wool, however, that opened up the inland plains, brought Australia its first wealth, and attracted new free settlers. Merino sheep were ideally suited to Australia's hot dry summers and mild winters, and by the late 1820s Australian wool was selling for high prices at the London auctions. The colony was "riding on the sheep's back," though this meant devastation for the Aboriginal people.

Penal Colonies

Van Diemen's Land was settled as a penal colony in 1803, became an entity separate from New South Wales in 1825, and was renamed Tasmania in 1856. The Swan River Colony, later Western Australia,

was settled as a free colony in 1829. In 1836, South Australia was also established as a free colony. The Port Phillip District, on the southeastern coast, received its first white settlers in 1834 and became the independent colony of Victoria in 1851. The Moreton Bay District was founded in 1824 and became the colony of Queensland. The Northern Territory was settled in 1824 as part of New South Wales, then given to South Australia in 1863 and separated in 1912. New Zealand was also part of New South Wales until 1840.

ABOVE The eleven ships of the First Fleet, carrying about 14,00 people and stores, sailed for 252 days and over 15,000 miles (24,000 km) to reach Botany Bay. Surprisingly, given the cramped conditions, only 48 people died on the way.

RIGHT The First Fleet consisted of two navy ships (*Sirius* and *Supply*), three supply ships, and six transport ships containing convicts. The cargo included a great deal of hardware (for building huts), and a supply of tents.

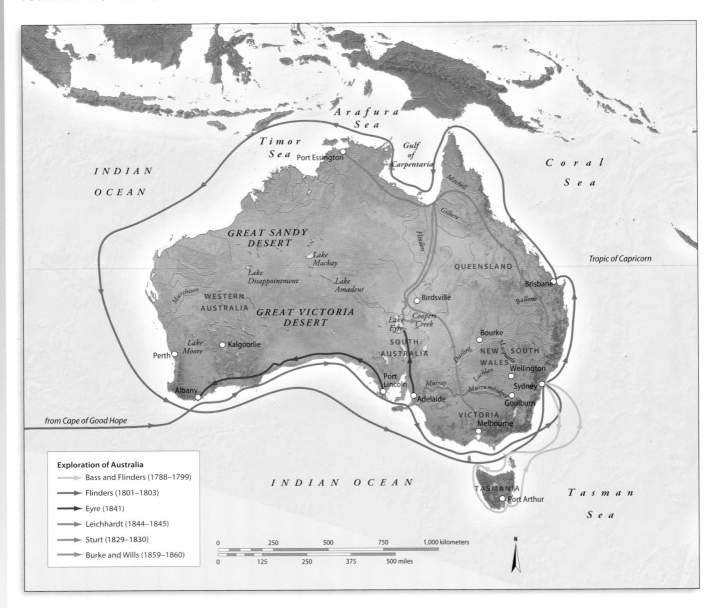

Exploration of Australia
- Bass and Flinders (1788–1799)
- Flinders (1801–1803)
- Eyre (1841)
- Leichhardt (1844–1845)
- Sturt (1829–1830)
- Burke and Wills (1859–1860)

ABOVE Even after it was colonized, it took some time, and several waves of seafarers and land explorers, to bring the Great South Land into focus.

RIGHT Charles Sturt (1795–1869) departs for the interior of Australia from Adelaide, 1844. Sturt led several expeditions to the interior, from both Adelaide and Sydney. While searching for the fabled "inland sea," he traced several westward-flowing rivers and established that they all merge into the Murray River.

RIGHT Disappointed by Botany Bay, the site first chosen for the colony, Governor Phillip and a party set off to explore other bays to the north, finding what Phillip called "the finest harbor in the world, in which a thousand sail of the line may ride in the most perfect security." This was Port Jackson (Sydney Harbour). Phillip decided to relocate the colony to this new site.

BELOW Ways of life that had sustained Australian Aborigines for millennia became more difficult to maintain as the colonies expanded, ignoring prior ownership of the land.

Wealth for Toil

Australia is quite a challenging and paradoxical country. It is the driest of inhabited continents, with a desert heartland. Yet it has tropical rainforests, winter snow on its southeastern mountains, rolling green hills, and temperate forests.

Luckily, what Australia lacks in reliable rainfall and arable soil it makes up for in mineral deposits. In the 1840s, silver and copper were found in South Australia, and small amounts of gold in New South Wales—though in 1848, when gold was discovered in California, many Australians raced across the Pacific to try their luck. Some, notably Edward Hargraves, returned to Australia with new knowledge of prospecting. Hargraves claimed to have soon found gold in New South Wales, though this claim was later disputed. In 1851, huge quantities were discovered in Victoria, and prospectors hurried to Australia from all over the globe. Payable gold was discovered in all colonies except South Australia. The last great rush of the century occurred near Kalgoorlie, Western Australia, in the 1890s. Gold transformed Australia and ensured its economic future. Its export helped to counter serious periodic depressions caused by drought or market forces.

A Free Land

The gold rushes also had negative side-effects which magnified problems caused by isolation, harsh terrain, and the new immigrant society. For most of the nineteenth century, Australia had more men than women, sometimes up to four times the number. All the same, Australia made significant social progress through the nineteenth century. Miners, angry at expensive license fees, staged the Eureka Stockade protest, an indication of a move to greater democracy. In the 1860s, land was opened up to small selectors, diluting the wealth and power of the squatters. Women gained the vote—in South Australia in 1895—and in all colonies by 1908, well before Britain. Education was made compulsory. Sports, theaters, and newspapers flourished. The stigma and social divisions caused by the convict era gradually faded.

The combined effects of the building of the Suez Canal in 1869, and the advance of the telegraph from the 1860s, linked Australia more closely to the rest of the world. Instead of news—whether business or personal—taking months to arrive from England, by the 1880s it could be transmitted in hours. By the end of the

nineteenth century, Australia was a different place from that of 1788. It was prosperous and productive, with cities, towns, agriculture, and industry. Gold and wool had built city mansions and country estates. Railways, extensive roads, and the telegraph had partly overcome distance and isolation. The gender balance had evened up, through female immigration and natural increase. Its separate colonies were self-governing and ready to combine in a new unified country, the Commonwealth of Australia.

> I love a sunburnt country,
> A land of sweeping plains,
> Of rugged mountain ranges,
> Of droughts and flooding rains.
> ~Dorothea Mackellar (1855-1968), Australian poet, from the second stanza of "My Country."

La Révolution–Liberté, Égalité, Fraternité, ou la Mort!

The French Revolution (1789-1799) is the most written-about event in human history. Arguably, no other historical period has altered human destiny so radically. In destroying the French monarchy, and in convulsing the institutions and organization of society as it was then known, the Revolution inaugurated the first great crisis of modernity.

The Revolution had many causes. But its most important cause by far was France's deepening financial crisis. The monarchy's many wars, coupled with general government mismanagement, had resulted in a massive national debt. It was in an attempt to relieve it, and to overcome the nobility's resistance to his economic reform measures, that in May 1789 King Louis XVI called the Estates General to meet for the first time in 175 years.

Estates General

Conflict soon arose within this body when the nobility wanted each of the three estates to meet and vote separately, since in this way nobles' votes would have the same weight as those of the clergy and the Third Estate. But the more numerous Third Estate wanted the Estates General to meet as one, so that the common people's voice could predominate.

When the Third Estate declared itself the National Assembly in June 1789, Louis XVI took the nobility's side and closed the hall in which the Third Estate met. Its members then gathered in a nearby tennis court and signed the Tennis Court Oath of June 1789, whereby they swore to continue meeting until they had drafted a constitution. This was an event unprecedented

> **I survived.**
> –Emmanuel Joseph Sieyès, when asked what he did during the French Revolution.

in French history—a political body had appointed itself to give France laws without the king's consent.

Storming of the Bastille

The year 1789 was one of very bad harvests and economic depression, and the government, now paralyzed, could not undertake its usual relief measures. Lower-class unrest broke out and crowds of Parisians began to arm themselves in defense. On July 14, one such crowd came to the Bastille, Paris' elite prison. When the governor refused to hand out the weapons cache, the crowd stormed the Bastille, and freed the

few prisoners. It also murdered the governor and a few officials.

Citizens' Rights

In the meantime the cry spread through the countryside that "the brigands are coming." It was the Great Fear of 1789, when peasants armed themselves against vagabonds but ended up destroying manors instead. On the "night of August 4," some aristocrats in the Assembly decided to meet peasants' demands and surrender their traditional privileges and abolish what remained of feudalism—formalized by the Assembly on August 26 by issuing the Declaration of the Rights of Man and of the Citizen.

Church and State

Of the Assembly's policies, perhaps the most significant was its quarrel with the Church. In 1790, the Assembly promulgated the Civil Constitution of the Clergy, which required French clergymen to swear allegiance to the state. Most clergy, obliged to choose between loyalty to the state and loyalty to the Church, refused the oath. A religious schism followed and for the next 12 years France would harbor two churches—one that was maintained by the state, and another that was obedient to Rome, and persecuted by the state.

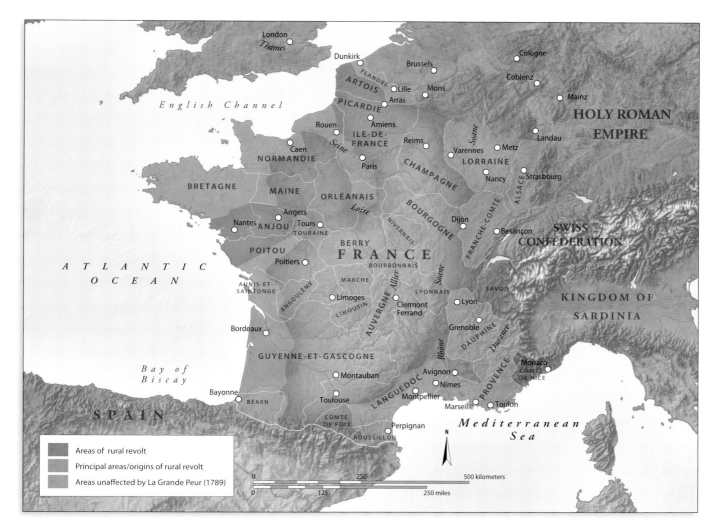

London
Thames
Dunkirk
Brussels
Cologne
FLANDRE
ARTOIS
Lille
Mons
Coblenz
PICARDIE
Arras
Mainz
English Channel
Amiens
Rouen
ILE-DE-
Varennes
Metz
Landau
FRANCE
Reims
Seine
LORRAINE
Caen
Paris
NORMANDIE
CHAMPAGNE
Nancy
Strasbourg
BRETAGNE
MAINE
Besançon
ORLÉANAIS
BOURGOGNE
ALSACE
Loire
Angers
Dijon
SWISS
Nantes
ANJOU
NIVERNAIS
FRANCHE-COMTE
CONFEDERATION
Tours
TOURAINE
BERRY
ATLANTIC
POITOU
FRANCE
OCEAN
Poitiers
BOURBONNAIS
Saône
AUNIS-ET-
MARCHE
SAINTONGE
Allier
SAVOIE
KINGDOM OF
ANGOULÊME
AUVERGNE
LYONNAIS
SARDINIA
Limoges
LIMOUSIN
Clermont
Lyon
Bordeaux
Ferrand
Grenoble
Bay of
Biscay
GUYENNE-ET-GASCOGNE
DAUPHINE
Durance
Monaco
Rhône
COMTE
Bayonne
Montauban
Avignon
PROVENCE
DE NICE
BÉARN
Nîmes
SPAIN
Toulouse
LANGUEDOC
Montpellier
Toulon
Marseille
COMTE
DE FOIX
Mediterranean
Perpignan
N
Sea
ROUSSILLON

Areas of rural revolt
Principal areas/origins of rural revolt
Areas unaffected by La Grande Peur (1789)

0   250   500 kilometers
0   125   250 miles

ABOVE Bad harvests in 1789 brought unrest among the peasantry, who then attacked the manor houses of the local landowners and destroyed civil records documenting their feudal obligations.

ABOVE LEFT Louis XVI preferred to spend his time hunting, relying heavily on his advisors for the running of the nation. However, his advisors were unable to prevail against the entrenched privileges of the aristocracy.

RIGHT Around six to seven thousand women marched from Paris to Versailles to protest against the high price and scarcity of bread. They presented their demands to the National Assembly there.

It was the Civil Constitution that convinced the pious King Louis XVI to reject the Revolution, since for him accepting it implied signing his own eternal damnation. Therefore, in June 1791, he and his family attempted to flee France, but he was caught at Varennes and the royal family returned to Paris under house arrest.

Constitution
In September 1791, the Constituent Assembly finally proclaimed the constitution, and dissolved itself. The Legislative Assembly, a body dominated by the Girondins, the most powerful faction of the radical Jacobins, succeeded it in October. The Girondins insisted on exporting the Revolution to the world, and silencing the increasingly clamorous anti-Revolutionary movement in Europe, which was particularly strong in neighboring Austria and Prussia. To achieve this, the Assembly declared war on Austria in April 1792.

1601 to 1900

LEFT Bad harvests in 1789 brought unrest among the peasantry. Afraid of mobs, Parisians began to arm themselves, and revolution began.

RIGHT *La Terreur* is the name given to the campaign of executions that took place across France in 1793–1794.

1789 The Estates General are called for the first time since 1614

May 5, 1789 Voting is to be by Estate and not by head, resulting in Third Estate meeting alone and later declaring itself the National Assembly

June 27, 1789 Louis XVI recognizes the validity of the National Assembly, ordering First and Second Estates to join Third

1791 Royal family flees to Varennes but is arrested and returned to Paris

1792 The tricolor cockade becomes compulsory headgear for men

1793 Louis XVI is guillotined after trial before the National Convention

1795 "La Marseillaise" is accepted as the French national anthem

Second Revolution

The war boded ill for the lower classes—if lost to the anti-Revolutionary powers, it could result in the restoration of feudal privileges. In the "second revolution" of August 1792, Parisian workers entered the Tuileries and imprisoned the royal family. Setting up a municipal government called the Commune, they forced the dissolution of the Assembly, the abrogation of the constitution, and the

ABOVE Marie Antoinette, Queen of France, being found guilty of treason, was guillotined on October 16, 1793.

RIGHT Maximilien Robespierre, radical revolutionary became a victim of the Reign of Terror himself, on July 28, 1794.

election of a republican Constitutional Convention made up entirely of Jacobins. About 1,100 priests and counter-revolutionaries were dragged out of prisons and murdered in the "September massacres."

Republic

The Convention met in September 1792, discarded the Gregorian calendar, and proclaimed Year I of the Republic. The next few months witnessed French military victories as the Republican army invaded Belgium, Savoy, and the left bank of the Rhine.

In this explosive atmosphere, Louis XVI was tried for treason, found guilty, and condemned to death by a majority of one. He was guillotined in January 1793. His

execution radicalized the Convention further as, with over half its members as regicides, it could not afford a return to the Old Regime.

Panic spread in April when French General Charles Dumouriez defected to Austria and the French were driven from Belgium. In May, the Commune, the Montagnards, and the sans-culottes organized a mass invasion of the Convention and arrested the Girondins.

The Terror of Robespierre

The Girondins' fall heralded the rise to power of Maximilien Robespierre. He aimed to win the war, repress anarchy and counter-revolution, and create a republic of virtuous citizens. To achieve these goals, he convinced the Convention to suspend indefinitely the newly drafted Constitution of 1793, and to institute the Reign of Terror (1793–1794).

In less than a year, 40,000 supposed "enemies of the Republic," including royalists, nobles, clerics, bourgeois, Girondins, Dantonists (right-wing Jacobins), counter-revolutionaries, Hébertists (radical "ultra-revolutionaries"), but particularly peasants and workers—who represented about 70 percent of the victims—were guillotined or otherwise summarily executed.

A group in the Convention conspired against Robespierre

and his associates, proscribing them and sending them to the guillotine in the *coup d'état* of the 9th of Thermidor, Year II (July 27, 1794). The Thermidorians then ended the Terror, closed the Jacobin Club, and prepared the new Constitution of 1795, which provided for yet another government—the Directory.

Europe (1798–1799)

Area of French Constitutional rule

French satellite states

Church lands to be absorbed by other German states

Boundary of French influence

Open Dictatorship

In 1797, the Directory suffered a crisis when France's first truly free republican election yielded a royalist victory. The government, terrified, turned to the army for help. Napoleon Bonaparte was then a brilliant young general who had conquered North Italy for France, and who wanted an expansionist republican regime at home in order to preserve his conquests. He sent to Paris his general, Augereau, whose troops stood by as the Directory canceled the election results. It was the *coup d'état* of Fructidor. Most of Italy, the Netherlands, and the German states remained French satellites as a result.

With the Directory now an open dictatorship, civil strife intensified and the economy remained unstable. Meanwhile, Bonaparte invaded Egypt in an attempt to strike at England indirectly. But England responded by forming the Second Coalition, a military alliance that retaliated successfully against France.

Taking advantage of this perceived French weakness, Bonaparte returned to Paris and colluded with dissatisfied members of the Directory. In the *coup d'état* of the 18th of Brumaire (November 9, 1799), the Directory disbanded.

Bonaparte became the First Consul of France's third Republican government, the Consulate.

The Little General

Born to a minor noble family in Corsica, Napoleon Bonaparte (1769–1821) rose to become one of the most powerful and controversial individuals in history.

1796 Napoleon marries the widow Josephine de Beauharnais

1799 Napoleon stages a coup d'état and installs himself as First Consul

1804 Napoleon crowns himself Emperor

1810 Marie Louise, Archduchess of Austria, marries Napoleon after his divorce from Josephine, who could not give him an heir

1815 Napoleon is exiled to the island of Saint Helena, dying in 1821

Taking advantage of the system of meritocracy that resulted from the French Revolution (1789–1799), in which ability carried greater weight than pedigree, Napoleon rose from a junior command in the French Army to the throne of an empire. He gained mastery over the government and the armed forces, and he enlisted the allegiance of the people necessary for the state to wage war.

For over a decade, Napoleon's dual role as head of state and commander in chief of the armed forces conferred on him enormous freedom to conduct the affairs of state. Political and military authority merged in the figure of Napoleon and he exploited this authority to its full extent.

Continental System

However, the undivided authority that Napoleon enjoyed as both military and political leader lacked the checks and balances that govern much of modern statecraft. The Imperial France of his design controlled a continent, but that design was drawn to suit not the realities of European politics, but more the ambitions of Napoleon himself.

Being stymied in his attempt to invade England during 1803 to 1804 and humiliated by the French Navy's defeat at Trafalgar led Napoleon, in 1806, to create the Continental System—a European blockade of British trade intended to undermine the British economy. Although Russia agreed in 1807 to implement the Continental System, Napoleon's attempt to destroy British commerce backfired.

France did not possess the means to wage an economic war against an adversary that dominated the sea lines of communication essential to its national survival.

Warfare

Napoleon had initiated revolutionary warfare supported by both institutional and tactical modernization. But after nearly a decade of war, other countries, such as Austria, Prussia, and Russia, began

> France has more need of me than I have need of France.
>
> –Napoleon Bonaparte, French military and political leader

to emulate France. The superiority Napoleon had enjoyed at the turn of the century no longer existed by the time he launched his wars in support of the Continental System. While Napoleon's tactical genius remained a potent force, the strategic advantage of having been the first to adopt the revolutionary means of waging war had passed from France.

Striking the Enemy

Napoleon reached the pinnacle of power because of the positive social and political consequences of the French Revolution, his valuable political connections, his considerable military and political ability, and his astounding success on the battlefield. His absolute power and dominion over Europe fueled smoldering resentments, blunted the ambitions of other states, and upended the balance of power.

Despite his brilliance in waging war and molding French society, Napoleon could not envision any policy except that of striking at the enemy's center of gravity. This had served him well in his rise to power and in creating the French Empire in Europe. That resounding success served to reinforce his convictions of the primary place of warfare in policy making.

Yet Napoleon's failure to align the means of reaching his objectives with the very worth of those objectives themselves led to his downfall and that of Imperial France. He sought goals that required means that were beyond the resources of France at the time.

ABOVE RIGHT Portrait of Napoleon as King of Italy, painted in 1805 by Koenig von Italien.

LEFT The magnificence of the French court is seen in this painting of the coronation of Napoleon and Josephine as Emperor and Empress of France. Pope Pius VII is shown on the far right.

RIGHT Josephine de Beauharnais, consort of Napoleon, who divorced him so that he could produce an heir. Despite their estrangement, Napoleon's last word was "Josephine".

ABOVE A magnificent young general in battle, Napoleon is seen here in the Battle of Rivoli, 1797, and his victory over Austria.

RIGHT Napoleon conducted a campaign in Northern Italy from 1796 to 1797, where he won territory from Piedmont across to Venice.

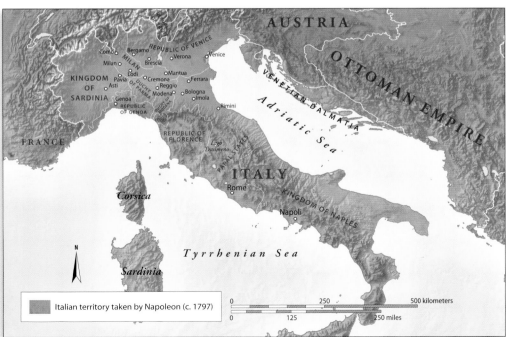

Italian territory taken by Napoleon (c. 1797)

TECHNOLOGY, TRADE, AND TRANSITION

Napoleonic Wars

The Napoleonic Wars (1805-1815) produced fundamental changes in Europe. During this period, France sought to defend its sovereignty and spread the ideals of the French Revolution abroad.

During this time, the monarchs of Europe attempted to take any advantage possible of French weakness and check the spread of revolution to their own lands. In response, they assembled military coalitions intended to defeat France.

Initially, the European powers achieved very little success, as France became militarily dominant in Europe. However, Napoleon's decision to invade Spain in 1808 and then Russia in 1812 over-extended his empire. By 1814, a coalition of Austria, Britain,

Prussia, and Russia invaded France and drove Napoleon into exile. Although he regained control of the French government in 1815 for 100 days, he suffered a final defeat at the Battle of Waterloo and was banished permanently to the island of St Helena.

Causes

There were three factors led to the Napoleonic Wars. First was the attempt by other European powers to exploit France's internal confusion in order to further their own territorial aspirations. A second factor was the widespread fear in

	British forces under Wellington
	British forces under Nelson
	French forces
✗	Major battles

France that the monarchy was conspiring with *émigrés* and foreign powers to reverse the gains of the Revolution. This fear led France to seek to destroy its supposed enemies. Napoleon's political power and his military prowess on the battlefield allowed him to make warfare his instrument of choice in solving problems at home and abroad. Finally, both France and the other Great Powers made a series of severe miscalculations about each other that pushed them closer to war.

LEFT Over a decade, Napoleon waged battles with the surrounding Great Powers, eventually losing Paris and being forced into exile.

1792-1791 Campaign of the First Coalition

1798-1801 Napoleon invades Egypt. His fleet is destroyed by Nelson.

1805 Third Coalition sees victory for the French with surrender at Ulm and a crushing victory over Russia and Austria

1808-1814 Peninsular War leaves Napoleon's army decimated

1812 Napoleon invades Russia in one of the worst military mistakes in history. The march to Moscow causes hardship and death. Eventually retreating back across plundered territory, the army crosses out of Russian territory with the loss of thousands of men.

RIGHT Napoleon reviewing troops in Vienna in 1805, after occupying the city following his victory over the Austrians at the Battle of Ulm. There were few losses on either side.

French Revolution (1789-1799)

The French Revolution laid the groundwork for the Napoleonic Wars. The Revolution ended France's traditional social and political system, which automatically accorded leadership to the nobility. The new system of merit opened doors to the lower classes, who responded enthusiastically. In the military, the *bourgeoisie* now filled the ranks of the officer corps, which had previously been dominated by the aristocracy. Henceforth, French officials were to be chosen on the strength of their merit, not bloodline. It is the former route on which Napoleon rode to power. The Great Powers viewed the political infighting in France that followed the Revolution and sought to reap benefits from it. Though less important, the monarchies of Europe also feared the ideational power unleashed by the Revolution. The monarchs had obtained power on the strength of tradition, not the ballot box. Were the twin ideologies of liberalism and nationalism to spread, the people might revolt and seize power. In response, they mounted a series of military coalitions in order to defeat France.

Grande Armée

Threatened with invasion, France adopted the *levée en masse* in 1793 —a conscription law that enabled it to raise an army of 750,000 men. However, during the following 10 years, mainly due to desertion, the French Army shrank in size but gained in experience and professionalism, while retaining its revolutionary fervor. By 1805, this force was known as the Grande Armée. Beyond its experience and professionalism, the Grande Armée also benefited from the new social and political system that had emerged in France. Led by Napoleon, France's army was comprised of citizens, not subjects. Their willingness to fight and die for flag and country contrasted sharply with the armies of France's rivals, which were comprised of mercenaries and members of the peasantry who were forcibly conscripted into service. France was thus able to harness the material and moral resources of the country in service of the national interest—it had become a nation under arms.

BELOW Titled *The Second of May, 1808*, this painting by Goya shows the Spanish uprising against the Marmeluke soldiers of Napoleon's occupying army.

ABOVE Napoleon during the "Hundred Days"—the phrase coined to describe the period in 1815 between his return to Paris from exile on the island of Elba and the return of Louis XVIII.

RIGHT This painting by Thomas Jones Barker shows the meeting of the Duke of Wellington of Britain and Field Marshall Blücher of Prussia, on the eve of victory at Waterloo in 1815.

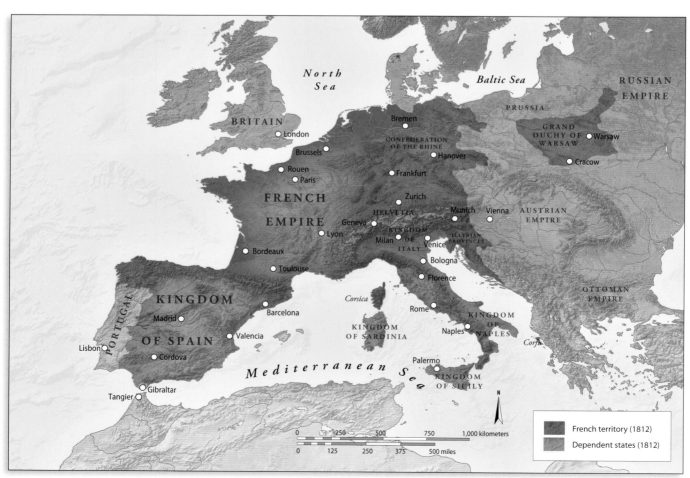

French territory (1812)

Dependent states (1812)

> In victory, you deserve Champagne. In defeat, you need it.
>
> –Napoleon Bonaparte (1769-1821), French military and political leader.

Objectives

The Grande Armée also achieved dominance over its rivals due to the military innovations introduced by Napoleon.

Breaking from the military customs of the day, France introduced a revolutionary style of warfare. The country adopted ambitious goals and provided the army with the means to achieve them. Instead of attempting to seize land in order to trade for other land, a tactic that had characterized the "age of limited war" (roughly 1648–1793), Napoleon recognized that the true objective of warfare was the destruction of the enemy's army, not the possession of his capital. The armies of the other great powers simply fell short of the Grande Armée.

Victories and Defeat

During the first decade of the nineteenth century, Napoleonic France met the security challenges that arose, racking up a series of stunning, though hard-fought, military victories over the other Great Powers of Europe. But this string of victories began to run

ABOVE RIGHT Following his massive defeat at the Battle of Waterloo (1815), Napoleon is seen fleeing from the scene.

LEFT By 1812, Napoleon controlled not only France's neighboring states but also held agreements and alliances with other territories.

RIGHT The Battle of Waterloo comprised four battles fought over three days. Napoleon beat back the Anglo-Dutch troops from Quatre-Bras, and the Prussians from Ligny and Wavre. But, on June 18, 1815, at the small Belgian town of Waterloo, his army was finally defeated by the combined forces of Wellington and Blücher.

out. In 1808, Napoleon's invasion of Spain led to a long and bloody guerilla war. In 1812, France invaded Russia. France's subsequent inability to defeat Russia handed Napoleon his biggest military and political setback. From 1812 to 1814, Austria, Prussia, Russia, the United Kingdom, Sweden, and

several Germanic states formed a coalition against France and eventually bore down on Paris.

Despite a series of stunning victories, Napoleon failed to halt the Allied tide and Paris eventually fell. Negotiations for peace failed, and in 1814 Napoleon abdicated the throne of France and was driven

into exile to the island of Elba. He briefly returned to power in 1815 for 100 days but was eventually defeated at the Battle of Waterloo and returned to exile on the island of St Helena.

After Napoleon's final exile, the Great Powers of Europe convened to restructure European politics. At this Congress of Vienna (1815), the conferees sought to prevent the rise of another dominant power, to uphold the balance of power, and to preserve the conservative social order. In pursuit of this, the Great Powers decided against weakening France or excluding it from the envisioned post-war international political system. Instead, they allowed France to retain its present borders and place a Bourbon monarch, Louis XVIII, on its throne. They also enlisted France in this security system, the Concert of Europe, intended to extinguish any spark of liberalism and nationalism before it became powerful enough to undermine or threaten the legitimacy of monarchical rule. Although the Concert of Europe successfully fulfilled its mission until mid-century, it collapsed due to conflicting interests among its members. However, Europe did enjoy a long period of relative peace until 1914 and the outbreak of World War I.

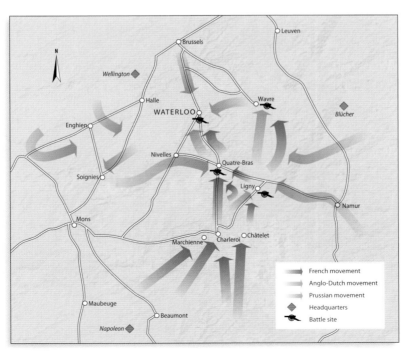

Workshop of the World

Philosophical enlightenment, together with Adam Smith's pathbreaking modern economics, made Britain a pioneer of the free society and the laissez-faire economy.

RIGHT Scottish engineer James Watt (1736-1819), whose innovations led to a highly improved steam engine in 1765, coined the word "horsepower." The watt, a standard unit of power, is named after him.

1761 With the opening of Bridgewater Canal, designed by James Brindley, barges can now carry coal from Worsley to Manchester

1777 Grand Trunk Canal opens, connecting the Mersey to the Trent and the industrial Midlands to the ports of Bristol, Liverpool, and Hull

1792 James Watt's assistant William Murdock lights his home with coal gas

1811-15 Laborers attack factories and break the machines out of fear of being replaced

1849 Monier develops reinforced concrete

Britain emerged as a preeminent economic power between the sixteenth and eighteenth centuries. Its economic rise rested on the foundations of its constitutional monarchy, the remarkable success of the English Reformation, and an agricultural revolution that had increased productivity and secured a rich food supply. In the space of just one hundred and fifty years, the population increased three-and-a-half times over.

The Age of Inventions

Crowning two hundred years of development, a series of separate but mutually reinforcing technological innovations in the last third of the eighteenth century were to transform industry. John Kay's 1733 invention of the flying shuttle boosted the productivity of weaving by 30 to 50 percent, at the same time boosting the demand for thread. The Society of Art offered an award in 1760 to create a more productive spinning machine. In 1764, James Hargreaves, a weaver and carpenter, created his eight-spindle "Spinning Jenny," which increased productivity by 8–10 times. Richard Arkwright, a barber, patented his water frame in 1769. This machine used waterpower to move 100 spindles. Then in 1785 Samuel Crompton—who had learned to spin yarn as a boy to

> Labor was the first price, the original purchase-money that was paid for all things.
> –Adam Smith (1723-1790), Scottish economist and philosopher.

support his family after his father died—combined Hargreaves' jenny and Arkwright's frame to develop his steam-powered "muslin mule," suitable for producing fine thread.

Mechanization Pays Off

Mechanized weaving was invented by Edmund Cartwright, a clergyman who patented his power loom in 1787. Four years earlier, James Bell had patented the roller printer machine that replaced the work of 40 hand-block printers. The process of whitening yarn in the sun, which took weeks or months, was also shortened to a few hours by using chlorine as a bleach, as invented by the French chemist Claude Louis Berthollet in 1784. Thanks to the mechanized textile factories, the overall price of textiles dropped to one-twentieth of what they had been pre-mechanization. Britain was soon supplying the entire world with textile products. In the 1780s,

LEFT James Hargreaves's "Spinning Jenny," a machine with eight wooden spindles, enabled one person to spin several threads at once.

cotton products made up 7 percent of total exports. By the 1840s, their share had climbed to 45 percent.

Steam Power

In 1705, Thomas Newcomen, an ironmonger and blacksmith, built a rudimentary 20-horsepower steam engine for use in mines to pump water. The turning point arrived with James Watt, an instrument maker, who established a small workshop at Glasgow University and started working to improve Newcomen's engine. By 1763, he had built a more efficient engine that was able to work continuously and move machines. He acquired patents for several consecutive innovations that led to a highly improved steam engine—five times more efficient than Newcomen's engine by 1784. In 1800, Britain possessed a capacity of about 10,000 horsepower. By 1815 this had increased to 210,000, and by 1850 to 1,290,000 horsepower.

Map legend:
- Coalfields
- Major railway links
- Shipbuilding centers
- Copper mines
- Metal manufacture
- Cotton mills
- Woolen mills
- Chemical manufacture (soap, salt, etc.)

Iron Innovations

Henry Cort, an ironmaster in a Portsmouth harbor mill, invented steam-powered rolling (1783), and the puddling furnace (1784), which together replaced slow and labor-intensive hammering. His use of combined puddling and rolling to de-carbonize pig iron and produce wrought iron in a single step decreased by two-thirds the amount of coal required to produce one ton of crude iron. In 1839, the engineer James Nasmyth invented the steam hammer. The modern iron industry was born in Britain.

While the textile, iron, and coal industries were transformed quickly, most other industries retained their traditional small scale for a few more decades. In 1841 most of the active population was engaged in agriculture. Mechanized industry really broke through in the second half of the century, then gradually spread to the Continent, ushering in the age of industrial capitalism.

ABOVE When Queen Victoria opened the Great Exhibition on May 1, 1851, her country was the world's leading industrial power, producing more than half its iron, coal, and cotton cloth. Birmingham alone was known as "the city of a thousand trades."

ABOVE LEFT Women and children sifting coal, the energy source so crucial to the industrialization process. Traditional power sources like wind and water could not supply the energy needs of industry. But coal could, and it was plentiful in Britain.

LEFT The workshop of James Watt in Heathfield, Birmingham, where he spent his time from 1790 until his death in 1819.

Revolt Against Spain

The early nineteenth century witnessed the end of three centuries of mostly peaceful Hispanic rule, and the creation of the modern Latin American republics following ruinous wars between 1808 and 1830.

RIGHT Simón Bolívar presenting the flag of liberation to the patriot forces after their victory at the Battle of Carabobo, in 1821.

1494 Treaty of Tordesillas divides the New World between Spain and Portugal

1500 Pedro Alvares Cabral claims the Brazilian "hump" for Portugal

1507 The name "America" is used for the first time by a German cartographer who publishes a map of the New World. He chooses the word in honor of Amerigo Vespucci (1454–1512)

1519-22 Cortés conquers the Aztec capital of Tenochtitlan

1823 United States issues the Monroe Doctrine warning against recolonization of the newly independent Spanish American republics

1846-48 Mexico is defeated by the United States which annexes the northern half of the country in the Treaty of Guadalupe Hidalgo

The roots of this process may be traced to the mid-eighteenth century. In particular, colonial disaffection with Spanish rule increased markedly during the era of the Bourbon reforms, an unremitting series of measures stretching from around 1740 to the 1790s.

Breaking Rank
In 1809, Upper Peru (Bolivia) broke ranks when the cities of La Paz and Chuquisaca (renamed Sucre in 1825) formed independent juntas. Then, in 1810, the Central Junta collapsed.

South Americans responded by creating ruling juntas in Río de la Plata (Argentina, Uruguay, Paraguay), Chile, New Granada (Colombia, Ecuador), and Venezuela. In Buenos Aires, the viceroy was deposed and war was declared on both Paraguay and Montevideo.

Paraguay emerged victorious, proclaimed its independence in 1811, and then settled down to an unbroken, relatively prosperous 26 years of dictatorship from 1814 to 1840. Argentina declared independence from Spain at the Congress of Tucumán in 1816.

Uruguay's birth was more protracted. The Banda Oriental was incorporated into Brazil from 1817 until 1828, when it became the Sovereign Republic of Uruguay.

Chile
After years of royalist repression, Chile was finally liberated in 1817 after the patriot victory at the battle of Chacabuco, following the extraordinary march by the Army of the Andes, led by José de San Martín, with Bernardo O'Higgins and his remnant Chilean army. Independence was declared in 1818 and O'Higgins made supreme director.

> He who serves a revolution ploughs the sea.
>
> –Simón Bolívar (1783-1830), leader of South American Independence movements.

Simón Bolívar
Simón Bolívar, the greatest of all Independence heroes, arrived in Caracas in 1812. After early military reverses, patriot forces defeated the royalists at the Battle of Boyacá in 1819, thereby liberating Bogotá and other provinces of New Granada. The patriot army under Bolívar then proved irresistible, crushing royalist forces at the Battle of Carabobo in 1821. Venezuela was now triumphantly independent. Less than a year later, it was joined by New Granada, with the Quito region liberated by Antonio José de Sucre at the battle of Pichincha. The Viceroyalty of New Granada now became the Republic of Colombia.

Peru
The road to Lima now stood open. Bolívar's expedition from the north coincided with San Martín's expedition from the south.

At a celebrated meeting between Bolívar and San Martín in Guayaquil in 1822, San Martín ceded command of the Peruvian expeditionary force to Bolívar. The Liberator arrived in Lima to be acclaimed as Dictator. With Peru seized, Upper Peru was the only remaining royalist redoubt, but fell to Bolívar's General Sucre in 1825. This victory was the capstone of independence in Spanish South America.

Mexico and Central America
The Plan de Iguala of February 24, 1821, proclaimed Mexico's independence, with Agustín de Iturbide appointed as commander of the army of the south. In 1822, with the support of his troops, Iturbide became emperor, but was ousted soon afterwards. Finally, the Constitution of 1824 established a federal republic.

In Central America, independence was reached raggedly. The five soon-to-be Central American states—Guatemala, Honduras, Nicaragua, Costa Rica, El Salvador—were disunited. When Iturbide fell in 1823, Mexican interest in the region lapsed, and the five

provinces declared themselves absolutely independent, but yoked together under the constitution of 1824 as the United Provinces of Central America. By 1830 each Province had declared its independence. The circle was complete as Mesoamerica, Central America, and Spanish South America reached fully-fledged nationhood almost simultaneously.

NORTH ATLANTIC OCEAN

Chihuahua

Monterrey

Gulf of Mexico

MEXICO

Tampico

Guadalajara

Mexico City

Acapulco

Oaxaca

Merida

CUBA

DOMINICAN REPUBLIC

HAITI

PUERTO RICO

Belmopan

BELIZE

BRITISH HONDURAS

Caribbean Sea

Guatemala

GUATEMALA

Honduras

San Salvador

EL SALVADOR

NICARAGUA

Managua

San Jose

COSTA RICA

Panama

PANAMA

Gulf of Panama

Medellin

Bogota

Cali

COLOMBIA

Quito

ECUADOR

Guayaquil

VENEZUELA

Valencia

Caracas

Georgetown

BRITISH GUIANA

Paramaribo

DUTCH GUIANA

Cayenne

FRENCH GUIANA

Manaus

Amazon

Santarem

Belem

San Luis

Fortaleza

Natal

Recife

Parnaiba

Trujillo

Port Velho

BRAZIL

Salvador

PERU

Lima

Cuzco

BOLIVIA

La Paz

Cuiaba

Brasilia

Goiania

Belo Horizonte

Sao Paulo

Rio de Janeiro

Santos

Curitiba

Arequipa

Santa Cruz

Sucre

Parana

Paraguay

PARAGUAY

Asuncion

Uruguay

Antofagasta

Chacabuco

Salado

Porto Alegre

Cordoba

CHILE

Santiago

Mendoza

Rosario

URUGUAY

Montevideo

Rio de la Plata

Buenos Aires

ARGENTINA

Concepcion

Colorado

Bahia Blanca

Puerto Montt

Comodoros Rivadavia

SOUTH ATLANTIC OCEAN

Punta Arenas

Dates of Independence

up to 1820
1821–1829
1830–1899
1900–1959
1960–1969
1970–1979
After 1980

RIGHT Countries in Latin America gained their independence in a flurry of wars and revolutions.

BELOW Miguel Hidalgo y Costilla, the Mexican Catholic priest who began the fight for Mexican independence, is called "Father of the Country."

N

0   1,000   2,000 kilometers

0   500   1,000 miles

307

1601 to 1900

Age of Empire

Princess Alexandrina Victoria, born to the Duke of Kent and Princess Victoria of Saxe-Coburg on May 24, 1819, became one of the most famous monarchs in history, although her uncle, King William IV of England, had hoped that she would not inherit the throne.

Victoria's parents were unpopular, but through dynastic mischance eighteen-year-old Princess Alexandrina became Queen Victoria when William IV died in June 1837. The young queen's marriage to her cousin, Prince Albert of Saxe-Coburg, had been planned from their childhoods, but fortunately Victoria fell in love with Albert, whom she married in 1840.

Albert, the Consort
Albert was never popular with the British people, mostly because he was German, but he was a conscientious consort who worked hard and guided Victoria well. Albert successfully planned and executed the Great Exhibition of 1851, the first international exhibition of industry, invention, and discovery.

England
Queen Victoria also relied on her ministers for support. Of her ten Prime Ministers she disliked William Gladstone intensely but admired Lord Melbourne. Her favorite Prime Minister was Benjamin Disraeli, who flattered her and flirted with her.

The industrial revolution was in full stride, fuelled by Britain's coal and iron reserves, aided by freedom from internal war and revolution. Nevertheless, poverty existed behind the glittering façade of Empire and industrial wealth. Radicals and Republicanists pressed their agendas, and Ireland demanded Home Rule. However, although Victoria was a conservative, political and social reform slowly came about during her reign. The seven attempts on her life were by unbalanced men rather than serious revolutionaries.

1847 *Ten Hours Act* is passed, restricting the working hours of children in factories

1852 The Victoria and Albert Museum in London is opened

1855 Balmoral Castle is completed

1858 Government of India is transferred to the British Crown

1863 First underground railway in London, between Paddington and Farringdon Street, opens on January 10

1876 Queen Victoria is named Empress of India

1891 New Scotland Yard is completed

1901 The population of London reaches 6.6 million

RIGHT In a photograph taken the year before she died, Queen Victoria poses with four of her 37 great-grandchildren. Prince Albert, seated on a cushion in the foreground, became King George VI, Queen Elizabeth II's father.

Empire
The British Empire doubled during Queen Victoria's reign. For more than two centuries Britain's traders and explorers had helped it acquire vast territories. During the 63 years of Victoria's rule, a conglomerate of disparate states spread across the globe were incorporated into a more consolidated whole. New Zealand, Canada, and Australia all gained responsible government but remained part of the British Empire. In 1876 Disraeli maneuvered to have Victoria proclaimed Empress of India, a title she craved.

Closer to home, the European powers challenged each other's rule throughout the nineteenth century. Britain tried to maintain peace with and among France, Austria, Germany, and Russia as alliances formed and re-formed. Britain and France were traditional enemies, while Britain and Germany mostly

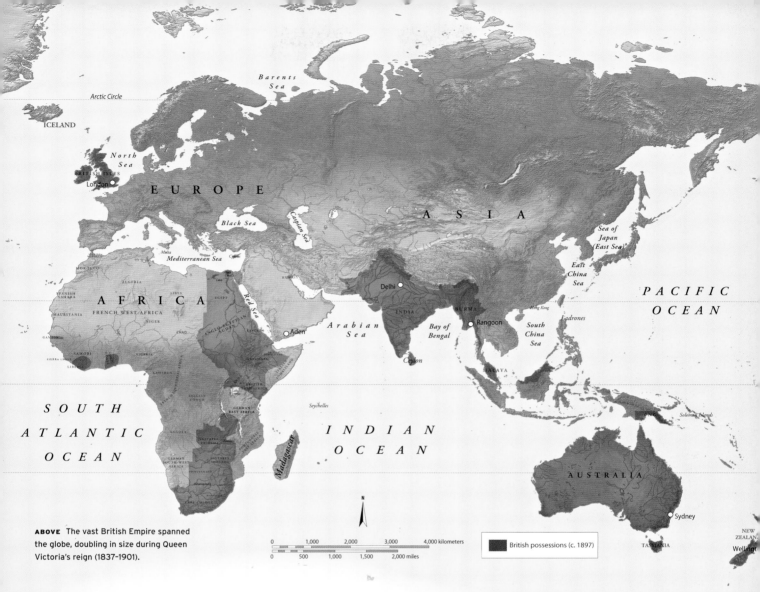

ABOVE The vast British Empire spanned the globe, doubling in size during Queen Victoria's reign (1837–1901).

British possessions (c. 1897)

agreed on matters of policy. The only major European war Britain was involved in between 1815 and 1914 was the unpopular Crimean War of 1853–1856.

Royal Connections

Victoria was a romantic who encouraged her children and grandchildren to marry for love, but royal marriages had political and strategic implications. Eight of Victoria's children married European royalty, while the other married a British Duke. Kaiser Wilhelm II of Germany was Victoria's grandson, and her granddaughter Alexandra of Hesse became Empress of Russia. Both Queen Elizabeth II and her husband the Duke of Edinburgh are descended from Queen Victoria.

When Prince Albert died in December 1861 Victoria retreated into intense mourning at her

> The important thing is not what they think of me, but what I think of them.
> –Queen Victoria of England (1819–1901).

favorite homes, Osborne House located on the Isle of Wight, and Balmoral in Scotland. The country became highly critical when her mourning lasted until 1887, exacerbated by scandal regarding her friendship with her Highland servant John Brown.

Eventually Victoria emerged into public life and her Golden Jubilee in 1887 was a major success. By the time of her Diamond Jubilee she had become a legendary and beloved figure, ruling a huge and prosperous empire. Victoria died at Osborne House on January 22, 1901, at the age of 81.

ABOVE Fashioned using bronze from cannons captured during the Crimean War, the Victoria Cross is Britain's highest military award for acts of bravery.

LEFT Queen Victoria's reign was Britain's longest, at 64 years.

Late Tsarist Russia

In 1801, the Romanov Dynasty had exerted autocratic rule over the complex Russian Empire for 200 years. Composed of different ethnic groups, it stretched from western Europe to Asia and from the frozen Arctic north to the temperate Black Sea in the south.

Alexander I

Alexander I, grandson of Catherine the Great, came to power in 1801, following the murder of his father, Paul, in an attempted coup. Despite being autocrats, tsars needed to retain the goodwill of the nobles, a tiny but powerful group. Most people were either state peasants or serfs who belonged to private land-owners. Tsars were reluctant to free the peasantry, fearing retaliation by the aristocracy. Nobles and gentry peopled the bureaucracy and the officer class of the army—in the early nineteenth century Russia had only a small middle class.

Russia developed an aggressive foreign policy and a large standing army. In 1812, Russia sided with Britain, Prussia, and Austria against French aggression. Napoleon's army advanced into Russia, which responded with retreat and with a "scorched earth" policy. Even Moscow was burned and the once-great French army was decimated in the bitter Russian winter of 1813.

Nicholas I

When Alexander died in December 1825, his brother Nicholas I succeeded, to be confronted by the Decembrist Revolt, a rebellion by army officers who wanted a constitution and an end to autocracy. They had been influenced by French revolutionary ideas, but there was no mass support for the revolt. Nicholas, whose motto was "Orthodoxy, Autocracy, Nationality," stopped the uprising and allowed little reform throughout his reign. In 1848–1849, he was disturbed by the political unrest in mainland Europe and even more determined to hold onto absolute rule. Later, foreign alliances changed and in 1854, Nicholas I fought and lost the Crimean War against France and Britain.

ABOVE Born Aleksandr Pavlovich Romanov, Tsar Alexander I died at the age of 47 after a 24-year reign. An enigmatic man, he became interested in mysticism in later life.

1812 Napoleon invades Russia; the people burn Moscow to prevent him gaining the spoils

1814 Napoleon is defeated in Russia

1855 Russia annexes Kazakhstan

1859 Russia annexes Chechnya

1867 Russia sells Alaska to the United States

1895 Vladimir Lenin is arrested for engaging in revolutionary activities

RIGHT Over a period of about 120 years, Russia expanded its territory to encompass a vast area, from Warsaw in the west to Vladivostok in the east.

> I do not rule Russia;
> ten thousand clerks do.
>
> —Nicholas I (1796-1855).

Alexander II

Nicholas' son, Alexander II (1855–1881), the Tsar Liberator, freed the serfs under the Emancipation Decree of 1861. The nobles lost some land, and serfs had to buy their land (using loans from the state) but were still bound to their village council. Nevertheless, both peasants and nobles complied with the arrangement. Emancipation forced changes to government systems, and Alexander II reformed the army and the judicial system.

However, by the middle of the nineteenth century a growing middle class was questioning autocratic government. The intelligentsia responded negatively to the

terms of the Emancipation Decree, leading to agitation for more change and ultimately to terrorism and revolution. The People's Will, a middle-class terrorist group, assassinated Alexander II in March 1881.

Under Alexander II, Fyodor Dostoyevsky wrote about life for the poorer classes, while Leo Tolstoy wrote of the aristocracy: *War and Peace* appeared in 1869 and *Anna Karenina* in 1877. Much of intellectual life was suppressed, but poems and novels provided an outlet for the circulation of ideas.

Alexander III

Industrialization and the spread of the railways prompted more change. A large urban working class pushed for reform, but Alexander III reacted to his father's assassination by reversing reforms of the previous decades. He tried to strengthen the autocracy and conquer all opposition. He promoted industrialization and built the Trans-Siberian railway, but development hurt agriculture. The population grew but agricultural methods remained unchanged and people

FAR LEFT Nicholas I was criticized by writers of the time, such as Nikolai Gogol and Ivan Turgenev, for his autocratic rule.

LEFT Tsar Nicholas II and his wife Tsarina Alexandra were executed by the Bolsheviks in 1918.

BELOW Napoleon receives Alexander I, along with Prussia's King Frederick William III and his wife Queen Louise, before the signing of the Treaties of Tilsit in July 1807.

became hungry. A policy of Russification resulted in persecution for minority groups, especially Jews.

Nicholas II

When in 1894 Nicholas II, the last tsar, inherited the throne, Russia was politically, socially, and economically backward compared to other European powers. When World War I came, both Nicholas and the country were overwhelmed by the huge drain on resources. In the upheaval of war and revolution, 300 years of Romanov rule ended.

PACIFIC OCEAN

Sea of Okhotsk

khotsk

Vladivostok

JAPAN

Tokyo

- ▨ Russian Empire (1796)
- ▨ Territorial gains (1855)
- ▨ Territorial gains (1914)
- — Main Trans-Siberian Railway

Voyage of the Beagle

Charles Darwin's five-year expedition aboard the HMS *Beagle*, resulted in a dramatic and permanent change in scientific thinking.

ABOVE Charles Darwin's health suffered due to overwork, but he was supported by his wife, Emma.

In September 1835, the *Beagle* reached the Galapagos islands. Darwin observed the impressive giant tortoises and thought they had been brought to the island for food. He saw marine iguanas in Stephen's Bay and mistakenly thought they were a South American spices. The crew feasted on Galapagos tortoises on the voyage to Tahiti.

RIGHT The *Beagle* spent five years exploring some of the most scientifically important parts of the natural world.

1839 Darwin marries Emma Wedgwood, granddaughter of the famous potter, and first cousin of Darwin. They will have 10 children.

1844 Charles Darwin writes an essay on natural selection, which is never published

1859 Darwin publishes *The Origin of the Species*

1882 Following his death, Charles Darwin is given a state funeral in Westminster Abbey

HMS *Beagle* departed from Devonport on December 27, 1831, under the command of Robert FitzRoy, with Charles Darwin aboard as the ship's naturalist. After a stop in the Cape Verde Islands, they proceeded westward across the Atlantic. Like James Cook's second and third voyages, the *Beagle* was loaded with chronometers—22 of them—with which to measure longitude and meridian distance, the distance traveled in a single day.

Phosphorescent Sea

On February 16, 1832, Darwin observed typical volcanic geological formations at St Paul's Rocks, an island some 350 miles (560 km) from Fernando Noronha where "the sea gave out light in flashes," a phosphorescence—now called bioluminescence—that Darwin attributed to the decomposition of organic particles.

The *Beagle* landed in Bahia, Brazil on February 28, 1832. While FitzRoy made a short detour to correct some charts, Darwin was left on shore, giving the 22-year-old naturalist his first experience of the tropics.

Argentine Coast

The next phase of the voyage, from August 1832 through March 1834 was along the Uruguayan coast, south to Tierra del Fuego and the Falkland Islands, the latter a contested British archipelago which was an important fueling stop along the India shipping route. There Darwin completed two sets of observations that caused him to reflect on the origins of species— the first was the presence of large fossil mammals in areas that demarcated the ranges of related, smaller, living species, suggesting descent with modification. The second was the overlapping ranges of closely related species, which also suggested common ancestry.

The *Beagle* was on the western coast of South America from June 1834 to September 1835. In March 1835, the crew witnessed a spectacular earthquake in Valparaiso. The voyagers then continued northward to Callao—the port of Lima, Peru was reached on July 19—before heading west into the Pacific and the Galapagos Islands, where it was based for about a month, from September 15 to October 20.

> It is a cursed evil to any man to become as absorbed in any subject as I am in mine
>
> Charles Darwin (1809-1882), English naturalist and geologist.

Galapagos

Contrary to common belief, Darwin did not discover evolution in the Galapagos Islands. What he suspected was that if the famous finches that differed slightly from one another from island to island were separate species, then the fixity of species was in doubt. But he believed these groups to be varieties, and, as a result, failed to label his specimens by island. Only after Darwin's return to England did the ornithologist John Gould demonstrate that the finches were, in fact, quite different species.

Pacific Ocean

Darwin saw his first coral atolls in the Tuamotu Archipelago on November 13, 1835, and some days later in Tahiti. From April 1 to 12, 1836, the *Beagle* stopped at Keeling

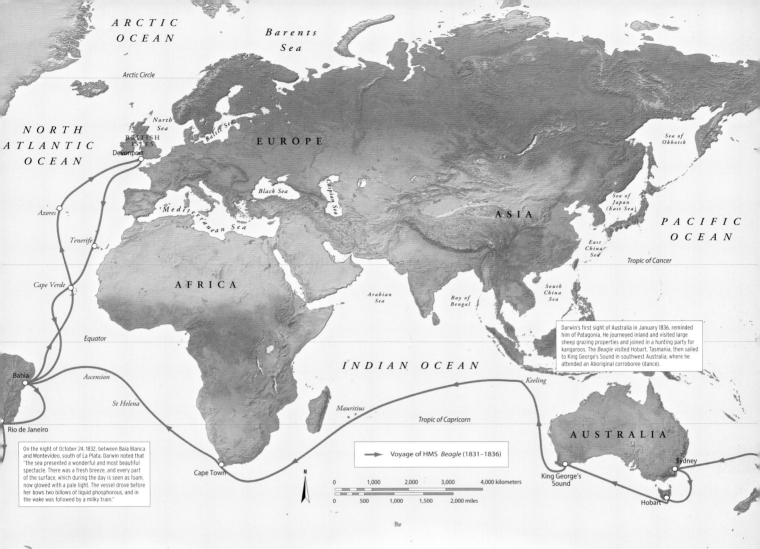

On the night of October 24, 1832, between Baía Blanca and Montevideo, south of La Plata, Darwin noted that "the sea presented a wonderful and most beautiful spectacle. There was a fresh breeze, and every part of the surface, which during the day is seen as foam, now glowed with a pale light. The vessel drove before her bows two billows of liquid phosphorous, and in the wake was followed by a milky train."

Darwin's first sight of Australia in January 1836, reminded him of Patagonia. He journeyed inland and visited large sheep grazing properties and joined in a hunting party for kangaroos. The *Beagle* visited Hobart, Tasmania, then sailed to King George's Sound in southwest Australia, where he attended an Aboriginal corroboree (dance).

→ Voyage of HMS *Beagle* (1831–1836)

RIGHT The *Beagle* spent over 18 months voyaging along the east coast of South America, stopping at many points, including Tierra del Fuego, as pictured here.

Island, an atoll in the Indian Ocean, the only reef Darwin investigated in detail. The last atoll he visited was at Mauritius later that month. Darwin's theory, which has stood the test of time, was that if coral reefs went a good way down, the ocean floor had been sinking, because coral cannot live deeper than 160 feet (50 m). So atolls must be the product of slow reciprocal processes of the uplifting of an island by volcanic action, the colonizing of its slope by polyps, and gradual subsidence into the sea.

The *Beagle* passed the Cape of Good Hope on May 31, 1836, stopped briefly at St Helena and Ascension Island, visited Bahia, Brazil on August 1, and crossed the Atlantic to the Cape Verdes and the Azores. The *Beagle* arrived home at Falmouth, on October 2, 1836.

1601 to 1900

The Opium War

The Opium War was fought between the British and the Qing dynasty in China from 1839 to 1842. It began when the Chinese resisted British attempts to reverse their trade deficit by importing more opium to sell on Chinese markets. China wanted this trade stopped.

> The expense of a war could be paid in time; but the expense of opium, when once the habit is formed, will only increase with time.
>
> ~Townsend Harris (1804-1878), first US Consul General to Japan.

BELOW In the last year of what is sometimes considered the Second Opium War (1856-1860), British forces destroyed the Summer Palace in Beijing, along with the Gardens of Perfect Brightness (pictured).

During the nineteenth century, Qing dynasty trade restrictions made trade in low-value consumer products uneconomic. Instead, Sino-British trade was dominated by valuable luxury items, such as tea from China, and silver from Britain. Due to the high demand for Chinese goods in Britain and the low demand for British goods in China, Britain had a large trade deficit and began searching for other commodities to sell. Seeing the immense potential of opium, Britain began production of the drug in India through the agency of a British government monopoly, the British East India Company.

A Growing Market

Large-scale importation of opium into China began in 1781, despite a previous British commitment to respect the Qing government's ban on the drug. When China had tried to stop the opium trade in 1729, about 200 chests of opium were being imported annually. By 1767, 1,000 chests were entering the country, and toward the end of the 1830s more than 10,000 chests were recorded. By the end of the 1800s there were about 15 million opium addicts and 30 million occasional users in China, notwithstanding the government's continued attempts to turn the tide. This situation reached a crisis point in the Opium War, the underlying aim of which was to force China to accept the import of British opium.

British Attack

The British first seized Hong Kong (at that time a minor outpost) as a base on August 23, 1839. Retaliating against the Qing emperor's decree that all other foreigners in China end assistance to the British, the British government and the East India Company resolved to attack Canton (Guangzhou). In June 1840, a deployment of 15 barracks ships, four steam-powered gunboats, and 25 smaller boats, with 4,000 marines, reached Guangdong. Marine head James Bremer demanded that the Qing government compensate Britain for losses caused by interrupted trade. When the Chinese refused, the British attacked. By January 1841, British forces controlled the high ground around Guangzhou and had overcome the Chinese at Ningbo and Chinghai. By the middle of 1842, they had defeated the Chinese at the mouth of the Yangtze, and had occupied Shanghai.

China Cedes Hong Kong

The war concluded in August 1842 when China agreed to sign the first Unequal Treaty (Treaty of Nanjing), committing the Qing government to fixed tariffs on British goods. As part of the treaty, Hong Kong was ceded to the British, and the ports of Guangzhou, Xiamen, Fuzhou, Shanghai, and Ningbo were thrown open to British merchants, who were now allowed to trade autonomously with Chinese merchants. The Qing government was also forced to compense the British for lost opium sales and war costs. In addition, in the Treaty of the Bogue in 1843, Britain was granted most-favored nation status, entitling it to any rights granted by the Qing

West versus East

Opium, a derivative of the poppy (*Papaver somniferum* L.), had traditionally been used in China for medicinal purposes. From the eighteenth century onwards, people began smoking pure opium sap in a pipe and its narcotic effects relieved both physical and emotional pain. Britain manufactured and distributed opium on a large scale in India, through the East India Company. The drug was seen as a way to improve the balance of payments with China.

The Opium War created lasting mistrust of Western society among the Chinese, and this kind of invasion was repeated in subsequent conflicts in China and the rest of Asia. Other European nations later used military force to instigate trade with China. From the time of the Opium War of 1839-1842 until the founding of the People's Republic of China (PRC) in 1949, various Western countries as well as Japan forced China to agree to a number of unequal treaties that enabled foreigners to establish themselves autonomously and commence dealings with privileged status in China. These rights were abolished with the creation of the PRC.

→ British attack routes, first Opium War (1840–1842)

⚓ Open ports for British trade (Treaty of Nanking, 1842)

→ Anglo-French attack route, second Opium War (1857–1860)

government to any other nation, plus extra-territorial privileges for British nationals at its treaty ports.

The Qing government had never been strong, and the Opium War brought the world's largest empire to its knees, demonstrating that the Qing government was no match for Western powers either in politics or in war. The undermining of China's imperial authority led to instability such as the Taiping Rebellion of 1850–1864, one of many that shook the last imperial dynasty of China to its foundations. For this reason the Opium War heralds the end of Qing rule, and marks the beginning of modern Chinese history.

ABOVE British warships wreaked havoc on coastal towns in China once war broke out. The recent innovation of steam power combined with sail and the use of iron in ships like the *Nemesis* made them very powerful and highly mobile.

LEFT Recreational use of opium began in China in the fifteenth century but was limited by its rarity and expense. Known to be addictive by the seventeenth century, it was also more accessible by then.

1729 The Qing government bans opium in China

1781 British merchants begin large-scale opium import from India

1821-1837 British merchants increase opium imports, trying to reverse trade imbalance with China

July 1839 20,000 chests of opium seized by Chinese. Sailors destroy Kowloon temple and kill a Chinese man.

August 1839 British take control of Hong Kong. Charles Elliot establishes a blockade of the Pearl River to prevent British merchant ships from reaching the mainland and trading with the Chinese.

June 1840 British marines headed by James Bremer, and ships from the British East India Company, sail to Kwangtung

June 1840 British attack and move north to Xiamen

January 1841 British defeat the Chinese at Ningbo

1842 British occupy the mouth of the Yangtze

1842 Shanghai is occupied without opposition

Land of the Long White Cloud

How did a small British colony come to occupy the whole of the islands known today as Aotearoa, or New Zealand?

ABOVE Maoris consider the head the most sacred part of the body and all high-ranking Maoris were tattooed. A bone chisel was used and special rituals were performed during the long process.

The British Crown had formally recognized Maori ownership of the land from the beginning of their involvement with New Zealand, and indeed, Maori people occupied most of the North Island at that time. Yet over the next four decades, the issues of land and sovereignty enflamed a series of bloody and complicated wars, known as the New Zealand Wars, the Maori Wars, or as *Te Riri Pakeha*—the White Man's Anger.

Land Sale

While in the early days the British Imperial government had insisted upon obtaining a whole tribe's consent to a land sale, under political pressure from settlers the rules changed. In March 1859, British Governor of New Zealand, Gore Browne, declared that a Maori chief had no right to interfere in land purchases as chief, but only as an immediate owner. The chief of one the tribes in the Taranaki region of the South Island, Wiremu Kingi, objected to this principle, and stood to block a proposed sale of his tribal lands around the lush Waitara River.

The tension over land was also about much more than land. Wiremu Kingi was involved in an ever-growing Maori unity movement, opposed to the sale of land, but also in favor of the creation of a Maori sovereign that would unite Maori tribes—a Maori King who stood against the British Queen. The Maori Wars quickly became not only about land, but also about sovereignty and *mana* (authority).

Skirmish

Fighting began in January 1860 when Wiremu Kingi obstructed the British in surveying new land. The Imperial troops invaded his *pa* (fortress), but they became a laughing stock, as the *pa* was empty. The Maori had control of the surrounding mountainous

In consideration thereof Her Majesty the Queen of England extends to the Natives of New Zealand Her royal protection and imparts to them all the Rights and Privileges of British Subjects.
–Article the third of the Treaty of Waitangi, 1840.

region and after a series of skirmishes, in which Maori fighters inflicted heavy casualties on the troops, an uneasy truce was called in April 1861.

LEFT British soldiers guard deserted trenches after the attempted attack on the Maori stronghold of Puke Wharangi Pah in April, 1864.

1840 The Treaty of Waitangi is signed by Maori chiefs and representatives of Queen Victoria

1841 New Zealand is declared a crown colony

1842 Auckland is proclaimed the capital of New Zealand

1865 Wellington replaces Auckland as capital of New Zealand

1893 New Zealand is the first country in the world to give women the vote

LEFT The Battle of Gate Pa in 1864 took place outside the British camp of Te Papa where Maoris built a fortress to provoke an attack. The British suffered their biggest defeat in the land wars and began peace negotiations soon afterward.

RIGHT Most of the major battles of the New Zealand wars took place on the North Island. Following the wars, the Maori chiefs continued resistance but in the end they lost sovereignty of much of the land on the North Island.

Imperial Victory

In 1863, the tensions exploded into renewed and even larger conflict. In May, troops were ambushed in Taranaki as they tried to occupy the land at the center of the conflict. The British Governor saw the ambush as illegal, and sought to "punish" the person who ordered it—Rewi Maniapoto, a leader of the King movement in Waikato.

As a result, the whole Waikato region was invaded by 20,000 troops, commanded by Duncan Cameron. The Imperial troops, facing a combined foe of around 5,000, swept down from Auckland, and took the Maori King's residence at Ngaruawahia. They took *pa* after *pa* by sailing down the Waikato River in gunboats and using Howitzer cannons on land.

One major consequence of the war was the colonial policy of confiscating land belonging to rebels as payment for the war. Unsurprisingly, this caused further resentment and bloodshed in the years ahead. In the late 1860s to early 1870s guerilla warfare ensued, not between the King movement and the Imperial troops (who went home to Britain in 1866), but

between colonial settler forces and various new Maori religious movements. Leaders like Titokawaru in the South Island, and Te Kooti on the North Island, inflicted heavy losses on settlers. Yet despite fierce resistance, the overall effect of the wars was to signal the end of Maori sovereignty, and the end of their ownership of the interior of the North Island.

317

Blight of Ireland

On the eve of the Irish famine, over 80 percent of the population lived in the countryside, many on small, near-subsistence farms. The principal food crop was the potato.

Ireland's poorest depended almost entirely on this nutritious tuber for their subsistence. The century preceding the potato famine was one of rapid population growth, even by contemporary European standards. Ireland's population more than trebled, from 2.6 million in 1750 to an all-time high of 8.5 million in 1845.

Fungus

In 1845, the Irish potato crop was affected by the appearance of a new fungus that had made its way from the Americas, *Phytophthora infestans*. Potatoes affected by the disease rotted in the soil, exuding a putrid odor. Between a quarter and a third of the entire potato harvest was lost.

The failure of the potato crop in 1845, unlike others that had preceded it, initiated a crisis unprecedented in Ireland's history. In 1846, the blight struck with much greater force than in 1845, decimating yields of potatoes per acre planted and causing total potato production in Ireland to fall as low as one-fifth the level of 1844. Overall potato production remained at a third or less of pre-famine levels into the early 1850s.

Death Toll

The demographic dimensions of the famine, though still a matter of debate even today, are staggering. Recent estimates put the number of deaths caused by the famine at more than one million, and Ireland forfeited perhaps another 400,000 births during those years.

Emigration

As a result of the famine, in excess of two million Irish men, women, and children emigrated in the decade 1845–1855. The famine years saw a major reorientation of the origins of Ireland's emigrants. The provinces of Ulster and Leinster, previously the source of most who left Ireland, were overtaken by the vast numbers of men and women who took flight from Connacht and Munster. The vast majority who left at this time were Roman Catholics and most of them went to the United States.

Many others made the shorter move to settle in Britain. Fewer famine emigrants departed for Australia, deterred by the greater fare and longer voyage. In the headlong rush to escape from Ireland little attention was paid to the welfare of those who went. The transatlantic voyage was perilous to the poorly clad and undernourished passengers, especially when undertaken in winter. Estimates suggest 30 percent of the poorest emigrants bound for British North America, and 9 percent of those sailing to the United States, died aboard the "coffin ships," or shortly after arrival in the New World.

Relief

British government efforts to provide relief during the Irish famine have been criticized ever since. Nineteenth-century writers frequently asserted that Britain forced Ireland to export grain that would otherwise have sustained its population. Without doubt, the relief efforts of Lord John Russell's Whig government were woefully inadequate. Its commitment to laissez-faire economics and the belief that Ireland and its people needed fundamentally to be reformed inhibited the provision of relief. The experience created an enduring legacy of bitterness toward Britain.

LEFT Published in the *London News*, this sketch shows a hungry woman with children scratching in the ground for edible potatoes.

> I could scarcely bear the fearful and strange smell, which came up so rank from the luxuriant crop then growing all around...
> –William Steuart Trench, *Realities of Irish Life*, second ed.
> (London: Longmans, Green and Co., 1869).

BELOW The port of New York and especially Ellis Island were the landing spots for Irish migrants escaping the famine.

Post-famine Migration
The massive outflow during the "Great Famine" did not end the hemorrhage of Ireland's population. Post-famine reforms sustained departures for decades to come. Between the end of the famine and 1921, approximately 4 million people left Ireland's shores for North America, Britain, or destinations within the British Empire.

CANADA

Québec

UNITED STATES OF AMERICA

New York

ATLANTIC OCEAN

Tropic of Cancer

Caribbean Sea

Equator

SOUTH AMERICA

Tropic of Capricorn

Destitution at Skibbereen
"We take the following from the *Cork Examiner* of Friday evening: 'Disease and death in every quarter...the population perceptibly lessened–death diminishing the destitution–hundreds frantically rushing from their home and country, not with the idea of making fortunes in other lands, but to fly from a scene of suffering and death...'" *The Vindicator, Belfast, December 23, 1846.*

Arctic Circle

IRELAND BRITAIN
Dublin   London

Black Sea

Mediterranean Sea

ASIA

AFRICA

Arabian Sea

Bay of Bengal

PACIFIC OCEAN

INDIAN OCEAN

AUSTRALIA

Convict migration
Approximately 40,000 convicts were transported directly from Ireland to the Australian colonies.

Sydney

Distribution of Irish-born in Major Destinations (1851)

Britain—3.5 percent of local population (727,300)
USA—4.1 percent local population (961,700)
Canada—9.2 percent local population (227,000)
Australia—17.4 percent local population (70,200)

N

0	1000	2000	3000	4000 kilometers
0	500	1000	1500	2000 miles

1800 *Act of Union* is passed making Ireland part of Great Britain

1817 Royal Canal is completed

1828 The *Catholic Emancipation Act* is passed

1838 The production of whiskey is reduced

1867 Thousands of Irish-Americans return home to fight for Irish Republican Brotherhood

1879-1881 Land War for the reform of tenancy laws

1892 The Irish Home Rule Bill is defeated again

ABOVE Because the voyage from Ireland to the United States was much shorter than the voyage to Australia, the majority of migrants headed to the US, creating cultural change in the major cities.

LEFT This painting by Erskine Nicol shows the devastation of the potato famine. Peasants, already living at near-subsistence level, lost their main food source when potatoes went rotten in the ground.

...Rode the Six Hundred

The Crimean War is probably best remembered by the immortalization of the Battle of Balaclava in the famous poem "The Charge of the Light Brigade" by Tennyson. His description of their ride "into the valley of Death" has made the charge a symbol of courage in warfare.

March 12, 1854
Alliance formed between Britain, France, and Turkey

September 14, 1854
Following Russia's withdrawal across the Danube, Allies invade the Crimea with the intent to capture Sebastopol and destroy the Russia fleet

September 20, 1854
Russians defeated at Alma with approximately 2,000 British casualties

October 17, 1854
Allied siege of Sebastopol begins

1854-55 British troops suffer badly after spending the winter holed up in Crimea. *The Times'* daily reports bring public outrage and Florence Nightingale pushes for improved hospital conditions and nursing care.

March 30, 1856 Peace in Crimea is concluded with the Treaty of Paris. Russia agrees to cease expansion into the Balkans and Scandinavia and the Black Sea is declared a neutral zone.

> Cossack and Russian
> Reel'd from the sabre stroke,
> Shatter'd and sunder'd.
> Then they rode back, but not,
> Not the six hundred
>
> –Alfred, Lord Tennyson (1809-1892),
> in *The Charge of the Light Brigade*, fourth verse.

The war's origins go back to 1699, with the Treaty of Karlowitz ending 300 years of Ottoman advance in the European continent. The great powers assisted local uprisings in the Balkans and contributed to the liberation of the peninsula from Ottoman rule in the nineteenth century. The allied British and French navies defeated the Ottomans in Navarino Bay in 1827 while assisting the Greek struggle for independence, and in a Russian ground offensive in the Balkan mountains in 1828.

The Lust for Power

The decline of Ottoman power increased the hunger of all the great powers to fill the ensuing vacuum. Russia conducted a series of military campaigns against Ottoman Turkey from the late seventeenth to the late nineteenth centuries. When Russia secretly offered an agreement for the partition of the Ottoman Empire by the great powers, Britain rejected it. Instead Britain changed sides and helped Ottoman Turkey against Russia.

Invasion

The turning point occurred when Russia gave an ultimatum to the sultan in March 1853, and after its rejection invaded the principalities of Wallachia and Moldavia—which later became Romania. In October 1853, the sultan declared war against Russia, and the British and French navies appeared at Constantinople. When the Russian Navy destroyed Ottoman ships on the Black Sea, the British and French navies entered to protect Turkish ships. In March, the two European great powers declared war against Russia and in September their troops landed in the Crimean Peninsula and launched an attack against Sebastopol.

The charge of the Light Brigade was a disastrous cavalry charge led by cavalry commander Lord Cardigan during the Battle of Balaclava on October 25, 1854, during the Russian attempts to break the siege of Sebastopol.

RIGHT The ill-fated charge of the Light Brigade at the Battle of Balaclava claimed the lives of 118 British troops and left 127 wounded.

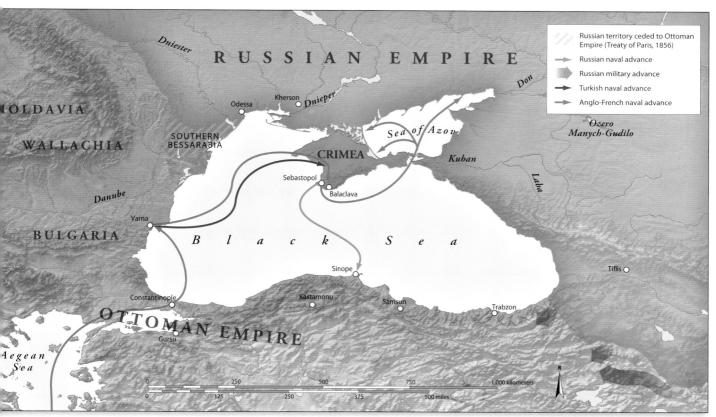

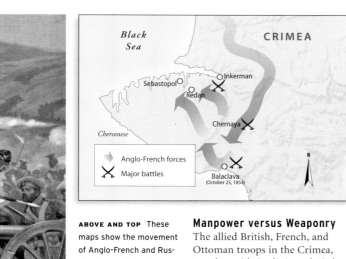

ABOVE AND TOP These maps show the movement of Anglo-French and Russian troops during the Crimean War (1854–1856), considered to be the world's first "modern" conflict.

RIGHT Officers of the 42nd Royal Highlanders, also known as the Black Watch, in camp during the Crimean War. The regiment played a pivotal role in the decisive Allied victory in the Battle of Alma in 1854.

Manpower versus Weaponry

The allied British, French, and Ottoman troops in the Crimea, together with Sardinia and Piedmont, counted altogether some 593,000 soldiers. The largest contingent was French, with a total of 309,000 troops.

Russia, one of the strongest European military powers, exhibited all of its genuine weaknesses in this situation and, with its lack of infrastructure and modern industry, was unable to quickly mobilize its vast military forces.

Although Russia ultimately had a numerical advantage, sending an army of 888,000 men to the Crimea, it remained inferior in modern weaponry. This was clear from the death toll—half the Russian troops died while the allied forces lost just 28 percent of their men. Russia decided to give up Sebastopol in September 1855 and was unable to prevail in the secondary fronts in the Caucasus and on the Baltic Sea.

Russian Withdrawal

Russia suffered a humiliating defeat on its own territory. It was forced to withdraw from Moldavia and Wallachia by September 1854, and also to give up southern Bessarabia and the mouth of the Danube. The goal to make the Black Sea part of Russian territorial waters also failed: it became demilitarized.

321

Italia

By 1861, out of a complex mismatch of imperial powers and rival provinces, there emerged a unified Kingdom of Italy.

Italy is best known today for its distinct geographic expression—the boot-like peninsula protruding into the Mediterranean Sea. In fact, around 200 years ago, the European statesman, Count Metternich, made the remark that Italy was nothing *but* a geographic expression, with no chance of becoming a political reality. Subjected since the time of the Roman Empire to the whims of a stream of imperial powers,

what we now know as Italy was broken into provinces and city-states—no centralized government bound these provinces together.

The Republican Empire

In 1795, Napoleon Bonaparte swept through Italy and established a Republican Empire that was to last only 20 years. With Napoleon's defeat in 1815, the great powers met at the Congress of Vienna to decide who would get what pieces of Napoleon's empire. Only the kingdom of Piedmont—the north-western province of Italy—retained self-rule. Piedmont also gained the coastal city of Genoa.

The Austrian Problem

In 1848, events in Europe again spilled over into Italy. A wave of revolutions swept across Paris, Germany, and Austria. Leaders of the growing Italian independence movement took the opportunity to wage wars of their own. Revolts occurred in Sicily, Venice, and Milan. The Kingdom of Piedmont

> Here we make Italy or we die.
> –Giuseppe Garibaldi (1807-1882), Italian general.

under King Charles Albert sought to expel Austria from the north. Austria, however, responded with superior military force.

Despite its losses Piedmont retained self-government. After the war a new king, Victor Emmanuel, and a new prime minister, Camillo di Cavour, were installed. They became in effect the political leaders of the independence and unity movement. Di Cavour, a cunning diplomat, realized that outside powers would be needed to help expel the Austrians from Italian soil. In a plan carefully organized with the French, he agreed to precipitate a war with Austria by mobilizing Piedmontese troops. When the Austrians responded to the threat, the French stepped in. The result, in 1859–60, was the Second War of the Risorgimento.

Italy Emerges

By March 1860, in a stunning series of elections, all the northern Italian provinces—except Venice, still held by Austria—had voted overwhelmingly to be annexed by Piedmont. The nation of Italy was beginning to take shape.

In April 1860, another rebellion broke out in Sicily. This provoked Giuseppe Garibaldi, a famed war hero and patriot of the north, to assemble soldiers to sail south and liberate Sicily. Garibaldi and his thousand red-shirts were more successful than anticipated—they liberated Sicily, then went on to free Naples as well. They too were submitted to the rule of Piedmont. The outer (eastern) Papal States were also allowed to join Piedmont following their own elections, but France insisted that Rome remain free from Italian control. The Kingdom of Italy was thus declared by the new Italian parliament on March 17, 1861, in the capital city of Florence.

The Return of Rome

In 1866, as a result of Italy aiding Prussia in a war against Austria, Venice was given to the Kingdom of Italy. When the Prussians went to war again, this time with France, the French were forced to recall their troops from Rome. Italian troops soon took the city, despite opposition mounted by the Pope's own troops. In an election in October 1870, Rome at last became part of a unified Kingdom of Italy. In 1871, it became the capital city.

1805 Napoleon declares himself Italian emperor

1814 Italy is divided into small provinces

1820-1850 Venice, Rome, and Tuscany declare themselves republics

1849 Republic of Rome taken over by French troops

1861 The Kingdom of Italy is established, excluding Rome, Venice, and San Marino. Victor Emmanuel II of Sardinia becomes king.

1870 Italian forces occupy Rome

1871 Rome is named the capital of Italy

Divisions of Italy (1815)
- Piedmont
- Lombardy
- Parma
- Venezia
- Modena
- Tuscany
- Papal States
- Lucca
- Kingdom of the Two Sicilies

FAR LEFT Hero of the Risorgimento, Giuseppe Garibaldi (1807–82), was dubbed the "Hero of Two Worlds" due to his military expeditions in both South America and Europe.

ABOVE The Venetian delegation arrives in Turin in 1866 to announce the result of a plebiscite held to confirm annexation of Venice to the Kingdom of Italy. Only 0.01 percent of voters were opposed.

ABOVE RIGHT Tuscan envoys present Victor Emmanuel II (1820–1878), King of Italy, with the *Act of Annexation of Tuscany to the Kingdom of Italy*, in the Council Chamber of the Palazzo Reale, Turin.

LEFT Following the defeat of Napoleonic France, the Congress of Vienna (1815) redrew the map of Europe. In Italy, the pre-Napoleonic patchwork of independent governments was for the most part restored.

RIGHT Charles Albert, King of Sardinia (whose kingdom was centered around Piedmont and Savoy), tried and failed to unify Italy. It did however unify under his son, King Victor Emmanuel II.

Kingdom of Sardinia at Congress of Vienna (1815)

Territory gained (1859–1860)

Territory gained (1860–1870)

Attack routes of Garibaldi (1860)

Major battles

American Civil War

The American Civil War (1861-1865), caused by tensions over slavery, shattered the fledgling nation's hard-won unity.

March 1861 Abraham Lincoln inaugurated as the sixteenth President of the United States

July 1861 The North begins a naval blockade of the South

July 1862 Union Army appoints Henry Halleck as general-in-chief

November 1863 Union forces push Confederate troop back at the Battle of Chatttanooga

July 1864 Confederate troops push to within five miles of Washington, DC

January 1865 Starving soldiers begin to desert the Confederate Army

April 1865 General Grant calls on General Lee to surrender

During the 1850s, the American political system and leadership proved incapable of resolving the nation's growing sectional tensions. The "Compromise of 1850" eased North-South tensions only temporarily, and the publication in 1852 of Harriet Beecher Stowe's *Uncle Tom's Cabin*, with its vivid descriptions of the horrors of slavery, convinced many Northerners that the abolitionists had been right to denounce slavery. During the mid-1850s, pro-slavery and anti-slavery settlers in Kansas clashed in the new territory.

Southern Secession

In late 1860, after Lincoln won the presidential election, long-standing tensions between the North and South boiled over. Led by South Carolina, a number of Southern states formally seceded from the United States, and established the Confederate States of America, under the reluctant leadership of Jefferson Davis. Southerners contended that, as they had entered the Union voluntarily, they could choose to leave it—the Northern view was that the Constitution was a sacred document, which bound the states together in an indivisible union. The Union, Lincoln asserted, was "perpetual." On April 12, 1861,

the Confederates attacked a Union force in Fort Sumter, in Charleston Harbor, South Carolina. The Civil War had begun.

Balance of Power

On paper, the Civil War was a quite uneven contest—the states of the North had more men, and included all the major industrial regions of the nation. The population of the North totalled nearly 21 million, while the Southern population, just over 9 million, included more than 3 million slaves. After considerable debate, the Border States of Maryland, Kentucky, Delaware, and Missouri joined the Union. But the South had a proud military tradition, would be fighting on its own territory, and would be exploiting internal lines of communication. Moreover, many US Army officers —including Robert E. Lee, who would go on to be considered one of the greatest generals in American military history—chose to serve the Confederacy, rather than the Union.

Early Battles

The outbreak of the war soon led to outpourings of patriotism in both the Union and Confederacy. Americans, North and South, believed their cause was righteous, and assumed that the war would

ABOVE The 1,050 members of the 7th Regiment of the New York State Militia marched off to war on April 19, 1861.

...that we here highly resolve that these dead shall not have died in vain, that this nation under God shall have a new birth of freedom, and that government of the people, by the people, for the people shall not perish from the earth
–Abraham Lincoln (1809-1865), sixteenth President of the United States, in the Gettysburg Address (1863).

be over quickly. From towns and farms, tens of thousands of men volunteered for military service. Because the Confederate capital of Richmond was just 65 miles (100 km) from Washington, DC, Union leaders had hoped to march quickly to Richmond and seize the seat of Confederate authority. But in July 1861, at the First Battle of Bull Run—known to the Southerners as the Battle of Manassas—the Confederate forces dispelled much of the early Northern optimism. As hundreds of spectators looked on, disorganized and dispirited Union forces were routed.

Confederate Successes

The Confederate army's resounding success at Bull Run set the scene for the early stages of the war. Although the Union's commander, George B. McClellan, managed an excellent

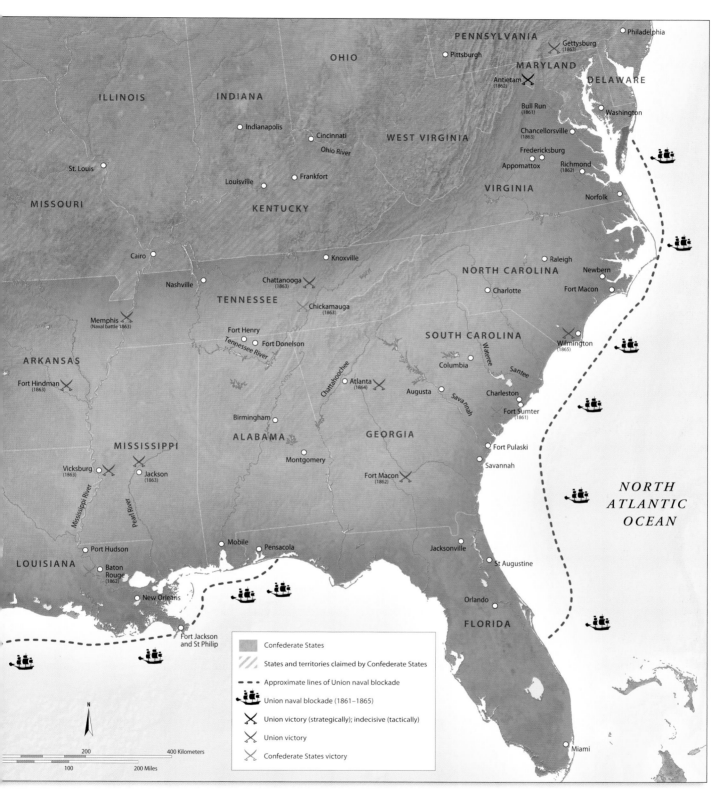

PENNSYLVANIA
Gettysburg (1863)
Philadelphia
Pittsburgh
OHIO
MARYLAND
DELAWARE
Antietam (1862)
INDIANA
Bull Run (1861)
Washington
ILLINOIS
Indianapolis
WEST VIRGINIA
Chancellorsville (1863)
Cincinnati
Ohio River
Fredericksburg
Richmond (1862)
Appomattox
St. Louis
Louisville
Frankfort
VIRGINIA
Norfolk
MISSOURI
KENTUCKY
Cairo
Knoxville
Raleigh
NORTH CAROLINA
Newbern
Nashville
Chattanooga (1863)
Charlotte
Fort Macon
TENNESSEE
Chickamauga (1863)
Memphis (Naval battle 1863)
Fort Henry
Fort Donelson
SOUTH CAROLINA
Wilmington (1865)
Tennessee River
Wateree
Columbia
Santee
ARKANSAS
Chattahoochee
Atlanta (1864)
Augusta
Charleston
Fort Hindman (1863)
Savannah
Fort Sumter (1861)
Birmingham
MISSISSIPPI
ALABAMA
GEORGIA
Fort Pulaski
Vicksburg (1863)
Jackson (1863)
Montgomery
Savannah
Mississippi River
Fort Macon (1862)
Pearl River
NORTH
ATLANTIC
OCEAN
Port Hudson
Mobile
Pensacola
Jacksonville
LOUISIANA
Baton Rouge (1862)
St Augustine
New Orleans
Orlando
Fort Jackson and St Philip
FLORIDA
Miami

Legend:

Confederate States

States and territories claimed by Confederate States

Approximate lines of Union naval blockade

Union naval blockade (1861–1865)

Union victory (strategically); indecisive (tactically)

Union victory

Confederate States victory

N

200   400 Kilometers
100   200 Miles

job of marshalling troops, and building up his army into a formidable force, he proved somewhat reluctant to use it. The Southern generals, by contrast, were more than willing to take the fight

directly to their foes. As McClellan's force moved tentatively southward during the early part of 1862, Confederate forces under the leadership of Robert E. Lee continued to resist fiercely. Despite having

pushed his force southward to within just 18 miles (30 km) of Richmond, McClellan then decided to retreat north. Lincoln, frustrated by McClellan's refusal to fight, sacked him.

ABOVE The Union North fought the Confederate South in the American Civil War which, at its heart, was all about the abolition of slavery.

RIGHT The Battle of Gettysburg was one of the turning points in the war, as Union troops triumphed over the tenacious Confederate forces.

FAR RIGHT Over a five-year period, the Union gradually eroded Confederate hold over its lands.

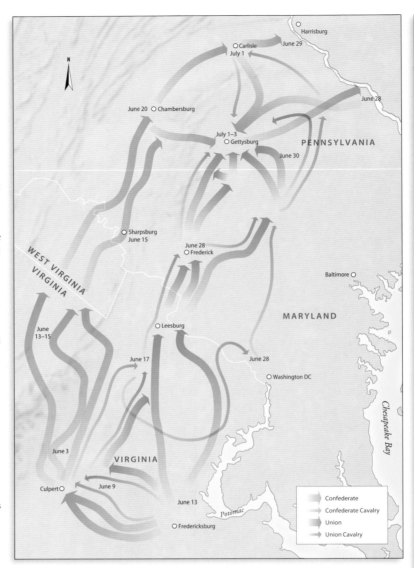

Leadership

At the Second Battle of Bull Run, in August 1862, Union forces suffered another costly defeat. Then at Antietam, Maryland, in September 1862, with McClellan back in command of Union forces, the North and South fought what would prove to be the bloodiest single-day battle of the Civil War. More than 4,500 men died at Antietam. Having had the good fortune to obtain details of Lee's plans, McClellan was optimistic that he would be capable of destroying the Southern armies seeking to gain a foothold in Union territory. But having obtained the military advantage, McClellan was unwilling to force the advantage, and Lee's armies were able to slip away. At the Battle of Fredericksburg, December 1862, and at the Battle of Chancellorsville, in May 1863, Union forces were again defeated by smaller Confederate armies. The Battle of Chancellorsville, however, also proved costly for the Confederates, when one of their most dashing leaders, Thomas "Stonewall" Jackson, was killed.

Gettysburg

For three days during July 1863, at the small southern Pennsylvanian town of Gettysburg, Union and Confederate forces fought the most decisive battle of the whole Civil War. Although the Confederate forces demonstrated characteristic tenacity, the Union forces held. And a bold, almost suicidal charge across open territory by Southern General George Pickett was driven back by Union armies. Unable to overcome the Union armies, Lee began withdrawing his forces. Again, however, the Union armies—by now under the leadership of General George G. Meade—failed to exploit their advantage, and the Confederate armies slipped back to the South.

Slavery

Although many Northerners had denied initially that they were fighting to free the slaves, abolitionists and the slaves themselves knew that the war was ultimately about slavery. After the Battle of Antietam, Lincoln issued the "Preliminary Emancipation Proclamation," which outlined the intent to emancipate those held as slaves on January 1, 1863.

Emancipation Proclamation

At the stroke of midnight, on the night of December 31, 1862, Lincoln's Emancipation Proclamation came into effect. Abolitionists and African Americans were jubilant. While the Proclamation was subsequently criticized on the grounds that it had not freed any of the slaves under Union control—it applied only to those states in rebellion from the Union—nevertheless there was recognition that the war was now unequivocally and irreversibly about the future of slavery.

Diplomacy

The Emancipation Proclamation, however, complicated Confederate diplomatic efforts immeasurably. Many Southerners had hoped that Britain, and other European powers, would give recognition to the Confederate States of America. In particular, they had hoped that the British need for Southern cotton would make many Britons sympathetic to the Confederacy. But Britain was able to secure sufficient cotton from European, Indian, and Egyptian sources. And in the wake of the Emancipation Proclamation, no British government of the day could possibly have granted recognition to the Confederacy, which was unambiguously fighting to defend slavery. Britain, after all, had emancipated its own slaves three decades earlier.

PENNSYLVANIA

Trenton

Harrisburg

NEW
JERSEY

OHIO

MARYLAND   Dover

Baltimore   DELAWARE

Annapolis

ILLINOIS

Columbus

Washington

INDIANA

Springfeild

Indianapolis

WEST
VIRGINIA

Richmond

St Louis   Frankfort   Charleston   Norfolk

VIRGINIA   Petersburg

Jefferson City

MISSOURI   KENTUCKY   Raleigh

Cumberland

Cairo   NORTH CAROLINA

Murfreesboro   Knoxville

Nashville   New Bern

Chattanooga

TENNESSEE   Wilmington

Columbia

Memphis   Cornith   SOUTH CAROLINA

Little Rock   Tennessee River

RKANSAS

Charleston

Atlanta

Port Royal

MISSISSIPPI   ALABAMA   GEORGIA

Savannah

Jackson   A T L A N T I C

Vicksburg   Montogomery

OUISIANA   O C E A N

Fernandina

Mobile   Jacksonville

Pensacola   Olustee

Baton Rouge   Tallahassee   St Augustine

bine Pass   New Orleans

FLORIDA

Gulf of Mexico

Fort Brooke   Tampa

Port St Lucie

Fort Lauderdale

Fort Myers

Naples   Miami

	Southern areas under Union control (1861)
	Confederate areas lost to Union (1862)
	Confederate areas lost to Union (1863)
	Confederate areas lost to Union (1864)
	Confederate areas lost to Union (1865)

N

0   250   500 kilometers

0   125   250 miles

ABOVE Ulysses S. Grant, commander of the victorious Union army, later seved two terms as US President.

LEFT The most decisive battle of the Civil War took place at Gettysburg. Confederate forces succumbed to those of the Union.

War at Sea

The Confederate failure to secure British recognition influenced the naval war with the Union, since during the early part of the conflict the Confederacy had purchased ships from the British. By 1863, however, the British Government intervened to prevent shipbuilders from supplying warships to the Confederate Navy. This made the task of the Confederate Navy even more difficult than it had hitherto been. The South did make several bold attempts to seize the naval advantage, by building "ironclad" ships, and then submarines, but neither initiative was sufficient to overcome the Union's advantages.

Controlling the Mississippi

The Union's supremacy at sea meant it was able to control the flow of Confederate goods from the Mississippi. But early on in the war, Union commanders also realized that control of the Mississippi, and other rivers along which much of Southern trade was conducted, would seriously impede the Southern war effort. In 1862, Union General Ulysses S. Grant seized Fort Henry, on the Tennessee River, and then Fort Donelson, on the Cumberland River. In April 1862, Union forces captured the city of New Orleans, at the mouth of the Mississippi. The focus then turned back toward Grant, who moved on the Confederate-controlled river port of Vicksburg. The ensuing siege captured national attention, and when the Confederate forces eventually succumbed to Grant in July 1863, Union forces had gained full control of the Mississippi River, along with much of the adjacent territory to the west.

Grant's Victory

As the Union General William T. Sherman was wreaking havoc in Georgia, Ulysses S. Grant's forces had advanced toward Richmond.

Robert E. Lee's Army of Northern Virginia, which for so long had held out against the numerically superior Union forces, found itself in an increasingly desperate situation. With the Southern economy in disarray, the slave system collapsing, and the Confederate Government of Jefferson Davis incapable of managing either the war or the economy, Southern efforts on the battlefield became increasingly futile. While many of his troops continued to believe in the cause of Southern independence, and although significant Confederate forces remained on the battlefield, by April 1865 it was evident to Lee, and to his political masters, that prolonging the war would serve no political or military purpose. On April 9, at Appomattox Courthouse, Virginia, Lee formally surrendered to Grant. Around the country, some vestiges of the Confederate Army fought on, but within a few weeks all resistance had ended. The Union had prevailed.

African American Soldiers

A key factor behind the Union's victory was the contribution made by black soldiers. When war broke out, Northern blacks offered their services to the Union, only to be informed their services were not needed. But from the outset of the war, African Americans made important contributions. In the South, slaves who ran away robbed the Southern economy of a vital labor supply, and also provided valuable labor and military information to the Union commanders. As a result, when the North reversed its policy and finally allowed African Americans to fight, over 186,000 blacks served in the Union Army. Though paid less than their white counterparts, often given menial duties, and threatened with execution if they were captured by their Confederate adversaries, when given opportunities to fight, the African Americans proved their courage as well as their loyalty to the Union.

Assassination and Legacy

After four long years of bloodshed and devastation, Abraham Lincoln sought a smooth reconciliation of the North and South. On the night of April 14, 1865, Lincoln attended the Ford Theater, in Washington, DC. As the President and his wife watched *Our American Cousin*, John Wilkes Booth shot Lincoln in the head. The President died the next day. Booth made his escape, but was tracked down and killed on April 26. Lincoln was the most famous of the 620,000 Americans who died as a consequence of the Civil War, which led to the Emancipation Proclamation, and ensured the survival of the Union. But the failure of post-Civil War attempts to "reconstruct" the South to grant equality to African Americans demonstrated that while slavery had been a Southern issue, racism was to become an American problem.

LEFT The Confederates had hoped for support from Britain in the form of warships. But Britain refused, helping to seal the Confederates' fate at sea.

BELOW President Lincoln with William Tecumseh Sherman, Ulysses S. Grant and David Porter, the men who headed the Union's military forces.

Oh Canada!

The year 1867 marked the birth of the Dominion of Canada. With the passing of the *British North America Act* in the British Parliament, the four provinces of New Brunswick, Nova Scotia, Ontario, and Quebec were constituted into a new nation.

RIGHT Both Canada and the United States of America displaced First Nations tribes in the drive to claim new territories.

The Act embodied the aspirations of British North American subjects determined to direct their own future. It was the culmination of a decision-making process that required constitutional amendments to the legislatures of each province. Debates and negotiations on the desirability of a Canadian nation, and the shape it should take, had led to two constitutional conferences in the region in 1864, in Charlottetown and Quebec.

Confederation

At a third conference in London in December 1866, the final form of the resolutions formulated in Quebec to define the terms of confederation was agreed upon by delegates from the four provinces. However, Prince Edward Island and Newfoundland elected not to join. The former did so when the liberals led by Alexander Mackenzie beat the conservatives in the federal elections of 1874. By then Manitoba (1870), the Northwest Territories (1870), and British Columbia (1871) had become the fifth, sixth, and seventh provinces of the Dominion. Newfoundland did not join until 1949, lagging behind the newly created Yukon Territory (1898) and the provinces of Alberta and Saskatchewan (1905). Nunavut,

1774 The *Quebec Act* recognizes both the French language and the Roman Catholic religion in the colony

1817 The Bank of Montréal, the first permanent bank in British North America, is founded

1836 Canada's first railway, the Champlain and St Lawrence Railroad, opens

1885 The Canadian Pacific Railway is completed

1896-1899 Gold is discovered in the Klondike, causing a gold rush of people hoping to earn their fortune

RIGHT This nineteenth-century engraving shows the city of Quebec as it was at the time of Confederation. The second constitutional conference was held here in October 1864.

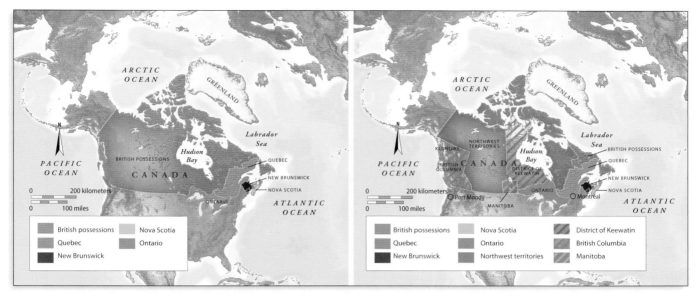

ABOVE The map on the left shows the Dominion of Canada in 1867; the map on the right shows Canada as it was in 1895 after the addition of four more provinces.

> We shall be Canadians first, foremost, and always, and our policies will be decided in Canada and not dictated by any other country.
> –John G. Diefenbaker, (1895-1979), thirteenth Prime Minister of Canada.

created in 1999, represents the last boundary change of the Dominion.

United States' Influence

Apart from the internal significance of 1867 as a watershed year in Canadian politics, the events that led to confederation were closely linked to developments in the United States of America. Although many obstacles had to be surmounted before the interests of the separate British North American colonies could be accommodated satisfactorily, confederation was undoubtedly intended to guard Canadian interests against the expansionism of their southern neighbor following the end of the Civil War in 1865.

Confederation provided a viable future at a point in history when the shadow of the United States loomed ever larger. And this shadow had grown since the 1803 Louisiana Purchase, which doubled the territory of the United States. The expedition by the Corps of Discovery led by Meriwether Lewis and William Clark in 1803–1806 courted the First Nations people encountered during their travels into trading with the Americans, rather than with the Hudson's Bay Company. Boundary disputes were finally settled in 1846, when the 49th parallel was established as the international boundary between the United States of America and Canada. It remained a porous border. Illegal American whiskey traders and commercial hunters regularly crossed the border in search of profit.

For Canada, Confederation inaugurated a new era of mutual cooperation that vowed to deliver increased prosperity through the creation of a larger home market.

Three years after confederation, Canada purchased the vast lands known as Rupert's Land and the Northwestern Territory from the Hudson's Bay Company. It created the North-West Mounted Police and charged it with the removal of the illegal American traders. In the following decade, it signed treaties with First Nations who occupied the purchased territories, advancing the great dream of a Dominion that would extend from sea to sea. In June 1886, the first passenger train of the Canadian Pacific Railway left Montréal bound for Port Moody, in British Columbia, a fitting testimony to the coming of age of the Canadian nation through its determination and capacity to respond to internal and external challenges.

RIGHT Spokane Indians, 1861. The first European settlement at Spokane Falls, in northwest USA, was a fur trading post.

TECHNOLOGY, TRADE, AND TRANSITION

The Boer War

The Afrikaners, believing fervently in God-given rights to their land and their independence, and the British, imbued with what they regarded as their imperial destiny, to preserve British honor and the Empire, proved worthy opponents in a bitter three-year war.

1890 Cecil Rhodes becomes Prime Minister of Cape Colony

1898 Paul Kruger reelected as president of Transvaal

1899 British ammunition train ambushed on its way to Ladysmith with Winston Churchill captured. He was the *London Morning Post* correspondent.

1900 British government annexes Transvaal

1901 Kitchener divides the country into sectors and erects barbed wire to protect the railways

ABOVE Refusing to surrender, and without reinforcements, British and Australian troops at Elands River were wiped out during a bungled campaign in 1901.

> We are not interested in the possibilities of defeat. They do not exist.
> –Queen Victoria of England (1819-1901), commenting on the Boer War.

BELOW Winston Churchill, later Prime Minister of Britain, as a war correspondent for the *London Morning Post*, during the Boer War.

Though at the beginning not all Afrikaners were for a war, just as in Britain there was opposition to hostilities in South Africa, the British government and the two Afrikaner (Boer) republics of the Transvaal—the South African Republic and the Orange Free State—were the protagonists in a conflict that ran from 1899 to 1902. The war raged between some 88,000 predominantly Afrikaner farmers, who had intimate knowledge of the local terrain and were armed with modern rifles, and a British army of about 500,000 trained soldiers, which had to maintain long lines of communication through hostile country. Despite the numbers, the Afrikaners initially proved more than a match for British forces.

Cause and Effect

The immediate cause of the conflict was the discovery of rich gold and diamond deposits, predominantly the gold of the Witwatersrand in the Transvaal, then the largest gold-mining complex in the world. The crisis also arose from the personalities on each side. The President of the South African Republic was Paul Kruger—a descendant of 200 years of Afrikaner settlers—who had been hostile to the influx of miners from outside. Working for the British cause in South Africa was Cecil Rhodes, erstwhile Premier of the Cape. The belligerence of the British Colonial Secretary, Joseph Chamberlain, in London, and the unimaginative British High Commissioner in South Africa, Lord Milner, added to this explosive mix.

Initial Success

President Kruger refused to grant political rights to the "Uitlanders"—non-Afrikaner—miners on the Rand, and the British strengthened their military garrisons in South Africa. The Afrikaners responded to the build-up of British strongholds by launching attacks into Natal and the northern Cape. At first, they were successful as the British were unprepared. Once hostilities had commenced, Afrikaners in the northern Cape joined these forces. In the meantime, British reinforcements were arriving from Britain and eventually Ladysmith was relieved. Boer

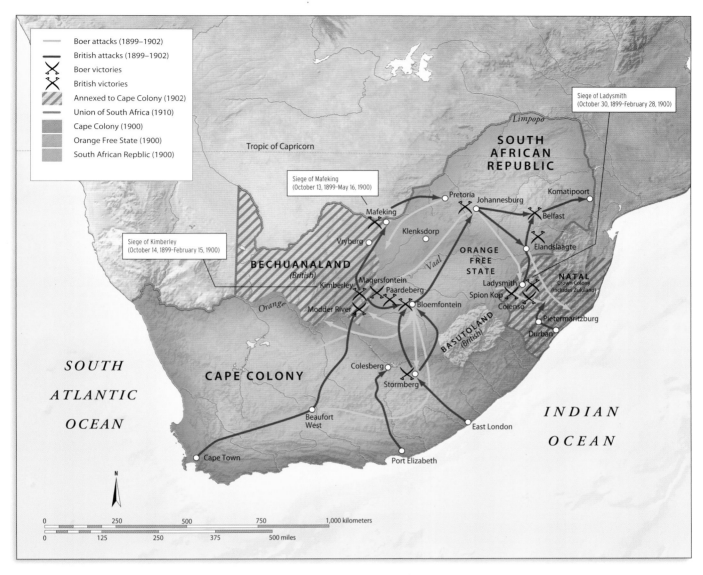

Legend:
- Boer attacks (1899–1902)
- British attacks (1899–1902)
- Boer victories
- British victories
- Annexed to Cape Colony (1902)
- Union of South Africa (1910)
- Cape Colony (1900)
- Orange Free State (1900)
- South African Repblic (1900)

Siege of Ladysmith (October 30, 1899–February 28, 1900)

Siege of Mafeking (October 13, 1899–May 16, 1900)

Siege of Kimberley (October 14, 1899–February 15, 1900)

Tropic of Capricorn

Limpopo

SOUTH AFRICAN REPUBLIC

Pretoria — Johannesburg — Komatipoort — Belfast — Elandslaagte

Mafeking — Klenksdorp

Vryburg

BECHUANALAND *(British)*

Vaal

ORANGE FREE STATE

Kimberley — Magersfontein — Paardeberg — Bloemfontein

Modder River

Orange

BASUTOLAND *(British)*

Ladysmith — Spion Kop — Colenso

NATAL Crown Colony *(includes Zululand)*

Pietermaritzburg — Durban

SOUTH ATLANTIC OCEAN

CAPE COLONY

Colesberg

Stormberg

Beaufort West

East London

INDIAN OCEAN

Cape Town

Port Elizabeth

N

| 0 | 250 | 500 | 750 | 1,000 kilometers |
| 0 | 125 | 250 | 375 | 500 miles |

forces were unable to defeat the disciplined British troops, who occupied Pretoria, Bloemfontein, and Johannesburg.

Reinforcements

President Kruger departed for Europe in 1900 and in his absence the nature of the war changed, under the skilful Afrikaner commanders left behind—notably de Wet and De La Rey. Boer commandos attacked British troops in their isolated bases and their lines of communication. The British had great difficulty in striking back at these mobile bands and, as a result, large rural parts of the Transvaal and Orange Free State were out of effective British control.

British forces—supported by renegade Boers from the Cape—commanded by Generals Lord

Kitchener and Lord Roberts then reinforced defenses along the railroads and adopted a "scorched-earth" policy of destroying the Afrikaner farms and seizing livestock. Boer commandos, under Jan Smuts—later a British general

in World War I—continued their raids against British forces deep into the Cape, to within a day's ride of Cape Town. But the British campaign gained the upper hand, and by early 1901 the Afrikaners sued for peace and to preserve

ABOVE Most action in the Boer War took place in the center of what is now the Republic of South Africa.

LEFT Under siege by the Boers at Ladysmith, British forces held out for almost four months, over the summer of 1899-1900, until relief arrived. This view from a sandbagged trench shows the heavy defenses.

their independence. Eventually they were forced to accept that the latter was not negotiable and in May 1902 the war came to an end by the Peace of Vereeniging, the British claiming complete control of all Afrikaner territory.

333

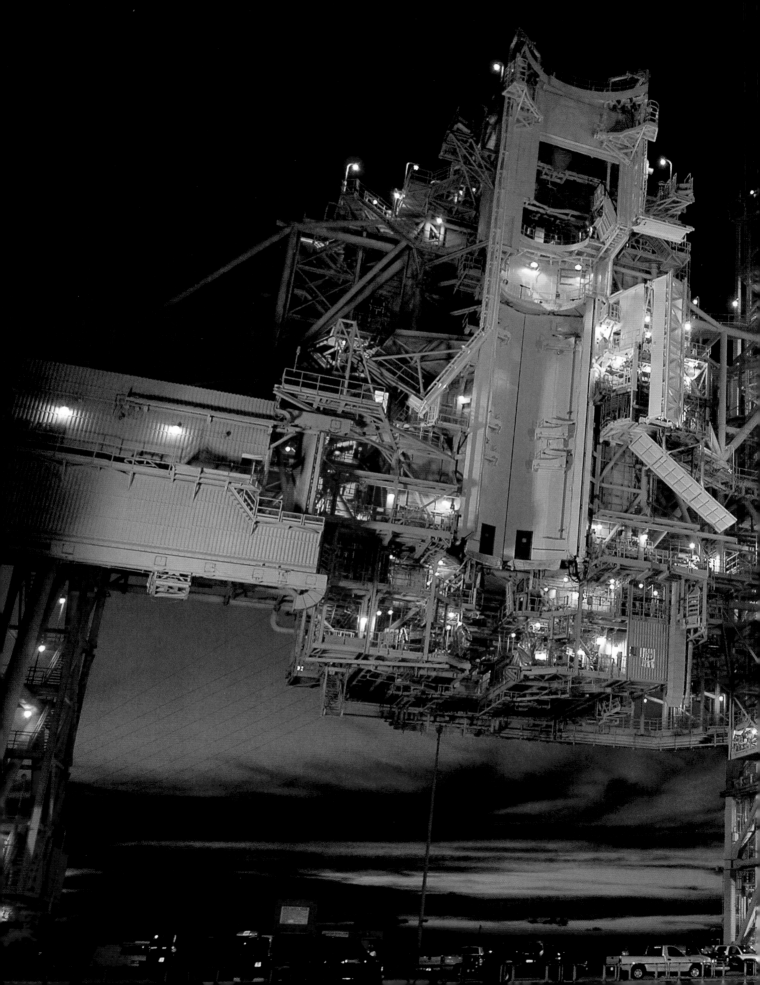

A Changing World

The twentieth century was a period of triumph and tragedy, marked by two world wars that changed the planet, and cultural turbulence that changed it even more.

In the summer of 1914, the already smoldering ashes of nationalism ignited in the Balkans when a Serb nationalist assassinated the archduke of Austria. Fearful that Slavic nationalism could quickly engulf the multi-ethnic Austrian Empire, Austria declared war against Serbia, which was supported by Russia. Austria was allied with Germany. Drawn into the war, Germany attacked France by invading neutral Belgium, and this brought Britain into the war as well. The escalating conflict led the United States to get involved too, by declaring war on both Germany and its allies in April 1917. In 1918, Germany sought peace, and at the Paris Peace Conference (1919), the political leaders of the victorious powers once again redrew the map of Europe.

Germany's domestic turmoil led to the rise of the Nazi Party under Adolf Hitler. After years of domestic crisis, Hitler was made chancellor in January 1933. Vowing to exact vengeance on the victors of World War I and to right what he saw as historical wrongs, Hitler ordered his army to attack Poland on September 1, 1939. This was the beginning of World War II. The deadliest conflict ever waged, it would cost over 60 million lives.

The combination of Britain, the Soviet Union, and the United States eventually defeated the forces of Italy and Germany in 1945. But there was a second theater of war. Responding to an embargo, Japan had attacked the US fleet at Pearl Harbor in December 1941. The resulting Pacific War ushered in the nuclear era when in early August 1945 the United States dropped atomic bombs on the cities of Hiroshima and Nagasaki. Japan surrounded days later.

The Grand Alliance collapsed after 1945, resulting in a Cold War. Fearful of Soviet actions, especially the communization of Eastern Europe, the main Western powers formed the North Atlantic Treaty Organization in April 1949 to deter the Soviet Union militarily. The Communist victory in China's civil war (1949) gave the Soviet Union a new ideological ally. The Cold War would last until the late 1980s when the Soviet Union collapsed. In the meantime, the two superpowers carried out their rivalry in the Third World, each supporting proxy allies that fought each other. This competition resulted in the Indochina War (1946–1954), the Korean War (1950–1953), and the Vietnam War (1959–1965).

Decolonization
Decolonization was one of the century's great forces, especially from 1945 to 1960. Peoples in colonized lands—Algeria, Angola, Cambodia, Indonesia, Iraq, Kenya, Laos—began to throw off their colonial masters. The creation of the state of Israel (1948) caused great strife in the Middle East because the land came at the expense of the Palestinians.

The Civil Rights Movement
The Civil Rights Movement (usually dated 1955–1965) in the United States was a non-violent struggle that saw black Americans demand an end to centuries of official and unofficial discrimination against them. The most famous figure of the movement was Dr Martin Luther King, who inspired millions, but was assassinated in 1968.

A Connected World
The end of the Soviet Union prompted the end of the Cold War and the liberation of millions of people from communist rule. The absolute sovereignty of the nation state was also challenged. The Maastricht Treaty (1992), an outgrowth of the Treaty of Rome (1957), laid legal foundations for the European Union (EU), a single market with guaranteed freedom of movement for all capital, goods, people, and services among its members.

Technological change was swift. As the century drew to a close and the Internet wove its electronic web around the world, many experts warned that international systems could grind to a halt because of a flaw in early computer design that failed to anticipate any year after 1999. This "Y2K bug" was seen as a ticking time bomb. But the century ended with widespread relief as this prediction failed to come true.

ABOVE Workers watch a thermonuclear detonation during Pacific tests. In the 1950s new hydrogen bomb designs were trialed, along with new, improved fission weapon designs.

RIGHT Many politicians have claimed credit for it, but the first section of the Berlin Wall was torn down by crowds on the morning of November 10, 1989.

LEFT Jacqueline Kennedy stands with her children Caroline Kennedy and John F. Kennedy, Jr and brothers-in law Ted (L) and Robert (R) at the funeral of her husband, John F. Kennedy, the first US president assassinated in over 60 years.

PREVIOUS PAGES Though flying machines were only invented in the first years of the twentieth century, they have come a long way since the early biplanes. As space shuttles like the *Atlantis* demonstrate, not even the sky is the limit.

Seeking Wealth

Much of the human movement seen during the twentieth century represents a continuation of trends set in motion during the eighteenth and nineteenth centuries.

The mechanization of agriculture reduced the need for farm workers, resulting in large-scale movements from the country to the city. Although these changes came quite slowly to southern and eastern Asia, along with most of Africa, by the century's end the demographic landslide appeared unstoppable and irreversible.

World

As in the eighteenth and nineteenth centuries, the growth of manufacturing provided a pull factor quite as powerful as the push from the countryside. Many moved to cities in search of higher pay and a better life. Some stayed within their countries of origin, bolstering urban growth, while others followed the now well-worn paths of migration to the Americas, southern Africa, and Australasia. The factors that had pushed Germans, Russians, and Poles into migration the previous century now afflicted the Mediterranean peoples. Southern Italians, Greeks, Maltese, Lebanese, and Turks sought new overseas homes, often sparking unfounded fears among previous arrivals of being overrun by dangerous invaders.

America and Africa

Less anticipated was movement away from the country in regions only recently opened to farming. The United States witnessed what was called the Great Migration of black farm workers and sharecroppers from the old Cotton Belt to Northern manufacturing cities (along with Dixieland jazz).

Similar phenomena could be observed at the same time in South America, where the impoverished *barrios* of Rio de Janeiro exploded on the hillsides above the glittering seafront playground of the rich. Or in South Africa, where the descendants of nineteenth-century Voortrekkers lost their rural footholds and streamed into the slums of cities, creating the so-called Poor White Problem. Or in Australia, where war veterans recently installed as Soldier Settlers on small farms found that agriculture on that scale no longer paid.

An entirely different set of population movements was set in motion by political developments—migration caused by fear or force. In the last two decades of the nineteenth century a round of European territorial annexations—the so-called Scramble for Africa—had laid down the territorial

> If a free society cannot help the many who are poor, it cannot save the few who are rich.
> ~John F. Kennedy (1917-1963), thirty-fifth President of the United States.

ABOVE LEFT Italian migrants wait to be processed at Ellis Island, New York, in 1905.

LEFT This map shows the percentage of population affected by HIV/AIDS in Africa, in 2002. The disease initially spread along the trucking routes.

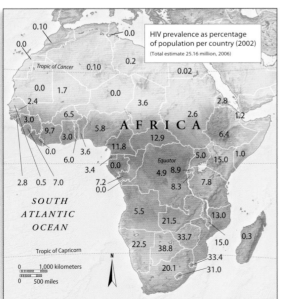

HIV prevalence as percentage of population per country (2002)
(Total estimate 25.16 million, 2006)

AFRICA

SOUTH ATLANTIC OCEAN

Tropic of Cancer
Equator
Tropic of Capricorn

0   1,000 kilometers
0   500 miles

ABOVE Sikh refugees from Lahore waiting to be resettled in Jalandhar, in 1947, after the partition of British India.

LEFT After World War II, Australia set up the "assisted passage scheme" whereby UK citizens could migrate for the cost of £10. The program attracted over one million migrants between 1945 and 1972.

1946 Hundreds of thousands of people cross from Eastern Europe to the United Kingdom, seeking escape from communism

1948 The *Displaced Persons Act* of 1948 permits approximately 200,000 displaced Europeans to immigrate to the United States

1972 Approximately 28,000 expelled Ugandans settle in the United Kingdom

1980 An amendment to US law abolishes western and eastern hemisphere immigration quotas and changes the total to 290,000 annually with a country maximum of 20,000

RIGHT Increasingly, people are driven to new countries in the hope of a better life. The number of foreign-born residents in a city alters the basic structure and opens up communities to new ideas and cultures.

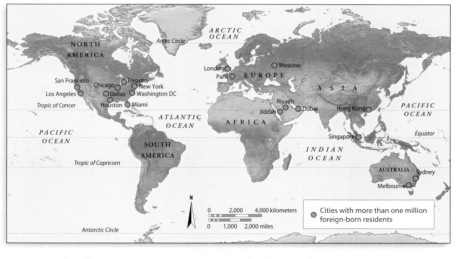

Cities with more than one million foreign-born residents

boundaries that can still be seen on the map of Africa. Having acquired their colonies, European masters set about making them pay. Taxes were imposed, payable only in cash, to force people out to work. These practices, along with the building of railways and seaports, created vast networks of labor migration—mostly male — that broke up families, ruptured tradition, and spread diseases ranging from tuberculosis to AIDS.

Russia
World War I and its aftermath set huge numbers of people in motion. The stresses of warfare destroyed the empires of Tsarist Russia, Austria-Hungary, and the Ottomans. Communist Russia would brook no opposition to its program of collectivizing agriculture. When Crimean Tartars and better-off farmers known as Kulaks resisted, they were rounded up and sent off to new homes in Siberia.

Asia Minor and Middle East
Like Humpty Dumpty, the Ottoman Empire fell into pieces that no one could put back together. In the Balkan and Arab worlds, new nations appeared, many with the idea that they must purge their territories of ethnic minorities. Britain's decision to sponsor a homeland for Jews in Palestine led, over decades, to mutual hostility between Muslims and Jews in a region that had seen mutual tolerance over centuries.

Germany
Worst of all, German disappointment at losing World War I and resentment against what they regarded as an unjust peace, fueled the Nazi movement. Hitler's determination to restore lost greatness through a new world war and the elimination of "impure races" not only caused the destruction of 6 million people, but also the movement of millions of others as postwar refugees.

The Lucky Country

An ancient land, with an ancient people, Australia, as we know it today, was founded under the influence of Britain.

In 1899, 16,000 Australians chose to fight for Britain in the Boer War—proof of the Australian colonies' commitment to the British Empire. On January 1, 1901, when the six states united to form the Commonwealth of Australia, the country remained under the British crown.

A Westminster System

The newly written constitution of 1901 reflected Australian interests while following British precedent. It created a Westminster system of government, with a lower house (House of Representatives) and an upper house of review (the Senate).

Prior to federation, the various colonies had operated as independent entities, and strong opposition to union remained in some quarters. Nevertheless, after a long campaign led mainly by three politicians—Alfred Deakin, Henry Parkes, and Edmund Barton—the six states federated, with Edmund Barton as the first Prime Minister. New Zealand, although it had close political ties with Australia, did not join the Commonwealth.

United under the Crown

Federation came about partly for racial reasons—it provided a united defense against perceived threats of invasion by non-European nations. White Australians were conscious of their position in a British settlement far from Europe and close to heavily populated Asian countries. Even today, Australia remains a constitutional monarchy with the British monarch the formal head of state, represented by the Governor-General, who performs ceremonial and formal executive duties. For years, Melbourne and Sydney vied to be the capital of Australia, but in 1927 the new city of Canberra, in the Australian Capital Territory within New South Wales, became the national capital.

Mateship

In many ways the new nation was progressive. Its industrial relations policies were based on fairness for workers, and in 1907 the principle of a basic wage was negotiated. Old age, sickness and widows' pensions also came into being. But in the early part of the twentieth century, Australia remained strongly pro-

British. During World War I, 417,000 men enlisted out of a population of 5 million—59,000 were killed and 174,000 wounded. The defining theater of war for Australia was the 1915 Gallipoli campaign in Turkey. Although it was ultimately a defeat, the Australians gained a reputation for bravery, sardonic good humor, and mateship. Anzac (Australian and New Zealand Army Corps) Day, April 25, became an important, almost sacred, day of commemoration in Australia.

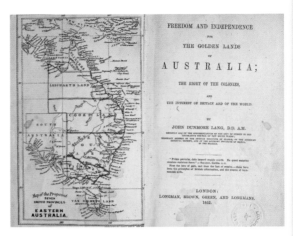

ABOVE John Dunmore Lang (1799-1878) was the first advocate of an independent Australian nation.

RIGHT This map shows Australia's agricultural belt and natural resources.

BELOW The Anzac legend, born on Sunday April 25, 1915, at Gallipoli, has done much to shape Australia's self-perception.

Tropic of Capricorn

340

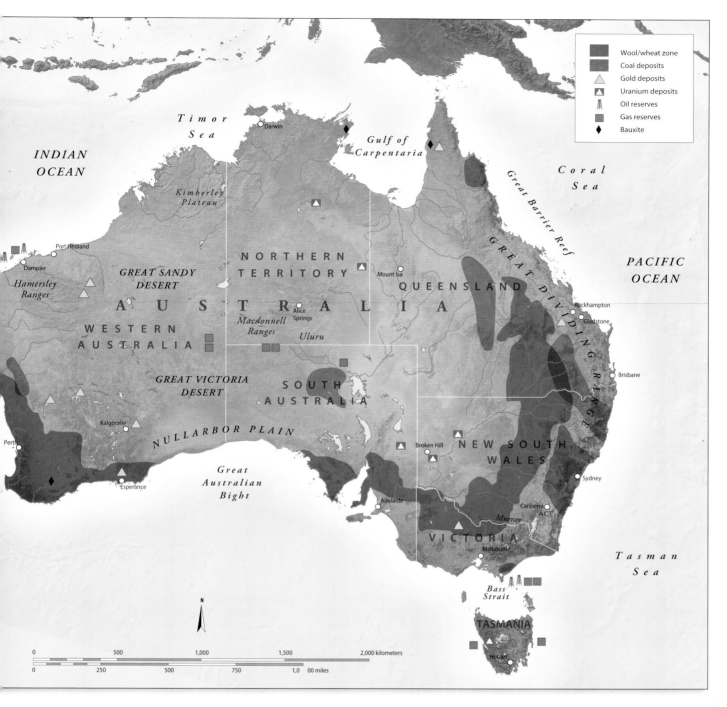

Legend:
- Wool/wheat zone
- Coal deposits
- Gold deposits
- Uranium deposits
- Oil reserves
- Gas reserves
- Bauxite

Timor Sea

INDIAN OCEAN

Darwin

Kimberley Plateau

Coral Sea

Great Barrier Reef

Gulf of Carpentaria

PACIFIC OCEAN

Port Hedland

Dampier

Hamersley Ranges

GREAT SANDY DESERT

NORTHERN TERRITORY

Mount Isa

QUEENSLAND

GREAT DIVIDING RANGE

Rockhampton

Gladstone

A U S T R A L I A

Macdonnell Ranges

Alice Springs

Uluru

WESTERN AUSTRALIA

Brisbane

GREAT VICTORIA DESERT

SOUTH AUSTRALIA

Kalgoorlie

Broken Hill

NEW SOUTH WALES

Perth

NULLARBOR PLAIN

Sydney

Esperance

Great Australian Bight

Adelaide

Canberra
ACT

Murray

Tasman Sea

VICTORIA

Melbourne

Bass Strait

N

TASMANIA

Hobart

| 0 | 500 | 1,000 | 1,500 | 2,000 kilometers |
| 0 | 250 | 500 | 750 | 1,0 00 miles |

Export Dependence

Between the wars, much of white Australia held dual loyalties—to England as the source of culture and history, but also to Australia, which was considered a sunny land of opportunity where everyone was equal. The economy was stable during the early twentieth century. Wheat joined wool as an important export, helped by the spreading of railways to the outer limits of agricultural areas. The railways helped other industries to remain viable, by keeping down transport costs. But the 1930s Great Depression hit Australia harder than most other countries. As an exporter of primary products dependent on international markets, the country suffered greatly—unemployment was over 30 percent. Australia's class system, never as rigid England's, existed nonetheless, and the Depression increased the divide between rich and poor.

The American Alliance

In 1939 when the world went to war, Australia once again followed Britain into battle. But there were differences this time. Australia was more concerned with the threat from Japan than with the threat from Germany (a fear realized when Darwin and Broome in the north were bombed), and when Singapore fell in 1942, Australia looked to the United States for support—a fundamental shift.

> Don't worry about the world coming to an end today. It's already tomorrow in Australia.
> –Charles M. Schulz (1922-2000), American cartoonist

RIGHT March 17, 1951: Bales of Australian wool are loaded onto a barge on arrival in Britain. In the early 1950s, record wool prices saw Australia's trade balance shift from a 21 percent deficit to a 26 percent surplus.

1911 Canberra is designated the capital city of Australia

1941 Australia allows the United States to use its shores as the base for its supreme command in the Pacific theater of the war

1975 The government of Gough Whitlam (Labor) is dismissed by the Governor-General after its budget is continually blocked by Opposition members of the upper house of Parliament

1986 The *Australia Act* comes into force, making Australian laws totally independent of Britain and disallowing any appeals to the Privy Council in London

1992 The *Citizenship Act* is amended to remove the swearing of an oath of allegiance to the British Crown

The Post-war Boom

Australia continued its cultural ties with Britain after World War II. The monarchy remained popular and Australia gave preference to British migrants. Young Australian travelers usually made London their base. However, in the second half of the twentieth century, trade and defense links with Britain faded and relationships with the United States, Japan, and in latter years China, became increasingly more important. When Britain joined the European Economic Community in 1973, Australia faced a watershed moment of rejection by its former protector. Trade with Asia became crucial.

Australia boomed economically after the war. Wool reached record prices in the 1950s and there was full employment. The birth-rate increased so significantly that the "baby boomers" have influenced economic and social life ever since. Garden suburbs steadily radiated out from the coastal cities.

On the political stage, various interest groups coalesced into the Labor and Liberal parties. Broadly speaking, Labor represents workers and urban intellectuals, whereas the Liberal party is conservative, representing middle-class suburbs and big business. The Liberal Party ruled from 1949 until 1972, perhaps reflecting a complacency born of prosperity and peace. Most people, whether in neat suburban houses, prosperous farmsteads, or thriving country towns, were satisfied with the *status quo* and approved conservative government regulations, such as no Sunday trading. Even so, on February 14, 1966, Australia adopted decimal currency and measurement, a change that moved it further from British influence.

Whitening Australia

Immigration was encouraged because its small population was believed to make Australia vulnerable to invasion. Over two million migrants arrived between 1947 and 1969. At first, because the infamous White Australia policy was in place, they came only from Britain, then Northern Europe. The next "New Australians" to be recruited were Southern Europeans, and in the

RIGHT Old Parliament House, Canberra, was the home of the Australian Federal Parliament from 1927 until 1988. When Parliament relocated to its new home on Capitol Hill, this heritage-listed building became a museum of Australian political and social history.

1970s Asian migrants, eventually followed by people from Middle Eastern countries. By late in the twentieth century black Africans were also included in immigration quotas. Australian Aborigines were not counted as citizens until 1967.

Summers of Discontent
From the late 1960s, many younger Australians began challenging the prevailing mood of content. They protested against their nation's involvement in the Vietnam War, and at the dismissal of the Labor Prime Minister, Gough Whitlam, by the Governor-General in 1975. The gay and women's liberation movements got underway, while Aboriginal protesters demanded land rights. Music and books from Britain and America articulated new ideas. The contraceptive pill made sexual freedom possible, and in 1975 divorce laws were reformed.

Republican Rumblings
Since 1975, power has alternated between Liberal and Labor governments. The economy has swung from boom to recession, but the hardships of the 1930s Depression have not been repeated. Wheat and wool remain important exports,

but have now been overtaken by minerals, particularly iron ore. Western Australia exports huge amounts of raw materials, fueled by demand from India and China, creating a strong economy.

Australia debated becoming a republic in 1999, but the referendum was rejected. In 1992, the Mabo decision recognized Aboriginal land title, and indigenous

people claimed an apology for past wrongs. The century ended with the success of the 2000 Sydney Olympics.

"A Sunburnt Country"
For years, eastern Australia has been suffering a prolonged and severe drought, stimulating much concern about climate change. Yet Australia's 20 million people live in

ABOVE Parliament House on Capital Hill in Canberra replaced Old Parliament House in 1988, the bicentenary of the founding of Australia. The forecourt mosaic comprises 90,000 pieces depicting a Possum and Wallaby Dreaming from Aboriginal culture.

LEFT Notwithstanding its short life and difficult end, the Whitlam government ushered in an era of great change and modernization in Australia. One of its innovations was universal health care, now regarded as a sacred right by many Australian citizens. Free education was another.

a rich and cosmopolitan country with much to offer. Though theirs is an isolated country, Australians are enthusiastic overseas travelers, and modern communications have brought the rest of the world much closer than before. Australia boasts 16 World Heritage sites, including Uluru, formerly Ayers Rock, the giant rock sitting in the middle of a plain in central Australia.

Russo-Japanese War

The Russo-Japanese war of 1904–1905 marked the historic first defeat of a European power by an Asian nation, and paved the way for Japanese imperialist expansion into China and the Pacific in the coming decades.

1904, February 7
The telegraph line at Port Arthur is cut

1904, February 8-9
The Japanese launch a surprise torpedo attack on the Russian fleet in Port Arthur

1904, February 9
Japanese occupy Seoul, Korea

1904, February 10
Japan declares war on Russia

At the beginning of the twentieth century, China appeared to the imperial powers to be a land of opportunity. It was also a land of competition between the powers. China was increasingly sliced into concessions, spheres of interest, and treaty ports by France, Britain, Russia, and Germany. But China soon became a flashpoint for the newest power seeking membership of the imperial club—Japan.

Competing Interests
Late in the nineteenth century, growing nationalist sentiment had turned into calls for the expansion of Japanese interests overseas. These hopes and visions of Japan's rising imperial strength were seen to be confirmed by Japan's 1894–1895 victory over China. But the war between China and Japan had only been stopped by the intervention of European powers, and this brought Russia into the picture. Under bargains made with a nearly bankrupt postwar China, Russia built railways through Manchuria linking their Trans-Siberian railway with Vladivostok, and also leased a military base at Port Arthur on the Liaotung Peninsula.

The Japanese tried to negotiate with the Russians to gain mutual recognition of their influence in the region, but this did not succeed. With the Russians not withdrawing according to their promise to the Chinese, Japan weighed its options.

ABOVE The end of the Russo-Japanese conflict is announced via newspaper to Russians in a Moscow fruit market, 1905. Popular discontent was on the increase.

Anglo-Japanese Alliance
The Anglo-Japanese alliance was formed in January 1902 with the aim of protecting both parties' interests in China. If Japan went to war with Russia, the guarantee of British protection would restrict involvement to Japan and Russia alone. With the subsequent breakdown of negotiations between Japan and Russia in 1904, this is exactly what happened.

Russo-Japanese Conflict
In an eerie foreshadowing of Pearl Harbor, the Japanese struck Russian ships at Port Arthur on February 8, 1904, before declaring war on February 10. Within a few weeks the towns to the north of Port Arthur had been taken, and the Japanese proceeded south with their eyes on this heavily fortified headland. Port Arthur was under siege until January 1905, at a cost of over 55,000 Japanese lives. When the Russians finally surrendered the fort, Japanese confidence was given a great boost.

Having landed several armies in Manchuria, to the north of the Liaotung Peninsula, and having marched north through Korea, the Japanese were met with strong

> The fields were quagmires and the roads were abominable. Finally, we lacked good maps.
> –Captain Englehardt, Nerchinski Cossak Regiment, in a lecture in 1905.

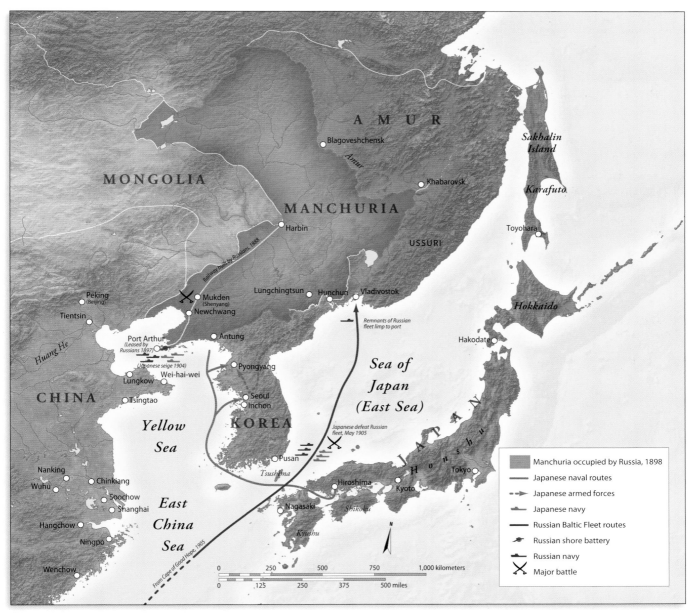

Map labels:
AMUR
Blagoveshchensk
Sakhalin Island
Karafuto
MONGOLIA
Khabarovsk
MANCHURIA
USSURI
Toyohara
Harbin
Railway built by Russians, 1898
Peking (Beijing)
Lungchingtsun
Hunchun
Vladivostok
Hokkaido
Tientsin
Mukden (Shenyang)
Newchwang
Remnants of Russian fleet limp to port
Huang He
Port Arthur (Leased by Russians 1897)
Antung
(Japanese seige 1904)
Pyongyang
Hakodate
Lungkow
Wei-hai-wei
Seoul
Inchon
Sea of Japan (East Sea)
CHINA
Tsingtao
KOREA
Yellow Sea
Japanese defeat Russian fleet, May 1905
Nanking
Pusan
Tsushima
Wuhu
Chinkiang
Soochow
Shanghai
Hiroshima
Kyoto
Tokyo
East China Sea
Nagasaki
Shikoku
Hangchow
Kyushu
Ningpo
JAPAN
Honshu
Wenchow
From Cape of Good Hope 1905
N

Scale:
0 250 500 750 1,000 kilometers
0 125 250 375 500 miles

Legend:
- Manchuria occupied by Russia, 1898
- Japanese naval routes
- Japanese armed forces
- Japanese navy
- Russian Baltic Fleet routes
- Russian shore battery
- Russian navy
- Major battle

Russian resistance at Mukden, Manchuria in March 1905. The battle involved armies of over 300,000 amassed on each side. It resulted in another very costly but strategically significant victory for the Japanese.

Others followed. Russia was separated from the theater of war by over 5,000 miles (8,000 km). Transportation of troops via the Trans-Siberian railway was patchy, and reinforcements were slow to arrive. Furthermore, Russia's main naval fleet was based in the Baltic Sea. The Russians decided to send this fleet around the long way on an 18,000-mile (29,000-km), six-month journey. This was decisive for the Japanese, who skillfully

ambushed the fleet and decimated it upon its arrival in the straits between Japan and Korea.

US-brokered Peace Talks

The United States, under President Theodore Roosevelt, was eager to see a peace settlement, and invited the powers to attend peace talks in Portsmouth, Maine in August 1905. After a month of talks, the Russians agreed to grant the Japanese their rail interests in Manchuria, and recognize Japan's special status in Korea. This would eventually lead to Japan's annexation of Korea in 1910, and pave the way for Japanese occupation of Manchuria in the 1930s.

ABOVE With their naval superiority established in the first few weeks of war, the Japanese were better able to transport troops.

RIGHT Russian warships being brought into Sasebo Harbor as captives of the Imperial Japanese Navy, flying the victor's flag.

FAR LEFT Japanese soldiers arrive in Korea to fight the Russians there. The Russians were not popular with the Koreans, who welcomed the Japanese.

The End of Imperialism

The collapse of China's 2,000 year-old system of government in 1911 may have appeared sudden. But the fall of the Manchurian Qing dynasty—the last of the dynasties—came after a century of internal and external pressures.

1894 Sun Yixian moves to Hawaii where he founds the Revive China Society

1905 Sun publishes his political philosophy *Three Principles of the People*, which appears in the first line of the national anthem of the Republic of China

1911 Sun returns to China after 15 years in exile in Europe, the United States, Canada, and Japan

1912 Sun Yixian is sworn in as the first provisional president of the Republic of China

Tropic of Cancer

LEFT The Boxers blamed China's troubles on Western intervention and the growth of the Christian religion in China. They took to the streets in violent protests, tearing up public infrastructure, and killing Christians.

The demise of dynastic rule in China had a lot to do with the encroachment of foreign powers on Chinese soil in the nineteenth century. In the Opium Wars of 1839–1842 and 1856–1860, the English had forced China to open its doors to opium from India in exchange for silver. During the late nineteenth century, the presence of foreign powers grew stronger and China was pressured by France, Germany, Russia, and Japan to allow them access to its territories and resources, and to grant them virtual sovereignty over ports.

Internal factors were also bringing pressure to bear on the government. During the nineteenth century, the Chinese population had grown, but food production

had not followed. Repressive and corrupt taxes enforced by the land-lords and gentry kept the majority of peasants desperately poor.

Rebellion and Revolution

The 1850s–1860s saw a wave of localized rebellions within China, the most famous being the Taiping Rebellion, in which a staggering 20–30 million people were killed. All these rebellions fused radical religious sentiment with a deep frustration at the corruption and inequality of dynastic rule. When the Chinese suffered a humiliating military defeat at the hands of Japan (1894–95), calls for reform were amplified. Between June and September 1898, the Emperor, in the Hundred Days Reform, decreed

changes to education, commerce, and civil service examinations.

Another answer to China's problems came from the "Boxers," the Yi He Tuan movement—Society of Righteous and Harmonious Fists. While initially condemning the uprising, Empress Dowager Ci Xi ordered Imperial troops to support the Boxers. The eventual quashing of the Boxers by European troops brought about the Boxer Protocol (1901), a humiliating package of reforms forced upon the Imperial government, including indemnities of 450 million taels. This debt alone crippled the Imperial government both financially and politically.

The decisive answer came in the form of nationalist revolution. One prominent revolutionary was

Dr Sun Yixian (Sun Yat-sen). Born in China, educated in Hawaii, and baptized into the Anglican Church, Sun called for a greater sense of nationalism among the Chinese, and sought a government based on the Three People's Principles—nationalism (China for Chinese), people's sovereignty (republicanism), and people's livelihood (redistribution of land). In 1905, while in Japan, Sun found himself heading a national revolutionary organization, the Tongmenhui.

In 1911, the Tongemnhui, who had been active in ongoing revolts in China's south, were involved in an accidental bomb explosion in Wuchang (present-day Wuhan). Government soldiers refused to move against them, and when the

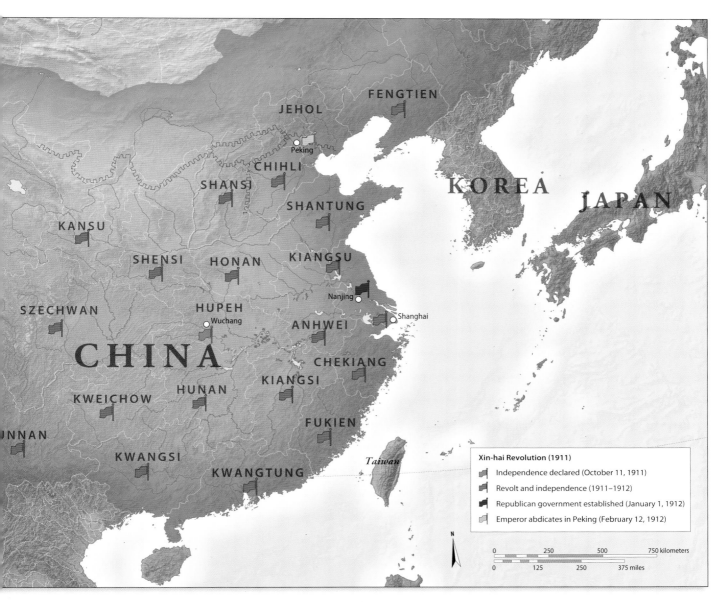

JEHOL

FENGTIEN

Peking

CHIHLI

SHANSI

SHANTUNG

KANSU

SHENSI

HONAN

KIANGSU

KOREA

JAPAN

SZECHWAN

HUPEH
Wuchang

ANHWEI

Nanjing

Shanghai

CHINA

CHEKIANG

HUNAN

KIANGSI

KWEICHOW

FUKIEN

UNNAN

KWANGSI

KWANGTUNG

Taiwan

Xin-hai Revolution (1911)

Independence declared (October 11, 1911)

Revolt and independence (1911–1912)

Republican government established (January 1, 1912)

Emperor abdicates in Peking (February 12, 1912)

N

0		250		500		750 kilometers
0	125		250		375 miles	

An individual should
not have too much freedom.
A nation should have
absolute freedom.

–Dr Sun Yixian (Sun Yat-sen) (1866-1925),
Chinese political and revolutionary leader.

government of Hupeh (present-day Hupei) province fell on October 11, the province declared independence from Imperial rule. This caused a domino effect of secessions in the provinces of southern and central China, as the military and middle classes fell in with the emerging nationalist movement. By November, 15 of China's 24 provinces had declared independence from the

Qing, and by January 1, 1912, a republican government headed by Sun Yixian was established in Nanjing. Support from northern China didn't come so easily, however.

The Last Emperor

The end of the Qing dynasty came as a direct result of the betrayal of a northern military general, Yuan Shikai. The Qing emperor could not stop the nationalists without Yuan. Holding the balance of power, he brokered a deal which brought the northern provinces into the new Republic of China, and delivered the emperor's abdication on February 12, 1912. China's long dynastic system had finally come to an end, but half a century of bloody revolution was only just beginning.

ABOVE The failure of the Imperial Court to enact adequate reform measures caused many reformists to rebel. The Xin Hai Revolution of 1911 began with the Wuchang rebellion, and ended the rule of the empire.

LEFT Sun Yixian (Sun Yat-sen) (1867-1925) became provisional president of the Republic of China in 1912. A uniting figure in the post-Imperial years, he remains unique among twentieth-century Chinese politicians for being widely revered in both mainland China and Taiwan.

Conquest of the South Pole

In the twentieth century, the South Pole remained one of the great challenges for explorers. In the end, the race turned to tragedy.

1773 Captain James Cook's second voyage of discovery is the first to cross the Antarctic Circle

1820 Russian Gottlieb von Bellingshausen is the first person to see the Antarctic continent

1902 Robert Scott, Edward Wilson, and Ernest Shackleton head for the South Pole but only reach latitude 82ºS before suffering snow blindness and having to return

1908 Shackleton and other explorers attempt to reach the South Pole, getting with 97 miles (155 km) before having to abandon the journey

1911 Norwegian explorer Roald Amundsen is the first man to reach the South Pole

1947 A US Navy base is set up at Little America in Antarctica. Aerial photographs and extensive mapping are done.

RIGHT Roald Amundsen's use of dog sleds instead of manpower enabled him to reach the pole ahead of Scott and return safely.

British explorer Robert F. Scott arrived in McMurdo Sound on January 4, 1911, just 11 days ahead of Norwegian explorer, Roald Amundsen, who was determined to beat Scott—the race to the South Pole was on. Neither man was inexperienced.

The Race

Amundsen landed at the Bay of Whales, 60 miles (100 km) closer to the Pole than Scott's base at Cape Evans. Both parties laid their supply depots during the winter of 1911. On reaching Beardmore Glacier, Scott ordered the dog teams back, leaving the remaining men to haul three 800 lb (360 kg) sledges on a torturous struggle up the 10,000 foot (3,000 m) glacier.

At the same time, Amundsen and his party of four men, 52 dogs and four 850 lb (385 kg) sledges, were 350 miles (560 km) further south after an easy ride being towed by the dogs. They covered 90 miles (150 km) in four days compared to Scott who managed 130 miles (200 km) in two weeks.

On the morning of December 14, 1911, Roald Amundsen and his team reached the South Pole while Scott was still struggling up the slopes of the Beardmore Glacier.

Scott and four men finally arrived at the Pole on January 17, 1912, only to find the Norwegian flag flying, much to their disappointment. On their return home the five men were plagued by frostbite, hunger, and exhaustion. On

March 21, within only 11 miles (18 km) of One Ton Depot, a blizzard set in, holding the men captive in their tents for a week, resulting in a total loss of life. Meanwhile, Amundsen and his team had reached the safety of their base on January 26, in good health and without mishap, having covered the 1,400 miles (2,250 km) in only 99 days.

Amazing Survival

With the race to the South Pole won, British explorer Sir Ernest Shackleton departed in August 1914, to cross the Antarctic continent on foot. Unfortunately, even before they reached land, their ship became trapped in drifting pack ice for the duration of the winter of 1915.

Eventually the men set off for land, dragging their lifeboats across the ice. Due to the backbreaking effort of hauling their supplies, they spent six months making camp on the drifting ice. They finally launched their three boats on April 9, 1916, landing on Elephant Island on April 15. Shackleton, seeking help, took one boat and five men on an 800-mile (1300 km) journey across the world's most dangerous sea to South Georgia for help. Landing on the west side of South Georgia, Shackleton and two men set out to cross a ridge of mountains, miraculously arriving at the whaling station on the east. Within hours a whaler set off to pick up the three men left on the other side of the island.

From May 26, Shackleton made three arduous attempts to rescue the remaining 21 men, finally succeeding on August 30 after they had spent four months of hardship and deprivation on Elephant Island, and two years after their departure from England.

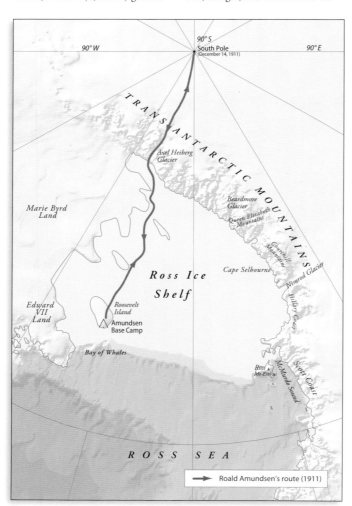

90° W

90° S
South Pole
(December 14, 1911)

90° E

TRANSANTARCTIC MOUNTAINS

Axel Heiberg Glacier

Beardmore Glacier

Queen Elizabeth Mountains

Marie Byrd Land

Churchill Mountains

Cape Selbourne

Nimrod Glacier

Ross Ice Shelf

Hillary Coast

Edward VII Land

Roosevelt Island

Amundsen Base Camp

Bay of Whales

Ross Mt Erebus

McMurdo Sound

Scott Coast

R O S S S E A

→ Roald Amundsen's route (1911)

South Pole
(January 17, 1912)

90° E

T R A N S A N T A R C T I C   M O U N T A I N S

Mt Darwin

Beardmore
Glacier

+ Evans dies
(February 17, 1912)

Churchill
Mountains

Cape
Selbourne

Nimrod Glacier

Hillary Coast

Ross Ice
Shelf

+ Oates dies
(March 17, 1912)

One Ton Depot
(Scott's final diary entry,
March 29, 1912)

Scott, Wilson,
and Bowers die +
(approximately
March 30, 1912)

Scott
Base Camp

Ross
Mt Erebus

McMurdo Sound

Scott Coast

R O S S   S E A

Victoria
Land

→ Robert Scott's route (1911–1912)

| 0 | 250 | 500 kilometers |
| 0 | 125 miles | 250 miles |

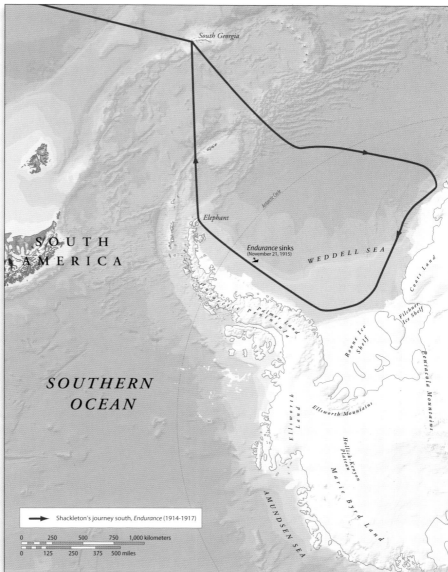

South Georgia

SOUTH
AMERICA

Elephant

Endurance sinks
(November 21, 1915)

W E D D E L L   S E A

Antarctic Circle

Palmer Land

Coats Land

Antarctic Peninsula

Ronne Ice
Shelf

Filchner
Ice Shelf

SOUTHERN
OCEAN

Ellsworth Land

Ellsworth Mountains

Pensacola Mountains

Hollick-Kenyon
Plateau

Marie Byrd Land

AMUNDSEN
SEA

→ Shackleton's journey south, Endurance (1914-1917)

| 0 | 250 | 500 | 750 | 1,000 kilometers |
| 0 | 125 | 250 | 375 | 500 miles |

LEFT A dog team watches as Shackleton's ship, *Endurance*, is caught in pack ice before reaching Antarctica. Seeking rescue, it took four months to return to the stricken men left behind.

ABOVE LEFT Scott and his party perished on the return from the South Pole, the last three dying within a day of supplies.

ABOVE Shackleton's journey south was fraught with problems, including the sinking of the *Endurance,* in November 1915.

HILLARY

New Zealander Sir Edmund Hillary (1919–2008) was the first man to reach the summit of Mount Everest with Tensing Norgay in 1953. He reached the South Pole in 1958. Having landed on the North Pole in 1985 in the company of Neil Armstrong, he became the only explorer to have stood at both poles and on the summit of the world. In the 1960s his concerns turned to the welfare of the Nepalese, helping build clinics, hospitals, and schools.

RIGHT Edmund Hillary and Tensing Norgay after the Everest climb. Hillary reached both poles as well.

Dividing the Spoils

As the nineteenth century drew to a close, European powers looked to the African continent in a last bid for empire. Entering the twentieth century, black Africa found itself divided into dozens of dominions under the control of a white Europe.

ABOVE This cartoon makes fun of Cecil Rhodes' idea of Britain controlling Africa from Cape Town to Cairo. In 1890, Rhodes became prime minister of Cape Colony.

Britain, closely followed by France, was eventually the most successful European power in achieving control over most of black Africa. British naval squadrons patrolled off Zanzibar and West Africa from the early 1800s, protecting colonies in Sierra Leone (1808), Gambia (1816), and the Gold Coast (1821) that served as bases for suppressing the slave trade and for stimulating commerce. Renewed assertions of British supremacy in the interior of southern Africa came with Britain annexing Griqualand West as a crown colony in 1871 and transferring it to the Cape Colony in 1881. This followed the diamond discoveries during the 1870s and successful wars against African kingdoms between 1878 and 1884 that led to

> I dream of an Africa which is in peace with itself.
> –Nelson Mandela, anti-apartheid activist and former President of South Africa.

a unified South Africa—with later expansion into Southern and Northern Rhodesia (1895 and 1911 respectively), and Nyasaland (1907). In Eastern Africa, Kenya became a colony much later, in 1920, though it had been under British domination since 1888. Uganda and Somaliland became British protectorates in 1894.

Other than Britain, the four main European powers involved in colonizing Africa were Belgium,

ABOVE The Italian-born French empire builder, Pierre de Brazza, added around 193,000 square miles (500,000 km²) to the French empire in central Africa.

Germany, France, and Portugal. The pioneer colonizer in central Africa was Leopold II, King of the Belgians, who ostensibly established his colony, called the Congo Free State, as a "private humanitarian venture," to limit the devastation of slaving and the liquor trade.

German Rival

The most immediate rival to Leopold in creating instant new colonies was Germany which, in the 1880s, claimed territory in South West Africa (now South West Africa/Namibia), Togoland, Cameroon, and part of the East African coast opposite Zanzibar—German East Africa or Tanganyika—and later, Rwanda and Burundi. In World War I, the Belgians effectively annexed both of the latter to their Congo colony and gradually incorporated them into a central colonial administration.

French Conqueror

During the latter part of the nineteenth century, France consolidated its hold on the whole of North Africa (except Libya and Egypt) by either conquering or establishing a dominant presence in Morocco, Algeria, and Tunis. In central Africa, the French explorer Pierre de Brazza aspired to join French coastal enclaves to the middle stretch of the Congo River, where the colonial capital was named Brazzaville in his honor. He also claimed territory for France as far east as the upper regions of the Nile. His endeavors brought France into competition not only with

1893 British South African Company occupies a new territory and calls it Rhodesia

1905 French explorer Pierre de Brazza dies in Dakar, Senegal

1908 Public outrage at the treatment of native Africans in the Congo leads the Belgian Parliament to annex Congo Free State and call it Belgian Congo

1910 The Cape Colony, Natal, the Transvaal, and the Orange Free State are united to become the Union of South Africa

1964 Nelson Mandela is sentenced to life imprisonment for treason

LEFT In March 1905, Pierre de Brazza made his final trip to the Congo. He died six months later on the journey home.

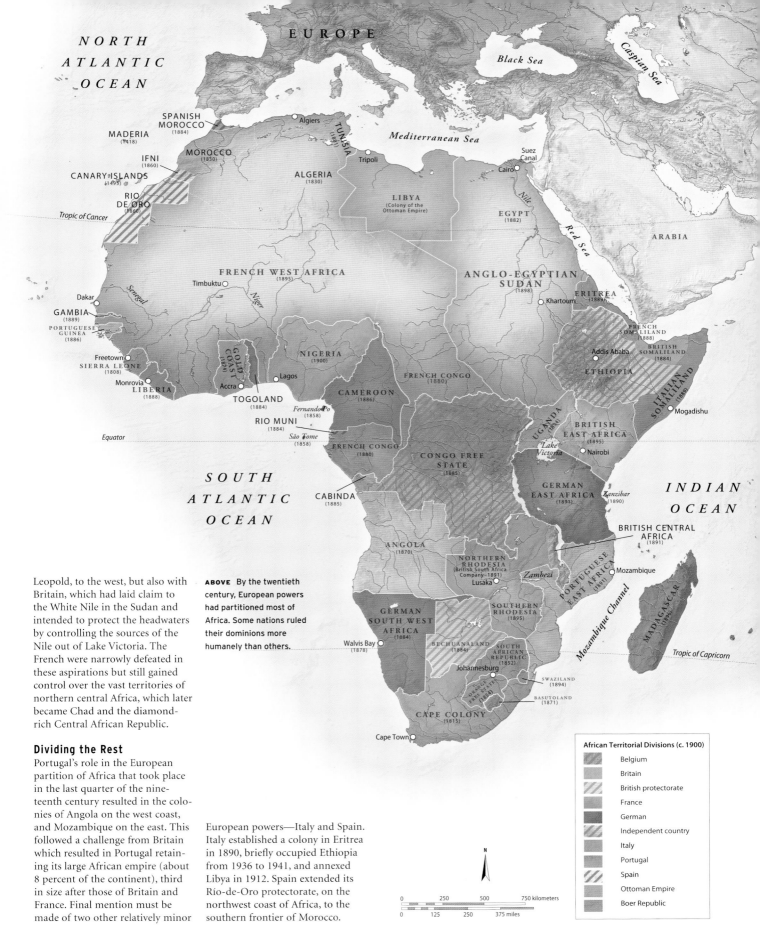

NORTH
ATLANTIC
OCEAN

EUROPE

Black Sea

Caspian Sea

Mediterranean Sea

SPANISH
MOROCCO
(1884)

Algiers

TUNISIA
(1881)

MADERIA
(1418)

Suez
Canal

IFNI
(1860)

MOROCCO
(1830)

Tripoli

Cairo

CANARY ISLANDS
(1495)

ALGERIA
(1830)

LIBYA
(Colony of the
Ottoman Empire)

EGYPT
(1882)

RIO
DE ORO
(1860)

ARABIA

Tropic of Cancer

FRENCH WEST AFRICA
(1895)

Red Sea

Nile

ANGLO-EGYPTIAN
SUDAN
(1898)

ERITREA
(1889)

Timbuktu

Senegal

Khartoum

Dakar

FRENCH
SOMALILAND
(1888)

Niger

GAMBIA
(1889)

NIGERIA
(1900)

Addis Ababa

BRITISH
SOMALILAND
(1884)

PORTUGUESE
GUINEA
(1886)

Freetown

GOLD
COAST
(1874)

FRENCH CONGO
(1880)

ETHIOPIA

SIERRA LEONE
(1808)

Lagos

Monrovia

Accra

LIBERIA
(1888)

TOGOLAND
(1884)

CAMEROON
(1886)

ITALIAN
SOMALILAND
(1889)

Fernando Po
(1858)

Mogadishu

RIO MUNI
(1884)

UGANDA
(1894)

BRITISH
EAST AFRICA
(1895)

São Tomé
(1858)

Equator

FRENCH CONGO
(1880)

CONGO FREE
STATE
(1885)

Lake
Victoria

Nairobi

SOUTH
ATLANTIC
OCEAN

CABINDA
(1885)

GERMAN
EAST AFRICA
(1891)

Zanzibar
(1890)

INDIAN
OCEAN

ANGOLA
(1870)

NORTHERN
RHODESIA
(British South Africa
Company—1891)
Lusaka

Zambezi

BRITISH CENTRAL
AFRICA
(1891)

Mozambique

GERMAN
SOUTH WEST
AFRICA
(1884)

SOUTHERN
RHODESIA
(1895)

PORTUGUESE
EAST AFRICA
(1891)

Mozambique Channel

MADAGASCAR
(1896)

Walvis Bay
(1878)

BECHUANALAND
(1884)

SWAZILAND
(1894)

SOUTH
AFRICAN
REPUBLIC
(1852)

Johannesburg

Tropic of Capricorn

ORANGE
FREE STATE
(1854)

BASUTOLAND
(1871)

CAPE COLONY
(1815)

Cape Town

Leopold, to the west, but also with Britain, which had laid claim to the White Nile in the Sudan and intended to protect the headwaters by controlling the sources of the Nile out of Lake Victoria. The French were narrowly defeated in these aspirations but still gained control over the vast territories of northern central Africa, which later became Chad and the diamond-rich Central African Republic.

Dividing the Rest

Portugal's role in the European partition of Africa that took place in the last quarter of the nineteenth century resulted in the colonies of Angola on the west coast, and Mozambique on the east. This followed a challenge from Britain which resulted in Portugal retaining its large African empire (about 8 percent of the continent), third in size after those of Britain and France. Final mention must be made of two other relatively minor

ABOVE By the twentieth century, European powers had partitioned most of Africa. Some nations ruled their dominions more humanely than others.

European powers—Italy and Spain. Italy established a colony in Eritrea in 1890, briefly occupied Ethiopia from 1936 to 1941, and annexed Libya in 1912. Spain extended its Río-de-Oro protectorate, on the northwest coast of Africa, to the southern frontier of Morocco.

African Territorial Divisions (c. 1900)

- Belgium
- Britain
- British protectorate
- France
- German
- Independent country
- Italy
- Portugal
- Spain
- Ottoman Empire
- Boer Republic

N

| 0 | 250 | 500 | 750 kilometers |

| 0 | 125 | 250 | 375 miles |

Europe—Readying for War

Over centuries, Europe gradually emerged as the center of the world as countries expanded their colonial empires, causing great power rivalry and alliances.

1901 to 2000

A colonial empire was considered the hallmark of greatness and prestige. Even little Belgium acquired the Belgian Congo, whose 900,000 square miles (2.3 million km²) of territory was several times the size of Belgium itself. Japan, emerging from its strict isolation in 1868, embarked on expansionism around the turn of the century, seizing small areas of Asia as well as Korea. Russia enlarged its empire: Toward the west, incorporating Finland and the Baltics; to the south in Central Asia; and to the east in Siberia by internal colonization of neighboring territories. Imperial Russian goals included the Balkans and rule over the Black Sea.

Germany's Challenge

A latecomer in the rivalry, Germany wanted to join the club of colonial powers. Its efforts, however, were stymied by Britain and France. Between 1885 and 1914, while Britain conquered 30 percent of Africa's territory, Germany's colonies covered only 9 percent. The traditional German idea of *drang nach Osten*, expansion toward the East; or, as the German-American philosopher Hannah Arendt called it, "continental imperialism," was well illustrated by building the Berlin–Constantinople railroad under German control and with German investments directed toward the Near East.

Expansionist ideologies were developed about *mission civilisatrice*, as the French called it; or, as Rudyard Kipling described British colonialism, the "white man's burden" of patronage for the "half child-half animal" subjects. British philosopher Herbert Spencer interpreted colonial conquest as "natural law" by introducing the concept of the "survival of the fittest,"

> If there is another war in Europe, it will come out of some damned silly thing in the Balkans.
>
> –Otto von Bismarck (1815-1898), Prussian Prime Minister and Founder of the German Empire.

1904 Russo-Japanese War breaks out; the Japanese occupy Seoul

1905 Tsar Nicholas II introduces his "October Manifesto" to establish reforms

1906 Britain forces Turkey to cede Sinai Peninsula to Egypt

1907 Dutch complete occupation of Sumatra

1907 Wilhelm II of Germany and Nicholas II of Russia meet at Swinemunde

1908 Leopold II of Belgium concedes his private possession of Congo to Belgium

1910 Revolution in Portugal—King Manuel II flees to England

1911 German gunboat *Panther* arrives in the Moroccan port of Agadir, creating an international crisis

1912 Treaty of Lausanne signed between Italy and France

ABOVE In 1910, nine European kings were photographed at Buckingham Palace, London, England. They had gathered for the funeral of Edward VII.

discovering social Darwinism before Darwin. The German Heinrich von Treitschke maintained that to make a mark in history a country must build a colonial empire.

Power Blocs

The rivalry, however, sharpened at the turn of the twentieth century as the great powers tried to build blocs of alliances to realize their interests. In 1879, Germany allied with Austria-Hungary, and in 1882 Italy joined to form the Triple Alliance. In 1894, France signed an agreement with Russia to encircle Germany and Austria-Hungary. The British-French Entente Cordiale settled their traditional conflict in 1904 to form a powerful alliance against the most dangerous new rival, Germany. In 1907, Britain and Russia ended their central Asian conflicts so that the encirclement of the central powers was accomplished. Several smaller

countries joined to one of the main blocs, and some of them, such as Italy and Romania, later changed sides to realize their goals.

Powderkeg

Conflicts erupted around the turn of the century at the margins of the world theater—the Spanish-American war in 1898, and the Russo-Japanese war in 1904–05. The two Moroccan crises with German involvement in Tangier and Agadir in 1905 and 1911 respectively presaged further European confrontation. Even local conflicts between marginal players became dangerous in this explosive situation. The rearrangement of the Balkans ignited several small wars

European and Balkan countries (1914)

0   250   500   750   1,000 kilometers
0 125 250 375 500 miles

N

in the late nineteenth century and two major Balkan wars in 1912–13. Finally, Austria-Hungary's Balkan expansion and incorporation of Bosnia-Herzegovina led to the explosion of the Balkan powder-keg—during Archduke Franz-Ferdinand's visit to Sarajevo in 1914, Gavrilo Princip, a Bosnian Serb nationalist, assassinated the archduke and his wife. The incident gave Germany an excellent oppor-tunity to push its Austrian ally.

The declaration of war against tiny Serbia led to the explosion of World War I, history's first mecha-nized warfare with trucks, tanks, airplanes, and submarines that led to the death of more than eight million people across Europe.

ABOVE The First Balkan War ended with the May 1913 Treaty of London. Disputes over the spoils of war led to the Second Balkan War, which concluded in August 1913 with the Treaty of Bucharest.

LEFT Macedonian rebels guarding the highway leading north to Salonika against Turkish troops in 1912. The first of the Balkan Wars resulted in Turkey's loss of Macedonia, with much of the territory divided between Bulgaria, Greece, and Serbia, and changing the balance of power in the region.

The Great War

In 1914, the balance of power that had, with some notable exceptions, maintained peace in Europe for over a century, failed to resolve the crisis ignited by the assassination of the Habsburg heir, Archduke Franz Ferdinand, on June 28 in the Bosnian city of Sarajevo.

1901 to 2000

1915 Germany stages a Zeppelin air raid on England

1916 Easter uprising in Ireland demands independence from Britain—leaders make deals with Germany ensuring an independent Ireland would get a fair hearing at the post-war peace talks

1916 Woodrow Wilson is re-elected President of the United States on the slogan: "He kept us out of the war"

1917 Tsar Nicholas II abdicates and a provisional government is established in Russia

1917 Woodrow Wilson asks Congress for a declaration of war with Germany. Kaiser Wilhelm II of Germany abdicates.

The conflict that evolved between the Triple Entente of Britain, Russia, and France, and the Central Powers of Germany and Austria-Hungary, fighting alongside their various friends, allies, and subjects brought unprecedented destruction across the continent and beyond.

Within weeks of Ferdinand's death, declarations of war had been made by Austria-Hungary against Serbia and Russia; Russia against Austria-Hungary and Germany; Germany against Russia, France, Belgium, and Britain; France against Germany; Britain against Germany; and Japan against Germany. Within months, the Ottoman Empire had also declared war against Britain, France, and Russia. By 1915, Bulgaria and Italy had also entered the war; by 1916, Romania and Portugal were involved; and by 1917, Greece and the United States of America had joined the Entente.

The war drew on the Imperial ties that would involve men and women from South Africa, Canada, Australia, and New Zealand; its protagonists utilized the human resources spawned by their colonial enterprises, bringing thousands of men from Africa and the Indian subcontinent; while the labor shortages brought on by war drew men from China, 500 of whom became casualties of the war when the French ship they were sailing on was torpedoed in 1917.

This truly was the first *world* war. In the four years of fighting, almost eight and a half million military losses were incurred. Approximately five million civilians lost their lives to the submarines' torpedoes, the Zeppelins' bombs, the passage of forces through the landscape of Belgium and northern France, the savage nature of the front that swept back and forth across Eastern and Southeastern Europe, the privation and sickness that followed the lines of refugees and the military policies of deliberate deprivation. Other casualties of the war included political entities. Four great empires—the Ottoman, German, Austro-Hungarian, and Russian—were felled by a combination of military losses, political failings, and economic and social upheaval.

For many historians, World War I has come to signify an abrupt and violent transition from the civilized European order of the nineteenth century to the turbulence of twentieth century history. For other historians, the war signifies, rather, the failure of the nineteenth century order presided over by the Concert of Europe—the powers of Britain,

Germany, France, Austria-Hungary, and Russia—to adequately confront the radical social changes taking place at home, the continental changes that saw the birth of new states such as Serbia, the decline of imperial powers such as the Ottoman Empire, and the intrinsically combative nature of the Concert's ambitions for territory and influence. This latter approach, with its appreciation of both the short-term impact of political assassination and the long-term build-up of tensions, suggests the need to begin, not with the belief that Ferdinand's death itself was a crisis of unique import, but that something was different about the negotiations and ultimata of the "July crisis"—something which meant that the European powers who had preserved peace during previous crises, or at least never engaged simultaneously in a conflict, were unable to do so in 1914.

ABOVE This 1913 photograph of King George V riding with Kaiser Wilhelm II shows no sign of the tensions soon to develop. They were both grandsons of Queen Victoria.

LEFT Archduke Franz Ferdinand and his wife Sophie in the Austro-Hungarian capital of Sarajevo, moments before being shot. His assassination on June 28, 1914, precipitated World War I.

> War is part of God's order. In it, Man's most noble virtues are displayed—courage and self-denial, devotion to duty, willingness to sacrifice oneself, and to risk life itself. Without war, the world would stagnate and lose itself in materialism.
>
> –Helmuth von Moltke the Elder (1800-1891), German master strategist.

LEFT Huge crowds gathered outside Buckingham Palace on August 4, 1914, the night before England declared war on Germany.

BELOW These images show British and German troops celebrating during a truce—known as the "Christmas Truce"—in December 1914. These truces continued between the French and Germans in 1915, and at Easter 1916, there was a truce on the Eastern Front.

Boiling Point

Gavrilo Princep was an obscure, sickly student when he fired the shot that "echoed around the world." He was one of a group of young conspirators who were mem-bers of a Serb nationalist militia, called The Black Hand. Princep's role as Franz Ferdinand's assassin came about almost by acci-dent—he found himself in posi-tion to take the shot only because the Archduke's driver had taken a wrong turn. Two years later, suffer-ing tremendous remorse for his actions due to the disproportionate consequences they inspired, Prin-cep died from tuberculosis in a Habsburg jail.

The Balkans had, for some years previous to the assassination, been regarded by the powers as the most likely European "Boiling Point." The competing powers of Russia and Austria-Hungary, and the declining Ottoman Empire had been a central preoccupation of professional diplomats since the late nineteenth century.

Austria-Hungary's 1908 annex-ation of Bosnia created such ten-sion as to justly be regarded as the first Bosnian crisis of the twentieth century. The possibility for war be-tween Serbia and Austria-Hungary in 1908 was very real, but a couple of key factors prevented outright Serbian belligerence. First, the Ger-mans—Kaiser Wilhelm specifical-ly—noted that they would fight with Austria if the need arose. Second, Russia alerted Serbia to its unwillingness to engage in conflict at the time, feeling unprepared to deal with a Germany prepared to, in the words of Wilhelm, fight like "a knight in shining armor."

In the years following 1908, all the powers of Europe readied for war, even as they proclaimed themselves committed to peaceful co-existence. The British and the Germans raced to build mightier navies; tensions arose over compet-ing colonial ambitions; the Russian Army was reorganized to facilitate rapid mobilization.

Thus, although the second Bos-nian crisis, like the first, stemmed from tensions between Serbia and Austria-Hungary, it happened when key powers were prepared for war. Austria issued Serbia with an ultimatum on July 23, just weeks after the shooting in Sarajevo, insisting that their agents should be allowed to pursue the assassins within Serbia, thereby impinging upon Serbian sovereignty as well as implicating direct Serbian con-nections to the assassination. As happened during the first Bosnian crisis, Germany announced full support for all Austrian action against Serbia. The Serbian gov-ernment ordered partial mobiliza-tion and waited to see what offers might transpire. On July 25, Russia offered its support in case of war— a significant departure from the first Bosnian crisis.

When Russian intentions were made clear, the likelihood of Ser-bia submitting to the Austro-Hungarian ultimatum diminished. Austria-Hungary officially declared war on Serbia on July 28, at which point Russia began to mobilize. Now the pressure was on Germany to avoid a war on two fronts—a war with an already mobilizing Russia and one with Russia's for-mal ally, France.

Germany issued an ultimatum to Russia and then to France, with war declarations following on August 1 against Russia, and on August 3 against France. Under Germany's Schlieffen Plan, timing speed was crucial. Also key to the

ABOVE LEFT In 1914, the poppy fields of Belgium were the scene of advanc-ing German infantry as they began occupation of the country.

LEFT Published in 1912, this *Punch* cartoon—titled "The Boiling Point"—por-trayed political leaders trying to control the Balkan troubles—depicted as a dangerously boiling cauldron.

TOP Despite the dreadful conditions in the trenches, French officers maintained their cultural love of fine dining.

LEFT Bulgarian troops attack Ottoman Empire's forces during the first Balkan War, in another example of the conflicts that were a precursor to World War I.

plan was the passage of German troops through Belgium into France. Belgium had warned Germany that they would not permit the maneuver and would consider the act of crossing their border an act of war. As the German army moved across Belgium on August 3, heading for France, Britain sent an ultimatum to Germany.

Britain was signatory to an old treaty declaring its commitment to the independence of Belgium, but this alone was not the reason for the decision to go to war. Other factors included a loose alliance—the Triple Entente with Russia and France—a long-standing colonial and naval rivalry with Germany, and a desire to satisfy public opinion—which increasingly favored war.

There was also the hope that a war would ease the social and political problems plaguing Britain at the time—suffragism, unions, and the Irish question. In the long term, of course, none of these problems were diminished in any way by the war. In the short term, they were eased as working-class men set aside the class war in favor of the Great War. Women turned their attention from the right to vote, and the question of Irish Home Rule was put aside, as Britain declared war on Germany on August 4, 1914.

The Western Front—"Impasse"

For 40 days the German attack on France appeared unstoppable. Overcoming a delay caused by British defense at Mons and Ypres, and Belgian defense at Liège, the three-pronged assault by the Kaiser's forces was finally halted by a desperate combined British and French defense at the River Marne that involved the commandeering of 600 French taxis to transport reserves. The Schleiffen Plan had almost succeeded in its aim of knocking the French out of the war in six weeks, but the failure of the German army to reach Paris and its ensuing entrenchment in northern France exposed a weakness in the German attack. Having failed in their original aim, the German forces were now far from Berlin and forced to sustain long communication and supply lines in order to support the Western Front.

The Western Front has had a powerful effect on the way in which The Great War has been remembered. The stagnation or immobility of the forces massed behind their lines, the horrifying spectre of No Man's Land, the visual impact of what artillery fire and mustard gas could do to the human body, and the sheer scale of the losses incurred, left powerful images and accounts.

Until the war ended in 1918, a war of attrition was waged along the lines that ran from Switzerland to the English Channel. During this time the lines barely moved, each "push" from French, German, or British forces resulting in massive loss of life, but little tactical advantage or territorial gain.

The scale of the slaughter was extraordinary. By the end of 1914, after only five months of fighting, the French had lost as many as 300,000 men.

In the major battles of the Western Front's history, tens of thousands were lost per hour, hundreds of thousands in single days of battles that sometimes lasted weeks. The British offensive at the Somme (1916) saw the 20,000 lives lost on the first day of fighting. After four months, the British had gained only 8 miles and lost over 95,675 men. German losses were even higher with 150,000 men lost during the same period. The seriously depleted French army lost a further 50,000. Support and morale waned, and recriminations against military hierarchies set in.

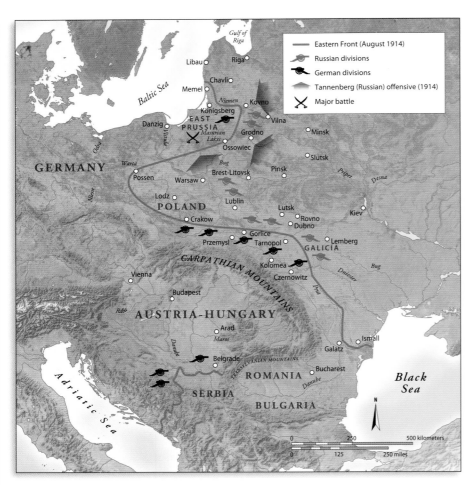

Map legend:
- Eastern Front (August 1914)
- Russian divisions
- German divisions
- Tannenberg (Russian) offensive (1914)
- Major battle

The Eastern Front

The Eastern Front was no less brutal than the Western Front, although it was certainly more mobile. The rapidity of the initial Russian advance into German and Austrian territory came as a shock, but the Germans recovered quickly with a victory at Masurian Lakes in Poland and, by May 1915, had broken the Russian line at Gorlice, capturing Warsaw and retaking the city of Lemberg, the Habsburg administrative capital in the Galician region.

Suffering under the pressure of the German momentum in 1915, the Russians appealed to the British to cause a distraction with an offensive elsewhere. To the south, the ill-fated Entente offensive at Gallipoli certainly preoccupied the Ottomans, but did little to slow the Germans. The Gallipoli campaign helped to convince Bulgaria that entry into the war on the side of the Central Powers was advisable and they joined Austria-Hungary in renewed attacks in Serbia throughout October–November

1915. The Serbs were unable to repel the offensive and over 300,000 troops began to retreat toward the Adriatic coast, facing rough terrain during inclement weather. Over 20,000 died in this mass exodus. In light of Serbia's defeat, and given the losses they themselves had experienced, by the end of 1915 Austria-Hungary was beginning to search for other powers who might be convinced of the benefits of peace. However, German successes in the east had whetted the nation's appetite for territorial conquest, with industrialists lobbying hard for a significant expansion of Germany's eastern holdings before the war was over.

German Advances

By the end of 1916, German submarines had sunk over one million tons of Entente shipping, including the British liner *Lusitania* in 1915, with over 1,000 deaths, among them 100 US citizens.

By 1917, Germany had declared unrestricted submarine warfare,

ABOVE The early days along the Eastern Front showed the stand-off between Russian and German divisions, prior to the German offensives.

ABOVE RIGHT On May 7, 1915, RMS *Lusitania*, a British liner, was hit by a torpedo from German U-boat *U-20*. The ship sank in just 18 minutes, and the tragedy showed that merchant shipping was no longer immune from attack.

RIGHT Australian and New Zealand Allied troops on board a transport ship headed for war. They landed on the Gallipoli Peninsula on April 25, 1915. The site was later named Anzac Cove, and April 25 is a national holiday in Australia and New Zealand to honor the memory of fallen soldiers.

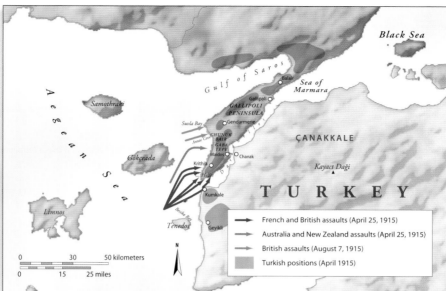

LEFT The battle for control of the Dardenelles took place between April 1915, and January 1916. Casualties on both sides totalled over 330,000.

Map legend:
→ French and British assaults (April 25, 1915)
→ Australia and New Zealand assaults (April 25, 1915)
→ British assaults (August 7, 1915)
▓ Turkish positions (April 1915)

0   30   50 kilometers
0   15   25 miles

BELOW The theaters of war on the Eastern Front extended from northern Russia to the Caucasus, and saw Russia engaged in battle with German and Austro-Hungarian forces.

and the German naval chief of staff promised the Kaiser that, thanks to their control of the Atlantic, not a single American soldier would set foot on the European continent. By July 1917, one million US troops had landed in Europe, due largely to the *Entente's* strategy of convoy shipping.

Russian Peace

The war was extremely unpopular in Russia, affecting the standing of the Tsar. The year 1917 meant revolution in Russia. The first step, although unseating the Tsar, did not affect the country's commitment to the war effort; but the second step, the Bolshevik Revolution, buoyed in part by resentment at the continuing hostilities, saw Russian seek peace with Germany. Negotiations between Russia and Germans began in December 1917,

and peace was finally settled in March 1918 with the Treaty of Brest-Litovsk.

Beginning of the End

The German confidence of 1917 could not withstand the American inclusion in Entente ranks, nor the increasing resistance to the war on the home front, with strikes and protests becoming regular features of Germany's domestic landscape by early 1918.

By 1918, when the Italians launched an offensive at Monte Grappe, the exhausted Austrians, who had been fighting a war of attrition against the Italians since 1915, were forced to retreat.

German successes against Russia and gains in the Treaty of 1918 could not conceal the cracks that were beginning to emerge in the Central Powers campaign. Major

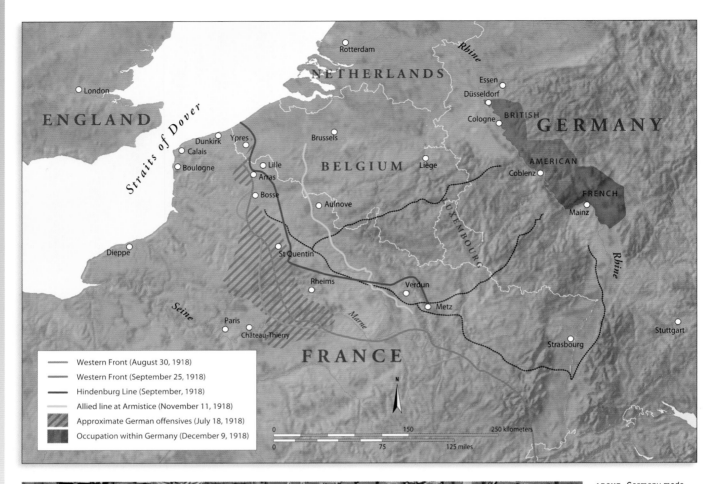

Western Front (August 30, 1918)
Western Front (September 25, 1918)
Hindenburg Line (September, 1918)
Allied line at Armistice (November 11, 1918)
Approximate German offensives (July 18, 1918)
Occupation within Germany (December 9, 1918)

ABOVE Germany made a last-ditch offensive late in the war along the Western Front. However, occupying forces were already stationed at railway heads ready to advance.

ABOVE RIGHT The Great War was the first conflict that saw the wide-scale use of poison gas as a weapon of war. Here, British casualties blinded by mustard gas in a German gas attack at Bethune, France, walk shoulder to shoulder to a medical post.

LEFT A massive outpouring of relief followed the signing of the Armistice on November 11, 1918. Crowds gathered in US cities to celebrate the end of the Great War.

German setbacks on the Western Front in June–July 1918 led to the later reminiscence by the then Chancellor, Count Georg von Hertling, that, "On the eighteenth [July] even the most optimistic amongst us knew that all was lost." By August, the Germans were fighting on merely in the hope of obtaining a better peace deal as their allies—first Bulgaria and then Austria-Hungary—sought to conclude their own war efforts in the best way possible. As the domestic political situation became increasingly unstable—with the threat of a socialist revolution growing daily—the need to conclude the hostilities was heightened. On November 10, Kaiser Wilhelm II abdicated, and at 5:30 a.m. on November 11 an armistice was signed with fighting to conclude at 11 a.m.—the need for symmetry costing several men their lives, such as Canadian George Price, killed by a German sniper two minutes before eleven.

1917 - 1918 Eastern Front

— Front line (January 1, 1917)
◄ Kerensky Offensive
✕ Russian victory—Kerensky Offensive (1–19, 1917)
◄ German counter offensive (July 19, 1917)
✕ German battle victories
— Front line at time of Armistice between Russia and Central Powers (December 1917)
▨ Area occupied by Central Powers after Treaty of Brest-Litovsk

0   250   500 kilometers
0 125 250 miles

The Cost

The war years spawned the first instance of genocide on the continent. World War I was the birthplace of tanks, unrestricted submarine warfare, and aerial bombing. It was the first time chemical weapons were used, and the devastation they caused resulted in the League of Nations banning their use in future wars. World War I cost each combatant a huge proportion of its young men and left a generation of brutalized, and often physically impaired, men who risked alienation as they tried to settle into post-war life. The war also ended with Germany's defeat and even more humiliating settlement at Versailles. It left a bitter taste in the mouths of those who had supported the war effort, who had suffered terrible losses, who resented the damage done to German prestige, and who held on to the achievements of World War I— as the great "might have been"— an ambition unrealized and des-tined to be resurrected under the leadership of a World War I veteran—Adolf Hitler.

ABOVE Nearing the end of The Great War, it is clear from this map that the German offensive was faltering despite some late advances.

RIGHT Returning soldiers were treated with honor marches in cities throughout Europe. Here, French troops march under the Arc de Triomphe in Paris in 1918.

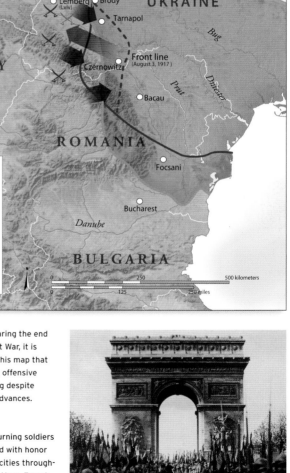

361

Russian Revolution

The year 1917 marked the end of three centuries of monarchical rule in Russia, and the founding of the world's first communist state—what would become the USSR.

The Russian Revolution was not in fact, one revolution, but many. Decades' worth of tension over authority, land ownership, and political accountability exploded in the hardships of war and hunger during the early twentieth century.

Peasant Unrest

The transition from monarchy to communism did not come peacefully or simply. In 1905, a first revolution took place amidst an expensive and unsuccessful war against the Japanese. Urban liberals demanded a government responsible to a *Duma* (parliament).

Food

World War I was meant to be over quickly. However, its length, futility, and brutality shocked everyone, not least the Russians. The drain on even the most basic of resources back home was just as significant as the lives lost at the front. In Petrograd in February 1917, workers were desperate. The city only had flour to last for around 10 days. The revolution that was to dethrone Tsar Nicholas II was thus begun by

women marching in the streets on the morning of February 23 (March 8 on the Western calendar) chanting "Bread! Bread! Bread!" Within 24 hours, over 200,000 workers had taken to the streets to express their frustration at living conditions, the ongoing war, and the seeming irresponsibility of the Tsarist regime.

Abdication

The soldiers of Petrograd had little incentive to suppress people who were just as disaffected by the war as they were. The officers in charge made little effort to enforce the will of a Tsar who had lost legitimacy with the people. Having lost the power of the military, Tsar Nicholas II's abdication came just days later, signaling the end of the 300-year-old monarchy.

The revolution of February and March 1917 was inconclusive, however. In place of the monarchy, liberal reformers sought to retain parliamentary democracy, but at the same time they were insistent on continuing the war against Germany. Meanwhile another power base had emerged in

> Revolutions are always verbose.
>
> –Leon Trotsky (1879-1940), Bolshevik revolutionary.

Petrograd. The Petrograd "Soviet" (Council) of Workers' Deputies had grown organically to become the center of political organization for workers, and commanded loyalty among soldiers. The period between March and November 1917 was thus known as the time of dual-government, or *dvoevlastie*.

Bolsheviks

Out of this state of near-anarchy arose a group of zealous Marxist intellectuals known as the Bolsheviks. They were the radical wing—opposed to the Mensheviks—of a movement called the Social Democrats, which in turn stood against the liberal reformism dominating the parliament.

Lenin

One of the most ardent leaders of the Bolsheviks, Vladimir Lenin,

1905 Bloody Sunday–Tsarist troops open fire on a peaceful demonstration in St Petersburg

October 1905 Russia experiences a general strike

1906 The new *Duma* is dissolved when it produces an anti-government majority

February 1917 After several days of protest in Petrograd, the government orders troops to open fire on demonstrators

June 3, 1917 The first All-Russia Congress of Workers and Soldiers Soviets opens

July 3 and 4, 1917 Workers and soldiers in Petrograd demand the Soviet takes power

October 1917 Bolsheviks overthrow Provisional government

ABOVE LEFT In May 1920, Lenin addresses Red Army troops leaving to fight against a Polish incursion.

RIGHT From 1918 to 1921, the Bolshevik Red Army fought a bitter civil war against the White Russian Army and its allies.

had been exiled from Russia, but took the opportunity afforded by the chaos of 1917 to return. Bolsheviks such as Lenin emphasized the role of an organized party "vanguard" that would interpret and represent the interests of the workers on their behalf, ushering in revolution. Though urban intellectuals themselves, leaders like Lenin and Leon Trotsky aimed to

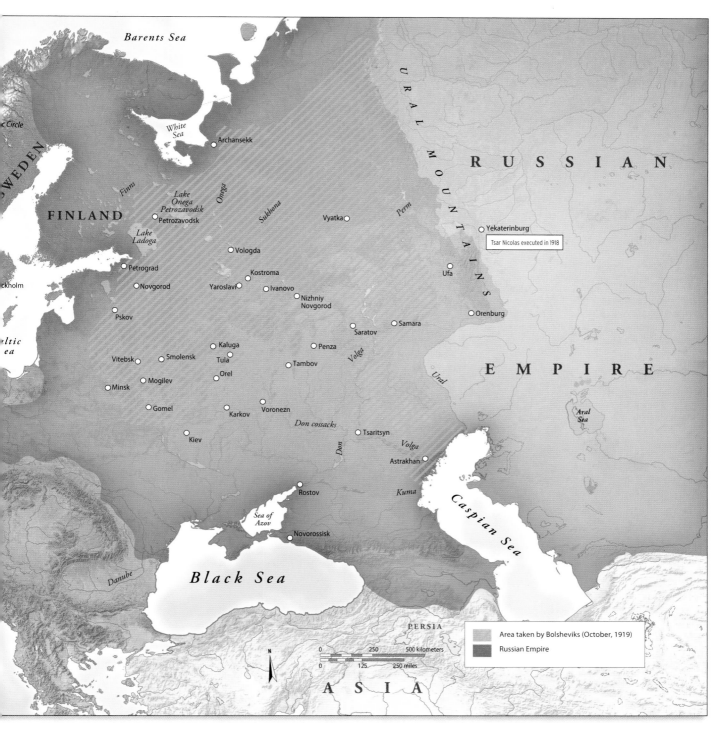

take leadership of the emerging workers' movement in Petrograd.

October Revolution

Having established political dominance in the Petrograd and Moscow Soviets, Lenin and Trotsky began to plan for another revolution. What became known as the October Revolution was surgically precise—communications centers, railway stations, and military posts were suddenly and simultaneously taken over on October 25, 1917 (November 7 on the Western calendar). Just after 9:30 pm revolutionaries stormed the Winter Palace, the home of the incumbent government, and set up the new "Soviet of People's Commissars," headed by Lenin. The new Bolshevik government quickly ended Russia's involvement in World War I; however, war did not end there.

Counter-revolutionary forces soon amassed a "White Army" and attempted to take power back from the Bolsheviks. The Bolsheviks, however, had skillfully consolidated their power through their *Cheka* police force and through control of information, and were centrally organizing the economy. They managed to conscript an army of over 5 million. This "Red Army" was massed against the White Army in a civil war lasting from 1918–21. France, Britain, and even the USA lent various amounts of military support to the White Army, but to no avail. The Reds emerged victorious and the new Union of Soviet Socialist Republics (USSR) was established in 1922.

Supply and Demand

Commonly called the Great Depression, the slow-down of the global economy during the early 1930s caused hardship and emotional catastrophe worldwide.

Economic development is not a linear process. A French dentist-turned-economist, Clement Juglar, first identified a regular nine- to eleven-year medium-term cycle caused by overproduction during prosperity that made a portion of the products unsaleable.

First Economists

Around the turn of the twentieth century, some British and Dutch economists recognized the existence of long-term cycles in the economy as well. The first economist to describe the phenomenon was the Russian Nikolai Kondratiev, who found 50- to 60-year-long cycles with about 25–30 years of upswing

BELOW A crowd of depositors outside the Union Bank in New York, June 30, 1931, after the bank failed to allow them to withdraw their savings.

and a similar downswing. Based on Kondratiev's idea, Joseph Schumpeter, the Austrian-born leading American economist of the twentieth century, gave a more exact explanation. He introduced the notion of "structural crisis," caused by "a whole set of technological changes," or industrial revolutions, that render the old leading sectors of the economy obsolete and declining, as new technologies pave the way for new leading sectors.

Global Catastrophe

The decades between the two world wars represent such a period of structural crisis, combined with a medium-term Juglar recession in the early years of the 1930s. This crisis between 1929 and 1933, which is usually referred to as the Great Depression, was the most serious economic crisis in modern economic history.

Black Thursday

The first sign of impending depression in the interwar economy appeared in the late 1920s when a major overproduction of grain—a 30–80 percent increase in output of basic agricultural commodities—led to dramatically declining prices. The combined average agricultural price level dropped by 30 percent, but grain prices fell by 60 percent. At the same time, credits and foreign investments dried up—in one year, from the middle of 1928,

> The Great Depression, like most other periods of severe unemployment, was produced by government mismanagement rather than by any inherent instability of the private economy.
>
> –Milton Friedman (1912-2006), American economist.

1924 The US stock market begins its spectacular rise while the rest of the economy languishes

1928 The average prices of US stocks rises 40 percent

1929 US stock market crash begins on October 24 ("Black Thursday") leading to "Black Tuesday" of October 29. Losses for the month total US$16 billion.

1930 US Federal Reserve cuts prime interest rate from 6 to 4 percent, GNP falls 9.4 percent. The US unemployment rate climbs from 3.2 to 8.7 percent. British unemployment rate reaches 20 percent.

1932-1933 Worst years of the Great Depression. US unemployment rises to 23.6 percent. Industrial stocks lose 80 percent of their value since 1930. Top tax rate is raised from 25 to 63 percent. Tariff of 10 percent introduced on all US imports except those from the British Empire.

1934 The US economy turns around—GNP rises 7.7 percent, and unemployment falls to 21.7 percent. Sweden is the first nation to recover fully, following a policy of Keynesian deficit spending.

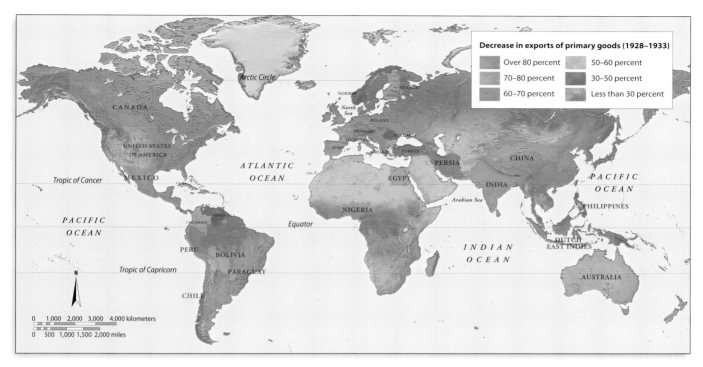

Decrease in exports of primary goods (1928–1933)

Over 80 percent | 50–60 percent
70–80 percent | 30–50 percent
60–70 percent | Less than 30 percent

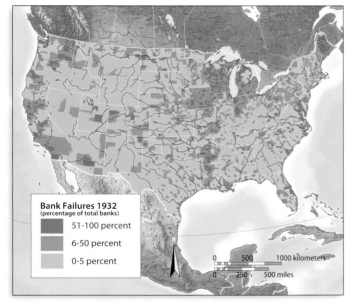

Bank Failures 1932
(percentage of total banks)

51-100 percent
6-50 percent
0-5 percent

ABOVE Depression led to massive drops in primary production worldwide, although it was overproduction in the early 1920s that precipitated the fall in global economies.

LEFT US bank failures increased through the years of the Great Depression, reaching their peak in 1932.

RIGHT US investors await the latest prices on New York's Wall Street, October 29, 1929—coined "Black Thursday." It was the day of the biggest fall in stock market history to that time.

American capital inflow to Europe declined by half, and in 1931 it stopped entirely. The collapse of the American Stock Exchange in late 1929—known as "Black Thursday"—marked a turning point. Between 1929 and 1933 the world's industrial output declined by 30 percent, and coal and iron production fell by 40–60 percent.

Economic Panic

Heavily indebted countries became unable to repay principal or interest. In July 1931, one of the leading German banks fell into bankruptcy and in two days the government ordered closure of all banks. The banking system, the powerhouse of the German economy since the mid-nineteenth century, collapsed. It was soon followed by the Central European banking giant, Viennese Creditanstalt, and the financial crisis spread like wildfire.

In 1931, Britain abandoned the gold standard and the British pound stopped serving as the world currency. Most national currencies became non-convertible.

Global Disintegration

The laissez-faire system (also called the "first globalization" during the half-century before World War I) disintegrated. Governments tried desperately to save farms and companies with subsidies and job-creating programs such as President Roosevelt's New Deal.

In 1936, John Maynard Keynes published his *General Theory of Employment, Interest, and Money,* explaining that supply and demand are not balanced in the market, and that economic growth might

be generated by additional employment to create additional demand. The traditional view that each supply creates corresponding demand—Say's Law—was no longer valid. In some of the crisis-ridden countries, populist, right-wing, fascist movements emerged and in several countries assumed control. The Great Depression polarized the world and stimulated war preparation throughout Europe. The world, as a consequence, shifted toward a new world war.

Jewel in the Crown

India is one of the youngest states formed from one of the oldest civilizations in world history. So how did the "jewel in Britain's crown" emerge to be one of the world's largest and most powerful independent nations?

1947 India gains independence

1948 Gandhi is assassinated

1949 The Indian Constitution is enacted

1950 India becomes a Republic

1952 The first general elections are held

The emergence of an independent India and Pakistan in 1947 came directly out of, and in response to, 90 years of British direct rule. The British East India Company was dissolved by the British in 1858, following the so-called "Indian Mutiny" or "Sepoy Rebellion" (*sepoy* means soldier), and British India thus passed directly into the hands of the British Crown.

Buying Loyalty

Having learnt some painful lessons about loyalty among the military and rulers, the Crown offered to preserve the 560 or so existing princedoms within India in exchange for loyalty to Queen Victoria as sovereign. To cement the process, land was taken from

those tried as rebels and distributed among the faithful ruling classes. The military was kept on side through a complex quasi-scientific system of caste classification that distinguished between "martial castes" and non-martial castes.

Indian Civil Service

Direct rule brought about a complex new structure of government and administration. A Secretary of State with an executive council based in Whitehall took administrative responsibility for British India, while a viceroy represented the Crown in the capital city of Calcutta, theoretically implementing Whitehall's policy. Three levels of government were organized within India—the viceroy and his

> [Gandhi] dresses like a coolie, forswears all personal advancement, lives practically on the air, and is a pure visionary. He does not understand details of schemes.
>
> –Secretary of State Edwin Samuel Montagu on Mahatma Gandhi, c. 1916.

executive council and legislative council, then provincial governors, and below them, district officials. This elaborate system was made to run by the Indian Civil Service. Indians were theoretically able to join their civil service, but had to travel to England to sit entrance examinations in order to do so.

RIGHT Supplying the textile mills of Northern England, raw cotton was a major export for British India. Export was limited to raw cotton only, due to stringent British trade conditions. After independence, India became a major competitor to British-produced textiles.

Industrialization

India was used to supply Britain with cotton and tea, while garments made in Lancashire mills were sold back to Indians with the aid of trade protections. When the opening of the Suez Canal in 1869 made the Britain–India trip only three weeks, Indian production was folded even more into the back-and-forth of British trade.

Education

Aside from industrial infrastructure, the British developed an educational and political infrastructure, which would be used against them to gain independence. In the cities, an emerging group of middle-class intellectuals began to articulate their ideas about the future of

India. These early nationalists had received British education and legal training—the British had created universities in Bombay, Calcutta, and Madras—and had influence in the emerging newspapers of the Indian provinces. They formed several political organizations to give expression to the various stripes of Indian nationalism. The Indian National Congress (INC), which had been founded in 1885, sought to reform British rule through means of constitutional change.

Nationalist Movement

The twentieth century saw the nationalist movement begin to radicalize, however. The most significant trigger occurred in 1905, when the British decided to partition the northeastern province of Bengal (including today's Bangladesh) creating a barrier between the Hindu-dominated Calcutta in the west of the province, and the Muslim-dominated east.

Frustrations erupted at what was perceived as another British attempt to "divide and conquer," and Indians across the subcontinent began to resort to a new weapon—economic boycott. All over the country the cry of *Swadeshi* was heard, meaning "of our own," or "buy Indian made." The production of Indian textiles began to challenge the dominance of British textiles, thus stimulating Indian industry; these textiles became symbols of revolution. By 1908, British imports to India had been cut by 25 percent.

LEFT Demand for tea in England initially provided the East India Company with a lucrative trade in this commodity. Their exclusive claim to this market came to an end with the relaxing of trade regulations and the establishment of local companies.

FAR LEFT During the 90-year period of British rule in India—known as the Raj—the English kept up their usual social activities.

RIGHT The Partition of India in 1947–creating the Union of India and East Pakistan, and granting independence to Burma and Ceylon in the following year.

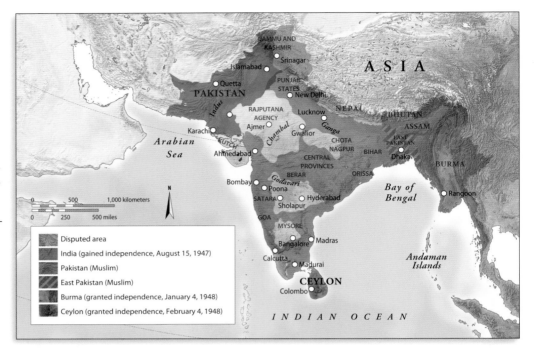

Map legend:
- Disputed area
- India (gained independence, August 15, 1947)
- Pakistan (Muslim)
- East Pakistan (Muslim)
- Burma (granted independence, January 4, 1948)
- Ceylon (granted independence, February 4, 1948)

Political Repression

The Great War of 1914–18 left Indians even more disillusioned with the British than they already were. They contributed more than 750,000 troops to the Allied cause, 36,000 of whom were lost in costly operations. While they were promised due reward for assisting the English in their battle for civilization against German "barbaric militarism," at home Indians were in fact subject to severe political repression, including mass arrests for unspecified reasons, banning of newspapers, and mass violence. The slaughter of some 400 protestors in Punjab in 1919 was emblematic of the problem.

Gandhi

In 1915, in this milieu of wartime turmoil, Mohandas K. Gandhi, otherwise known as Mahatma ("good soul") Gandhi, re-entered the country. Born in Gujarat in the northwest of India, Ghandi had trained in law in London and practiced law for the Indian population of Durban, in South Africa. Gandhi was deeply affected by his experience of segregation in South Africa, and it was there that he first experimented with *Satyagraha*— "holding fast to the truth," or civil disobedience—as a form of political action. Soon after his return, Gandhi became a leader in the Indian National Congress.

Salt March

Since before World War I, the Indian nationalist movement had been calling for *Svaraj* (self-rule) as their goal. While this was a shared aim, ideas about how to attain it differed. Gandhi became a national and global icon for turning his methods of *Satyagraha* and *Ahimsa* (non-violence) into a national strategy, mobilizing millions of Indians in civil disobedience campaigns. The first wave of these was in 1920–1922, in which Indians once again resorted to boycotting British goods and institutions. After spending the mid-1920s in prison, Gandhi emerged to lead another wave of protest in 1930, famously marching against the British-imposed salt tax. To protest the tax, which hit the very poorest of Indians in order to finance the British administration, Gandhi walked 240 miles (390 km) to the coast to be the first person to illegally take salt from the sea.

India Act

The British government began to show signs of listening, and held a series of round table discussions in London, to which Gandhi and other leaders were invited. While no real agreements were reached, the British eventually passed the *Government of India Act* in 1935, which provided a constitutional basis for elections and the autonomous rule of the provinces.

Quit India Campaign

When Britain went to war again in 1939, India was dragged reluctantly along as well. Insisting that without unity there would be no independence, in 1942, in protest, Gandhi mobilized Indians into a "Quit India" campaign. Black flags and angry slogans plastered the cities telling the British to leave.

Meanwhile, Gandhi's insistence on unity met with opposition from Muslim Indians. The Muslim League, under the articulate leadership of Muhammad Ali Jinnah, feared a potential loss of power if a Hindu-dominated Indian state emerged. They lobbied the British for a separate independent Muslim Indian state in the northwest of India, taking in part of the northern Punjab province. The name "Pakistan" was proposed, meaning "Land of the Pure." (It had been coined by Muslim Indian students in 1930 in Cambridge.)

The British were reluctant to partition India, as were Gandhi and the Congress. Yet in 1946, following many years of painful diplomatic effort, the goal of one India was deemed unfeasible by the British, and the partition of India and Pakistan was finally agreed, to come into effect on August 15, 1947.

LEFT Mahatma Gandhi led the 1930 Salt March from Ashram Ahmedabad to the Arabian Sea.

RIGHT Mourners climb a telegraph pole to witness Gandhi's funeral procession in February 1948. Gandhi was assassinated by Nathuram Godse, a fanatical Hindu.

Path to Dictatorship

On January 30, 1933, President Hindenburg offered the Chancellorship of Germany to Adolf Hitler. Hitler's ascent to the position of Chancellor, however, had less to do with his or the Nazis' popularity than with a miscalculation on the part of those political elites who engineered his success.

Despite a decline in the popularity of Hitler's party, the NSDAP (*Nationalsozialistische Deutsche Arbeiter Partei*/The National Socialist German Workers' Party), at the 1932 elections, Hitler remained leader of the biggest party in the Reichstag. The proposal of a right-wing coalition was predicated on the understanding that traditional conservatives—such as Hindenburg and an ex-Chancellor, Franz von Papen (1932)—could manipulate Hitler, using him and his supporters to defeat the communist menace and unite a nation suffering the effects of the Great Depression and political upheaval.

Popular Vote

Less than a month after Hitler's appointment, an arsonist set fire to the Reichstag in Berlin. Declared a communist plot by Hitler and his followers, the effect of this event was revealed in elections conducted a week later when the Nazis managed to secure 44 percent of the popular vote. By March 9, political opponents were being taken to a new concentration camp near the Bavarian town of Dachau.

1919 Hitler is given the job of lecturing returning German prisoners of war on the dangers of communism and pacifism. He joins the German Workers' Party.

1923 Hitler and his storm troopers attempt to kidnap the leaders of the Bavarian government at a beer hall. He is accused of treason and sentenced to five years' jail with parole in six months.

1925 After release from jail in 1924, Hitler again begins to threaten the government in his speeches and is banned from public speaking for two years

1929 Hitler meets his lifelong mistress, Eva Braun

1932 Adolf Hitler is granted German citizenship

LEFT In August 1927, nationalist leaders met with Adolf Hitler at Nuremberg. The government had lifted its ban on the Nazi Party in May.

> By the skillful and sustained use of propaganda, one can make a people see even heaven as hell or an extremely wretched life as paradise.
> –Adolf Hitler (1889–1945), Austrian-born German dictator and politician.

RIGHT Hitler salutes members of the Nazi Party at a rally in Nuremberg in 1927. The annual Nuremberg Rallies were exercises in propaganda and intimidation.

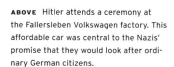

German territory (1938)

Sudetenland (1938)

Rhineland demilitarized zone (1938)

Austria (1938)

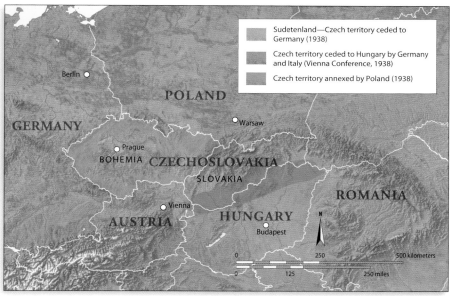

Sudetenland—Czech territory ceded to Germany (1938)

Czech territory ceded to Hungary by Germany and Italy (Vienna Conference, 1938)

Czech territory annexed by Poland (1938)

ABOVE Hitler attends a ceremony at the Fallersleben Volkswagen factory. This affordable car was central to the Nazis' promise that they would look after ordinary German citizens.

Enabling Act

The path to dictatorship was being swiftly laid, and on March 23, 1933, when the Reichstag passed the *Enabling Act*—giving the Chancellor the ability to pass laws without parliamentary approval for a period of four years—it was all but complete. The collaborative vision of von Papen and Hindenburg had, within three months, been extinguished and replaced by the singular vision of a dictator.

Adolf Hitler

Born April 20, 1889, in the Austrian town of Braunau, Hitler was the son of a bureaucrat. A restless youth who was prone to fantasy, he spent an unhappy period during early adulthood in Vienna attempting to realize his artistic ambitions.

When World War I broke out, Hitler was in Munich. He fought for Germany and was awarded both a 1st and 2nd class Iron Cross.

After the war, Hitler joined and, by 1921, was leader of the NSDAP, a party that relied heavily on his skills as an orator. In 1923, the failed Beer Hall Putsch in Munich saw Hitler jailed for treason; however, his imprisonment lasted less than a year and he used the time to pen his infamous quasi-autobiographical *Mein Kampf.*

Hitler's Regime

Once established, Hitler's regime extended its power rapidly through a combination of popularity and fear. On June 30, 1934, the Night of the Long Knives helped purge the party of its old "muscle"— the SA Brownshirts—in favor of the new face of the regime, the SS Blackshirts and the *Gestapo.* Oppression of political opponents, homosexuals, and Jews, among others, continued in the 1930s. The Nuremberg Laws (1935) institutionalized Nazi anti-Semitism,

and *Kristallnacht* (1938)—night of broken glass—indicated the vulnerable position of Germany's Jews.

Violent episodes helped to diminish opposition to the regime. And projects such as the German Autobahns (1933–34) and the people's car, the Volkswagen (1938), events such as the Berlin Olympics (1936), and the annual Nuremberg Rallies, programs such as workers' holidays, and Nazi associations, helped to place Nazism and the *Führer* at the center of everyday life.

By 1938, Hitler's territorial aims were becoming evident, with the annexation of Austria to the German Reich, followed by annexation of the Sudetenland. On August 31, Hitler issued Directive No. 1 for the attack on Poland. On September 1, 1939, German forces crossed the border. War in the east would also provide impetus to the "Final Solution" of Hitler's other most consistent theme—the "Jewish problem."

TOP Part of Germany for most of its history, the Sudetenland became part of Czechoslovakia after World War I, despite the opposition of its citizens.

ABOVE The Munich Agreement allowed Hitler to take Sudetenland, and Hungary and Poland to take border districts from Czechoslovakia.

World at War

Encompassing nearly every country in the world, World War II was a war of technology and brute force. Lasting six years, it would involve around 100 million personnel, and led to the death of over 60 million people.

Drôle de Guerre

By the time the Nazi German army marched into Poland on September 1, 1939, Adolf Hitler's regime had already annexed all of Austria and the Sudetenland (1938), created the "protectorate" of Bohemia and Moravia (March 1939), and captured Lithuanian Memel (March 1939).

In spite of a British and French guarantee of Polish safety, which had been signed in March 1939, promising action within 15 days of invasion, there was little attempt by either country to alleviate the suffering of the besieged nation. Indeed, a French politician of the time described the war during this period (between the September 1939 invasion of Poland and the May 1940 invasion of France) as a "phony war"—a *drôle de guerre* —because, in spite of declarations of war against Germany, neither the British nor French had truly become engaged in the conflict.

LEFT At the outbreak of World War II, British schoolchildren were evacuated to the country for safety—just one example of the many changes war brought to civilian life.

Fall of France

By May of 1940, the Third Reich had begun to turn its attention to the Low Countries. It took only 18 days for Germany to secure the surrender of Belgium on May 28, by which time German forces had already crossed the French border —May 14. The fall of France took less than five weeks, the Wehrmacht employing their Panzer division to full effect in a Blitzkrieg—lightning war—that saw Paris fall on June 16. When France fell, the French World War I hero, Marshal Pétain, negotiated the capitulation that saw him become leader of a government that was put in charge of approximately one-third of France, located in the south of the country and centered on the city of Vichy. The remainder of France fell under the direct control of the Nazis. Vichy France was to last two years before Hitler took command of its occupation.

Dunkirk

British losses at Dunkirk were huge, as the British Expeditionary Force, having desperately tried to halt the German advance, made their escape across the English Channel—the rescue effort was awesome in scale.

September 3, 1939
Neville Chamberlain announces that Britain is at war with Germany. This is followed by declarations of war from Australia, India, and New Zealand.

May 10, 1940
Winston Churchill is called on to form a wartime coalition government

August 24, 1940
Germany bombs London. Churchill orders the bombing of Berlin in retaliation.

May 4, 1942
The Battle of the Coral Sea begins, the first battle where enemy ships never sight each other

February 3, 1945
Berlin is heavily bombed by the Allies

September 2, 1945
Japan signs the articles of surrender on board the USS *Missouri*

RIGHT A flotilla of small vessels was needed to help evacuate the British Expeditionary Force and French troops from France at Dunkirk. Churchill called it Britain's "darkest hour."

FAR LEFT German troops crossed into France on May 14, 1940, and in just over a month Paris had fallen to the Nazis.

LEFT Warsaw, Poland, was the scene of some of the most awful destruction of World War II, beginning with the German invasion in 1939. In 1944, the people of the city rose up against the Nazis, but the uprising was cruelly put down.

The British experience of being driven out of France was described by Britain's new Prime Minister, Winston Churchill, as the nation's "darkest hour." But it was very soon to be joined by the "spirit of the Blitz," as Britain began to weather the German bombing campaign, and "Britain's finest hour," during the Battle of Britain, in what was to become the desperate defense of Europe's last democracy.

By April 1941, the German army had moved into the Balkan region in order to staunch the flow of failures by Germany's Axis ally Italy. Signs of a split in the Nazi-Soviet alliance then began to show, as Joseph Stalin signed a "Friendship Treaty" with Yugoslavia on April 5, the day before the Nazis began bombing Belgrade. Yugoslavia fell to the Nazis after 11 days of relentless German attack.

By the end of May, the Nazis had control of Greece, while the Balkans region appeared to be under Axis control. It was time to recommence the *Drang nach Osten*—drive into the east—that had begun with the annexation of the Sudetenland and the invasion of Poland. But Hitler's aim this time was monumental, as outlined in his Instruction 21, issued on December 18, 1940—the invasion of the Soviet Union.

> We must be very careful not to assign to this deliverance the attributes of a victory. Wars are not won by evacuations.
>
> –Winston Churchill (1874-1965), British Prime Minister, to Parliament, June 4, 1940, the day after Dunkirk

Operation Barbarossa

On June 22, 1941, the Germans, along with representatives from their allies—the Italians, Hungarians and Romanians—commenced Operation Barbarossa, the invasion of the Soviet Union. The hostilities involved 156 German division and over 3 million men. It was the start of a campaign that would last years and account for 75 percent of all German World War II casualties. The bold invasion of the USSR contained within it the core Nazi theme of *lebensraum*, and the brutality with which the Germans attempted to capture their "living space" is evidenced by their treatment of POWs and local populations, a brutality that had been outlined in their *Generalplan Ost*. This plan dictated that local populations would have no freedom, that they would be used as slave labor, or allowed to starve to death. POWs would be killed or allowed to starve—by February 1942, of the 3.9 million soldiers captured by the Germans, 2.8 million were dead. Leningrad (St Petersburg) and Moscow would be completely destroyed. Ethnic Germans would be brought in to populate and control occupied territories.

The German invasion had also shifted the continental alliances significantly, with the USSR joining the Allies as a logical consequence of the Axis offensive.

For the Nazis, success needed to be immediate and enduring as there was no plan for replacement men or equipment should they fail. And, certainly, in the opening two weeks of the invasion it appeared as though the plan would work. However, by late July the campaign was starting to falter due to the vast reality of the Russian reserves and their determination. A pause ensued as the Germans, throughout August, resupplied, and on September 5, the Red Army experienced its first victory at Yelnya.

By the end of 1941, the Nazis' invading forces were faced with the

Operation Barbarossa June–October, 1941

———	German front line (June 22–August 31, 1941)
———	German front line (October, 1941)
➤	German advance lines
⚔	Russian troop concentrations
➤	Russian counter attacks

frigid reality of the Russian winter, leading to a call for German civilians to donate warm clothing to the soldiers stationed on the eastern front. This request was the first blow to German confidence.

Nevertheless, the war continued to rage in the USSR. German troops laid siege to the city of Leningrad in the north from September 1941 to January 1944. Renewed attacks from the center in late 1941 saw the Wehrmacht reach to within 50 miles (80 km) of Moscow, and the capital was evacuated. Meanwhile, in the south, the Germans enjoyed some success before the Soviets managed to establish a front at the city of Stalingrad—in July 1942.

Stalingrad

By September 1942, Stalingrad was under siege from all directions, the Germans capturing most of the city and starting a slow house-by-house

advance that set up a landscape full of snipers and traps. But Russia had retained its vast capacity for putting more and more men into battle, as well as its industrial output, while the Germans were suffering from the length of their supply and communication lines.

By November 1942, the Germans fighting within the city were certain that an attempted breakout was the best plan, but Hitler insisted they hold until reinforcements arrived. But a new Soviet offensive from November 25 destroyed the Germans' ability to hold the city and, by February 2, 1943, the commanding officer in Stalingrad, General von Paulus, was forced to sign a surrender. Stalingrad had cost over one million lives—the biggest single battle loss in world history. The effect of the German defeat was monumental. To the Allies, it felt like the tide had turned.

ABOVE Operation Barbarossa was the name the Germans gave to their plan to invade Russia. It was a close-run thing, and in the end the Germans were driven back, but not before millions died.

North Africa

The German campaign in North Africa was also stretched to full capacity under the leadership of Erwin Rommel. Rommel captured Tobruk on June 21, 1942, and enjoyed success at the 1st Battle of El Alamein, near Cairo, from July 1 to July 27, 1942. However, shortly after the Battle of Stalingrad had reached its height, the 2nd Battle of El Alamein, from October 23 to November 5, 1942, signaled a crushing blow to Germany's North African campaign. A few months later, German and Italian troops surrendered in North Africa, and the sense of German invincibility began to fade rapidly.

ABOVE Allied forces battled the German army across North Africa. Both sides had their share of successes and failures, but in the end the Allies triumphed.

RIGHT The Nazi machine devised one of the most horrible plans in the history of warfare—the "Final Solution"—the extermination of Jews and other minorities.

Genocide

On July 31, 1941, the Head of Reich Security Main Office (RSHA) had obtained permission to organise a "solution" to the problem of Jews in Nazi-controlled Europe. The plan —the "Final Solution of the Jewish Question" or *Endlösung*—put aside all delays such as the relocation and placing in ghettoes of Jewish populations that had previously been enacted, and instead outlined the goal of extermination, in what has come to be known as the Holocaust, or *Shoah*.

In January 1942, a conference was held at Wannsee that authorized the plan and set in motion its

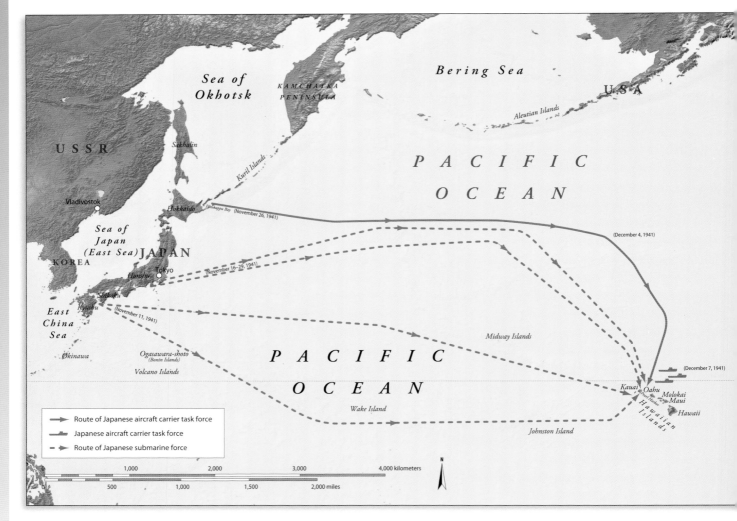

Route of Japanese aircraft carrier task force

Japanese aircraft carrier task force

Route of Japanese submarine force

ABOVE Japan's audacious long-range attack on the US fleet at Pearl Harbor, Hawaii, was the opening shot in the Pacific theater of World War II.

RIGHT Japan's grand plan was to establish a "Greater East Asia Co-Prosperity Sphere." Within months of joining the war, Japanese forces had overrun much of Southeast Asia.

LEFT The USS *Arizona* was left a smoking, sunken wreck by the surprise attack on Pearl Harbor. Many other ships were hit too, but most were soon repaired and back in action.

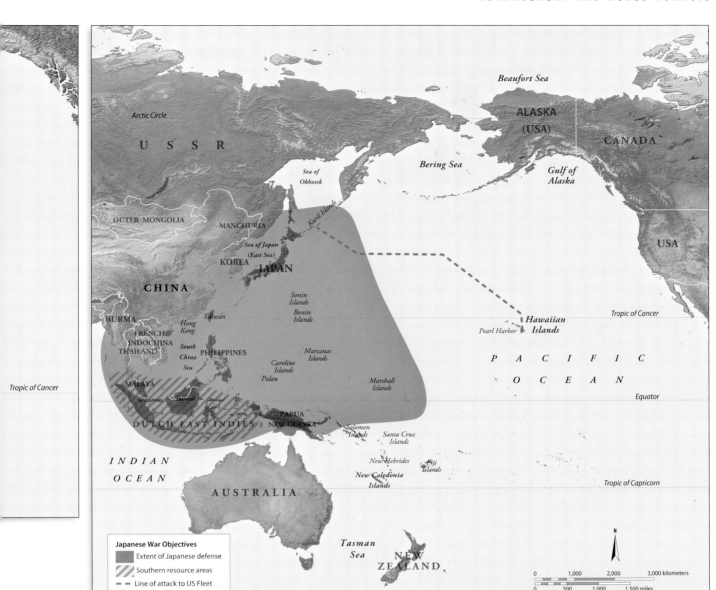

Japanese War Objectives
- Extent of Japanese defense
- Southern resource areas
- Line of attack to US Fleet

organization. Death camps were to be constructed at Chelmno, Belzec, Sobibór, Treblinka, and at Auschwitz-Birkenau. Train timetables were to be rearranged according to the needs of the final solution, and personnel were to be trained— diverted, if necessary, from other, military, tasks.

Around 11 million people were put to death through a combination of mobile killing units (*Einsatzgruppen*), deliberate policies of starvation and other deprivations in the ghettoes and concentration camps, and the gruesome death camps with their capacity to gas thousands of people on a daily basis. Of all those killed, approximately 6 million were European Jews.

By December of 1942, the Allies were fully aware of the atrocities being carried out, with British Foreign Secretary Anthony Eden informing the House of Commons about the mass execution of Jews. Help, however, was not forthcoming, the British and Americans preferring to talk about vengeance for these crimes to be pursued after the war, rather than propose that any action be taken during it.

Pearl Harbor
On December 7, 1941, one of the key changes in the progress of the war occurred when the Japanese bombed the American naval fleet at Pearl Harbor. In spite of clear support for the British war effort

from US President Franklin D. Roosevelt, there had been, prior to the Japanese attack, no desire on the part of Congress to become embroiled in any war—let alone another European war. The Japanese attack was quickly followed on December 8 by US and British declarations of war on Japan. Hitler made the surprising move of formally declaring war on the United States on December 11, and was joined in this move by Italy's leader, Mussolini. War in Asia and the Pacific had begun, and with it US involvement in Europe.

The Japanese imperial forces moved swiftly through East and Southeast Asia, capturing Hong Kong, Malaya, Burma, and then

Singapore from the British, the Dutch East Indies, Indochina from the French, and the Philippines. They were less successful in capturing and then defending the Pacific islands, suffering heavy losses at the Battle of the Coral Sea in May 1942, and a comprehensive defeat at the Battle of Midway that June. Following this, the Allies—which in the Pacific involved forces from the USA, Australia, New Zealand, and Britain—began to fight by land, by sea, and by air in order to hold their positions and bring the war closer and closer to Japan. By early 1944, their combined forces were within easy striking distance, and they commenced a bombing campaign in June of that year.

377

V-E Day

On July 9 and 10, 1943, the Allies landed in Sicily. The fall of Mussolini opened the way for Italian negotiations with the Allies and, on September 8, Italy surrendered. As a consequence the Germans moved in, occupying Rome on September 11, 1943. On October 13, Italy declared war on Germany, and the Italians fought alongside the Allied forces until they took Rome on June 5, 1944.

The day after the Germans lost Rome, the D-Day landings began in Normandy. A huge force of over 150,000 men—British, Canadian, and American troops, alongside Poles, Free French, and others—landed on the beaches of Normandy on June 6, 1944. With support from heavy aerial bombings, the men managed to get a firm foothold in France by August 21, after four years of Nazi occupation.

Warsaw

On August 1, 1944, the Polish Home Army, buoyed by the Allied victories in the west, and believing they had the support of the Soviets, started the Warsaw uprising. But after two months of fighting in and around the Polish capital —and with no Red Army support forthcoming—the uprising was defeated on October 2, 1944. Adolf Hitler, ever vindictive, issued an order for Warsaw to be leveled.

Paris

During the intervening period, Paris had been liberated. This was on August 25, 1944. Over the following weeks, approximately 11,000 collaborators were killed by their fellow French citizens. The leading Vichy figures were arrested and condemned to death, although the new French leader, Charles de Gaulle, commuted Marshal Pétain's sentence to life imprisonment.

Battle of the Bulge

On December 16, 1944, Germany commenced a ground offensive at Ardennes on the Belgian–German border. What would later become known as the Battle of the Bulge had begun. Over one million troops—Germans, British, and Americans —fought at Ardennes. For the US, Ardennes was to be the site of their greatest military losses in Europe—81,000 casualties.

On January 17, 1945, the USSR's Red Army captured Warsaw and,

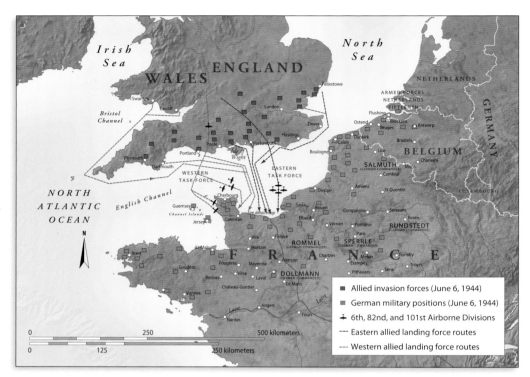

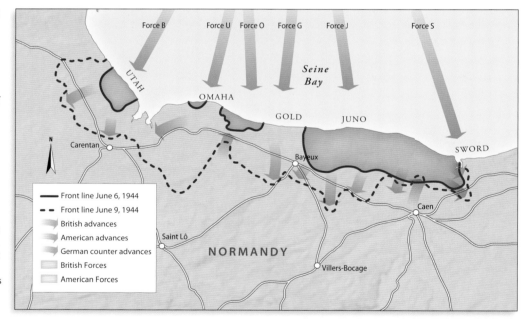

by January 26, had liberated those few survivors remaining at Auschwitz. British and American bombers then began a vast and merciless air attack on German cities, killing tens of thousands of civilians in the firestorms that followed the saturation bombing.

The death of US President Franklin D. Roosevelt on April 12, 1945, was a blow to the Allies, but by April 21 the Soviets had reached Berlin. Further south, Mussolini

was fleeing his Republic, but was captured by partisans and, along with his mistress, killed on April 28. Europe's first fascist dictator was dead. Two days later he was joined by the second, as Adolf Hitler and his wife, Eva Braun, committed suicide in their bunker in Berlin.

German capitulation followed quickly after Hitler's death, with unconditional surrender achieved on May 7 and May 8—known as V-E Day: Victory in Europe.

TOP The Allied D-Day assault in June 1944 was preceded by a vast deception plan to keep the Nazis in the dark about where the invasions would come. This clever ploy meant that the German command were not prepared for the combined air and land assault.

ABOVE The D-Day landings in Normandy formed the single largest military operation in history, as hundreds of thousands of Allied troops opened the second front in the European theater of the war.

Hiroshima and Nagasaki

Meanwhile Japan had been on the receiving end of episodes of Allied bombing similar to those conducted against Germany. In March 1945, the Americans had commenced mass aerial bombings of key cities. Over 125,000 people were killed in the capital city of Tokyo alone, as firestorms swept through the city after each bombing raid.

The Americans, now under the leadership of President Harry S. Truman, believed that, although they would win the Pacific war in time, the most important thing was to avoid tactics, such as a massive land invasion of the Japanese home islands, that could easily cost large numbers of American lives.

Thus, at the highest levels of the US government and military, the decision was taken to employ the most radical development ever in military technology—the atom bomb. On August 6, the first bomb was dropped on Hiroshima. Then, on August 9, a second bomb was dropped on the city of Nagasaki. Over 100,000 people were killed immediately in both cities. The cities were utterly destroyed and fallout from the bombs—which produced awful radiation sickness —would continue to kill for years. The effect of the tactics, though, was immediate and comprehensive—the Japanese agreed to an unconditional surrender on August 14 and, on September 2, the Allies celebrated V-J—Victory over Japan— Day. World War II was over.

ABOVE LEFT Winston Churchill, Franklin D. Roosevelt, and Joseph Stalin met at Yalta, in the Crimea, in February 1945. The conference was held to discuss the make-up of post-War Europe.

ABOVE American and Russian troops greeted each other joyously as their forces met up in Germany.

LEFT The controversial Allied bombing raids on the historic German city of Dresden, a non-military target, left it in smoking ruins.

The Long March to Revolution

Within 100 years, China has risen from "semi-colony" to superpower. But who decided what kind of China would enter the world stage? How did the fall of dynastic rule in 1911 result in the founding of a communist state in 1949?

1928 Chiang Kai-shek defeats the northern warlords and takes Beijing

—

1934 Mao Tse-tung leads the Long March of the communist Red Army into the north

—

1946 Civil war rages between Chiang and Mao, with Chiang helped by the USA and Mao helped by the Soviet Union

—

1949 Mao Tse-tung proclaims the People's Republic of China. Zhou En-lai is appointed premier of Communist China, while Mao retains the chairmanship of the Communist Party.

BELOW Some of the 8,000 survivors of the Long March made by Mao Tse-tung and his followers from southern to northern China.

In February 1912, military general Yuan Shikai became President of the new Republic of China, having been instrumental in bringing the Qing dynasty to an end. Yet the Republic was perhaps doomed right from the start. While the rhetoric of the first president, Dr Sun Yuxian, and his revolutionary Tongmenhui party, had been about constitutional government and land equalization, these ideas had not been translated into practice during the revolution.

Chaos

Constitutional rule would have meant submitting the power of the presidency and military to the rule of law. For Yuan, who was both the president and military chief, this was not at all desirable. In fact, the opposite was the case. Yuan tried to reinstate himself as emperor in 1915, and restore dynastic rule. It was under Yuan that the governance of China rapidly devolved into a tumultuous period marked by the rise of warlords.

Cultural Movement

Ideas about democratic revolution had not gone away completely, however. The New Cultural movement of the early 1900s saw many intellectuals calling for a radical overhaul of Chinese politics, education, and culture.

A moral and intellectual watershed moment had emerged during May 1919. The "May 4" movement protested the seeming betrayal of the Chinese people by the western powers in the Treaty of Versailles. They had fully expected an end to all foreign intervention in China under the new League of Nations. But in the diplomatic wheeling and dealing of Versailles, the Japanese were handed the German "sphere of influence" in Manchuria.

ABOVE Propaganda played a huge role in the rise of the Communist Party in China. This poster from 1950 shows crowds rejoicing on the People's Republic National Day.

New Politics

Out of the near anarchy of the Chinese political system, and from the hotbed of revolutionary sentiment in the cities, there emerged two strong parties devoted to the nationalist democratic revolution in China—the Chinese Communist Party (CCP), and the Guomindang (or Nationalist Party or KMT, after Kuomintang).

The Soviets (after the Russian revolutions of 1917–1922) were interested in strengthening the Chinese Communist Party and the Guomindang in their revolutionary cause. In fact, they encouraged the two sides to work together in a "United Front." The United Front set about the task of fomenting revolution and uniting China. Tragedy struck, however, and Sun Yixian, suffering from stomach cancer, died in 1925 while he was in Beijing. The leadership thus passed to the dynamic young military general, Chiang Kai-Shek.

In 1926, Chiang's military started a "Northern Expedition" to try to unite China under a Guomindang government. They were successful. Within a year, Chiang held the entire south, and then sought to shift his government to Nanjing.

> China should bury head to work diligently for 10 years and then raise head to face Japan.
>
> Yuan Shikai (1859–1916),
> President of the Republic of China.

The rest of the country was taken in a second phase of the Northern Expedition in 1927.

When Communist leaders suggested moving the government from Nanjing to Wuhan, Chiang suspected a threat to his power. As a result, a long campaign of "purging" of the communists was undertaken, beginning with the Shanghai massacre of 1927. For the next two decades the communists, led by Mao Tse-tung, and the KMT were bitter enemies as each sought to shape China's future. Mao and his forces made a strategic retreat into the north—the famous Long March—but in the end, Chiang fled, leaving Mao to declare the People's Republic of China in 1949.

Communist areas
Early Communist military groups
"Long March"—First Front Army (1934-1935)

MONGOLIA

GOBI DESERT

MANCHURIA

Harbin

Changchun

NINGXIA

Paotow

Tatung

Mukden

Chinchow
(Jinzhou)

Anshan

Sea
of
Japan
(East Sea)

SHANXI

Peking
(Beijing)

Tientsin
(Tianjin)

Tangshan

Port Arthur
(Lushun)

KOREA

JAPAN

QINGHAI

Lanchow
(Lanzhou)

GANSU

Yan'an

Taiyuan

HEBEI

Tsinan
(Jinan)

SHANDONG

Yellow
Sea

Loyang
(Louyang)

Kaifeng

Hsu-Chou
Suchow

JIANGSU

Xian

SHAANXI

C   H   I   N   A

HENAN

4th army
(Communist)

Nanking
(Nanjing)

Soochow
(Xuzhou)

Shanghai

SICHUAN

Yangtze

HUBEI

Wuhan

ANHUI

Hangchow
(Hangzhou)

Chengtu

Chungking
(Changqing)

West Hunan

Kiukiang

JIANGXI

ZHEJIANG

East
China Sea

Zunyi

Changsha

Nanchang

10th army
(Communist)

Kweiyang

HUNAN

Hengyang

Ruijin

Foochow
(Fuzhou)

GUIZHOU

Juikin
Soviet
(Self governing)

FUJIAN

Kunming

YUNNAN

Amoy

Taiwan

Tropic of Cancer

BURMA

GUANGXI

GUANGDONG

Shantou
Soviet
(Self governing)

Canton
(Guangzhou)

Hong Kong

Hainan

South
China
Sea

ABOVE The one in ten
who survived the Long
March traveled more than
5,600 miles (9,000 km)
in 12 months.

FRENCH
INDOCHINA

PHILIPPINES

N

0   250   500   750   1,000 kilometers
0   125   250   375   500 miles

The Cold War

The Cold War was the dominant theme in international relations for nearly five decades. As the "Free World" (led by the United States) and the Communist Bloc (led by the Soviet Union) faced off after World War II, the world became divided into two opposing camps.

1949 NATO is ratified

1949 The Russian blockade of Berlin ends

1955 The Communist Warsaw Pact is formed

1989 The Berlin Wall opens after 28 years

1989 The Communist governments of Bulgaria, Czechoslovakia, and Romania fall

1990 Boris Yeltsin elected to the presidency of Russia

1990 East and West Germany are reunited

1991 The Warsaw Pact comes to an end

ABOVE RIGHT A high point of the Cold War was the signing of a treaty between the major powers that banned most nuclear weapons tests.

RIGHT A line of West Berliners watches as a plane delivers food and other goods to their blockaded city, part of the Berlin Airlift supplied by the American and the British.

The Cold War had its origins in the deep ideological differences between communist and capitalist systems. The Soviet notions of collective ownership and atheism horrified the Americans and others, and relations between the Soviet Union and Western countries were further strained by Russian attempts to encourage communist revolutions around the world.

"Iron Curtain" in Europe

Following World War II, when the Soviet Army had liberated much of Eastern Europe from the Nazis, Soviet leader Joseph Stalin was determined to establish communist regimes throughout the region, partly to ensure that Russia would be protected from another German invasion. These communist governments did not always enjoy popular support, and by 1946, when former British Prime Minister Winston Churchill declared that an "iron curtain" had "descended across the continent," Europe was effectively split between pro-communist governments in the east, and liberal-democratic governments elsewhere.

Tensions in Europe

America's goal was to "contain" the spread of communism. In 1948, under the historic Marshall Plan, the US promised to give economic

aid to European countries on the assumption that, if those nations were economically sound, their populations would be far less likely to support communism.

In June 1948, the Soviet Union blockaded Berlin, a city located deep within the Soviet-controlled section of eastern Germany, but divided between pro-Western areas, and a Communist section. Unable to supply Berlin by road or rail, the West responded by launching the Berlin Airlift, which kept Berlin supplied until the Soviets lifted the blockade in May 1949.

Fall of China

Despite massive US aid supplied to Chiang Kai-shek's anti-communist forces, in 1949 Mao's armies defeated Chiang, who retreated to the island of Formosa (Taiwan). The fall of China sent shockwaves through the United States, and fueled suspicions that sections of the State Department were either incompetent or disloyal. Playing on those fears, Senator Joseph McCarthy gained national prominence by accusing government officials, and many others, of being "soft" on communism.

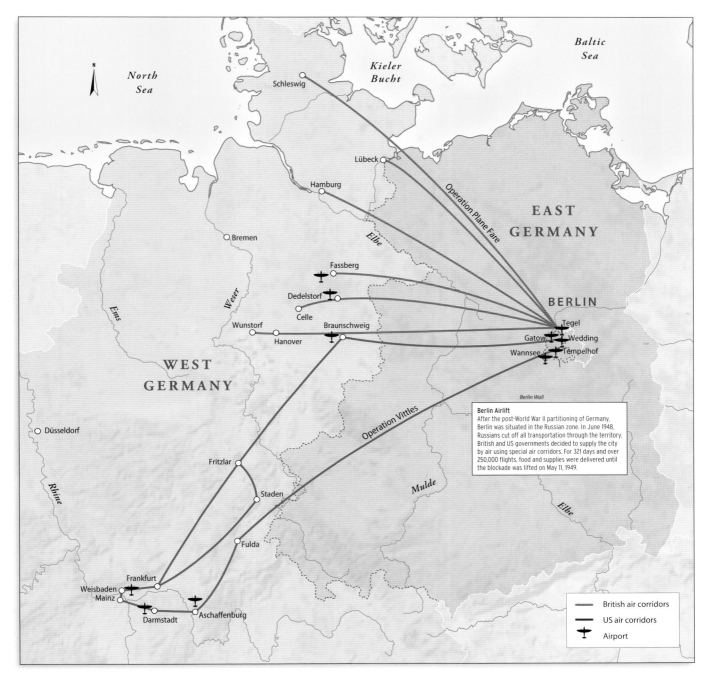

Berlin Airlift
After the post-World War II partitioning of Germany, Berlin was situated in the Russian zone. In June 1948, Russians cut off all transportation through the territory. British and US governments decided to supply the city by air using special air corridors. For 321 days and over 250,000 flights, food and supplies were delivered until the blockade was lifted on May 11, 1949.

British air corridors
US air corridors
Airport

Korean War

In June 1950, the Cold War turned very hot indeed, when North Korea attacked South Korea, forcing its army to retreat into the southernmost part of the Korean Peninsula. The United States, with the support of the United Nations, sent troops to the aid of South Korea. Initially outnumbered, the Americans were defeated in the first conflict of the war. But the United States soon poured vast forces into the theater, gaining significant ground. However, in October 1950, Chinese forces joined in the conflict to support their North Korean allies. The US and UN forces retreated, and from mid-1951 until an armistice was signed in July 1953, the war became a bloody stalemate.

Global Cold War

The Korean War might have been the hottest conflict of the Cold War during the 1950s, but it was by no means the only one.

France was engaged in war with the nationalist-communist forces led by Ho Chi Minh in the French colonies of Indochina. Vietnam, like Korea, was divided between a non-communist south and the communist north. Throughout the 1960s and 1970s, the United States spent billions of dollars, and sent hundreds of thousands of troops, in an unsuccessful effort to prevent the collapse of South Vietnam to the nationalist-communist forces.

In 1959, the pro-Western regime in Cuba fell to Fidel Castro, who aligned Cuba with the communist world. US efforts to "contain" communism were only a partial success.

ABPVE In June 1948, the Soviets sealed off Berlin, so the West began the Berlin Airlift, which lasted until May 1949.

> We're eyeball to eyeball, and I think the other guy just blinked.
> Dean Rusk (1909-1994), US Secretary of State.

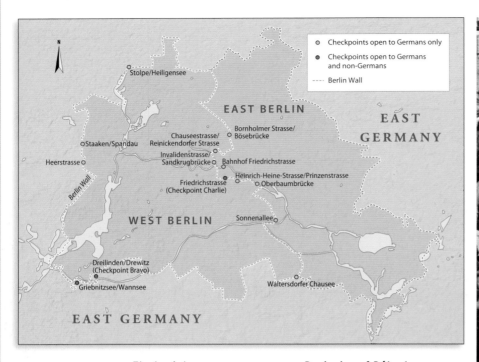

ABOVE For 28 years, the city of Berlin was divided into Soviet and Western halves by the Berlin Wall.

BELOW *Polzunov*, one of the Soviet freighters carrying nuclear missiles back to Russia from Cuba, was escorted by the American destroyer *Vesole* at the end of the Cuban missile crisis.

Flashpoint

In October 1962, US President John F. Kennedy learned that Fidel Castro was allowing the Soviets to construct missile bases in Cuba, which would have enabled the Russians to launch a nuclear strike. Kennedy responded by placing a naval "quarantine" around Cuba, to prevent additional Russian supplies and materiel reaching the island. With Russian and US forces on high alert, the world watched anxiously. When the Russian ships chose to turn around, rather than risk confrontation with the US Navy, the whole world breathed a sigh of relief. The Russians agreed to dismantle their bases, while the US undertook to not invade Cuba.

Beginning of Détente

The Cuban Missile Crisis was the moment of greatest tension during the Cold War. In its aftermath, the American and Soviet leaders began to realize the folly of the policy of Mutual Assured Destruction, by which both sides were prevented from attacking the other by the knowledge that such an attack would lead to a nuclear holocaust. Nikita Khrushchev, who had succeeded Stalin as leader of the Soviet Union, declared his support for communist insurgencies around the world, but he also understood that it was vital to establish and maintain a dialogue with the US. Plans had been made for a summit meeting in 1959, but after a US spy-plane, piloted by Francis Gary Powers, was shot down over the USSR, the summit was deferred. Despite deep differences over the future of the divided city of Berlin, the ongoing dialogue between the Soviet Union and the West gradually began to improve.

Détente

When Richard Nixon became US President in early 1969, he was determined to improve relations with both the major communist powers. In February 1972, he went to China to meet with Mao Tse-tung, and in June he traveled to Moscow to meet with the Soviet leader, Leonid Brezhnev. The US and the USSR then began a series of negotiations—the Strategic Arms Limitations Talks—whose intention was to put a limit on the number of nuclear weapons in the world.

Cold War Revived

In December 1979, in a surprise move, the Soviet Union sent troops into neighboring Afghanistan. Thus began a long and bloody conflict that many in the West considered to be "Russia's Vietnam." Just as the Americans had been unable to win in Vietnam, so too did victory prove elusive for the Soviet Union's forces in Afghanistan. The Soviet invasion helped convince many Americans— including Ronald Reagan, who became president in 1981—that the Soviet Union was an "evil empire" to be confronted at every turn.

LEFT A long row of East German cars pass through Checkpoint Charlie to an enthusiastic welcome from West Berliners after the opening of the Berlin Wall in November 1989.

BELOW The financial drain of the Cold War, and the US's proposed Star Wars space-based system, were major reasons behind the Soviet Union's push to end the Cold War.

During the 1980s, the US and the Soviets engaged in a "Second Cold War," which saw more confrontation around the world, and massive expenditure on military equipment. At the same time, however, President Reagan was able to establish a dialogue with Mikhail Gorbachev, who took over as Soviet leader in 1985. When he realized the extent of the costs of waging the Cold War, Gorbachev began to negotiate arms reduction treaties with the US, and began to liberalize the Soviet economy. Finally, all Russian military forces withdrew from Afghanistan in 1989.

End of the Cold War
In December 1989, with communist regimes throughout Eastern Europe faltering, and with the Wall separating East Berlin from West Berlin being dismantled, Gorbachev and US President George H. W. Bush declared the Cold War was officially over. While Russia and the United States continued to have their differences, the deep ideological divisions that characterized the Cold War had passed.

Although the two superpowers had managed to avoid going to war, and avoided a nuclear holocaust, the numerous "hot spots" around the globe had led to the deaths of many millions of people.

RIGHT More than half a million Afghans died in their 10-year fight against the Soviet invasion. Although poorly armed, the resistance fighters eventually forced the Soviets to withdraw in 1989.

Land of the Free

Since World War II, the international power of the United States has rested on its economy, which is based on rich agriculture, abundant raw materials, and one of the world's best education systems.

1952 Dwight D. Eisenhower is elected 34th President of the United States as the Cold War begins influencing economic and political decisions

—

1960 John F. Kennedy begins the "New Frontier" domestic program to federally fund education, and medical care for the aged

—

1964 Kennedy's successor, Lyndon B. Johnson, tackles poverty with the *Economic Opportunity Act*

—

1971 Richard Nixon imposes wage and price controls and indexes Social Security to inflation

—

1981 Ronald Reagan lifts the domestic price of petroleum and lowers the tax on oil companies. He ends the Oil Windfalls tax in 1988.

—

1997 Bill Clinton enacts the *Taxpayer Relief Act* reducing federal taxes

The modern US economy had its origins in the post-Civil War period, when dramatic industrialization and growth were fueled by an influx of immigrants. By 1900, the US enjoyed the world's most productive economy. The Allied victory in World War I was based in part on America's industrial and agricultural output, and finance. During the 1920s the American economy headed in two divergent directions—while the urban, industrial economy appeared to boom, the rural and agricultural sectors felt left behind.

ABOVE Symbolic of the "bull" market, this bronze charging bull stands outside the New York Stock Exchange.

RIGHT During the last decade of the twentieth century, US residents began to move southwest. Note the large population increases in Nevada and Arizona.

New Deal

Following the 1929 Stock Market Crash, both sectors fell into depression. President Franklin D. Roosevelt's New Deal went some way toward addressing the economic crisis, and alleviating the suffering associated with the Depression, but it was the wartime demand for goods in 1939–1945 that revived the economy. Roosevelt described the US as the "arsenal

of democracy," and the Allies' wartime victories rested in large measure on the remarkable productivity of the US economy. When World War II ended in 1945, the US faced several challenges. Millions of service personnel returned to civilian life; there was a shortage of housing and consumer goods; there were fears of unemployment and inflation; and some of the women who had joined the paid workforce for the first time were very keen to remain there.

Happy Days—the 1950s

The postwar US economy was based on its extraordinary industrial production and its rich agricultural harvest. During the 1940s and 1950s, the US led the world in both sectors. Industrial strength was based particularly in the northeast and mid-west regions, and also in California, which had boomed during World War II. US agriculture led the way in the application of technology and

> There is nothing wrong with America that cannot be cured by what is right with America
>
> –Inauguration speech by President Bill Clinton, January 1993.

CANADA

MONTANA
12.9

NORTH
DAKOTA
0.5

MINNESOTA
12.4

WISCONSIN
9.6

MICHIGAN
6.9

MAINE
3.8

VERMONT
8.2

NEW
HAMPSHIRE
11.4

NEW
YORK
5.5

MASSACHUSETTS
5.5

RHODE
ISLAND
4.5

CONNECTICUT
3.6

NEW JERSEY
8.9

DELAWARE
17.6

MARYLAND
10.8

WASHINGTON DC
-5.7

SOUTH
DAKOTA
8.5

WYOMING
8.9

NEBRASKA
8.4

IOWA
5.4

ILLINOIS INDIANA
8.6   9.7

OHIO
4.7

PENNSYLVANIA
3.4

WEST
VIRGINIA
0.8

VIRGINIA
14.4

UNITED STATES

COLORADO
30.6

KANSAS
8.5

MISSOURI
9.3

KENTUCKY
9.7

OF

AMERICA

NEW MEXICO
20.1

OKLAHOMA
9.7

ARKANSAS
13.7

TENNESSEE
16.7

NORTH
CAROLINA
21.4

SOUTH
CAROLINA
15.1

ALABAMA
10.1

GEORGIA
26.4

MISSISSIPPI
10.5

LOUISIANA
5.9

TEXAS
22.8

FLORIDA
23.5

MEXICO

*Gulf
of
Mexico*

Tropic of Cancer

Cuba

N

| 0 | 250 | 500 | 750 | 1,000 kilometers |

| 0 | 125 | 250 | 375 | 500 miles |

Change in Resident Population (1990–2000)

39.6 percent or more

26.4 to 39.5 percent

13.2 to 26.3 percent

0 to 13.1 percent

No change

(Map shows the percentage increase in population
by state from 1990 to 2000, based on US Census
Bureau figures)

ABOVE The US economy is heavily dependent on its highway system, which is the most dynamic in the world. Illustrated here is the fine network of excellent major roads that link the country.

BELOW As the country with the highest per capita car ownership, US reliance on oil is massive. Texas, the seat of US oil production, is the home of five of the world's biggest refineries, working 24 hours a day.

science, and the US exported vast quantities of agricultural produce. Encouraged by stable banking and financial structures, a trade union movement that emphasized cooperation rather than conflict, and a political system that was conducive to economic growth, many Americans believed their economy would continue to grow, perhaps indefinitely. Yet there were significant inequalities in the US economy during the post-war period.

The Southern states continued to be cursed by a relatively underdeveloped economy. There was less industry in the South, and southern agriculture was neither as productive nor as technologically advanced as elsewhere in the US.

Cold War and the Military-Industrial Complex

Much of the economic growth of the 1950s was based on military expenditure. As the US faced the communist Cold War challenge, it spent vast sums developing, building, and maintaining new weapons systems. This expenditure reflected the close relationship between the government and private companies, which benefited from the government investment.

Economic and Social Challenges of the 1960s

By the 1960s, social critics and economists were calling on the government to address the inequalities in American life. In *The Other*

America (1962), Michael Harrington proved that despite the culture of prosperity, millions of Americans were living below the poverty line. John F. Kennedy took some steps toward overcoming inequality, but it was Lyndon B. Johnson who took the most dramatic steps to provide people with opportunities to climb the economic ladder. Declaring a "War on Poverty," Johnson channeled millions of dollars into education, housing, health care, and social and economic programs. Although he was criticized for fostering a culture of dependence, and while his "Great Society" did not solve all of America's woes, it did provide very real support for many people.

RIGHT The heart of the US economy has to be the New York Stock Exchange on Wall Street which is the largest in the world by dollars traded. This scene shows the trading floor.

LEFT President Roosevelt's New Deal policy in the 1930s to rejuvenate the country included a Civilian Conservation Corps whose job it was to reforest National Parks. Here the Reforestation Army clears debris in St Joe National Forest, Idaho.

Challenges of the Vietnam War

At the same time as Johnson was waging war on poverty, his administration was increasingly focused on the war in Vietnam. Johnson was reluctant to raise taxes to help pay for the war and, especially after the US was humiliated by the Tet Offensive of 1968, it was clear that the war was distracting the US from the task of social reform at home. The war in Vietnam exposed the limits of American economic as well as military power.

Oil Crisis of the 1970s

The limits of US economic power became clearer during the early 1970s, when Arab nations cut oil production. Heavily dependent on imported oil, the US suffered as gas shortages frustrated motorists and affected productivity.

With oil in short supply, and many industries under threat from international competition, Americans realized their economy was vulnerable to international processes which politicians could not control.

Boomtime—The Reagan Years

Promising to restore American prosperity, and re-establish its international reputation, which had not recovered from Vietnam, Ronald Reagan won the Presidency in 1980. His economic policies were vague and the first year of his administration was marked by a continuing economic decline. When the situation improved during 1982–83, particularly in the "Sunbelt" states of the West, and parts of the South, the recovery was as much a result of international developments as it was a consequence of Reagan's policies. Believing that if wealthy Americans generated even more wealth, the benefits would "trickle down," Reagan delivered tax cuts to those at the top.

Despite the appearance of prosperity, many Americans felt economically vulnerable. And despite the collapse of the Soviet Union, and images of American victory in the Cold War, Reagan's successor, George H. W. Bush, was incapable of addressing that sense of vulnerability, which was exacerbated by Americans' fears that Japan, and a unified Europe, were on the verge of overtaking the US.

Contemporary Times

During the 1990s, the Clinton administration went a long way toward reducing government debt, and took steps to overcome the social and economic inequalities that had deepened during the 1980s. Yet the American economy continued to face many challenges.

China loomed as both a place of opportunity, as well as a rival. Billions of dollars worth of cheap goods were imported from China to the US. Similarly, despite continuing American advances in computers and electronics, and the associated revolution in information technology, the US has no monopoly in those areas.

Most troubling for many Americans, the attacks of September 11, 2001 exposed the US to the horrors of international terror. During the early twenty-first century, as the "War on Terror" threatened to become a "War without End," Americans worried about the long-term fate of their nation.

The US economy has tackled a number of challenges, some of which are yet to be resolved. Yet it would be wrong to underestimate the capacity of the economy to adapt. Although the US might not long remain the world's greatest economic power, it will continue to be a dynamic powerhouse of new ideas, technology, and wealth creation, as well as a beacon of hope and opportunity for millions of people around the world. Symbolic of that dynamism is the fact that if the state of California were to secede and become a nation in its own right, it would have the fifth largest economy in the world.

A New Europe

On May 2, 1989, something extraordinary happened—Hungarian border guards cut holes in the border fence between Hungary and Austria.

> Everyone pushes a falling fence.
> —Chinese proverb.

At midnight on September 11, 1989, Hungary officially opened its border. The consequence was a rush of East Germans, long trapped in Hungary, heading west. Tens of thousands gathered in Leipzig on October 11, sparking fears of heavy repression. But there was no bloodshed as SED (Socialist Unity Party of Germany) moderates paved the way for a peaceful demonstration and SED extremists were left to deal with the reality of isolation as Moscow announced that it would not be supporting the regime—in other words, the German Democratic Republic must determine its fate without Soviet intervention.

The Wall Falls

On November 9, 1989, the SED District Secretary announced moves intended to liberalize travel rules. Thousands of East Germans, thinking the border to the west was being opened, rushed to border crossings where they were allowed to pass by border guards. Germans from the west rushed to meet those from the east, passing back and forth across the border. Others began to take to the wall with sledgehammers, or climbing the once impenetrable barrier. Footage of this momentous event was beamed around the world. East and West Germany were still two different countries,

the Soviet Union still existed, and to all intents and purposes people were still living in a world divided by ideology, but on November 9, 1989, it seemed apparent that radical changes were coming.

Velvet Revolutions

As communism collapsed in the German Democratic Republic, it also collapsed in Czechoslovakia, Hungary, Poland, Romania, Bulgaria, Albania and, most dramatically, in Yugoslavia. However, so peaceful was the transition generally from communism to democracy that the movements have been dubbed "Velvet Revolutions."

In Poland, Lech Wałesa, leader of the Solidarity movement that had emerged in 1980, only to fall victim to the Soviet-backed communist regime in 1981, triumphed in the 1990 elections—after showing promising signs in the partially free elections of 1989. Wałesa thus became the first democratic President of Poland since 1926.

In Czechoslovakia, peaceful mass protests in 1989 were quickly followed by free elections in 1990 in which Vaclav Havel, the playwright and long-time dissident, was elected President.

In 1989 in Bulgaria, the Union of Democratic Forces was created,

1984 Various Western countries boycott the 1984 Moscow Olympics

1985 Mikhail Gorbachev is elected leader of the Soviet Union

1986 US President Ronald Reagan and Soviet leader Gorbachev hold summit talks in Reykjavik, Iceland, to discuss arms control

1987 On a visit to Berlin, President Reagan challenges, "Mr Gorbachev, tear down this wall!"

1987 The Intermediate-Range Nuclear Forces Treaty is signed in Washington, DC

RIGHT On November 18, 2006, around 25,000 people gathered to commemorate the 1991 siege of Vukovar in Croatia, during the 1991–1995 war with the Yugoslav Federation.

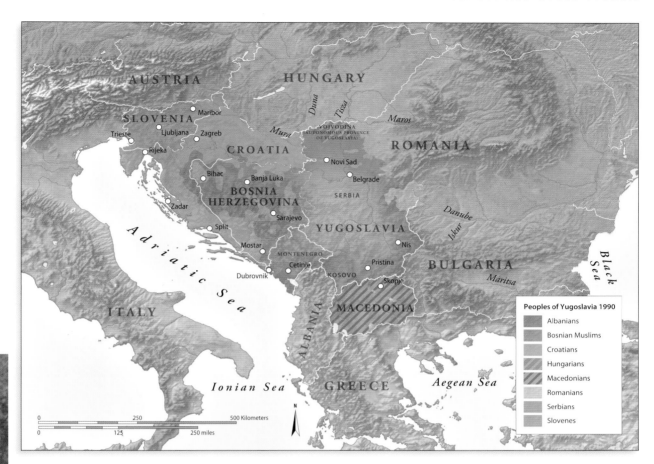

Peoples of Yugoslavia 1990
- Albanians
- Bosnian Muslims
- Croatians
- Hungarians
- Macedonians
- Romanians
- Serbians
- Slovenes

but an economic crisis saw the reformed communists elected in 1990. Reformed communists also enjoyed success in Albania. Political freedom was allowed in 1990, but the 1991 elections saw an alliance of communists and their allies win, with the last communist leader, Ramiz Alia, re-elected.

In Romania, the much-hated figures of Nicolae Ceauşescu and his wife Elena became victims of an uprising that began on December 21, 1989, and concluded with their "trial" and execution four days later. Brutal as the Romanian experience was, however, it was in Yugoslavia that the transition resulted in utter disaster.

Yugoslavia–A Special Case

In January 1990, the Federal League of Communists—the executive governing body that convened the communist parties of Yugoslavia—ceased to exist. Yugoslavia comprised six republics—Serbia, Croatia, Slovenia, Bosnia-Herzegovina, Macedonia, and Montenegro—and two autonomous provinces—Kosovo and Vojvodina.

At any Congress, since the constitutional changes in 1974, each republic and province would command a vote. Elections in all republics in 1990 result in mixed political outlooks, with Croatia and Slovenia clearly heading toward democracy and independence. On June 25, 1991, Slovenia and Croatia declared their independence.

Fighting had already broken out at several crisis points in Croatia. The Slovenian declaration led to the Yugoslav army being sent to enforce the Serbian desire for retaining Yugoslavia. After 10 days fighting ceased and Slovenian independence was assured. The Serb-Croat war and the disintegration of Yugoslavia had begun.

ABOVE This breach in the Berlin Wall was seen across the world in November 1989. The wall had stood since August 1961.

TOP The break-up of Yugoslavia into smaller countries mainly followed ethnic boundaries.

Sea of Azov

Bosnia-Herzegovina

In Bosnia-Herzegovina, the free elections of 1990 had resulted in a republic divided by ethnic politics. The Muslim Party of Democratic Action won most votes, followed by the Herzegovinian arms of the Croatian Democratic Union and Serbian Democratic Party.

On March 3, 1992, the Bosnian government, following in Slovenian and Croatian footsteps, declared independence. The Bosnian Serb response was immediate, creating a breakaway state within Bosnia on March 27, 1992, (Republika Sprska—RS, centered around Banja Luka; not to be confused with Republic of Serbian Krajina, RSK, centered around Knin in Croatia). Violence began on April 1, with the siege of Sarajevo on April 5. The war in Bosnia lasted until the signing of the Dayton Peace Accords on December 14, 1995.

Violence was to break out again in the former Yugoslavia in 1998 and 1999 between Serbia and the largely Albanian population of Kosovo. Serb actions in Kosovo, their refusal to broker a peace deal, evidence of massacres, and globally available images of thousands of Albanian refugees fleeing Serb forces, encouraged the West to take much hastier action than in 1991–1995. NATO began bombing targets in Kosovo, Serbia, and Montenegro on March 24, 1999. By June 20, 1999, Serbian forces withdrew.

LEFT President Ronald Reagan meeting with Mikhail Gorbachev in 1986 to discuss arms control.

USSR

Learning from the experience of earlier attempted revolutions within theEastern Bloc, Soviet leader Leonid Brezhnev clamped down on all reformist tendencies, setting the USSR on the road to two decades of stability and stagnation. In 1980, a Polish trade union, Solidarity, won the formal right to strike and recruit members. Its immense popularity rattled both the local communists and the USSR, with Moscow moving to have it suppressed by promising support to a local commander, General Wojciech Jaruzelski, who carried out a coup on December 13, 1981, and declared martial law.

But in 1985 a new generation took center stage with the leadership of Mikhail Gorbachev. His reforms, *Perestroika* (restructuring) and *Glasnost* (openness), were supposed to allow for the massive rebuilding and reinvigoration of the USSR but instead they contributed to its demise. When the stirrings of democratic revolutions commenced, the most important distinction between the movements in 1989–1990, and earlier mutterings about liberalization and democracy, was that Moscow did nothing. Gorbachev, presiding over a dying political monolith, issued the "Sinatra doctrine"—permission, in a way, for each nation to "do it their way."

Germany Reunites

The German way included the reunification of the country. By January 1990, it was clear that Moscow would not—indeed could not—intervene to prop up the GDR government. Helmut Kohl, leader of the Federal Republic of Germany (FRG) obtained Gorbachev's open support for the commencement of a process that could end with reunification. An initial step was the proposal of a monetary union that, it was hoped, would help pave the way to unification itself as well as to stem the steady flow of eastern migrants heading westward.

Unification was the issue that dominated the first free elections held in the GDR (March 1990). The electorate was not interested in caution. The success of the East German Alliance parties made clear the ambitions of ordinary GDR citizens—unity, democracy, prosperity—"flourishing landscapes," in fact. Meanwhile, fears were being voiced, particularly by Britain and Poland, about the potential for a reunited Germany to once again wreak havoc across the continent.

R U S S I A

Volga

Budennovsk

Cherkessk

KARACHAY
CHERKESSIA

Kodori Gorge   KABARDINO-   Nalchik
                      BALKARIA   Kuma
ABKHAZIA   CHECHNYA-
                                          INGUSHETIA
Gudauta   Sukhumi   Mestia   Ingush   Grozny
                                 NORTH   Makhachkala
                                 OSSETIA

B l a c k
                      GEORGIA   Tskhinvali   Chechen
S e a   SOUTH   DAGESTAN
            Poti   OSSETIA   Derbent

            Batumi   Tbilisi   Kuba
            Ajaria

                                          Armenians   Kura
            T U R K E Y   Azeris   Sumgait
                                 ARMENIA   Baku
                                          Lake   AZERBAIJAN
                      Yerevan   Sevan
                                          NAGORNO-KARABAKH
                                          (INDEPENDENT)
                                          Stepanakert
                                    Shusha

                                 NAKHICHEVAN
                                 (AZERBAIJAN)   N
                      Nakhichevan   Araks

C a s p i a n   S e a

	Georgia at independence (April, 1991)
	Armenia at independence (September, 1991)
	Azerbaijan at independence (October, 1991)
	Chechnya-Ingushetia at independence (November, 1991)
→	Movement of refugees

0 _____ 250 kilometers
0 _____ 125 miles

The British Prime Minister, Margaret Thatcher, convened a meeting of experts to explore the likelihood of re-emerging German nationalism. Poland, meanwhile, was concerned with the specific issue of the German-Polish border determined at the close of World War II, a border they wanted confirmed by the new and emerging united Germany.

Generally, however, German unification was, after the March 1990 elections, accepted as inevitable. Monetary union occurred on July 1, 1990, with unification on October 3, occurring under Article 23 of the FRG Basic Law, which allowed states (Landes) to join the FRG.

The GDR simply dissolved itself and each of the former GDR states joined the Federal Republic of Germany.

ABOVE The move to independence in the Caucasus in 1991 caused a massive migration of people in and out of different areas.

LEFT The central residential area of the southern Serbian town of Aleksinac after it was hit by a NATO missile on April 6, 1999.

RIGHT A woman places flowers at the memorial, Mitino Cemetery, erected to the victims of the 1986 Chernobyl nuclear reactor meltdown. The disaster compounded the downward spiral of the Russian economy.

BELOW The break-up of Eastern Europe meant a change in boundaries for many countries. It especially altered the influence of the USSR.

Soviet Union Collapse

The USSR was economically exhausted by years of poor economic growth, war in Afghanistan, the 1986 Chernobyl disaster, the space and weapons race with the USA, and maintaining control of the feuding socialist republics within the USSR. Meanwhile, it was becoming increasingly clear that Gorbachev's reforms were not having the desired effect. Massive shortages of basic goods, rising debt and inflation, public criticism of the Communist Party, hostilities and rising nationalism in the Baltic states, the Ukraine, and the Caucasus, were having a huge impact on the ability of the communists to maintain control of the Union.

It was decided to open the political system up to multiple

Gorbachev was elected both the first and, as it turns out, last president of the USSR by the Congress of People's Deputies. His previous position was First Party Secretary.

The push for further liberalization—both public and political—appeared to be resolved on June 12, 1991, when former Party elite Boris Yeltsin was elected president of the Russian Soviet Federated Socialist Republic with 57 percent of the popular vote. Yeltsin became the first popularly elected president in Russian history, but was still expected to co-exist with Gorbachev, who remained the leader of the Union.

Yeltsin took office on July 10, promising economic reform, but not the rapid introduction of a market economy that elsewhere,

parties and hold elections, and the article in the Soviet constitution that guaranteed the monopoly of the CPSU (Communist Party of the Soviet Union) was subsequently removed. Like the GDR, the USSR held March 1990 elections, and

in the former GDR and Poland, for example, was proving electorally unpopular—being generally accompanied by price rises and massive unemployment. Gorbachev, on the other hand, moved forward with market reforms and democratization—his program for both being approved by the CPSU Central Committee on July 26.

Gorbachev hoped that the democratization of Russia and the maintenance of the Union could continue side by side. To that end, he had earlier been prepared to use force, instructing the suppression of the Lithuanian independence movement, resulting in the death of between 15 and 20 Lithuanians in January 1991. By the time Yeltsin took power, it was clear that certain battles to retain the Union were lost.

ABOVE LEFT Soviet President Mikhail Gorbachev (right) congratulating Boris Yeltsin on his investiture as President of the Russian Federation, July 10, 1991.

BELOW Newly elected Russian president Boris Yeltsin stands on top of an armored vehicle in front of the Russian Federation White House, addressing soldiers during the abortive coup of 1991.

On July 30, Yeltsin signed a treaty recognizing the independence of Lithuania. Gorbachev continued to fight to retain some kind of Union, proposing a new Union Treaty that would allow for voluntary membership. Yeltsin, however, wanted the Union dissolved completely. A Communist coup was attempted on August 19, 1991, in Moscow. The coup sought to reverse the changes made under Gorbachev to the Soviet Union, and forestall the new flexible Union Treaty. The enduring image from the short-lived coup attempt (it was quashed by August 21) is that of Yeltsin on a tank proceeding down a street in Moscow. Gorbachev was not in Moscow during the coup and was held under house arrest—it was Yeltsin who emerged triumphant as the man who had resisted efforts to reverse the introduction of political and economic changes and heroically fought off attempts to take the USSR back to the old days of Brezhnev-style rule.

As result of the coup, on August 23 the Communist Party was suspended. Although restored to his position as President of the Union, Gorbachev's position was extremely weak.

The responsibilities for the political provinces of the Union were absorbed, bit by bit, into the folds of Russian government. On December 21, 11 republics signed agreements creating the new Commonwealth of Independent States (CIS). Gorbachev was now a president without a party or a union. On December 25, he resigned, and the history of the Soviet Union officially met its end.

RUSSIAN FEDERATION

Ural

KAZAKHSTAN

Volga

Dnieper

Caspian Sea

Black Sea

CHECHNYA
Grozny

GEORGIA
NAGORNO-KARABAKH
AZERBAIJAN

ARMENIA

Territory dominated by Soviet Union to 1989
Unified with Federal Republic of Germany in 1990
Yugoslavia to 1991
Independence declared in 1991
Boundary of Soviet Union to 1991

The Promised Land

On May 14, 1948, the Israeli Declaration of Independence announced the new Jewish State of Israel, on land where the kingdoms of Israel, Judah, and Judea had once been.

The foundation of the new Jewish state was the culmination of many centuries of unrest and dispersal across Europe for millions of Jews, brought about by both mistrust and religious persecution. During the early twentieth century, mutual mistrust was aroused when the Zionist claim to the Holy Land as the rightful possession of the Jewish people (to the exclusion of its Muslim and Christian inhabitants) aroused great fear and suspicion among the Arab Palestinians.

> Israel has created a new image of the Jew in the world—the image of a working and an intellectual people, of a people that can fight with heroism.
>
> –David Ben-Gurion (1886–1973), first signatory to the Israeli Declaration of Independence and first Prime Minister of Israel.

Palestinian Mandate

During World War I, following the defeat and dismemberment of the Ottoman Empire, the British Government's Balfour Declaration of 1917 promised a homeland for the Jews—in flagrant contradiction of the Arabs being promised independent homelands as a reward for assisting the Allies during the war. As part of the post-war agreement between France and Britain over areas of influence in the Middle East, the British established a mandate over Palestine, and its High Commissioner in Jerusalem tried to suspend further Jewish immigration. He noted that all cultivable land was seen as occupied, and any of this land being sold to Jews would create a class of landless Arabs. His recommendation was rejected. Over the next decade, Zionist aims became increasingly strident, and in 1936–39, the Palestinian Arabs attempted a nationalist revolt, which was forcibly crushed by the British.

Restricted Ownership

After 1940, the mandatory authority restricted Jewish land ownership to specific zones inside Palestine, but there was much illegal buying (and selling) within the 65 percent restricted to Arabs. Thus, when a partition plan was announced in 1947 it included land that was held illegally by Jews, incorporated as a *fait accompli* inside the borders of the Jewish state. The United States was the principle supporter of partition under heavy pressure from American Jewish interests, urging the United Nations to overlook the basic principle of upholding the right of all people—in this case

ABOVE The medieval mythical character known as the Wandering Jew is said to have offended Jesus Christ, who condemned the man to walk the Earth alone forever.

1909 Tel Aviv, the first modern all-Jewish city, is founded

1917 Ottoman rule is ended by British conquest

1922 Britain is granted a mandate over Palestine by the League of Nations

1925 The Hebrew University of Jerusalem is established on Mount Scopus

1939-1945 Holocaust in Europe with over 6 million Jews killed

RIGHT This illustrated plan of the holy city of Jerusalem was published in 1572, in *Civitates Orbis Terrarum* by Braun and Hogenberg.

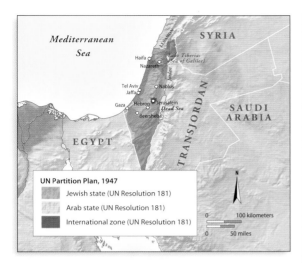

UN Partition Plan, 1947

Jewish state (UN Resolution 181)

Arab state (UN Resolution 181)

International zone (UN Resolution 181)

the Arabs who formed two-thirds of Palestine—to self-determination.

Military Creation

Jewish resistance to the British mandate had begun before World War II. Military thinking shaped the Zionist policies aimed at creating and developing a Zionist presence in Palestine. From the outset, the Jewish state was a military creation. Armed force was the main means of carrying out any plan. In 1944, Lord Moyne, the British Minister Resident in Egypt, was assassinated in Cairo by two members of a Zionist organization, the Stern Gang. There were numerous other attacks against the British presence. In December 1947, the British Government announced its withdrawal by May 13, 1948. The following day, independence was declared.

Aftermath

Palestinians in Jerusalem and Jaffa called a general strike against partition, which was followed by fighting that mushroomed into all-out war. The Jews had occupied most Arab cities before the British withdrawal. Arabs began to flee in terror; about 700,000 Palestinians were dispossessed. The second phase of the war commenced with the entry of the five generally ill-equipped Arab armies into Palestine, immediately after the state of Israel was proclaimed. In negotiations after the 1948–49 wars, Syria, Egypt, Lebanon, and the Palestinians attempted to secure what they had lost in the war—a Palestinian state alongside Israel. This did not eventuate and the scene was set for the later conflicts between Israel and its Arab neighbors.

ABOVE This map shows the division of land under the November 1947 UN Partition Plan for Palestine. Both Jews and Arabs were unhappy with it.

RIGHT Jewish refugees from the war in Europe arrive by ship at Haifa in January 1948.

BELOW Zionist pioneer settlers enjoy the sun at Rana'ana camp in what would the following year be the State of Israel.

Islam and the Middle East

Islam—the faith at the center of what was once the world's pre-eminent civilization—faced great challenges in the emerging post-colonial world order of the twentieth century.

> Islam is not only a religion, but a way of life. And at its heart lie the sacred principles of tolerance and dialogue.
> –King Hussein I of Jordan (1935-1999).

ABOVE Israeli Prime Minister Yitzhak Rabin (left) and Palestinian leader Yasser Arafat won the Nobel Peace Prize in 1994.

Nowhere was this more pronounced than in the traditional heartland of the Middle East, where the vestiges of the Ottoman Empire gave way to modern states and new forms of secular identities. The end of the Ottoman Empire was not the end of colonial rule, however. France and Britain expressed their intentions in the Sykes-Picot agreement of 1916—the French would hold Syria (including Lebanon), and the British would administer Palestine and regions around the Jordan, then east to include Mesopotamia (Iraq).

League of Nations

Under the League of Nations these divisions were formalized into "mandates," overseen by European powers until they were considered capable of self-government. The mandate system thus created artificial states with artificial boundaries. The new kingdom of Iraq, for example, grouped three distinct regions, both religious and ethnic—the Shiite Muslims in the province of Basra, Sunni Muslims in the province around Baghdad, and the Kurdish population of the north.

In addition to formal mandates, the European powers exercised a *de facto* colonization in other parts of the Middle East. In Iran—a distinctly Shiite nation—the British had gained "concessions" to access the country's oil supply as early as 1901, through the Anglo-Persian Oil company, later British Petroleum (BP). While not formal colonization, the British (and Russians) nonetheless shaped the governance of Iran, from the 1906 revolution to the installation of a pro-Western Shah (king) in World War II.

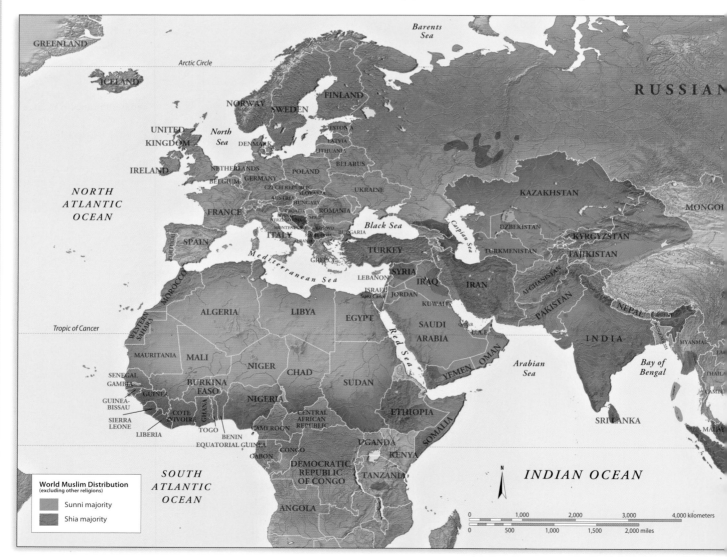

World Muslim Distribution
(excluding other religions)

- Sunni majority
- Shia majority

Arab Nationalism

In the climate of decolonization after World War II, the Middle East saw the rise of a new and strident Arab nationalism, fusing ethnic Arab identity, Islamic faith, and western forms of nationalist ideology. This found expression in the Arab League, formed in 1945 between seven key Arab states, and in the policies of socialist governments like that of Egyptian president Gamal Abdel Nasser, who famously nationalized the Suez Canal in 1956.

LEFT Followers of the Muslim religion are present within a vast number of countries, even in Hindu-dominant countries such as India. Sunni is the largest denomination of Islam.

1961 Syria gains independence

—

1971 Qatar and the United Arab Emirates gain their independence

—

1979 A peace treaty between Egypt and Israel is finalized at Camp David

—

1979 Iran forms a new government under the Ayatollah Khomeini

—

1991 A multi-national force launches an air attack on Iraq following its invasion of Kuwait

After violence on both sides, the new State of Israel declared independence in 1948, resulting in a declaration of war by the Arab League. The war was a humiliating defeat for the Arab states, and Israel's territory actually expanded. The same result was repeated in 1967 and 1973. The unresolved problems of the Palestinian refugees of 1948 and the territories conquered in the 1967 war have continued to cast a shadow across the whole Middle East region.

This fostered the emergence of the Palestinian Liberation Organization (PLO) under Yasser Arafat. But following Israel's war with Lebanon in 1982, and the emergence of a new Islamic radicalism, more extreme terror organizations emerged—Hezbollah in Lebanon, and Hamas in Palestine.

Military Governments

Apart from the Arab-Israeli conflict, the Middle Eastern states have had to deal with the vast socio-political changes. Across the region, huge population growth, along with improvements in education and health care, led to large-scale urbanization and the ruin of traditional rural ways of life and work. These new social conditions prompted radical responses. The pro-Western regime in Iran lasted until 1979, until its unpopularity, along with alleged cruelty and corruption, led to its overthrow by advocates of traditional Shiite modes of government. Elsewhere, civilian rule appeared weak compared to alternative military government, resulting in dictatorships such as in Iraq with Saddam Hussein's Baath ("renaissance") Party.

RIGHT Women in support of Iraq in the Gulf War of 1991 hold up posters of Palestinian leader Yasser Arafat and Iraqi military dictator Saddam Hussein.

399

The Rise and Fall of Apartheid

For over 40 years the official South African government policy of *apartheid* (Afrikaans for "separateness") dictated the economic, residential, and educational opportunities of the black and colored population of South Africa, while brutally suppressing their opposition to it.

Apartheid was a policy promise given in 1948 by the South African National Party when it came to power. Yet it was not an entirely new idea. One of the earliest laws of the South African Union was the 1913 *Native Land Act*, under which black Africans could only settle in restricted areas—totaling around 10 percent of South African land.

RIGHT During the 1920s, workers were needed for labor in South Africa's valuable diamond mines. Restrictions were imposed preventing non-white persons from holding skilled positions.

Flash Point
Industrial relations became a flash-point for racial tension too. In the seething election atmosphere of 1948, the proposed program of apartheid held electoral appeal, vowing to protect white employment, control city growth, and bolster Afrikaans language and culture.

Homelands
The National Party was elected, and soon Prime Minister D. F. Malan and his successor, H. F. Verwoerd, introduced a swathe of legislation that classified and registered everyone according to their race.

Mandela
Born in 1918 in Umtata in today's Eastern Cape Province, Nelson Mandela was the son of a counselor to a Thembu chief. Mandela and his colleague, Oliver Tambo, started the first black legal practice in South Africa in Johannesburg.

African National Congress
Mandela and Tambo became deeply involved with the African National Congress (ANC), a political organization founded in 1912 to promote racial equality through democratic process. In 1944, Mandela helped the ANC to organize its Youth League. By 1951, he was Vice-President of the ANC.

During the early 1950s, the ANC were committed to change through non-violence. However, by the 1960s, some held the view that non-violence was inadequate. In 1960, police fired on about 5,000 protesters at Sharpeville, killing 69 people in the infamous Sharpeville massacre. In the reprisals that followed, the ANC and their more extreme rival, the Pan African Congress, were both banned.

In 1962, Mandela and his colleagues founded the military arm of the ANC, the *Umkhonto we Swize* or "Sword of the Nation," an organization devoted to sabotage. Mandela left for Algeria to be trained in the ways of guerilla warfare. On his return, he was arrested and imprisoned for five years for unlawfully leaving the country—but while in prison, following the arrest of fellow ANC militants, he was found guilty of treason and sentenced to life imprisonment. Mandela was kept on Robben Island from 1964 until 1982, then moved to a maximum security prison near Johannesburg.

International Condemnation
International pressure began to mount on the South African government in the form of sporting boycotts, economic sanctions, and expulsion from the UN General Assembly. Mandela only increased in worldwide appeal the longer he was imprisoned. His seventieth birthday was celebrated by tens of thousands of people at London's Wembley Stadium in his absence.

De Klerk
Finally, the political climate within South Africa changed with the rise of F. W. De Klerk as leader of the Nationalist party at the end of the 1980s. In 1990, he lifted the ban on the ANC, and gave Mandela unconditional release. Nelson Mandela walked free to worldwide cheers.

Nobel Peace Prize
For their efforts in facilitating the drafting of a new constitution in 1992—reconciling Zulu interests, ANC interests, and white interests—Mandela and De Klerk were awarded the Nobel Peace Prize in 1993. In 1994, they formed joint government after the ANC won a two-thirds majority in the first ever non-racially restricted election.

1959 The South African parliament passes new laws creating separate Bantustans (homelands) for major black groups

1965 Rhodesia (Zimbabwe) gains its independence with only whites represented

1974 South Africa is expelled from the United Nations

1983 White farmers are allowed arms to protect themselves from black dissidents

1990 De Klerk lifts the ban on the African National Congress (ANC)

1990 Nelson Mandela is freed

1991 Mandela becomes President of the African National Congress

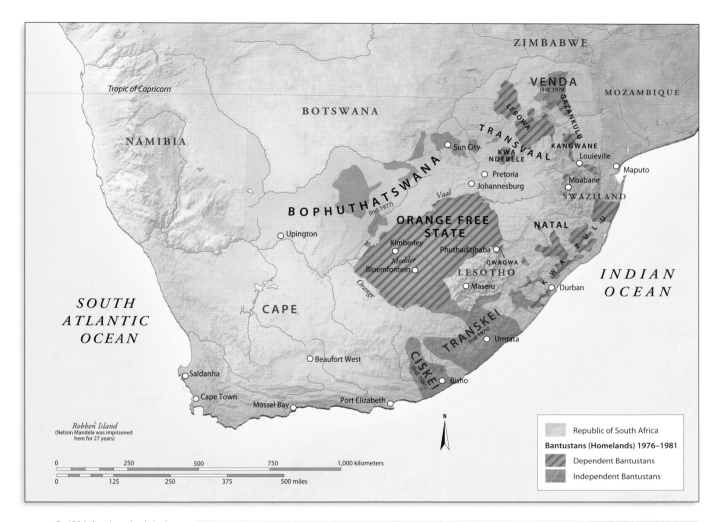

Map legend:

Republic of South Africa

Bantustans (Homelands) 1976–1981

Dependent Bantustans

Independent Bantustans

Robben Island
(Nelson Mandela was imprisoned here for 27 years)

0   250   500   750   1,000 kilometers

0   125   250   375   500 miles

ABOVE By 1986, four homelands had accepted independence from the South African government: Transkei (1976), Bophuthatswana (1977), Venda (1979), and Ciskei (1981). Both dependent and independent homelands have now been incorporated into the new South Africa.

> For to be free is not merely to cast off one's chains, but to live in a way that respects and enhances the freedom of others.
>
> –Nelson Mandela, anti-apartheid activist and former President of South Africa.

LEFT In December 1993, Nelson Mandela and F. W. De Klerk jointly received the Nobel Peace Prize in Oslo, Norway.

RIGHT Nelson Mandela and his wife Winnie celebrate his release from prison in February 1990. His freedom signaled the end of apartheid.

De-kulakization to Glasnost

From revolution in 1917, the Soviet Union fought long and hard to become an industrialized nation equal to the Western powers. But the political changes necessary to bring this about brought immense suffering to the population and decades of suspicion from the West.

The late 1920s marked a turning point in the history of the Soviet Union. The first decade after the Bolshevik Revolution (1917) saw several reorientations embodied by "war communism," market-oriented New Economic Policy, and infighting for leadership after the death of Lenin in 1924, and concluded with the rise of Joseph Visarionovich Stalin as Secretary General of the Bolshevik Party and head of the Soviet state.

LEFT Lenin (left) suffered a series of strokes from 1922 and died in January 1924. He had hoped Leon Trotsky, rather than Stalin (right), would succeed him.

RIGHT This map shows the USSR's extent before its collapse. Gorbachev announced his resignation and the nation's dissolution in December 1991.

Stalinism

In 1925, Stalin called for socialism at home rather than a worldwide revolution. He ordered a rapid modernization program that would move Russia from the periphery of the civilized world to the center of a new civilization. In December 1929 he seized absolute power with a propaganda campaign that hailed him as "the Lenin of today." In his speech on agrarian policy Stalin announced "de-kulakization," elimination of the well-to-do peasantry. As a consequence, about 10 million people were deported and killed.

Forced industrialization was also launched. The entire economy was run by the state and prices were fixed. Investments were financed from the state budget, and grew fivefold in the summer of 1929.

These heroic efforts brought great suffering to the population. Famine, starvation, and mass terror characterized the 1930s. Opposition to Stalin's policy was ruthlessly eliminated. From the late 1920s a series of show trials frightened the people. Resisting peasants, the army officer corps, and Stalin's rivals in the top Bolshevik leadership (such as Trotsky, Zinoviev, Kamenev, and Bukharin) were all purged, assassinated, or accused of treason, tried, and executed.

Industrialization

The Soviet Union, however, under the shield of a bloody, modernizing dictatorship, realized its over-ambitious industrialization program and gradually emerged as an industrial power. When Hitler attacked the Soviet Union in the summer of 1941, a massive evacuation of industry from European Russia—mostly land occupied by Nazi Germany—to Siberia further strengthened the industrial potential of the country. The Western powers entered into an alliance with Stalin, and the Soviet Union, though suffering an unprecedented death toll of 20–30 million people,

1924 Lenin dies and is succeeded by Joseph Stalin

1940 Leon Trotsky is assassinated in Mexico City

1953 Stalin dies and is succeeded by Nikita Khrushchev

1961 Yuri Gagarin becomes the first cosmonaut

1961 The Soviet Union builds a wall between East and West Berlin

1964 Khrushchev is replaced by Leonid Brezhnev

1985 Mikhail Gorbachev becomes the new leader of the Soviet Union

1990 Boris Yeltsin is elected president of the new Russian Federation

1999 Yeltsin resigns and appoints Vladimir Putin as his successor

HOLOAVIA

Mediterranean Sea

> Without glasnost there is not, and there cannot be, democratism, the political creativity of the masses and their participation in management.
>
> –Mikhail Gorbachev, last head of state of the USSR, Nobel Peace Prize winner 1990.

LEFT Russians march through the streets of Vladivostok in 1922 in support of their new leaders, Lenin and Trotsky.

FAR RIGHT Retiring Russian President Boris Yeltsin (right) leaves the Kremlin, shaking hands with Prime Minister and acting President Vladimir Putin (left).

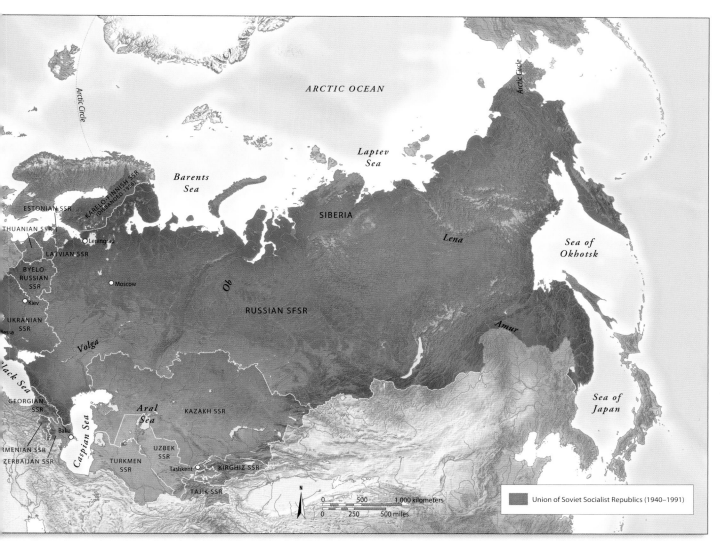

ARCTIC OCEAN

Laptev Sea

Barents Sea

KARELO-FINNISH SSR (DISBANDED 1956)

ESTONIAN SSR

THUANIAN SSR

Leningrad

LATVIAN SSR

SIBERIA

Lena

BYELO-RUSSIAN SSR

Moscow

Kiev

Sea of Okhotsk

UKRANIAN SSR

Ob

RUSSIAN SFSR

Volga

Amur

Black Sea

GEORGIAN SSR

Aral Sea

KAZAKH SSR

Sea of Japan

Baku

Caspian Sea

RMENIAN SSR

ZERBAIJAN SSR

TURKMEN SSR

UZBEK SSR

Tashkent

KIRGHIZ SSR

TAJIK SSR

N

| 0 | 500 | 1,000 kilometers |
| 0 | 250 | 500 miles |

Union of Soviet Socialist Republics (1940–1991)

played the decisive role on German soil in the defeat of Adolf Hitler.

Cold War

Between 1945 and 1948, Stalin "sovietized" Central and Eastern Europe (the nations that were liberated from Nazi occupation by the Soviet army) and built up a huge buffer zone, the Soviet Bloc. His successors continued his policy and did not hesitate to launch military interventions if revolutions or radical reforms in their sphere of interest endangered their rule. This happened in Hungary in 1956, in Czechoslovakia in 1968, in Poland in 1981, and in Afghanistan in 1979.

Perestroika

The deadly arms race with the West absorbed Soviet technological potential and exhausted resources. Nevertheless, reforms to keep up with modern needs were rejected

in favor of orthodox ideological considerations. By the 1980s, when Mikhail Gorbachev introduced reforms under *perestroika* (reconstruction) and *glasnost* (openness), it was too late.

Collapse

Some of the satellite countries revolted and state socialism collapsed in Poland and Hungary, and then throughout Central and Eastern Europe in 1989. In 1991, the Soviet Union also collapsed. The multinational country disintegrated and was replaced by 15 independent successor states. In Russia, the first decade after the collapse was debilitating. Strong centralized power, including the oppression of opposition, was re-established only after 2000 under President Vladimir Putin when rapidly increasing oil prices helped stimulate new economic growth and stabilization.

"Police Action"

The Korean War was the twentieth century's forgotten war. It is also the twenty-first century's unfinished war.

1950 The UN Security Council demands North Korea cease attacks on the South. UN forces come under the command of General Douglas MacArthur.

1951 The USSR delegate to the United Nations proposes a truce, but months later, North Korea breaks off talks.

1952 The UN proposes an exchange of POWs. The idea is rejected by North Korea.

March–April 1953 Fighting becomes more intense, with heavy casualties on both sides. Sick and wounded POWs are exchanged.

July 1953 Peace talks resume, and a ceasefire is signed

> Together we will be stronger than the USA and England... If war is unavoidable, then let it be now.
> –Joseph Stalin, writing to Mao Tse-tung, October 1950.

In 1945, with Japanese surrender imminent, Russian troops entered the northern part of the Korean peninsula to round up surrendering Japanese troops. The USA did the same in the south and, after the Japanese surrender, the country was controlled by these foreign forces.

38th Parallel
An arbitrary line was put forward by the Americans to divide the Soviet's region in the north from US responsibility in the south. Agreed upon by President Truman and Marshall Stalin, the line was to become known as the 38th Parallel.

War
Neither government, however, was content merely to govern on its side of the 38th Parallel. Elections led to violent skirmishes at the border, and 100,000 Koreans were killed even before the war proper began. But the war started on Sunday, June 25, 1950, when before dawn, North Korean troops launched a mass surprise attack on the South.

This invasion was considered an act of aggression by the UN Security Council—but without the vote of Russia or the inclusion of China—and a "police action" was agreed upon, whereby UN troops would come to the aid of the South and restore its territory.

United Response
The US-led UN forces responded with stealth and force, landing hundreds of miles behind enemy lines at the western port of Inch'on in the middle of September 1950. They then moved inland to liberate the southern capital of Seoul, and were soon joined by the American forces from Pusan, who successfully blocked the North Korean forces.

TOP LEFT The Korean War mixed tactics from both world wars, including heavy bombing missions by the US Air Force.

LEFT US-led forces landed in September 1950, liberating Seoul, but Chinese forces assisted the North to drive the UN back.

KOREAN WALL

The 38th Parallel was suggested as the line of separation in Korea by a group of US army officials who sought a territorial division with Russia on the eve of Japanese surrender in 1945. Given one night—August 10, 1945—to come up with their ideas, their resources included a *National Geographic* map marked with longitude and latitude. The line chosen coincided with no existing political or geographic divides, and intercepted numerous rivers, roads, and rail-tracks. It was perhaps the Asian equivalent of the Berlin Wall.

ABOVE UN vehicles recrossing the 38th Parallel on withdrawal from Pyongyang.

Within weeks, UN forces had secured South Korea and restored the 38th Parallel border. The war could have ended here.

But the UN faced the dilemma of settling on the original objective of restoring the 38th Parallel line, or pressing north in pursuit of the North Korean armies. China, now under control of Mao Tse-tung's Communist government, warned the Americans and British, through an Indian diplomatic channel, that entry into North Korea would not be tolerated. President Truman and the USA decided to call their bluff, however, and went in full pursuit northward. They were very successful in driving back the North Korean troops, and made it to the Yalu River at the Chinese border.

The tide of the war changed drastically as a "volunteer" force

ABOVE AND RIGHT North Korea moved forward in early 1951 and took Seoul. The battle then raged back and forth, until an armistice was reached in 1953.

of 200,000 Chinese troops entered Korea and sent the UN forces backward. Repeated waves of attacks almost forced American troops into the sea. Eventually, heavy UN airpower and extreme cold of −4° F (−20° C) took their toll on the Chinese, and the UN troops were able to recover and hold their line.

By early summer 1951, the line had stabilized near the 38th Parallel. Despite inching back and forward it remained largely the same until the armistice on July 27, 1953, with the final line lying just north of the 38th Parallel. To this day, the war has not officially ended.

North and South

1901 to 2000

The Vietnam War (1959-1975) began long before the United States and other countries sent in their troops. The real cause was the threat of communism to a suspicious West. The result was a war with few winners.

Vietnam—along with two of the other Indochinese nations, Cambodia and Laos—was colonized by France during the nineteenth century. The Vietnamese nationalists fought to expel the French, whose rule brought economic exploitation, religious and cultural domination, and terror. By the 1920s, the most important nationalist was Ho Chi Minh.

Communist Conspiracy

When Japan surrendered in 1945, Ho declared Vietnam an independent nation. As the superpower Cold War got hotter, however, Franklin D. Roosevelt's successor, President Harry S. Truman, could not afford to antagonize France, whose support he needed in Europe, and which was determined to reclaim its Indochinese empire. Particularly after 1949, when Mao Tse-tung's communists triumphed in China, Americans assumed Ho was part of a global communist conspiracy. For his part, Ho had worked with the Americans during World War II, knew that Roosevelt opposed colonialism, and hoped the US would support Vietnamese independence.

> You can kill ten of my men for every one I kill of yours, but even at those odds, you will lose and I will win.
> –Ho Chi Minh to the French in the late 1940s.

The 17th Parallel

The Viet Minh defeat of France at Dien Bien Phu in May 1954 ended all French authority in Indochina. France agreed to withdraw from Vietnam, which was temporarily partitioned at the 17th Parallel. Ho's Viet Minh took charge of the north, while Ngô Dình Diem—who had links to the US—became the dominant figure the south.

Along with a majority of the Vietnamese populace, Ho rejected the division and, beginning in 1959, his forces renewed their struggle to reunify Vietnam. The US, ignoring the growing Soviet-Chinese rift, remained convinced that Ho was part of a worldwide communist monolith. By late 1963, President John F. Kennedy had dispatched over 16,000 American advisors to assist Diem's struggling regime.

Frustrated with the regime, however, the US did not prevent a November 1963 coup led by sections of the South Vietnamese military. But Diem's demise did not bring any order to South Vietnam, and it was not until 1965, when Nguyen Van Thieu and Nguyen Cao Ky assumed control, that there existed any semblance of stability.

Johnson Takes Command

Meanwhile the assassination of John F. Kennedy in November 1963 had made no substantial difference to American policy. Kennedy's successor, Lyndon B. Johnson, stated he was not "about to send American boys 9 or 10,000 miles away from home to do what Asian boys ought to be doing for themselves."

However, Johnson was also not prepared to let South Vietnam fall. In August 1964, following a clash between American and North Vietnamese naval forces off the coast of

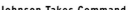

1950 The Viet Minh gets assistance from China while the US pledges military aid to France to help the fight in Vietnam

1954 Geneva Accords create a ceasefire and the French withdraw from the country. The border between north and south is established on the 17th parallel.

1960 The National Liberation Front—Viet Cong—is established in South Vietnam

1965 First US troops arrive in Vietnam

1968 Hundreds of Vietnamese civilians are killed by US troops in My Lai village

1969 Nixon orders the first withdrawal of US troops

1970 Nixon says US troops will attack in Cambodia, creating worldwide protests

1972 The North Vietnamese cross the 17th parallel to attack South Vietnam

1973 Last foreign troops leave Vietnam

1975 The South surrenders to the Communists

LEFT An American heavy artillery piece blasts a 175mm projectile toward North Vietnamese forces. Despite pouring enormous military resources into the Vietnam conflict, in the end the US and its allies were not successful in defeating the communists.

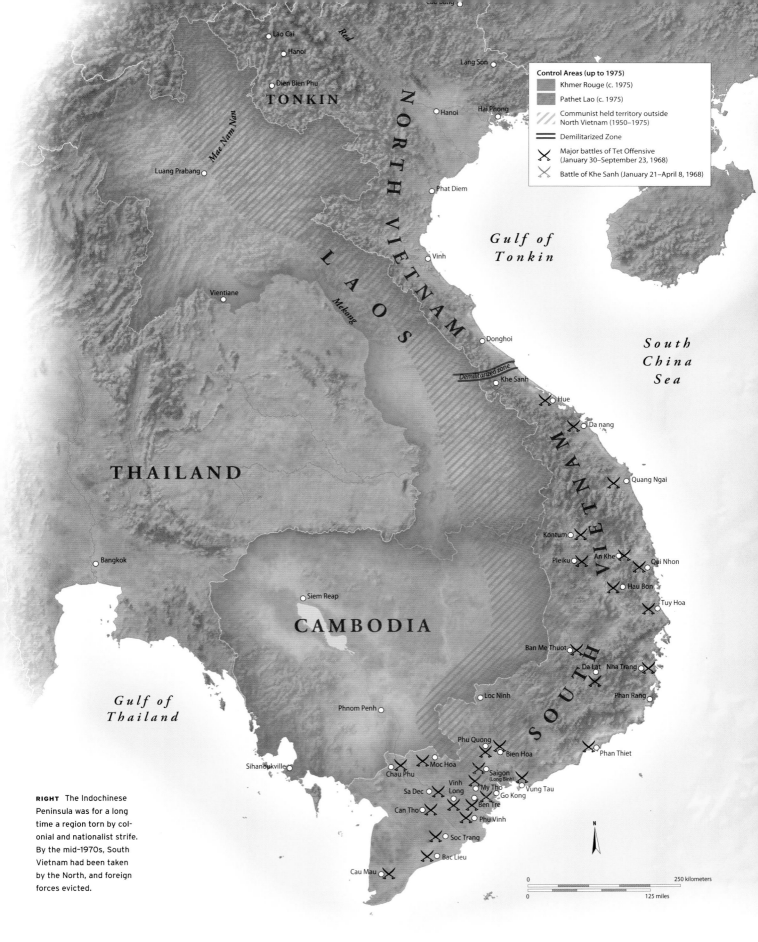

Cao Bang

Lao Cai

Hanoi

TONKIN

Dien Bien Phu

Lang Son

Mae Nam Nan

Hanoi

Hai Phong

NORTH VIETNAM

Luang Prabang

Phat Diem

Control Areas (up to 1975)

Khmer Rouge (c. 1975)

Pathet Lao (c. 1975)

Communist held territory outside
North Vietnam (1950–1975)

Demilitarized Zone

Major battles of Tet Offensive
(January 30–September 23, 1968)

Battle of Khe Sanh (January 21–April 8, 1968)

*Gulf of
Tonkin*

L A O S

Vientiane

Vinh

Mekong

*South
China
Sea*

Donghoi

Demilitarized zone

Khe Sanh

Hue

Da nang

THAILAND

Quang Ngai

Kontum

Pleiku

An Khe

Qui Nhon

Bangkok

Hau Bon

Tuy Hoa

Siem Reap

CAMBODIA

Ban Me Thuot

Da Lat   Nha Trang

*Gulf of
Thailand*

Loc Ninh

Phan Rang

SOUTH VIETNAM

Phnom Penh

Phu Quong

Bien Hoa

Phan Thiet

Sihanoukville

Moc Hoa

Chau Phu

Saigon
(Long Binh)

Vung Tau

Vinh
Long

My Tho

Sa Dec

Go Kong

Ben Tre

Can Tho

Phu Vinh

Soc Trang

Bac Lieu

Cau Mau

RIGHT The Indochinese
Peninsula was for a long
time a region torn by colonial and nationalist strife.
By the mid-1970s, South
Vietnam had been taken
by the North, and foreign
forces evicted.

N

0   250 kilometers

0   125 miles

407

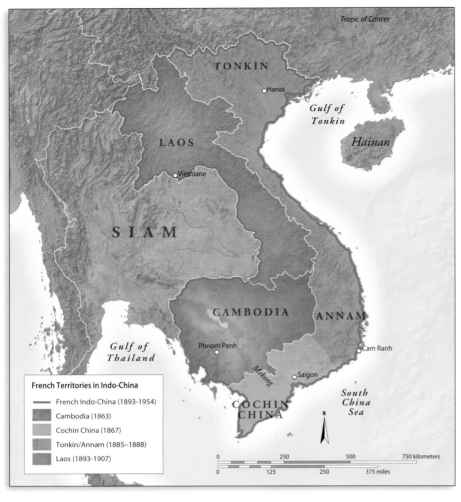

ABOVE France had long been a colonial power on the Indochinese peninsula. It was partly in response to this foreign rule that the conflict that would evolve into the Vietnam War began.

RIGHT It wasn't just US forces that backed South Vietnam. Other countries contributed forces too, such as these Australian soldiers marching through Sydney before leaving for Vietnam.

North Vietnam, Johnson secured from the US Congress the Gulf of Tonkin Resolution.

American commanders hoped airpower would force Ho to the negotiating table. But they underestimated the Vietnamese commitment to reunification, and while the "Rolling Thunder" bombing campaign laid waste to vast areas of Vietnam, killing tens of thousands, it did little to help the South Vietnamese defeat communist Viet Cong guerrillas and their North Vietnamese allies.

Waging War
Johnson decided in mid-1965 to send American ground troops to Vietnam. This helped prevent the defeat of South Vietnam that year, and during 1966 and 1967, as tens of thousands of additional US troops—along with others from allies including South Korea, Australia, and New Zealand—were sent to Vietnam, US commanders claimed they were winning the war

of attrition. But the communists matched the Allied escalation. With growing US casualties, and frustrated by the enemy's guerrilla tactics, many Americans started to grow disillusioned.

Antiwar Protest
Leaders of the antiwar movement in the US denounced the brutal misapplication of American force in Vietnam, where military commanders were relying heavily on firepower to achieve their objectives. There was a big contradiction between the stated aim of "saving" South Vietnam, and the damage and suffering caused by the war.

Tet Offensive
Americans had been assured their forces were winning the war, but in early 1968 the communist forces launched a series of coordinated attacks, the Tet Offensive, right across South Vietnam. Images of Viet Cong forces attacking the American Embassy in the South

Vietnamese capital of Saigon were seen on television screens all over the US. While the attacks did not prompt the kind of mass uprisings that communist leaders had hoped they would, and although communist forces suffered dreadful casualties as the American and South Vietnamese forces fought back, the Tet Offensive was an important and pivotal moment in the war.

Map labels: TONKIN, Hanoi, Gulf of Tonkin, Hainan, LAOS, Vientiane, SIAM, CAMBODIA, ANNAM, Phnom Penh, Cam Ranh, Gulf of Thailand, Mekong, Saigon, South China Sea, COCHIN CHINA, Tropic of Cancer

French Territories in Indo-China
— French Indo-China (1893–1954)
Cambodia (1863)
Cochin China (1867)
Tonkin/Annam (1885–1888)
Laos (1893-1907)

In part, the war was a contest between North Vietnam and South Vietnam. But it was also a civil war, since a majority of the Vietnamese —South, as well as North—knew that South Vietnam was a nation in name only, nothing more than an exercise in nation-building on the part of the US.

Nixon's Withdrawl Policy

Nineteen sixty-eight brought an election year to the US. With his Vietnam policies discredited, Johnson withdrew from the presidential election. The Democrats nominated Hubert Humphrey, who was narrowly defeated by the Republicans' Richard Nixon. Promising "peace with honor," Nixon announced the policy of "Vietnamization," whereby South Vietnamese forces assumed primary responsibility for the war. This enabled Nixon to begin withdrawing American troops from Vietnam, which defused the anti-war movement. Nixon also sent his National Security Advisor, Henry

Kissinger, to Paris, for secret negotiations with the North Vietnamese.

At the same time, however, as Nixon was withdrawing American troops from Vietnam and seeking a negotiated end to the war, he also expanded the war by first bombing, and then sending American troops into Cambodia, where communist forces had long since found sanctuary from the Americans and South Vietnamese.

The decisive defeat dealt to the South Vietnamese forces when they entered Laos in 1971 exposed the limits of the Vietnamization policy, and helped to persuade the communist leadership that the time was now ripe to launch a conventional military attack on South Vietnam.

At the time that attack was initiated in 1972, only a handful of American troops remained in South Vietnam, and the communist assault was repelled only after a massive American aerial bombing campaign.

The Fall of Saigon

Thwarted on the battlefield, the communists decided they could wait until the US had withdrawn all its forces from South Vietnam. Just prior to the 1972 presidential election in the US, Kissinger announced that a negotiated settlement to the war was in sight. Soon after Nixon won the election, negotiations collapsed. Nixon responded by launching a renewed bombing assault on North Vietnam, and in early 1973 the Paris Peace Agreement was eventually signed.

Under the terms of the accord, the US agreed to withdraw all its forces from Vietnam. South Vietnamese leaders worried they would be abandoned by the US should the communist forces renew their assault. In early 1975, North Vietnam launched an offensive against South Vietnam. Gerald Ford, who became President after Nixon had resigned on account of his involvement in the Watergate scandal, understood that after more than

ABOVE LEFT America's involvement in the Vietnam War sparked massive, and sometimes violent, protests at home. The war became increasingly unpopular.

TOP RIGHT The American Embassy in Saigon had to be evacuated in April 1975 as victorious North Vietnamese forces entered the city.

ABOVE American Secretary of State Henry Kissinger and Vietnamese politician Le Duc Tho signed the Paris Peace Agreement in 1973. Both men were later awarded the Nobel Peace Prize, but Le Duc Tho refused to accept it.

a decade of war, billions of dollars, and nearly 60,000 American deaths, most Americans were in no mood to commit more forces to Vietnam. Despite a massive influx of US materiel, the South Vietnamese were no match for their communist adversaries, and in April 1975 Saigon fell. After thirty long years of war, Vietnam was reunified.

Cuban Affairs

The United States had a long history of involvement in Cuban affairs. The Cuban Revolution of 1959, and America's opposition to Fidel Castro's government, set the stage for the darkest hour of the Cold War.

ABOVE A Cuban military court was established to try captured US-backed exiles who took part in the Bay of Pigs invasion. Some were executed, others were eventually repatriated to the US.

BELOW The Cuban Missile Crisis arose from the Soviet decision to site nuclear missiles on the Caribbean island, within easy reach of the US.

Kennedy's Plans

In January 1961, John F. Kennedy became President of the US. Having promised to resist communist aggression, he agreed with Eisenhower that the US should support the plan to overthrow Castro, who, during 1961, more openly declared his communist allegiances and aligned himself more closely with the Soviet Union. So the US drew up plans to invade Cuba and oust Castro's regime. But with assistance from Soviet intelligence, and using information gathered from within the exile community in the US, the Cuban government learned of the plans for the invasion.

Bay of Pigs Invasion

After a bombing mission using aircraft supplied by the CIA, on April 17, 1961, a force of 1,500 Cuban exiles was landed at the Bay of Pigs, on the south coast of Cuba. Having lost the vital element of surprise, however, the invading forces very soon found themselves in trouble.

On April 20, surviving members of the invading force surrendered to Cuban government troops. Over 100 of the exiles had been killed.

Soviet Deployment

Following the Bay of Pigs mission, relations between the US and Cuba understandably remained tense. Increasingly, Cuba had allied itself to the Soviet Union, which was very happy to have a friend in the Caribbean, especially one so geographically close to the US. In April 1962, Soviet leader Nikita Khrushchev raised the possibility of placing missiles in Cuba.

US Reaction

On October 15, 1962, American reconnaissance flights identified the construction of Soviet missile facilities in Cuba. Kennedy's first step was to assemble the Executive Committee of the National Security Council (EXCOM), which was charged with planning a response to the Soviet challenge.

> It shall be the policy of this Nation to regard any nuclear missile launched from Cuba against any nation in the Western Hemisphere as an attack by the Soviet Union on the United States, requiring a full retaliatory response upon the Soviet Union.
>
> –John F. Kennedy in his address to the nation, October 22, 1962.

The World Holds its Breath

With US forces on the highest alert, on October 22 President Kennedy made a televised address to the American people—and, by extension, to the world. Describing the Soviet build-up in Cuba as a direct challenge to the US, he declared that any attack on the US from Cuba would be regarded as an attack from the USSR. He also announced the "quarantine" of Cuba by a naval blockade. Khrushchev said that Kennedy's actions were leading to "the abyss of a world nuclear-missile war," and that Soviet ships would run the blockade.

There were significant moves behind the scenes. An official from the Soviet Embassy in Washington asked a US journalist to relay a message to the US Administration, that the Soviet Union would be willing to agree to withdraw their missiles from Cuba if the US pledged publicly to not invade Cuba.

Cuban Missile Sites
Intermediate-Range Ballistic Missile (IRBM)
Medium-Range Ballistic Missile (MRBM)

ABOVE Not willing to try a second invasion, the US put a naval blockade around Cuba to prevent the Soviets from landing more missiles.

ABOVE RIGHT The naval blockade was successful in calling the Soviets' bluff, and they recalled their ships.

RIGHT The ill-fated Bay of Pigs invasion pitted US-based Cuban exiles against Fidel Castro's forces.

1959 Fidel Castro assumes power after the Cuban Revolution

June 1961 Kennedy and Khrushchev hold summit talks in Vienna

October 14, 1961 Joint Chiefs of Staff advise Kennedy to make an air strike on Cuba

October 23, 1961 Kennedy receives letter from Khrushchev stating a serious threat to peace. Robert Kennedy speaks with the Russian Ambassador.

October 24, 1961 All Russian ships, except one, reverse their course to Cuba

October 27, 1961 Kennedy sends Khrushchev a letter stating that the US will not invade Cuba if Khrushchev removes his missiles

October 28, 1961 Khrushchev announces his agreement to withdraw all missiles from Cuba

Resolution

During this very confused period, Kennedy's closest advisor was his brother, Robert Kennedy. There had been contradictory messages from the Soviet leadership. The first was the Soviet proposal to remove its missiles from Cuba. The second was a demand that the US remove its own missiles from Turkey. Robert Kennedy proposed that the US should respond to the first message and disregard the second, less conciliatory message. The end result was that, on October 28, Khrushchev announced his willingness to remove the Soviet missiles from Cuba.

Legacies

John F. Kennedy's cool leadership won him wide praise, and helped establish his reputation as a President who was willing to resist communist aggression.

Perhaps the most valuable legacy of the Cuban Missile Crisis was that it led to some thawing of the Cold War. A "hot line" was installed between Moscow and Washington to ensure that future crises could be resolved by the countries' leaders. The aftermath of the crisis also saw the start of negotiations that would lead to the signing of the treaty banning atmospheric testing of nuclear weapons.

Independent States

When the British left the Indian subcontinent in 1947, they left two countries delineated by religious differences—largely Hindu India, and basically Muslim Pakistan, a country in two sections separated by 1,000 miles (1,600 km)

ABOVE Yahya Khan, President of Pakistan from 1969 to 1971. Following Pakistan's defeat, he surrendered his powers and died in 1981 after a stroke.

From 1956 Pakistan's two parts were formally known as East and West Pakistan. In addition to distance, the country was divided by language and ethnicity. These divides were made worse by political and economic disparity. East Pakistan, making up half the population, was represented as only five provinces in the national assembly, while West Pakistan felt under-resourced and over-burdened by the central government.

Pakistan Election
In the first popular election, held in December 1970, the Awami League of Sheik Mujibur Rahman, supporting increased self-government for East Pakistan, won 160 of the East's 162 seats. The numbers should have made him Prime Minister of Pakistan. However, the country had

been under military rule for 13 years, and the incumbent President, Yahya Khan, faced with requests that the new prime minister not be an East Pakistani, ordered talks and postponed the change of government. Strikes and protests broke out in East Pakistan.

Bangladesh Atrocities
East Pakistan proclaimed itself as the independent republic of Bangladesh on March 25, 1971, after talks broke down in the provincial capital of Dhaka. However, sixty thousand West Pakistani troops had been left in Bangladesh, and at midnight they opened fire on student quarters and other sleeping civilian targets in Dhaka, beginning a spree of violence and killing. Mujibur Rahman was arrested at 1:00 A.M., escorted by tanks. With-

out their own military or police force for protection, Bengalis were forced to flee. Within a month, a million refugees had crossed the border into India, and continued to do so at a rate of 60,000 a day. Over the course of the conflict, around 10 million refugees spilled into India. Foreign intervention was not quickly forthcoming. The Nixon administration, as a part of its Cold War strategic interests in the region, continued to supply arms to Pakistan.

> The struggle this time is for our freedom. The struggle this time is for our independence.
> —Mujibur Rahman, (1920–1975), from a speech in Dhaka on March 7, 1971.

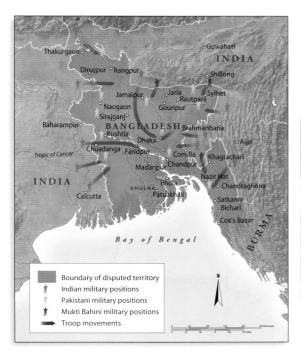

1971 India recognizes the Democratic Republic of Bangladesh, while Pakistan breaks off diplomatic relations

1971 Following defeat in the Bangladesh war Pakistan develops a nuclear weapons program

1974 Pakistan officially recognizes Bangladesh

1980 General Ziaur Rahman of Bangladesh is assassinated by army officers

1982 Hussein Mohammed Ershad seizes power in Bangladesh, in a bloodless coup

April 1991 A cyclone in Bangladesh kills approximately 131,000 people. Thousands of survivors die from hunger and water-borne disease, while about nine million are left homeless.

ABOVE Local resistance fighters known as the Mukti Bahini (trained and amed by India) joined with Indian forces to defeat Pakistan.

LEFT Daughter of Sheikh Mujibur Rahman, Sheikh Hasina Wazed attracts supporters of the Awami League in 1991. She was Prime Minister of Bangladesh from 1996 to 2001.

In November 1971, Indian troops crossed the border and attacked Pakistani positions inside Bangladesh. Within weeks they cut off the Pakistanis in Dhaka, encircling the city. Meanwhile, following Pakistani air attacks on India, the Indians invaded West Pakistan on December 4. The surrender of Pakistani forces in Bangladesh came on December 15, 1971.

Mujibur Rahman was released from prison on December 21, and returned to Dhaka where he was

to become Prime Minister of the People's Republic of Bangladesh until August 1975, when he and his family were shot in a military coup. While Bangladesh reached independence in 1971, the hard world of international alliances meant that recognition from other nations was slow to come. The USA tarried until 1972, and China vetoed the admission of Bangladesh to the United Nations, withholding its own recognition of the country until 1975.

ABOVE Covering the largest river delta in the world, Bangladesh is subject to flooding, bringing poverty and economic hardship.

BELOW Millions of people were left homeless following the atrocities in the Pakistan–Bangladesh conflict. Here refugees wash their clothes in the river at Dhaka, in 1971.

KISSINGER'S MYSTERY ILLNESS

During his visit to Bangladesh in July 1971, US Security advisor Henry Kissinger was mysteriously delayed by an "intestinal infection" during talks with the Pakistani leader, Yahya Khan. In fact, Kissinger flew in secret to Beijing to begin making plans with the Chinese for President Nixon's historic China visit.

ABOVE Security advisor, Henry Kissinger, briefs President Nixon and Secretary of State, William Rogers, following his trip to China.

Desert Storm

The immediate cause of the First Gulf War was Iraq's occupation of the state of Kuwait situated on the Gulf at the border of Iraq in August 1990.

Iraq sought cancellation of debts owed to Kuwait, arguing that it had incurred the debts in the cause of protecting Gulf states in the Iraq–Iran war of 1980–1989. Moreover, Saddam Hussein accused Kuwait of drilling diagonally to reach Iraqi oil through the Ramaila oilfield situated at the border. These economic questions were expanded into geopolitical ones, as Saddam claimed Kuwait was originally and rightfully an Iraqi territory—"the 19th province of Iraq." When the Kuwaitis—ruled by Emir Sheikh Jabir al-Sabah—refused to accede to the Iraqi demands, Saddam decided to invade.

International Condemnation

The reaction of the international community was immediate. UN Security Council Resolution 660 called for an immediate and unconditional Iraqi withdrawal from Kuwait. While diplomatic answers were being sought by members of the Arab League, and even the Soviet Union, the USA responded to a Saudi call for defense of its territory, and sent naval and military forces to Saudi Arabia in Operation Desert Shield.

Meanwhile, US President George H. W. Bush argued for a UN Security Council resolution authorizing use of any necessary means for expelling Iraq from Kuwait. He succeeded and UN Security Council Resolution 678 gave Saddam the deadline of January 15, 1991, for withdrawal.

LEFT General Norman Schwarzkopf offers words of encouragement to US Marines about to embark on their ground war offensive against Iraq.

RIGHT The encircling tactic of the Allied forces against the Iraqis during the First Gulf War led to a swift victory for the coalition.

SAUDI
ARABIA

Arab Allies

Despite significant opposition to the war inside and outside the US, a sizable coalition was mustered, including, significantly, Egypt, Syria, and Saudi Arabia. Great Britain and France contributed military forces, numbering 25,000 and 5,500 respectively.

Air Attack

When the January 15 deadline came and went, Operation Desert Storm began with massive

January 17, 1991
War begins at 2:38 am Baghdad time when Apache attack helicopters destroy Iraqi radar sites

January 22, 1991
Iraqi troops begin blowing up Kuwaiti oil wells

January 25, 1991
Iraqi troops dump millions of gallons of crude oil into the Gulf

February 13, 1991
Bombing raid by US forces kills 400 Iraqi civilians in an air raid shelter

February 24, 1991
Allied forces invade Iraq and Kuwait. The US Army is first to enter Iraqi territory.

February 26, 1991
Saddam Hussein orders withdrawal from Kuwait. Allied aircraft bomb retreating troops and about 10,000 are killed on the "Highway of Death."

March 17, 1991
US troops begin to arrive home

RIGHT During their withdrawal from Kuwait in early 1991, Iraqi troops set fire to more than 600 oil wells, dealing a devastating blow to Kuwait's petroleum-based economy.

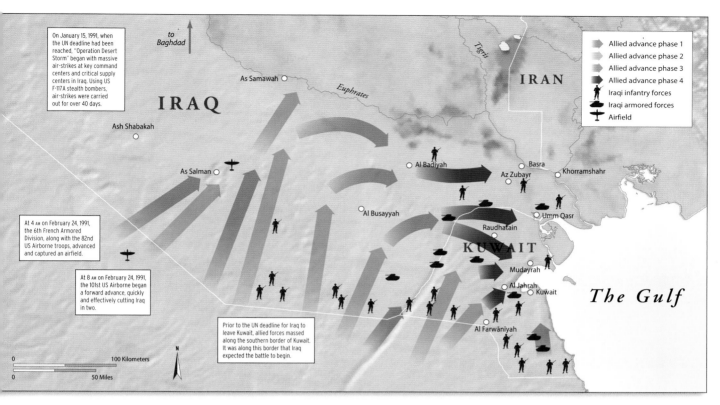

On January 15, 1991, when the UN deadline had been reached, "Operation Desert Storm" began with massive air-strikes at key command centers and critical supply centers in Iraq. Using US F-117A stealth bombers, air-strikes were carried out for over 40 days.

At 4 AM on February 24, 1991, the 6th French Armored Division, along with the 82nd US Airborne troops, advanced and captured an airfield.

At 8 AM on February 24, 1991, the 101st US Airborne began a forward advance, quickly and effectively cutting Iraq in two.

Prior to the UN deadline for Iraq to leave Kuwait, allied forces massed along the southern border of Kuwait. It was along this border that Iraq expected the battle to begin.

to Baghdad

IRAQ

IRAN

Euphrates

Tigris

As Samawah

Ash Shabakah

As Salman

Al Badiyah

Basra

Az Zubayr

Khorramshahr

Al Busayyah

Umm Qasr

Raudhatain

KUWAIT

Mudayrah

Al Jahrah

Kuwait

Al Farwaniyah

The Gulf

Allied advance phase 1
Allied advance phase 2
Allied advance phase 3
Allied advance phase 4
Iraqi infantry forces
Iraqi armored forces
Airfield

0   100 Kilometers
0   50 Miles
N

air-strikes aimed at key Iraqi command posts, communications centers, and power supplies. The newcomers to the war were the F-117A stealth bombers, and Tomahawk cruise missiles launched from ships in the Gulf. The air-strikes were carried out in over 100,000 sorties over 40 days. The Iraqi Air Force offered no opposition, having been moved to neighboring Iran for protection, leaving the coalition with free access to bomb.

Missile Response
The most significant form of counter-attack from the Iraqis came in the form of long-range SCUD missile attacks. On January 18, eight such missiles were fired from Iraq into Israel in the hope of provoking Israeli retaliation—two landing in Tel Aviv, and three near Haifa. On January 20, a successful SCUD hit was made on a US station in Riyadh, causing casualties for the coalition.

Land Attack
The commander of the coalition, General Norman Schwarzkopf, had planned an encircling tactic in which coalition forces would not only push through Kuwait but also outflank the Iraqi troops from the west. On February 24, the land attack was launched. It lasted only 100 hours. The encircling tactic was successful in cutting off the Iraqi troop columns retreating from Kuwait to Basra. These

regular Iraqi troops were exposed helplessly to devastating land and air fire.

Surrender
President Bush pulled back from his aim of deposing Saddam Hussein and destroying his Republican Guard, fearing a costly occupation with no "exit strategy." Iraq agreed to the UN's terms for a ceasefire on March 3, but on their way out sabotaged Kuwaiti oil wells.

We would have been forced to occupy Baghdad and, in effect, rule Iraq...There was no viable "exit strategy" we could see, violating another of our principles.
–President George H. W. Bush on why he didn't seek to eliminate Saddam Hussein.

LEFT Located across the border in Saudi Arabia, the US Army 1st Cavalry's M270 Multiple Launch Rocket System (MLRS) fires a long-range missile into an Iraqi-held position in Kuwait.

Hello World

Only a little over 2 percent of the world regularly uses the Internet, yet it has changed the way the world works, thinks, and communicates. It is truly the people's voice.

People send e-mail, instant messages, buy and sell goods on Amazon.com and eBay, look for information on Google, and use Facebook for social networking. Sitting in front of the personal computer and making contact with people and institutions on every continent became part of everyday life by the turn of the twenty-first century.

Getting There

These everyday activities are the results of a series of revolutionary technological inventions. The wartime creation of the first room-sized mainframe computers to break German coded military messages, and the ENIAC to build the atomic bomb, ignited a new technological revolution.

Several related innovations between the 1960s and 1990s made it possible to store thousands of documents electronically. Networks and ways to store and send information already existed, but the invention of the World Wide Web created the easiest way to access them, becoming the flagship of the communications revolution.

Big Blue vs Apple

The appearance of the personal computer in 1974 was another turning point. The first microprocessor-based computer was produced in France in the 1970s, but then Apple and IBM took over. Instead of the first giant computers weighing tons, desk and later laptop computers gradually became household gadgets. By the late

1990s, every other person in the United States and every fifth person in Europe had a computer.

WWW

The Internet and the World Wide Web are often confused, but they are not the same. The Internet (or interconnected networks) is like a freeway system, a system of interconnected networks of computers, while the Web is like a truck service with a vast fleet of loaded trucks carrying information. The Web is only one of the services accessible via the Internet that is the network of the networks.

World Standard

By the end of the 1980s the Internet managed to contact the previously existing different

public computer networks and become a world standard. In September 2007, 1,244 billion people used the Internet, although only 2 percent of the world population uses it on a regular basis. The lingua franca of the Internet is English—31 percent of the users communicate in English, 16 percent in Chinese, 9 percent in Spanish, 7 percent in Japanese, and 5 percent in both German and French. However, 37 percent of Internet users are in Asia, 27 percent in Europe, 19 percent in North America, and 9 percent in Latin America.

Organic Connection

The Internet is a central institution of the communication revolution. Its decentralized system has trans-

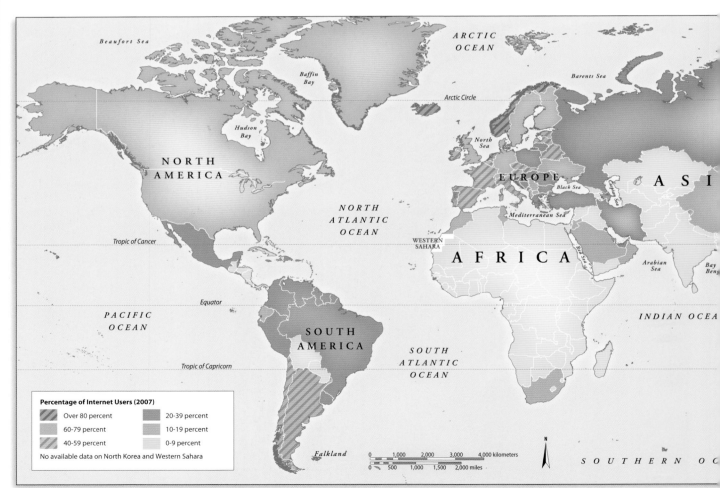

Percentage of Internet Users (2007)

- Over 80 percent
- 60-79 percent
- 40-59 percent
- 20-39 percent
- 10-19 percent
- 0-9 percent

No available data on North Korea and Western Sahara

RIGHT Via the power of the Internet students in a classroom in Zambia receive a conservation message about the black rhinoceros from an instructor at Frankfurt Zoo, Germany.

formed personal communication. At the beginning critics suggested that the Internet would bring into being an isolated virtual world attracting users away from the "real world" of reading and meaningful conversation with family and friends. In reality, the Internet became part of the real world, assisting social networking, more frequent contact with friends, and even more reading. It created free and rapid information flow despite efforts in dictatorial countries to impose Internet censorship.

The Internet made it possible to work from home, outsource jobs to other countries, and assist in collaborative work by people of different nations and locations. In less than two decades the Internet has conquered almost the entire world.

LEFT The number of Internet users worldwide has rapidly increased during the past five years.

> You affect the world by what you browse.
> –Tim Berners-Lee, English computer contractor who worked with Robert Cailliau to create the World Wide Web.

BELOW A drop in the ocean: The four layers of the World Wide Web suspended in the "deepest" layer of individual sites, accessed only by knowing the exact address.

WORLD WIDE WEB

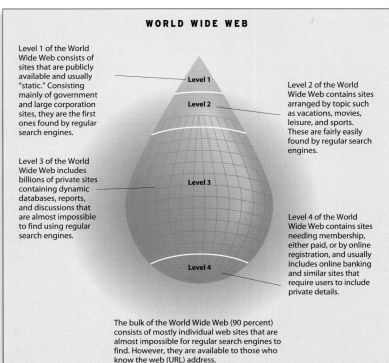

Level 1 of the World Wide Web consists of sites that are publicly available and usually "static." Consisting mainly of government and large corporation sites, they are the first ones found by regular search engines.

Level 2 of the World Wide Web contains sites arranged by topic such as vacations, movies, leisure, and sports. These are fairly easily found by regular search engines.

Level 3 of the World Wide Web includes billions of private sites containing dynamic databases, reports, and discussions that are almost impossible to find using regular search engines.

Level 4 of the World Wide Web contains sites needing membership, either paid, or by online registration, and usually includes online banking and similar sites that require users to include private details.

The bulk of the World Wide Web (90 percent) consists of mostly individual web sites that are almost impossible for regular search engines to find. However, they are available to those who know the web (URL) address.

October 1, 1969 The first ARPANet message sent: "lo". Trying to spell login, but the system crashed.

March 1972 First basic e-mail programs written by Ray Tomlinson. "@" sign chosen for its "at" meaning.

1976 Apple Computer founded by Steve Jobs and Steve Wozniak

1980 Tim Berners-Lee writes program called "Enquire Within," predecessor to the World Wide Web

1981 IBM announces its first Personal Computer. Microsoft creates DOS.

1983 Domain Name System (DNS) designed by Jon Postel, Paul Mockapetris, and Craig Partridge; .edu, .gov, .com, .mil, .org, .net, and .int created.

1984 William Gibson writes "Neuromancer." Coins the term "cyberspace." Apple Computer introduces the Macintosh on January 24.

March 15, 1985 Symbolic.com becomes the first registered domain

1990 Tim Berners-Lee creates the World Wide Web

1999 "Surfing the Internet" is coined by Jean Armour Polly

February 2007 Apple surpasses one billion iTunes downloads

April 2007 Search engine Google surpasses Microsoft as "the most valuable global brand," and also is the most visited Web site

Unequal World

The continuing advance of technology has indelibly marked the twenty-first century, but not all countries nor all peoples have shared in the spoils.

This spread of technology could potentially empower millions by providing them the opportunity to quickly and cheaply collaborate with others worldwide using a personal computer and Internet access.

The Internet also places private information at risk. Most companies offering search engines store records of search queries, with most of the public either accepting or unaware of such practices.

Healthcare

Technology is also affecting healthcare issues. The collection and collation of DNA samples enables researchers to unlock puzzles about the human body. The genome of an organism (its hereditary information) could be used to treat or prevent diseases before they pose a serious problem.

The tragedy of HIV/AIDS combined with poverty in Africa and elsewhere has reached a new level of awareness worldwide. Retroviral drugs can increase a sufferer's life span substantially, but their high cost limits widespread use.

Hunger

Hunger has soared in a world of plenty, as global food prices have spiked, leaving millions with too little to eat. Many blame the increased use of biofuels for motor fuels. This greater demand for food crops inflates their prices, which disproportionately harms the poor.

Environment

The global environment has received much attention this century, as science has linked weather volatility, resource scarcity, disease, and the extinction of species to human activity. Highly developed countries, like the United States, contribute heavily to the production of greenhouse gasses. But the emerging economies of China and India also harm the environment and may do much more damage in the years to come as their economies grow.

Economy

The world's economy remains highly dependent on petrol. For economic and environmental reasons, much effort has been expended on developing alternative sources of energy, including water, wind, and solar power. An increasingly popular source is biofuels, controversially derived from food crops.

Politics

There have also been important geopolitical changes. The steep rise in the price of oil has provided an economic boost to Russia, which has raised the standard of living of its middle class significantly. China's economic reforms and increasing status as a center for mass production position it to become dominant later in the century. India is another country with great economic and military potential. Its competition with China in these two areas will ensure that Asia remains a region of great geopolitical significance.

Terrorism

Terrorism, though not a new tactic on the political horizon, has adopted a higher profile this century.

On September 11, 2001, suicide bombers crashed jet planes into buildings symbolizing American economic and military might, killing and injuring thousands. The United States responded by invading Afghanistan, which was providing safe harbor for al-Qa'eda, the militant Islamic group that masterminded the attacks.

The United States proclaimed that it was opening a second front in its global war on terror (GWOT) by invading Iraq in 2003. The Iraq War toppled the regime of Saddam Hussein, but the successor government has failed to unify the nation's competing ethnic groups and solve the ongoing civil strife.

GWOT also indicates the limits of traditional military technology, as America's superiority in this area has yet to produce a victory. Conversely, information technology has greatly benefited the insurgents by allowing them to communicate with cells worldwide by the use of the Internet and instant messaging, and by creating and disseminating high production-quality recruiting videos.

The digital divide has increasingly segmented the planet between those who have access to the technology and the skills to manipulate it and those who do not, thus reinforcing existing racial, social, and economic inequities.

ABOVE Robert Mugabe's Zanu-PF party have presided over a dramatic decline in Zimbabwe's fortunes. Inflation is rampant and food shortages are at critical levels.

LEFT Years of civil strife, refugee movements, wars, and drought have left more than 200 million Africans, like this Kenyan woman accepting food in Nairobi, dependent on international aid.

RIGHT The devastating cyclone that tore through Myanmar on May 2, 2008, left hundreds of thousands dead and two million homeless. Weather volatility is predicted to increase as a result of global warming.

PREVIOUS PAGES A child lies down on a peace flag lining St Peter's Square, Vatican City, as demonstrators demand the release of Italian hostages held in Iraq during 2004.

Push and Pull of People

In general, as countries become increasingly developed there is a fall in the rate of growth of the population. In 2007, the global fertility rates ranged from about four children per female in developing countries to about one child in the most developed.

By the twenty-first century there had been numerous improvements in medical care and basic sanitation that had affected most parts of the world through an increase in life expectancy. In countries where the fertility rate—the average number of children born to the average woman—had not fallen, this caused an increase in the population size. There seems to be an inverse relationship between the level of development in a country and the rate of population growth.

Effects of Migration

The early twenty-first century is seeing an array of views about the virtues of migration. Supporters would argue that it is beneficial from an economic perspective, particularly for countries with a relatively small population or labor

We estimate that there are at least 190 million migrants in the world.
–United Nations Population Division (2005).

force. Proponents of migration also highlight the benefits of migration from developing to developed countries, whereby migrants can provide a boost to aging societies, because most migrants are nearer the beginning of their working career.

Those against migration claim that there is an additional state welfare cost as migrants have to be supported in the same way as the existing population and that migrants can crowd out domestic labor by taking jobs that would

RIGHT Some of the 6,000 people rushing to be sworn in as US citizens prior to July 30, 2007, when the cost of Green Cards and naturalization fees rose considerably.

BELOW The number of people migrating per country is indicated here with a minus showing the average number leaving. Positive numbers indicate the average number of arrivals.

otherwise be filled by the indigenous population. A more general concern about immigration pertains to cooperation between the migrants and existing populations and the desire to avoid social

conflict. Such tensions came to a head in Paris during the 2006 riots between the indigenous population and the African and Arab youth, whose parents had emigrated to France.

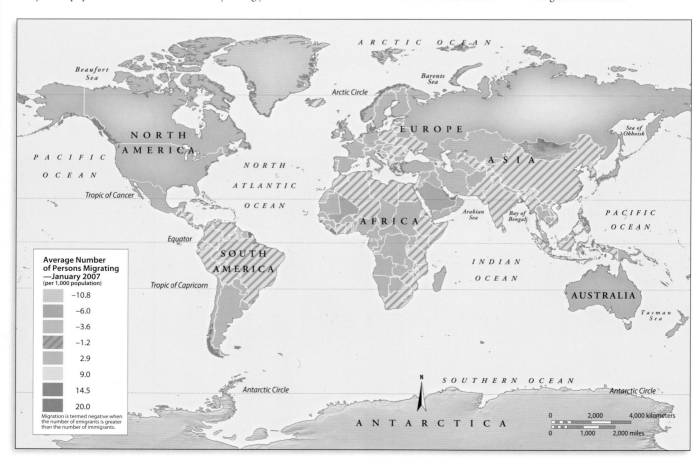

Average Number of Persons Migrating —January 2007 (per 1,000 population)

	−10.8
	−6.0
	−3.6
	−1.2
	2.9
	9.0
	14.5
	20.0

Migration is termed negative when the number of emigrants is greater than the number of immigrants.

2007, July World population is 6,602,224,175

2007 World population average age is 28 years

2007 World birth rate is 20.09 births per 1,000 population. Death rate is 8.37 deaths per 1,000 population.

2007 World average life expectancy is 65.82 years

2007 World literacy rate is 82 percent. Two thirds of the 785 million illiterate people in the world are women.

LEFT This mass naturalization ceremony took place at DisneyWorld, Florida, where 1,000 people braved the weather to recite the Pledge of Allegiance on July 4, 2007.

Reasons for Migration

Understanding the reasons for migration helps to clarify the movement of populations in the twenty-first century. These reasons can be considered in terms of push and pull factors.

Push factors represent reasons why the population might want to leave their original location and can include factors from social unrest or war to a shortage of economic opportunities.

Pull factors are features of the new country that make it attractive for immigrants, such as civil liberties or political freedom. Attractive for an extra array of pull factors are countries like Australia, UK, and USA, which tend to offer better security, health, and education systems than many immigrants have in their country of origin.

Effects of War

In the most extreme cases, certain populations can be forced to migrate for reasons of personal safety. In this situation, migrants are often referred to as refugees or asylum seekers.

As a result of the invasion of Iraq more Iraqis have lost their homes than any other nation, and

about two million of them have fled Iraq, as of 2007. The UN estimates that 40 percent of Iraq's middle class have fled, which includes all kinds of people who have been forced to leave by militia.

Jordan's immigration rate of 0.63 percent was one of the highest during the early twenty-first century, a direct result of the high proportion or Iraqi refugees the country has received.

ABOVE Because of overcrowding in the school, children must be taught outdoors and bring their own supplies in Devannapet, India. Lack of indoor space also restricts computer access for the children. Demand for education is growing steadily.

Buying Power– Europe and the Euro

Although it has been an example of successful regional integration, one of the primary concerns with the idea of a European Union has been the problem of defining the notion of "Europe," both geographically and politically.

1949 France, Great Britain, and the Benelux countries make plans for a Council of Europe

1951 The Treaty of Paris is signed by Belgium, France, Germany, Italy, Luxembourg, and the Netherlands

1954 The Council of Ministers of the Council of Europe adopt the blue flag and twelve-star emblem

1978 The European Council establishes the European Monetary System based on central currency

1983 A draft treaty is presented to the European Parliament establishing the European Union

1993 The Single European Market comes into force

2002 Euro coins and notes enter circulation

RIGHT "Into the EU as farmers, not as beggars." Czech farmers protested for more government aid during 2002 because they did not expect to receive the same level of subsidy enjoyed by farmers with existing EU membership.

The European Union had its beginnings in the aftermath of World War II. Throughout the second half of the twentieth century, the growth and development of European integration was centered on the political and economic stability of the region.

The Beginnings of Union
One of the first successful proposals for European cooperation came in the 1951 Treaty of Paris, which created the European Coal and Steel Community (ECSC). Its founding members—France, West Germany, Belgium, Italy, Luxembourg, and the Netherlands—declared it "a first step in the federation of Europe."

In 1967, the ECSC was joined by the European Atomic Community (EURATOM) and the European Economic Community (EEC) in the Merger Treaty, which created a single set of institutions for the three communities—these are now collectively referred to as the European Communities (EC).

The Middle Years
In 1973, the EC enlarged to include Denmark, the Republic of Ireland,

and the United Kingdom. Norway had negotiated to join at the same time but a national referendum rejected membership. The first direct democratic elections of members of the European Parliament were held in 1979. In 1981, Greece joined, and in 1986, Spain and Portugal. During this period, the collective nations increasingly presented a united front to the rest of the world. In 1990, after the withdrawal of Soviet control and support, the former East Germany became part of the EC

> Therefore I say to you:
> Let Europe arise!
> –Winston Churchill ending his address at the University of Zurich, 1946.

in a newly reunited Germany. This was a significant moment in the evolution and expansion of the integration effort.

Maastricht Treaty
In 1991, the beginning stages of Eastern amalgamation into the EC called for formal criteria to be established for candidate nations to fulfil. These conditions, which were referred to as the "Copenhagen Criteria," were agreed at the European Council Summit at Maastricht in December 1991. The treaty of European Union, now referred to as the Maastricht Treaty, was signed on February 7, 1992, and entered into force on November 1, 1993.

EU Expansion
In 1995, Austria, Sweden, and Finland joined the EU. The 1997 Amsterdam Treaty amended the Maastricht Treaty in areas such as democracy and foreign policy. The Amsterdam Treaty was followed by the Treaty of Nice in 2001, which

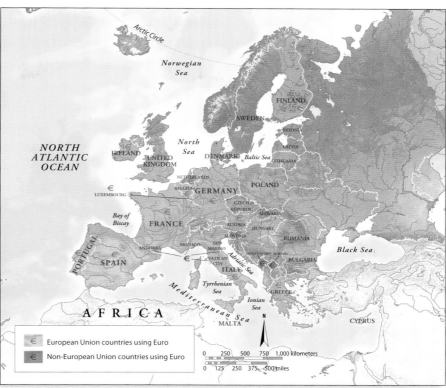

European Union countries using Euro

Non-European Union countries using Euro

0 250 500 750 1,000 kilometers
0 125 250 375 500 miles

ABOVE In 2006, a red-and-white sea of trade unionists demonstrated in Berlin against wage dumping in the European Union. The protest was to demand protection for the German job market against cheap labor from Eastern Europe.

ABOVE LEFT Former French president François Mitterrand casts his vote in the 1992 referendum on the Maastricht Treaty for a united Europe. Voter turnout was relatively low.

Founding members of EU
Countries joining EU in 1995
Countries joining EU in 2004
Countries joining EU in 2007
Candidate countries

0 500 1,000 kilometers
0 250 500 miles

ABOVE Although the euro is the EU unit of currency, some member nations prefer to keep their own currency, as part of their individual cultural identity.

LEFT Each member of the EU must meet the Copenhagen criteria, which specify particular political and economic requirements.

revised the Rome and Maastricht Treaties to allow the EU to cope with enlargement to the East.

Preparations for the Euro

The "euro" was established by the provisions in the 1992 Maastricht Treaty on European Union, which was used to establish an economic and monetary union. In order to participate in the new currency, member states had to meet strict criteria such as a budget deficit of less than 3 percent of their gross domestic product (GDP), a debt ratio of less than 60 percent of GDP, low inflation, and interest rates close to the EU average. The Single market went into force in January 1993. The decision was made in 1995 to call the new currency the "euro."

Twenty-first Century

The European Union is made up of 27 independent sovereign countries which are known as member states. They are: Austria, Belgium, Bulgaria, Cyprus, the Czech Republic, Denmark, Estonia, Finland, France, Germany, Greece, Hungary, Ireland, Italy, Latvia, Lithuania, Luxembourg, Malta, the Netherlands, Poland, Portugal, Romania, Slovakia, Slovenia, Spain, Sweden, and the United Kingdom.

Its political centers are Brussels, Luxembourg, and Strasbourg, and it is governed by three institutions—the European Commission, the European Parliament, and the Council of the European Union. Although European integration is still controversial, the EU's motto remains "United in Diversity."

Islamic Fundamentalism

Islamic fundamentalism emerged during the 1970s from a combination of new thoughts, significant events, and unfolding social conditions.

CANADA

UNITED STATES OF AMERICA

New York

Washington DC

Aircraft hijacks and attacks on Washington DC and New York City, September 11, 2001.

NORTH ATLANTIC OCEAN

Tropic of Cancer

Equator

SOUTH AMERICA

Tropic of Capricorn

1979 Revolution in Iran sees the Shah overthrown. Ayatollah Khomeini takes control and introduces strict Islamic practices.

1982 An uprising by a Muslim Brotherhood is suppressed by Syrian forces but thousands are killed

1989 Osama bin Laden founds the al-Qa'eda network

1996 Taliban in Afghanistan restrict women's role in Islamic society

2000 Prime Minister of Israel, Ariel Sharon, visits the al-Aqsa Mosque accompanied by armed police and riot forces, beginning the second Arab intifada

2001 Taliban leader Mullah Omar invokes outrage when calling for destruction of all pre-Islamic statues and shrines in Afghanistan

One of the great trends in the Middle East since the 1980s has been the rise of piety and religious politics, and Islam is now seen to offer many people an alternative political and social system to other ideologies, especially the secular ones that previously dominated Middle Eastern politics. An aspect of the growth of Islam has been the rise of Islamic fundamentalism.

Types

Islamic fundamentalism consists of three main variants. The first is those who are literally fundamentalist in interpreting scripture, believing that society is impious and wicked and, as a result, needs to return to the core or fundamental principles of Islam. Such people are usually not violent, though some argue that this view foreshadows violence.

A second variant takes this fundamentalist interpretation further, arguing for the inseparability of religion and politics and thus the creation of an Islamic nation-state. This approach often is found in groups and parties with a strong social justice agenda.

A third variant goes further still, adopting a radical or violent approach to the promotion of Islam. Some seek to remove a leader through revolution or violence, while others reject the

ABOVE Many Afghani families seek refuge outside their own country as a result of violence and threats from the fundamentalist Taliban regime.

> Call [the community] to jihad ('holy war') for the sake of God Almighty and call her to motivate people for it.
> –Osama bin Laden, message to clerics in the mid-1990s.

state completely and want to replace it with a political and legal system based on Islamic law—*shari'a*. Some go even further, arguing that the entire concept of nation-states is foreign to Islam and divides Muslims from each other. This view may seek to replace the state with a pan-Islamic community, or to replace secular institutions with religious ones.

International Context

Some fundamentalists draw their ideas from intellectuals such as Hassan al-Banna or Sayyid Qutb, early Egyptian Muslim Brothers. Much scholarship now exists that emerged from the debate started by al-Banna and promoted by Qutb and other thinkers.

Events since the 1970s have further strengthened the profile and appeal of Islamic fundamentalism. The 1978–1979 Iranian revolution was the first time a secular system was replaced with an "Islamic state." This was followed by the USSR's invasion of Afghanistan in 1979. The conflict that followed attracted many Muslims from around the world, and the success of these *mujahideen*—holy warriors—against the Soviet superpower helped legitimise Islamic fundamentalism.

The end of the Cold War increased US involvement in the Middle East, which added to the grievances expressed by many Islamic fundamentalists. Many saw the 1991 and 2003 wars

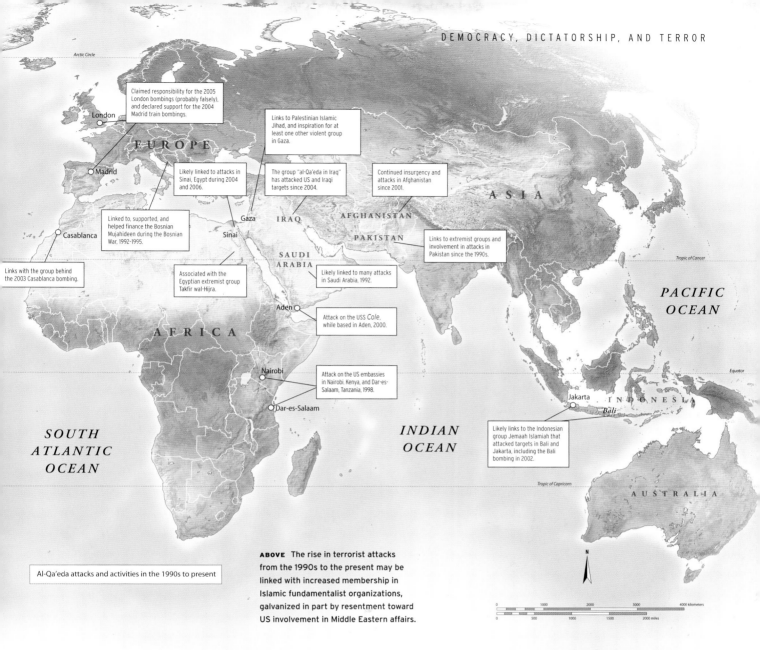

Claimed responsibility for the 2005 London bombings (probably falsely), and declared support for the 2004 Madrid train bombings.

Links to Palestinian Islamic Jihad, and inspiration for at least one other violent group in Gaza.

Likely linked to attacks in Sinai, Egypt during 2004 and 2006.

The group "al-Qa'eda in Iraq" has attacked US and Iraqi targets since 2004.

Continued insurgency and attacks in Afghanistan since 2001.

Linked to, supported, and helped finance the Bosnian Mujahideen during the Bosnian War, 1992-1995.

Links to extremist groups and involvement in attacks in Pakistan since the 1990s.

Links with the group behind the 2003 Casablanca bombing.

Associated with the Egyptian extremist group Takfir wal-Hijra.

Likely linked to many attacks in Saudi Arabia, 1992.

Attack on the USS *Cole*, while based in Aden, 2000.

Attack on the US embassies in Nairobi, Kenya, and Dar-es-Salaam, Tanzania, 1998.

Likely links to the Indonesian group Jemaah Islamiah that attacked targets in Bali and Jakarta, including the Bali bombing in 2002.

Al-Qa'eda attacks and activities in the 1990s to present

ABOVE The rise in terrorist attacks from the 1990s to the present may be linked with increased membership in Islamic fundamentalist organizations, galvanized in part by resentment toward US involvement in Middle Eastern affairs.

against Iraq as "crusades" by the West against a Muslim country, and as attempts to gain control of the region and its oil. In the minds of some, including many fundamentalists, the region is under attack from the West, particularly the US, which justifies a *jihad*—holy war—in response. Violent fundamentalists, including for example al-Qa'eda, have used this argument to rationalize attacks on their governments and the West as a whole.

RIGHT Floral tributes crowd the steps of Parliament House in Melbourne, Australia, in memory of those killed in the Bali bombings of October 2002, instigated by Islamic fundamentalists of Indonesia.

> It is sheer foolishness, in addition to being wholly un-Islamic, to imagine that Islam can be established through violent or offensive means...
>
> –Waris Mazhari, editor *Tarjuman Darul Uloom.*

ABOVE In Gaza City, the Palestinian political party Hamas holds a female rally against the peace conference taking place in the US city of Annapolis, 2007. The conference proposed a two-state solution to the Israeli-Palestinian conflict.

RIGHT The distribution of predominantly Islamic populations worldwide is centered around the Middle East and North Africa where the religion arose.

- 90–100 percent Islamic
- 70–89 percent Islamic
- 50–69 percent Islamic
- 30–49 percent Islamic
- 10–29 percent Islamic
- 0–9 percent Islamic

Changing Social Context

Over this same tumultuous period, social and economic conditions in the Middle East have changed. Regional economic performance has declined, compared with the 1970s. Population growth is among the highest in the world, as is unemployment, which sits at a regional average of 15 percent.

Governments therefore have lost their legitimacy—and these governments are often secular. Some came to power through coups, promising but not delivering democracy and greater equity.

More conservative monarchies in the region face fundamentalist opposition, too. Osama bin Laden has often criticized the Saudi royal family for being corrupt, and other fundamentalists criticize their governments for failing to build a strong and pious society, or for not sharing oil wealth fairly.

Appeal

It is impossible to put a figure on how many people in the Middle East or elsewhere should be called "Islamic fundamentalists," but in countries where Islamist parties or groups operate relatively freely, they usually gain significant, but not majority, support. They are numerous enough to worry many governments in the region.

The lure of Islamic fundamentalism comes from the promise of something new for the disenfranchised or embittered. This is where the decline in support for existing governments has been most important. Many fundamentalist groups also build up their support through vocal opposition to Israel and support for the Palestinians. Palestinian Hamas and Islamic Jihad are examples, as is Hezbollah—the Party of God—in Lebanon. Hamas and Hezbollah have both military and social wings, the former engaging in violence, and the latter to demonstrate piety and build support.

Still others, especially al-Qa'eda and other violent international groups, derive support from a fear of foreign cultural and military penetration. Some of these are anti-Western, specifically anti-American in their rhetoric or actions, while others are worried about the corrupting influence of foreign culture, such as international companies, consumer brand names, and foreign social values.

Future

The future of Islamic fundamentalism depends on two things. The first is how well mainstream governments and leaders respond to economic and social conditions—a failure in these areas will give further opportunities and legitimacy to fundamentalists.

The second is the success or failure of fundamentalists that do gain power, and their ability to deliver what they promise and to seem successful compared to the governments they replace.

OSAMA BIN LADEN

Perhaps the most famous violent Islamic fundamentalist of all is Osama bin Laden, the founder and chief of al-Qa'eda. Al-Qa'eda is actually a conglomeration of extremist Islamic groups, formed in 1988, with many of its initial members veterans of the fight against the Soviets in Afghanistan in the 1980s. Bin Laden was born in Saudi Arabia, probably in 1957. He had a devout childhood, despite his family being extremely wealthy due to connections with the Saudi royals. While he was a student, he grew increasingly interested in religion, and developed the view, shared with many fundamentalists, that a return to Quranic law and a war of *jihad* was necessary. He was involved in fighting the Soviets in Afghanistan during the 1980s. In the 1990s, he moved about, from Saudi Arabia to Sudan in 1992 and then to Afghanistan in 1996. Bin Laden and al-Qa'eda were involved in terrorist attacks in the Middle East and Africa after this time, most spectacularly the 2001 attacks on the United States. Since then he has been in hiding. His effectiveness has been reduced by the War on Terrorism, and some now see bin Laden and al-Qa'eda as more important as symbols than as an actual person and organization.

2001 to Present

Nine-Eleven

The death of 3,000 Americans at the hands of 19 al-Qa'eda operatives in New York, Washington DC, and Pennsylvania traumatized a watching public, sent shockwaves around the globe, and changed the course of world history.

RIGHT The horrific ruins of the Twin Towers are still smoldering after collapse. Surrounding buildings and indeed most of lower Manhattan were damaged by debris.

BELOW RIGHT This aerial view of the Pentagon in Washington DC shows the outer building completely penetrated. Fire spread through surrounding offices after the crash.

September 11, 2001

8:46 A.M. Jet fighters are scrambled from Otis Air National Guard Base in Massachusetts

9:08 A.M. The FAA bans all takeoffs going to or through New York airspace and shuts down all airports and civilian flights

9:31 A.M. President George W. Bush makes a statement from Florida calling the crashes an "apparent terrorist attack"

9:45 A.M. The FAA orders all airborne aircraft in the US to land at the nearest airports

9:48 A.M. The White House West Wing and the Capitol building are evacuated

2:51 P.M. The US Navy dispatches missile destroyers to New York and Washington DC

8:30 P.M. President Bush addresses the nation from the Oval Office

On the morning of September 11, 2001, 19 hijackers boarded four domestic US flights with the intention of flying the planes into specified buildings in New York City and Washington DC. At 8:48 A.M. American Airlines Flight 11, from Boston to Los Angeles, crashed into the 96th floor of the North Tower of the 110-story World Trade Center buildings in downtown Manhattan.

Within 18 minutes, a second flight from Boston to Los Angeles crashed into the 78th floor of the South Tower—the "twin" to the North Tower. As television cameras rolled, 10,000 gallons (38,000 liters) of flaming airplane fuel caused such fierce heat as to melt the steel supports of the high-rise buildings. At 9:59 A.M. the South Tower collapsed; the North Tower followed within 30 minutes.

Meanwhile, at 9:40 A.M. a third plane, American Airlines Flight 77, from Dulles Airport near Washington DC, crashed into the Pentagon, home of the US Defense Department, across the Potomac River from the White House. One hundred twenty-five staff were killed.

A fourth flight was hijacked and probably intended for attacking the White House. United Airlines Flight 93, instead, crashed into a field in Somerset County near Pittsburgh in Pennsylvania. Passengers on the flight had cell phone contact with family on the ground. Learning of the other attacks, some passengers decided to overpower the hijackers in order to prevent the plane from hitting its intended target.

Including the hijackers, all 265 passengers and crew on the four flights perished. At the World Trade Center site, an estimated 2,830 people are thought to have died, including 343 firefighters and police.

RIGHT The South Tower of the World Trade Center implodes as the North Tower begins to burn. The heat of the jet fuel melted the metal stanchions that supported the buildings.

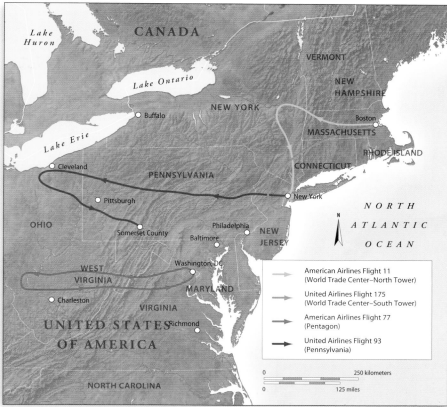

The attacks that September came amid a succession of attacks that were coordinated by Osama bin Laden, a Saudi national at the head of the underground Islamic terrorist network al-Qa'eda. Leading up to the attacks, the Central Intelligence Agency and the Federal Bureau of Investigation had separate and uncoordinated intelligence on al-Qa'eda movements. A general warning had been issued about a possible attack on US soil. On August 6, a briefing given to President George W. Bush was entitled, "Bin Laden Determined to Strike in US."

Effects

The attacks of 2001 drastically changed the politics of the United States both domestically and in its relationship with the world. Culturally, the attacks caused an outpouring of patriotism as "United We Stand" banners plastered cities. Laws were quickly passed extending and integrating the powers of the federal government for matters of national security.

The *USA Patriot Act* of October 2001 strengthened the investigative powers of the Justice Department, and a totally new Department of

ABOVE The disaster of the 9/11 hijackings had consequences for all airlines. In an effort to prevent the bankruptcy of the airlines, the September 11th Victim Compensation Fund was founded. Those joining the action agreed not to sue. Average payout was $1.8 million.

LEFT The people of New York chose to honor the victims of 9/11 with a symbol of the Twin Towers. Here, memorial lights pierce the sky above New York on the fifth anniversary.

Homeland Security was established in 2003, combining many agencies.

War on Terrorism

In response to the attacks, President Bush declared an open-ended "war on terrorism." The USA issued an ultimatum to the Taliban government of Afghanistan insisting that they hand over the al-Qa'eda leader. When Taliban head, Mohammed Omar, refused, the USA attacked

Afghanistan, supported by NATO. In an historic first, NATO had recognized the attacks of September 11 as an attack on all NATO members.

By early December, the US, NATO, and the warlords had defeated Taliban troops, forcing them to withdraw into Pakistan. The US had successfully ousted the Taliban, but failed to produce Osama bin Laden.

Our war on terror begins with al-Qa'eda, but it does not end there. It will not end until every terrorist group of global reach has been found, stopped, and defeated.

–President George W. Bush, during an address to Congress and the American people, September 20, 2001.

The Goldilocks Zone

The Sun is our star giving us warmth and life and Earth sits perfectly in the "Goldilocks zone" of "just right" temperature. But if we continue to thicken the natural greenhouse blanket that keeps our planet safe, we will destroy the parts of our world that sustain life itself.

The climate system consists of the atmosphere, land surface, snow and ice, oceans and other water bodies, as well as living things.

This system evolves in time due to influences from internal and external drivers that include natural phenomena such as volcanic eruptions and solar variations, along with human-induced changes in atmospheric composition such as the increase of greenhouse gases.

The Driving Force

Solar radiation powers and drives the climate system and, due to the Earth being a sphere, the tropics receive more energy than higher latitudes. Consequently, energy is transported from the equatorial areas to higher latitudes through atmospheric and oceanic circulations, including storm systems. Energy in the form of "latent heat" is needed to evaporate water from the sea or land surface, and this energy is released when water vapor condenses in clouds.

Due to the Earth's rotation, the atmospheric circulation patterns tend to be biased towards east-west. Embedded in the mid-latitude, westerly winds are large-scale weather systems that act to transport heat toward the poles. These weather systems are the familiar migrating low- and high-pressure systems and their associated cold and warm fronts.

Changing the Balance

Generally speaking, the radiation balance of the Earth can be influenced by changing the incoming solar radiation, such as by changes in Earth's orbit or in the Sun itself; changing the fraction of solar radiation that is reflected, such as by variations in cloud cover, atmospheric particles, or vegetation; and altering the long wave radiation from Earth back towards space, such as by changing greenhouse gas concentrations.

For example, as rising concentrations of greenhouse gases warm Earth's climate, snow and ice begin to melt. This melting reveals darker land and water surfaces that used to be covered by snow and ice, and these darker surfaces absorb more of the Sun's heat, causing more warming, which causes more melting, and so on, in a self-reinforcing cycle. This reaction cycle strengthens the primary warming caused by rising levels of greenhouse gases.

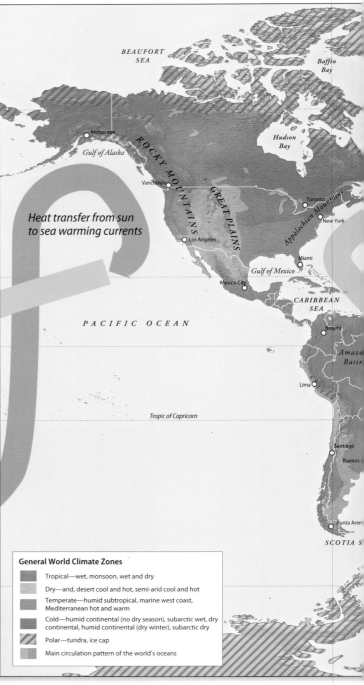

Heat transfer from sun to sea warming currents

General World Climate Zones

- Tropical—wet, monsoon, wet and dry
- Dry—arid, desert cool and hot, semi-arid cool and hot
- Temperate—humid subtropical, marine west coast, Mediterranean hot and warm
- Cold—humid continental (no dry season), subarctic wet, dry continental, humid continental (dry winter), subarctic dry
- Polar—tundra, ice cap
- Main circulation pattern of the world's oceans

LEFT More than 25,000 bicyclists take part in Earth Day, April 20, 2008, in Budapest, Hungary.

RIGHT Engraving of Joseph Fourier (1768-1830), mathematician, who is credited with discovering that gases in the atmosphere might increase the surface temperature on Earth.

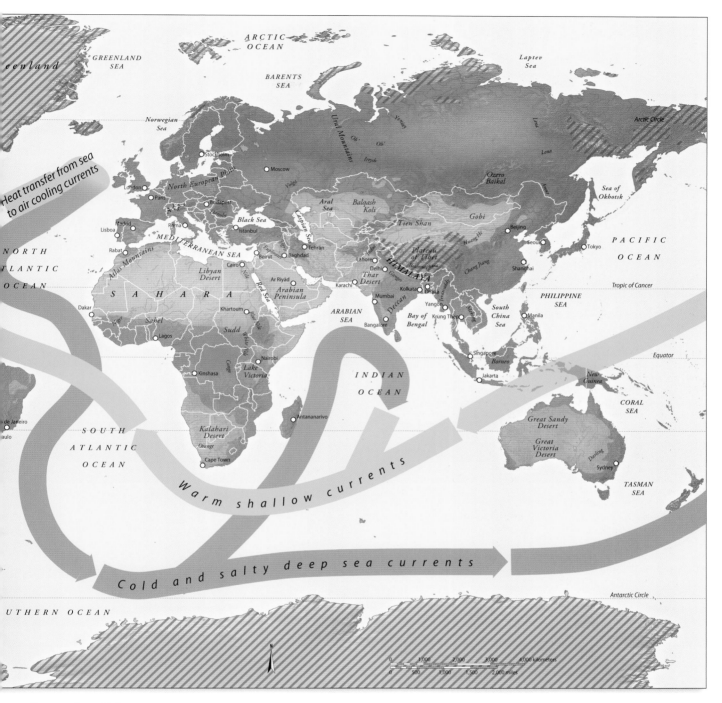

Temperature Rising

About a third of the sunlight that reaches our atmosphere is reflected back out into space by light colored areas of the Earth's surface, mainly snow, ice, and deserts. The rest of the reflectivity is due to clouds and small particles in the atmosphere known as "aerosols."

The warmth of the Earth's surface is due to the presence of greenhouse gases—water vapor, carbon dioxide, and other gases— that act as a partial blanket for the long wave radiation coming from the surface. This blanketing is known as the natural greenhouse effect. Devoid of this, temperatures would be much lower than they are, and life as we know it would not be possible. Instead, owing to these natural greenhouse gases, the Earth's average temperature is a more hospitable 60°F (16°C).

In terms of climate change, meaning a change in average air temperature and precipitation, literature indicates that global mean surface temperatures have increased 0.5-1.0°F since the late nineteenth century. The twentieth century's 10 warmest years all occurred in the last 15 years of the century. Furthermore, evidence shows that most of the warming is associated with human activity, particularly burning of fossil fuels, which has made the blanket of greenhouse gases around the earth "thicker."

ABOVE This map clearly shows the effect of ocean streams and currents on the sea temperatures and thus on weather patterns on Earth. As water is pushed up through warmer and shallower areas, it heats up. The inverse applies as currents move into cooler climates.

AEVI VETERIS, TYPVS GEOGRAPHICVS.

ABOVE This ancient map of the world in 1606, from *Theatrum Orbis Terrarum*, by Abraham Ortelius, shows the weather and population zones.

Burning the Planet

Fossil fuels burned to run cars, buses, and trucks, heat homes and businesses, and power industry are responsible for about 98 percent of US carbon dioxide emissions, 24 percent of methane emissions, and 18 percent of nitrous oxide emissions. Increased agriculture, deforestation, landfills, industrial production, and mining also contribute a significant share of emissions. These human activities have altered the chemical composition of the atmosphere through the buildup of greenhouse gases.

Atmospheric concentrations of CO_2 have increased by nearly 30 percent, methane concentrations have more than doubled, and nitrous oxide concentrations

> We are upsetting the atmosphere upon which all life depends.
> –David Suzuki, Canadian environmentalist and activist.

have risen by about 15 percent over the last 120 years. These increases have enhanced the heat-trapping capability of Earth's atmosphere.

Scientists expect the average global surface temperature could rise 1–4.5°F (0.6–2.5°C) in the next 50 years, and 2.2–10°F (1.4–5.8°C) in the next century, with significant regional variation. Evaporation will increase as the climate warms, which will increase average global precipitation. Soil moisture is likely to decline in many regions, and very intense rainstorms are likely to become more frequent. Sea level is also rising worldwide by about 0.07 inches (2 mm) per year.

Human activities are depositing CO_2 into the air, through burning fossil fuel or wood, as well as adding CFC (chlorofluorocarbon) compounds, used in refrigeration. CFCs are greenhouse gases and destroyers of ozone. Records show that the amount of CO_2 in the atmosphere has increased by about 35 percent in the industrial era primarily due to the combustion of fossil fuels

and removal of forests. Estimating future emissions is hard, as there is still great uncertainty as to what extent warming will take place and where its effects will be felt, because this will depend on demographic, economic, technological, policy, and institutional developments.

The intergovernmental panel reaffirmed that human emissions are very likely to cause serious climate change and developed several emissions scenarios including one, depending on what steps people took to restrict emissions, showing that by the end of the twenty-first century we could expect the planet's average temperature to rise anywhere between about 1.4–6°C (2.5–11°F).

Scientists indicated that failing ice sheets could initiate severe changes in climate and showed that the warming was itself starting to cause changes that would generate still more warming.

Millions live in very vulnerable locations such as floodplains or in shantytowns on exposed hillsides.

1750 Before the Industrial Revolution, the atmosphere holds 280 parts per million of CO_2

1824 Jean Baptiste Joseph Fourier describes the greenhouse effect

1979 First World Climate Conference

1997 Treaty parties approve Kyoto Protocol mandating emission cuts by industrial nations, an approach rejected in advance by US Senate

2004 CO_2 levels reach a record 379 parts per million. Russia gives crucial ratification to Kyoto Protocol.

2005 Kyoto Protocol takes effect on February 16

2007 UN Climate Change Summit takes place in Bali bringing together representatives of over 180 countries agreeing to adoption of the Bali roadmap and the launch of the Adaptation Fund as well as decisions on technology transfer and on reducing emissions from deforestation

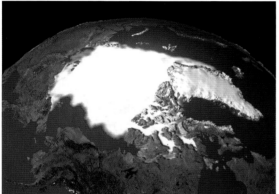

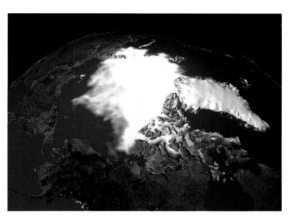

In the past, humans migrated in response to changes in habitat—but the space for migration is getting smaller every day.

Finally, a simple rise in standards of living in countries like India and China, which is a reality, will involve a significant increase in fossil fuel consumption. Therefore, the amount of CO_2 in the atmosphere will inevitably rise further in the coming decades.

Buying Time
Against this background there is a critical need to accelerate developments toward lower energy-intensive economies in the developed world. This will help to decelerate the increase in greenhouse gases in the atmosphere and "buy extra time" for conversion to economies that are based on sustainable energy sources. As well, many behavior changing actions can be taken.

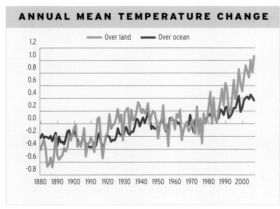

ABOVE LEFT AND RIGHT These contrasting NASA images of the Arctic ice-cap in 1979 (left) and 2003 (right) show the decrease in solid ice at about 9 percent per decade. The reason for this drop in can be found by observing the graph (left) which shows the increase in land surface temperatures over the last century.

Issues relating to the unrelenting growth of the population and potential environmental refugees deserve serious attention Some predict that by 2050 as many as 150 million people may be displaced by the impact of global warming and sea level rise—up to 26 million people from coastal regions in Bangladesh, 73 million people in China, and about 20 million in India.

Other climatic factors with the potential to stimulate migration may increase gradually over many decades, allowing affected countries to make adjustments to ameliorate the effects. Government actions will be a critical determinant.

Policies should plan for the future against extreme weather events and possible climate changes to ensure a safe environment, sustainable development, and sufficient food production all over the world.

435

War in Afghanistan

The war in Afghanistan began with American and British air strikes in October 2001, following the refusal of the ruling Taliban regime to hand over Osama bin Laden, a Saudi Arabian held responsible for the September 11 attacks in the United States.

1994 The Taliban movement begins in Afghanistan

1996 Civil war breaks out in Afghanistan. The Taliban force the government out of Kabul.

1998 Taliban take control of Mazar-e Sharif

2001 Osama bin Laden and the al-Qa'eda organization claim responsibility for the attacks on the US on September 11

October 7, 2001 The United States begins aerial bombing of Taliban strongholds in Afghanistan

Although Afghanistan possesses a population of less than 32 million, mostly very poor people, and few natural resources, its geographic location has placed it at the center of great power rivalry for a very long time. Zahir Shar, last king of Afghanistan, who came to the throne in 1933, was forced into exile after a 1973 coup led by a former prime minister, General Mohammed Daud. When Daud himself was overthrown and killed in a 1978 coup, power struggles ensued among shifting coalitions of secular, ethnic, and Islamic conservative political forces. Soon after the Soviets sent in troops in 1979 to assist one of the factions, they found themselves engaged in a war of occupation, which they could not win and from which they could not withdraw without a massive loss of prestige.

Western Protest

US President Jimmy Carter led a boycott of the 1980 Moscow summer Olympics in protest against the Soviet invasion while his successor, President Ronald Reagan, inaugurated a policy of open support for anti-Soviet forces.

In addition to the billions of dollars' worth of covert military aid supplied by the United States, support for the *mujahideen* guerilla fighters in Islamic countries, particularly those that are Islamic fundamentalists—also flowed in from Saudi Arabia, Pakistan, China, and Iran.

Taliban

Even after a peace accord negotiated in 1988 and the departure of Soviet troops, fighting continued until in 1991 the US and USSR, by mutual agreement, ended all military aid to rival factions. All attempts to unite the *mujahideen* in a single government faltered. Eventually, a fundamentalist Islamic organization known as the Taliban—meaning "religious students"—seized control of the capital city, Kabul, in 1996, and gradually extended its rule over much of the rest of Afghanistan.

In 1998, US President Bill Clinton authorized selective missile strikes on suspected bases of Osama bin Laden, whose al-Qa'eda organization had been accused of bombing US embassies in Africa. But it was the Taliban's refusal to hand over Osama bin Laden after the

September 11, 2001, attacks on the US that provoked a full-scale invasion. US President George W. Bush made it clear that the US fight against terrorists included "those who harbor them."

US–British Invasion

It took only weeks for the joint US–British forces to take Kabul and the other major cities. The arrival of NATO forces in Kabul in August 2003 was the first time these forces had been deployed outside Europe. Other milestones were the election of Hamid Karzai as president in 2004 and the first parliamentary elections in over 30 years. And still there was no peace.

Opium

When the Taliban were in power, they had conducted a religiously inspired war on drugs that had

BELOW Strategic maps outline the US military operations and targets during the offensive in Afghanistan.

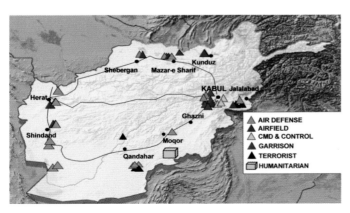

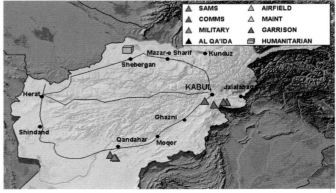

LEFT Members of an Afghan *mujahideen* group rest in their camp at Jegdalay in Kabul Province, Afghanistan, 1988.

RIGHT A B-1B Lancer Strategic Bomber, part of the US Air Force 28th Air Expeditionary Wing, bombs targets in Afghanistan during 2001.

BELOW Most of Afghanistan's opium fields were eliminated on religious grounds during the early Taliban regime, but insurgents soon nurtured their reemergence when profits from illicit drug sales could finance lucrative weapons deals.

BELOW RIGHT Confiscated opium products. High-tech laboratories convert 90 percent of Afghanistan's home-grown opium into heroin before it is smuggled around the world.

virtually eradicated the opium fields by the year 2000. However, as military requirements took precedence over ideology, Taliban insurgents were grateful for the guns and ammunition that the proceeds of illicit drug dealing could buy. By 2007, Afghanistan was once again one of the world's leading opium producers.

Negotiations

Adding to and complicating the war effort for the occupying forces was the absence of a clear objective. By 2008, the pursuit of Osama bin Laden and al-Qa'eda had dropped down the agenda. While keeping the Taliban out of power remained a key aim, it was reported that behind-the-scenes efforts were being made to negotiate with Taliban commanders. When peace might be declared and foreign forces withdrawn remained unclear.

The misery in war-torn Afghanistan is reminiscent of images from the Thirty Years' War.
–Jürgen Habermas, German philosopher and sociologist.

China—The New World Power

With its massive population of over 1.3 billion and the meteoric rise of its economy, the People's Republic of China is often referred to as an emerging superpower. With its burgeoning private sector, China is the world's fastest growing economy.

2001 to **Present**

2000 China launches Chinasat-22 (Zhongxing-22) communication satellite

2000 Government starts long-distance resettlement schemes to move more than 1.5 million people from the Three Gorges Dam project area

2001 After much negotiation, China becomes a member of the World Trade Organization

2003 The first fiber optic network connection across Russian-Chinese border is established

2006 CNOOC, one of China's largest oil and gas producers, buys a stake in a Nigerian offshore oil and gas field

2008 Beijing hosts the Games of the XXIX Olympiad

Over the last 25 years, China's economy has changed dramatically, from a centrally planned system closed to international trade, to a booming market-oriented economy. Living standards have improved and there is greater individual freedom for the Chinese people. China has a workforce of over 800 million people.

Trade

Since 2006, China has been the second largest economy in the world, after the United States, measured on a purchasing power parity basis. Having opened up to the rest of the world at the end of the twentieth century, China plays a significant role in international trade today. It is the third largest importer and the second largest exporter in the world, the world's largest consumer of steel and concrete, and the world's second largest importer of petroleum.

As the world's fastest-growing economy, China is the largest oil consumer after the United States, and is the world's biggest producer and consumer of coal. At the same time the country spends billions of dollars to purchase foreign energy supplies. In efforts to secure more stable energy supplies, China is investing in energy and resource projects around the world. It is also pursuing renewable energy projects and putting in place energy efficiency targets.

In 2001, China joined the World Trade Organization (WTO), an important step towards paving the way for increased trade and foreign investment from the West. China is also a member of the Asia-Pacific Economic Cooperation (APEC). Direct foreign investment has been steadily rising and is an important contributing factor in the growth of urban jobs.

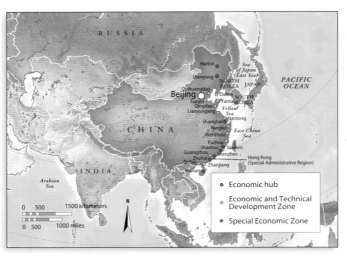

ABOVE China has set up special economic zones that enjoy easing of trade restrictions and other financial benefits designed to assist industry.

RIGHT The vast population of China is becoming more concentrated in the urban and fertile areas of the country as the economy expands.

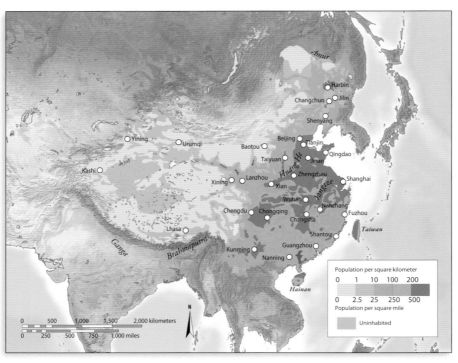

RIGHT China's capital city of Beijing has a population of more than 17 million people. Despite rising car pollution in the city, the bicycle is still the major means of transport. Like many of the city's roads, Changan Avenue is crowded with bikes in rush hour.

While global trade was sluggish at the turn of the century, China's trade continued to out-perform the rest. Global companies are rushing to do business with Chinese companies and participate in the phenomenal growth being experienced. But despite industrial growth, agriculture remains the major occupation.

Today, being the biggest developing countries in the world, China and India are both committed to developing their economy and raising their people's living standards.
–Li Peng, Premier of China (1987-1998).

Foreign Exchange

In July 2005, China revalued its currency by 2.1 percent against the US dollar. In 2007, China recorded the largest current account surplus in the world—US$380 billion. At the end of 2007, China's foreign exchange reserve was almost US$1.5 trillion, making it the largest in the world.

The economic reforms that China has been implementing since the late 1970s have enabled 400 million Chinese to rise above the poverty line.

In 1981, 53 percent of the Chinese population was living in poverty. By 2004, this had already been reduced to 10 percent.

Media and Censorship

The Chinese government closely monitors media organizations and even Internet censorship is meticulous, with international giants like Google and MySpace, known for revolutionizing information flow in the West, making concessions in order to do business there. By 2007, there were 172 million Internet users in China.

Telephone services, both domestic and international, are becoming more readily available and China has over 500 million cell phone users.

Currently most television broadcasts are state run with children's channels being mandatory.

ABOVE Now completed, this dam on the Yellow River formed the Lijiaxia Reservoir in Qunghai Province. It is used for leisure boating and sightseeing.

LEFT Kwai Chung Container Terminal in the New Territories, Hong Kong, is one of the busiest container ports in the world. Hong Kong is officially the Hong Kong Special Administrative Region of the People's Republic of China.

Coalition of the Willing

From a superficial perspective, the invasion of Iraq appeared to be a rerun of the 1990 Gulf War. At a deeper level, however, the 2003 invasion was very different.

August 2003 Saddam's cousin Ali Hassan al-Majid ("Chemical Ali") is captured

December 14, 2003 Saddam Hussein is captured in Tikrit

June 2004 After an interim government is formed, Saddam Hussein is handed over to Iraqi custody

August 2005 A draft constitution is approved by Shia and Kurdish representatives but the Sunni reject it

November 2006 Saddam Hussein is found guilty of crimes against humanity and sentenced to death. He is hanged in December.

May 2007 The leader of al-Qa'eda in Iraq, Abu Ayyub al-Masri, is killed

February 2008 Iraqi parliament passes legislation that allows former officials of the Baath party to hold public office

Following a military coup in 1958 that deposed the monarchy, Iraq became a republic. Further coups eventually resulted in a one-party state under the Arab Socialist Baath Party.

Following the resignation of President Ahmad Hasan al-Bakr in 1975, Vice-President Saddam Hussein succeeded to the presidency, an office he was to hold for the next 28 years.

In September 1980, war broke out with neighboring Iran—a conflict that would result in the deaths of an estimated one million people

> In Iraq, a dictator is building and hiding weapons that could enable him to dominate the Middle East and intimidate the civilized world, and we will not allow it.
>
> —George W. Bush, President of the United States.

before a cease-fire in 1988 ended hostilities under the aegis of a UN Iran-Iraq Military Observer Group.

On August 2, 1990, Iraq invaded a much smaller neighbor, Kuwait, which Saddam accused of tapping into Iraqi oil reserves.

Iraq's defiance of international condemnation led eventually to a UN-sponsored, multi-national invasion spearheaded by the US military, on January 16, 1991. By the beginning of March, when Saddam Hussein accepted terms for a ceasefire, the Iraqi military forces had been largely destroyed.

Saddam remained president, his powers much diminished. To protect Kurdish Iraqis in danger of persecution, the UN created a "safe haven" in Northern Iraq. A "no-fly zone" in southern Iraq, policed by British and American warplanes, aimed to provide similar protection for Shiite Muslim groups in that region who had reason to fear Saddam would punish

ABOVE Taken down by Iraqi civilians, with the help of US marines, the toppling of a massive statue of Saddam Hussein in Baghdad on April 9, 2003, is an iconic image of the conflict.

RIGHT Following the US invasion, hundreds of civilians left Baghdad as hostilities increased. This group, their vehicle loaded with produce, was attempting to enter the beseiged city of Basra in March 2003.

them for their demonstrated hostility to his regime, which was dominated by Sunni Muslims. Thus a de facto tripartite division began to appear along the faultlines of the long-suppressed provincial boundaries laid down by the Ottomans.

Airstrikes

Throughout the 1990s tensions remained high, with UN sanctions preventing export of Iraqi oil in place until 1995. A partial resumption was permitted under UN Security Council Resolution 986, which allowed some exports in order that the country might buy medical and food supplies—the so-called "oil for food" scheme.

The administration of US President Bill Clinton repeatedly charged that Iraq was failing to comply with UN directives for the dismantling of weapons programs. In 1996, the US expanded the area of the southern

"no-fly zone" almost as far as the country's capital, Baghdad.

Following Iraq's decision in October 1998 to suspend any cooperation with the UN Commission charged with overseeing the dismantling of nuclear and other weapons of mass destruction, British and American warplanes bombed a number military targets in "Operation Desert Fox." Further airstrikes were conducted early in 2001, when George W. Bush succeeded Clinton as US President.

Axis of Evil

The Bush administration stepped up its verbal onslaught on Iraq following the September 11, 2001 al-Qa'eda attacks on US targets, even though there was no apparent link to Saddam's regime.

The President's State of the Union Address on January 29, 2002, identified Iraq, along with North Korea and Iran, as "an axis of evil,

arming to threaten the peace of the world. By seeking weapons of mass destruction these regimes pose a grave and growing danger." Bowing to Bush's pressure, Iraq allowed the UN's chief weapons inspector, Hans Blix, to lead a team of inspectors back into the country in November 2002.

Coalition of the Willing

Over the next few months US President Bush and British Prime Minister Tony Blair struggled unsuccessfully to get UN Security Council backing for a further armed intervention.

Some other members of the Security Council held back on the ground that Hans Blix needed time to ascertain whether weapons of mass destruction were indeed being stockpiled by Saddam's regime. When it became apparent that France and Russia would not approve military action before a

ABOVE Iraqi leader Saddam Hussein's defiance of a US ultimatum to step down from power resulted in the bombing of Baghdad, commencing on March 20, 2003. The world watched as this ancient and historic town came under attack.

definitive report, the US and Great Britain determined to act on their own, in conjunction with whatever nations chose to join a "Coalition of the Willing."

Invasion

On March 17, 2003, President Bush issued an ultimatum, threatening invasion unless Saddam Hussein and his sons vacated their offices and left Iraq within 48 hours. In the absence of a positive response, American missiles began slamming into Baghdad on March 20. US and British armed forces marched across the southern borders of Iraq the next day.

In place of "Operation Desert Storm," Bush promised a campaign of "Shock and Awe." The coalition forces swept rapidly toward Baghdad. On April 9, a worldwide audience watched footage of Saddam Hussein's statue being dragged from its pedestal by a jubilant crowd.

If the coalition forces had expected some high-ranking Iraqi official to stage a public surrender, they were disappointed. The Iraqi military simply melted away, taking much of their light weaponry. With 55 top members of Saddam's government put on "Iraq's Most Wanted" list, coalition commanders found no one willing to hand over the reins. Instead, a former American diplomat, Paul Bremer, was installed as administrator. One of his first acts was to bar all members of the former ruling Baath Party from holding any positions in the new regime. A necessary consequence was that the government of the country passed into the hands of the invaders. A prediction once made about Iraq by US Secretary of State, Colin Powell appeared to be coming true: "You break it, you own it."

Administration
Without any publicly announced plan for the future government of the country, coalition troops were left to perform most administrative functions. Although the UN Security Council bowed to facts on the ground by recognizing Bremer's administration and lifting all

LEFT US Army patrols leave the Al-Tuwaitha nuclear facility east of Baghdad following an inspection in June 2003.

BELOW Coalition troops move into position in preparation for the takeover of Basra airport on March 22, 2003.

economic sanctions, it had no formal role. Meanwhile, military forces scouring the countryside could find none of the weapons of mass destruction whose existence had been the rationale for the invasion.

While the coalition partners explored ways to institute some form of legitimate and democratic government, the security situation within Iraq rapidly deteriorated. Armed gangs began staging hit and run attacks on coalition troops and public places. By July 2003, the US commander acknowledged that his forces faced a guerilla war on the streets. The Insurgency, as it was called, soon began hitting oil wells

and pipelines which the coalition was counting on to help finance rebuilding. The capture of Saddam Hussein in December 2003 made no difference—the insurgents stepped up their attacks. Millions of Iraqis moved, as refugees, to neighboring countries.

Religious Rivals
One of the greatest obstacles to restoring peace was the widening of the cracks that had been opening throughout the 1990s between Kurds in the north, Sunnis in the center, and Shiites in the south of the country. Although Shiites welcomed the fall of Saddam, they

showed no enthusiasm for allowing their Sunni religious rivals to dominate the new Iraq. Moqtada Sadr, a Shiite leader in the south, began forming his own armed militias, which openly clashed with coalition forces in April 2004.

Self-rule
By 2004, the US had managed to find a sufficient number of Iraqis willing and able to take part in an interim government. Sovereignty was formally handed over to Prime Minister Iyad Allawi in June. In January 2005, elections were held to pick members of a national assembly and as many as eight

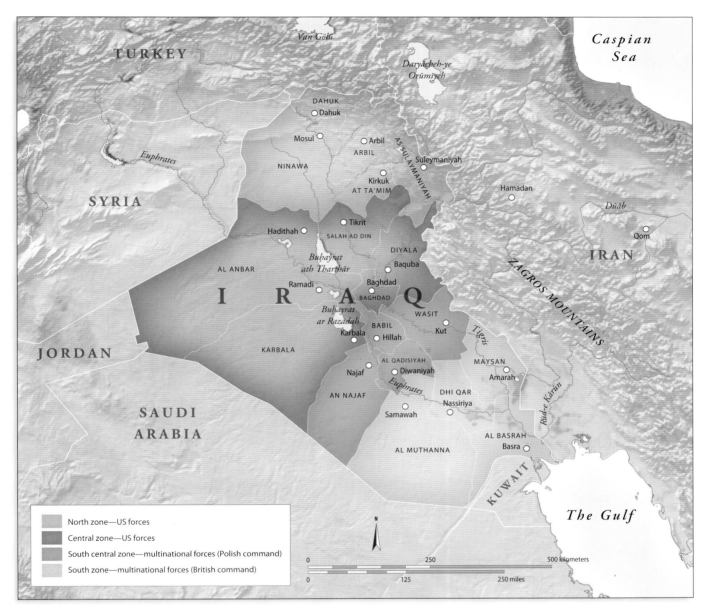

Map legend:

- North zone—US forces
- Central zone—US forces
- South central zone—multinational forces (Polish command)
- South zone—multinational forces (British command)

million people may have cast ballots. Further progress was signaled by a referendum on a new constitution in October 2005 and parliamentary elections in January 2006.

Troop Withdrawal

As time went on, the Coalition of the Willing shrank, as important military contingents such as those from Spain and Italy were called home. When Britain handed over security in Basra Province to Iraqi forces in December 2007, it seemed that the main coalition partner with the US might be on the way out. The Labor Government of Australian Prime Minister Kevin Rudd also signaled its intention to withdraw all combat troops.

Cost

A much-vaunted US troop "surge" had quelled violence in and around Baghdad, but suicide bombings and armed attacks by insurgents continued in many places. In a book published in February, 2008, a Nobel Prize-winning American economist, Joseph Stiglitz, and co-author Linda Bilmes, estimated the war had cost far more than the $US500 billion claimed by the White House. Their estimate of direct and indirect costs was $US3 trillion dollars. Whatever the true figure, the Iraq War had indisputably become America's second most expensive war, after World War II, and its second longest, after Vietnam.

ABOVE The different zones set up by invasion forces roughly correspond to Kurdish, Shiite, and Sunni-dominated regions within Iraq.

RIGHT The bombing of Baghdad continues to this day. A double car bomb near the Islamic Supreme Council in February 2008 caused this powerful explosion.

Deadly Wave

Created by a megathrust earthquake in the seafloor, the tsunamis that surged around the perimeter of Asia in December 2004 caused more human suffering than thought possible in this modern world.

LEFT This aerial shot taken on January 16, 2004, shows the complete devastation in Banda Aceh, the region closest to the epicenter.

RIGHT Three weeks after the tsunami, an Acehnese man sits on the debris of what was his home in Lamjame, on the outskirts of Banda Aceh.

BELOW RIGHT The Indo-Australian Plate shifted in the Boxing Day earthquake, unleashing a destructive tsunami.

> This is an unprecedented global catastrophe and it requires an unprecedented global response.
> —Kofi Annan, Secretary General of the United Nations (1997-2007).

On December 26, 2004, a series of devastating tsunamis, collectively termed the Boxing Day or Asian Tsunami, struck along the coasts of most of the landmasses bordering the Indian Ocean.

The tsunami was generated by the Indian Ocean earthquake, also known as the Sumatra-Andaman earthquake, on the same day at 07.58 A.M. local time, with the epicenter off the west coast of Sumatra, Indonesia.

HOW AND WHY?

A tsunami is a chain of fast moving waves that are generated when water in the ocean is rapidly displaced by sudden upheaval either from an earthquake, a volcanic eruption or a landslip. Tsunamis are not detectable in the open sea. Tsunami waves, however, can travel across the ocean at speeds of up to 600 mph (1,000 k/ph), destroying people and the environment.

The earthquake that triggered the Indian Ocean tsunamis of 2004 is estimated to have released the energy of 23,000 Hiroshima-type atomic bombs. When the earthquake occurred, forceful movements of sections of the earth's crust, known as tectonic plates, displaced large amounts of water. The 2004 earthquake was the result of the sliding of the portion of the Earth's crust called the Indian Plate under the section called the Burma Plate. This caused a rupture that was about 600 miles (1,000 km) long and vertically displaced the seafloor above the rupture by about 10 yards (10 m). Above the affected seafloor the great volume of the ocean was displaced along the line of the rupture, causing the deadly tsunamis.

Exact numbers vary but somewhere between 170,000 and 190,000 people are thought to have perished in the disaster, killed by waves of up to 100 ft (30 m) that inundated the coastal areas. More than 40,000 people are still officially listed as missing, although this figure could be as high at 120,000.

Magnitude

The Sumatra-Andaman earthquake lasted only about 10 minutes and measured 9.0 on the Richter scale, vibrating the entire planet.

Within 15 minutes of the earthquake, the tsunami struck Aceh province in Sumatra, approximately 150 miles (250 km) from the epicenter. Fifteen minutes later it reached the Andaman and Nicobar islands, and then Malaysia. One and a half hours later, it wreaked havoc on the beaches of Thailand and an hour after that the tsunami swept Sri Lanka and the southeast coast of India. Maldives was next and seven hours after the earthquake, the tsunami pounded on the coast of East Africa, some 2,800 miles (4,500 km) from Sumatra.

The 2004 Indian Ocean earthquake was the fifth largest quake recorded, the largest in the last 40 years, and precipitated the single worst tsunami ever.

Casualties

It is reported that about one-third of those killed in the tsunami were children, due both to the large child population in many of the affected regions, and because children were the most vulnerable when struck by the giant waves of water. As many as four times more women than men were killed in some regions because they were waiting on the beach for fishermen to return. Many fishing boats at some distance from the coast rode out the waves. Most of those who were affected by this tragic course of nature were caught unawares.

Unexpected Outcome

One positive outcome of the tsunami was the washing away of sand from the ruins of a 1,200-year-old lost port city at Mahabalipuram on India's south coast, swallowed by the sea hundreds of years ago.

1755 In November, a massive earthquake in the Atlantic causes an enormous tsunami to wash across the harbor of Lisbon, Portugal. Over 100,000 people are killed.

1883 The volcanic explosion of Krakatoa in Indonesia causes tsunamis across the Pacific and Indian oceans and as far away as the English Channel. They kill over 36,000 people.

1896 An earthquake off the coast of Japan triggers a massive tsunami that washes over Sanriku, killing over 26,000 people

1960 A tsunami and the resulting flooding caused by an earthquake in Chile brings the death of 61 people on Hilo, Hawaii. Seven hours later, the tsunami kills 200 people in Japan.

1976 A massive tsunami resulting from an earthquake near the Philippines sweeps away more than 5,000 people, with thousands missing

1998 Although a relatively small quake, the tsunami resulting from the earthquake in New Guinea causes 40 ft (12 m) waves to wash across the coast, killing around 2,200 people

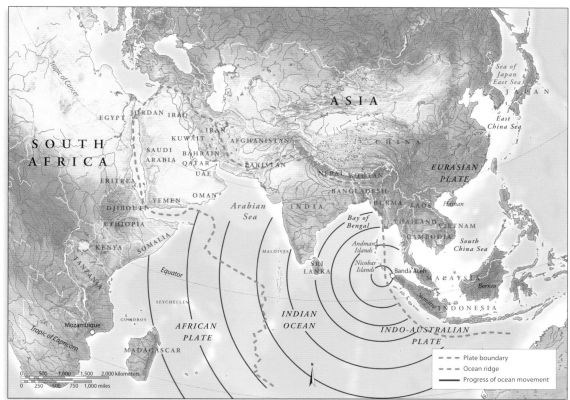

Australia—Becoming a Global Economy

Over the last decade, despite its tiny population and vast areas of uninhabited land, Australia has begun a determined globalization of its economy, concentrating on its geographic position in Asia.

Australia's economic growth since 2001 has been impressive, and has contributed to the nation's overall competitiveness in the globalized market. Structural reform to taxation, industrial relations, and the privatization of some state-owned companies has helped to augment the growth of the economy. The "Resources Boom" that has occurred due to the combination of exploitation of mineral resources and new markets such as China and India, has also had a significant impact on the changes to the country's growth and trade during this time.

> To the stolen generations,
> I say the following:
> as Prime Minister of Australia,
> I am sorry.
> –Kevin Rudd, Prime Minister of Australia, in his apology speech on the opening day of the new Parliament, February 13, 2008.

Living Standards

Australia's economic growth has been greatly increased by structural reform aimed at globalizing the economy and encouraging international competitiveness. These reforms began in the 1980s, but continue to have effect in recent years. Australian households have benefited from the economic growth generated by the resources boom, with living standards increasing steadily since the 1990s.

This has been coupled, however, with an increase in the real estate market and decreasing housing affordability, particularly in Western Australia, where interstate migration is at an all time high, placing incredible demand on housing. Also in Western Australia, the mining boom has resulted in large numbers of people relocating to remote areas to work in the resources sector.

Because Australia's trade is now directed toward mineral export, the nation has been positioned to benefit greatly from the global commodities boom. Investment in mining is significant, which has increased demand for productivity. The privatization of state-owned businesses, such as Telstra, the country's largest telecommunications company, has been implemented in the last decade.

Changing Markets

Australia is the seventeenth largest economy in the world. Traditionally, Australia has been considered as largely a producer of agricultural commodities, minerals, and energy, and these have played a very significant role in the nation's economic growth. Until the middle of the twentieth century over half of all Australia's exports went to Europe, in particular the United Kingdom.

However, in the second half of the twentieth century Australia's trade markets moved from Europe and the United States, to Asia, where energy and mineral commodities took on an increased demand in countries such as Japan and China.

Exports and Imports

Australia's main merchandise exports are iron ore, coal, gold, crude petroleum (mainly LNG), thermal coal, alumina, aluminum, and beef and veal. The main destinations for exports are Japan, China, South Korea, India, USA, New Zealand, Taiwan, Singapore, UK, and Thailand.

Australia's natural abundance of resources has been at the heart of a resources boom in recent years. The recent and very marked increase in global demand for Australia's minerals has produced the largest export boom in Australia's history, and has been highly influential in creating large profits. The country's terms of trade are at their highest in 50 years. Lack of ports and rail workers have, however, limited the ability to export the resources as fast as demand requires.

Australia's main imports are passenger motor vehicles, crude and refined petroleum, computers, and medicaments, mainly sourced from China, the United States, Japan, Singapore, and Germany.

Agriculture

Agriculture makes a significant contribution to the GDP, not only directly through export but also through the development and maintenance of communities and infrastructure solely linked to particular industry and areas.

Australia is the world's largest wool-producing country and one of the great wheat exporters.

Trade

The global commodity boom created a favorable environment for Australian trade, which continues to be in a good position to export minerals. One of the most significant developments to shape Australia's economy was the introduction of the Australian-United States Free Trade Agreement, which came into force on January 1, 2005.

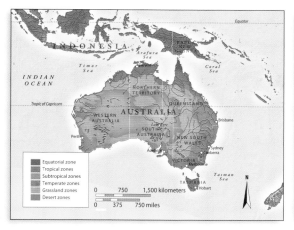

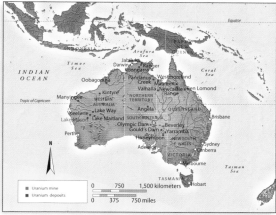

2000 Australia hosts the Games of the XXVIII Olympiad in Sydney—the most popular games ever

2001 Commonwealth of Australia celebrates 100 years since Federation

2003 Australia is included in the United States's "Coalition of the Willing" that sends troops to Iraq to overthrow the dictatorship of Saddam Hussein

2004 The *Human Rights Act 2004* is passed by Parliament

2007 Kevin Rudd is elected Prime Minister—the first change of government in more than a decade

ABOVE LEFT Australia's climate is one of the most ideal in the world with most of the populated regions sitting in a temperate zone.

RIGHT Australia is one of the world's leading uranium exporters, despite having only three operating mines.

RIGHT The population of Australia lives mostly along the coast. The interior has very sparse populations scattered over huge stations (ranches).

LEFT The original Ranger open-cut mine in Kakadu National Park in the Northern Territory was discovered in 1969. A share of the profits go to the traditional Aboriginal land owners.

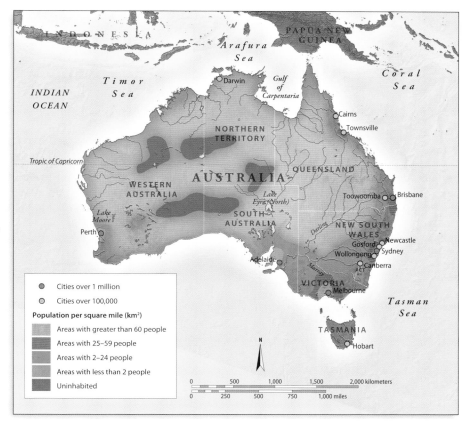

THE STOLEN GENERATION

The term "stolen generation" is used to describe the generation of Aboriginal and Torres Strait Islander children who were taken from their families by official government policy under the *Aborigines Protection Act* of 1909. The practice continued until 1969. Incomplete records made it almost impossible for children to trace their families. In 2008, after years of controversy, the Australian Government chose to express a national apology to those affected. Kevin Rudd, the Australian Prime Minister, made his "sorry" speech on the opening day of Parliament on February 13, 2008. Witnessed by Aboriginal elders and many of those torn from their families, the open expression of regret did much to heal the wounds caused by the forced removal.

LEFT Watched live by most of the country, Kevin Rudd's historic "sorry" speech was a watershed in Australia. This huge crowd waves the traditional Aboriginal flag as they watch on a giant screen.

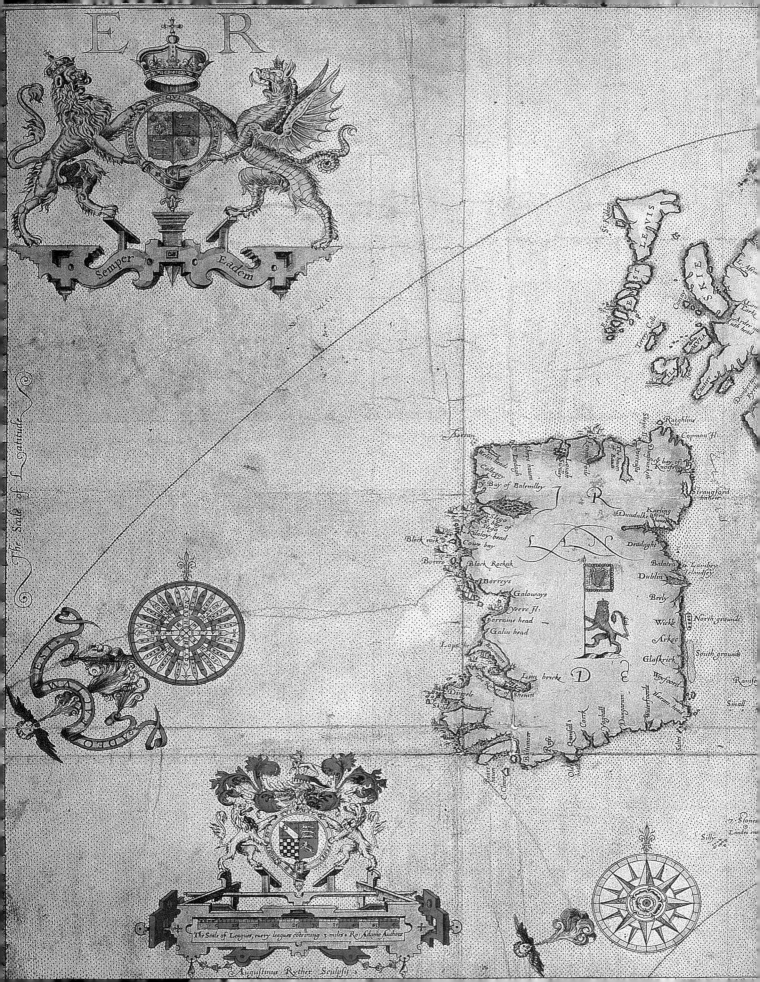

E R

Semper Eadem

DIEV ET MON DROIT

The Scale of Latitude

St Kilda

LEVIS

SKIE

I R LAND

Astran
Ratghline
Copman fl.

Sligo haven
College
ye Bay of Balenilley
Strangford haven

Kaysing
Dundalke ford

Black rock
Borris
Dradught

Black Rockuk
Balatra Lainsbey Ielandsy
Dublin

Borreys
Galowsye
Brely

Yeere fl.
orraine head
Galin head
Wicke
North grounds

Lope flie
Arker
South grounds

Glaskrick
Ranse

Law bricke
Wexford
Small

Dingle
Shenut

D

Dunmore
Carr
Vogall

Kinfall
Dungarum
Waterford haven

7 Stones
Landes ende

Silly

The Scale of Leagues, every leagues containing 3 miles. Ro: Adams Authors

Augustinus Ryther Sculpsit

NORMANDIE
FLANDERS
HOLLAND
BRABANTE
PICARDIE
FRISLANDE
LONDON
BRISTOL
YORKE
Aberdin
Kendall
Lancaster
Chester
Hartlepoole
Scarbrough
Boston
Yarmouth
Harwich
Colchester
Bergen
Antwerpe
Calais
Boulonge
Abbeuielle
Diepe
The Spanishe fleete
The English fleete
HONI SOIT QUI MAL Y PENSE

Timeline

c. 150,000 BCE	*Homo sapiens* appear in Northeast Africa.
c. 71,000 BCE	Mount Toba on Sumatra erupts, possibly causing the change in climate.
c. 70,000–10,000 BCE	Ice Age inhibits the spread of humans in Europe, Northern Asia, and North America.
c. 60,000 BCE	Migration to the Australian continent takes place.
c. 32,000 BCE	Cremated skeleton of "Mungo Man" found at Lake Mungo, New South Wales, Australia.
c. 30,000 BCE	Humans settle in Japan.
c. 13,000 BCE	Early settlements appear in North America, probably via the Bering Strait from Siberia through Alaska.
c. 10,000 BCE	The climate improves enough for colonization to increase in Europe.
c. 9500 BCE	Grains begin to be grown along the Nile.
c. 8000 BCE	People migrating to the Nile region form societies.
c. 6000 BCE	Rowing boats and small ships are built in Egypt.
c. 5700 BCE	Towns develop in Egypt.
5000 BCE	Evidence of early human culture.
4750 BCE	The first temple of Ashur is built, marking the beginning of the Assyrian calendar.
c. 4600 BCE	Cities and towns develop in the Indus Valley.
c. 4400 BCE	Pottery is evident during the Halaf period; also some evidence of metal.
c. 4400 BCE	Finely woven linen and cloth is evident.
4300-3200 BCE	Chalcolithic cultures develop.
4200 BCE	Susa is founded in western Persia.
c. 4000 BCE	Evidence of cosmetics and alchemy.
c. 3900 BCE	Southern Mesopotamia culture established with temples and early architecture.
c. 3800 BCE	State and city organizations develop in China.
c. 3500 BCE	Musical instruments appear.
3500-2700 BCE	Early Harappan civilization begins.
c. 3400 BCE	Gawra and Ninevite periods.
c. 3300 BCE	Earliest hieroglyphic writing.
c. 2950 BCE	Memphis becomes the capital of Egypt.
2750 BCE	Tyre is established as a major settlement.
c. 2700 BCE	The first Greek and Etruscan city-states emerge.
2700-1900 BCE	Middle Harappan civilizations continue to develop.
2589-2560 BCE	The Great Pyramid is built.
2500 BCE	Hinduism begins in India.
c. 2000 BCE	The first palaces are built on Crete.
2000 BCE	The game of chess—shatranj—develops in Persia.
2000 BCE	Stonehenge is built.
1900-1500 BCE	Late Harappan (Lothal, Bet Dwarka) civilizations.
c. 1850 BCE	First invasions by Myceneans.
c. 1800-1200 BCE	Mayan civilization begins to emerge.
c. 1628 BCE	Volcanic eruption of Thera.
c. 1640 BCE	Period of classical art and literature.
c. 1500-1200 BCE	Exodus. Jews wander in the desert.
c 1500 BCE	The Phoenicians settle Cyprus.
c. 1500 BCE	The Myceneans conquer Crete.
c. 1425 BCE	The palace of Knossos is destroyed.
c. 1327 BCE	Tutankhamun dies.
1307 BCE	Adad—Nirari I establishes the first Assyrian Empire.
c. 1200 BCE	Rise of Olmec and Maya civilizations.
1200 BCE	Tyre becomes the chief Phoenician city. The Trojan wars begin.
1200-1050 BCE	Occupation of the Promised Land.
1200-900 BCE	The earliest Vedas are compiled.
1050-920 BCE	Jews—united under Saul, David, and Solomon—form a capital at Jerusalem.
c. 1000 BCE	Hinduism begins to gain followers in southern India.
c. 970 BCE	Temple of Solomon built.
935 BCE	Ashur-Dan II establishes the Assyrian Empire from Egypt to the Caspian Sea, under one rule.
c. 860 BCE	Princess of Tyre, Jezebel, marries Ahab, King of Israel.
c. 854 BCE	The Phoenicians are defeated by the Assyrians.
813 BCE	Carthage is founded.
c. 800-400 BCE	First stirrings of Inca culture in South America.
776 BCE	Coroebus of Elis wins the first stade (sprint) race and becomes the first winner in the Olympics. Hippias of Elis (c.460 BCE–399 BCE) calculated from inscriptions recording Olympic victories that the first Olympic Games must have been held in 776 BCE.
752 BCE	A wreath from the sacred olive tree is awarded for the first time to an Olympic victor.
722 BCE	Assyria conquers Israel.

720 BCE	At the 15th Olympiad, a new event, the Dolichos—long race—is introduced. Acanthus of Sparta is the first winner and Orsippus probably ran in the nude for the first time.
c. 715 BCE	Egypt is briefly conquered by the Assyrians.
609 BCE	The Assyrian Empire collapses after a successful attack by Medes, Scythians, and Babylonians.
604–562 BCE	The Hanging Gardens of Babylon are built.
594 BCE	Athens starts a special training program designed to stop the dominance of Spartan athletes at Olympia.
587 BCE	Judah becomes a province of Babylonia.
586 BCE	Nebuchadnezzar II conquers Phoenicia.
581 BCE	Nebuchadnezzar II burns Jerusalem.
539 BCE	Cyrus conquers Babylonia, absorbing it into the Persian empire. Captive Jews are set free.
c. 538 CE	Buddhism is introduced to Japan via Korea.
525 BCE	The Persians conquer Egypt.
521 BCE	Darius becomes King of Persia and expands the empire west beyond the Indus River.
509 BCE	The Roman Republic is established.
c. 500 BCE	Numerous Hindu texts are composed including—Shrauta, Sutras, Mahabharata, and Puranas.
490 BCE	Greeks defeat the Persians in the battle of Marathon.
483 BCE	Buddha dies at Kusinara.
480 BCE	Greeks defeat the Persians in the battle of Salamis.
c. 472 BCE	Theater begins to thrive in Athens. Many of the Greek tragedies are written over the next few decades.
472 BCE	The Olympic Games are extended to five days duration.
432 BCE	Construction of the Parthenon is completed.
431 BCE	Spartans invade Attica. Plague of Athens begins.
429 BCE	Death of Pericles. Plague continues.
424 BCE	Battle of Delion. Athens is defeated by the Thebans.
421 BCE	The Peace of Nicias.
411 BCE	Subversion of democracy in Athens with political assassinations and reign of terror.
410 BCE	Alcibiades victorious in the Aegean.
406 BCE	Antiochos is defeated by Lysander in battle of Notium (Cape Rain). Alcibiades is deposed. Spartans offer peace.
405 BCE	Siege of Athens begins.
404 BCE	Starvation compels surrender in Athens.
c. 400 BCE	Polynesian travelers arrive in Marquesas.
c. 400 BCE	Panini composes Sanskrit grammar—Ashtadhyayi.
399 BCE	Master philosopher Socrates dies.

388 BCE	Plato, founds his Academy—a school of philosophy—in Athens.
343 BCE	Aristotle is invited to become Alexander's teacher in Macedonia.
338 BCE	Phillip II of Macedonia defeats the combined Greek army of Chaeronea.
336 BCE	Phillip II of Macedonia is assassinated; his son Alexander succeeds him as king.
336–323 BCE	Alexander the Great reigns as King of Macedon. A palm branch is introduced as the immediate symbol of victory at the Olympic Games.
332 BCE	Alexander is crowned Pharoah of Egypt at the capital Memphis.
331 BCE	Alexander the Great conquers Persia.
331 BCE	Alexander burns the royal palace at Persepolis following a heavy drinking bout.
c. 331 BCE	The city of Alexandria is founded by Alexander.
327 BCE	Alexander marries the Bactrian princess, Rhoxane.
323 BCE	Alexander dies.
310 BCE	Rhoxane and her son Alexander IV are imprisoned and murdered.
304 BCE	Chandragupta takes control of the Indus region by trading 500 war elephants.
300 BCE	Use of iron increases across Africa.
280 BCE	The Colossus of Rhodes is built and the Lighthouse of Alexandria is completed.
276–194 BCE	Eratosthenes produces an early map of the world.
250 BCE	Canon of Buddhist scriptures is selected by a general council of Buddhist monks held in Patna.
218 BCE	Carthagian general Hannibal conquers Spain, crosses the Alps with elephants to defeat the Romans in north Italy, but retreats.
206 BCE–9 CE	Period known as the Western or Former Han with the capital Ch'ang-an in the present-day Shaanxi Province.
c. 200 BCE	Trading with Arabia, Indians begin to spread the word of Buddha.
195 BCE	After defeat by the Romans, Hannibal flees to Tyre and then to Ephesus to join Antiochus III of Syria.
192 BCE	Hannibal assists Antiochus III to land in Greece.
189 BCE	Hannibal is defeated by the Romans at Thermopylae and Magnesia before fleeing to Crete and then back to Asia Minor to assist Prusias I of Bithynia.
c. 183 BCE	Hannibal takes poison—long carried in a ring—in Bithynia, rather than be extradicted by the Romans.
150 BCE	Mayans establish walled city of El Mirador.
120 BCE	Two golden statues of Buddha are presented to the Chinese Emperor Han Wudi.

c. 101 BCE	Emperor Wudi regains control of territory lost in southern China and the northern part of Vietnam. He also sets up commands in Korea. He seizes horses and gives China control of trade routes—the Silk Roads.
58–51 BCE	Caesar and the Romans conquer Gaul.
55–54 BCE	Romans invade Britain.
45 BCE	The Julian calendar is introduced.
43 BCE	Following the assassination of Caesar, the third Roman civil war breaks out. Octavian, Antony, and Lepidus form the Second Triumvirate.
31 BCE	After ending their peace, Octavian defeats Antony and Cleopatra in the Battle of Actium.
30 BCE	Antony and Cleopatra commit suicide and Egypt becomes a province of Rome.
27 BCE	Octavian becomes Augustus Caesar, Emperor of Rome.

CE—TIMELINE OF HISTORY IN THE CURRENT ERA (1–1300)

c. 1 CE	Populations in the Basin of Mexico expand.
c. 6 BCE	Birth of Jesus.
25–220 CE	The Eastern Han period, China is ruled from Luoyang, a new capital in present-day Henan Province.
c. 26 CE	John the Baptist begins his missionary work.
c. 27 CE	Jesus begins his ministry.
c. 30 CE	Jesus is crucified.
c. 46 CE	Paul begins his missionary journeys and spreads the word of Christianity.
50 BCE	Mayan city of Cerros is built and abandoned 100 years later and its people return to fishing and farming.
50 CE	The first Buddhist stupa is constructed at Sanchi, India.
57 CE	Paul writes his Letter to the Romans.
60 CE	Peter, the apostle of Jesus Christ, dies.
62 CE	In Britain, the Romans defeat the Iceni, a tribe led by warrior queen Boadicea.
68 CE	The building of the White Horse Temple officially establishes Buddhism in China.
100 CE	Camels introduced to North Africans for trans-Saharan trade.
c. 100 CE	Lombards settle along the lower Elbe.
100–200 CE	People along the east African coast start trading with Romans and Arabs.
132 CE	Paper, water clocks, sundials, and astronomical instruments are developed.
c. 135 CE	Roman governors ban circumcision.
c. 150–300 CE	Grid pattern established at Teotihuacan.

166 CE	Reported arrival of an emissary from Andun (the emperor Marcus Aurelius Antoninus) bringing ivory, rhinoceros horn, and tortoiseshell, suggesting a link to Rome.
192 CE	Commodius is murdered by the Praetorian Guard.
c. 200–533 CE	Vandals establish a kingdom along the Danube River.
224 CE	Ardashir, descendant of the priest Sassan, seizes the throne of Persia and becomes the first Sassanid king.
235–285 CE	The Romans are continuously at war with the Persians during this period. There are also Barbarian raids on Rome.
238 CE	Goths cross the Danube.
250–275 CE	Franks begin raids through the Western Empire.
c. 250 CE	The Pyramid of the Moon, at Teotihuacan, is decorated with wall paintings. Single-story buildings, mainly occupied by craftsmen are built. About 2,000 apartment compounds will make up the city. Teotihuacan controls most of the essential trade in obsidian in central Mexico.
c. 300 CE	First Polynesian people arrive in Hawaii from the Marquesas.
312 CE	Constantine the Great defeats Marcus Aurelius at the Mulvian Bridge.
313 CE	Constantine and Licinius, the Eastern ruler, agree to end persecutions. Christianity is legalized.
324 CE	Constantine establishes Byzantium as his new capital and moves his court.
330 CE	Constantine renames the town of Byzantium to "New Rome, which is Constantine's City." It became known as Constantinople.
335 CE	Emperor Constantine builds the Church of the Holy Sepulcher in Jerusalem.
336 CE	Constantine the Great dies.
350 CE	Crops such as bananas and yams begin to grow in east Africa.
361–363 CE	Roman emperor Julian the Apostate attempts to ban Christianity. He dies while fighting the Parthians.
375 CE	Ostrogoths are conquered by the Huns.
380 CE	Christianity is made the official religion of the Roman Empire.
380 CE	Buddhist monks carve two huge Buddhas into the rock face at Bactria, Afghanistan.
400 CE	Inca tribe first mentioned in Peruvian myths and legends.
400 CE	Maya highlands fall under the domination of Teotihuacan.
410 CE	Visigoths sack Rome.
455–476 CE	Barbarians become Roman generals and puppet emperors.
460 CE	King Firuz of Persia persecutes Jews, who emigrate to Arabia.
499 CE	Hindu mathematician Aryabhata writes the first book on algebra—Aryabhatiya.
500 CE	Japan adopts the Chinese alphabet.
500 CE	Tikal becomes the first great Maya city.

FROM 500 CE	Language changes cause a shift in High German consonants that separates it from other Germanic languages.
527 CE	Justinian rules the Byzantine Empire.
c. 538 CE	Buddhism is introduced to Japan via Korea.
555 CE	The Ostrogoths disappear.
c. 560 CE	Justinian returns the treasure of Jerusalem, plundered by the Romans in 70 CE, to the Church of the Holy Sepulchre in Jerusalem.
570 CE	Birth of Mohamed.
600 CE	The civilization at Teotihuacan is destroyed by an unknown event. Tikal becomes the largest city-state in Mesoamerica, with 500,000 inhabitants.
607 CE	Prince Shotoku of Japan builds a Buddhist temple in the Asuka Valley.
c. 610 CE	Mohamed has a vision in a cave near the city of Mecca.
624 CE	Caravans from Mecca are attacked by Muslims.
625 CE	Citizens of Mecca defeat Muslims at Uhud.
630 CE	Muslims capture Mecca.
632 CE	Death of Mohamed, who is succeeded by Abu Bakr.
632 CE	Abu Bakr declares war on the Roman and Persian (Sassanid) empires.
636 CE	Arabs gain control of most of Palestine from the Byzantine Empire.
645 CE	Reforms called the Taika no Kaishin strengthen the emperor's power in Japan.
646 CE	Egypt is conquered by the Arabs.
c. 650 CE	Teotihuacan falls, Mesoamerica loses its unifying force.
c. 650 CE	Qur'an is recorded by order of Caliph Uthman.
650 CE	Arabs conquer the whole of Persia.
c. 661 CE	Damascus becomes the capital of the Umayyad Caliphate.
700 CE	The Arabs conquer Tunis.
710 CE	New capital founded at Nara, Japan. Buddhism is taught in the hope of bringing a peaceful society.
c.720 CE	King Ine of Wessex builds a stone church at Glastonbury Abbey.
c.729 CE	The Northumbrians sign a peace treaty with the Picts.
745 CE	Plague breaks out in Iraq, upper Mesopotamia, and Syria.
747 CE	Abu Muslim of the Abbasids begins revolution.
749 CE	The Abbasids gain control of Persia.
749-750 CE	The Caliphate of the Umayyads is ended by revolution.
751 CE	Pepin the Short becomes King of the Franks.
754 CE	Baghdad becomes the capital of the Abbasid Caliphate.
755 CE	Al-Mansur has Abu Muslim murdered.

789 CE	The first Viking attack on England.
794 CE	Heiankyo (Kyoto) becomes home of the imperial court.
798 CE	Viking attacks on France begin.
800 CE	The Great Migration-the first Polynesian peoples land in New Zealand.
800 CE	Charlemagne is crowned as Holy Roman Emperor by Pope Leo III.
802 CE	Jayavarman II declares independence from Java.
810 CE	King Godfred of Denmark is murdered.
c. 813 CE	The magnificent Oseberg Viking ship is built.
814-40 CE	Louis the Pious succeeds Charlemagne as Holy Roman Emperor.
827 CE	The Saracens conquer Sicily.
831 CE	Danish Vikings invade Ireland.
835 CE	The Isle of Sheppey comes under Viking attack.
843 CE	Treaty of Verdun partitions the Carolingian Empire.
844 CE	A Viking raid on Seville is repulsed.
858 CE	Emperor begins the rule of the Fujiwara clan.
866 CE	Danish Vikings establish the kingdom of York, England.
870 CE	Treaty of Mersen allows the Frankish kingdoms to absorb the fragmented middle lands to the east and west.
871 CE	Alfred the Great becomes King of Wessex and the Danish advance is halted in England.
882 CE	Saracens base established at Garigliano, Campania, Italy.
898 CE	Magyars make a raid into Italy.
900 CE	The Mayans establish Chichen Itza as main center.
903 CE	Good King Wenceslaus, Duke of Bohemia, is born.
936 CE	Otto the Great is crowned King of Germany.
955 CE	Otto I defeats the Hungarians in the Battle of Lechfeld.
955 CE	John XII becomes pope at age 18 and rules for nine years.
c. 955 CE	Archbishop Oda of Canterbury rebuilds Canterbury Cathedral.
962 CE	Otto I is crowned Emperor of the Romans, beginning the Holy Roman Empire.
966 CE	Duke Mieszko I of Poland converts to Christianity when he marries Dabrowka of Bohemia.
983 CE	Vikings establish a settlement in Greenland under Erik the Red.
c. 988-989 CE	Vladimir, prince of Kievan Rus', having adopted Orthodox Christianity, commissions the creation of religious icons and architecture.
997 CE	St Adalbert of Bohemia is martyred.
997 CE	King Stephen rules over the Arpad Dynasty of Hungary.

c. 1000	An early Andean culture of Huari uses complex irrigation systems to cultivate crops.
1000	Château de Goulaine vineyard in the Loire Valley, France, is founded. It is thought to be one of Europe's oldest continuous family businesses.
c. 1000–1100	Marrakech is founded on the junction of a trade route running southward to the Niger River and eastward to Cairo.
c. 1000–1500	Stone statues on Easter Island are carved out of volcanic ash.
1004	Muhammad of Ghazni defeats the armies of a Hindu confederacy. He annexes the Punjab and introduces Islam.
1009	Ly Cong Uan founds the Ly Dynasty, and establishes Vietnam as an independent state.
1016	King Cnut (Canute) defeats the English.
1016	Airlangga becomes the founding ruler of the Kingdom of Mataram, greatest of the medieval Southeast Asian island empires.
1019	Yaroslav is made Grand Prince of Kiev.
1026	Muhammad of Ghazni sacks the Samnath Temple.
1037	Construction of the St Sofia Cathedral in Kiev begins.
c. 1044	Book published with a written formula for gunpowder as well as describing an early form of the compass.
1052	Edward the Confessor founds Westminster Abbey.
1054	The Roman Catholic Church and Eastern Orthodox Church go their separate ways.
1055	The foundation charter for the abbey at Tihany in Hungary is the earliest writing in the Hungarian language.
1067	Construction begins on the Tower of London.
1072	Princes Boris and Gleb of Russia are canonized.
1082	The Almoravids, led by Youssef bin Tachfin, capture the city of Algiers.
1095	Pope Urban II calls for the First Crusade.
1099	Jerusalem is captured by Crusaders. El Cid, the great Moorish leader is killed.
1100–1200	Serbs occupy already inhabited parts of northern and eastern Albania.
c. 1100	Rise of the Toltec empire.
c. 1100	Chinese kilns begin to mass produce ceramics for the imperial court.
1100	Boleslaw Krzywousty divides Poland among his sons.
1115	Jurchen warriors from Manchuria defeat the Khitan Liao Dynasty, and establish the Jin Dynasty in northern China.
1125	German princes abolish heredity claims to the throne and establish an election system.
1127	Jurchen soldiers besiege the capital of the Song Dynasty in China and kidnap the emperor and other members of the imperial court.

1135	Mongols raid northern China.
1138	In England, the Battle of the Standards is fought between English and Scottish forces.
1141	The Battle of Samarkand is fought between the Seljuks and Qara-Khitai.
1143	Portugal becomes an independent kingdom.
1146	The first mention of Moscow appears in documents.
1150	Suryavarman II trades elephant tusks and feathers with China in return for gold. He dies in battle in the same year.
1155	Frederick Barbarossa is proclaimed Holy Roman Emperor.
1155	A map of western China—the oldest known printed map—is produced.
1156	The first Kremlin walls are built in Moscow.
1163	Construction of Notre Dame Cathedral in Paris is begun.
1181	King Jayavarman VII takes the throne of the Khmer Empire. The empire will expand and be at its most powerful during his reign.
1185	In Japan, Minamoto samurai warriors win the civil war by defeating the Taira clan in a great naval battle.
1186	The monastery at Ta Prohm, Cambodia, is finished. Inscriptions say it took thousands of servants to maintain it.
1189	Richard I is crowned King of England, then leaves on crusade. His brother John makes overtures to the throne in his absence.
1190–1191	Prithviraj defeats the Muslim troops beyond Punjab. Muhammad of Ghur is severely wounded.
1191	Richard I of England is captured near Vienna.
1192	Second battle of Tarain, in India. Muhammad of Ghur captures the fortress of Uch.
1192	Minamoto no Yoritomo becomes the first Shogun of the Kamakura dynasty, unifying Japan.
1193	Muhammad of Ghur establishes a kingdom in India with its capital in Delhi.
1194	After release at Mainz, Richard I returns to England and captures Nottingham Castle thus ending John's attempts to take the throne. Richard is again crowned King of England.
1195	Aztecs arrive in Valley of Mexico.
1200 CE	Manco Capac is the first ruler of the small city-state of Cuzco.
1200	The Anasazi tribe begin building cliff dwellings in southwest Colorado, USA.
1202–1204	The Fourth Crusade is undertaken.
1206	Muhammad of Ghur is murdered. With no successor, his throne is in disarray until Qutb-ud-din Aibak returns to India and declares himself Sultan.
1206	Genghis Khan becomes supreme ruler of all Mongol tribes.

1210	Iltutmish treats infidels according to the liberal Hanafi school of thought, which puts a strong emphasis on human reason.
1215	Mongols attack northern China and continue their quest south.
1215	King John I signs the Magna Carta.
1223	Mongols have first victory over Kievan Rus'.
1224	Genghis Khan splits his empire into khanates, to be ruled by his four sons.
1227	Genghis Khan dies and is succeeded by Ogedei, who moves the Mongol capital to Karakorum.
1227	Zen Buddhism is introduced into Japan by a monk called Dogen.
1235	In Africa, Sundiata Keita emerges victorious from the Battle of Kirina and establishes the Mali Empire.
1237	Mongol forces under the leadership of Batu Khan invade Russia.
1241	Ogedei dies and the Mongols retreat from Europe. Ogedei's widow Toregene takes over as regent.
1242	Batu Khan establishes the Kipchak Khanate, which is known in Russia as the "Golden Horde."
1245	Cottage weavers in Flanders go on strike against cloth merchants.
1250	Florence becomes a major center for commerce and industry.
1250	Aztecs settle near Lake Texcoco.
1251	Kubilai becomes governor of the southern territories of the Mongol empire.
1253	Kubilai attacks Yunnan and destroys the kingdom of Dali.
1258	The Mongols conquer Baghdad.
1259	Arik Boke, Kubilai's younger brother is pronounced the Great Khan.
1260	Kubilai is appointed Khan and declares Buddhism the state religion. Mongols are defeated for the first time in Palestine.
1263	Kubilai eventually wins after three year's battle with his brother and is declared the Great Khan.
1267	Kubilai Khan moves the Mongol capital to Dadu (present-day Beijing).
1271	Marco Polo begins his journey to China.
1273	Rudolf I, founder of the Habsburg Dynasty, becomes King of Germany.
1274 AND 1281	Kubilai Khan attempts invasion of Japan but is repelled with the influence of the divine wind (kamikaze).
1279	Kubilai Khan proclaims himself emperor of China.
1291	Three valleys in central Switzerland unite against the Habsburgs.
1299	Osman I establishes the Ottoman Empire.
1300	Paris is the largest city in the world with a population 200,000 to 300,000.

1300	People from the Mississippi region of America build the earthen city of Cahokia.
c. 1300	Rise of Mexica culture and Aztec empire.
c. 1300	Archeological evidence that the first Polynesian peoples landed in New Zealand—the Great Migration.

CE—TIMELINE OF HISTORY IN THE CURRENT ERA (1301–1600)

1302	The Peace Treaty of Caltabellota brokered between the Angevins and the Aragonese ends the 20-year-long War of the Sicilian Vespers.
1303	King Philip IV of France kidnaps Pope Boniface VIII over the right to tax French clergy.
1305	Papal seat moves to Avignon.
1312	Mansa Musa becomes king of Mali Empire.
1317	Ottoman emperor, Osman I, lays siege to the city of Bursa.
1320–1346	The Black Death ravages China and the Middle East.
1325	Explorer and scholar, Ibn Battuta, then aged 20, begins his travels.
1325	Tenochtitlan is founded in Mesoamerica and the first temple is built.
1326	After an extended battle, Bursa surrenders and is made capital of the Ottoman Empire.
1326	Isabella, daughter of Philip IV of France and Queen of England, begins to recruit mercenaries from amongst the nobility of France.
1326	The Hindu kingdom of Vijayanagara is established in southern India by brothers Harihara and Bukka Sangama.
1326	Ibn Battuta arrives in Mecca for the hajj.
1328	Edward III of England and Philippa of Hainault are married.
1328	After studying in Mecca for a year, Ibn Battuta travels the Red Sea to Aden, then East Africa.
1338	Edward III of England invades France—beginning the Hundred Years' War.
1340	The English fleet defeat the French at the Battle of Sluys.
1346	The marksmanship of English longbowmen plays a vital role in the English victory over the French at Crécy.
1346	In Germany, Charles IV of Luxembourg is elected Holy Roman Emperor.
1346	Edward III closes all English ports, to prevent news of his planned invasion of France from leaking out.
1346	The Black Death reaches the Crimea, including Kaffa.
1347	The plague spreads throughout Europe, killing roughly one third of the population.
1348	The plague strikes France.

1348, AUGUST	The Black Death enters England through the port of Bristol.
1348, SEPTEMBER	London is struck by the plague.
1348, DECEMBER	Evidence of the plague begins to disappear in Italy.
1349	Jews are expelled from Zurich, Switzerland.
1349	The Black Death continues to spread through England and into Ireland.
1351	Ibn Battuta travels to West Africa and Timbuktu.
1352	English Parliament limits the king's powers of conscription.
1355	The Black Prince sails to Bordeaux.
1368	Zhy Yuanzhong defeats the Mongols and establishes the Ming Dynasty.
1368	The renovation of the Great Wall of China is begun.
1399	Timur destroys Delhi—in the process committing some of the worst atrocities in history.
1400–1500	Incas begin to expand and conquer other tribes.
c. 1400	The Toraja people arrive in Sulawesi and settle on the banks of the Sa'dan River.
c. 1400	Swahili cities begin to appear on the east coast of Africa.
1411	Sigismund becomes the Holy Roman Emperor.
1419	Prince Henry the Navigator establishes an observatory and navigation school at Sagres.
1421	Construction begins on the Forbidden City in Beijing.
1424	A Portuguese navigation chart is produced showing a land called Antilia near the West Indies.
1428	Aztecs form Triple Alliance with Texcoco and Tlacopan peoples.
1429	Joan of Arc rides into Orléans with a small escort. The siege of the city comes to an end three weeks later.
1431	Invasion by Thai armies sees the end of the Khmer civilization at Angkor Thom with the court eventually moving to Phnom Penh.
1439	Portuguese claim the Azores Islands.
c. 1439	Portuguese explorers reach the Gold Coast (Ghana), greatly influencing the patterns of trade.
c. 1441	The trade in human lives begins with countries outside Africa.
1451	Sailors from Portugal regularly visit the Senegal River.
1452, APRIL 15	Leonardo da Vinci is born.
1453	The fall of Constantinople signals the end of the Byzantine era, and the rise of the Ottoman Empire.
1455	First battle of St Albans begins the Wars of the Roses.
1460	Prince Henry the Navigator dies.
1461	York defeats Lancaster at the Battle of Mortimers Cross. King Henry VI is ousted, replaced by Edward IV.

1462	Margaret of Anjou captures castles in Northumberland with the help of the French.
1464	Second phase of the Wars of the Roses begins with a battle at Hexham.
1465	Henry IV is captured at Clitheroe by Yorkists.
1467	Rival daimyo vying for power spark the breakout of the Onin Wars.
1469	Leonardo da Vinci moves to Florence as Lorenzo de Medici becomes ruler.
1471	Henry IV is imprisoned in the Tower of London and killed.
c. 1477–1484	A young Christopher Columbus begins his adventures sailing in merchant vessels to Iceland.
1479	After a four-year war, Spain agrees to a Portuguese trade monopoly along the west coast of Africa.
1483	Edward IV of England dies. Richard, Duke of Gloucester, locks away his heir Edward V and his younger brother Richard. Neither boy is ever seen again.
1485	Richard III is killed at the Battle of Bosworth. Henry Tudor comes to the throne as Henry VII, marking the beginning of the Tudor Dynasty.
1487	Battle of Stoke ends Wars of the Roses.
1492	Columbus discovers the Americas. He also notes the first recorded reference to tobacco.
1494	Spain and Portugal sign the Treaty of Tordesillas establishing a demarkation 370 leagues west of the Azores. Portugal claims new land discovered in the east and Spain claims the west.
1497	Leonardo da Vinci paints *The Last Supper*.
1498	Michelangelo, aged 24, begins his *Pieta*, completing it one year later.
1498	Portuguese navigator Vasco da Gama becomes the first European to reach India by sea.
1500	Pedro Alvares Cabral claims the Brazilian "hump" for Portugal.
c. 1500	The Kingdom of Kongo reaches its peak along the path of the Congo River.
1500	Portuguese explorer Diego Diaz discovers the island of Madagascar.
1502	Shah Ismail I, having defeated his rival Alwand of the White Sheep, founds Persia's Safavid Dynasty.
1504	Leonardo da Vinci paints *Mona Lisa*. Michelangelo creates the massive statue of *David*, originally begun 40 years earlier by Agostino di Duccio.
1504	Sikander Khan of India founds a new town named Agra and raises the status of the Sultan's office.
1505	Ferdinand Magellan sails to India on his first voyage.
1507	The name "America" is used for the first time by a German cartographer who publishes a map of the New World. He chooses the name in honor of Amerigo Vespucci (1454–1512).

1508	Michelangelo begins painting the ceiling of the Sistine Chapel. He completes the composition four years later.
1509	On the death of his father, Henry VIII comes to the English throne.
1510	The Portuguese establish a trading colony at Goa, the first permanent European settlement in Asia.
1512	Joining a force against the Moroccan stronghold of Azamour, Ferdinand Magellan is wounded and has a limp for the rest of his life.
1513	Spanish explorer, Vasco Nunez de Balboa, crosses the isthmus of Panama and claims the Pacific Ocean for Spain.
1513	Spanish explorer Ponce de Leon discovers Florida.
1514	Approximately 1,500 Spanish immigrants settle in Panama.
1517	Sikander begins construction of the Moth ki Masjid in Delhi.
1517	Ferdinand Magellan travels to Spain and joins with Portuguese cosmographer Rui Faleiro to renounce their nationalities and offer their services to King Charles I of Spain.
1519	Leonardo da Vinci dies in Amboise, France.
1519	Cortés conquers Mexico and captures Moctezuma II.
1519	Magellan's crew observe the Large Magellanic Cloud (LMC) and the Small Magellanic Cloud (SMC) during their voyage in the southern hemisphere.
1519-22	Cortés conquers the Aztec capital of Tenochtitlan.
1520	Moctezuma II is ruler of the Aztecs with the empire at its height.
1520	Chocolate from Mexico arrives in Spain for the first time.
1521	Ferdinand Magellan heads a voyage to circumnavigate the world. He dies on the way and his crew complete the voyage.
1522	Luther's New Testament translation appears in German.
1523	Calvin begins study in Paris and is soon influenced by Lutheran teaching.
1523	Turkeys are introduced to Spain and Europe from America by the conquistadors.
1524	Italian Giovanni da Verrazzano, is the first European to discover present-day New York.
1524-1525	Luther and Erasmus debate the freedom of the will.
1525	Civil war breaks out between Huascar and Atahualpa of the Incas, dividing the vast empire.
1526	Ibrahim Khan, the last Lodi leader, is killed in the Battle of Panipat.
1533	Henry VIII of England splits with the Roman Catholic Church.
1534	Jacques Cartier lands on the Gaspé Peninsula and claims the land for France. He sails inland up the St Lawrence River and names the surrounding territory "Kanata," meaning village in the Huron-Iroquois language.
1535	On a return voyage to France, Cartier loses 25 men to scurvy.
1536	Calvin's Institutes of the Christian Religion are published at Basel.
1539	Olaus Magnus, Swedish historian, produces a map of the world.
1541	On his third voyage, Cartier meets with de Roberval who was commanded to take charge of the colonization of Canada. Cartier warns him of the severe weather.
1541	Spanish explorer Hernando de Soto discovers the Mississippi River.
1542	Gonzalo Pizarro, younger brother of Francisco reaches the mouth of the Amazon River after having sailed its length as far as the Andes Mountains.
1543	De Roberval returns to France, abandoning the territory of Canada due to the harshness of the weather.
1545	The Council of Trent begins.
1545	Cartier publishes tales of his explorations.
1547	The Navy Royal, as it was known then, has a fleet of 58 vessels.
1547	Ivan IV is crowned the first Tsar of Russia.
1551	Ottoman forces invade and conquer Tripoli.
1554	Mary I of England marries Philip II of Spain.
1557	Portuguese traders found the port city of Macau, the first European trading enclave in China.
1558	England's Mary I dies and is succeeded by her half-sister Elizabeth who refuses to marry Philip of Spain.
1564	Michelangelo dies after designing the dome at St Peter's Basilica.
1564	French settlement is established in Florida, south of Jacksonville.
1565	The first Spanish settlement in the Philippines is established in Cebu City.
1566	Suleyman, Sultan of the Ottomans, dies.
1570	Nagasaki becomes the first Japanese port open to overseas trade.
1571	The Spanish fleet overcomes the Ottomans in the Battle of Lepanto, ending their supremacy in the Mediterranean.
1583	Jesuit missionary Matteo Ricci arrives in China.
1583	John Davis first proposes his expedition to find the Northwest Passage.
1584	Sir Walter Raleigh dispatches an expedition to explore the east coast of North America for settlement. The Outer Banks (North Carolina) are chosen.
1586	Sir Richard Grenville is assigned to further explore the possible colony. Ralph Lane was left in charge.
1587	Sir Walter Raleigh attempts a second expedition to North America.
1587	John White becomes governor of the newly-established Roanoke Colony but after returning to England for supplies, he found the colony deserted two years later.

1588, August	After years of political conflict, the English fleet destroys the Spanish Armada, killing 600 Spaniards and injuring around 800.
1588, October 23	After avoiding the English off the coast of Ireland, the remaining Spanish Armada returns to Santander.
1588	During the pursuit of the Spanish Armada up the English Channel, Drake forgoes duty in order to plunder the Spanish galleon *Rosario*, known to be carrying funds to pay the Spanish Army.
1589	Richard Hakluyt writes *The Principall Navigations, Voiages and Discoveries of the English Nation*, detailing eyewitness accounts of England's colonization.
1589	Drake fails in an attempt to capture Lisbon with a navy of 150 ships.
1589	After completing three unsuccessful attempts to find the Northwest Passage, John Davis joins Thomas Cavendish on his last voyage.
1590	Toyotomi Hideyoshi successfully unites Japan.
1592	After leaving Cavendish's expedition, Davis goes on to discover the Falkland Islands.
1592	Samurai forces dispatched by Japanese Shogun Hideyoshi invade Korea.
1595	Elizabeth I sends Drake to seize treasure from a wrecked Spanish galleon at La Forteleza.
1596	Sir Francis Drake dies of dysentery off the coast of Panama and is buried at sea.
1596	On his third voyage, Willem Barents's ship gets caught in packice and the crew use timber from the ship to build a lodge.
1597	By June, the ice has still not loosened and Willem Barents's crew took to two small boats to escape. Barents died seven days later. His lodge was discovered in 1871.
1598	The Edict of Nantes is issued, allowing religious freedom to French Huguenots after years of persecution.
1600	West Timor is seized by the Netherlands.
c. 1600	Japan begins to reunify after almost 100 years of civil war.
1600	The British East India Company is founded.
1602	The Dutch East India Company is founded.

CE—TIMELINE OF HISTORY IN THE CURRENT ERA (1601–1900)

1608	Samuel de Champlain founds the city of Québec.
1610	After several previous voyages, Henry Hudson once more sails for an English trading company, and discovers the bay and the strait that will bear his name.
1611-1613	Disputed seafaring trade routes see Denmark and Sweden engage in the Kalmar War.

1615	The Privy Council of Britain sanctions the transportation of convicts to West Indian colonies and Virginia.
1616	The Jurchens are unified and the state of Jin/Qing in northeastern China is established.
1616	William Baffin, English maritime explorer, arrives at the bay named for him—Baffin Bay.
1616	Landing on Run, smallest of the Banda Islands, British merchant seaman Nathaniel Courthope persuades the residents to enter an alliance with England over nutmeg. Combining forces, they hold off the Dutch for over four years.
1619	One hundred homeless children are sent to Virginia.
1619	Ferdinand II is elected Holy Roman Emperor.
1620	In Europe, the Catholic League and the Protestant Union enter into the Treaty of Ulm pledging not to battle each other.
1620	A group of English Puritans known as the Pilgrims land in North America after a 65-day voyage from Portsmouth, England in the *Mayflower*.
1621	Under Dutch control, Jakarta is renamed Batavia.
1622	Leading the Protestant forces, Christian of Halberstadt is defeated by Count von Tilly and Fernandez de Cordova.
1626	Count von Tilly wins a crushing victory against the Danes at Lutter-am-Bamberg.
1631	French and Swedish forces enter into the Treaty of Barwalde.
1631	Mumtaj, third wife and beloved favorite of Shah Jahan, dies giving birth to their fourteenth child while accompanying her husband on a military campaign in Burhanpur. The court is ordered into mourning for two years.
1632	Shah Jahan orders the building of the Taj Mahal as a monument to his wife. Its construction takes 20 years to complete.
1632	Count von Tilly dies at Ingoldstadt, Bavaria, from wounds received in the battle of Rain.
1634	Abel Tasman is second-in-command of an expedition to Formosa in which half the crew dies during the voyage.
1634	Charles I creates a "ship money" levy in order to build up the navy. The tax becomes the main cause of the English Civil War.
1636	Hong Taiji of China changes the name of his people from Jurchen to Manchu meaning "pure."
1637	Manchus invade Korea.
1638	Shogun Iemitsu forbids any shipbuilding in Japan.
1640-41	Tasman voyages to Japan and then southern Sumatra, where he makes a trade treaty with the sultan.
1641	Shogun Iemitsu bans all foreigners, except Chinese and Dutch.
1642	Tasman claims formal possession of Anthoonij Van Diemen's Land (Tasmania) for the Dutch. Later he sights New Zealand.

1642	England is plunged into civil war, as the parliamentarian "Roundhead" forces and the royal "Cavalier" forces engage in battle.
1643	Tasman's voyage takes him past Tonga and then Fiji.
1644	Manchus invade northern China and take Beijing, overthrowing the Ming Dynasty and establishing the Qing Dynasty.
1648	Shah Jahan moves the court to the new capital Delhi, India.
1648	The Peace of Westphalia brings about the end of the Thirty Years War.
1649	Abel Tasman, charged with unlawfully hanging a crew member, has his commission suspended.
1649	Charles I of England is found guilty of treason and executed on January 30. His son and heir, Charles, is forced into exile in Europe. Oliver Cromwell becomes Lord Protector of England.
1655	Massachusetts Bay Colony Puritans punish the first Quakers and later ban them from holding their meetings.
1657	Shah Jahan of India becomes seriously ill and his sons struggle for power.
1660	Louis XIV marries Maria Teresa, daughter of Spanish king Philip IV.
1660	The monarchy is restored as Charles II takes back the throne left vacant since his father's execution in 1649.
1664	New Amsterdam becomes New York after Stuyvesant's surrender to the English.
1665	Louis XIV commissions architect Claude Perrault to design the eastern wing of the Palais du Louvre, then a royal palace.
1665	The King of the Kongo Empire, António I, is killed by the Portuguese at the Battle of Mbwila.
1666	Shah Jahan dies and is buried next to his beloved wife Mumtaj, in the Taj Mahal.
1666	The Great Fire of London consumes much of the city.
1667	In North America, a peace treaty is signed between the Iroquois people and the French.
1670	Hudson's Bay Company is chartered.
1671	At a ceremony held in Sault Ste Marie, the French lay claim to all land lying west of Montreal, in North America.
1676	Tobacco planter, Nathan Bacon, asks permission to attack the Susquehannock Indians who are raiding settlements. When permission is refused, the colonists burn Jamestown and kill many Indians.
1682	Château de Versailles is opened.
1683	Ottomans lose the Battle of Vienna, which marks the end of expansion.
1684	The Charter of Massachusetts Bay is revoked after criticism reaches England.
1684	Changamire Dombo resists the Portuguese traders and starts to establish his Rozvi Empire.

1685	Following the death of Maria Teresa in 1683, Louis XIV marries Françoise d'Aubigne.
1699	Peace treaty at Maine ends hostilities between the Abenaki Indians and the Massachusetts' colonists.
1707	England and Scotland unite under one ruler and one Parliament.
1709	Russia score a victory over Sweden at the Battle of Poltava.
1711	Russia's Peter the Great establishes laws to allow the governing Senate to pass laws in his absence.
1713	The War of the Spanish Succession is ended by the Treaty of Utrecht. Philip V remains King of Spain, but Spanish territories in other parts of Europe are given up.
1719	The newly-established principality of Liechtenstein declares its independence.
1721	The Great Northern War ends with the Treaty of Nystad. Peter is declared Emperor of Russia.
1722	Easter Island is discovered by Dutch explorer Jacob Roggeveen.
1727	The Treaty of Kiakhta defines the boundary between the Chinese and the Russian empires.
1728	Vitus Bering discovers the passage between Russia and Alaska.
1729	The Qing government bans opium in China.
1736	Emperor Qianlong ascends the Chinese throne, inaugurating the golden age of the Qing Dynasty.
1746	The British Army defeat Scottish Highlander clansmen at the Battle of Culloden.
1750	Before the Industrial Revolution, the atmosphere holds 280 parts per million of CO_2.
1755	In November, a massive earthquake in the Atlantic caused an enormous tsunami across the harbor of Lisbon, Portugal. Over 100,000 people are killed.
1755	James Cook joins the navy, hoping that participation in the Seven Years' War will advance his career.
1756	Great Britain declares war on France, formalizing the existing conflict in the American colonies and starting the Seven Years' War.
1757	James Cook gains his Master's certificate and is qualified to navigate and captain a ship of the Royal Navy.
1759–1765	HMS *Victory* is built. It is the oldest naval ship still in commission. *Victory* sits in dry dock at Portsmouth, UK.
1761	With the opening of Bridgewater Canal, designed by James Brindley, barges can now carry coal from Worsley to Manchester.
1765	The Treaty of Allahabad gives the East India Company control of much of India.
1768	Gorkha King Prithvi Narayan Shah becomes first king of Nepal.

1770	Captain James Cook claims the east coast of Australia for Great Britain.
1773	Captain James Cook's second voyage of discovery is the first to cross the Antarctic Circle.
1774	The very First Continental Congress is held.
1774	The *Québec Act* recognizes both the French language and the Roman Catholic religion in the colony.
1775	The American Revolution begins.
1775	James Cook is promoted to the rank of Captain and given honorary retirement from the Royal Navy. In addition he is made a Fellow of the Royal Society.
1776	James Cook is promoted from the rank of Master to Commander in the Royal Navy.
1776, July 8	Liberty Bell in Philadelphia rings to call out the people for a historic public reading of the Declaration of Independence.
1777	Grand Trunk Canal opens connecting the Mersey to the Trent and connecting the industrial Midlands to the ports of Bristol, Liverpool, and Hull.
1781	British merchants begin large-scale opium import from India.
1783	John Adams helps write the peace treaty with England.
1787	The revolutionary US Constitution is adopted by the people of the new United States.
1788	The 11 ships of the First First arrive in Australia.
1789	The Bill of Rights becomes the first ten amendments to the US Constitution.
1789	George Washington becomes the first President of the United States, John Adams is Vice-president, Thomas Jefferson is Secretary of State, and Alexander Hamilton is Secretary of the Treasury.
1789	In France, the Estates General are called for the first time since 1614. Voting in France is to be by Estate and not by head, resulting in Third Estate meeting alone and later declaring itself the National Assembly.
1789, June 27	Louis XVI recognizes the validity of the National Assembly, ordering First and Second Estates to join Third.
1789, July 14	Parisians storm the Bastille.
1790	The US Congress passes an act requiring two years' residency before citizenship.
1790	Congress meets in the temporary capital of Philadelphia. The US Supreme Court meets for the first time.
1791	French royal family flees to Varennes but is arrested and returned to Paris.
1791-1792	Campaign of the First Coalition—the major European powers, concerned at events in France, join forces to protect their nations from a similar fate to that of France, which is in the grip of revolution.
1792	The first trade union in the US is formed by shoemakers.
1792	The French tricolor cockade becomes compulsory headgear for men.

1792	James Watt's assistant William Murdock lights his home with coal gas.
1793	Eli Whitney invents the cotton gin, speeding up the production of cotton for export.
1793	Louis XVI of France is guillotined after trial before the National Convention.
1795	"La Marseillaise" is accepted as the French national anthem.
1796	Napoleon marries the widow Josephine de Beauharnais.
1797	Mount Fuji erupts.
1798-1801	Napoleon invades Egypt. His fleet is destroyed by Nelson.
1799	Napoleon stages a coup d'état and installs himself as First Consul.
1800	Washington DC is chosen as the capital of the United States.
1800	*Act of Union* is passed, making Ireland part of Great Britain.
1803	Matthew Flinders circumnavigates the continent of Australia.
1803	The French government sells its Louisiana Territory to the USA.
1804	Napoleon crowns himself Emperor of France.
1805	Third Coalition sees victory for the French with surrender at Ulm and a crushing victory over Russia and Austria.
1805	Napoleon declares himself Italian Emperor.
1805	Admiral Horatio Nelson leads the British Royal Navy to victory against France and Spain at the Battle of Trafalgar. He is fatally wounded.
1807	British Parliament votes to abolish the trade in slaves.
1808	US Congress prohibits the importation of African slaves.
1808	The Rum Rebellion breaks out in Australia after Governor Bligh tries to stop the barter and sale of spirits. It results in Bligh being returned to England.
1808-1814	Peninsular War leaves Napoleon's army decimated.
1810	Marie Louise, Archduchess of Austria, marries Napoleon after his divorce from Josephine, who could not give him an heir.
1810	South American Wars of Independence begin. Colombia and Mexico gain independence.
1811	The British fleet captures Batavia in the Dutch East Indies, and wrests control of Java from the Dutch.
1811-15	In England, laborers attack factories and break up the machines out of fear of being replaced.
1812	America declares war on British North America.
1812	Napoleon invades Russia in one of the worst mistakes in military history. The march to Moscow caused hardship and death. The Russians burn Moscow to prevent Napoleon gaining the spoils. Eventually retreating back across plundered territory, the army crosses out from Russian territory with the loss of thousands of men.

1813	Persia signs the Treaty of Gulistan, ceding Baku, Karabagh, and other territories to the Russian Empire.
1814	Italy is divided into small provinces.
1814	Napoleon is defeated in Russia.
1814	The Treaty of Ghent marks the end the War of 1812 between the UK and USA.
1815	The French forces are defeated at the Battle of Waterloo.
1815	Napoleon is exiled to the island of St Helena, dying in 1821.
1815	The Congress of Vienna reshapes Europe after Napoleon's defeat. It establishes the German Confederation, guarantees the neutrality of Switzerland, and bans the trading of slaves by its signatories.
1817	The Bank of New South Wales opens in Sydney, Australia.
1817	The Royal Canal—connecting Ireland's Liffey River with the Shannon River—is completed.
1817	The Bank of Montréal, the first permanent bank in British North America, is founded.
1818	USA and Britain establish the boundary between Canada and the USA.
1819	US Federal legislation requires the notation of passenger lists.
1820	Russian Gottlieb von Bellingshausen is the first person to see the Antarctic continent.
1820–1850	Venice, Rome, and Tuscany declare themselves republics.
1821	El Salvador, Guatemala, Honduras, Nicaragua, and Peru all gain independence from Spain.
1821	The American Colonization Society purchases land around Cape Mesurado in West Africa to enable "free people of color" from the USA to settle there.
1821–1837	British merchants increase opium import trying to reverse trade imbalance with China.
1823	United States issues the Monroe Doctrine warning against recolonization of the newly independent Spanish American republics.
1824	Jean Baptiste Joseph Fourier, describes the greenhouse effect.
1825	Bolivia declares separation from Peru, and Uruguay from Brazil.
1825	Indonesians revolt against the Dutch colonists in the Java War.
1826	Following British victory in the First Anglo-Burmese War, the Treaty of Yandaboo secures British control of Assam.
1827	Russia, France, and Britain unite to destroy the Turkish and Egyptian armada at the Battle of Navarino.
1828	The Catholic Emancipation Act is passed.
1830	Revolutionary unrest in France, Italy, Germany, and Poland.
1830	Belgium wins independence from the Netherlands.

1831	The Navy Board is abolished and the Admiralty takes charge of the Royal Navy.
1831	The Sydney Herald is first published—later The Sydney Morning Herald.
1833	The penal colony of Port Arthur is founded in Tasmania.
1835	More than 10,000 Boers leave Cape Colony to found the republics of Natal, Transvaal, and Orange Free State. This mass migration becomes known as "The Great Trek."
1836	Canada's first railway, the Champlain and St Lawrence Railroad, opens.
1837	Victoria becomes Queen of the United Kingdom of Great Britain and Ireland.
1838	The production of whiskey is reduced in England.
1838–1839	Cherokee Native Americans are forced to relocate; they move westward on the brutal "Trail of Tears."
1839 July	20,000 chests of opium are seized by the Chinese. Sailors destroy Kowloon temple and kill a Chinese man.
1839 August	British take control of Hong Kong. Charles Elliot establishes a blockade of the Pearl River to prevent British merchant ships from reaching the mainland and trading with the Chinese.
1840	British marines headed by James Bremer, and ships from the British East India Company, sail to Kwangtung.
1840	The Treaty of Waitangi is signed in New Zealand by Maori chiefs and representatives of Queen Victoria.
1840 June	British attack and move north to Xiamen, China.
1840	Act of Union unites upper and lower Canada.
1841	New Zealand is declared a crown colony.
1841 January	British defeat the Chinese at Ningbo.
1842	British occupy the mouth of the Yangtze.
1842	Shanghai is occupied by the British without opposition. The signing of the Treaty of Nanking confirmed the opening of a number of Chinese ports for trade.
1842	Auckland is proclaimed the capital of New Zealand.
1842	The border dispute between America and Canada is settled with the signing of the Webster-Ashburton Treaty.
1845–1850	Potato blight causes famine, and begins mass migration to Britain and the USA.
1846-48	Mexico is defeated by the United States that annexes the northern half of the country in the Treaty of Guadalupe Hidalgo.
1847	In England, the Ten Hours Act is passed restricting the working hours of children in factories.
1848	Revolutions are staged in Italy, France, Hungary, Austria, Germany, Switzerland, and Denmark.
1849	Monier develops reinforced concrete.
1849	Republic of Rome taken over by French troops.
1851	Frederick Douglass publishes the first series of newspapers.

1852	The Victoria and Albert Museum in London is opened.
1852	Transvaal becomes an independent Boer Republic.
1853–1856	Crimean War—the Ottomans and their allies fight Russia to control the Middle East.
1854	The US Supreme Court upholds slavery.
1854	In southern Africa, Britain returns Orange Free State to the Boers.
1854	The Treaty of Kanagawa opens trade between USA and Japan.
1854, MARCH 12	Alliance formed between Britain, France, and Turkey.
1854, SEPTEMBER 14	Following Russia's withdrawal across the Danube, Allies invade the Crimea with the intent to capture Sebastopol and destroy the Russia fleet.
1854–55	British troops suffer badly after spending the winter holed up in Crimea. The Times' daily reports bring public outrage and Florence Nightingale pushes for improved hospital conditions and nursing care.
1854, SEPTEMBER 20	Russians are defeated by Allied forces at Alma.
1854, OCTOBER 17	Allied siege of Sebastopol begins.
1855	Balmoral Castle is completed.
1855	Russia annexes Kazakhstan.
1856, MARCH 30	Peace in Crimea is concluded with the Treaty of Paris. Russia agrees to cease expansion into Balkans and Scandinavia and the Black Sea is declared a neutral zone.
1858	The first trans-Atlantic cable is completed.
1858	Government of India is transferred to the British Crown.
1859	Russia annexes Chechnya.
1859	Darwin publishes The Origin of the Species.
1860	In New Zealand, war breaks out between Maori and settlers, starting over a decade of fighting over land and sovereignty (known as the "New Zealand Wars").
1861	The Kingdom of Italy is established excluding Rome, Venice, and San Marino. Victor Emmanuel II of Sardinia becomes King.
1861–1865	American Civil War.
1861, MARCH	Abraham Lincoln inaugurated as the sixteenth President of the United States.
1861, JULY	In the United States, the North begins a naval blockade of the South.
1862	The US Homestead Act grants citizens title to 160 acres, encouraging naturalization.
1862	Emancipation Proclamation issued by US President Abraham Lincoln. It comes into effect the following year.
1862, JULY	Major General Henry Halleck is appointed general-in-chief of the Union Army.
1863	US Emancipation Proclamation comes into force.
1863	First underground railway in London—between Paddington and Farringdon Street—opens on January 10.
1863, NOVEMBER	Union forces push Confederate troops back at the Battle of Chatttanooga.
1864, JULY	Confederate troops push to within five miles of Washington DC.
1865	Thirteenth Amendment to the Constitution of the United States proposed. The amendment stated that: "Neither slavery nor involuntary servitude, except as a punishment for crime whereof the party shall have been duly convicted, shall exist within the United States, or any place subject to their jurisdiction."
1865	Wellington replaces Auckland as the capital of New Zealand.
1865, JANUARY	Starving soldiers begin to desert the Confederate Army.
1865, APRIL	General Grant calls on General Lee to surrender in the American Civil War.
1867	Russia sells Alaska to the United States for $7.2 million.
1867	Thousands of Irish-Americans return home to fight for Irish Republican Brotherhood.
1868	The emperor is restored to power and Japan becomes a nation with one ruler.
1868	The Spanish Revolution begins.
1870	Italian forces occupy Rome.
1870	Emperor Napoleon III is deposed and Third Republic is declared.
1871	Rome is named the capital of Italy.
1874	In West Africa, the Anglo-Ashanti War is ended with the signing of the Treaty of Fomena.
1876	At the Battle of Little Big Horn, the 7th Cavalry—commanded by General George Custer—is obliterated; 265 troopers face 3,500 Indian warriors led by chiefs Sitting Bull and Crazy Horse.
1876	Queen Victoria is named Empress of India.
1877	Britain annexes Boer Republics of southern Africa.
1877	Russia declares war on the Ottoman Empire in order to liberate the Balkans.
1878	The Treaty of Berlin divides the Balkans, following the Russo-Turkish War.
1879–1881	Land war for reform of tenancy laws.
1882	Following his death, Charles Darwin is given a state funeral in Westminster Abbey.
1883	The volcanic explosion of Krakatoa in Indonesia causes tsunamis across the Pacific and Indian oceans and as far away as the English Channel. They kill over 36,000 people.
1885	The Canadian Pacific railroad is completed.
1885 ·	Three months of negotiations by 15 nations divides Africa among the colonial powers.

1890	Cecil Rhodes becomes Prime Minister of Cape Colony.
1890	In the USA, the cavalry massacres hundreds of Sioux at Wounded Knee.
1891	New Scotland Yard is completed.
1892	Ellis Island in New York Harbor, is established as a screening station for immigrants.
1892	The Irish Home Rule Bill is defeated again.
1893	British South African Company occupies a new territory and calls it Rhodesia.
1893	New Zealand is the first country in the world to give women the vote.
1894	Sun Yixian moves to Hawaii where he founds the Revive China Society.
1895	Japan rises to world power status after victories in the Sino-Japanese and Russo-Japanese wars.
1895	Vladimir Lenin is arrested for engaging in revolutionary activities.
1896	An earthquake off the coast of Japan triggers a massive tsunami that washes over Sanriku, killing over 26,000 people.
1896–1899	Gold is discovered in the Klondike, causing a gold rush of people hoping to earn their fortune.
1898	Paul Kruger is re-elected as president of Transvaal.
1898	Spain cedes Cuba, Puerto Rico, Guam, and the Philippines to the USA for $20 million.
1899	In South Africa, a British ammunition train ambushed on its way to Ladysmith is captured, with Winston Churchill, the *London Morning Post* correspondent, on board.
1899	Boxer Uprising rebels besiege foreign legations in Peking for 100 days before being defeated.
1900	British government annexes Transvaal.

CE–TIMELINE OF HISTORY IN THE CURRENT ERA (1901 TO THE PRESENT)

1901	The population of London reaches 6.6 million.
1901	In Australia, the separate British colonies unite to form the Commonwealth of Australia. Edmund Barton is the first prime minister.
1901	Britain annexes the Ashanti kingdom on Africa's Gold Coast.
1901	Italian Guglielmo Marconi transmits wireless telegraphic signals from Cornwall to Newfoundland, a distance of 2,232 miles (3,593 km).
1901	In South Africa, Kitchener divides the country into sectors and erects barbed wire to protect the railways.
1901	Death of England's longest reigning monarch, Queen Victoria. She held the throne for 64 years. Edward VII ascends the throne.

1902	Robert Scott, Edward Wilson, and Ernest Shackleton head for the South Pole but only reach latitude 82ºS before suffering snow blindness and having to return.
1903	Serbian Army officers assassinate King Alexander and Queen Draga and install Prince Karageorgevitch as leader.
1903	Following Panama's secession from Colombia, the USA signs a treaty with the new state, which opens the way to a canal being built under US control.
1904	Russo-Japanese War breaks out.
1904, FEBRUARY 8	The Japanese launch a surprise torpedo attack on the Russian fleet in Port Arthur.
1904 FEBRUARY 9	Japanese occupy Seoul, Korea.
1904 FEBRUARY 10	Japan declares war on Russia.
1905	Sun publishes his political philosophy *Three Principles of the People*, which appears in the first line of the national anthem of the Republic of China.
1905	French explorer Pierre de Brazza dies and is buried in Dakar, Senegal.
1905	Tzar Nicholas II introduces his "October Manifesto" to establish reforms.
1905	Bloody Sunday—Tsarist troops open fire on a peaceful demonstration in St Petersburg.
1905, OCTOBER	Russia experiences a general strike.
1906	Britain forces Turkey to cede Sinai Peninsula to Egypt.
1906	In Russia, the new Duma is dissolved when it produces an anti-government majority.
1907	Dutch complete occupation of Sumatra.
1907	Wilhelm II of Germany and Nicholas II of Russia meet at Swinemunde.
1908	Shackleton and other explorers attempt to reach the South Pole, getting within 97 miles (155 km) before having to abandon the journey.
1908	Public outrage at the treatment of native Africans in the Congo leads Belgian Parliament to annex Congo Free State and call it Belgian Congo.
1908	Leopold II of Belgium concedes his private possession of Congo to Belgium.
1909	Tel Aviv, the first modern all-Jewish city is founded.
1910	Cape Colony, Natal, Transvaal, and Orange Free State are united to become the Union of South Africa.
1910	Revolution in Portugal—King Manuel II flees to England.
1911	Canberra is designated the capital city of Australia.
1911	Sun returns to China after almost 15 years in exile in Europe, United States, Canada, and Japan.
1911	German gunboat *Panther* arrives in the Moroccan port of Agadir, creating an international crisis.
1911	Norwegian explorer Roald Amundsen is the first man to reach the South Pole.

1912	The White Star liner *Titanic*, on its maiden voyage, strikes an iceberg and sinks. Almost 1,600 people perish.
1912	Sun Yixian is sworn in as the first provisional president of the Republic of China.
1912	Treaty of Lausanne signed between Italy and France.
1912	First Balkan War—following Montenegro's lead, Bulgaria, Serbia, and Greece declare war on Turkey.
1912	Albania declares independence from the Ottoman Empire, after 500 years of external rule.
1913	In London, on May 30, Turkey signs a treaty with the Balkan League members (Bulgaria, Greece, Montenegro, and Serbia), ending the eight-month First Balkan War. Turkey is compelled to cede large amounts of territory to the Balkan Peninsula. Tensions remain, and before long, the Second Balkan War commences. On August 10, Bulgaria signs a peace treaty with the Balkan states, but the unrest in this region is a factor in the outbreak of The Great War (World War I).
1914	World War I begins—Britain declares war on Germany on August 3–4 as German troops invade Belgium. In November, England, France and Russia declare war on supposedly neutral Turkey, after German ships were allowed through the Dardanelles, then bombarded Russian Black Sea ports.
1915	Germans stage a Zeppelin air raid on England.
1915	Allied troops land at Gallipoli in Turkey, on April 25. On December 20, they withdraw, in the wake of the failure to take Turkish positions and indifference from London.
1916	Germany switches its focus from the Eastern to the Western Front, launching into battle at Verdun. One million German troops are pitted against 200,000 French defenders.
1916	Easter uprising in Ireland, demanding independence from Britain.
1916	On July 1, at the Battle of the Somme, over 58,000 British casualties are sustained, one-third fatalities, in the first day of the new Western Front offensive.
1916	Woodrow Wilson is re-elected President of the United States on the slogan: "He kept us out of the war."
1917	Tsar Nicholas II abdicates and provisional government is established in Russia.
1917	Woodrow Wilson asks Congress for a declaration of war with Germany. Kaiser Wilhelm II of Germany abdicates.
1917	Ottoman rule is ended by British conquest.
1917	Puerto Rico becomes a US protectorate, with all citizens awarded American citizenship.
1917, February	After several days of protest in Petrograd, Russia, the government orders troops to open fire on demonstrators.
1917, April 6	The USA declares war against Germany.
1917, June 3	The first All-Russia Congress of Soviets of Workers and Soldiers opens.
1917, october	In Russia, the Bolsheviks overthrow the provisional government.
1917	Croatian, Montenegrin, Serbian, and Slovenian politicians sign the Corfu Declaration, providing for the establishment of a new nation, Yugoslavia, at the end of the war.
1918	Hostilities on the Eastern Front cease with the signing of the Treaty of Brest-Litovsk.
1918	Revolution breaks out in Austria and Hungary after Emperor proclaims reorganization of the monarchy. The Habsburg dynasty comes to an end.
1918, November 11	World War I comes to an end at 11:01 a.m. as Germany surrenders.
1918	Iceland proclaims independence from, but retains ties with, Denmark.
1918	After two centuries of stagnation, the Ottoman Empire ends with the Armistice of Mudros in which it lost its Middle East territories, large areas of Anatolia, and almost all of Thrace.
1919	Hitler is given the job of lecturing returning German prisoners of war on the dangers of Communism and pacifism. He joins the German Workers' Party.
1920	The Treaty of Trianon redefines Hungary's borders. The German, Austrian, Russian, and Turkish empires have all been radically redrawn since the end of the Great War.
1920	The British government partitions Ireland into two separate territories, following Bloody Sunday (November 21), when 26 people were killed.
1921	With the help of White Russian troops, Mongolia expels the Chinese after 200 years.
1921	Southern Ireland becomes a free state under the dominion of Britain. The eight counties forming Ulster in the North shall remain part of the United Kingdom.
1922	Britain is granted a mandate for Palestine by the League of Nations.
1923	After Hitler and his storm troopers attempted to kidnap the leaders of the Bavarian government at a beer hall, he is accused of treason and sentenced to five year's jail with parole in six months.
1924	The US stock market begins its spectacular rise while the rest of the economy languishes.
1924	Lenin dies and is succeeded by Joseph Stalin.
1925	After release from jail, Hitler again begins to threaten the government in his speeches and is banned from public speaking for two years.
1925	The Mediterranean island of Cyprus becomes a colony of the British Empire.
1925	The Hebrew University of Jerusalem is established on Mount Scopus.
1928	The average prices of US stocks rises 40 percent.
1928	Chiang Kai-shek defeats the northern warlords and takes Beijing.
1929	Richard E. Byrd and three others become the first to fly over the South Pole.

1929	More than half of all Americans are living below a minimum subsistence level. US Stock market crash begins on October 24 leading to "Black Tuesday" of October 29 when losses were the greatest. Losses for the month total US$16 billion, an astronomical sum in those days.
1930	US Federal Reserve cuts prime interest rate from 6 to 4 percent. The GNP of the United States falls 9.4 percent from the year before. The US unemployment rate climbs from 3.2 to 8.7 percent. British unemployment rate reaches 20 percent.
1932	Japan declares Manchuria to be an independent state.
1932	The military seizes power, making Siam a constitutional monarchy.
1932	King Ibn Saud unites the kingdoms of Hejaz and Nejd as the Kingdom of Saudi Arabia.
1932	Iraq gains independence from its British-imposed rule under a treaty granting the UK certain privileges.
1932	Adolf Hitler is granted German citizenship.
1933	Hitler becomes Dictator of Germany after the Reichstag grants him full powers, less than two months after being appointed Chancellor of Germany.
1932–1933	Worst years of the Great Depression. US unemployment rises to 23.6 percent. Industrial stocks have lost 80 percent of their value since 1930. Top tax rate is raised from 25 to 63 percent. Tariff of 10 percent introduced on all US imports except those from the British Empire.
1933	Paraguay declares war on Bolivia.
1934	The US economy turns around—GNP rises 7.7 percent, and unemployment falls to 21.7 percent. A long road to recovery begins. Sweden is the first nation to recover fully from the Great Depression. It has followed a policy of Keynesian deficit spending.
1934	Germany and Poland sign a 10-year non-aggression pact following a period of tension.
1934	Friendship treaties are signed between Saudi Arabia and Britain, and between Britain, India, and Yemen.
1934	Following the death of President Paul von Hindenburg, Adolf Hitler proclaims himself Führer of Germany, making him both Head of State and Chancellor. The armed forces are forced to swear an oath of allegiance.
1934	The communist Red Army, led by Mao Zedong, commences a 6,000-mile (9,654-kilometer) march, retreating from southeastern China after being encircled by General Chiang Kai-shek's nationalist forces and suffering heavy losses.
1935	Persia officially changes its name to Iran to gain favor with Germany; "Iran" means "Aryan."
1936	Abyssinia is taken by Italy, crumbling under the weight of the massive offensive as Italy seizes the capital, Addis Ababa.
1936	Prince Albert is proclaimed King George VI after his brother Edward VIII abdicates the British throne.
1937	The Chaco War between Bolivia and Paraguay ends.

1937	The new Irish Constitution comes into force and the Irish Free State officially becomes Eire.
1938	Oil is discovered in Saudi Arabia.
1938, SEPTEMBER 30	The Munich Agreement, made by Germany, Italy, Britain, and France, allows Hitler to take Sudetenland, and Hungary and Poland to take border districts from Czechoslovakia. Another resolution is signed to resolve future disputes between Britain and Germany peacefully.
1938, OCTOBER 5	Hitler's army marches into Czechoslovakia.
1938	The Japanese capture the southern city of Canton.
1939, MARCH 16	The German Army occupies Prague and Czechoslovakia becomes a Nazi protectorate.
1939, MAY 22	Mussolini signs a military pact with Hitler, obligating Italy to fight alongside Germany.
1939, AUGUST 23	Hitler and Stalin sign a Nazi–Soviet pact of non-aggression that divides Eastern Europe between Germany and USSR.
1939, SEPTEMBER 1	German forces invade Poland from Germany in the west, East Prussia in the north, and Czechoslovakia in the south.
1939, SEPTEMBER 3	Neville Chamberlain announces that Britain is at war with Germany. This is followed by a declaration from Australia, India, and New Zealand. South Africa declares war on Germany on September 6, joined by Canada on September 10.
1939, SEPTEMBER 17	USSR invades Poland from the east.
1939–1945	Holocaust in Europe with over 6 million Jews killed.
1940	Leon Trotsky is assassinated in Mexico City.
1940, FEBRUARY 20	Hitler orders his U-boat captains to attack all shipping, Allied vessels and neutral ships alike.
1940, MARCH 13	Russia defeats Finland following its 200,000-strong invasion on January 2; a peace treaty is signed in which Finland loses territory.
1940, MAY 10	After invading Norway and Denmark on April 9, Germany now invades Luxembourg, Belgium, Netherlands, and France—on the same day that Winston Churchill becomes British Prime Minister.
1940, MAY 10	Winston Churchill is called on to form a wartime coalition government in Britain.
1940, AUGUST 24	Germany bombs London. Churchill orders the bombing of Berlin in retaliation.
1941	Australia allows the United States to use its shores as the base for its supreme command in the Pacific theater of the war.
1941	By April 30, most of Greece is under German and Italian occupation; German forces took Athens on April 26.
1941, JUNE 22	Germany invades the USSR, breaking the Nazi–Soviet pact.
1941, JUNE 28	Albania declares war on USSR. Allied troops take Damascus.
1941, DECEMBER 7	Japanese planes make a surprise attack on the US fleet at Pearl Harbor.
1941, DECEMBER 8	The USA, Britain, Australia, and New Zealand declare war on Japan.

1942, FEBRUARY 15	Singapore falls to the Japanese.
1942, MAY 4	The Battle of the Coral Sea begins. It is the first battle where enemy ships never sight each other.
1943, AUGUST 17	Allies occupy Sicily. With North Africa, this gives them control of the Mediterranean Sea.
1943, SEPTEMBER 12	Italy surrenders unconditionally to the Allied forces.
1944, JANUARY 27	The Siege of Leningrad is fully lifted; over 640,000 people died during the 900 days of the siege.
1944, FEBRUARY 3	Berlin is heavily bombed by the Allies.
1944, JUNE 6	Allied forces storm Normandy on the French coast.
1945, APRIL 30	Hitler and newly-wed wife, Eva Braun, commit suicide.
1945, MAY 7	Germany signs its surrender after the foreign minister gives notice in a radio broadcast.
1945, AUGUST 6–9	The United States drops atomic bombs on Hiroshima and Nagasaki.
1945, SEPTEMBER 2	Japan signs the articles of surrender on board the USS *Missouri*.
1946	Hundreds of thousands of people cross from Eastern Europe to the United Kingdom, seeking escape from communism.
1946	Civil war between Chiang and Mao continues, with Chiang helped by the USA and Mao helped by the Soviet Union.
1946	The Philippines gain independence from the USA.
1947	A US Navy base is set up at Little America in Antarctica. Aerial photographs and extensive mapping are done.
1947	India gains independence.
1948	The *Displaced Persons Act* of 1948 permits approximately 200,000 displaced Europeans to immigrate to the United States.
1948	Gandhi is assassinated.
1948	Burma is granted independence by Britain on January 4. A month later, Ceylon (Sri Lanka) also gains independence.
1948	From Tel Aviv, Jews proclaim the Nation of Israel.
1949	The Indian Constitution is enacted.
1949	Mao Zedong proclaims the People's Republic of China. Zhou Enlai is appointed premier of Communist China, while Mao retains the chairmanship of the communist party.
1949	NATO is ratified.
1949	The Russian blockade of Berlin ends.
1949	France, Great Britain, and the Benelux countries make plans for a Council of Europe.
1949	Mao Zedong officially proclaims the establishment of the Communist People's Republic of China.
1950	India becomes a Republic.
1950	War breaks out after North Korean communists invade South Korea.

1950	The Viet Minh gets assistance from China while the US pledges military aid to France to help the fight in Vietnam.
1950	In December, the Dalai Lama flees Chinese-occupied Tibet following the invasion of his country on October 21.
1951	The USSR delegate to the UN proposes a truce. Months later, North Korea breaks off talks.
1951	The Treaty of Paris is signed by Belgium, France, Germany, Italy, Luxembourg, and the Netherlands.
1952	Dwight D. Eisenhower is elected 34th President of the United States as the Cold War begins influencing economic and political decisions.
1952	The first general elections in India are held.
1952	In the Korean conflict, the UN proposes an exchange of POWs. It is rejected by North Korea.
1953	Stalin dies and is succeeded by Nikita Khrushchev.
1953	Korean War—fighting becomes more intense, with heavy casualties on both sides. Sick and POWs are exchanged.
1953	Coronation of Queen Elizabeth II.
1953 JULY	Peace talks resume, and a ceasefire is signed. An armistice signed by the United Nations, Korea, and China on July 27, ends three years of war.
1954	The Council of Ministers of the Council of Europe adopt the blue flag and twelve-star emblem.
1955	The Warsaw Pact is formed.
1956	Pakistan is declared an Islamic Republic.
1956	Israeli forces invade Egypt. They enter via the Sinai Peninsula and head toward the Suez Canal.
1957	The Gold Coast and Togoland become Ghana, gaining independence from Britain; Tunisia abolishes its monarchy to become a republic.
1957	Treaty of Rome is signed by France, West Germany, Italy, Belgium, Netherlands, and Luxembourg to create the European Economic Community (EEC).
1958	The French-ruled African countries of Mali, Mauritania, Congo, Chad, and Gabon are made republics.
1959	The South African parliament passes new laws creating separate Bantustans (homelands) for major black groups.
1959	Fidel Castro assumes power after the Cuban Revolution.
1959	Alaska is admitted as the 49th state of the USA, with Juneau as its capital.
1959	Dr Mary Leakey discovers the oldest hominid skull. "Nutcracker Man" dates back at least 1.8 million years.
1960	The National Liberation Front—Viet Cong is established in South Vietnam.
1960	Congo gains independence after 75 years of Belgian rule. Mali, British Somaliland, and Madagascar all became self-governing this year.
1960	John F. Kennedy is elected president of the USA.

1961	Syria gains independence.
1961	Yuri Gagarin becomes the first cosmonaut.
1961	The Soviet Union builds a wall between East and West Berlin.
1961, June	Kennedy and Khrushchev hold summit talks in Vienna.
1961, October	Joint Chiefs of Staff advise Kennedy to make an air strike on Cuba. Kennedy receives letter from Khrushchev stating a serious threat to peace. Kennedy sends Khrushchev a letter stating that the US will not invade Cuba if Khrushchev removes his missiles. Khrushchev announces his agreement to withdraw all missiles from Cuba.
1962	Seven days of escalating tension bring the world to the brink of nuclear confrontation before the USA and USSR reach a compromise.
1963, November 22	President John F. Kennedy is assassinated.
1964	Nelson Mandela is sentenced to life imprisonment for treason.
1964	Kennedy's successor, Lyndon B. Johnson tackles poverty with the *Economic Opportunity Act*.
1964	Khrushchev is replaced by Leonid Brezhnev.
1964	The Palestine Liberation Organization (PLO) is founded.
1964	Kenya becomes a republic.
1965	Rhodesia (Zimbabwe) gains its independence with only whites represented.
1965	The first US troops arrive in Vietnam.
1967, June 10	The six-day war against Syria and Egypt comes to an end as Israel finally observes a UN ceasefire.
1968	Martin Luther King is assassinated in Memphis on April 4. Less than 2 months later, Presidential candidate Robert Kennedy is shot down by Palestinian militant Sirhan Sirhan.
1969	Nixon orders the first withdrawal of US troops.
1969	Neil Armstrong walks on the Moon, watched by millions of television viewers.
1969	Colonel Muammar Gaddafi becomes premier of Libya after a bloodless coup brings the 18-year rule of King Idris to an end.
1970	Nixon says US troops will attack in Cambodia, creating worldwide protests.
1970	Gambia and Rhodesia become republics.
1971	Qatar, United Arab Emirates, and Bahrain gain independence.
1971	India recognizes the Democratic Republic of Bangladesh, while Pakistan breaks off diplomatic relations.
1971	Following defeat in the Bangladesh War, Pakistan develops a nuclear weapons program.
1971	General Idi Amin seizes power in Uganda while President Obote is abroad.
1972	The North Vietnamese cross the 17th parallel to attack South Vietnam.
1972, March	First basic e-mail programs written by Ray Tomlinson. "@" sign chosen for its "at" meaning.
1973	The US and Vietnamese combatants in the Vietnam War sign a peace accord.
1974	South Africa is expelled from the United Nations.
1974	Pakistan officially recognizes Bangladesh.
1974	Westminster brings Northern Ireland under direct rule again.
1975	The Australian government of Gough Whitlam (Labor) is dismissed by the Governor General after its budget is continually blocked by the Opposition in the upper house of Parliament.
1975	South Vietnam surrenders to the Communists.
1975	Juan Carlos de Borbón becomes king of Spain following the death of General Franco, who had led the country since 1936.
1976	Apple Computer founded by Steve Jobs and Steve Wozniak.
1976	Seychelles gains independence from Britain after 162 years.
1976	In Tangshan, China, an estimated 242,000 people are killed in an earthquake registering 8.2 on the Richter scale.
1977	Djibouti gains independence from France.
1978	The European Council establishes the European Monetary System based on a central currency.
1978	The first non-Italian pontiff for over four centuries is elected. Karol Wojtyla, from Poland, will be known as John Paul II.
1979	A Peace Treaty between Egypt and Israel is finalized at Camp David.
1979	Revolution in Iran sees the Shah overthrown. Ayatollah Khomeini takes control and introduces strict Islamic practices.
1979	First World Climate Conference.
1979	Margaret Thatcher becomes Europe's first female prime minister.
1979	In Afghanistan, the build-up of Soviet troops has become an invasion, culminating in the fall of the government in Kabul.
1980	General Ziaur Rahman of Bangladesh is assassinated by army officers.
1980	Simmering hostilities between Iraq and Iran explode into a full-scale war.
1980	Tim Berners-Lee writes program called "Enquire Within" predecessor to the World Wide Web.
1981	IBM announces its first personal computer. Microsoft creates DOS.
1981	Egyptian leader, Anwar Sadat, is assassinated.
1982, April–June	Falklands War between UK and Argentina.
1982	Hussein Mohammed Ershad seizes power in Bangladesh, in a bloodless coup.

1983	Domain Name System (DNS) designed by Jon Postel, Paul Mockapetris, and Craig Partridge. .edu, .gov, .com, .mil, .org, .net, and .int created.
1983	US troops invade Grenada in an effort to restore democracy.
1983	A draft treaty is presented to the European Parliament establishing the European Union.
1984	Brunei achieves independence after 95 years of British rule.
1984	Various Western countries boycott the 1984 Moscow Olympics.
1984	William Gibson writes "Neuromancer." Coins the term "cyberspace." Apple Computer introduces the Macintosh on January 24.
1984	Indira Gandhi is assassinated by her Sikh bodyguards.
1985	Mikhail Gorbachev is elected leader of the Soviet Union.
1985, MARCH 15	Symbolic.com becomes the first registered domain.
1986	The *Australia Act* comes into force, making Australian laws totally independent of Britain and disallowing any appeals to the Privy Council in London.
1986	The Chernobyl nuclear reactor melts down, releasing massive amounts of deadly radiation.
1987	On a visit to Berlin, President Reagan challenges: "Mr. Gorbachev, tear down this wall!"
1987	The Intermediate-Range Nuclear Forces Treaty is signed in Washington DC.
1988	After 8 years of fighting, Soviet troops begin to withdraw from Afghanistan.
1988	The Iran–Iraq war comes to an end.
1989	The Berlin Wall opens after 28 years.
1989	The Communist governments of Bulgaria, Czechoslovakia, and Romania fall.
1989	Osama bin Laden founds the al-Qa'eda network.
1990	East and West Germany are reunited.
1990	De Klerk lifts the ban on the African National Congress (ANC).
1990	Nelson Mandela is released from jail after serving 27 years.
1990	Boris Yeltsin is elected president of the new Russian Federation.
1990	Tim Berners-Lee, creates the World Wide Web.
1990	Lithuania declares its independence.
1991	The Warsaw Pact comes to an end.
1991	A multi-national force launches an air attack on Iraq following its invasion of Kuwait.
1991	Mandela becomes President of the African National Congress.
1991, FEBRUARY 13	Bombing raid by US forces kills 400 Iraqi civilians in an air raid shelter.
1991, FEBRUARY 24	Allied forces invade Iraq and Kuwait. The US Army is first to enter Iraqi territory.
1991, FEBRUARY 28	US President Bush announces the end of the war to liberate Kuwait.
1991, APRIL	A cyclone in Bangladesh kills approximately 131,000 people. Thousands of survivors die from hunger and water-borne disease, while about nine million are left homeless.
1991	Georgia declares independence after 70 years of Soviet rule.
1991	The Madrid protocol governing Antarctica comes into effect, designating the continent as a natural reserve, devoted to peace and science.
1992	The European Commission recognize Croatia and Slovenia as independent states.
1993	The Single European Market comes into force.
1993	Czechoslovakia splits into two separate entities—Czech Republic and Slovakia.
1993	Benazir Bhutto is reinstalled as Prime Minister of Pakistan—three years after being ousted.
1994	In South Africa, Nelson Mandela is made Head of State.
1994	The Taliban movement begins in Afghanistan.
1995	Croatian, Bosnian, and Serbian leaders sign a peace accord ending three years of bloody conflict.
1996	Civil war breaks out in Afghanistan. The Taliban force the government out of Kabul.
1997	The British hand back Hong Kong to China.
1997	Treaty parties approve Kyoto Protocol mandating emission cuts by industrial nations, an approach rejected in advance by US Senate.
1998	Taliban take control of Mazar-e Sharif.
1998	Although a relatively small quake, the tsunami resulting from the earthquake in New Guinea caused 40 ft (12 m) waves to wash across the coast, killing around 2,200 people.
1999	Yeltsin resigns and appoints Vladimir Putin as his successor.
1999	In Canada, the new territory of Nunavut is established, with its capital located at Iqaluit.
1999	UN peacekeepers enter East Timor to control violence by pro-Indonesian militia since elections in early September.
2000	Prime Minister of Israel, Ariel Sharon, visits the al-Aqsa Mosque accompanied by armed police and riot forces, beginning the second Arab intifada.
2000	China launches Chinasal-22 (Zhongxing-22) communication satellite.
2000	Chinese government starts long-distance resettlement schemes to move more approximately 1.5 million people from the Three Gorges Dam project area.
2000	Australia hosts the Games of the XXVIII Olympiad in Sydney—the most popular games ever.

2000	Vast numbers in Australia take part in the People's Walk for Reconciliation over the Howard government's failure to say sorry to the "Stolen Generation" of Aboriginal children who were taken from their parents.
2001	Commonwealth of Australia celebrates 100 years since Federation.
2001	In Nepal, Crown Prince Dipendra shoots dead nine members of the royal family, before shooting himself.
2001, SEPTEMBER 11	The World Trade Center is destroyed when two hijacked aircraft smash into the twin towers. A third plane hits the Pentagon; the death toll is estimated to be approximately 3,000.
2001	Osama bin Laden and the al-Qa'eda organization claim responsibility for the attacks on the US on September 11.
2001, OCTOBER 7	The United States begins aerial bombing on Taliban strongholds in Afghanistan.
2001	After much negotiation, China becomes a member of the World Trade Organization.
2002	Euro coins and notes enter circulation.
2003	The first fiber optic network connection across the Russian-Chinese border is established.
2003	Australia is included in the United States' "coalition of the willing" that sends troops to Iraq to overthrow the dictatorship of Saddam Hussein.
2003, DECEMBER 14	Saddam Hussein is captured in Tikrit.
2004	Cyprus, Czech Republic, Estonia, Hungary, Latvia, Lithuania, Malta, Poland, Slovakia, and Slovenia join the European Union.
2004	CO_2 levels reach a record 379 parts per million. Russia gives crucial ratification to Kyoto Protocol.
2004, JUNE	After an interim government is formed in Iraq, Saddam Hussein is handed over to Iraqi custody.
2004	Striking on Boxing Day, a tsunami leaves coastal communities from Sri Lanka to Indonesia devastated; more than 200,000 people perish.
2005	Bush ratifies the Dominican Republic-Central America Free Trade Agreement.
2005	Kyoto Protocol takes effect on February 16.
2005, AUGUST	In Iraq, a draft constitution is approved by Shia and Kurdish representatives but the Sunni reject it.
2005	German cardinal Joseph Ratzinger becomes the new pontiff, Benedict XVI.
2005	In Dublin, Ireland, the IRA announces an end to its 30-year armed campaign and that it will pursue its objectives by political means.
2006	CNOOC, one of China's largest oil and gas producers, buys a stake in a Nigerian offshore oil and gas field.
2006, NOVEMBER	Saddam Hussein is found guilty of crimes against humanity and sentenced to death. He is hanged in December.

2007	World population is 6,602,224,175. World population average age is 28 years. World birth rate is 20.09 births per 1,000 population. Death rate is 8.37 deaths per 1,000 population. World average life expectancy is 65.82 years. World literacy rate is 82 percent—two-thirds of the 785 million illiterate people in the world are women.
2007	Kevin Rudd is elected Prime Minister of Australia— the first change of government in more than a decade.
2007	UN Climate Change Summit takes place in Bali bringing together representatives of over 180 countries agreeing to adoption of the Bali roadmap and the launch of the Adaptation Fund as well as decisions on technology transfer and on reducing emissions from deforestation.
2007, FEBRUARY	Apple surpasses one billion iTunes downloads.
2007, APRIL	Search engine giant Google surpasses Microsoft as "the most valuable global brand", and also is the most visited Web site.
2007, MAY	The leader of al-Qa'eda in Iraq, Abu Ayyub al-Masri, is killed.
2007	Benazir Bhutto—who had served as Prime Minister of Pakistan on two occasions—is assassinated.
2008	Australian Prime Minister Kevin Rudd delivers the land-mark "Sorry" speech, apologizing to Australia's "Stolen Generation" for their treatment.
2008, FEBRUARY	Iraqi parliament passes legislation that allows former officials of the Baath party to hold public office.
2008	A massive earthquake hits China, claiming 70,000 lives; Myanmar (Burma) is hit by a cyclone, which claims an estimated 80,000 lives.
2008	Kosovo declares its independence.
2008	The monarchy is ousted and Nepal becomes a republic.
2008	Beijing hosts the Games of the XXIX Olympiad.

aliuaroi · Pro.serica nel cha Ausari
taio Fiume ga mons

queciã
fu
piada
queciafu

fiume
qutan.

Iarizu

Lago

Gatanfu

Soto el regno de nã
gin son 12
citade, lezu

nangin.

Prouicia de nãgin
oue. regno

El ca
moia

fuzzuzach

In questa citade
se fa gra quatita
de pani doro e de seda

Quanzu

IMPERIO e tri
umpho no
bilissimo
del chataio

Questo excellentissin
potentissimo iperador e
ha.lx.re de corona sot
dominio quado el ua
el senta i un caro dora
lio ornado de cole el pr
le qual e iextimabile. e
caro ine menado dauno
te biãcho. e ha.iiij.re di pu
del suo regno uno per cãto
che regeno questo caro. e.lx
tri li uano auanti. con assai
numero de homeni darme dã
nanti e dadrieto e qui sono
tuti piaceri çentileçe e costu
mi del mõdo.

INDEX TO PEOPLE AND PLACES

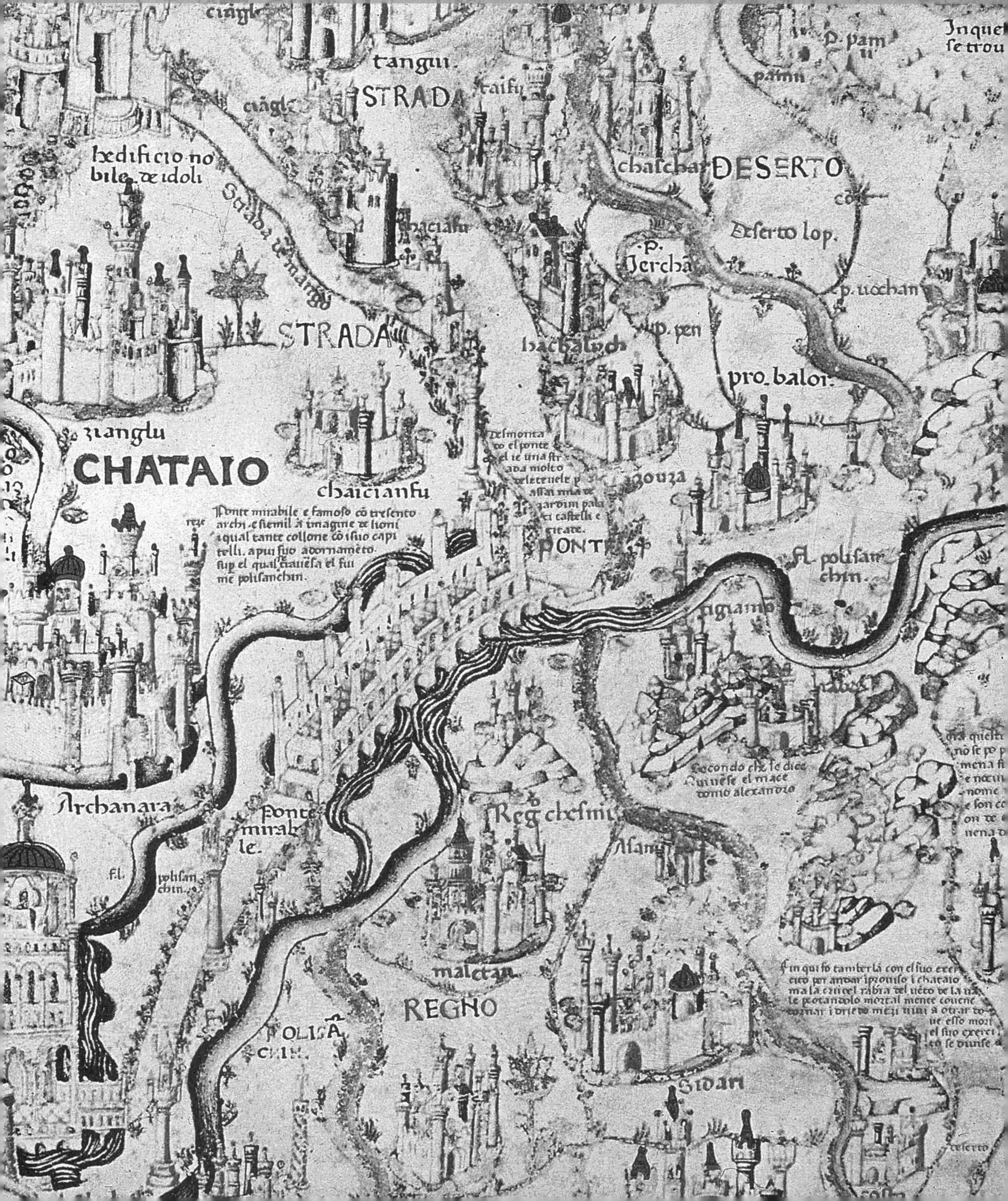

Index to People and Places

Page numbers in *italics* refer to photographs and illustrations

Index to Maps

Contributors

CHIEF CONSULTANT

Dr Geoffrey Wawro

Dr Geoffrey Wawro is General Olinto Barsanti Professor of Military History and the Director of the Military History Center at the University of North Texas. He is co-editor of the Cambridge Military Histories, and is the author of *The Austro-Prussian War: Austria's War with Prussia and Italy in 1866*, *Warfare and Society in Europe, 1792–1914*, and *The Franco-Prussian War: The German Conquest of France in 1870–71*. Dr Wawro is a host and consulting historian with the History Channel and a member of the History Book Club Review Board.

CONSULTANTS

Zoë Anderson

Zoë Anderson is a doctoral candidate in the Discipline of History at the University of Western Australia. Her thesis re-examines issues of immigration in Australia in the 1970s and 1980s, with emphasis on cultural citizenship. Her research interests are nationalism and cultural belonging, theories of sexuality, ethnicity and bodies, and the politics of biomedicine. She has taught history units at all levels at UWA, and was awarded a UWA Teaching Internship in 2006. Publications include *Reconstruction: Studies in Contemporary Culture*. She was previously a member of the editorial board on *Limina: Journal of Historical and Cultural Studies* and in April 2007 presented a paper at the American and Popular Culture Association Conference, Boston, Massachusetts.

Carolina Armenteros

Carolina Armenteros is a Postdoctoral Research Fellow at the University of Cambridge. She is specialized in European political, social, and religious thought c. 1748–1914, with a special emphasis on France. She earned her Bachelor's and Master's degrees in History from Stanford University and wrote her doctoral dissertation at Cambridge on the contribution that the counterrevolutionary thinker Joseph de Maistre made to the rise of historicism in the early nineteenth century. Her major current project investigates the intersection between educational and republican thought in France during the Enlightenment and Revolution, focusing especially on Rousseau's philosophy and its eighteenth-century interpretations.

Serwan M. J. Baban

Serwan Baban is Professor of Environmental Geoinformatics at Southern Cross University. He obtained his PhD in Environmental Remote Sensing from the prestigious School of Environmental Sciences at the University of East Anglia, UK, in 1991. His research interests are in Geosciences, Environmental Science, and in Geoinformatics (Environmental Remote Sensing and GIS). He has published over 80 papers in international and national journals, international conference proceedings, and in books, as well as consultancy reports. Serwan is an academic referee for scientific papers for a wide range of national and international journals. He is Director and founder, The Centre for Geoinformatics Research and Environmental Assessment Technology (GREAT), and a Fellow of the Royal Geographical Society, Geological Society, and the Remote Sensing and Photogrammetry Society.

Anthony J. Barker

Tony Barker is a Senior Honorary Research Fellow in the School of Humanities at the University of Western Australia, where he taught global and British imperial history from 1973 until 1983 and then mainly American history until his retirement as an Associate Professor in 2004. A graduate of Sheffield University, he has an MA in colonial American history from Sydney University (1969) and a PhD in the history of British racial attitudes from the University of London (1972). He is the author of seven published books, including *Slavery and Antislavery in Mauritius 1810-33: The Conflict Between Economic Expansion and Humanitarian Reform Under British Rule* (London: Macmillan, 1996).

Ivan T. Berend

Ivan Berend is a Distinguished Professor, Department of History, UCLA. Previously he was professor of economic history at the Budapest University of Economics. He was also President of the Hungarian Academy of Sciences (1985–90) and the International Committee of Historical Sciences (1995–2000). He is a member of the British Academy and five other European academies of sciences. During his career he has published 26 books and 175 studies. Among them is a trilogy on nineteenth- and twentieth-century Central and Eastern Europe, *The European Periphery and Industrialization, 1780-1914*, 1984; *An Economic History of 20ᵗʰ Century Europe*, 2006.

David Cahill

David Cahill is a Professor of Modern History at the University of New South Wales, Sydney. He has taught at the University of Liverpool, the University of Bielefeld, Macquarie University, and in 2007 was visiting professor at the École des Hautes Études en Sciences Sociales, Paris. In 2003 he was awarded the Conference on Latin American History Prize. He is cur-

rently finalizing a biography of José Gabriel Túpac Amaru, and researching new projects on the Church in the Independence era, and the ethnohistory of Southern Peru and Bolivia. Among his many publications are *From Rebellion to Emancipation in the Andes: Soundings from Southern Peru, 1750-1830* (2002). His "Genocide from Below: The Great Rebellion of 1780–82 in the Southern Andes", in Dirk Moses (ed), *Empire, Colony, Genocide: Conquest and Subaltern Resistance in World History* (Berghahn Books, New York), was published in 2008.

Malcolm Campbell

Malcolm Campbell is Associate Professor of History at the University of Auckland, New Zealand, where he teaches Irish and Australian history. A graduate of the University of New South Wales, he has published widely on the history of Ireland, Irish emigration, and the Irish Diaspora. His most recent book, *Ireland's New Worlds: Immigrants, politics and society in the United States and Australia, 1815–1922* is published by the University of Wisconsin Press. He is currently writing a book on the Irish in the Pacific World between 1760 and 1945.

Emma Cavell

Originally from Australia, Emma Cavell completed her DPhil in Medieval History at Balliol College, Oxford, before being elected to a research fellowship at the University of Cambridge in October 2006. Her research includes medieval British frontiers, women's burial in England, and women's rights under the common law of England. She is currently writing a monograph exploring the interaction of gender, status, and locality in shaping the lives of the aristocratic women of the medieval March of Wales. Dr Cavell has also worked on the early Tudor period, specializing in the activities and writings of late fifteenth-century English heralds.

Dr Robert Coenraads

Dr Bob Coenraads is a consultant geoscientist, and the author of four books and over 30 scientific publications. He has led archeology, natural history, and geology field trips to various corners of the globe, including the magnificent Olmec, Maya, and Aztec sites of Mexico, active volcanoes of the Pacific region, and a number of fabulous gem mines. During his 30-year exploration career, travel to some of the world's poorest regions has sparked a strong humanitarian interest. Dr Coenraads is currently the President of FreeSchools World Literacy—Australia, and has established a support network to provide free education for underprivileged children in Bihar State, India. It is his firm belief that a solid education for all, not just a privileged few, is the key to solving the world's major problems including overpopulation, hunger, and poverty.

Sally Cove

Sally Cove has a PhD in History and European Studies from the University of New South Wales where she has been a lecturer in Modern European History for the past three years, teaching courses on World War I, World War II, the Cold War, Balkan History, and the history of modern European culture. She has published work on the historiographical treatment of the interwar Polish-Jewish Left and the autobiographical writing of young Polish-Jews of the interwar period. Sally's current research is preoccupied primarily by the history of young people's writing during times of conflict.

Michael Creswell

Before joining the faculty at Florida State University, Professor Michael Creswell was the Annenberg Visiting Assistant Professor of History at the University of Pennsylvania. He has also served as an adjunct professor of strategy for the US Naval War College. A graduate of Indiana University and the University of Chicago, where he received his PhD, Michael has also studied at the École Nationale d'Administration, the Institute International D'Administration Publique, and the Université de Dijon. A specialist on international politics, the Cold War, and military affairs, he is the author of *A Question of Balance: How France and the United States Created Cold War* Europe (Harvard, 2006). His next book will examine how France rebuilt its army after World War II.

Michael Crouch

Michael Crouch was born and brought up in North Africa and Kenya. After army service in Southern Rhodesia (Zimbabwe) he completed four years at Cambridge and Oxford Universities and participated in two archeological expeditions to Libya during vacations. He then worked as a political officer with the British Overseas Service in Aden and the Protectorates for nearly 10 years. A fluent Arabic speaker, he has lived in Western Australia since 1967 and worked in the areas of commerce, heavy industry, education, and management consulting. He has written numerous articles and four books. In his spare time he records books for the visually impaired. Michael is currently working on a PhD at the University of Western Australia, on English female tertiary education in the 1890s.

Chris Dixon

Dr Chris Dixon is an Associate Professor of History at the University of Queensland, where he teaches courses on American History. He holds BA (Hons) and MA degrees from the University of Western Australia, and a PhD from the University of New South Wales. He has previously taught at the University of NSW, Sydney University, Massey University, and the University of Newcastle. His current research interests include the cultural and social history of the Pacific War, and the role of African Americans in the Vietnam War. Chris has many major publications including *Perfecting the Family: Antislavery Marriages in Nineteenth-Century America* (1997), *Black America and Haiti: Race, Nationality and Emigration in the Nineteenth Century* (2000), *Conflict in the Pacific 1937–1951* (2005)—co-authored with Roger Bell and Sean Brawley; and *Conflict in Indochina, 1954–1979* (2005), which he co-authored with Sean Brawley and Jeffrey Green.

Peter Edwell

Peter Edwell lectures on Roman, Hellenistic and Near Eastern History in the Department of Ancient History at Macquarie University, Sydney, Australia. He completed a PhD in Ancient History in 2005 and recently published a book on the Middle Euphrates in the Roman period. Dr Edwell has traveled and researched extensively in the Middle East and Europe and is presently researching and writing a book on the wars between Rome and Sasanian Persia.

Norman Etherington

Norman Etherington completed his BA, MA and PhD at Yale University. After 20 years in the History Department at the University of Adelaide, he was invited to take up a Chair in History at the University of Western Australia. As a teacher, he pioneered instruction in Global and African History. As a researcher in the fields of British Empire and African History, he has published eight books as well as 80 journal articles and book chapters. His most recent books include *The Great Treks: the Transformation of Southern African History* (2001), *Missions and Empire* (2005), and *Mapping Colonial Conquest: Australia and Southern Africa* (2007).

William R. Fowler

William Fowler is an anthropologist and historian who is interested in the pre-Columbian and Colonial-period cultures of Mexico and Central America. William has conducted archeological and archival research in Mexico, Guatemala, El Salvador, and Spain. His main area of research interest lies in the initial encounters between European and Native American populations at the time of the Conquest for the first few generations of the Early Colonial period. He is currently working on a book about his research at the first *villa* of San Salvador, El Salvador, a conquest town dating from 1528 to 1545.

Thomas Glick

Thomas Glick is Professor of History and Geography at Boston University, Massachusetts, USA, where he teaches the history of science and technology. He is the author of *Irrigation and Society in Medieval Spain* (1970; 2nd Spanish edition, 2003), *Islamic And Chris-tian Spain in the Early Middle Ages* (2nd ed., 2005), and *From Muslim Fortress to Christian Castle: Social and Cultural Change in Medieval Spain* (1995; rev. Spanish ed., 2006).

Jonathan A. Grant

Jonathan Grant is Associate Professor of Russia History at Florida State University in Tallahassee, Florida, USA. He earned his PhD from the University of Wisconsin in 1995. He is the author of two monographs: *Big Business in Russia* (University of Pittsburgh Press, 1999) and *Rulers, Guns, and Money, The Global Arms Trade in the Age of Imperialism* (Harvard University Press, 2007). Jonathan teaches a variety of courses on Eurasian history including tsarist Russia, the Soviet Union, the Ottoman Empire, Central Asia, and the Balkans.

Matthew Gray

Matthew Gray joined the Centre for Arab & Islamic Studies (Middle East & Central Asia) (CAIS) at the Australian National University as Sheikh Hamdan bin Rashid al-Maktoum Senior Lecturer and Graduate Academic Adviser in January 2005, where he teaches courses on Middle Eastern politics, the Arab-Israeli conflict, Gulf security, and Middle Eastern economic development and political economy. He has held various positions with the Australian Government, most recently as Director Middle East & Africa at the Department of Immigration and Multicultural and Indigenous Affairs. His most recent publications include contributions to "Islam in the Iraqi and Afghan Constitutions: A Comparative Perspective", *Global Change, Peace & Security*, Volume 19, Number 1 (February 2007); and "Development Strategies and the Political Economy of Tourism in Contemporary Jordan", in George Joffé (ed), *Jordan in Transition, 1990-2000* (London: Hurst & Company, 2002).

Hart, Sue

Sue Hart has had a long and varied career as a teacher, freelance writer, and recruitment consultant. As a full-time mature-age student she is currently completing her PhD in Australian history. Her thesis topic is *Widowhood and Remarriage in Colonial Australia*. Under the name Sue Hart-Byers she has had three non-fiction books published: *Jane Austen's Universal Truths*, *Secrets of Successful Step-families*, and *Snobs, Nobs and Yobs: A Classy Guide to Australia*. She has also had numerous travel and lifestyle articles published in Australian newspapers. Sue's writing and research interests are primarily centered on the nineteenth century, especially colonial Australia. Another area of expertise and interest is the lives of the nineteenth-century writers of fiction for girls. Sue has written a treatment for a documentary based on the diaries of three nineteenth-century women writers.

Kerry Hickson

Kerry Hickson is a British Academy postdoctoral fellow based in the Cambridge Group for the History of Population and Social Structure at the University of Cambridge. Her research focuses on historical demography, public health, and economic history. Her work includes *The Contribution of Improved Health to Economic Development in Twentieth Century England and Wales* and *The Standard of Living Gains Generated by the Elimination and Amelioration of Tuberculosis in Twentieth Century England and Wales*. Much of her recent work explores the value of health gains in the USA and the contribution of healthcare systems and therapy to twentieth-century gains in health.

B. Dexter Hoyos

Dexter Hoyos has lectured on Roman history and Latin studies at Sydney University since 1972. His scholarly interests include Roman and Carthaginian history, and the teaching of fluent Latin reading skills. His most recent book is *Truceless War: Carthage's Fight for Survival, 241–237 BC* (Leiden, 2007).

Hans Hummer

Hans Hummer received his PhD in medieval history from the University of California at Los Angeles in 1997 and currently is an Associate Professor of History at Wayne State University in Detroit, Michigan. He specializes in the social and political history of the Frankish realms in early medieval Europe. His book, *Politics and Power in Early Medieval Europe: Alsace and the Frankish Realm, 600–1000* (Cambridge: Cambridge University Press, 2005) was awarded the David Pinkney prize by the Society for French Historical Studies for the best book in French history by a North American scholar in 2006.

Cynthia Lane

Cynthia Lane is a postgraduate student of History at the University of Western Australia working on her doctoral thesis entitled: *Travellers' Imaginings of Southern Western Australia 1850 to 1914*, which will be a contribution to the cultural history of Australia. She completed her Bachelor of Arts Degree with First Class Honors, writing a thesis in British history on *Cornwall and the Industrial Revolution 1690 to 1865* at Edith Cowan University, publishing an article from her research in the journal *Cornish Studies Thirteen*. During 2007 she has also completed a Postgraduate Teaching Internship Scheme, submitting a research paper, comparing Teaching and Learning at Universities and Vocational Colleges, to the Teaching and Learning Forum Conference 2008.

Jessica Lenney

Jessica completed her degree in History, Anthropology, and Archeology at The University of Western Australia. She achieved an Honors degree in medieval history in 2006.

Cecilia Leong-Salobir

Cecilia Leong-Salobir is a doctoral candidate in history with a thesis titled *A taste of Empire—Food, the Colonial Kitchen and the Role of Servants in India, Malaysia and Singapore c. 1858–1963*. Cecilia graduated with a Bachelor of Arts with Honors (History) and Graduate Diploma in Education from the University of Western Australia, Perth, Western Australia. Her research interests are in food history, global history, Asian and imperial history and the history of race and racism. Her publications include *Sabah—The First 100 Years; Labuan—Past and Present*; and *Children of Sabah*. She has worked as a journalist, civil servant. and schoolteacher and has lived in Malaysia, Brunei, New Zealand, Tanzania, the Sudan, Germany, England, and Indonesia and is now resident in Australia.

Sophie Loy-Wilson

Sophie Loy-Wilson (BA Hons, Class I) is a PhD Candidate at the University of Sydney where she is completing a thesis on Australia–China relations 1914–1939, with a particular focus on cosmopolitanism in Sydney and Shanghai. Sophie speaks Mandarin Chinese and in 2006 submitted an honors thesis on Chinese Australian resistance to the White Australia Policy in 1930s Sydney. This work received the Pioneers Prize for History in 2007, and an article based on the thesis will be published in History Australia in 2009.

Janette McWilliam

Janette McWilliam is a Roman Historian of the Late Republic and Early Empire. Her particular research interests lie in Roman legal and social history, Roman epigraphy, and Roman art. She is currently completing a research project on representations of children in Roman art. Janette is also developing a blended learning course for the teaching of introductory Latin to adult beginners for University of Queensland.

Ryota Nishino

Ryota Nishino was born and raised in Yokohama, Japan. Attracted to the dramatic end to apartheid in South Africa, he left Japan and studied for his first degree in history at Rhodes University, Grahamstown, South Africa. He then taught Social Studies, History, and Japanese at a rural high school in New Zealand for a few years. He went on to study for his doctorate in History at the University of Western Australia, Perth, Australia. The subject matter of his research was a comparative history of history textbooks and policy changes in history education in Japan and South Africa from 1945 to 1995. He currently lives and works in New Zealand.

Prashant Prasad

Prashant Prasad was educated at Normanhurst Boys High School in New South Wales, Australia, where he was one of the top ancient history students. After high school, he began a conjoint degree of Arts and Law majoring in Ancient History at the University of Auckland. His studies include the Egyptian, Greek, and Roman periods of history.

Sonia Puttock

Sonia Pottock is a lecturer in Classics and Ancient History at the University of Queensland, Australia. She is also Director of the RD Milns Antiquities Museum, also at the university. Her main areas of interest are the art, archeology, and religion of Greece, Rome, and Roman Britain.

Damodar SarDesai

Damodar SarDesai is former Chairperson of South and Southeast Asian Studies, Vice-Chair and Chair of the Department of History, and the first holder of the Doshi Chair in Indian History at the University of California Los Angeles (UCLA). He is currently Emeritus Professor of History at UCLA. He was also the Director, University of California's Education Abroad Program in New Delhi. Professor SarDesai was the President of the Asiatic Society of Bombay from 1989–99. He is the recipient of numerous honors and awards including the Lifetime Achievement Award from the California State University, Long Beach in 2005 and the Global Goan Award from the Government of Goa, India, in 2007. Among the 15 books he has written or edited are *India, The Definitive History*, Boulder, Colorado, Westview Press, 2007 and *Vietnam, Past and Present*, Boulder, Colorado, Westview Press, 2005, fourth edition.

Jamie Smith

Jamie Smith is Assistant Professor of History at Alma College and Co-Director of Women's Studies. She earned her PhD from the University of Toronto in 2007 after defending her dissertation, "Navigating Absence: Law and the Family in Genoa, 1380-1402." Research interests include gender and family in premodern Europe, premodern legal history, exile in the Italian context, and Genoese colonial expansion in the Mediterranean.

Alice Stevenson

Alice Stevenson is an archeologist specializing in the prehistory (Predynastic) of Egypt (4000–3100 BCE). She earned her MPhil and PhD at the University of Cambridge and currently works for the Egypt Exploration Society in London, as well as the University of Cambridge, Institute of Continuing Education, where she teaches courses on the archeology of ancient Egypt. She has published widely on the ancient burial practices and grave goods of early Egypt, together with archeological theory and practice. Alice also holds a Masters in Museum Studies and has worked extensively with Egyptology collections in UK museums.

Tom Stevenson

Tom Stevenson was born and raised in Sydney, Australia. He was educated at the Universities of Sydney and Oxford, PhD (Sydney) 1990 in Roman History. Currently he is a lecturer in Classics and Ancient History at the University of Queensland after previously holding appointments at Sydney (1990) and Auckland (1991–2003) Universities. He is a specialist in Roman history of the Middle and Late Republican periods, especially the public careers of Cicero and Julius Caesar. His ancillary interest is in ancient art, athletics, and the Seven Wonders of the Ancient World. He has published on a wide variety of topics, notably on Roman politics and religion, the Parthenon Frieze, and the Statue of Zeus of Olympia. Tom teaches Greek language, Latin language, and both Greek and Roman history at the University of Queensland.

Denis Stonham

Denis Stonham is a freelance writer, editor, and consultant specializing in maritime historical topics. In 1969, he joined the staff of the National Maritime Museum, Greenwich, where he was a curator for 22 years. During his time there he was co-author, with Basil Greenhill, the museum's director, of the book *Seafaring Under Sail*, a history of the merchant seaman. Since leaving the National Maritime Museum, Denis has been involved in a number of projects and was editor of the magazine *Maritime Heritage*. Other work has included research and preparation of texts for the new Museum in Docklands, which describes the history of London as a port, and research and consultancy on behalf of a riverside London borough. His articles have appeared in the magazines *Windjammer* (of which he is editor) and *Archive*, and in the programs for successive International Festivals of the Sea, in Britain.

G. Bruce Strang

Bruce Strang lives in Thunder Bay, Ontario, Canada, with his wife Nancy Hennen and their two sons, Sean (almost 3) and Marc (almost 1), and their black cat Felix. Bruce is an Associate Professor in the Department of History at Lakehead University, where he teaches modern European history. He is the author of *On the Fiery March: Mussolini Prepares for War*, and he is currently working on a manuscript on Italian economic and political reconstruction after World War II. He also writes on Italian and British foreign policy and the origins of World War II.

Mike Thompson

Currently completing a PhD in American History at the University of Sydney, Australia, Mike Thompson has taught, written, and researched in the fields of US politics, religion, and history. Mike holds a First Class Honors degree in History from the University of Sydney and he is currently an academic tutor for the Department of History. His research, which focuses on thinkers and their responses to war, peace, and world crisis during the twentieth century, has been published in the *American Quarterly*.

Blanca Tovías

Blanca Tovías is a Research Associate in the School of History and Philosophy, University of New South Wales, Australia. Her research focuses on both North American and Latin American History and Literature, with particular emphasis on the history of native peoples of the Americas under colonial rule. Blanca has conducted research in historical archives in Canada, the United States, and Mexico. She was awarded her PhD in 2007 for a dissertation on Resistance and Culural Revitalization among the tribes of the Blackfoot Confederacy of Canada and the USA, 1870–1920. Among her publications are *New World, First Nations: Native Peoples of Mesoamerica and the Andes under Colonial Rule* (2006) and *Élites Indígenas en los Andes: Nobles, Caciques y Cabildantes bajo el Yugo Colonial* (2003), both of which were co-edited with David Cahill, and "Fur and Skin Trades in the Americas", in Thomas Benjamin (ed.), *Encyclopedia of Western Colonialism since 1450* (2006).

Chad Van Dixhoorn

Chad Van Dixhoorn is a Research Fellow of Wolfson College, Cambridge, and a postdoctoral fellow of the British Academy. He is a member of the Faculty of History of the University of Cambridge where he teaches and researches in the Reformation and post-Reformation periods. His special interest is in the theology and history of creeds and councils. He is currently serving as general editor of *The Minutes and Papers of the Westminster Assembly, 1643–1652*, a signally important early modern text, unique in the history of Christianity. An 880,000 word critical edition of the manuscript is due to be published by Oxford University Press in the near future.

Elisabeth van Houts

Elisabeth van Houts is a specialist in the history of the Central Middle Ages with a special interest in the Anglo-Norman period, Latin historiography, and the history of women and gender. Among Elisabeth's most recent books are *The Gesta Normannorum Ducum of William of Jumieges, Orderic Vitalis and Robert of Torigni*, (two volumes) Oxford Medieval Texts, (Oxford 1992, 1996); *Memory and Gender in Medieval Europe, 900–1200* (Basingstoke, 1999); *History and Family Traditions in England and the Continent, 1000–1200* (Aldershot, 1999); *The Normans in Europe* (Manchester, 2000); and *Medieval Memories. Men, Women and the Past, 700–1300* (Harlow, 2001).

Jelle van Lottum

Jelle van Lottum is ESRC Postdoctoral Fellow at the Cambridge Group for the History of Population and Social Structure at the University of Cambridge. He is the author of *Across the North Sea—The Impact of the Dutch Republic on International Labour Migration, c. 1550–1850* (Amsterdam, 2007), and wrote several articles on migration and labor markets in the early modern period and the nineteenth century.

Richard von Glahn

Richard von Glahn is Professor of History at the University of California, Los Angeles, USA. Trained in middle imperial (Tang-Song) Chinese economic history at UC Berkeley and Yale, he has taught Chinese history and world history at UCLA since 1987. He is the author of *The Country of Streams and Grottoes: Expansion, Settlement, and the Civilizing of the Sichuan Frontier in Song Times* (Harvard, 1987); *Fountain of Fortune: Money and Monetary Policy in China, 1000–1700* (California, 1996); and *The Sinister Way: The Divine and the Demonic in Chinese Religious Culture* (California, 2004); and is co-editor of *The Song-Yuan-Ming Transition in Chinese History* (Harvard, 2003) and *Monetary History in Global Perspective, 1470–1800* (Ashgate, 2003).

Steven A. Wernke

Steven Wernke is an archeologist and historical anthropologist with interests in community, landscape, imperialism, and culture change during prehispanic and colonial times in the Andean region of South America. His research combines archeological field research from the Andean highlands and documentary research from Spanish colonial archives to provide an integrated view of cultural continuity and transformation in the years leading up to and following the Spanish invasion of the Americas. Recent publications include *Negotiating Community and Landscape in the Peruvian Andes: A Trans-Conquest View* (*American Anthropologist*, 2007) and *The Politics of Community and Inka Statecraft in the Colca Valley, Peru* (*Latin American Antiquity*, 2006).

Picture Credits

Key: (t) top of page; (tl) top left of page; (tr) top right of page; (b) bottom of page; (bl) bottom left of page; (br) bottom right of page; (l) left side of page; (r) right side of page; (c) center of page; (cl) center left of page; (cr) center right of page.

Getty

Getty Images: 97(t), 388(t), 441(l); Abid Katib / Getty Images: 427(l); ADEK BERRY/AFP/Getty Images: 444(l); AFP/Getty Images: 382(t), 385(b), 399(t), 403(b), 413(t), 429(b); After James Rattray: 153(b); Allan Tannenbaum/Time Life Pictures/Getty Images: 401(b); Allocca/Timepix/Time Life Pictures/Getty Images: 430(bl); Andrea Sperling: 33(l); Andreas Rentz/Getty Images: 424(tr); Andries Beeckman: 195(t); Angelo Cavalli: 33(b); Antoine Rivalz: 143(t); Attributed to James Herring: Front cover image; Attributed to Liu Kuan: 148(t); Bill Fitzpatrick/White House/Time Life Pictures/Getty Images: 392(c); Bobby Haas: 27(b); Boucicaut Master and workshop: 151(b); British Library: 86(b); Carl Mydans/Time & Life Pictures/Getty Images: 384(b); Central Press/Getty Images: 408(r); Charles Le Brun: 13(b); Courtesy USAF/Getty Images): 437(b); Dante Gabriel Rossetti: 179(r); Dave Watt/ Keystone/Getty Images: 408(t); David Levenson/Getty Images: 400(b); David McNew/Getty Images: 422(r); Diane-Lu Hovasse/AFP/Getty Images: 395(b); Digital Vision Keren Su: 240(t); Digital Vision Travel Ink: 439(b); Dirck Halstead/Getty Images: 409(t); Dmitri Kessel/Time Life Pictures/Getty Images: 397(t); Dorling Kindersley John Woodcock: 288(c); Eduardo Javier Ramon Cano de la Pena: 3(r); EPA Photos DPA Files/AFP/Getty Images: 385(t); Eric Feferberg/AFP/Getty Images: 392(t), 394(t); Evening Standard/Getty Images: 379(b); Fox Photos/ Getty Images: 365(r), 372(l), 372(r); Francois-Hubert Drouais: 13(tl); Fred Ramage/Getty Images: 379(tr); Garrick Club: 302(l); General Photographic Agency: 356(t); Gerard Cerles/AFP/Getty Images: 424(c); Gerard Malie/AFP/Getty Images: 391(r); Henry Guttmann/Getty Images: 372(b); Hideo Kurihara: 342(b); HLA HLA HTAY/AFP/Getty Images: 421(b); Hughes & Mullins/Hulton Archive: 308(b); Hugo Jaeger/Timepix/Time Life Pictures/Getty Images: 371(t); Hulton Archive: 77(r), 147(b), 154(r), 195(r), 199(b), 217(b), 219(r), 222(t), 223(b), 236(b), 241(b), 245(t), 245(r), 271(b), 277(r), 281(l), 281(r), 290(r), 294(tr), 304(c), 305(b), 316(r), 318(c), 328(r), 337(b), 342(t), 344(t), 347(b), 352(l), 353(b), 354(r), 357(t), 359(r), 359(b), 364(b), 366(b), 367(r), 370(c), 370(b), 432(br), 436(r),; HultonArchive/ Illustrated London News/Getty Images: 86(t); Imagno/Getty Images: 298(t); Jack Esten/Stringer:Hulton Archive: 393(b); Jason Hawkes/Getty Images: 432(bl); Jewel Samad/AFP/Getty Images: 445(t); Joos van Gent: 012(t); Kenneth Garrett/National Geographic/Getty Images: 038(c); Keystone/Getty Images: 349(r), 373(t), 375(t), 404(l), 406(b), 410(l), 412(l); Keystone/Hulton Archive/Getty Images: 343(c); Lodovico Venuti: 9(c); Los Alamos National Laboratory/Time & Life Pictures/Getty Images:337(l); Louie Psihoyos: 23(t), 26(t); Mai/Mai/Time Life Pictures/ Getty Images: 430(t), 430(br), 436(bl), 436(br); Mansell/Mansell/Time & Life Pictures/Getty Images: 218(b), 234(b), 358(t), 368(b); Marco Di Lauro/Getty Images: 418(t); Margaret Bourke-White/Time & Life Pictures/Getty Images: 339(r), 369(t); Mark Peters/ Liaison: 421(l); Massoud Hossaini/AFP/Getty Images: 437(bm); Matt Stroshane/Getty Images: 423(t); Michel Gangne/AFP/Getty Images16(b); MPI/Getty Images: 409(r); Museo Capitolino Rome / Gianni Dagli Orti: 76(r); National Geographic David Evans: 3(t); National Geographic/Getty Images: 22(b), 417(t); Novgorod School: 96(t); Panoramic Images: 118(r); Paula Bronstein/Getty Images: 426(c); Peter Macdiarmid/Getty Images: 420(t); Photodisc StockTrek: 414(b); Photographer's Choice RF DKAR Images: 230(l); Pictorial Parade/Hulton Archive/Getty Images: 413(l); Popperfoto/Getty Images: 7(t), 359(l), 413(b); Ralph Morse/Time & Life Pictures/Getty Images: 385(r); Randy Wellz: 21(b); Richard I'Anson: 343(r); Riser Eightfish: 386(t); Riser William Lesch: 388(b); Robert Harding World Imagery Robert Francis: 446(b); Robert Lackenbach/Time Life Pictures: 339(l); Robert Nickelsberg/Getty Images: 412(b), 423(r), 440(t), 442(b); Robert W. Kelley//Time Life Pictures/Getty Images: 410(r); Rodrigo Buendia/AFP/Getty Images: 26(l); Rosemary Calvert: 27(t); Sean Gallup/Getty Images: 424(b); Shah Marai / AFP / Getty Images: 437(bl); Sir John Gilbert: 178(b); Slava Katamidze Collection/ Getty Images: 402(b); Spencer Platt/Getty Images: 389(t), 440(b) Staff/AFP/Getty Images): 336(t); Stephen Alvarez: 207(r); Stock Montage/Stock Montage/Getty Images: 304(c); Stone Robin Smith: 343(t); Stringer/AFP/ Getty Images: 390(b); Stuart Hannagan/Getty Images: 426(b); Taxi Keren Su: 120(b); The Bridgeman Art Library A. Benini: 83(t); The Bridgeman Art Library After Joris Hoefnagel: 15(t) The Bridgeman Art Library Anonymous: 312(l); The Bridgeman Art Library Antonio Lafreri: 137(t); The Bridgeman Art Library Bridgeman Art Library: 146(l); The Bridgeman Art Library Charpentier: 14(b) The Bridgeman Art Library Chinese School: 129(r), 184(t), 184(br), 185(b); The Bridgeman Art Library English School: 218(t); The Bridgeman Art Library Flemish School: 141(b); The Bridgeman Art Library French School: 14(br), 15(r), 235(t), 295(br); The Bridgeman Art Library George Catlin: 330(t); The Bridgeman Art Library Gerard Mercator: 247(b); The Bridgeman Art Library Indian School: 216(b); The Bridgeman Art Library Islamic School: 116(l); The Bridgeman Art Library Italian School: inside front cover; The Bridgeman Art Library Jean Antoine Theodore Gudin: 234(c), 286(r); The Bridgeman Art Library Jean-Marc Nattier: 270(c); The Bridgeman Art Library Juan de la Cosa: 5(r); The Bridgeman Art

Library Persian School: 154(b), 263(b); The Bridgeman Art Library Samuel Thomas Gill: 293(b); The Bridgeman Art Library Sebastien Leroy: 292(b); The Bridgeman Art Library Thomas Jones Barker: 302(r) The Bridgeman Art Library Willem Blaeu: 194(b); The Bridgeman Art Library William Aiken Walker: 262(b); The Bridgeman Art Library Xanthus Russell Smith: 328(b) The Bridgeman Art Library: 160(b), 281(t); The Bridgeman Art Library: 47(t), 47(b); The Image Bank Archive Holdings Inc.: 361(b); The Image Bank Keren Su: 439(t); Three Lions/Getty Images: 361(t), 380(b); Time & Life Pictures Margaret Bourke-White: 400(r); Time & Life Pictures/Getty Images: 15(c), 16(l), 199(t), 320(b), 399(b), 402(c), 414(c); Time Life Pictures/ Mansell/Time Life Pictures/Getty: 354(b), 355(t), 355(b), 359(t); Time Life Pictures/ National Archives/Time Life Pictures/Getty Images: 405(t); Time Life Pictures/US Army Signal Corps/Time Life Pictures/Getty Images: 360(b), 379(l); Timothy A. Clary/AFP/tty Images): 442(t); Tony Vaccaro/Hulton Archive/Getty Images: 382(b); Topical Press Agency/Getty Images: 359(r); U.S. Navy/Newsmakers: 376(b); Veneto-Byzantine School: 94(t); Vitaly Armand/AFP/Getty Images: 395(t); Walter Bibikow: 108(r); Wathiq Khuzaie/Getty Images: 443(r); William West/AFP/Getty Images: 447(b); Yaakov Saar/GPO: 398(t); Yugoslav Army/RL: 393(b); Zoltan Kluger/GPO via Getty Images) Getty Images Europe:397(b)

Art Archive

Art Archive: 29(b), 37(b), 48(b), 70(t), 141(r), 193(r), 233(b), 246(t), 246(b), 247(t), 253(t), 254(r), 259(t), 274(b), 277(l), 284(t), 293(t), 313(b), 316(l), 316(b), 321(r), 324(l), 333(c), 338(t), 340(t), 350(l), 356(b), 362(t), 367(b); Accademia Venice / Alfredo Dagli Orti: 174(t); Alcazar Seville / Gianni Dagli Orti: 224(t) Alcazar Seville/Gianni Dagli Orti: 227(b); Alfredo Dagli Orti: 41(r), 66(t), 70(b), 137(b), 181(r); Anagni Cathedral Italy / Alfredo Dagli Orti]:122(c); Antenna Gallery Dakar Senegal / Gianni Dagli Orti: 218(t); Antochiw Collection Mexico / Mireille Vautier: 166(b), 180(b), 207(t); Archaeological Museum Aleppo Syria / Gianni Dagli Orti: 54(c); Archaeological Museum Sparta / Gianni Dagli Orti: 68(l); Archaeological Museum Teheran / Gianni Dagli Orti: 63(c); Archaeological Museum Tipasa Algeria / Gianni Dagli Orti: 58(t); Arquivo Nacional da Torre do Tombo Lisbon / Gianni Dagli Orti: 238(b); Biblioteca Augustea Perugia / Alfredo Dagli Orti:165(b); Biblioteca d'Ajuda Lisbon / Gianni Dagli Orti: 210(b), 239(t); Biblioteca Estense Modena / Alfredo Dagli Orti: 172(b); Biblioteca Nacional Mexico / Gianni Dagli Orti: 220(t); Biblioteca Nazionale Marciana Venice / Alfredo Dagli Orti:396(b); Biblioteca Nazionale Marciana Venice / Gianni Dagli Orti: 134(t), 135(c); Bibliothèque des Arts Décoratifs Paris / Gianni Dagli Orti: 15(t), 28(t), 34(c), 57(b), 117(b), 171(bl), 220(b), 330(b); Bibliothèque Inguimbertine Carpentras / Gianni Dagli Orti: 72(b) Bibliothèque Municipale Dijon / Gianni Dagli Orti: 346(l); Bibliothèque Nationale Paris: 176(b), 314(b); Bibliothèque Universitaire Geneva / Gianni Dagli Orti: 203(r) Bodleian Library Oxford: 110(t), 150(l), 166(t), 434(l); British Library / Eileen Tweedy: 182(l); British Library: 97(b), 99(b), 108(c), 138(l), 149(t), 156(t), 160(l), 177(t), 186(b), 242(b), 244(l), 260(b), 284(b), 290(b); British Museum / Alfredo Dagli Orti: 42(r); British Museum / Harper Collins Publishers: 222(b); British Museum: 184(bl), 204(r), 291(b); Buffalo Bill Historical Center, Cody, Wyoming / 21.78: 288(b); Chateau de Blerancourt / Gianni Dagli Orti: 278(c); Chiaramonti Museum Vatican / Alfredo Dagli Orti: 70(r); Christopher Lay: 120(t); Conservatoire des Arts et Métiers Paris / Marc Charmet: 304(r); Culver Pictures: 261(r), 264(c), 276(b), 311(tr), 328(l), 329(b), 332(b), 349(b); Doges' Palace Venice / Alfredo Dagli Orti: 234(l); Doges' Palace Venice / Gianni Dagli Orti: 17(l); Domenica del Corriere / Alfredo Dagli Orti : 251(l), 344(b), 356(r); Egyptian Museum Cairo / Gianni Dagli Orti: 39(t), 39(r), 41(l), 42(c); Eileen Tweedy: 309(r), 332(c); Fishmonger's Company / Eileen Tweedy: 275(l); Galleria d'Arte Moderna Florence / Gianni Dagli Orti: 323(r); Galleria d'Arte Moderna Rome / Alfredo Dagli Orti: 83(b); Galleria degli Uffizi Florence / Alfredo Dagli Ort: 105(r), 191(b), 200(r); Galleria Nazionale dell'Umbria Perugia / Alfredo Dagli Orti: 89(c); General Archive of the Indies Seville / Gianni Dagli Orti: 238(r); Gianni Dagli Orti: 36(t), 59(b), 60(b), 62(r), 68(b), 80(b), 98(b), 102(b), 111(l), 157(b), 216(t), 229(t), 350(b), 396(r); Gift of Mrs Robert I Littlejohn / Museum of the city of New York/ 33.169.1: 318(r); Gioviana Archives Florence / Gianni Dagli Orti: 88(l); Gutenberg Museum Mainz / Gianni Dagli Orti: 175(l); Haghia Sophia Istanbul / Alfredo Dagli Orti]: 115(b); Hamburg Staatsarchiv / Harper Collins Publishers: 161(b); Harper Collins Publishers: 283(b); Hellenic Institute Venice / Alfredo Dagli Orti: 74(t); Imperial War Museum: 340(b), 358(b); Jan Vinchon Numismatist Paris / Gianni Dagli Orti: 92(c); Laurie Platt Winfrey: 133(l); Luxor Museum, Egypt / Gianni Dagli Orti: 42(b); Magdalene College Cambridge / Eileen Tweedy: 273(b) Malmaison Musée du Chateau / Gianni Dagli Orti: 299(b); Marc Charmet: 294(b); Marine Museum Lisbon / Gianni Dagli Orti: 226(t), 229(b); Miramare Museum Trieste / Alfredo Dagli Orti: 309(b); Mireille Vautier: 106(b), 188(t), 206(bs), 209(t); Monastery of the Rabida, Palos, Spain / Gianni Dagli Orti: 231(b), 232(t); Musée Archéologique Naples / Gianni Dagli Orti: 80(c); Musée Calvet Avignon/Gianni Dagli Orti: 205(r); Musée Carnavalet Paris / Alfredo Dagli Orti: 248(t), 296(b); Musée Carnavalet Paris / Gianni Dagli Orti: 243(t), 250(t); Musée Condé Chantilly / Gianni Dagli Orti: 92(l), 113(r), 130(b); Musée d'art et d'histoire Geneva / Gianni Dagli Orti: 75(b); Musée de la Marine Paris / Gianni Dagli Orti: 272(l); Musée de Laon France / Alfredo Dagli Orti: 162(l); Musée des Arts Africains et Océaniens / Alfredo Dagli Orti: 350(l); Musée des Arts Africains et Océaniens / Gianni Dagli Orti: 52(t), 242(t); Musée des Arts Décoratifs Paris / Alfredo

Dagli Orti: 131(r); Musée des Beaux Arts Grenoble / Gianni Dagli Orti: 90(b); Musée des Beaux Arts Lausanne / Gianni Dagli Orti: 200(b); Musée des Beaux Arts Orléans / Alfredo Dagli Orti: 268(l); Musée du Château de Versailles / Gianni Dagli Orti: 145(r), 158 (b), 177(r), 211(t), 268(r), 268(c), 278(b), 296(l), 296(t), 297(t), 298(b), 299(t), 311(b); Musée du Louvre Paris / Alfredo Dagli Orti: 63(t), 148(t); Musée du Louvre Paris / Gianni Dagli Orti: 39(tr), 40(t), 50(bl), 50(br), 55(b), 88(t), 93(b); Musée Fénaille Rodez / Gianni Dagli Orti: 20(t); Musée Guimet Paris / Alfredo Dagli Orti: 106(c); Musée Guimet Paris / Gianni Dagli Orti: 64(t), 65(c), 126(r), 129(l); Musée Rolin Autun France / Alfredo Dagli Orti: 63(b); Museo Bolivar Caracas / Gianni Dagli Orti: 306(t); Museo Civico Modigliana Italy / Alfredo Dagli Orti: 322(l); Museo Civico Revoltella Trieste / Alfredo Dagli Orti : 251(b); Museo Civico Trieste / Alfredo Dagli Orti: 101(b); Museo Correr Venice / Alfredo Dagli Orti: 164(t), 191(l); Museo de Arte Antiga Lisbon / Gianni Dagli Orti: 236(t); Museo de Santa Cruz Toledo: Museo del Prado Madrid: 301(b); Museo del Risorgimento Venice / Gianni Dagli Orti: 323(l); Museo della Civilta Romana Rome / Gianni Dagli Orti: 91(b); Museo Nacional de Historia Lima / Mireille Vautier: 196(t); Museo Naval Madrid / Gianni Dagli Orti: 227(t); Museo Pedro de Osma Lima / Mireille Vautier: 198(c); Museo Tridentino Arte Sacra Trento / Alfredo Dagli Orti: 203(t); Museum der Stadt Wien / Alfredo Dagli Orti: 303(t); Museum der Stadt Wien / Gianni Dagli Orti: 168(b); Museum der Stadt Wien: 301(t); Museum of the City of New York / 29.100.1304: 275(b); National Anthropological Museum Mexico / Gianni Dagli Orti: 180(l); National Gallery Budapest / Alfredo Dagli Orti : 134(b); National History Museum Mexico City / Gianni Dagli Orti: 306(b) National Library Cairo / Gianni Dagli Orti: 152(l), 187(c); National Library of Australia: 259(b); National Museum Karachi / Alfredo Dagli Orti: 48(l); New York Public Library / Harper Collins Publishers: 193(l); Niedersachsisches Museum: 84(c); Okugawa Art Museum Nagoya / Laurie Platt Winfrey : 133(b) Oriental Art Museum Genoa / Alfredo Dagli Orti: 133(t); Palazzo Leoni- Montanari Vicenza / Gianni Dagli Orti: 32(t), 124(b); Palazzo Pitti Florence / Alfredo Dagli Orti: 103(b), 169(b), 208(t); Palazzo Pubblico Siena / Gianni Dagli Orti: 171(br); Pastrana church Spain / Gianni Dagli Orti: 228(l); Prehistoric Museum Moesgard Højbjerg Denmark / Gianni Dagli Orti: 21(l), 136(l); Private Collection / Gianni Dagli Orti: 56(b); Private Collection / Philip Mould: 145(c); Private Collection Beirut / Alfredo Dagli Orti: 057(t); Private Collection Italy / Gianni Dagli Orti: 174(c); Private Collection Paris / Gianni Dagli Orti: 254(b), 266(b); Private collection Washington / Laurie Platt Winfrey: 264(t); Royal Palace Caserta Italy / Gianni Dagli Orti : 74(b); Russian Historical Museum Moscow / Alfredo Dagli Orti /.Culver Pictures: 310(l), 311(tl); Russian Historical Museum Moscow / Alfredo Dagli Orti: 270(l); Saint Sebastian Chapel Lanslevillard Savoy / Gianni Dagli Orti: 67(c); San Vitale Ravenna Italy / Alfredo Dagli Orti]: 112(l); San Zeno Maggiore Verona Italy / Alfredo Dagli Orti: 60(c); Sheffield City Art Galleries / Eileen Tweedy: 319(b); Simon Bolivar Amphitheatre / Alfredo Dagli Orti: 252(c); Staatliche Glypothek Munich / Alfredo Dagli Orti: 73(r); Stadtmuseum Aachen / Alfredo Dagli Orti: 131(b); Sucevita Monastery Moldavia Romania / Alfredo Dagli Orti: 71(l), 104(l); Topkapi Museum Istanbul / Gianni Dagli Orti: 100(c), 102(c), 165(l), 214(l); Turkish and Islamic Art Museum Istanbul / Alfredo Dagli Orti: 116(b); University Library Istanbul / Gianni Dagli Orti: 119(t); University Museum Cuzco / Mireille Vautier: 190(t); Vatican Museum Rome: 68(t), 69(t); Victoria and Albert Museum London / Eileen Tweedy: 315(b); Victoria and Albert Museum London / Sally Chappell: 331(b); William Sewell: 380(r); Zeller Collection Turin / Gianni Dagli Orti: 235(tl);

NASA

334(t); Defense Meteorological Satellite Program (DMSP) Special Sensor Microwave Imager (SSMI): 435(c); The Hubble Heritage Team (AURA/STScI/NASA): 240(b);

Captions for double pages images in the endmatter

Pages 448–449 When retreating from battle, the Spanish Armada took a long route home, sailing north and around England and Ireland. On their retreat down the west coast of Ireland, many of their ships sank. This sixteenth-century engraving by Augustine Ryther done in 1590, is of a map of the British Isles by Robert Adams that shows the voyage. It can be seen in the National Maritime Museum, London, UK.

Pages 470–471 Part of a world map by Fra Mauro drawn around 1459, this section shows the empire of Genghis Khan including Cathay—China as it is known today. The Fra Mauro world map is drawn on parchment and shows a circular image with south at the top. It is considered one of the marvels of medieval cartography and can be found at the Bibliotec Nazionale Marciana, in Venice, Italy.

Pages 494–495 This seventeenth-century illustration shows monarchs in full regalia surveying their kingdoms which are represented as globes supported by cherubs.

Pages 506–507 The Catalan Atlas produced in 1375 consists of paintings on vellum depicting various aspects of discovery including travel, astronomy, and cosmography. One of the leaves covers the journeys of Marco Polo. Here in close-up is a section showing Marco Polo and his family in a camel caravan traveling to the east.